HIV/AIDS Primary Care Guide

HIV/AIDS
Primary Care Guide

Clinical Content Editors:
Jeffrey Beal, MD
Clinical Director, Florida/Caribbean AIDS
Education and Training Center

Joanne J. Orrick, PharmD, BCPS
Clinical Assistant Professor,
University of Florida

Managing Editor:
Kimberly Alfonso, MAcc
Assistant Director,
Florida/Caribbean AIDS Education
and Training Center

Associate Editor
Pediatrics/Adolescents:
Mobeen Rathore, MD
Professor, University of Florida,
Jacksonville

Crown House Publishing Company LLC
www.chpus.com

2006

Published by
Crown House Publishing Company, LLC
4 Berkeley Street
Norwalk, CT 06850
www.chpus.com

and
Crown House Publishing Ltd
Crown Buildings
Bancyfelin, Carmarthen, Wales SA33 5ND, UK
www.crownhouse.co.uk

DISCLAIMER
Recognizing the rapid changes that occur in this field, readers are encouraged to consult with their local experts or research the literature for the most up-to-date information to assist in individual treatment decisions for their patient. This text in its entirety, as well as additional HIV/AIDS care and treatment chapters, can be found at the Florida/Caribbean AETC website: www.faetc.org. The online chapters are reviewed and updated on a regular basis. The reader is encouraged to visit this site and view updates as they become available.

10 Digit ISBN: 1-845900278
13 Digit ISBN: 978-184590027

LCCN: 2006922110

Manufactured in the United States of America

There are trees that seem to wither at the end of autumn,
There are also evergreens,
Among us are people who are like evergreens,
They keep hope alive in themselves and radiate hope for the rest of us.
They teach us that AIDS is a fightable disease
And that we are powerful people.
They teach us how to be survivors, evergreens.

— The Color of Light

Contents

Section I: HIV Basics

Section II: Treatment

Section III: Systemic Manifestations

Section IV: Management of Co-Existing Conditions

Section V: Pediatrics/Adolescents

Section VI: Special Populations and Other Issues

Foreword

Michael D. Knox, PhD
Distinguished Professor and Director
Florida/Caribbean AIDS Education and Training Center
University of South Florida

The constantly changing HIV epidemic and evolving treatments for people living with HIV continue to present challenges to healthcare providers worldwide. Recent trends related to the complexities and rapid changes in medical care are particularly relevant to assessing the value of continuing HIV/AIDS education. Such changes and trends include:

1. Strategies for treatment continually change as new drugs are regularly approved and new drug-drug interactions are identified.
2. The US Department of Health and Human Services has published 42 different treatment guidelines since 1998.
3. There are multiple opportunistic infections and co-existing conditions that clinicians are challenged to prevent, evaluate, and treat.
4. The complexity and chronic nature of HIV disease requires clinicians to know how to individualize care for each patient and as the patients are living longer, new issues are arising.
5. The wide range of available treatment options, the high pill burden, and strict requirements for consistent adherence to medication regimens present unique treatment challenges.

A testament to the importance of continuing clinical education to address the epidemic, these facts help to clarify the critical role that the federally funded AIDS Education and Training Centers (AETCs) play in improving HIV care. Clearly, training and the dissemination of emerging information on treatment strategies are more important than ever. While treatments are significantly reducing the annual rate of death due to AIDS, too many Americans continue to acquire HIV infection — over 40,000 per year.[1] All healthcare providers require continual training to ensure that they are up to date on treatment guidelines, as well as proficient at HIV risk assessment, testing, and behavior change methods for those at risk or already infected with HIV.

Funded by the US Health Resources and Services Administration, the AETCs meet training needs through a geographically dispersed network of more than 130 clinical training sites, most located at leading academic medical centers. The AETC Program is the continuing education arm of the Ryan White CARE Act that funds treatment for HIV-infected patients in the US. The medical literature has documented that HIV/AIDS patients treated by experienced HIV healthcare providers obtain the best clinical outcomes and their patients have reduced mortality and increased longevity.[2,3,4] AETCs provide this experience through intensive clinical training that allows community clinicians to learn by working side-by-side with HIV experts. The AETCs help to create, expand, and improve the workforce of HIV care providers throughout the country to assure that persons with HIV disease have access to the best possible care. Training activities are designed following a needs assessment at the clinical level. Emphasis is placed on interactive, hands-on training and clinical consultation to assist providers with complex issues related to the management of HIV/AIDS in specific patients. To access a map showing the AETC serving each region, go to http://hab.hrsa.gov/educating.htm and click on "11 Regional Centers."

AETCs are mandated to train healthcare personnel in the diagnosis, treatment, and prevention of HIV disease. Through a variety of mechanisms the AETCs network provides the essential function of keeping medical providers updated on the latest technologies available to serve their patients. Training is targeted to providers who treat traditionally underserved and hard to reach populations including minorities, the poor, the homeless, rural communities, incarcerated persons, community and migrant health centers, and Ryan White CARE Act funded sites. As part of this network, the Florida/Caribbean AIDS Education and Training Center provides state-of-the-art continuing education, training, and consultation on prevention and treatments for HIV/AIDS to healthcare professionals throughout Florida, Puerto Rico, and the US Virgin Islands. Targeting physicians, physician assistants, nurses, nurse practitioners, dental providers, and pharmacists, the AETC offers educational experiences in a variety of formats including workshops, expert consultation, hands-on supervised clinical training, case conferences, and specialty conferences. Over 80 medical experts, including many with international reputations, serve as faculty members. Since the Florida/Caribbean AETC was formed in July 2002, it has provided over 50,000 hours of training and consultation to more than 60,000 healthcare workers throughout the region. The AETC is part of the University of South Florida Center for HIV Education and Research founded in 1988.

AETCs work intensively with HIV clinic staff through repeated educational interactions. The Florida/Caribbean AETC, for example, reviews medical records to evaluate the treatment provided and designs practical training plans for the clinic based on the findings. The Florida/Caribbean AETC, with training sites at the University of South Florida, University of Florida, University of Miami, University of Puerto Rico, Florida A&M University, and the University of the Virgin Islands, provides a variety of educational programs. Clinical mini-residencies are offered to physicians who have an interest in learning more about the diagnosis, early management, and on-going treatment of HIV disease. This opportunity, in the form of a preceptorship, is also available to nurses, physician assistants, and pharmacists. For more than 15 years, the Center has offered its annual HIV conference each spring, which attracts hundreds of participants from across the region. Frequent clinical conferences and workshops are available throughout the region to reach specialized groups and rural providers. Professionals can receive advice and support in the use of antiretroviral treatment and other issues related to specific patients through the AETC's consultation service. A newsletter, "HIV CareLink," is emailed monthly to over 1,000 healthcare workers treating patients with HIV. Special bulletins with urgent clinical information are disseminated as necessary through this same listserv. Pocket guides are produced to provide a quick reference for healthcare providers as they see patients.

This *HIV/AIDS Primary Care Guide* is the curriculum for the Florida/Caribbean AETC and is the underlying knowledge base for all of its education, training, and consultation programs. The *Primary Care Guide* is also used by Ryan White clinics as a standard of care throughout the region. We owe a debt of gratitude to editors Dr. Jeff Beal, Dr. Joanne Orrick, and Ms. Kimberly Alfonso who edited this massive volume and to the faculty of the Florida/Caribbean AETC and other experts who researched and wrote the chapters and to USF Center staff who managed the process, including Michael Ikeya who contributed to the graphic design.

Knowledge in this field is rapidly changing. This means that many of the chapters that deal with drugs, side effects, and treatment guidelines may soon be out of date. Each chapter will be revised as necessary and be available on the Center's website as individual PDF files that can be downloaded. To learn more about the Florida/Caribbean AETC, please visit our website **www.faetc.org**.

References

1.   Knox MD. AIDS Prevention Leadership. *Journal of HIV/AIDS and Social Services* 2005; 4(3).

2   Kitahata M M, Koepsell T D, Deyo R A, Maxwell C L, Dodge W T, Wagner E H, Physicians' experience with the acquired immunodeficiency syndrome as a factor in patients' survival, *NEJM* Mar 14, 334(11), 701-6, 1996.

3.   Coker RJ, Poznansky, MC. Physician experience and survival of patients with AIDS. *NEJM* Aug 1, 335(5), 1999.

4.   Laine, C, et al. The relationship of clinical experience with HIV and survival of women. *AIDS* March 5, 1998: (12)4:417–424.

Introduction

This text represents the collective efforts of 25 of the Florida/Caribbean AIDS Education and Training Center (AETC) faculty and 37 guest authors. The faculty represents a diverse group of HIV care providers. This guide is organized into 6 sections covering HIV and AIDS care and treatment of the child, adolescent, and adult. The text is targeted for the front-line clinician and is formatted to allow for the rapid identification of practical treatment information. Still, recognizing the rapid changes that occur in this field readers are encouraged to consult with their local experts or research the literature for the most up-to-date information to assist in individual treatment decisions for their patient. As an example of the frequency with which treatment information changes, three new DHHS Guidelines were issued in the weeks before the deadline for submission of this book to the publisher. We revised just-written chapters to include these changes. Chances are good that by the time you read this, there will already be newer Guidelines.

The success of antiretroviral therapy is resulting in not only an improved quality of life, but also an improved life expectancy for our patients. With these changes come new challenges. Clinicians are pressed to better manage the primary care needs of their patients. Patients co-infected with Hepatitis B and C need careful consideration for treatment. Complications of medication therapies need to be evaluated and treated, as do problems associated with the aging of our patients such as hypertension, heart disease, diabetes, etc. As more medications are required, closer observation is needed to prevent serious drug interactions.

As editors, we would like to recognize the contributions of the staff of the Florida/Caribbean AIDS Education and Training Center Central Office for their assistance with research, editing, and formatting of this text. We would also like to thank our elected officials and HRSA for their continued support and funding of the Ryan White Care Act and the nationwide efforts of all of the AETCs. We would like to thank all of the authors of the book for their hard work, dedication, and contribution to making this a valuable resource for HIV clinicians. We thank as well our spouses, significant others, and families who supported us in the extensive work required in preparing this text.

Special recognition and thanks are extended to several key faculty of the AETC: Dr. Michael Knox and Dr. Martha Friedrich for their encouragement and support through this process and Dr. Mobeen Rathore for his leadership as Associate Editor of the Pediatric/Adolescent section of this book.

This text in its entirety, as well as additional HIV/AIDS care and treatment chapters, can be found at the Florida/Caribbean AETC website: www.faetc.org. The online chapters are reviewed and updated on a regular basis. The reader is encouraged to visit this site and view updates as they become available.

This book is dedicated to the AETC faculty across the United States and the Caribbean and to our patients who continue to challenge us to remain committed to the effort. Our patients' courage, perseverance, and love of life inspire us to keep abreast of the continual changes in this field to provide the best treatment possible. Collectively, our lives have been forever changed by the patients for whom we have cared[JKH1][JKH2].

Jeffrey Beal, MD
Joanne J. Orrick, PharmD, BCPS
Kimberly Alfonso, MAcc
March, 2006

Contributors

Kimberly Alfonso, MAcc (University of South Florida, 1995). Ms. Alfonso is the Assistant Director of the Florida/Caribbean AIDS Education and Training Center and served as Managing Editor for this publication.

Rafael Alfonso, DDS (University of Maryland, 1982). Dr. Alfonso is in private practice and a Ryan White Title I provider in Miami, Florida.

David Ashkin, MD (New York Medical College, 1986). Dr. Ashkin is Medical Executive Director of A.G. Holley State Hospital. He also serves as the State TB Controller for the Florida Department of Health and is an Assistant Professor of Medicine with the University of Miami, School of Medicine. He also serves on the faculty of the Florida/Caribbean AIDS Education and Training Center.

Jeffrey Beal, MD (University of Missouri at Kansas City, 1979). Dr. Beal is the Clinical Director of the Florida/Caribbean AIDS Education and Training Center. He is also an Associate Professor at the University of South Florida and Medical Director for the Ryan White Title III program at Hendry and Glades County Health Department, Florida. In addition, Dr. Beal is the Senior Physician at Lee County Health Department, Florida.

David Beall, PhD, Microbiology and Cell Science (University of Florida, 1995). Dr. Beall is Head of Mycobacteriology Laboratory at the Florida Department of Health, Bureau of Laboratories, Jacksonville, Florida.

Kevin T. Belasco, DO, MS. Dr. Belasco is a current Resident in Dermatology at Sun Coast Hospital in Largo, Florida.

Berry Bennett, MPH. Mr. Bennett is the Retrovirology Administrator at the Florida Department of Health, Florida Bureau of Laboratories, Jacksonville, Florida.

Kimberley Brown, PharmD. Dr. Brown is an Assistant Professor in the Department of Pediatrics, Pediatric Infectious Diseases and Immunology at The Rainbow Center for Women, Adolescents, Children and Families at the University of Florida, Jacksonville, Florida.

Patricia M. Bryan, RN, BSN, MPH (Florida International University, 1997). Ms. Bryan is a Florida/Caribbean AIDS Education and Training Center Coordinator/Trainer in the Department of Obstetrics and Gynecology, University of Miami, School of Medicine, Miami, Florida.

Tracina Bush is an Epidemiologist for the Florida Department of Health, Bureau of HIV/AIDS, Tallahassee, Florida.

Daniela Chiriboga, MD. Dr. Chiraboga works in the Department of Pediatrics at the University of South Florida, College of Medicine, Tampa, Florida.

Charles F. Clark, MD (John Hopkins University, 1964), **MPH.** Dr. Clark is an inpatient physician in psychiatry at Lutheran Medical Center, Wheatridge, Colorado.

Marcus A. Conant, MD (Duke University, 1961). Dr. Conant is Medical Director at Conant Medical Group, San Francisco, California.

Amanda Cotter, MD (Trinity College, Ireland, 1994), **MSPH.** Dr. Cotter is an Assistant Professor and the Director of the Perinatal HIV Service in the Department of Obstetrics & Gynecology, University of Miami, Miller School of Medicine, Miami, Florida. Dr. Cotter also serves on the faculty of the Florida/Caribbean AIDS Education and Training Center.

Susan S. Davis, ARNPC, MSN. Ms. Davis is a Nurse Practitioner in Employee Health at Memorial Hospital, Miramar, Florida.

Jeri A. Dyson, MD. Dr. Dyson is a physician practicing at the University of Florida, Jacksonville, Florida.

Michael G. Dow, PhD, Psychology (Pennsylvania State University, 1983). Dr. Dow is a Professor in the Department of Mental Health Law and Policy, Louis de la Parte Florida Mental Health Institute at the University of South Florida, Tampa, Florida.

Patricia Emmanuel, MD (University of Florida College of Medicine, 1986). Dr. Emmanuel is an Associate Professor of Pediatrics and Head of the Division of Pediatric Infectious Disease at the University of South Florida, College of Medicine, Tampa, Florida. She is also the Medical Director for the University of South Florida HIV Program for Children and Adolescents. Dr. Emmanuel serves on the faculty of the Florida/Caribbean AIDS Education and Training Center.

Luis A. Espinoza, MD (UNIV/NAC Federico Villarreal, 1986). Dr. Espinosa is an Assistant Professor of Clinical Medicine for the Clinical Immunology Section, Division of Infectious Diseases, University of Miami, School of Medicine, Jackson Memorial Hospital, Miami, Florida.

Karen V. Farrell RN, BSN, RM. Ms. Farrell is the Executive Nursing Director and Director of Education at A.G. Holley State Hospital, Lantana, Florida.

Tanira Ferreira, MD. Dr. Ferreira is Senior Physician at A.G. Holley State Hospital, Lantana, Florida.

Cade Fields-Gardner, MS, RD. Ms. Fields-Gardner is Director of Services at The Cutting Edge in Cary, Illinois.

Lawrence B. Friedman, MD (University of Missouri at Kansas City, 1980). Dr. Friedman is Professor and Director of Adolescent Medicine, University of Miami School of Medicine, Miami, Florida. Dr. Friedman also serves on the faculty of the Florida/Caribbean AIDS Education and Training Center.

Carol M. Fulton, MSN, ARNP, CPNP. Ms. Fulton is a Pediatric Nurse Practitioner at the University of Florida, Department of Pediatrics, The Rainbow Center for Women, Adolescents, Children and Families at the University of Florida, Jacksonville, Florida. Ms. Fulton also serves on the faculty of the Florida/Caribbean AIDS Education and Training Center.

Sandra G. Gompf, MD, FACP (University of South Florida College of Medicine, 1991). Dr. Gompf is Assistant Clinical Professor, Division of Infectious and Tropical Diseases, Department of Internal Medicine, University of South Florida College of Medicine, and Section Chief, James A. Haley VA Hospital, Tampa, Florida. Dr. Gompf also serves on the faculty of the Florida/Caribbean AIDS Education and Training Center.

Manuel Guerra, MD. Dr. Guerra is Senior Attending Physician in the Division of Hematology/Oncology, Department of Medicine, Mercy Hospital, Miami, Florida.

Marcella Hamilton, RN, JD (Stetson University College of Law, 1996). Ms. Hamilton serves as a legal consultant for the Florida/Caribbean AIDS Education and Training Center.

Elena S. Hollender, MD (Universidad Autonoma de Santo Domingo, Dominican Republic, 1982). Dr. Hollender is Director of Clinical Services at A.G. Holley State Hospital, Lantana, Florida.

Asim A. Jani, MD, MPH, FACP (University of South Florida, College of Medicine, 1987). Dr. Jani is an Assistant State Epidemiologist for the Virginia Department of Health & Clinical Assistant Professor at Virginia Commonwealth University, Richmond, Virginia. Dr. Jani is also an Internal Medicine, Infectious Diseases & HIV Medicine, and Tri-County Infectious Disease Consultant at Orlando Internal Medicine, Infectious Diseases and HIV Medicine.

Michael D. Knox, PhD, Psychology (University of Michigan, 1974). Dr. Knox is a Distinguished Professor of Mental Health Law and Policy, Medicine, and Global Health at the University of South Florida, Tampa, Florida. He is also Director of the USF Center for HIV Education and Research and the Florida/Caribbean AIDS Education and Training Center.

Michael Lauzardo, MD (University of Florida, 1991). Dr. Lauzardo is the Deputy TB Controller for the state of Florida and is an Adjunct Assistant Professor in the Division of Pulmonary and Critical Care Medicine at the University of Florida, Gainesville, Florida. Dr. Lauzardo is also on the faculty of the Florida/Caribbean AIDS Education and Training Center.

Kathy Letro, RD, LD/N. Ms. Letro serves as a registered dietician in the Pediatric Infectious Diseases and Immunology, Rainbow Center for Women, Adolescent, Children and Families at the University of Florida, Jacksonville, Florida.

Spencer Lieb, MPH. Mr. Lieb is an Epidemiologist for the Florida Department of Health, Bureau of HIV/AIDS, Tallahassee, Florida.

D. Stewart MacIntyre, MD. Dr. MacIntyre is a Clinical Professor of Infectious Disease at the University of Miami School of Medicine, Miami, Florida.

Lorene Maddox, MPH. Ms. Maddox is an Epidemiologist for the Florida Department of Health, Bureau of HIV/AIDS, Tallahassee, Florida.

Igor Melnychuk, MD. Dr. Melnychuk is currently a Fellow in the Division of Infectious Disease and Tropical Medicine at the University of South Florida, Tampa, Florida.

Lynette J. Menezes, PhD, Public Health (University of South Florida, 2003). Dr. Menezes is Director of International Programs and Assistant Professor in the Division of Infectious Diseases and International Medicine at the University of South Florida, Tampa, Florida.

Jose N. Moreno, MD (University of Puerto Rico, 1967). Dr. Moreno is a Professor of Clinical Medicine in the Division of Infectious Diseases at the University of Miami School of Medicine, Miami, Florida. Dr. Moreno also serves on the faculty of the Florida/Caribbean AIDS Education and Training Center.

Jeffrey P. Nadler, MD, FACP (New York Medical College, 1975). Dr. Nadler is a Professor of Medicine in the Division of Infectious and Tropical Diseases, Department of Internal Medicine at the University of South Florida, College of Medicine, Tampa, Florida. Dr. Nadler also serves on the faculty of the Florida/Caribbean AIDS Education and Training Center.

Eknath Naik, MD (University of Bombay, 1991), **PhD, Epidemiology** (University of Alabama at Birmingham, 1999). Dr. Naik is an Assistant Professor in the Department of Epidemiology and Biostatistics at the University of South Florida, College of Public Health and in the Division of Infectious Diseases, Department of Internal Medicine, University of South Florida, College of Medicine, Tampa, Florida. He is the Director of Centers for Health, HIV/AIDS Research and Training in India. Dr. Naik also serves on the faculty of the Florida/Caribbean AIDS Education and Training Center.

Masahiro Narita, MD. Dr. Narita serves at the Tuberculosis Control Program, Department of Public Health, Seattle and King County, Washington.

Robin D. Nolen, MSW. Ms. Nolen is an Adherence Facilitator and Health Educator in Orlando, Florida.

Joanne J. Orrick, PharmD (University of Florida, 1997), **BCPS**. Dr. Orrick is a Clinical Assistant Professor at the University of Florida, Gainesville, Florida. Dr. Orrick also serves on the faculty of the Florida/Caribbean AIDS Education and Training Center.

Frank Paula, MSN, ARNP. Mr. Paula is a Nurse Practitioner at Mercy Hospital in Miami, Florida.

JoNell Efantis Potter, PhD, Nursing, ARNP (University of Miami, 2003). Dr. Potter is Division Director for Research and Special Projects, Assistant Professor in Clinical Obstetrics and Gynecology, University of Miami School of Medicine, Miami, Florida. She also serves on the faculty of the Florida/Caribbean AIDS Education and Training Center.

Ana M. Puga, MD (Ponce School of Medicine, 1990). Dr. Puga is the Medical Director for the Comprehensive Family AIDS Program, Children's Diagnostic and Treatment Center, Fort Lauderdale, Florida. Dr. Puga also serves on the faculty of the Florida/Caribbean AIDS Education and Training Center.

Iván Meléndez-Rivera, MD, FAAFP, AAHIVS. Dr. Meléndez-Rivera is Assistant Professor in the Family Practice Department, Ponce School of Medicine and Family Practice Residency, Dr. Pila Hospital. Dr. Meléndez is Director and Founder of Centro ARARAT, Inc., a non-profit multidisciplinary HIV organization in Ponce, Puerto Rico. He also serves on the faculty of the Florida/Caribbean AIDS Education and Training Center.

Mobeen H. Rathore, MD. Dr. Rathore is Professor and Assistant Chair of the Department of Pediatrics, and Chief of Infectious Disease and Immunology at the University of Florida, Health Science Center, Jacksonville, Florida. Dr. Rathore also serves on the Florida/Caribbean AIDS Education and Training Center faculty.

Allen E. Rodriguez, MD. Dr. Rodriguez is an Associate Professor of Clinical Medicine in the Clinical Immunology Section, Division of Infectious Disease, University of Miami School of Medicine, Jackson Memorial Hospital, Miami, Florida.

Gwendolyn B. Scott, MD (University of California, 1972). Dr. Scott is Professor and Director of the Division of Infectious Diseases and Immunology, Department of Pediatrics, University of Miami, School of Medicine, Miami, Florida. Dr. Scott also serves on the faculty of the Florida/Caribbean AIDS Education and Training Center.

David Simpson, MD (University of Maryland, 1991). Dr. Simpson is a Professor of Neurology, Director of Clinical Neurophysiology Laboratories, and Director of the Neuro-AIDS Program, Mount Sinai Medical Center, New York.

Charurut Somboonwit, MD (Srinanakharinwirot University, Thailand, 1995). Dr. Somboonwit is Senior Physician at the Polk County Health Department, and an Assistant Professor in the Division of Infectious Diseases and Tropical Medicine at the University of South Florida, Tampa, Florida.

Jerry Jean Stambaugh, PharmD. Dr. Stambaugh is Pharmacy Director at the AG Holley State Hospital, Lantana, Florida.

Anne Stewart, PhD, Nursing, ARNP. Dr. Stewart is Immunology Clinic Manager and a member of the Faculty at Florida Southern College, Orlando, Florida.

Carol Stewart, DDS, MS (Indiana University, 1980). Dr. Stewart is Associate Professor in the University of Florida College of Dentistry, Gainesville, Florida, and the Dental Director of the Florida/Caribbean AIDS Education and Training Center.

Stephen N. Symes, MD (Howard University, 1989). Dr. Symes is Assistant Professor in the Department of Medicine, Division of Clinical Immunology and Infectious Diseases, University of Miami School of Medicine, Miami, Florida.

Lee Tavel, RPh, serves as a Pharmacist for the Orange County Health Department, Florida Department of Health, Orlando, Florida.

Nicoletta Tessler, PsyD. Dr. Tessler is a Licensed Psychologist in the Department of Psychiatry and Behavioral Sciences at the University of Miami, Miller School of Medicine, Miami, Florida.

Michael Thompson, PharmD, BCNSP (University of Michigan, 1978). Dr. Thompson is Assistant Dean for Clinical Affairs and Professor of Pharmacy Practice in the College of Pharmacy and Pharmaceutical Sciences, Florida Agricultural and Mechanical University, Tallahassee, Florida. Dr. Thompson also serves on the faculty of the Florida/Caribbean AIDS Education and Training Center.

Deslyn Thornhill, MPH. Ms. Thornhill is an Epidemiologist for the Florida Department of Health, Bureau of HIV/AIDS, Tallahassee, Florida.

John F. Toney, MD (Marshall University, 1981). Dr. Toney is an Associate Professor of Medicine in the Division of Infectious and Tropical Diseases, Department of Internal Medicine, University of South Florida, College of Medicine, Tampa, Florida. He is the Medical Director of the Florida STD/HIV Prevention Training Center. Dr. Toney is also on the faculty of the Florida/Caribbean AIDS Education and Training Center.

Todd S. Wills, MD (University of South Florida, 1998). Dr. Wills is an Assistant Professor in the Division of Infectious Diseases, Department of Internal Medicine, University of South Florida, College of Medicine, Tampa, Florida. He is Assistant Director of the Florida STD/HIV Prevention Training Center. Dr. Wills is also on the faculty of the Florida/Caribbean AIDS Education and Training Center.

Section I

HIV Basics

1

Epidemiology of HIV/AIDS

Lorene Maddox, MPH
Tracina Bush
Deslyn Thornhill, MPH
Spencer Lieb, MPH
Epidemiologists
Florida Department of Health, Bureau of HIV/AIDS (HSDHIV)
Tallahassee
Marcella Hamilton, RN, JD
Faculty, Florida/Caribbean AIDS Education and Training Center

The Worldwide Pandemic

The United Nations estimates that as of December 2004, 39.4 million people worldwide were living with HIV, including 17.6 million women and 2.2 million children under the age of 15 (Figure 1).[1]

At the end of 2003, The US Centers for Disease Control and Prevention (CDC) estimated 1,039,000 to 1,185,000 persons in the United States were living with HIV/AIDS, with 24–27% undiagnosed and unaware of their HIV infection. US 2004 data are not yet available.[2] In the 33 areas of the United States with integrated HIV and AIDS surveillance since at least 1999, the number of new cases of HIV/AIDS has shown a minimal increase from 2000 through 2003.[3] An approximate increase of 1% was estimated from the end of the year 2002 through 2003.[3] However, for this same time period, the estimated number of AIDS cases has increased by 9% in the Northeast, 6% in the South, and 4% in the Midwest, while the West has shown a decline of 3%.[3] California, Florida, and New York accounted for 38% of AIDS cases reported to the CDC in 2003.[3]

According to the CDC, individuals aged 25 to 34 years accounted for 27% of HIV/AIDS cases diagnosed in 2003.[3] Of AIDS cases diagnosed in 2003, the age group of individuals aged 35 to 44 years accounted for 41%.[3] Moreover, from 2000 to 2003, the estimated number of HIV/AIDS cases increased in several age groups, including those individuals aged 13 to 14, 15 to 24, 45 to 54, 55 to 64, and 65 years and older.[3]

Figure 1. Adults and Children Living with HIV/AIDS

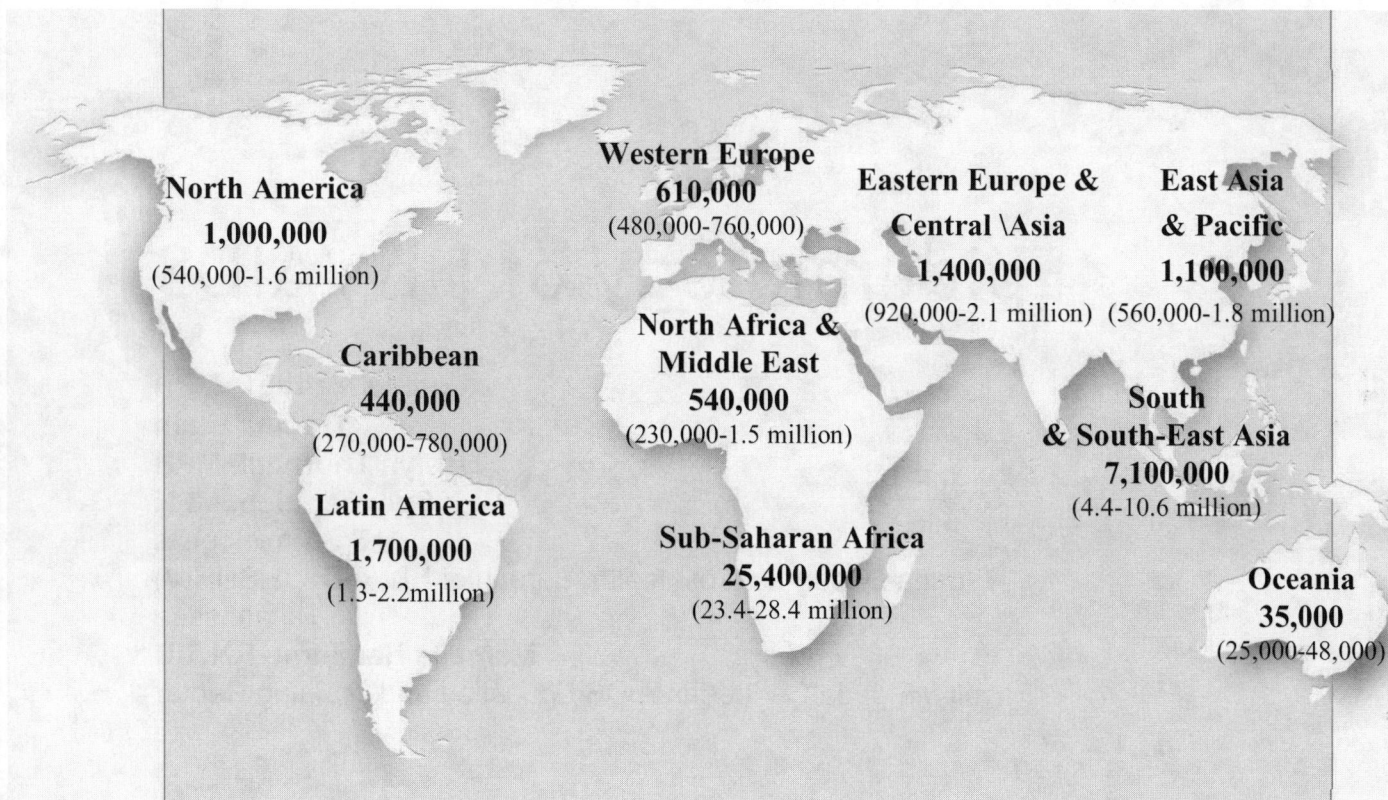

North America
1,000,000
(540,000-1.6 million)

Western Europe
610,000
(480,000-760,000)

Eastern Europe &
Central \Asia
1,400,000
(920,000-2.1 million)

East Asia
& Pacific
1,100,000
(560,000-1.8 million)

Caribbean
440,000
(270,000-780,000)

North Africa &
Middle East
540,000
(230,000-1.5 million)

South
& South-East Asia
7,100,000
(4.4-10.6 million)

Latin America
1,700,000
(1.3-2.2million)

Sub-Saharan Africa
25,400,000
(23.4-28.4 million)

Oceania
35,000
(25,000-48,000)

During this same time period, the estimated number of HIV/AIDS cases rose among whites, Hispanics, and Asian/Pacific Islanders, but decreased among blacks.[3] In contrast, from 1999 through 2003, the estimated number of AIDS cases decreased among whites, while reflecting increases among blacks, Hispanics, Asians/Pacific Islanders and American Indians/Alaska Natives.[3] Blacks continue to remain disproportionately affected by HIV infection, accounting for 50% of all HIV/AIDS cases diagnosed in 2003.[3]

With regard to mode of transmission, for the years 2000 through 2003, the estimated number of HIV/AIDS cases increased yearly in the populations of men having sex with men (MSM) and heterosexual adults and adolescents, but at the same time decreased among injection drug users (IDUs), MSM who also were IDUs, and children.[3] From 2000 through 2003, males continued to represent the highest proportion of HIV/AIDS cases, accounting for a 5% increase during this time, while the estimated number of HIV/AIDS cases for females decreased by 2%.[3] In comparison, from 1999 through 2003, the estimated number of AIDS cases increased approximately 15% among females and 1% among males.[3] Males represented 72% of HIV/AIDS cases among adults and adolescents in 2003.[3] Of HIV/AIDS cases diagnosed in 2003, MSM and persons exposed though heterosexual contact represented 79% of the total number.[3]

In the United States, with advancements in treatment for HIV infection, deaths from AIDS have decreased 3% from 1999 through 2003 while the number of persons living with AIDS increased by an estimated 30%.[3]

Table 1. AIDS Summary Statistics, Cumulative US (as of 12/31/03)*

	UNITED STATES	
	# OF CASES	% DEAD**
NO. ADULT/ADOLESCENT CASES	892,875	58%
NO. PEDIATRIC CASES (<13 years)	9,348	55%
TOTAL CASES	902,223	58%
EXPOSURE CATEGORY (ADULTS)	# OF CASES	% OF TOTAL
MALE TO MALE CONTACT	401,392	45%
INJECTION DRUG USER (IDU)	218,196	24%
MALE TO MALE CONTACT/IDU	57,998	6%
HEMOPHILIAC	5,448	1%
HETEROSEXUAL CONTACT	111,147	12%
TRANSFUSION RELATED	9,295	1%
NONE OF THE ABOVE	89,399	10%
RACE/ETHNICITY (ALL CASES)** (***)	# OF CASES	% OF TOTAL
WHITE (NON-HISPANIC)	367,121	41%
BLACK (NON-HISPANIC)	349,375	39%
HISPANIC	165,051	18%
OTHER/UNKNOWN	9,673	1%
SEX (ADULTS ONLY)	# OF CASES	% OF TOTAL
MALE	729,478	82%
FEMALE	163,396	18%

*Source: CDC HIV/AIDS Surveillance Report, Volume 15. CDC has published updated cumulative US AIDS case reports as of 12/31/04 of 911,053 Adults/Adolescents and 9,388 Peds <13 years old, Total 920,441. Breakdown of 2004 US cases by Exposure Category, Race/Ethnicity and Sex are not yet available.

** These numbers do not represent actual cases in persons who died with AIDS or who have a diagnosis of AIDS. Rather, these numbers are point estimates of cases in persons who died with AIDS or diagnosed with AIDS that have been adjusted for delays in reporting of deaths. The estimates have not been adjusted for incomplete reporting.

*** US race total does not include Pediatric cases (n=9,348).

Other races include Asian/Pacific Islander or American Indian/Alaska Native, Native Hawaiian, Multiracial or Other race.

Table 2. Reported AIDS Cases by State (as of December 2004)*

REPORTING STATE	ADULT/ADOLESCENT		CHILDREN	
	# OF CASES	% OF TOTAL	# OF CASES	% OF TOTAL
CALIFORNIA	134,889	15%	649	7%
FLORIDA	95,285	10%	1,504	16%
GEORGIA	28,190	3%	223	2%
ILLINOIS	30,825	3%	281	3%
MARYLAND	27,238	3%	314	3%
MASSACHUSETTS	18,165	2%	210	2%
NEW JERSEY	46,461	5%	766	8%
NEW YORK	164,536	18%	2,358	25%
PENNSYLVANIA	30,408	3%	353	4%
TEXAS	64,132	7%	390	4%
REMAINDER OF U.S.**	270,924	30%	2,340	25%
TOTAL CASES	911,053		9,388	

*Source: Statistics and Management Branch, DHIV/AIDS, CDC. Data provisional.

**Remainder of US AIDS cases also include US Territory data.

These territories include Guam, US Pacific Islands, Puerto Rico and US Virgin Islands.

Table 3. HIV Summary Statistics, Cumulative US (as of 12/31/03)*

	UNITED STATES	
	# OF CASES	
NO. ADULT/ADOLESCENT CASES	216,486	
NO. PEDIATRIC CASES (<13 years)	4,579	
TOTAL CASES	221,065	
EXPOSURE CATEGORY (ADULTS)	# OF CASES	% OF TOTAL
MALE TO MALE CONTACT	72,745	34%
INJECTION DRUG USER (IDU)	31,133	14%
MALE TO MALE CONTACT / IDU	8,623	4%
HEMOPHILIAC	584	0%
HETEROSEXUAL CONTACT	41,152	19%
TRANSFUSION RELATED	1,016	0%
NONE OF THE ABOVE	61,233	28%
RACE/ETHNICITY (ALL CASES)****	# OF CASES	% OF TOTAL
WHITE (NON-HISPANIC)	76,354	35%
BLACK (NON-HISPANIC)	106,383	48%
HISPANIC	29,595	13%
OTHER/UNKNOWN	2,310	1%
SEX (ADULTS ONLY)	# OF CASES	% OF TOTAL
MALE	152,739	71%
FEMALE	63,740	29%

*Source: CDC HIV/AIDS Surveillance Report, Volume 15. CDC has published updated cumulative U.S. HIV case reports as of 12/31/04 of 227,081 Adults/Adolescents and 4,858 Peds <13 years old, Total 231,939. Breakdown of 2004 U.S. cases by Exposure Category, Race/Ethnicity and Sex are not yet available.

Data only from those states where HIV is reportable. Includes only persons reported with HIV infection who have not developed AIDS.

**** US race total does not include Pediatric cases (n=9,348).

Other races include Asian/Pacific Islander or American Indian/Alaska Native, Native Hawaiian, Multiracial or Other race.

Table 4. Reported HIV Cases by State (as of December 2004)*

REPORTING STATE (DATE OF HIV REPORTING)	ADULT/ADOLESCENT # OF CASES	% OF TOTAL	CHILDREN # OF CASES	% OF TOTAL
FLORIDA (July 1997)	33,016	15%	335	7%
LOUISIANA (Feb 1993)	7,963	4%	138	3%
NEW JERSEY (Jan 1992)	16,287	7%	432	9%
NEW YORK (Dec 2000)	37,191	16%	1,893	39%
NORTH CAROLINA (Feb 1990)	12,268	5%	132	3%
OHIO (June 1990)	7,679	3%	95	2%
SOUTH CAROLINA (Feb 1986)	6,946	3%	93	2%
TENNESSEE (Jan 1992)	6,810	3%	89	2%
TEXAS (Feb 1994)	20,570	9%	393	8%
VIRGINIA (July 1989)	9,139	4%	88	2%
REMAINDER OF U.S.**	69,212	30%	1,170	24%
TOTAL CASES	227,081	100%	4,858	100%

*Source: Statistics and Management Branch, DHIV/AIDS, CDC. Data provisional.
**Remainder of States where HIV is reportable as of 12/02: Alabama, Alaska, Arizona, Arkansas, Colorado, Idaho, Indiana, Iowa, Kansas, Michigan, Minnesota, Mississippi, Missouri, Nebraska, Nevada, New Mexico, North Dakota, Oklahoma, South Dakota, Utah, W. Virginia, Wisconsin and Wyoming.
Connecticut has confidential HIV infection reporting for pediatric cases only. Washington reports symptomatic infection and name-to-code-based system.
California, District of Columbia, Hawaii, Illinois, Kentucky, Maryland, Massachusetts, Rhode Island and Vermont report HIV on a code-based system. Delaware, Maine Montana, and Oregon report on a name-to-code-based system. New Hampshire has other type of reporting.
Includes only persons reported with HIV infection who have not developed AIDS.

References

1. Joint United Nations Programme on HIV/AIDS and World Health Organization, AIDS epidemic update, December 2004.

2. Glynn M, Rhodes P. Estimated HIV prevalence in the United States at the end of 2003. National HIV Prevention Conference; June 2005; Atlanta. Abstract 595.

3. CDC: *HIV/AIDS Surveillance Report*, 2003 (Vol. 15). Atlanta: US Department of Health and Human Services, CDC; 2004:1–46. Available at http://www.cdc.gov/hiv/stats/2003surveillanceReport.pdf.

2

HIV Testing

Berry Bennett, MPH
Retrovirology Administrator
Florida Bureau of Laboratories, Jacksonville

Introduction

Since its widespread introduction in 1985, HIV testing is perhaps most associated with antibody testing, either for serostatus determinations or for screening blood and tissue donations. Clearly, HIV testing began and remains today the protector of our nation's blood supply as well as the overseer of the HIV pandemic. While these applications are still essential, HIV testing is now used to determine incidence (recent seroconversions), used in rapid test formats, and potentially as a tool for acute infection detection. In addition to antibody detection, HIV testing also includes a number of HIV disease management assays used in disease prognosis or to monitor and optimize an HIV patient's antiretroviral therapy.

HIV disease management assays are designed for use with HIV positive individuals after the diagnosis is confirmed.

The following is a brief description of HIV testing technology available in most clinical and reference laboratory settings. It is not meant to be a comprehensive listing of all technologies commercially available. The guide is intended to broaden one's base knowledge, aid in laboratory requests, and to theorize about future developments.

Diagnostic Tests

ENZYME IMMUNOASSAY (EIA) OR ENZYME-LINKED IMMUNOSORBENT ASSAY (ELISA)

- To date, the EIA format is still the primary HIV antibody screening test. Most of these assays are laboratory-based and have a Clinical Laboratory Improvement Amendment (CLIA) complexity status of moderately complex.
- Several assays are FDA approved and available for clinical samples such as human sera, plasma, dried blood spots, cadaveric serum, oral fluids, and urine.
- Assays are available to assess HIV-1 and HIV-2 separately or in combination. The assays on the market today are considered 3rd generation and perform well in detecting the majority of the HIV-1

Group M (Major) subtypes. In addition, several HIV-1 and HIV-1/2 screening assays have added antigenic proteins to detect HIV-1 Group O (Outlier) antibodies.

- These assays have a high degree of sensitivity and specificity.
- The EIA itself has evolved over the past 19 years. The original assays were whole viral lysates, incorporating all of the viral antigenic proteins on a reaction surface. Some are still used today; however, assays that incorporate a recombinant and/or synthetic peptide antigenic matrix have a broader utility.
- The EIA technology of today has increased specificity without compromising sensitivity. This aspect greatly reduces false positive screenings. Future EIAs are expected to continue sensitivity and specificity enhancements drawing near to the sensitivity and specificity associated with molecular testing.

Supplemental Testing in the Confirmation Process

WESTERN BLOT AND IMMUNOFLUORESCENT ANTIBODY ASSAY (IFA)

- The historic standard of practice for HIV diagnostic testing involves a confirmation test on non-negative screenings.
- This is sometimes referred to as supplemental testing in the confirmation process.
  - The Western Blot and the IFA are considered supplemental assays and are suitable for this confirmation process.
  - Currently only one HIV-1 IFA assay is FDA approved for diagnostic use.
  - IFA use is minimal in reference and state laboratories; however, it is a common support assay in the HIV home collection kit market.
  - The Western Blot procedure is the most recognized confirmation assay.
  - There are currently 2 manufacturers with FDA-approved blots for human sera/plasma/dried blood spots. There is also one Western Blot in the US approved for oral fluid testing, and one for urine testing.
  - Western Blot and IFA assays generally have a higher degree of specificity than EIAs.
  - The major problems with these assays are their subjective interpretations and a window period as seen with any antibody detection assay.

Figure 1. Synthetic Peptide or Recombinant HIV-1/2 Testing Algorithm

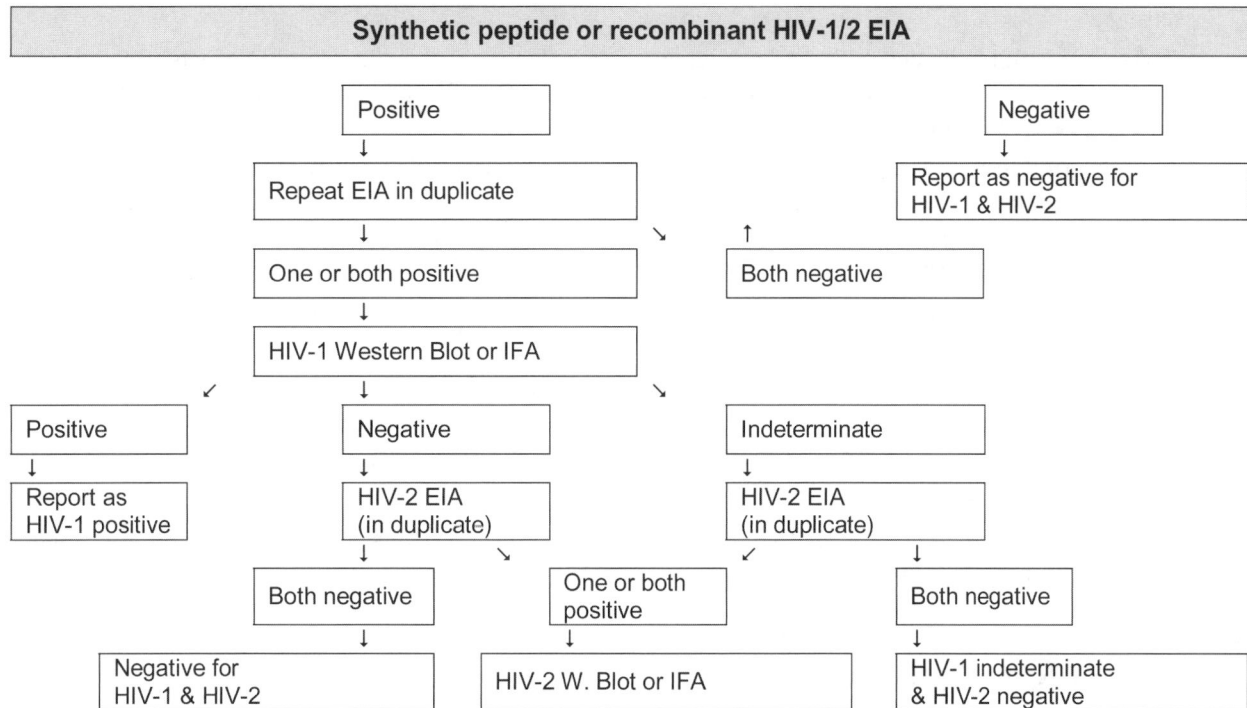

Synthetic peptide or recombinant HIV-1/2 EIA

Positive → Repeat EIA in duplicate → One or both positive → HIV-1 Western Blot or IFA

Negative → Report as negative for HIV-1 & HIV-2

Both negative →

From HIV-1 Western Blot or IFA:
- Positive → Report as HIV-1 positive
- Negative → HIV-2 EIA (in duplicate)
- Indeterminate → HIV-2 EIA (in duplicate)

HIV-2 EIA (in duplicate) [Negative branch]:
- Both negative → Negative for HIV-1 & HIV-2
- One or both positive → HIV-2 W. Blot or IFA

HIV-2 EIA (in duplicate) [Indeterminate branch]:
- Both negative → HIV-1 indeterminate & HIV-2 negative

QUALITATIVE POLYMERASE CHAIN REACTION (PCR)

- A procedure that is rapidly becoming more acceptable in reference laboratory settings is the qualitative PCR (Polymerase Chain Reaction). Availability, however, is sometimes difficult.
  - Qualitative PCR is not FDA approved for diagnostic use.
  - PCR has the capability to significantly reduce the pro-viral window period associated with antibody testing from approximately 22 days to 12 days.
  - Because it is a nucleic acid amplification test, it has a high degree of specificity.
  - At present, qualitative PCR is primarily used in occupational exposure incidents, resolving multiple indeterminate HIV antibody status, and with suspected perinatal transmission cases.
- In March 2002, the FDA approved a nucleic acid test (NAT) to detect HIV RNA and HCV RNA in pooled donor samplings, for use in US blood centers. The eventual mandatory use of this assay will sharply reduce or eliminate the need for p24 Antigen testing on blood donations. In November 2002, the blood centers were allowed to use a discriminatory HIV (dHIV) NAT test. It is anticipated that one, if not both, of these assays will eventually become available outside the blood bank setting. In July 2004, the CDC funded several studies to determine the performance and feasibility in conducting pooled NAT testing in public health populations, resulting data to be available in 12 to 18 months.

ALTERNATIVE FLUID TESTING

- Recent introduction of alternative fluids as suitable samples has allowed testing to go beyond a clinic setting.
    - Oral fluid (mucosal transudate) testing is a valuable tool for outreach projects. At present, there is only one FDA approved oral fluid EIA (12/1994) and one FDA approved oral fluid Western Blot (6/1996) for diagnostic use.
    - Urine testing is commonly used in the insurance market. At present, there is only one FDA approved urine EIA (8/1996) and one FDA approved urine Western Blot (5/1998) for diagnostic use. Calypte Biomedical is the sole manufacturer of these urine-based HIV-1 diagnostic assays.
    - These alternative fluid assays capture IgG antibodies as do traditional samples (blood and dried blood spots).
    - The noninvasive sample collection of oral fluid and urine prove to be assets of this technology.
    - Both alternative fluids tend to decrease the chance of occupational exposure among health care workers.
    - At present, these alternative fluid EIAs and Western Blots are not approved for donor screening.

RAPID HIV ANTIBODY DETECTION

- Perhaps the diagnostic service of the future will be rapid HIV antibody detection.
- Rapid HIV antibody detection is a generic term for assays capable of yielding a result in usually 40 minutes or less.
- These assays usually incorporate recombinant or synthetic peptide antigenic proteins in a self-contained testing device
- Two (2) formats are commonly used in rapid test designs:
    - Immunoconcentration devices — sometimes referred to as flow through, patient's sample and reagents pass through an antigenic matrix from top to bottom.
    - Immunochromatographic strip devices — sometimes referred to as lateral flow, patient's samples and reagents pass over the antigenic matrix via capillary action.
- These devices are safe, easy to use, and easy to interpret in most cases.
- At present, these devices are designed for serum, plasma, finger-stick whole blood, and oral fluid samples.
- Currently there are 2 rapid assays in the U.S. approved for diagnostic use **with** a CLIA complexity level of **waived**, OraQuick ADVANCE HIV-1/2 (2/2003) and Uni-Gold Recombigen HIV (7/2004). This is significant in that it allows testing to be performed in non-traditional settings by a wider range of health care professionals, as long as specific training and quality assurance measures are observed. The waived status **does not** allow these assays to be a home test. Also, 2 rapid assays (SUDS, 5/1992 & Reveal, 4/2003) are FDA approved for diagnostic use with a CLIA complexity level of **moderately complex**. The latter assays are restricted for use in CLIA certified laboratories. In addition to these 4 assays, several national and international clinical trials are underway that may yield numerous other assays for use in the next couple of years.
- These assays will be instrumental in occupational exposure incidents, in the labor and delivery setting without documented HIV status, outreach, and in clinics with poor client return rates.

- At present, ONLY the OraQuick rapid test is approved for alternative fluids, specifically oral fluids, in addition to its serum, plasma, and whole blood claim. A specific script is required to report positive results from a CLIA waived rapid test and to initiate collection of an additional specimen for traditional supplemental testing. Please refer to the latest edition of Counseling and Testing guidelines and state policies.

HOME COLLECTION KIT

At present, HIV testing is **not** an at home process. The closest procedure to this at home concept is a home collection kit that is commercially available and FDA approved as a "Testing Service" (7/1996). It amounts to a self-dried blood spot collection by the user and submission to a specific testing facility via mail or courier service. There is only one market source to date for this service. Testing proves to be reliable and results are relayed to the anonymous user by telephone, after the user initiates the request.

P24 ANTIGEN

- P24 Antigen testing has been a component of the blood bank algorithm since 1996.
- It was implemented in conjunction with the antibody assays in an effort to close the pro-viral window period by approximately 6–7 days.
- Antigen tests are designed to detect free, non-complexed, HIV antigens in peripheral blood.
- Because of less than desired sensitivity, it is unclear if this assay will remain in most algorithms when NAT becomes more common and accepted. Blood bank centers are already beginning to replace p24 antigen testing with NAT.
- The assay is available through most reference laboratories.
- A new procedure has been developed that incorporates p24 antigenic proteins into a real-time Immuno-PCR process. Investigators anticipate the research-based assay may detect HIV-1 viral loads as low as 2 RNA copies/ml blood. The assay remains under investigation and is not FDA approved at this time.

CULTURE

- Culture is still available through some commercial reference laboratories.
- Culture is costly and time consuming; however, its value is extremely important in phenotypic evaluations.

HIV Disease Management Testing (Also see Chapter 4, Initial Encounter and Subsequent Visits and Chapter 5, Antiretroviral Therapy)

IMMUNOPHENOTYPING (CD4/CD8 EVALUATION)

- For many years the only assessments of an HIV/AIDS patient's prognosis or therapeutic efficacy were the clinical condition and CD4/CD8 values from flow cytometry
- CD4/CD8 absolute counts, ratios, and percentages of total lymphocytes continue to play a major role in disease management.
- It is important to realize that CD4/CD8 testing is not a diagnostic tool for HIV, it is considered to be a marker test only. However, absolute CD4+ cell counts of < 200 cells/mm^3 or < 14% meet the definition of AIDS (class 3).

- Flow Cytometry is the most common method to achieve this assessment; however, the FDA has approved 2 alternative methods commonly referred to as single platform methods. These methods demonstrate excellent correlation to Flow Cytometry, are easy to use, and are less expensive.

PLASMA HIV RNA –VIRAL LOAD

- A viral load assessment is a generic term for an HIV RNA quantitative test, or plasma HIV RNA
- There are generally 2 formats: target amplification and signal amplification. Each format has good performance data. However, it is recommended that a patient's continued viral load testing be measured using one format only. Quantitative values of target versus signal do not necessarily correlate, especially at lower detection limits.
- Currently, 2 target amplification procedures (Amplicor Monitor, 3/1999 and Nuclisens QT, 11/2001) and one signal amplification procedure (Quantiplex bDNA, 9/2002) are FDA approved for viral load monitoring.
- Viral loads are normally reported as number of HIV RNA copies/mL of peripheral blood.
- Clinical guidelines concerning initial therapy, change of therapy, etc. are based in most part on sequential viral load results. Generally, significant changes must be $\geq$ 3-fold or $\geq$ 0.5 log_{10} RNA from baseline or previous test.
- Most reference laboratories and some clinical laboratories have the capability to perform viral loads.

GENOTYPING AND PHENOTYPING (See Chapter 8, Antiretroviral Resistance Testing and Therapeutic Drug Monitoring)

Antiretroviral resistance testing is the STANDARD OF CARE in the management of HIV infected individuals. Clearly, the disease management assays that are receiving the most attention today are HIV genotyping, phenotyping, and "virtual phenotyping." The growing numbers of single and multi-drug resistant strains of HIV has accented the need for these assays. In addition to the clinical significance, these assays are becoming a valuable public health instrument in monitoring the prevalence of non-wild type transmission among drug naïve patients as well as HIV-1 subtype (clade) identifications.

Chapter 8 provides more details as to why resistance develops the clinical advantages and disadvantages of resistance testing, as well as interpretational support. The Department of Health and Human Services (DHHS) established guidelines for the use of resistance testing in February 2002 (updated March 23, 2004). This information is available at http://www.aidsinfo.nih.gov.

Table 1. Genotyping vs. Phenotyping

Genotyping	• **Genotyping** is a nucleic acid mapping of specific regions of the HIV genome. There are extensive databases that demonstrate relationships between certain amino acid codon locations and resistance to a particular antiretroviral drug. • Genotyping is essentially an extraction of HIV RNA combined with qualitative RT-PCR procedure and carried onto protease and reverse transcriptase sequencing. • At present, 2 HIV-1 Genotyping kit procedures are FDA approved for patient monitoring. • Due to the complexity of the genotyping procedure, only large reference laboratories, hospitals, and some public health laboratories are performing it routinely.
Phenotyping	• Phenotype is the *in vitro* manifestation of a particular HIV-1 genetic makeup (genotype). • **Phenotyping** is the process of evaluating the numerous antiretroviral drugs against a particular HIV genotype in an *in vitro* environment. The significance of this is that phenotypic assessments opposed to any other assay are most closely associated to the actual conditions within each infected patient. • Because of the extensive culturing and drug sensitivity aspects, phenotyping is expensive and time consuming. • The procedure is usually a contracted service offered by some of the larger commercial reference laboratories. • There is currently no FDA-approved phenotypic procedure. • Because of the high costs associated with traditional phenotyping, one commercial laboratory is marketing a service called the **virtual phenotype.** It is a comparison of a specific genotype to a large database of historical genotype-phenotype results. NOTE: a virtual phenotype is not a phenotype.

References

1. Carpenter CJ, Fischl MA, et al. Antiretroviral therapy for HIV infection in 1998: Updated recommendations of the International AIDS Society – USA Panel. *JAMA* 1998; 280:78–86.

2. CDC. HIV counseling, testing and referral—standards and guidelines. Atlanta: CDC, Revised, November 9, 2001: 50(RR19);1–58.

3. CDC. Interpretation and use of the Western Blot assay for serodiagnosis of human immunodeficiency virus type 1 infections. *MMWR* 1989; 38(Supp 7): S4–S6.

4. CDC. Public health service guidelines for counseling and antibody testing to prevent HIV infection and AIDS. *MMWR* 1987; 36:509–515.

5. CDC. Technical guidance on HIV counseling. *MMWR* 1993; 40(RR-2).

6. CDC. Update: HIV counseling and testing using rapid tests—United States, 1995. *MMWR* 1998; 47:211-215.

7. Elbeik T, Charlebois E, Nassos PI, Kahn J, Hecht R, Ng V, Yajko D, Hadley K. Evaluation of clinical performance and cost comparison of Bayer Diagnostics and Roche Diagnostics HIV-1 viral load testing methods. Poster presentation: APHL Conference on Human Retrovirus Testing. 1999; Albuquerque, New Mexico.

8. Fredrichs RR, Hatoon MT, Eskes N, Lewin S. Comparison of saliva and serum for HIV surveillance in developing countries. *Lancet* 1992; 340:1496–1499.

9. Hirsch MS, Conway B, et al. Antiretroviral drug resistance testing in adults with HIV infection. *JAMA* 1996; 279:1984–1991.

10. Joint United Nations Programme on HIV/AIDS. The importance of simple/rapid assays in HIV testing. *Wkly Epidemiol Rec* 1998; 73:321–328.

11. Nolte FS, Boysza J, Thurmond C, Clark WS, Lennox JL. Clinical comparison of an enhanced-sensitivity branched-DNA assay and reverse transcription-PCR for quantitation of HIV Type 1 RNA in plasma. *J Clin Microbiology* 1998; 36(3):716–720.

12. Florida Medicaid. Antiretroviral Resistance Testing, Standards for Medicaid Reimbursement. Available at: http://www.fdhc.state.fl.us. Accessed October 25, 2004

13. Panel on Clinical Practices for Treatment of HIV Infection for DHHS and Kaiser Family Foundation. Guidelines for the Use of Antiretroviral Agents in HIV-Infected Adults and Adolescents. February 4, 2002. Available at: http://www.dhhs.gov. Accessed October 25, 2004.

14. FDA. Licensed/Approved HIV, HTLV and Hepatitis Tests. Available at: http://www.fda.gov/cber/products/testkits. Accessed October 25, 2004.

15. D'Aquila RT, Schapiro JM, et al. Drug Resistance Mutations in HIV-1. Available at: http://www.resistance@iasusa.org. Accessed October 25, 2004.

16. Medmira. Press release – Reveal HIV-1 rapid test. Available at: http://www.medmira.com. Accessed October 25, 2004.

17. OraSure Technologies. [Press release—October 20, 2004] OraQuick HIV-1 rapid test. Available at: www.orasure.com.

18. Gen-Probe, Inc. [Press release—November 20, 2002] FDA Approves Expanded Uses for Gen-Probe's HIV-1/HCV Assay. Available at: http://www.gen-probe.com. Accessed October 25, 2004.

19. Trinity Biotech, [Press Release—June 30, 2004] Uni-Gold Recombigen HIV Test. Available at: http://www.trinitybiotech.com. Accessed October 25, 2004.

3

Pathophysiology of HIV Infection

Jeffrey P. Nadler, MD, FACP
Professor of Medicine
University of South Florida College of Medicine, Tampa

Introduction

An understanding of the pathophysiology of HIV infection is important in order to appreciate how the virus targets the immune system and causes damage that may become sufficiently severe to result in clinical illness, defined as AIDS in its most advanced stage. It also explains the dynamics of viral reproduction and thus the need for continuous potent suppressive antiviral therapy. Finally, HIV pathophysiology explains where and how antiviral agents work.

Course of HIV Infection

The most common mode of transmission of HIV involves deposition of HIV on mucosal surfaces, especially the genital mucosa and intestinal epithelium. Direct inoculation into the blood through intravenous (IV) needle sharing is also a common mode of HIV transmission. Following successful transmission of HIV from one individual to another, the course of subsequent infection is quite variable and dependent on a number of factors. These factors include characteristics unique to the virus itself as well as a variety of cellular immune responses and other features of the host. Despite this variability, a common pattern of HIV disease development has been recognized to occur in individuals in whom no specific therapeutic intervention is implemented. Acute or primary HIV infection (PHI) is followed by a variable period of time during which viral replication persists and an inexorable progressive immunologic decline results. Throughout most of this period, the patient may be entirely asymptomatic. However, the end result of consequent immunologic deterioration is a state of profound immune suppression that renders the infected individual susceptible to a multitude of opportunistic infections and malignancies. The magnitude of ongoing viral replication during the aforementioned clinically quiescent phase is the primary determinant of the length of time necessary to progress from acute HIV infection to AIDS. Thus, the course of HIV infection in the untreated individual can be viewed as a spectrum of disease progressing through various stages. The initial acute infection usually is followed by an asymptomatic stage of variable duration before culminating in symptomatic disease or AIDS.

ACUTE OR PRIMARY HIV INFECTION

Up to 70% of patients with primary HIV infection develop an acute mononucleosis-like syndrome that usually occurs within 2 to 6 weeks following initial infection.[1] Also known as the acute retroviral syndrome (ARS), these signs and symptoms occur as a result of initial infection and dispersion of HIV, and consist of a typical, though non-descript, clinical syndrome. The manifestations are protean, but most commonly include fever, fatigue, myalgias, rash, lymphadenopathy, headache, and sore throat[2] (see Table 1). "Cold" symptoms such as runny or stuffy nose are conspicuously absent, helping to differentiate ARS from influenza or other viral respiratory conditions. Duration of this stage is usually less than 14 days but may become protracted, lasting several weeks or even months. Severe and prolonged illness has been correlated with more rapid disease progression and hence a worse prognosis.[3,4] Because of important prognostic and therapeutic implications, a possible diagnosis of acute HIV infection should be entertained in any patient presenting with a mononucleosis-like syndrome, especially if risk factors for acquisition of the virus are present. Appropriate patient exposure history and diagnostic tests should therefore be obtained in this setting. HIV infection should also be considered in any patient presenting with a sexually transmitted disease.

Table 1. Clinical Manifestations of the Acute Retroviral Syndrome

SYMPTOMS	PHYSICAL EXAM FINDINGS	LABORATORY ABNORMALITIES
Fever	Lymphadenopathy	Leukopenia
Fatigue	Pharyngitis, with or without exudates	Elevated hepatic transaminases
Headache	Rash, usually maculopapular	Cerebrospinal fluid pleocytosis consistent with aseptic meningitis
Diarrhea	Thrush	
Nausea and vomiting	Hepatosplenomegaly	
Weight loss	Oral ulcers	
Neurologic symptoms	Genital ulcers	
Sore throat		
Myalgias		
Arthralgias		
Night sweats		

Asymptomatic HIV Disease

Following acute HIV infection with viral dissemination and the subsequent appearance of HIV-specific immune responses, the infected individual enters into a second stage of infection. This phase may or may not be completely asymptomatic depending upon a number of factors. The term clinical "latency" has been used previously to designate this stage of disease. However, this terminology is not entirely accurate since a true stage of latency, where viral replication is temporarily halted, is never really attained[5]. Instead, replication of virions continues unabated in various tissue compartments while a progressive depletion of CD4+ lymphocytes ensues. The rate of progression of this immunologic decline is dependent in large part on the effectiveness of the initial host response to contain the infection. Following an initial drop in plasma viremia that occurs, a virologic *set-point* is established for a given individual. This viral load may remain fairly constant for several years following initial infection. Persons with the highest viral loads sustain the most rapid rates of progression to symptomatic disease and clinical AIDS[6]. Thus, viral load is one of the principal determinants of duration of this stage of illness (See Figure 1).

Figure 1: Likelihood of Developing AIDS by 3 Years After Becoming Infected with HIV Type 1

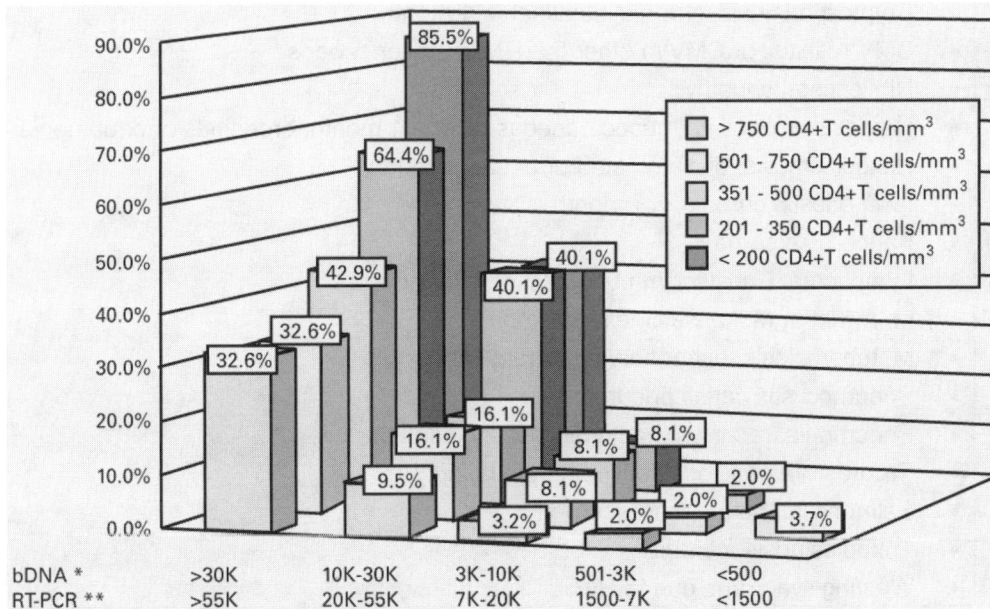

Plasma Viral Load (copies/mL, thousands)
*b-deoxyribonuceic acid
**Reverse transcriptase-polymerase chain reaction

Source: Mellors JW, Munoz A, Gigorgi JV, et al. Plasma viral load and CD4+ cell lymphocytes as prognostic markers of HIV-1 infection. Ann Intern Med 1997;126(12):946-954[7]

Symptomatic HIV Disease or Acquired Immunodeficiency Syndrome

As a consequence of the inevitable deterioration of the immune system, the infected individual suffers from immunologic dysregulation. The end result is vulnerability to a diverse array of opportunistic infections and neoplasms as well as an increased incidence of immune-mediated diseases. Autoimmune phenomena include HIV-associated thrombocytopenia and HIV nephropathy. These disease manifestations may occur at any point following acute infection and prior to significant CD4+ lymphocyte depletion. They are thought to occur as a result of disordered B-cell regulation since B-lymphocytes are highly dependent on immunocompetent inducer T-lymphocytes for their proper function. Improperly activated B-cells synthesize and release large quantities of nonfunctional immunoglobulins with a resultant increase in immunologic sequelae. However, the majority of problems related to HIV infection occur as a direct result of the loss of cell-mediated immunity that accompanies the destruction of CD4+ helper T-lymphocytes. Individuals who experience declines in their CD4+ cell counts to fewer than 200 cells/mm^3 are designated as having AIDS, even in the absence of any AIDS-defining illness (see Table 2). This designation reflects the increased likelihood of HIV-related problems that accompany progressively lower CD4+ cell counts. Once AIDS develops, the immune system is sufficiently compromised that the patient is unable to control infections with opportunistic pathogens that would normally not proliferate, and also becomes vulnerable to the development of several malignancies and other conditions that define clinical AIDS (Table 2). If untreated, the average patient with AIDS dies within one to three years.

Table 2. 1993 Revised CDC Case Definitions of AIDS-Defining Illnesses

Source: *MMWR* 41(RR-17); December 18, 1992

- Candidiasis: esophageal, tracheal, or bronchial
- Coccidiomycosis, extrapulmonary
- Cryptococcosis, extrapulmonary
- Cervical cancer, invasive
- Cryptosporidiosis, chronic intestinal (> 1 month)
- CMV retinitis, or CMV in other than liver, spleen, nodes
- HIV encephalopathy
- Herpes simplex with mucocutaneous ulcer > 1 month, bronchitis or pneumonia
- Histoplasmosis: disseminated or extrapulmonary
- Isosporiasis, chronic, > 1 month
- Kaposi's sarcoma
- Lymphoma: Burkitt's, immunoblastic, primary in brain
- M. avium or M. kansasii, extrapulmonary
- M. tuberculosis, pulmonary or extrapulmonary
- Pneumocystis carinii pneumonia
- Pneumonia, recurrent bacterial (≥ 2 episodes per year)
- Progressive multifocal leukoencephalopathy
- Salmonella bacteremia, recurrent
- Toxoplasmosis, cerebral
- Wasting syndrome due to HIV

There is a strong correlation between the absolute or percentage CD4+ lymphocyte counts and the risk of various infections. For example, non-specific symptoms such as lymphadenopathy, fever, night sweats, and intermittent diarrhea often occur when the CD4+ count declines below normal levels ($\sim$ < 500 cells/mm^3). Oral candidiasis, bacterial pneumonias, tuberculosis, and non-Hodgkin's lymphomas are first clinically recognized with increasing frequency at CD4+ counts of 200–350 cells/mm^3. *Pneumocystis* pneumonia (PCP), caused by *Pneumocystis jiroveci (formerly Pneumocystis carinii)* is most commonly seen with CD4+ counts < 150–200 cells/mm^3. Fungal esophagitis, cryptococcal meningitis, and disseminated endemic fungal diseases usually occur at counts < 100 cells/mm^3, while disseminated mycobacterial and cytomegalovirus infection usually do not become clinically apparent until CD4+ counts fall to less than 50 cells/mm^3. In general, the more profound the degree of immunosuppression, the more susceptible a given individual becomes to different infectious or neoplastic diseases. Unless treatment is initiated prior to this development, the infected host will usually succumb to one or more of these pathologic processes.

Currently available therapies have significantly altered the prognosis for HIV-infected patients and the overall course of HIV infection.[8] Adequate viral suppression facilitates some degree of immune reconstitution[9] and/or prevents progression of disease. Depending on when in the course of infection the diagnosis is made and therapy initiated, additional life expectancy may be as long as 36 or more years, which can be very close to normal.[10] An appreciation of how antiretroviral therapy has revolutionized HIV management and the course of disease may only be gained by first acquiring a thorough understanding of some of the structural aspects of the virus itself, and the pathogenesis of HIV infection.

Structural composition and genomic organization of the HIV virion

HIV virions consist of an inner nucleoprotein core surrounded by an outer envelope which in turn is composed of a lipid bilayer studded along its surface by the 2 major viral envelope proteins, gp 120 and gp 41.[11] The outer membrane proteins are primarily responsible for mediating binding to the CD4+ cells and chemokine receptors, which is an essential step to membrane fusion and resultant infectivity. This process is the target of an approved drug and numerous investigational agents. The viral core is comprised of 2 copies of single-stranded genomic RNA and several proteins involved in the process of viral replication. These proteins include the p24 capsid protein, the p17 matrix protein, and the p6 and p7 nucleocapsid proteins. The matrix protein essentially lines the inner surface of the lipid bilayer and probably plays an important role in maintaining structural integrity of the virion. The capsid protein surrounds the inner core of the virion forming a shell around the genomic material. Within this shell are found the nucleocapsid proteins, which are bound directly to the RNA molecules, along with several enzymes that participate in replication of the virus, including reverse transcriptase, integrase, and protease.[12]

HIV is a member of the Lentivirinae subfamily of retroviruses. Notable characteristics of this subfamily of viruses include their predilection to cause hematopoietic and nervous system involvement, their capacity to cause immune suppression and autoimmunity, host species specificity, their ability to cause persistent viremia, and their association with a stage of clinical latency.[13,14] Several other lentiviruses exist, most of them causing various clinical syndromes in animals. The one most similar to HIV is the simian immunodeficiency virus (SIV). This virus is capable of causing an AIDS-like illness in monkeys and has been used in animal studies to gain insight into the pathogenesis of HIV infection.

Complexity of the viral genome is a distinguishing feature of the lentiviruses. While most retroviruses contain at least 3 genes, *gag, pol,* and *env*, the lentiviruses contain an additional six genes (*vif, vpu, vpr, tat, rev,* and *nef*). *Gag* codes for the core proteins whereas *env* codes for the envelope proteins. *Pol* encodes the major enzymes involved in viral replication, reverse transcriptase, protease, and integrase. It is these enzymes that serve as the primary targets at which most currently available and investigational antiretroviral agents have been aimed. The remainder of the above genes found in the HIV genome are translated into proteins that perform a variety of functions, such as promotion and enhancement of viral infectivity, or the degradation and down-regulation of CD4 receptors that is necessary for efficient virion budding.

Pathogenesis of HIV infection

Transmission and early pathogenesis of infection

Although HIV can be transmitted in a number of ways, the most common mode is sexual transmission across the genital mucosa.[15] Whether or not successful transmission of the virus occurs is highly dependent on the viral load of the infected individual. Indeed, the chief predictor of the risk of heterosexual transmission of HIV is the viral load.[16] Once the virus is transmitted to a non-infected host, a transient high level viremia develops[17,18] during which the virus becomes widely disseminated throughout the body.[19] Within one week to three months after infection, an HIV-specific cellular immune response is initiated. This response is associated with a marked decline in levels of plasma viremia and temporally corresponds to the onset of symptoms of acute HIV infection. It is felt that many of the symptoms of acute HIV infection may be related to this virally directed immune response.[20] These symptoms usually resolve as the level of plasma viremia decreases. During this initial stage, viral replication is partially attenuated by these HIV-specific immune responses, but is never completely interrupted and remains detectable in various tissue compartments, especially lymphoid tissue.[21]

When HIV is introduced onto a mucosal surface, it attaches to CD4+ T-lymphocytes or macrophages (or dendritic cells in the skin). Studies in Rhesus monkeys acutely infected with the simian immunodeficiency virus have allowed scientists to glean important insights into the pathogenesis of early infection.[22] Following sexual transmission of the virus across the genital mucosa, it appears from these studies that the earliest cellular targets of the virus are tissue dendritic cells (also known as Langerhans' cells) found within the cervicovaginal epithelium. These dendritic cells subsequently fuse with CD4+ lymphocytes that in turn migrate via regional lymphatics to draining lymph nodes. Within only a few days of transportation to these regional lymph nodes, hematogenous dissemination and seeding of various tissue compartments ensues. Lymph nodes throughout the body or their tissue equivalent (such as Peyer's patches in the intestine) will eventually harbor the virus.

Alternatively, HIV may be introduced directly into the bloodstream and filtered through regional lymph nodes. The virus reproduces in the lymph nodes and progeny are released. Some of the progeny viruses may bind to and infect adjacent CD4+ T-lymphocytes; others may bind to follicular dendritic cells in the lymph nodes, from which location they may be presented to circulating cells with appropriate receptors. The receptor is the CD4 helper/inducer T-lymphocyte receptor. Viral entry is complex, and is described below in the discussion of the viral life cycle.

Figure 2 – The Life Cycle of HIV

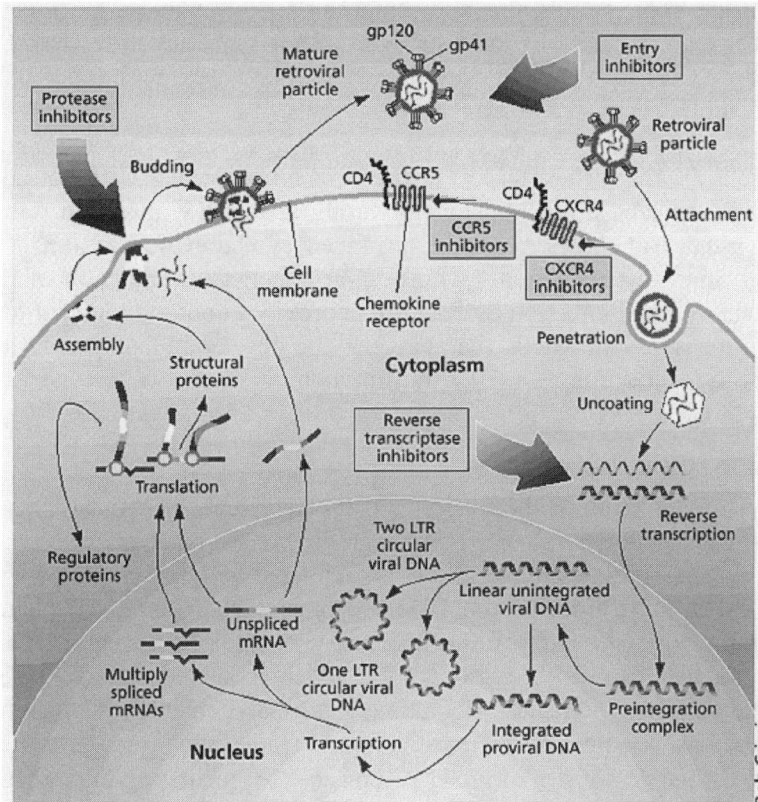

LIFE CYCLE OF HIV (See Figure 2)

It is important to review the life cycle of HIV in order to understand some of the approaches to therapy and the remaining challenges, such as dealing with integrated pro-virus. Before HIV can cause infection, free virions must first bind to a receptor and then penetrate into the host cell. After internalization of the HIV virion is complete, the HIV RNA is then converted into a complementary DNA copy with the help of the enzyme, *reverse transcriptase*. This DNA is then incorporated into the host cell genome to make use of that cell's genetic machinery in replicating itself and in manufacturing new virions capable of infecting other cells.

Attachment of the HIV virion to specific receptors

Initial HIV infection occurs when the virion binds to a specific combination of receptors located on the host cell. CD4+ lymphocytes and macrophages serve as the primary cellular targets of HIV[23]. In this setting, CD4, which is primarily concentrated on T-lymphocytes, acts as a receptor that preferentially binds to the gp120 surface envelope protein[24]. However, the recognition that some CD4+ monocytes were not susceptible to HIV infection[25] led investigators to postulate the existence of some other cell surface factor necessary for virus entry. It soon became evident that binding of gp120 to CD4 by itself was insufficient to result in viral penetration[26]. Subsequent investigations revealed that in order for cell entry to occur, a secondary receptor or coreceptor was required[27]. In this regard, several of the chemokine receptors, especially the CCR5 and CXCR4 receptors, have been implicated as the facilitating secondary receptors permitting the viral entry process. The chemokines are a family of cellular signaling proteins, universally present in humans, but with sufficient polymorphisms to perhaps explain in part the differential propensity to infection between individuals. Identification of these chemokine receptors as cofactors for viral entry improved our understanding of this process as well as the concept of cellular tropism[28,29,30,31].

Both macrophage-tropic and T-cell tropic viruses exist, each requiring a different surface chemokine receptor. For macrophage-tropic strains, this coreceptor is CCR5,[32] whereas for T-cell tropic strains it is CXCR4.[33] Viruses that require CCR5 as their surface chemokine receptor are termed R5 viruses while viral strains that need CXCR4 for viral entry are known as X4 viruses. Both types of viruses are capable of infecting and replicating in activated primary CD4+ T-cells.

Tissue dendritic cells are the earliest targets of the virus and express CCR5 but not always CXCR4.[34] R5 viruses are the predominant strain transmitted during acute HIV infection. However, later in the course of infection, usually in the presence of advanced symptomatic disease, X4 strains are more common.[35] The observation that individuals who bear a homozygous mutation of the gene coding for CCR5 are very resistant to initial infection by R5 viruses provides important insight into the essential role of CCR5 in HIV transmission. Ultimately, therapies may be developed that attempt to block chemokine function and thus help to reduce or prevent HIV transmission.

Internalization of the HIV virion

Following attachment of the virus to the target cell, the viral envelope must then fuse with the cell membrane of the host cell to allow viral entry. Although the precise mechanisms involved in this process remain incompletely understood, membrane fusion is facilitated by interactions with the gp 41 envelope protein. After the viral gp 120 binds to the CD4 receptor, a conformational change is induced that presents portions of the virus to part of the secondary chemokine receptor. This leads to further conformational changes that expose the viral gp 41, which then undergoes a coiled-coil interaction, bringing the virus and cell close together, facilitating viral insertion into and fusion with the host cell membrane.[36] These details remain under investigation. Fusion inhibitors have been developed that specifically target the fusogenic domain of gp 41 responsible for mediating this process. T-20 (Fuzeon®) is a gp 41 fusion inhibitor recently approved by the FDA. There are numerous investigational agents targeting gp 120, gp 41, and the chemokine receptors.

Once the viral coat proteins are fused with the host cell, the HIV virion is internalized and the viral RNA (2 single strands per virion) is exposed to viral reverse transcriptase (RT). This enzyme facilitates the production of complementary DNA (cDNA) strands, which become double stranded and are transferred to the host cell nucleus. The double-stranded cDNA binds into a pre-integration complex that is transferred across the nucleopore and then translocated to a position adjacent to the host cell genome.

The double-stranded DNA replica is then integrated into the host cell genome. These latter steps require the enzymatic derivative of the *pol* gene, viral *integrase*. Reverse transcriptase, which is also an enzymatic product of the *pol* gene, is an RNA-dependent DNA polymerase that is capable of promoting the synthesis of a strand of DNA from an RNA template that is then digested by viral RNAase. However, reverse transcriptase is prone to committing errors and HIV lacks typical histone repair enzymes, so that the incorporation of several incorrect base pairs during each round of HIV replication occurs.[37,38] These inaccuracies in coding lead to tremendous nucleotide sequence variation between strains and considerable viral heterogeneity, called the "quasispecies mixture."[39] Reverse transcriptase is the target of the nucleoside, nucleotide, and non-nucleoside RT inhibitors. Inhibitors of HIV integrase are a goal of clinical research efforts.

Production and release of new virions

Subsequent activation of the host cell, with activation of its reproductive machinery, produces new HIV RNA, some of which is genomic and some of which is translated into a large HIV polyprotein. This polyprotein is cleaved by viral enzymes into regulatory and structural components that are subsequently assembled around genomic HIV RNA that buds from the host cell. HIV protease completes the cleavage of the polyprotein into fully functional proteins, resulting in mature, infectious new HIV virions. This last step is an important one, and it is the protease enzyme that has been specifically targeted by the most potent of the antiretroviral agents yet discovered, the protease inhibitors.

Therapeutic implications

Review of selective features of the life cycle of HIV explains the rationale underlying the development of current antiretroviral agents, and the attempts to find new therapeutic targets. The first therapeutic class of antiretroviral agents was the inhibitors of the reverse transcriptase enzyme. Mammalian cells do not contain or use reverse transcriptase. This enzyme is specific to the infecting HIV and is thus a good therapeutic target if the agents do not interact with other host cell proteins. Reverse transcriptase inhibitors (RTIs) include the nucleoside reverse transcriptase inhibitors (NRTIs), the non-nucleoside reverse transcriptase inhibitors (NNRTIs), and most recently a nucleotide RTI. To be effective at inhibiting viral replication, nucleoside and nucleotide reverse transcriptase inhibitors must be phosphorylated to an active triphosphate intracellular form. After incorporation into the elongating DNA strand they act as either a chain terminator or as competitive blockers of the normal deoxynucleoside triphosphates.[40] NNRTIs act by interfering with template-primer actions at the site of potential natural nucleotide binding. Unfortunately, because of the error-prone nature of the reverse transcriptase enzyme, a significant number of HIV mutants are generated, especially following multiple cycles of viral replication. Some of these mutants will exhibit resistance to one or more of these agents, and these mutant strains will rapidly proliferate in the presence of only a single drug.[41,42,43] Combinations of reverse transcriptase inhibitors are significantly more effective,[44] especially when they are used in conjunction with some of the newer more powerful agents.[45] This is presumably accomplished by presenting a higher genetic barrier, i.e., multiple mutations, in order for resistance to occur.

Another potential target in the viral life cycle, HIV protease, has been exploited for therapeutic purposes. Protease inhibitors (PIs) proved to be the most significant advance in the therapy of HIV infection. HIV protease inhibitors are effective because the viral protease is quite distinct from mammalian proteases, and selective inhibitors have been developed. Combinations of these agents have additive or synergistic suppressive effects on HIV reproduction. However, despite the advances attained through the use of combination therapies, the inherent mutability of HIV, together with difficulties in maintaining rigid patient adherence to these complex antiviral regimens, lead to the almost inevitable emergence of resistant viruses. Therefore, other potential therapeutic options must be explored.

Other antiretroviral agents under investigation include: inhibitors of the binding process, interfering with the gp 120-CD4 interaction or the interaction with the chemokine receptors, agents that may interfere with the assembly or budding process, integration inhibitors, and inhibitors of the viral regulatory proteins that mediate the post-translational events in the reproductive cycle. Consideration is also being given to immunologic interventions. Attempts to enhance the cell-mediated anti-HIV immune response and/or induce anti-HIV antibodies with therapeutic and preventive vaccines and other manipulations of viral reproduction are under investigation. Also under investigation is the use of immunologic or biologic response modifiers to establish more normal immune regulation and function.

CELLULAR AND VIRAL DYNAMICS OF HIV INFECTION

The dynamics of HIV infection are such that infected lymphocytes are killed at a faster rate than new cells can be generated to replace them, resulting in a progressive diminution of helper lymphocytes. Further immune dysfunction results from loss of the T-cell inducer function, leading to dysregulation of B-cell function. In addition, the continued cycles of HIV infection maintain an immunologically activated state, which contributes to a predisposition to the development of opportunistic infections and other conditions by "blunting" the host's ability to respond to secondary immunologic stimuli.

The ongoing viral production and T-lymphocyte depletion occur over variable periods of time until sufficient damage is done to result in clinical AIDS. This time period of asymptomatic viremic cycles may be as short as a few months or as long as several decades. The average time from initial infection to the development of AIDS is over nine years in the absence of antiretroviral therapy. During this period the patient is producing new virions that are infectious to sexual and/or blood-sharing partners.

The dynamics of HIV infection have been defined in the past few years. It is estimated that the average patient with HIV produces 1-10 billion viral particles daily.[46,47] The half-life of free virions is just over one hour; that of active, acutely infected T-lymphocytes about one day. A second compartment of longer-lived cells, such as macrophages and follicular dendritic cells and HIV sequestered in protected tissues, has a half-life of up to several weeks. If these were the only compartments harboring HIV and antiretroviral agents could freely penetrate, it would be theoretically possible to eliminate HIV infection with sufficiently potent and sustained antiretroviral therapy administered for about 2 to 3 years. This was one justification for the more aggressive approach to initiating therapy once protease inhibitors became available and provided the clinician with a tool to achieve the theoretically necessary degree of antiretroviral potency in combination regimens. If the infection could potentially be eliminated, the risk of side effects, inconvenience, and poor tolerability of therapy for many patients was perhaps acceptable. This was especially the case for those patients who were already symptomatically ill.

More recently, an additional compartment for HIV has been demonstrated. This third compartment is the pool of integrated HIV in resting, long-lived memory lymphocytes.[48] While this pool may only be up to 1 million cells, these cells may have half-lives of up to several years. Their activation can re-populate the patient's lymphatic system with large quantities of HIV (based on the rapid replication dynamics of HIV noted above) up to decades later, with new cycles of viral proliferation and immune damage. (The situation has been complicated by the theory that a reservoir of proviral DNA may lie elsewhere.) It is unreasonable to expect patients to fully adhere to complex, often marginally tolerable or toxic antiretroviral therapies for the *many* years it would probably take for this compartment to be totally depleted by antiretroviral therapy alone. Further, it is now recognized that the potency and penetration into tissue compartments of available therapies is unlikely to be sufficient to achieve the necessary complete, sustained viral suppression required to facilitate resolution of the infection. Conversely, the potential for immune recovery is substantial even in later stages of HIV,[49] so the imperative to maximally preserve immune function with early intervention is lessened. Thus, recent recommendations about when to initiate antiretroviral therapy have become more conservative (see Chapter 5, Antiretroviral Therapy).

HIV-SPECIFIC IMMUNE RESPONSES

Both humoral and cellular immune responses are mounted against HIV infection.[50] The primary role of humoral immunity is in the production of neutralizing antibodies,[51] but antibody-dependent cellular cytotoxicity also contributes by prompting natural killer cells to eliminate HIV-infected cells displaying viral envelope proteins on their surfaces.[52] HIV-specific cytotoxic CD8+ T-lymphocytes play a major role in containing the magnitude of initial HIV infection.[53] However, these cytotoxic T-lymphocytes may have a dual role in their response to HIV infection. They have a beneficial role in their initial immune response to the virus, at which time they help to clear the infection, but later in the course of disease they may be involved in the continued destruction of HIV-infected cells, thereby contributing to the progressive decline of CD4+ lymphocytes (see below).

The immune response to acute HIV infection is typically sufficient to clear the initial viremia and thus lead to resolution of any symptoms that are directly attributable to the virus, but is rarely sufficient to permanently eliminate the infection. Antibodies are produced that help clear free virions. However, HIV bound to follicular dendritic cells or present in sequestered compartments may be protected from immune clearance. In addition, HIV that has entered quiescent cells or, more importantly, HIV whose genome is integrated into that of long-lived memory T-lymphocytes (noted above) is generally inaccessible to immunological clearance. HIV is produced from these sites for years after the initial establishment of infection, with each new cycle of viremia resulting in further immune and dysregulation damage.

MECHANISMS OF CD4+ T-CELL DEPLETION AND DYSFUNCTION

The T-lymphocyte infection eventuates in destruction of these lymphocytes through mechanisms that are still to be defined, but which likely include cell lysis. The infected lymph node architecture is also destroyed over a period of months to years, with prominent loss of the follicular network. The trafficking cells that become infected are distributed to lymph nodes and lymphatic collections throughout the body. This process typically occurs within days to weeks of the initial infection. Untreated HIV-infected patients eventually develop a state of profound immunosuppression that occurs as a result of both quantitative as well qualitative defects in CD4+ lymphocytes.

Direct virologic mechanisms

Direct HIV-mediated cytopathic effects include single-cell killing and syncytia formation.[54] Single-cell killing may occur as a result of either over accumulation of unintegrated viral DNA or interruption of cellular protein synthesis. Syncytia formation involves a complex process whereby potentially large numbers of uninfected CD4+ lymphocytes become fused with HIV-infected cells. This cascade of events occurs in such a way that only one infected cell may potentially account for the deaths of several hundred uninfected cells. Although the regulation of this process has been largely elucidated *in vitro*, no convincing data has ever verified its importance as a significant mechanism of CD4+ T -cell depletion *in vivo*. Nevertheless, the recognition that viral isolates with syncytia-inducing properties most commonly appear at the time of most rapid decline of CD4+ T-cells lends some support to the hypothesis that syncytia may play a significant role *in vivo*.[55,56,57]

Indirect nonvirologic mechanisms

These mechanisms include autoimmune mechanisms, anergy, superantigens, apoptosis, and virus-specific immune responses. Autoimmune responses may be evoked due to the shared structural homology between major-histocompatibility-complex (MHC) class II molecules and the gp 120 and gp 41 proteins of HIV[58, 59] Cellular and humoral immune responses directed toward these HIV proteins may cross-react against self-HLA antigens on T-lymphocytes with consequent immune-mediated destruction of these cells.

The role of anergy in contributing to CD4+ lymphocyte dysfunction has been demonstrated by showing that after the binding of anti-gp 120 antibodies to the CD4 molecule, the CD4+ T-cells become refractory to further stimulation.[60] This abnormal presentation of gp 120 by other CD4+ T-cells could induce anergy in already activated CD4+ T-cells.

The presence of superantigens in HIV infection has been debated.[61] Superantigens are microbial or viral antigens capable of potent activation of large numbers of T-cells. If present in HIV infection, superantigens most likely utilize their propensity for profound T-cell activation to render activated T cells more susceptible to HIV infection.

Programmed cell death, or apoptosis, contributes to elimination of autoreactive T-cells and may also cause death in cells that have been stimulated repeatedly by a specific antigen.[62] Finally, HIV-specific immune responses (antibody-dependent cellular cytotoxicity, cytotoxic T-lymphocytes, etc.) not only play a major role in the control of HIV replication but also may inadvertently contribute to T-cell depletion as previously described.

Conclusion

HIV is an unusually dynamic and unexpectedly complex retroviral pathogen. Further knowledge of the means by which this virus causes disease is needed to improve the approach to therapy, prolong the wellness of the infected individual, and develop improved approaches to the prevention of HIV infection.

References

1. Dorrucci M, Rezza G, Vlahov D, et al. Clinical characteristics and prognostic value of acute retroviral syndrome among injecting drug users: Italian seroconversion study. *AIDS* 1995; 9:597–604.

2. Kahn JO, Walker BD. Current concepts: Acute human immunodeficiency virus type 1 infection. *NEJM* 1998; 339:33–39.

3. Dorrucci M, Rezza G, Vlahov D, et al. Clinical characteristics and prognostic value of acute retroviral syndrome among injecting drug users: Italian seroconversion study. *AIDS* 1995; 9:597–604.

4. Henrard DR, Phillips JF, Muenz LR, et al. Natural history of HIV-1 cell-free viremia. *JAMA* 1995; 274:554–558.

5. Pantaleo G, Graziosi C, Fauci AS. The immunopathogenesis of human immunodeficiency virus infection. *NEJM* 1993; 328:327–335.

6. Mellors JW, Rinaldo CR Jr, Gupta P, White RM, Todd JA, Kingsley LA. Prognosis in HIV-1 infection predicted by the quantity of virus in plasma. [Erratum, *Science* 1997; 275:14.] *Science* 1996; 272:1167–1170.

7. Mellors JW, Munoz A, Gigorgi JV, et al. Plasma viral load and CD4+ cell lymphocytes as prognostic markers of HIV-1 infection. *Ann Intern Med* 1997; 126(12):946–954.

8. Palella FJ, Delaney KM, Moorman AC, Loveless MO, Furhrer J, Satten GA, Aschman, DJ, Holmberg SD. Declining morbidity and mortality among patients with advanced HIV infection. *NEJM* 1998; 338:853–860.

9. Autran B, Carcelain G, Li TS, et al. Positive effects of combined antiretroviral therapy on CD4+ T cell homeostasis and function in advanced HIV disease. *Science* 1997; 277:112–116.

10. Justice AC, Chang CH, Fusco J, West N. Extrapolating long-term HIV/AIDS survival in the post-HAART era. 39th Annual Interscience Conference on Antimicrobial Agents and Chemotherapy (ICAAC); September 26–29, 1999; San Francisco. Abstract.

11. Gelderblom HR, Hausmann EH, Ozel M, et al. Fine structure of human immunodeficiency virus and immunolocalization of structural proteins. *Virology* 1987; 156:171.

12. Geleziunas R, Greene WC. Molecular insights into HIV-1 infection and pathogenesis. In: *The Medical Management of AIDS*. Sande M, Volberding P, eds. Philadelphia: WB Saunders, 1999, 23.

13. Letvin NL. Animal models for AIDS. *Immunol Today* 1990; 11:322.

14. Haase AT. Pathogenesis of lentivirus infections. *Nature* 1986; 322:130–136.

15. Royce RA, Sena A, Cates W Jr, Cohen MS. Sexual transmission of HIV. *NEJM* 1997; 336:1072–1078.

16. Quinn TC, Wawer MJ, Sewankambo N, Serwadda D, Chuanjun L, Wabwire-Mangen F, Meehan M, Lutalo T, Gray R. Viral load and heterosexual transmission of human immunodeficiency virus type 1. *NEJM* 2000; 342:921–929.

17. Daar ES, Moudgil T, Meyer RD, Ho DD. Transient high levels of viremia in patients with primary human immunodeficiency virus type 1 infection. *NEJM* 1991; 324:961–964.

18. Clark SJ, Saag MS, Decker WD, et al. High titers of cytopathic virus in plasma of patients with symptomatic primary HIV-1 infection. *NEJM* 1991; 324:954–960.

19. Tindall B, Cooper DA. Primary HIV infection: host responses and intervention strategies. *AIDS* 1991; 5:1–14.

20. Cossarizza A. T-cell repertoire and HIV infection: facts and perspectives. *AIDS* 1997; 11:1075–1088.

21. Graziosi C, Pantaleo G, Kotler DP, Fauci AS. Dissociation between HIV expression in peripheral blood versus lymphoid organs of the same patients. *Clin Res* 1992; 40:333A. Abstract.

22. Spira AI, Marz PA, Patterson BK, et al. Cellular targets of infection route of viral dissemination after an intravaginal inoculation of simian immunodeficiency virus into rhesus macaques. *J Exp Med* 1996; 183:215–225.

23. Fauci AS. Multifactorial nature of human immunodeficiency virus disease: Implications for therapy. *Science* 1993; 262:1011.

24. Dalgleish AG, Beverly PC, Clapham PR, et al. The CD4 antigen is an essential component of the receptor for the AIDS retrovirus. *Nature* 1984; 312:763.

25. Chesebro B, Buller R, Portis J, Wehrly K. Failure of human immunodeficiency virus entry and infection in CD4-positive human brain and skin cells. *J Virol* 1990; 64:215–221.

26. Maddon PJ, Dalgleish AG, McDougal JS, et al. The T4 gene encodes the AIDS virus receptor and is expressed in the immune system and the brain. *Cell* 1986; 47:333.

27. Feng Y, Broder CC, Kennedy PE, Berger EA. HIV-1 entry cofactor: functional cDNA cloning of a seven-transmembrane, G protein-coupled receptor. *Science* 1996; 272:872–877.

28. Alkhatib G, Combadiere C, Broder CC, et al. CC CKR5: A RANTES, MIP-1α, MIP-1β receptor as a fusion cofactor for macrophage-tropic HIV-1. *Science* 1996; 272:1955.

29. Choe H, Farzan M, Sun Y, et al. The β-chemokine receptors CCR3 and CCR5 facilitate infection by primary HIV-1 isolates. *Cell* 1996; 85:1135.

30. Deng H, Liu R, Ellmeire W, et al. Identification of a major co-receptor for primary isolates of HIV-1. *Nature* 1996; 381:661.

31. Feng Y, Broder CC, Kennedy PE, Berger EA. HIV-1 entry cofactor: Functional cDNA cloning of a seven-transmembrane, G protein-coupled receptor. *Science* 1996; 272:872.

32. Dragic T, Litwin V, Allaway GP, et al. HIV-1 entry into CD4+ cells is mediated by the chemokine receptor CC-CKR-5. *Nature*.1996; 381:667–673.

33. Berger EA, Doms RW, Fenyo E-M, et al. A new classification for HIV-1. *Nature* 1998; 391:240.

34. Zaitseva M, Blauvelt A, Lee S, et al. Expression and function of CCR5 and CXCR4 on human Langerhans cells and macrophages: implications for HIV primary infection. *Nat Med* 1997; 3:1369–1375.

35. Schuitemaker H, Koot M, Kootstra NA, et al. Biological phenotype of human immunodeficiency virus type 1 clones at different stages of infection: progression of disease is associated with a shift from monocytotropic to T-cell tropic virus population. *J Virol* 1992; 66:1354.

36. Chan DC, Kim PS. HIV entry and its inhibition. *Cell* 1998; 93:681.

37. Preston BD, Poiesz BJ, Loeb LA. Fidelity of HIV-1 reverse transcriptase. *Science* 1988; 242:1168–1171.

38. Roberts JD, Bebenek K, Kunkel TA. The accuracy of reverse transcriptase from HIV-1. *Science* 1988; 242:1171–1173.

39. Domingo E, Martinez-Salas E, Sobrino F, et al. The quasispecies (extremely heterogeneous) nature of viral RNA genome populations: biological relevance. *Gene* 1985; 40(review):1–8.

40. Arts EJ, Wainberg MA. Mechanisms of nucleoside analog antiviral activity and resistance during human immunodeficiency virus reverse transcription. *Antimicrob Agents Chemother* 1996; 40:527.

41. Frost SD, McLean AR. Quasispecies dynamics and the emergence of drug resistance during zidovudine therapy of HIV infection. *AIDS* 1994; 8:323.

42. Emini EA, Graham DJ, Gotlib L, et al. HIV and multidrug resistance. *Nature* 1993; 364:679.

43. St. Clair M, Martin JL, Tudor WG, et al. Resistance to ddI and sensitivity to AZT induced by a mutation to HIV-1 reverse transcriptase. *Science* 1991; 253:1557.

44. Fischl MA, Stanley K, Collier AC, et al. Combination and monotherapy with zidovudine and zalcitabine in patients with advanced HIV disease: The NIAID AIDS Clinical Trials Group. *Ann Intern Med* 1995; 122:24.

45. Collier AC, Coombs RW, Schoenfeld DA, et al. Treatment of human immunodeficiency virus infection with saquinavir, zidovudine, and zalcitabine. AIDS Clinical Trials Group. *NEJM* 1996; 334:1011.

46. Coffin JM. HIV population dynamics in vivo: Implications for genetic variation, pathogenesis, and therapy. *Science* 1995; 267:483–489.

47. Ho DD, Neumann AU, Perelson AS. Rapid turnover of plasma virions and CD4 lymphocytes in HIV-1 infection. *Nature* 1995; 373:123–126.

48. Finzi D, Hermankova M, Pierson T, et al. Identification of a reservoir for HIV-1 patients on highly active antiretroviral therapy. *Science* 1997; 278:1295–1298.

49. Autran B, Carcelain G, Li TS, et al. Positive effects of combined antiretroviral therapy on CD4+ T cell homeostasis and function in advanced HIV disease. *Science* 1997; 277:112–116.

50. Fauci AS, moderator. Immunopathogenic mechanisms in human immunodeficiency virus infection. *Ann Intern Med* 1991; 114:678–693.

51. Bolognesi DP. HIV antibodies and vaccine design. *AIDS* 1989; 3(Supp 1):S111–118.

52. Fauci AS, moderator. Immunopathogenic mechanisms in human immunodeficiency virus infection. *Ann Intern Med* 1991; 114:678–693.

53. Walker BD, Chakrabarti S, Moss B, et al. HIV-specific cytotoxic T lymphocytes in seropositive individuals. *Nature* 1987; 328:348–351.

54. Garry RF. Potential mechanisms for the cytopathic properties of HIV. *AIDS* 1989; 3:683–694.

55. Schuitemaker H, Koot M, Kootstra NA, et al. Biological phenotype of human immunodeficiency virus type 1 clones at different stages of infection: progression of disease is associated with a shift from monocytotropic to T-cell tropic virus population. *J Virol* 1992; 66:1354.

56. Tersmette M, deGoede RE, Al BJ, et al. Differential syncytium-inducing capacity of human immunodeficiency virus isolates: frequent detection of syncytium-inducing isolates in patients with acquired immunodeficiency syndrome (AIDS) and AIDS-related complex. *J Virol* 1988; 62:2026.

57. Koot M, Keet IP, Vos AH, et al. Prognostic value of HIV-1 syncytium-inducing phenotype for rate of CD4+ cell depletion and progression to AIDS. *Ann Intern Med* 1993; 118:681.

58. Golding H, Robey FA, Gates FT, et al. Identification of homologous regions in human immunodeficiency virus I gp 41 and human MHC class II β1 domain: Monoclonal antibodies against the gp 41-derived peptide and patients' sera react with native HLA class II antigens, suggesting a role for autoimmunity in the pathogenesis of acquired immune deficiency syndrome. *J Exp Med* 1988; 167:914.

59. Golding H, Shearer GM, Hillman K, et al. Common epitope in human immunodeficiency virus-1 gp41 and HLA class II elicits immunosuppressive autoantibodies capable of contributing to immune dysfunction in HIV-1 infected individuals. *J Clin Invest* 1989; 83:1430.

60. Mittler RS, Hoffman MK. Synergism between HIV gp 120 and gp 120-specific antibody in blocking human T cell activation. *Science* 1989; 245:1380.

61. Janeway C. Mls: Makes a little sense. *Nature* 1991; 349:459–461.

62. Pantaleo G, Fauci AS. Apoptosis in HIV infection. *Nature Med* 1995; 1:118.

Section II

Treatment

4

Initial Encounter
and
Subsequent Visits

Sandra G. Gompf, MD, FACP
Assistant Clinical Professor
Division of Infectious and Tropical Diseases
University of South Florida College of Medicine, Tampa
Section Chief
James A. Haley Veterans Hospital, Tampa

Introduction

Perhaps no other encounter with a healthcare provider is fraught with as much anxiety as a patient's initial visit for evaluation of HIV infection. The newly diagnosed patient is often quite anxious, fearing a terminal illness, sometimes intimidated by the prospect of "toxic" therapies. The experienced patient "switching" providers often arrives wary of the new provider's level of experience and expertise in the rapidly evolving field of HIV medicine. Both patients need the same level of reassurance. The initial encounter is also a vital visit for the healthcare provider, providing a foundation of data upon which all future visits will build. Data collected at this time will determine the plan of care, including education, antiretroviral drug therapy, immunization schedules, preventive strategies for opportunistic infections, and psychosocial support. Spanning the first and second visits, this chapter provides the basis for the initial evaluation of the new HIV-infected patient.

Initial Visit

COMPLETE HEALTH HISTORY AND PHYSICAL EXAM

History

- Diagnosis
  - Date of first positive HIV test; documentation of positive ELISA and Western Blot
  - Lowest CD4+ count in the past (CD4+ cell nadir), for staging purposes (See Table 1)

- – Highest viral load in the past
- – Most recent CD4+ cell count and viral load, if known
- – Past history of antiretroviral (ARV) therapy
- HIV risk factors and behaviors
  - – Sexual partners and their risk behaviors
  - – Men having unsafe sex with other men
  - – Sharing needles/syringes for injecting drugs/steroids
  - – Having a sexual partner who shares needles/syringes
  - – Trading sex for anything
  - – Receiving blood transfusions, especially before 1985
  - – Hemophilia or blood disorders treated with blood products
  - – Receiving tissue/organs/semen, especially before 1985
  - – Being in jail/prison
  - – Victim of sexual assault/rape/sexual abuse
- Past medical history
  - – PPD testing dates and results. Prior history of tuberculosis therapy or prophylaxis
  - – Chickenpox or shingles
  - – Hepatitis A, B, C; sexually transmitted diseases (especially syphilis)
  - – Gynecologic history in women, including Pap screens and cervical dysplasia
- Evidence of Mild Immune Deficiency (CD4+ cell count 200–500 cells/mm^3)
  - – Oral candidiasis (thrush)
  - – Recurrent vaginal candidiasis
  - – Recurrent herpes zoster/shingles, especially > 1 dermatome
  - – Recurrent herpes simplex
  - – Neurologic abnormalities, such as Bell's palsy
  - – Tuberculosis
- Evidence of Severe Immune Deficiency —
  CD4+ cell count < 200 cells/mm^3; and/or % < 14): AIDS-Defining Illnesses (See Table 3)
  - – Pneumocystis carinii pneumonia (PCP)
  - – Disseminated mycobacterium avium complex (MAC)
  - – Kaposi's sarcoma (KS)
  - – Cytomegalovirus
  - – Cryptococcosis
  - – Toxoplasmosis
  - – Any other AIDS-defining illness
- Vaccine history
  - – Hepatitis A
  - – Hepatitis B
  - – Influenza
  - – Pneumovax®
  - – Tetanus
- Social history
  - – Living arrangements, social supports, financial resources, domestic violence, depression
  - – Ongoing or historical tobacco, alcohol, and IV drug use

- Prior travel to or residence in areas endemic for histoplasmosis (Ohio and Mississippi River valleys, Central and South America) and coccidioidomycosis (Southwestern deserts)
        - Refer to appropriate service agencies, when indicated
- Thorough review of systems

Physical exam

- Weight (changes or trends)
- Skin (seborrhea, psoriasis, tinea, candida, KS)
- Funduscopic eye exam (retinopathy)
- Oropharyngeal (thrush, oral hairy leukoplakia, periodontal disease, ulcerations, angular cheilitis)
- Cardiopulmonary (cardiomyopathy, pneumonia)
- Abdominal (hepatosplenomegaly, masses)
- Women: Pap, bimanual pelvic and rectal (cervical dysplasia, candidiasis, condylomata), breast exam, consider anal cytology
- Men: genital and rectal (ulcers, anal fissures, condylomata), consider anal cytology
- Neurologic/mental status (dementia, neuropathy)
- Lymphatic (generalized lymphadenopathy, lymphoma). Complete nodal exam: auricular, preauricular, submental, submandibular, anterior and posterior cervical, supraclavicular, infraclavicular, axillary, epitrochlear, inguinal, femoral, popliteal nodes

Labs

- Baseline CBC, differential and platelet count
- Urinalysis
- Syphilis serology
- Chemistries, including liver enzymes, BUN, creatinine, albumin
- Hepatitis A, B, and C serology
- Baseline toxoplasma IgG and (optional) cytomegalovirus IgG
- PPD skin test
- CD4 (% and absolute), CD8, and CD4/CD8 ratio
- HIV viral load (by RNA PCR or bDNA)
- G6PD if clinically indicated (black men [10%], black women [1–2%], or men from Mediterranean areas — Italians, Greeks, Sephardic Jews, Arabs, or in men from India or Southeast Asia)
- Chest x-ray (baseline and for TB screening)

Counseling and education

- Transmission and prevention for positives
- Notification of sexual and/or needle/syringe sharing partners; safer sex/needling practices. Counsel and encourage Public Health Department assistance for partner notification
- Avoidance of sharing razors, toothbrushes, other potential sources of body fluid transmission
- Preventive healthcare, healthy lifestyles, substance abuse counseling
- Guidelines for good nutrition (refer to dietician as appropriate)
- Discuss fears, anxieties, barriers to adherence
- For women, discuss fertility and preconception planning, if indicated. (See Table 4 — Immunizations, and Special Situations, below)

- Written materials should be provided whenever possible
- Conclude with a positive message about the benefits of HAART therapy and prophylactic medications

General care plan

- Discuss plan of care, frequency of visits, what to do in case of emergencies, hospital coverage

Determine next appointment date

- Approximately 2 weeks after initial visit

Second Visit

Determine level of immunosuppression (CD4, CD8, H and P)

Determine HIV activity (viral load)

Discuss labs/action indicated

- If VDRL/RPR reactive: treat as appropriate based on history and clinical findings. Consider evaluation for other sexually transmitted diseases
- Abnormal liver enzymes: question alcohol consumption and drug use. Consider opportunistic infections. Consider Hepatitis B and C viral load evaluation if liver enzymes are persistently elevated and unexplained even if antibody testing is negative
- See Table 4 for management of + Hepatitis A and B serologies; if Hepatitis B surface antigen positive or Hepatitis C antibody positive, counsel regarding potential infectivity and evaluate further
- + PPD (≥ 5 mm induration): do chest x-ray and manage as appropriate based on history and clinical findings
- See Tables 1 and 2 for interpretation and use of CD4 and viral load

Begin vaccinations as indicated (see Table 4)

- Remember to schedule vaccinations at least 2 to 4 weeks before drawing HIV viral load evaluations. Vaccines can temporarily elevate HIV viral load.

Counseling and education (reinforce issues discussed at first visit)

- Concerns/psychosocial issues
- Disclosure to partners, prevention of transmission
- Case management services, substance abuse counseling services
- Partner/spouse/family issues
- Advance directives, healthcare proxy/power of attorney, as appropriate
- Good long-term prognosis with adequate monitoring and adherence to ARV therapy

General care plan

- Plan of care based on CD4+ cell count and viral load
- Discuss course of therapy, prophylaxis
- Discuss possible side effects, keeping a symptom log, adherence

Determine next appointment date (see Table 2)

Subsequent Visits

Discuss medication side effects, adherence

Revisit counseling issues as needed, including psychosocial

Discuss prevention for positives giving at least one prevention message every visit

CBC with diff, LFTs, viral load and CD4 cell counts q 4 weeks until stable, then q 3 to 6 months (see Table 2)

Update immunizations (see Table 4)

Follow-up PPD, chest x-ray, RPR annually

Preventive healthcare

- Pap smears/mammography in women
- Ophthalmologic evaluation q 6 to 12 mos if CD4+ cell count < 100 cells/mm^3 (in office ophthalmologic evaluation is adequate if a dilated exam is done; patients with symptoms of visual change, flashes or bursts of light, or abnormal findings on Amsler grid evaluation as well as those with hemorrhages and exudates on funduscopic evaluation should be referred to a Retinal Specialist). See Figure 1 for copy of Amsler grid.
- Dental care

Figure 1. Amsler Grid

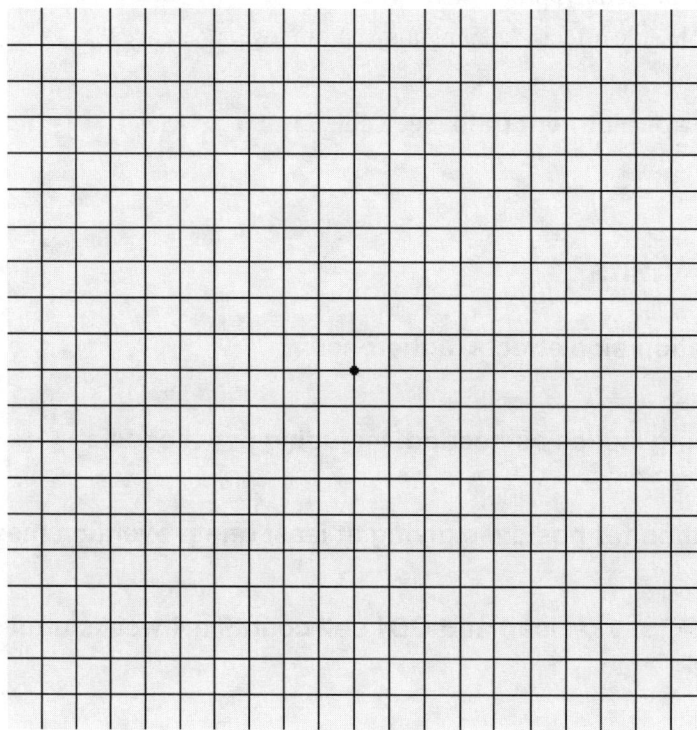

Table 1. AIDS Surveillance Case Definition for Adolescents and Adults, 1993

CD4 CELL CATEGORIES	CLINICAL CATEGORIES		
	A Asymptomatic or PGL (persistent generalized lymphadenopathy) or Acute HIV Infection	B Symptomatic* (not A or C)	C** AIDS-Defining Illness (see Chapter 3, Table 2)
> 500/mm³ (>29%)	A1	B1	C1
200-499/mm³ (14%-28%)	A2	B2	C2
< 200/ mm³ (<14%)	A3	B3	C3

*Conditions due to HIV infection or mild immunodeficiency, including bacillary angiomatosis, thrush, recurrent or refractory vulvovaginal yeast, cervical dysplasia/carcinoma in situ, oral hairy leukoplakia, shingles > 2 episodes / > 1 dermatome, idiopathic thrombocytopenic purpura, listeriosis, pelvic inflammatory disease, peripheral neuropathy, fever $\geq 38.5°C$, diarrhea > 1 month; refer to Section IV – Management of Co-Existing Conditions.
**Shaded areas define AIDS diagnosis (AIDS-Defining Illness +/- CD4 < 200/ mm³).

Table 2. CD4 Counts (Assess Immunity and Determine Plan of Therapy)

CD4 CELL COUNT	> 350 cells/mm³	200–350 cells/mm³	< 200 cells/mm³	< 100 CELLS/mm³
Symptoms	None to mild immune deficiency symptoms	None to mild immune deficiency symptoms	None to severe immune deficiency symptoms	None to severe immune deficiency symptoms
Treatment	Antiretroviral therapy based on most current guidelines			
Prophylaxis			PCP prophylaxis	PCP prophylaxis + toxoplasmosis prophylaxis (if Toxo IgG +) MAC prophylaxis, (some defer to CD4 < 50 cells/mm³)
Immunizations	See Table 4			
Labs	**No ART:** CBC/diff, CD4, HIV viral load q 3-6 mos **Upon initiation of ART:** CBC/diff, Chemistries, liver enzymes, CD4, HIV viral load at 4–6 wks **On stable ART:** CBC/diff, Chemistries, liver enzymes, CD4, HIV viral load q 3–4 mos			

Table 3. Risk for Progression to AIDS-Defining Illness Among a Cohort of Men Who Have Sex with Men, Predicted by Baseline CD4[+] T-Cell Count and Viral Load[*]

CD4 ≤ 200 cells/mm³ Plasma Viral Load (copies/mL) [†]		Percentage of AIDS-defining illness [‡]			
bDNA	RT-PCR	n	3 years	6 years	9 years
≤ 500	≤ 1,500	0 [§]	-	-	-
501 - 3,000	1,501 - 7,000	3 [§]	-	-	-
3,001 - 10,000	7,001 - 20,000	7	14.3	28.6	64.3
10,001 - 30,000	20,001 - 55,000	20	50.0	75	90.0
> 30,000	> 55,000	70	85.5	97.9	100.0
CD4 201 – 350 [∞] cells/mm³ Plasma Viral Load (copies/mL) [†]		Percentage of AIDS-defining illness [‡]			
bDNA	RT-PCR	n	3 years	6 years	9 years
≤ 500	≤ 1,500	3 [§]	-	-	-
501 - 3,000	1,501 - 7,000	27	0	20.0	32.2
3,001 - 10,000	7,001 - 20,000	44	6.9	44.4	66.2
10,001 - 30,000	20,001 - 55,000	53	36.4	72.2	84.5
> 30,000	> 55,000	104	64.4	89.3	92.9
CD4 > 350 cells/mm³ Plasma Viral Load (copies/mL) [†]		Percentage of AIDS-defining illness [‡]			
bDNA	RT-PCR	n	3 years	6 years	9 years
≤ 500	≤ 1,500	119	1.7	5.5	12.7
501 - 3,000	1,501 - 7,000	227	2.2	16.4	30.0
3,001 - 10,000	7,001 - 20,000	342	6.8	30.1	53.5
10,001 - 30,000	20,001 - 55,000	323	14.8	51.2	73.5
> 30,000	> 55,000	262	39.6	71.8	85.0

*Adapted for this report from data from the Multicenter AIDS Cohort Study (MACS) (Source: Mellors JW, Rinaldo CR Jr, Gupta P, et al. Prognosis in HIV-1 infection predicted by the quantity of virus in plasma, *Science* 1996;272: 1167-70. [Erratum: *Science* 1997; 275:14]; adapted by Alvaro Muñoz, PhD, John Hopkins University, Baltimore, MD 2001).

† MACS numbers reflect Plasma HIV RNA values obtained by version 2.0 bDNA testing. RT-PCR values are consistently 2 – 2.5-fold higher than first-generation bDNA values, as indicated. The version 3.0 bDNA assay provides similar HIV-1 RNA values as RT-PCR, except at the lower end of the linear range (< 1,500 copies/mL). The Organon Teknika NucliSen® HIV-1 QT assay, an in vitro nucleic acid amplification test for HIV RNA, has been approved by the Food and Drug Administration for monitoring the effects of antiretroviral therapy among adults with baseline HIV RNA of > 28,000 copies/mL.

‡ In the reference study, AIDS was defined according to the 1987 CDC definition, which did not include asymptomatic persons with CD4[+] T-cells counts < 200 cells/mm^3.

§ Too few subjects were in the category to provide a reliable estimate of AIDS risk.

∞ A recent evaluation of data from the MACS cohort of 231 persons with CD4[+] T-cell counts > 200 and < 350 cells/mm^3 demonstrated that of 40 (17%) persons with plasma HIV RNA < 10,000 copies/mL, none progressed to AIDS by 3 years (Source: Phair JP, Mellors JW, Detels R, Margolick JB, Muñoz A. Virologic and immunologic values allowing safe deferral of antiretroviral therapy. *AIDS* 2002; 16(18): 2455-2459). Of 28 individuals (29%) with plasma viremia of 10,000–20,000 copies/mL, 4% and 11% progressed to AIDS at 2 and 3 years, respectively. Plasma HIV RNA was calculated as RT-PCR values from measured bDNA values.

Table 4. Immunizations

VACCINE	TYPE/ROUTE	INDICATION/IMMUNIZATION SCHEDULE
Hepatitis A	Inactive viral antigen/IM	One-time series, if HAV IgG – and: HCV Antibody +, male having sex with males, IV drug use, chronic liver disease, residence or impending travel to endemic area. Vaccinate with first dose; second dose is given 6 months from first.
Hepatitis B	Inactive viral antigen/IM	One-time series, if hepatitis B sAntigen, B sAntibody, and B cAntibody negative. Give 1 dose, then repeat @ 1 month and 6 months from first dose. Repeat HB sAntibody 1–6 months after last dose; consider repeat series if negative, giving 2 more doses one month apart. If no response, no further vaccination recommended.
Hepatitis A/B (TwinRx®)	Inactive viral antigen/IM	One-time series, if criteria are met for both hepatitis A and B immunization. Give 1 dose, then repeat @ 1 month and 6 months from first dose. Repeat HB sAntibody 1–6 months after last dose; consider repeat series if negative, giving 2 more doses one month apart. If no response, no further vaccination recommended.
Influenza	Inactivated viral components/IM	Annually, as early as possible prior to flu season. Inhaled live attenuated influenza vaccine (FluMist®) has not been evaluated for use in immunocompromised individuals. Since shedding is possible for 3 weeks after administration, HIV-infected parents should be counseled to use only inactivated influenza vaccine in their children.
Pneumovax®	Capsular polysaccharide (23 types)/IM	One time repeat 5–6 years after the first vaccine is given. Consider waiting until CD4 cell count is > 200 cells/mm^3 prior to vaccinating or repeat vaccination when CD4 > 200 cells/mm^3). No further immunization recommended.
Measles-mumps-rubella(MMR)/measles-rubella (MR)	Live attenuated virus/SC	One-time series, in individuals who are **not** severely immunodeficient (see **NOTE**), indicated for all adults born in/before 1957, and ALL women of childbearing potential regardless of birth year. 0.5mL SC in upper arm x 2 doses, 28 days apart. Women must not be pregnant at the time of administration, and must be counseled to avoid pregnancy x 3 mos after series.
Tetanus-diphtheria	Inactivated toxins/IM	q 10 yrs (boost @ 5 yrs if tetanus-prone injury)

NOTE: In general, **live vaccines**, including *oral* polio vaccine, varicella zoster (chickenpox), BCG, *oral* typhoid, yellow fever vaccine, vaccinia (smallpox vaccine), and *inhaled* influenza vaccine (FluMist®) are **contraindicated** in HIV-infected patients. MMR/MR is contraindicated HIV-infected patients who are severely immunodeficient [age <12mos: CD4 <750 cells/mm^3 (<15%); age 1-5yo: CD4 <500 cells/mm^3 (<15%); age ≥ 6yo:CD4 < 200 cells/mm^3 (<15%). Per American College of Immunization Practices, varicella vaccine may be included in routine immunizations of asymptomatic or mildly symptomatic HIV-infected children in CDC class N1 or A1 with age-specific CD4+ T-lymphocyte percentages of greater than or equal to 25%; see Post-exposure Prophylaxis below.

SPECIAL SITUATIONS

Post-exposure Prophylaxis for Varicella

- HIV-infected adults who DO NOT give a history of chickenpox or shingles, or documented varicella immunization or documented serologic immunity to varicella zoster, should be considered non-immune. Varicella immune globulin (VZIG) may be given within 4 days of exposure to chickenpox or shingles. Exposure of non-immune HIV-infected adults to individuals who have received varicella vaccine does not require administration of VZIG, however, avoidance of close or household contact with a vaccinee for 6 weeks should be considered, whenever feasible.

- Given that many HIV-infected adults are becoming parents or considering parenthood, varicella serology may be considered prior to conception for those who do not recall a history of chickenpox, shingles, or documented vaccination. This information may be helpful in providing anticipatory guidance regarding exposures.

- Because immune globulin (IG) products may impair the production of protective antibody after immunization, varicella vaccine should not be given until 5 months after the administration of varicella IG.

Post-exposure Prophylaxis for Measles and Rubella

- HIV-infected individuals exposed to measles should receive IG regardless of their previous vaccination status. IG in usual doses may not be effective for immunocompromised persons, thus the usual dose is doubled, or 0.5 mL/kg administered intramuscularly (up to a maximum of 15 mL).

- The effectiveness of IG for preventing mumps or rubella is unknown, and its use is not recommended at this time.

- For those who are not immune to measles, mumps, or rubella, MMR vaccine should not be given until 6 months after the administration of IG.

Exposure to FluMist®

- No data exists as yet regarding the duration for which an immunocompromised individual should avoid contact with a recipient of the live influenza vaccine, however, 3 weeks where feasible seems prudent.

References

1. Gallant JE. The HIV-Patient – The initial encounter, clinical update. *Medscape* May 7, 2002; 12 screens. Available at: http://www.medscape.com/viewprogram/660. Accessed August 20, 2004.

2. Gallant JE. The seropositive patient – the initial encounter, HIV Clinical Management Vol. 1. *Medscape* January 19, 2000; 12 screens. Available at: www.medscape.com/Medscape/HIV/ClinicalMgmt/CM.v01/public/index-CM.v01.html. Accessed August 20, 2004.

3. Infectious Diseases Society of America (US). Primary care of patients infected with HIV, Practice Guidelines. *Clin Infec Dis* 1998; 26: 275–276.

4. Merigan TC Jr, Bartlett JG, Bolognesi D, eds. *Textbook of AIDS Medicine*. 2nd ed. Baltimore, MD: Williams and Wilkins, 1999.

5. USPHS guidelines for the use of antiretroviral agents in HIV-infected adults and adolescents, March 23, 2004; 23 screens. Available at: www.aidsinfo.nih.gov. Accessed August 20, 2004.

6. Measles, mumps, and rubella — vaccine use and strategies for elimination of measles, rubella, and congenital rubella syndrome and control of mumps: Recommendations of the Advisory Committee on Immunization Practices (ACIP), May 22, 1998 / 47(RR-8);1–57. Available at http://www.cdc.gov/mmwr/preview/mmwrhtml/00053391.htm#00003188.htm. Accessed August 20, 2004.

7. Prevention of varicella. Updated recommendations of the Advisory Committee on Immunization Practices (ACIP), *MMWR Recomm Rep* May 28, 1999; 48(RR-6):1–5. Available at http://www.cdc.gov/mmwr/preview/mmwrhtml/rr4806a1.htm. General recommendations on immunization: recommendations of the Advisory Committee on Immunization Practices [ACIP], *MMWR* 1994; 43[No. RR-1]:1–38). Available at www.cdc.gov/mmwr/preview/mmwrhtml/rr5102a1.htm. Accessed August 20, 2004.

8. Bartlett JG, Gallant JE. *The Medical Management of HIV Infection.* Baltimore, MD: Johns Hopkins University, 2003. Available at http://hivinsite.ucsf.edu/pdf/kbr-zoster.pdf. Accessed August 20, 2004.

5

Antiretroviral Therapy

Jeffrey Beal, MD
Clinical Director
Florida/Caribbean AIDS Education and Training Center
Associate Professor USF Center for HIV Education and Research
Joanne J. Orrick, PharmD, BCPS
Clinical Assistant Professor, University of Florida Colleges of Nursing and Pharmacy
Gainesville
Faculty, Florida/Caribbean AIDS Education and Training Center

Introduction

Highly active antiretroviral therapy or HAART (more recently referred to as combination antiretroviral therapy or CART) generally consists of 3 or more antiretroviral agents used in combination to attempt to decrease the patient's plasma HIV viral load to undetectable levels. The widespread availability and use of HAART (CART) in the United States has been successful in both decreasing the progression to AIDS and deaths due to AIDS.

The goals of antiretroviral therapy are:

- Improvement in quality of life
- Reduction of HIV-related morbidity and mortality
- Maximal and durable suppression of viral load
- Restoration and/or preservation of immunologic function

This chapter reviews guidelines and recommendations for the use of antiretroviral agents in adults and adolescents (defined as patients in late puberty or Tanner Stage V). Please refer to Chapter 30, Antiretroviral Therapy in Children for the management of HIV in pediatric patients.

Available Antiretroviral Guidelines

Several guidelines have been released regarding the use of antiretroviral medications in adults, adolescents, children, and pregnant women.

To obtain copies of the guidelines, order online or download from AIDSinfo (a Service of the Department of Health and Human Services) at www.aidsinfo.nih.gov

There are also guidelines available from the International AIDS Society-USA Panel. These guidelines entitled Treatment for Adult HIV Infection. The 2004 Recommendations from the International AIDS Society-USA Panel are available online at http://www.iasusa.org/pub/arv_2004.pdf.

IMPORTANT COMMENT: CHOOSING ANTIRETROVIRAL AGENTS (REGARDLESS OF PRIOR TREATMENT STATUS)

Upon the collaborative decision to start or even "change" antiretroviral therapy, the clinician and patient should discuss the risks and benefits of therapy in an informed consent paradigm. They should also attempt to define "success" and "failure" as clearly as possible and consider identifying the subsequent one to two regimens in the inevitability of initial regimen failure.

Initiation of Antiretroviral Therapy in the Antiretroviral Naïve Patient

The ARV-naïve patient has the most options for choosing antiretroviral agents and the greatest chance of achieving reductions in viral loads to undetectable levels for the longest duration of time.

It is clear that treatment should be offered to any person with symptomatic AIDS and patients with a CD4+ count < 200 cells/mm^3 with or without clinical AIDS.

Treatment should also generally be offered to all patients with a CD4+ cell count between 200 and 350 cells/mm^3, regardless of the viral load.

The decision to initiate therapy in patients with CD4+ cell counts > 200 cells/mm^3 should take several factors into account including:

- Readiness of the patient to begin therapy
- Degree of immunodeficiency — determined by CD4+ cell count
- Risk of disease progression — determined by serial trend of CD4 cell count and HIV RNA viral load over time
- Potential benefits and risks of initiating therapy in asymptomatic individuals
- Probability of patient adherence to prescribed regimen

Combination antiretroviral therapy can lead to complications and unwanted adverse effects; the risks and benefits should be considered prior to the initiation of therapy.

Starting therapy should not be based on one CD4+ cell count/viral load determination. Confirmation of CD4+ cell count/viral load values should be done before initiating therapy.

The following table contains the recommendations from the DHHS Guidelines for initiation of therapy in adults or adolescents chronically infected with HIV (HIV infection > 6 months):

Table 1. Indications for the Initiation of Antiretroviral Therapy in the Chronically HIV-Infected Adult or Adolescent

CLINICAL CATEGORY	CD4+ CELL COUNT	PLASMA HIV VIRAL LOAD	RECOMMENDATION
Symptomatic (AIDS, thrush, unexplained fever)	Any value	Any value	Treat
Asymptomatic, AIDS	CD4+ Cell Count < 200 cells/mm^3	Any value	Treat
Asymptomatic	CD4+ Cell Count > 200 but ≤ 350 cells/mm^3	Any value	Treatment should generally be offered, though controversy exists
Asymptomatic	CD4+ Cell Count > 350 cells/mm^3	≥ 100,000 copies/mL (RT-PCR or bDNA)	Some experts would recommend initiating therapy, recognizing that the 3-year risk of developing AIDS in untreated patients is >30%. In the absence of very high levels of plasma HIV RNA, some would defer therapy and monitor CD4+ cell count and level of plasma HIV/RNA more frequently. Clinical outcomes data after initiating therapy are lacking.
Asymptomatic	CD4+ Cell Count > 350 cells/mm^3	< 100,000 copies/mL (RT-PCR or bDNA)	Many experts would defer therapy and observe, recognizing the 3-year risk of developing AIDS in untreated patients is < 15%

SOURCE: Table 4 in Guidelines for the Use of Antiretroviral Agents in HIV-Infected Adults and Adolescents. *MMWR* 1998; 47(RR-5). Updated as the Living Document, October 6, 2005. Available at http://www.aidsinfo.nih.gov.

Table 2. Risks and Benefits of Early Therapy

BENEFITS	RISKS
Earlier suppression of viral replication Preservation of immune function Prolongation of disease-free survival	Drug-related reduction in quality of life Greater cumulative drug-related adverse effects
Lower risk of resistance with complete viral suppression	Earlier development of drug resistance (if viral suppression is not optimal) Risk of transmission of resistant virus (if viral suppression not optimal)
Possible decreased risk of HIV transmission	Limitation in future antiretroviral treatment options Unknown durability of current available therapy

SOURCE: Guidelines for the Use of Antiretroviral Agents in HIV-Infected Adults and Adolescents. *MMWR* 1998; 47(RR-5). Updated as the Living Document, October 6, 2005. Available at http://www.aidsinfo.nih.gov.

Choosing an Antiretroviral Regimen in the ARV-Naïve Patient

The following table contains the DHHS recommendations for the selection of antiretroviral agents in the treatment-naïve patient.

These are to be considered as guidelines only and should not replace clinical judgment of the practitioner in selecting appropriate regimens for specific patient situations.

Issues to consider when selecting an antiretroviral regimen:

- Patient's daily routine and social support as they relate to his/her ability to adhere to a particular regimen
- Side-effect profile of the medications including evaluation of concomitant medical conditions that may increase risk of certain adverse effects
- Drug interactions with other medications the patient is taking.

Table 3. Recommended Antiretroviral Agents for Initial Treatment of the Antiretroviral Naïve Adult or Adolescent

NNRTI-BASED REGIMENS	
Preferred	• **Efavirenz[1] + (Lamivudine[2] or Emtricitabine[3])+ (Zidovudine[2] or Tenofovir[3])**
Alternative	• Efavirenz[1] + (Lamivudine[4] or Emtricitabine) + (Abacavir[4] or Didanosine or Stavudine[5]) • Nevirapine[6] + (Lamivudine[2,4] or Emtricitabine[3]) + (Zidovudine[2] or Stavudine[5] Didanosine or Abacavir[4] or Tenofovir[3])
PI-BASED REGIMENS	
Preferred	• **Lopinavir/ritonavir + (Lamivudine[2] or Emtricitabine) + Zidovudine[2]**
Alternative	• Atazanavir[7] + (Lamivudine[2,4] or Emtricitabine[3]) + (Zidovudine[2] or Stavudine[5] or Abacavir[4] or Didanosine or Tenofovir[3,7]) • Fosamprenavir ± Ritonavir[8] + (Lamivudine[2,4] or Emtricitabine[3]) + (Zidovudine[2] or Stavudine[5] or Abacavir[4] or Tenofovir[3] or Didanosine) • Indinavir + Ritonavir[8] + (Lamivudine[2,4] or Emtricitabine[3]) + (Zidovudine[2] or Stavudine[5] or Abacavir[4] or Tenofovir[3] or Didanosine) • Lopinavir/ritonavir + (Lamivudine[4] or Emtricitabine[3])+ (Stavudine[5] or Abacavir[4] or Tenofovir[3] or Didanosine) • Nelfinavir + (Lamivudine[2,4] or Emtricitabine[3]) + (Zidovudine[2] or Stavudine[5] or Abacavir[4] or Tenofovir[3] or Didanosine) • Saquinavir (HGC or tablets) + Ritonavir[8] + (Lamivudine[2,4] or Emtricitabine[3]) + (Zidovudine[2] or Stavudine[5] or Abacavir[4] or Tenofovir[3] or Didanosine)
TRIPLE NRTI REGIMEN – Only when an NNRTI- or PI-based regimen cannot or should not be used as first line therapy	
Alternative	• Abacavir + Lamivudine + Zidovudine[9]

SOURCE: Table 5 in Guidelines for the Use of Antiretroviral Agents in HIV-Infected Adults and Adolescents. *MMWR* 1998; 47(RR-5). Updated as the Living Document, October 6, 2005. Available at http://www.aidsinfo.nih.gov.

1. Except for women in first trimester of pregnancy or women with high pregnancy potential due to teratogenic possibility
2. Lamivudine (3TC) + Zidovudine (AZT) available in combination as Combivir®
3. Emtricitabine (FTC) + Tenofovir (TDF) available in combination as Truvada®
4. Abacavir (ABC) + Lamivudine (3TC) available in combination as Epzicom®
5. Higher incidence of lipoatrophy, hyperlipidemia, and mitochondrial toxicities with stavudine
6. Note: Higher incidence of hepatotoxicity in women with pre-nevirapine CD4+ cell counts > 250 cells/mm^3 and in men with pre-nevirapine CD4+ cell counts > 400 cells/mm^3
7. Boosted atazanavir regimen (300 mg qd + ritonavir 100 mg qd) recommended with tenofovir or in PI-experienced patients
8. Low-dose ritonavir for boosting; See Table 8 (Combination Dose Adjustments) for dose recommendations
9. Abacavir + Lamivudine + Zidovudine available in combination as Trizivir®

Table 4. Antiretroviral Regimens and Components that are Not Recommended

ANTIRETROVIRAL REGIMENS OR COMPONENTS NOT RECOMMENDED *AT ANY TIME*	
Agent(s)	**Comments**
Monotherapy	Zidovudine monotherapy may be considered for use in pregnant women to prevent perinatal transmission if pre-treatment VL controlled < 1000 copies/mL*; combination therapy is preferred
Two-agents drug combinations	Rapid development of resistance. Inferior to regimens with 3 or more drugs. If virologic goals are achieved, some clinicians may choose to continue
Abacavir + Tenofovir + (Lamivudine or Emtricitabine)	High rate of early virologic non-response seen in ARV-naïve patients
Tenofovir + Didanosine + (Lamivudine or Emtricitabine)	High rate of early virologic non-response seen in ARV-naïve patients
Stavudine + Zidovudine	Both thymidine analogs; antagonistic
Stavudine + Zalcitabine	Additive peripheral neuropathy
Didanosine + Zalcitabine	Additive peripheral neuropathy
Lamivudine + Zalcitabine	*In vitro* antagonism
Didanosine + Stavudine	Increased risk of toxicities such as lactic acidosis and pancreatitis; May be considered when no other options available and potential benefits outweigh the risks. Reports of fatalities when used in pregnancy
Emtricitabine + Lamivudine	Similar resistance profile; no potential benefit
Amprenavir oral solution	Contains large amounts of propylene glycol; contraindicated in pregnancy, children < 4 years old, renal or hepatic failure, and those taking metronidazole or disulfiram or ritonavir oral solution
Amprenavir oral solution + Ritonavir oral solution	Should not be combined due to propylene glycol content of amprenavir solution/alcohol content of ritonavir solution
Amprenavir + Fosamprenavir	Amprenavir is the active component of both drugs; no benefit in combination
Atazanavir + Indinavir	Potential for additive hyperbilirubinemia
Saquinavir hard gel capsule or tablet (Invirase®) as single PI	Must be combined with other PIs such as ritonavir or lopinavir/ritonavir due to poor bioavailability
Efavirenz in 1st trimester of pregnancy or in women with pregnancy potential	Teratogenic; consider use only when no other options available and potential benefits outweigh the risk*
Nevirapine Initiation in women with CD4 > 250 in men with CD4 > 400	Higher incidence of symptomatic hepatic events; use only if potential benefits outweigh risks
ANTIRETROVIRAL COMPONENTS NOT RECOMMENDED AS PART OF *INITIAL THERAPY*	
Agent(s)	**Comment**
Zalcitabine + Zidovudine	Inferior efficacy; higher rates of adverse effects
Tenofovir + Didanosine + NNRTI	High rate of early virologic failure and rapid development of resistance
Delavirdine	Inferior efficacy; inconvenient dosing
Amprenavir (boosted or unboosted)	High pill burden
Indinavir (unboosted)	Inconvenient dosing; meal restrictions
Ritonavir as sole PI	High pill burden; GI intolerance
Saquinavir soft gel capsules (Fortovase,® unboosted)	High pill burden; inferior efficacy
Tipranavir/Ritonavir	Lack of data in treatment-naïve patients
Enfuvirtide	No data in treatment-naïve patients; requires bid injections

SOURCE: Tables 8 and 9 in Guidelines for the Use of Antiretroviral Agents in HIV-Infected Adults and Adolescents. *MMWR* 1998; 47 (RR-5). Updated as the Living Document, October 6, 2005. Available at http://www.aidsinfo.nih.gov.

*WHEN CONSTRUCTING AN ARV REGIMEN FOR A PREGNANT WOMAN, PLEASE CONSULT PUBLIC HEALTH SERVICE TASK FORCE RECOMMENDATIONS FOR THE USE OF ARV DRUGS IN PREGNANT WOMEN AT http://aidsinfo.nih.gov/guidelines/default_db2.asp?id=66

Class Sparing Strategies in the Initiation of Therapy (Drug Sequencing)

The table below summarizes the advantages and disadvantages of various class sparing regimens. Regimens that spare the use of PIs and NNRTIs have thus far been shown to have inferior efficacy to PI- or NNRTI-based regimens. The choice between initiation of a PI- or NNRTI-based regimen is made a on a case by case basis taking into account patient characteristics including concomitant diseases states and medications as well as patient and provider preference.

Table 5. Advantages and Disadvantages of Class Sparing Regimens

Protease Inhibitor Sparing Regimens (NNRTI-Based)	
PROS	CONS
• Avoid PI-related adverse effects such as GI intolerance • Less lipodystrophy and dyslipidemia than PI-based regimens • Simple regimens overall compared to PI regimens • Efficacy well-documented	• Class resistance usually conferred by single mutation (K103N) • Many drug interactions
NNRTI Sparing Regimens (PI-Based)	
PROS	CONS
• With "newer" PI formulations and "boosted" protease regimens (e.g., with mini-dose ritonavir + another PI) pill burdens can be lowered and tolerability may be improved • Multiple mutations required for resistance • Efficacy well-documented	• Potential concern for long term protease inhibitor related toxicity e.g., lipodystrophy, possible bone disease, hepatotoxicity – however this is debated and it has not been clearly shown such toxicity is "class-specific" to protease inhibitors • Risk of resistance and cross resistance development exists – especially at higher viral load values • Many drug interactions
PI and NNRTI Sparing Regimens	
PROS	CONS
• Simple regimen • Avoids PI and NNRTI adverse effects • No CYP-mediated drug interactions	• Inferior efficacy/lack of long-term efficacy data • Toxicity of nucleosides • Risk of cross resistance would make subsequent nucleoside backbone regimens difficult

SOURCE: Guidelines for the Use of Antiretroviral Agents in HIV-infected Adults and Adolescents. MMWR.1998; 47 (No. RR-5). Updated as the Living Document, October 6, 2005. Available at http://www.aidsinfo.nih.gov.

Monitoring Antiretroviral Therapy

The success or failure of antiretroviral therapy should be monitored by the clinical status of the patient as well as laboratory markers.

CLINICAL

• The development of signs or symptoms, such as fever, weight loss, candidiasis, oral hairy leukoplakia, or other opportunistic infections, is suggestive of therapeutic failure regardless of the patient's viral load or CD4+ cell count.

LABORATORY

- Viral load
  - The viral load should be checked at baseline, 1 month after starting therapy and every 3 to 4 months thereafter.
  - For a successful regimen, the viral load should generally decrease by 1 $\log_{10}$ by 2 to 8 weeks and should be undetectable (< 50 copies/mL) after 4 to 6 months. An occasional patient still on a successful regimen can take longer to achieve an undetectable viral load but the trend of the viral load should be continually downward.

Logs and Absolute Numbers

Logs and Absolute Numbers

log	copies/mL	log	copies/mL	log	copies/mL	log	copies/mL	log	copies/mL	log	copies/mL	log	copies/mL
		1.0	= 10	2.0	= 100	3.0	= 1,000	4.0	= 10,000	5.0	= 100,000	6.0	= 1,000,000
0.1	= 1	1.1	= 13	2.1	= 126	3.1	= 1,259	4.1	= 12,589	5.1	= 125,893	6.1	= 1,258,925
0.2	= 2	1.2	= 16	2.2	= 158	3.2	= 1,585	4.2	= 15,849,	5.2	= 158,489	6.2	= 1,584,893
0.3	= 2	1.3	= 20	2.3	= 200	3.3	= 1,995	4.3	= 19,953	5.3	= 199,526	6.3	= 1,995,262
0.4	= 3	1.4	= 25	2.4	= 251	3.4	= 2,512	4.4	= 25,119	5.4	= 251,189	6.4	= 2,511,886
0.5	= 3	1.5	= 32	2.5	= 316	3.5	= 3,162	4.5	= 31,623	5.5	= 316,228	6.5	= 3,162,278
0.6	= 4	1.6	= 40	2.6	= 398	3.6	= 3,981	4.6	= 39,811	5.6	= 398,107	6.6	= 3,981,072
0.7	= 5	1.7	= 50	2.7	= 501	3.7	= 5,012	4.7	= 50,119	5.7	= 501,187	6.7	= 5,011,872
0.8	= 6	1.8	= 63	2.8	= 631	3.8	= 6,310	4.8	= 63,096	5.8	= 630,957	6.8	= 6,309,573
0.9	= 8	1.9	= 79	2.9	= 794	3.9	= 7,943	4.9	= 79,433	5.9	= 794,328	6.9	= 7,943,282
												7.0	= 10,000,000

copies/mL refers to viral load

  - Viral loads must be drawn and processed correctly to obtain accurate results. The specimen should be drawn in a PPT or EDTA tube with completion of initial processing within 4 hours of the lab draw. The tubes are to be spun and the serum separated and frozen within this 4-hour window.

- CD4+ Cell Count
  - The CD4+ cell count should be checked at baseline, 1 month after starting therapy and every 3 to 6 months thereafter.
- Unfortunately, there are several reasons why patients may not achieve an optimal response. Among these are:
  - The patient may have a very high baseline viral load. Patients with loads of 1,000,000 copies/mL of HIV RNA will still have a load of 10,000 copies/mL after a 100-fold reduction in viral titer.
  - The patient may not be taking the drugs as prescribed.
  - The virus may be resistant to one or more of the drugs.

VIRAL LOAD/CD4+ CELL COUNT DISCORDANCE

- Discordance between the trends in CD4+ cell count and viral load can be seen in up to 20% of patients.
- The viral load should generally be used to assess the success or failure of therapy; however, a falling CD4+ cell count should also be considered as a potential sign of treatment failure.

Treatment of the ARV-Experienced Patient

The clinician should log and maintain a thorough medication history to determine antiretroviral agents used in the past and reasons for discontinuation of each agent (e.g., discontinued due to adverse effects versus treatment failure), as well as results of all resistance testing.

CHANGING ANTIRETROVIRAL THERAPY

General principles

- Always confirm within 30 days of failure of a regimen with a second viral load determination before making any changes in therapy.
- Try to determine the reason for failure. Adherence issues need to be addressed before any changes in therapy are made! A complete history and physical examination should be performed to rule out inter-current illness such as a viral URI as a cause of a transient rise in viral load. Vaccinations as well can cause a transient rise in viral load within 14 days of their administration.
- When considering a change in therapy due to virologic failure, resistance testing (either genotyping or phenotyping) should be done while the patient is still on therapy. Seek expert opinion or utilize an up-to-date resource (e.g., Stanford University HIV Drug Resistance Database: http://hivdb.stanford.edu) to interpret the results of testing.
- When changes are made, try to change at least two and preferably three drugs unless genotype or phenotype result suggests otherwise.
- Avoid switching to drugs to which there will be predictable cross-resistance (e.g., nevirapine to efavirenz; indinavir to saquinavir).

HEAVILY ARV TREATMENT EXPERIENCED PATIENT-SALVAGE REGIMENS

- Predictors of virologic failure exist: prior antiretroviral therapy, higher baseline peak viral load values, lower baseline/nadir CD4+ cell count, nonadherence.
- Review antiretroviral drug history carefully.
- Avoid "canceling" drug options without getting detailed history of name of drug, dosing pattern, duration of therapy, side-effects experienced and specific management, and sequencing.
- Assess past and present adherence patterns (identify barriers to successful adherence **first** and attempt to correct these before starting "new" salvage regimens).
- Include resistance testing with expert consultation "early" on in suspected drug failure while patient is on failing regimen.
- Consider therapeutic drug monitoring (specialized cases and expert consultation) to not miss possible "non-drug" related factors such as malabsorption or nonadherence leading to virologic failure.
- Consider referring to available clinical trials for salvage regimen or "newer" agents — visit www.clinicaltrials.gov.

Resistance Assays (See Chapter 8, Antiretroviral Resistance Testing and Therapeutic Drug Monitoring)

Discontinuation of Antiretroviral Therapy

Antiretroviral therapies are capable of producing serious and even life-threatening side-effects as described in the following pages and in Chapter 9, Metabolic Complications of HAART.

Although patients tolerate these products relatively well during the early stages of HIV infection, during the later stages the toxicities may be substantial and may outweigh the benefits.

The cessation of antiretroviral therapy is a matter of clinical judgment. In general, the patients most likely to benefit from cessation are those who are unable to tolerate any combination of drug and have not sustained either clinical or laboratory evidence of improvement on the antiretroviral agents, and have exhausted all drug options. All attempts should be made to continue on a tolerable regimen as studies have shown there is a survival benefit to maintaining the patient on antiviral therapy even though not adequately suppressing their virus.

Antiretroviral Agents

Currently four classes available:

Nucleoside/Nucleotide Reverse Transcriptase Inhibitors (NRTIs)

- Competitively inhibit reverse transcriptase enzyme (prevent viral RNA→DNA)
- Require *in vivo* phosphorylation to be active
- Nucleo*tide* analog: tenofovir; requires less *in vivo* phosphorylation to be active
- Nucleo*side* analogs: zidovudine, didanosine, zalcitabine (to be discontinued in 2006), stavudine, lamivudine, abacavir, emtricitabine

Non-nucleoside Reverse Transcriptase Inhibitors (NNRTIs)

- Noncompetitively inhibit reverse transcriptase enzyme
- NNRTIs: nevirapine, delavirdine, efavirenz

Protease Inhibitors (PIs)

- Inhibit protease enzyme preventing formation of mature proteins
- PIs: indinavir, ritonavir, saquinavir, nelfinavir, amprenavir, lopinavir/ritonavir, atazanavir, fosamprenavir, tipranavir

Fusion Inhibitors

- Bind to gp 41 of HIV particle preventing fusion with CD4+ cell
- T-20 (enfuvirtide) is currently the only fusion inhibitor available

- See Table 6 for Antiretroviral Dosage Forms, Dosing (usual adult doses), and Adverse Effects. Also, refer to the appendix for drug information sheets that are designed to be patient education handouts.

- See Table 7 for Antiretroviral Medication Storage Requirements
- See Table 8 for Dual NRTI, Boosted PI, Dual PI, PI/NRTI, and PI/NNRTI Dosage Adjustments
- See Table 9 for Renal Dosage Adjustments of Antiretroviral Agents
- See Table 10 for Hepatic Dosage Adjustments of Antiretroviral Agents
- See Table 11 for PI and NNRTI Interactions with Oral Contraceptives
- See Chapter 6 of this text or the website www.hiv-druginteractions.org for additional information on antiretroviral drug interactions

Table 6. Antiretroviral Dosage Forms, Dosing, and Adverse Effects

NUCLEOSIDE REVERSE TRANSCRIPTASE INHIBITORS **Class Adverse Effects: Lactic acidosis with hepatic steatosis**				
DRUG NAME	DOSAGE FORMS	USUAL ADULT DOSE	FOOD EFFECT	ADVERSE EFFECTS
Abacavir (Ziagen®, ABC)	300 mg tablets, 20 mg/mL solution	300 mg bid or 600 mg qd	Take with or without food	Hypersensitivity reaction: fever, rash, nausea, vomiting, diarrhea, abdominal pain, malaise, fatigue, respiratory symptoms
Didanosine (Videx®, Videx EC®, ddI)	25, 50, 100, 150, 200 mg non-enteric coated chewable tablets; 100, 125, 200, 250, 400 mg delayed release capsules with enteric-coated beadlets; 2g and 4g per bottle powder for oral solution (generic formulation available)	≥ 60 kg: 200 mg bid or 400 mg qd (250 mg qd when with tenofovir) < 60 kg: 125 mg bid or 250 mg qd (200 mg qd when with tenofovir)	Take ½ hour before or 2 hours after a meal (can be taken with or without food when used with tenofovir)	Pancreatitis, peripheral neuropathy, nausea, diarrhea (diarrhea more common with buffered, non-enteric coated formulation)
Emtricitabine (Emtriva®, FTC)	200 mg capsules, 10 mg/mL solution	200 mg qd (capsule) or 240 mg qd (solution)	Take with or without food	Generally well-tolerated; hyperpigmentation of palms and soles (6%) more common in Black and Hispanic patients; emtricitabine also has activity against hepatitis B; severe acute exacerbations of hepatitis B can be seen when emtricitabine is discontinued in HIV/hepatitis B co-infected patients, monitor hepatic function closely for several months after discontinuation in hepatitis B co-infected patients.
Lamivudine (Epivir®, 3TC)	150, 300 mg tablets, 10 mg/mL solution	150 mg bid or 300 mg qd	Take with or without food	Generally well-tolerated; lamivudine is also used in the treatment of hepatitis B infection; severe acute exacerbations of hepatitis B can be seen when lamivudine is discontinued in HIV/hepatitis B co-infected patients, monitor hepatic function closely for several months after discontinuation in hepatitis B co-infected patients.
Stavudine (Zerit®, d4T)	15, 20, 30, 40 mg capsules, 1 mg/mL solution	≥ 60 kg: 40 mg bid < 60 kg: 30 mg bid	Take with or without food	Peripheral neuropathy, pancreatitis
Zidovudine (Retrovir®, AZT, ZDV)	100 mg capsules; 300 mg tablets; 50 mg/5 mL solution; 10 mg/mL intravenous injection	300 mg bid or 200 mg tid	Take with or without food	Bone marrow suppression (neutropenia and/or anemia), GI intolerance, headache, insomnia, asthenia
COMBINATION PRODUCTS				
Combivir® (zidovudine/ lamivudine, AZT/3TC)	300/150 mg tablets	1 tab bid	Take with or without food	See zidovudine and lamivudine
Epzicom® (lamivudine/abacavir, 3TC/ABC)	300/600 mg tablets	1 tab qd	Take with or without food	See lamivudine and abacavir
Trizivir® (zidovudine/ lamivudine/ abacavir, AZT/3TC/ABC)	300/150/300 mg tablets	1 tab bid	Take with or without food	See zidovudine, lamivudine, and abacavir
Truvada® (emtricitabine/tenofovir, FTC/TDF)	200/300 mg tablets	1 tab qd	Take with or without food	See emtricitabine and tenofovir
NUCEOTIDE REVERSE TRANSCRIPTASE INHIBITOR				
Tenofovir Disoproxil Fumarate (Viread®, TDF)	300 mg tablets	300 mg qd	Take with or without food	Nausea, vomiting, diarrhea, flatulence, rare cases of nephrotoxicity; tenofovir also has activity against hepatitis B; severe acute exacerbations of hepatitis B can be seen when tenofovir is discontinued in HIV/hepatitis B co-infected patients, monitor hepatic function closely for several months after discontinuation in hepatitis B co-infected patients.

NON-NUCLEOSIDE REVERSE TRANSCRIPTASE INHIBITORS
Class adverse effects: rash, increased transaminase enzymes

DRUG NAME	DOSAGE FORMS	USUAL ADULT DOSE	FOOD EFFECT	ADVERSE EFFECTS
Efavirenz (Sustiva®, EFV)	50, 100, 200 mg capsules, or 600 mg tablet	600 mg qhs	Take capsules with or without food; avoid taking with high fat meals; Tablets should be taken on an empty stomach	Rash (1.7%), Central nervous system effects (may include dizziness, somnolence, insomnia, abnormal dreams, confusion, abnormal thinking, impaired concentration, amnesia, agitation, depersonalization, hallucinations, and euphoria) - usually resolves after 2-4 weeks, increased transaminase enzymes, false positive cannabinoid test; teratogenic
Delavirdine (Rescriptor®, DLV)	100, 200 mg tablets	400 mg tid; 4 100 mg tablets can dispersed in ≥ 3 oz water to create slurry; 200 mg tablets should be taken as intact tablets; separate from buffered preparations of didanosine by 1 hour	Take with or without food	Rash (4.3%), increased transaminase enzymes, headaches
Nevirapine (Viramune®, NVP)	200 mg tablet, 50 mg/5mL suspension	200 mg qd x 14 days, then 200 mg bid	Take with or without food	Rash (7%), increased transaminase enzymes, hepatitis (hepatotoxicity more common in women with CD4$^+$ count > 250 and men with CD4$^+$ count > 400, use with extreme caution; monitor LFTs closely in all patients for at least the first 18 weeks of therapy) Often administered as 400 mg qd after induction of 200 mg qd although not FDA approved.

PROTEASE INHIBITORS
Class adverse effects: hyperglycemia, lipodystrophy, lipid abnormalities (except atazanavir), increased bleeding episodes in hemophilliacs

DRUG NAME	DOSAGE FORMS	USUAL ADULT DOSE	FOOD EFFECT	ADVERSE EFFECTS
Amprenavir (Agenerase®, APV)	50 capsules, 15 mg/mL solution (cap and soln. not interchangeable on mg. per mg. basis)	Rarely used in adults due to availability of fosamprenavir	Take with food; avoid high fat meals	Nausea, vomiting, diarrhea, rash, oral paresthesias, increased transaminase enyzmes
Atazanavir (Reyataz®, ATV)	100, 150, 200 mg capsules	400 mg qd **or** ATV 300 mg qd with ritonavir 100 mg qd (Should be boosted with ritonavir in all PI-experienced patients and when used with tenofovir)	Take with food	Nausea, vomiting, diarrhea, jaundice, scleral icterus, increased indirect bilirubin, increased transaminase enzymes
Indinavir (Crixivan®, IDV)	100, 200, 333, 400 mg capsules	800 mg q8h **or** 800 mg bid with ritonavir 100-200 mg bid	Take 1 hr before or 2 hrs after meals (can take with food when combined with ritonavir or can take with skim milk or low fat meal)	Nephrolithiasis, nausea, headache, asthenia, blurred vision, dizziness, rash, metallic taste, thrombocytopenia, alopecia, increased indirect bilirubin
Fosamprenavir (Lexiva®, f-APV)	700 mg tablet (delivers 600 mg of amprenavir)	1400 mg bid or 1400 mg qd with ritonavir 200 mg qd (PI-naïve) or 700 mg bid with ritonavir 100 mg bid (PI-naïve or experienced)	Take with or without food	Nausea, vomiting, diarrhea, rash (19%), oral paresthesias, increased transaminase enzymes, caution with sulfa allergy
Lopinavir/ritonavir (Kaletra®, LPV/r)	200/50 mg tablets, 400/100 mg/5 mL solution	2tabs or 5 mL (400/100 mg) bid (PI-naïve or experienced) 4 tabs or 10 mL (800/200 mg) qd (PI-naïve)	Tablets can be taken with or without food; Solution should be taken with food	Nausea, vomiting, diarrhea, asthenia, alopecia, increased transaminase enzymes
Nelfinavir (Viracept®, NFV)	250 mg, 625 mg tablets; 50 mg/g oral powder	1250 mg bid	Take with food	Diarrhea

Ritonavir (Norvir®, RTV)	100 mg capsules 600 mg/7.5 mL solution	600 mg bid (requires dose escalation) Rarely used as sole PI; See Table 8 for ritonavir-boosted PI regimens	Take with food	Nausea, vomiting, diarrhea, circumoral paresthesias, hepatitis, pancreatitis, asthenia, taste perversion, increased triglycerides, transaminases, CPK, and uric acid levels (side effects less common/severe when used in low doses for boosting)
Saquinavir Hard Gel Capsules, tablets (Invirase®, SQV-HGC, tablets)	200 mg capsules, 500 mg tablets	1000 mg bid + ritonavir 100 mg bid (Should only be used with a ritonavir-containing regimen)	Take with or without food	Nausea, diarrhea, headache, increased transaminase enzymes; less GI adverse effects than Fortovase®, may take with food to decrease GI side effects
Tipranavir capsules (Aptivus®, TPV)	250 mg capsules	500 mg bid + ritonavir 200 mg bid (should only be used with a ritonavir-containing regimen)	Take with food (high fat meal preferred)	Hepatotoxicity-monitor LFTs, closely, contraindicated in patients with moderate to severe hepatic dysfunction (Child-Pugh Class B, C); Rash-8-14% of patients (may be more common in women taking estrogen-containing medications), diarrhea, nausea, vomiting, caution with sulfa allergy

FUSION INHIBITORS

DRUG NAME	DOSAGE FORMS	USUAL ADULT DOSE	RECONSTITUTION/ ADMINISTRATION	ADVERSE EFFECTS
Enfuvirtide (Fuzeon®, T-20)	Powder, 90 mg/1mL after reconstituted	90 mg SQ bid	Reconstitute with Sterile Water for Injection to produce 90mg/mL Inject in upper arm, upper leg or stomach. Rotate injection sites; May store reconstituted vial in refrigerator for 24 hours	Injection site reactions, usually mild to moderate, occur in 97% of patients (itching, swelling, redness, pain, tenderness, induration, nodules, cysts); severe injection site reactions and hypersensitivity reactions can be seen; bacterial pneumonia more common in T-20 treated patients

Source: Tables 10–13 in Guidelines for the Use of Antiretroviral Agents in HIV-infected Adults and Adolescents. *MMWR* 1998; 47 (No. RR-5) Updated as the Living Document, October 6, 2005 http://www.aidsinfo.nih.gov

[1]Once daily lopinavir/ritonavir should only be used in PI-naïve patients and should not be used in patients receiving concomitant efavirenz, nevirapine, amprenavir, fosamprenavir, or nelfinavir

Table 7 – Antiretroviral Medication Storage Requirements

MEDICATION	STORAGE	COMMENTS
Nucleoside/nucleotide reverse transcriptase Inhibitors		
Abacavir (Ziagen®) tablets or solution	20-25°C/68-77°F	Excursions to 15-30°C/59-86°F permitted
Abacavir/lamivudine (Epzicom®)	20-25°C /68-77°F.	Excursions to 15-30°C/59-86°F permitted
Abacavir/lamivudine/zidovudine (Trizivir®)	20-25°C /68-77°F.	Excursions to 15-30°C/59-86°F permitted
Didanosine solution (Videx®)	After reconstitution of powder b pharmacy, refrigerate 2-8°C/36-46°F	Good for 30 days
Didanosine enteric-coated (Videx EC®)	20-25°C /68-77°F.	Excursions to 15-30°C/59-86°F permitted
Emtricitabine (Emtriva®) capsules	20-25°C /68-77°F.	Excursions to 15-30°C/59-86°F permitted
Emtricitabine (Emtriva®) solution	Refrigerate 2-8°C/36-46°F	OK if used within 3 mos if stored at 25°C/77°F; Excursions to 15-30°C/59-86°F permitted
Emtricitabine/Tenofovir (Truvada®)	20-25°C /68-77°F.	Excursions to 15-30°C/59-86°F permitted
Lamivudine tablets (Epivir®)	20-25°C /68-77°F.	Excursions to 15-30°C/59-86°F permitted
Lamivudine solution (Epivir®)	20-25°C /68-77°F	
Lamivudine/zidovudine (Combivir®)	2-30°C/36-86°F	
Stavudine capsules (Zerit®)	20-25°C /68-77°F	Excursions permitted to 15-30°C/59-86°F
Stavudine solution (Zerit®)	After reconstitution of powder at pharmacy, refrigerate 2-8°C/36-46°F	Good for 30 days
Tenofovir (Viread®)	20-25°C /68-77°F	Excursions to 15-30°C/59-86°F permitted
Zidovudine tablets, capsules, or solution (Retrovir®)	15-25°C/59-77°F	

MEDICATION	STORAGE	COMMENTS
Non-nucleoside Reverse Transcriptase Inhibitors		
Delavirdine (Rescriptor®)	20-25°C /68-77°F.	Protect from high humidity
Efavirenz (Sustiva®)	20-25°C /68-77°F	Excursions to 15-30°C/59-86°F permitted
Nevirapine tablets or suspension (Viramune®)	20-25°C /68-77°F	Excursions to 15-30°C/59-86°F permitted
Protease Inhibitors		
Amprenavir capsules or solution (Agenerase®)	20-25°C /68-77°F	Excursions to 15-30°C/59-86°F permitted
Fosamprenavir (Lexiva®)	20-25°C /68-77°F	Excursions to 15-30°C/59-86°F permitted
Indinavir (Crixivan®)	15-30°C/59-86°F	Store in original container with desiccant
Lopinavir/ritonavir tablets (Kaletra®)	20-25°C/68-77°F	Excursions to 15-30°C/59-86°F permitted
Lopinavir/ritonavir solution (Kaletra®)	Refrigerate 2-8°C/36-46°F	OK if used within 2 mos stored at ≤ 25°C/77°F
Nelfinavir (Viracept®)	15-30°C/59-86°F	
Ritonavir capsules (Norvir®)	Refrigerate 2-8°C/36-46°F	OK if used within 1 mos stored at ≤ 25°C/77°F
Ritonavir solution (Norvir®)	20-25°C/68-77°F	Do not refrigerate
Saquinavir hard gel capsules or tablets (Invirase®)	20-25°C /68-77°F	Excursions to 15-30°C/59-86°F permitted
Tipranavir (Aptivus®)	Refrigerate 2°-8°C (36°-46°F)	OK if used within 2 mos stored at ≤ 25°C/77°F; Excursions to 15-30°C/59-86°F permitted

Table 8. Dual NRTI, Boosted PI, Dual PI, PI/NRTI, PI/NNRTI Combination Dose Adjustments

COMBINATION	DOSAGE RECOMMENDATION
didanosine + tenofovir [1]	≥ 60 kg: ↓ ddl dose to 250 mg qd
	< 60 kg: ↓ ddl dose to 200 mg qd
atazanavir + ritonavir	ATV 300 mg qd + RTV 100 mg qd (PI-exp or naive)
atazanavir + tenofovir	ATV 300 mg qd + RTV 100 mg qd + TDF 300 mg qd
atazanavir + efavirenz	ATV 300 mg qd + RTV 100 mg qd + EFV 600 mg qd
fosamprenavir + efavirenz	f-APV 700 mg bid + RTV 100 mg bid + EFV 600 mg qd
fosamprenavir + ritonavir	fos-APV 1400 mg qd + RTV 200 mg qd (PI-naïve)[2]
	fos-APV 700 mg bid + RTV 100 mg bid (PI-naïve or exp)
indinavir + ritonavir	IDV 800 mg bid + RTV 100 mg bid (PI-naïve)
	IDV 800 mg bid + RTV 200 mg bid (PI-exp)
indinavir + efavirenz or nevirapine	IDV 1000 mg q8h (or IDV 800 mg bid + RTV 200 mg bid) with EFV or NVP standard dose
lopinavir/ritonavir + efavirenz or nevirapine	↑ KAL dose to 600/150 mg (3 tabs) bid with EFV or NVP standard dose
saquinavir + ritonavir[3]	saquinavir 1000 mg bid + RTV 100 mg bid
saquinavir + lopinavir/ritonavir[3]	saquinavir 1000 mg bid + KAL 400/100 mg (2 tabs) bid

Source: Table 21 in Guidelines for the Use of Antiretroviral Agents in HIV-infected Adults and Adolescents. *MMWR* 1998; 47 (No. RR-5) Updated as the Living Document, October 6, 2005 http://www.aidsinfo.nih.gov

[1] CAUTION: early failure seen with combination of TDF + ddl when used with NVP or EFV
[2] fosamprenavir + ritonavir qd should not be used in PI experienced patients
[3] Invirase® should only be used in combination with ritonavir or Kaletra®

Table 9. Renal Dose Adjustments[1]

NRTIs	
Didanosine[2]	≥ 60 kg: CrCl 30-59: (buffered) 100 mg bid or 200 mg qd, (EC) 200 mg qd; CrCl 10-29: (buffered) 150 mg qd, (EC) 125 mg qd; CrCl <10 or HD[3] or CAPD: (buffered) 100 mg qd, (EC) 125 mg qd < 60 kg: CrCl 30-59: (buffered) 75 mg bid or 150 mg qd, (EC) 125 mg qd; CrCl 10-29: (buffered) 100 mg qd, (EC) 125 mg qd; CrCl < 10 or HD[3] or CAPD: 75 mg qd (use non-EC formulation)
emtricitabine	CrCl 30-49: 200 mg cap q48h or 120mg soln. q24h; CrCl 15-29: 200 mg cap q72h or 80 mg soln. q24h; CrCl < 15 or HD[3]: 200 mg cap q96h or 60mg soln. q24h
lamivudine	CrCl 30-49: 150 mg qd; CrCl 15-29: 150 mg x 1 then 100 mg qd; CrCl 5-14: 150 mg x 1 then 50 mg qd; CrCl < 5 or HD[3]: 50 mg x 1 then 25 mg qd
stavudine	≥ 60 kg: CrCl 26-50: 20 mg q12h, CrCl ≤ 25 or HD[3]: 20 mg q24h; < 60 kg: CrCl 26-50: 15 mg q12h, CrCl ≤ 25 or HD[3]: 15 mg q24h
tenofovir	CrCl 30-49: 300 mg q48h; CrCl 10-29: 300 mg twice weekly; CrCl < 10 or HD[3]: 300 mg q week
Tenofovir + Emtricitabine (Truvada®)	CrCl 30-49 one tab q48h; CrCl < 30 combo product cannot be used; see dosing for individual agents
zidovudine	CrCl < 15 or HD[3]: 100 mg TID
Combivir® Trizivir® Epzicom®	These combo products should not be used if CrCl < 50 mL/min; see dosing for individual agents

[1]There are no renal dose adjustment recommendations for ABC, PI's, NNRTI's, and T-20
[2] Didanosine buffered tablets no longer available in US.[3]Dose after HD on HD days

Source: Table 14 in Guidelines for the Use of Antiretroviral Agents in HIV-Infected Adults and Adolescents. *MMWR* 1998; 47(RR-5) Updated as the Living Document, October 6, 2005 http://www.aidsinfo.nih.gov.

Creatinine Clearance Calculation:[2]

$$CrCl = \frac{(140\text{-age}) \times (IBW\ in\ kg)}{72 \times Serum\ Cr} \times (0.85\ if\ female)$$

Estimate Ideal Body Weight (IBW) in kg:
Males: IBW = 50 kg + 2.3 kg for each inch over 5 feet.
Females: IBW = 45.5 kg + 2.3 kg for each inch over 5 feet.

Note: If Actual Body Weight (ABW) is less than the Ideal Body Weight (IBW), use ABW for calculating the Creatinine Clearance.

[2] Source: Sande MA, Eliopoulos GM, Moellering RC, Gilbert DN, eds. *The Sanford Guide to HIV/AIDS Therapy 14th edition.*[A3] Sperryville, VA.: Antimicrobal Therapy, Inc. 2005.

Table 10. Hepatic Dose Adjustments[1,2]

√RTIs	
Abacavir[2]	Mild (Child-Pugh 5-6): 200 mg bid Moderate/Severe: Contraindicated
√NRTIs	
Delavirdine or efavirenz	Use with caution-no recommendation
nevirapine	Avoid use with moderate to severe hepatic impairment
PIs	
amprenavir	Child-Pugh 5-8: 450 mg bid; Child-Pugh 9-12: 300 mg bid
atazanavir	Child-Pugh Class B: 300 mg qd; Class C: not recommended
fosamprenavir	Child-Pugh 5-8: 700 mg bid; Child-Pugh 9-12: Not recommended. Ritonavir boosting not advised with hepatic disease
indinavir	Mild to moderate insufficiency with cirrhosis: 600 mg q8h; no data in severe hepatic impairment
lopinavir/ritonavir	Use with caution; no dosing information available
nelfinavir	Use with caution; no dosing information available
ritonavir	No adjustment for mild impairment; no data for moderate/severe impairment-use with caution
saquinavir	Use with caution; no dosing information available
tipranavir	Use with caution; contraindicated with moderate/severe (Child-Pugh Class B & C)

Source: Table 14 in Guidelines for the Use of Antiretroviral Agents in HIV-Infected Adults and Adolescents. *MMWR* 1998; 47(RR-5). Updated as the Living Document, October 6, 2005 http://www.aidsinfo.nih.gov[A4]
[1] GlaxoSmithKline (2004, August). Ziagen® (abacavir Sulfate) tablets Prescribing Information (MG-028). [Electronic document]. Retrieved on November 8, 2005 from http://us.gsk.com/products/assets/us_ziagen_tablets.pdf.
[2] There are no hepatic dose adjustment recommendations for other NRTIs and T-20

Child-Pugh Score (add scores for each category to determine class)

Score	1	2	3
Encephalopathy*	None	Grade 1-2	Grade 3-4
Ascites	None	Mild or controlled by diuretics	Moderate or refractory to diuretics
Albumin	> 3.5 g/dL	2.8-3.5 g/dL	< 2.8 g/dL
Total Bilirubin or	< 2 mg/dL	2-3 mg/dL	> 3 mg/dL
Modified Total Bilirubin**	< 4 mg/dL	4-7 mg/dL	> 7 mg/dL
Prothrombin time	< 4	4-6	> 6
or INR	< 1.7	1.7-2.3	> 2.3

*Grade 1: mild confusion, anxiety, restlessness, fine tremor, slowed coordination; Grade 2: drowsiness, disorientation, asterixis; Grade 3: somnolent but rousable, marked confusion, incomprehensible speech, incontinent, hyperventilation; Grade 4: coma, decerebrate posturing, flaccidity
**Modified Total Bilirubin used to score patients with Gilbert's Syndrome or taking IDV or ATV
Class A: Score 5-6; Class B: Score 7-9; Class C: Score > 9
Source: Table 14 in Guidelines for the Use of Antiretroviral Agents in HIV-Infected Adults and Adolescents. *MMWR* 1998; 47(RR-5). Updated as the Living Document, October 6, 2005 http://www.aidsinfo.nih.gov[A5]

Table 11. PI and NNRTI Interactions with Combination Oral Contraceptives

PI	Interaction	Recommendation
ATV	Ethinyl estradiol AUC ↑ 48%; norethindrone AUC ↑ 110%	Use lowest effective dose or alternate form of contraception
F-APV	APV leads to ↑ in norethindrone and ethinyl estradiol levels and APV levels ↓ 20%	Do not co-administer; alternate form of contraception recommended
IDV	Noethindrone levels ↑ 26%; Ethinyl estradiol levels ↑ 24%	No dosage adjustment recommended
LPV/RTV	Ethinyl estradiol levels ↓ 42%	Use additional or alternate form of contraception
NFV	Noethindrone levels ↓ 18%; Ethinyl estradiol levels ↓ 47%	Use additional or alternate form of contraception
RTV	Ethinyl estradiol levels ↓ 40%	Use additional or alternate form of contraception
SQV	No data	Use additional or alternate form of contraception
TPV/RTV	Ethinyl estradiol levels ↓ 50%	Use additional or alternate form of contraception; women taking estrogens may be at increased risk of TPV-associated rash
NNRTI		
DLV	Potential for increase in ethinyl estradiol levels	Clinical significance unknown
EFV	Ethinyl estradiol levels ↑ 37%;	Use additional or alternate form of contraception
NVP	Ethinyl estradiol levels ↓ 20%	Use alternate or additional form of contraception

Source: Table 20 a and 20 b in Guidelines for the Use of Antiretroviral Agents in HIV-Infected Adults and Adolescents. *MMWR* 1998; 47(RR-5). Updated as the Living Document, October 6, 2005 http://www.aidsinfo.nih.gov).

References

1. Yenni PG, Hammer SM, Hirsch MS, Saag MS, Schechter M, et al. Treatment of adult HIV infection. 2004 Recommendations from the International AIDS Society—USA Panel. *JAMA*. 2004; 292:251-265.

2. Guidelines for the use of antiretroviral agents in HIV-infected adults and adolescents. *MMWR* 1998; 47(RR-5). Updated as the Living Document, October 6, 2005. Available at http://www.aidsinfo.nih.gov.

3. Report of the NIH panel to define principles of therapy of HIV infection. *MMWR* 1998; 47:1-41.

4. Public Health Service Task Force Recommendations for the Use of ARV Drugs in Pregnant Women. Available at http://aidsinfo.nih.gov/guiedlines/default_db2.asp?id=66.

Please see the following APPENDIX for Patient Medication Information

PATIENT MEDICATION INFORMATION

Agenerase®
(Amprenavir, APV)

Agenerase® is a type of anti-HIV drug called a Protease Inhibitor ("PI"). When taken with other anti-HIV drugs it can lower the amount of HIV in the blood (called "viral load") and increase the number of CD4 cells (a type of immune cell in the blood). Therefore, it can slow the damage to the immune system caused by HIV and delay symptoms of advanced HIV infection/AIDS.

You should always use anti-HIV drugs in combination with one another as a "cocktail." If you are starting a new regimen, do not start the meds until you receive all of them from the pharmacy.

Remember to call your pharmacy 5 days ahead for refills so that the pharmacist can order the medications for you!

How to take Agenerase®:
Due to the availability of Lexiva® (Fosamprenavir), Agenerase is rarely used in adult patients. Agenerase® is usually combined with another PI (e.g., Norvir®) to decrease the number of pills you are required to take. Agenerase® can be taken with or without food but you may want to take with food to decrease chance for upset stomach. However, avoid meals high in fat as this can significantly decrease the amount of Agenerase® in your bloodstream. Separate doses of Agenerase® from antacids by at least one hour.

Your healthcare professional should know if you have any of the following conditions before prescribing Agenerase®:
• liver or kidney disease (including Hepatitis B or C infection)
• diabetes
• high cholesterol
• pregnant or trying to be pregnant
• breastfeeding
• hemophilia

Side effects:
Serious side effects include:
• severe rash or rash accompanied with fever, blistering, oral lesions, swelling of eyelids, muscle or joint pain
• Increased blood sugar (thirst, frequent urination, increased appetite)
Call your healthcare provider immediately if you get any of these side effects.

Minor side effects include:
• nausea, vomiting, diarrhea
• increased cholesterol
• tingling sensation around mouth
• changes in fat distribution
• minor rash or itching
Let your healthcare provider know about these side effects if they do not go away or if they bother you.

Drug Interactions:
Combining certain drugs may alter their action or produce unwanted side effects. Tell your healthcare provider or pharmacist about all other drugs you're taking, including non-prescription medicines, herbal products, and nutritional supplements; if you are a frequent user of drinks with caffeine or alcohol; if you smoke; or if you use illegal drugs. Because Agenerase® Capsules and Oral Solution contain large amounts of vitamin E, you should not take additional vitamin E while taking Agenerase.® Check with your healthcare provider before stopping or starting any of your medications.

Things to watch for while taking Agenerase®:
• Similar to all PIs, Agenerase® can cause an increase in blood sugar (increased thirst, frequent urination, increased appetite, or hunger). You should notify your healthcare provider if you develop these symptoms.

Storage Conditions:
Store at controlled room temperature between 20–25°C (68–77°F). Excursions permitted to between 15–30°C (59–86°F). Avoid leaving medications in damp and/or hot environments such as the bathroom or hot car.

If you have any questions, please don't be afraid to ask your healthcare provider, pharmacist, or nurse for help.

PATIENT MEDICATION INFORMATION

Aptivus®
(Tipranavir, TPV)

Aptivus® is a type of anti-HIV drug called a Protease Inhibitor (PI). It interferes with the replication of the human immunodeficiency virus (HIV), the virus that causes AIDS. When taken with other anti-HIV drugs it can lower the amount of HIV in the blood (called "viral load") and increase the number of CD4 cells (a type of immune cell in the blood). Therefore, it can slow damage to the immune system caused by HIV and delay symptoms of advanced HIV infection/AIDS.

You should always use anti-HIV drugs in combination with one another as a "cocktail." If you are starting a new regimen, do not start the meds until you receive all of them from the pharmacy.

Remember to call your pharmacy 5 days ahead for refills so that the pharmacist may order the medications for you!

How to take Aptivus®:
- Take with food to increase the amount of Aptivus® that enters your bloodstream and to decrease stomach upset
- Must be taken with Norvir® to get enough Aptivus® in your bloodstream
- Usual adult dose is 2 Aptivus® capsules with 2 Novir® capsules twice daily

Your healthcare professional should know if you have any of the following conditions before prescribing Aptivus®
- liver or kidney disease (including hepatitis B or C infection)
- diabetes
- pregnant or trying to be pregnant
- breastfeeding
- hemophilia

Side effects:
Serious side effects include:
- yellowing of skin/eyes
- severe rash or rash accompanied with fever, blistering, oral lesions, swelling of eyelids, muscle or joint pain
- Increased blood sugar (thirst, frequent urination, increased appetite)

Call your healthcare provider immediately if you get any of these side effects.

Minor/moderate side effects include:
- minor rash or itching
- nausea, vomiting, diarrhea, heartburn
- changes in fat distribution
- increased cholesterol

Let your healthcare provider know about these side effects if they do not go away or if they bother you.

Drug Interactions:
Combining certain drugs may alter their action or produce unwanted side effects. Tell your healthcare provider or pharmacist about all other drugs you're taking, including non-prescription medicines, herbal products, and nutritional supplements; if you are a frequent user of drinks with caffeine or alcohol; if you smoke; or if you use illegal drugs. Check before stopping or starting any of your medications.

Things to watch for while taking Aptivus®:

- The major toxicity of Aptivus®/Norvir® is liver toxicity. Your healthcare provider will monitor your liver function by checking your liver enzymes with your blood work. Notify your healthcare provider if you have liver disease including hepatitis B or C infection. Drinking excessive amounts of alcohol can also be harmful to your liver. Let your healthcare provider know how much alcohol you drink.
- Similar to all PIs, Aptivus® can cause an increase in blood sugar (increased thirst, frequent urination, increased appetite, or hunger). You should notify your healthcare provider if you develop these symptoms.
- Aptivus®/Norvir® can decrease the effectiveness of oral birth control pills and other hormonal methods of birth control. Use alternate/additional forms of birth control methods.

Storage Conditions:
Aptivus® capsules should be kept in the refrigerator between 2–8°C (36–46°F) if possible but can be stored outside of the refrigerator between 15–30°C (59–86°F) for up to 60 days. Avoid leaving medications in damp and/or hot environments such as the bathroom or hot car.

If you have any questions, please don't be afraid to ask your healthcare provider, pharmacist, or nurse for help.

PATIENT MEDICATION INFORMATION

Combivir®
(Lamivudine, 3TC + Zidovudine, AZT)

Combivir® is a combination of two anti-HIV drugs called Epivir® (lamivudine) and Retrovir® (zidovudine). These are a type of anti-HIV drug called a Nucleoside Reverse Transcriptase Inhibitors (NRTIs or "Nukes"). When taken with other anti-HIV drugs it can lower the amount of HIV in the blood (called "viral load") and increase the number of CD4 cells (a type of immune cell in the blood). Therefore, it can slow the damage to the immune system caused by HIV and delay symptoms of advanced HIV infection/AIDS.

You should always use anti-HIV drugs in combination with one another as a "cocktail." If you are starting a new regimen, do not start the meds until you receive all of them from the pharmacy.

Remember to call your pharmacy 5 days ahead for refills so that the pharmacist can order the medications for you!

How to take Combivir®:
Combivir® can be taken with or without food. If it upsets your stomach, take with food.

Your healthcare professional should know if you have any of the following conditions before prescribing Combivir®:
* anemia
* dental disease
* liver or kidney disease (including hepatitis B or C infection)
* vitamin B12 or folic acid deficiency
* pregnant or trying to be pregnant
* breastfeeding
* recent radiation therapy

Side effects:
Serious side effects include:
* unusual weakness, fatigue, pale skin
* abnormal bleeding
* fever or chills, sore throat
* muscle pain
* persistent nausea, vomiting, stomach discomfort, decreased appetite, tiredness, weakness, shortness of breath (signs of lactic acidosis rare, but serious potential adverse effect of all Nukes)
Note: Lamivudine (a component of Combivir®) is also used in the treatment of hepatitis B infection; severe acute exacerbations of Hepatitis B can be seen when lamivudine is discontinued in HIV/Hepatitis B co-infected patients; liver function must be monitored closely for several months after discontinuation of lamivudine if you are co-infected with Hepatitis B.
Call your healthcare provider immediately if you get any of these side effects.

Minor/moderate side effects include:
* nausea, diarrhea
* headache
* nail or skin discoloration
* Let your healthcare provider know about these side effects if they do not go away or if they bother you.

Drug Interactions:
Combining certain drugs may alter their action or produce unwanted side effects. Tell your healthcare provider or pharmacist about all other drugs you're taking, including non-prescription medicines, herbal products, and nutritional supplements; if you are a frequent user of drinks with caffeine or alcohol; if you smoke; or if you use illegal drugs. Check with your healthcare provider or pharmacist before stopping or starting any of your medications.

Storage Conditions:
Store between 2–30ºC (36–86ºF). Avoid leaving medications in damp and/or hot environments such as the bathroom or hot car.

If you have any questions, please don't be afraid to ask your healthcare provider, pharmacist, or nurse for help.

PATIENT MEDICATION INFORMATION

Crixivan®
(Indinavir, IDV)

Crixivan® is a type of anti-HIV drug called a Protease Inhibitor ("PI"). When taken with other anti-HIV drugs it can lower the amount of HIV in the blood (called "viral load") and increase the number of CD4 cells (a type of immune cell in the blood). Therefore, it can slow the damage to the immune system caused by HIV and delay symptoms of advanced HIV infection/AIDS.

You should always use anti-HIV drugs in combination with one another as a "cocktail." If you are starting a new regimen, do not start the meds until you receive all of them from the pharmacy.

Remember to call your pharmacy 5 days ahead for refills so that the pharmacist can order the medications for you!

How to take Crixivan®:
- Take on empty stomach or with a light meal (e.g. dry toast with jelly, coffee with skim milk, corn flakes with skim milk). When taken in combination with Norvir® or Kaletra® it can be taken with a full meal).
- Drink at least 5 to 6 glasses (8 ounces each) of water each day
- Antacids should be taken at least 1 hour apart from Crixivan®

Your healthcare professional should know if you have any of the following conditions before prescribing Crixivan®:
- liver or kidney disease (including Hepatitis B or C infection)
- diabetes
- high cholesterol
- pregnant or trying to be pregnant
- breastfeeding
- hemophilia

Side effects:
Serious side effects include:
- blood in the urine, pain in your side or back
- Increased blood sugar (thirst, frequent urination, increased appetite)
Call your healthcare provider immediately if you get any of these side effects.

Minor/moderate side effects include:
- headache
- nausea, diarrhea, upset stomach
- changes in taste
- hair loss
- yellowing of skin or eyes
- changes in fat distribution
- increased cholesterol
- skin rash

Let your healthcare provider know about these side effects if they do not go away or if they bother you.

Drug Interactions:
Combining certain drugs may alter their action or produce unwanted side effects. Tell your healthcare provider or pharmacist about all other drugs you're taking, including non-prescription medicines, herbal products, and nutritional supplements; if you are a frequent user of drinks with caffeine or alcohol; if you smoke; or if you use illegal drugs. Check before stopping or starting any of your medications.

Things to watch for while taking Crixivan®:
- Crixivan® has caused kidney stones in some patients. Drink at least 5 to 6 glasses of water each day. This helps reduce the chances of forming kidney stone. You should promptly notify your healthcare provider if you develop kidney pains (e.g., middle to lower back pain), blood in the urine, or difficulty passing urine.
- Similar to all PIs, Crixivan® can cause an increase in blood sugar (increased thirst, frequent urination, increased appetite). You should notify your healthcare provider if you develop these symptoms.

Storage Conditions:
Store at room temperature between 15–30°C (59–86°F). Crixivan® capsules are sensitive to moisture and should be dispensed in the original container with the desiccant "pillow." Some data indicates that Crixivan® capsules are stable in prescription vials for 7 days so you can fill a pillbox one week at a time along with your other medications.

If you have any questions, please don't be afraid to ask your healthcare provider, pharmacist, or nurse for help.

PATIENT MEDICATION INFORMATION

Emtriva®
(Emtricitabine, FTC)
Emtriva® is a type of anti-HIV drug called a Nucleoside Reverse Transcriptase Inhibitor (NRTI or "Nuke"). When taken with other anti-HIV drugs it can lower the amount of HIV in the blood (called "viral load") and increase the number of CD4 cells (a type of immune cell in the blood). Therefore, it can slow the damage to the immune system caused by HIV and delay symptoms of advanced HIV infection/AIDS. Emtriva® is similar to Epivir® (lamivudine) and shares resistance patterns with Epivir®.

You should always use anti-HIV drugs in combination with one another as a "cocktail." If you are starting a new regimen, do not start the meds until you receive all of them from the pharmacy.

Remember to call your pharmacy 5 days ahead for refills so that the pharmacist may order the medications for you!

How to take Emtriva®:
- Usual adult dose is 200 mg (1 capsule) or 240 mg (24 mL) once daily
- Can be taken with or without food. If it upsets your stomach, take it with food.

Your healthcare professional should know if you have any of the following conditions before prescribing Emtriva®:
- breastfeeding
- liver or kidney disease (including hepatitis B or C infection)
- pregnant or trying to be pregnant

Side effects:
Serious side effects include:
- persistent nausea, vomiting, stomach discomfort, decreased appetite, tiredness, weakness, shortness of breath (signs of lactic acidosis rare, but serious potential adverse effect of all Nukes)

Note: Emtriva® also has activity against Hepatitis B; severe acute exacerbations of hepatitis B can be seen when Emtriva® is discontinued in HIV/Hepatitis B co-infected patients; liver function must be monitored closely for several months after discontinuation of Emtriva® if you are co-infected with Hepatitis B.
Call your healthcare provider immediately if you get the above side effects.

Emtriva® is generally well tolerated.
Minor side effects include:
- hyperpigmentation or darkening of the skin on the palms or soles (more common in African American and Hispanic patients)
Let your healthcare provider know about these side effects if they do not go away or if they bother you

Drug Interactions:
Combining certain drugs may alter their action or produce unwanted side effects. Tell your healthcare provider or pharmacist about all other drugs you're taking, including non-prescription medicines, herbal products, and nutritional supplements; if you are a frequent user of drinks with caffeine or alcohol; if you smoke; or if you use illegal drugs. Check with your healthcare provider or pharmacist before stopping or starting any of your medications.

Storage Conditions:
Store Emtriva® capsules at controlled room temperature between 20–25ºC (68–77ºF). Excursions permitted to between 15–30º C (59–86º F). Store Emtriva® solution in refrigerator at 2-8ºC (36-46ºF) OK if used within 3 mos if stored at 25ºC (77ºF). Avoid leaving medications in damp and/or hot environments such as the bathroom or hot car.

If you have any questions, please don't be afraid to ask your healthcare provider, pharmacist, or nurse for help.

PATIENT MEDICATION INFORMATION

Epivir®
(Lamivudine, 3TC)

Epivir® is a type of anti-HIV drug called a Nucleoside Reverse Transcriptase Inhibitor (NRTI or "Nuke"). When taken with other anti-HIV drugs it can lower the amount of HIV in the blood (called "viral load") and increase the number of CD4 cells (a type of immune cell in the blood). Therefore, it can slow the damage to the immune system caused by HIV and delay symptoms of advanced HIV infection/AIDS.

You should always use anti-HIV drugs in combination with one another as a "cocktail." If you are starting a new regimen, do not start the meds until you receive all of them from the pharmacy.

Remember to call your pharmacy 5 days ahead for refills so that the pharmacist can order the medications for you!

How to take Epivir®:
Epivir® can be taken with or without food. If it upsets your stomach, take it with food.

Your healthcare professional should know if you have any of the following conditions before prescribing Epivir®:

- liver or kidney disease (including Hepatitis B or C infection)
- pregnant or trying to be pregnant
- breastfeeding

Side effects:
Epivir® is generally well tolerated.
Serious side effects include:
- persistent nausea, vomiting, stomach discomfort, decreased appetite, tiredness, weakness, shortness of breath (signs of lactic acidosis rare, but serious potential adverse effect of all Nukes)

Note: Epivir® is also used in the treatment of Hepatitis B infection; severe acute exacerbations of Hepatitis B can be seen when Epivir® is discontinued in HIV/Hepatitis B co-infected patients; liver function must be monitored closely for several months after discontinuation of Epivir® if you are co-infected with Hepatitis B.

Call your healthcare provider immediately if you get the above side effects.

Minor/moderate side effects include:
- skin rash
Let your healthcare provider know about these side effects if they do not go away or if they bother you.

Drug Interactions:
Combining certain drugs may alter their action or produce unwanted side effects. Tell your healthcare provider or pharmacist about all other drugs you're taking, including non-prescription medicines, herbal products, and nutritional supplements; if you are a frequent user of drinks with caffeine or alcohol; if you smoke; or if you use illegal drugs. Check with your healthcare provider or pharmacist before stopping or starting any of your medications.

Storage Conditions:
Store at controlled room temperature between 20–25ºC (68–77ºF). Excursions permitted to between 15–30ºC (59–86º F). Avoid leaving medications in damp and/or hot environments such as the bathroom or hot car.

If you have any questions, please don't be afraid to ask your healthcare provider, pharmacist, or nurse for help.

PATIENT MEDICATION INFORMATION

Epzicom®
(Lamivudine, 3TC + Abacavir, ABC)

Epzicom® is a combination of two anti-HIV drugs called Epivir® (lamivudine) and Ziagen® (abacavir). These are a type of anti-HIV drug called a Nucleoside Reverse Transcriptase Inhibitor (NRTI or "Nuke"). When taken with other anti-HIV drugs it can lower the amount of HIV in the blood (called "viral load") and increase the number of CD4 cells (a type of immune cell in the blood). Therefore, it can slow the damage to the immune system caused by HIV and delay symptoms of advanced HIV infection/AIDS.

You should always use anti-HIV drugs in combination with one another as a "cocktail." If you are starting a new regimen, do not start the meds until you receive all of them from the pharmacy.

Remember to call your pharmacy 5 days ahead for refills so that the pharmacist can order the medications for you!

How to take Epzicom®:
Epzicom® can be taken with or without food. If it upsets your stomach, take it with food.

Your healthcare professional should know if you have any of the following conditions before prescribing Epzicom®:

- anemia
- liver or kidney disease (including hepatitis B or C infection)
- pregnant or trying to be pregnant
- breastfeeding
- history of abacavir (Ziagen®) hypersensitivity reaction/allergy

Side effects:
Serious side effects include:
- persistent nausea, vomiting, stomach discomfort, decreased appetite, tiredness, weakness, shortness of breath (signs of lactic acidosis rare, but serious potential adverse effect of all Nukes)
- **hypersensitivity reaction**
You may be having this reaction if: 1) you get a skin rash or 2) you get 1 or more symptoms from at least 2 of the following groups: 1-fever; 2-nausea, vomiting, diarrhea, stomach pain; 3-extreme tiredness, achiness, general ill feeling; 4-sore throat, shortness of breath, cough

It is important to stop taking Epzicom® and call your healthcare provider immediately if you experience these side effects. If you must stop treatment with Epzicom® because you have had a hypersensitivity reaction, NEVER TAKE EPZICOM® or TRIZIVIR® or ZIAGEN® AGAIN.

Note: Lamivudine (a component of Epzicom®) is also used in the treatment of Hepatitis B infection; severe acute exacerbations of Hepatitis B can be seen when lamivudine is discontinued in HIV/hepatitis B co-infected patients; liver function must be monitored closely for several months after discontinuation of lamivudine if you are co-infected with Hepatitis B.
Call your healthcare provider immediately if you get the above side effects.

Minor side effects include:
- skin rash
Let your healthcare provider know about these side effects if they do not go away or if they bother you.

Drug Interactions:
Combining certain drugs may alter their action or produce unwanted side effects. Tell your healthcare provider or pharmacist about all other drugs you're taking, including non-prescription medicines, herbal products, and nutritional supplements; if you are a frequent user of drinks with caffeine or alcohol; if you smoke; or if you use illegal drugs. Check with your healthcare provider or pharmacist before stopping or starting any of your medications.

Things to watch for while taking Epzicom®:
- Epzicom® can cause a serious hypersensitivity (allergic) reaction in some patients. You must be familiar with the possible side effects above and immediately call you healthcare provider if they occur.

Storage Conditions:
Store at controlled room temperature between 20–25°C (68–77°F). Excursions permitted to between 15–30°C (59–86°F). Avoid leaving medications in damp and/or hot environments such as the bathroom or hot car.

If you have any questions, please don't be afraid to ask your healthcare provider, pharmacist, or nurse for help.

PATIENT MEDICATION INFORMATION
Fuzeon®
(Enfuvirtide, T-20)

Fuzeon® is the first in a new class of anti-HIV drugs known as fusion Inhibitors. It inhibits the entry of the human immunodeficiency virus (HIV) into the CD4 cells (a type of immune cell in the blood) that HIV attacks. It works by blocking HIV's ability to infect healthy CD4 cells. This means that the HIV cannot enter the cell and then it cannot multiply. This is because HIV needs the DNA in the host cell so it can multiply.

You should always use anti-HIV drugs in combination with one another as a "cocktail." If you are starting a new regimen, do not start the meds until you receive all of them from the pharmacy.

Remember to call your pharmacy 5 days ahead for refills so that the pharmacist may order the medications for you!

How to take Fuzeon®:
The usual dose is 90 mg twice a day, given as a 1 ml subcutaneous (just below the skin) injection into the upper arm, thigh, or abdomen. Each injection should be given at a site different from the last place you injected. Never inject a dose where there is still an injection site reaction from an earlier dose. You should not inject your medicine into moles, scar tissue, bruises, or your navel. The injection comes as a powder and you will need to mix with the sterile water provided. This mixing needs to be done using aseptic technique and you will be provided instructions by your nurse or pharmacist.

Your healthcare professional should know if you have any of the following conditions before prescribing Fuzeon®:
• pregnant or trying to be pregnant
• breastfeeding

Side effects:
Serious side effects include:
• **hypersensitivity (allergy)** – Although rare, you may experience trouble breathing, fever, nausea, vomiting, skin rash, blood in your urine, and/or chills.
Call your healthcare provider immediately if you get any of the above side effects.
Minor/moderate side effects include:
• reactions at the injection site(s) – itchiness, swelling, redness, pain or tenderness, hardened skin, or bumps. These reactions can appear within the first week of treatment and generally do not get worse with continued use of Fuzeon.® Reactions at an individual injection site usually last for less than 7 days.
• to minimize injection site reactions, massage the area and/or apply heat to area.
Let your healthcare provider know about these side effects if they do not go away or if they bother you.

Drug Interactions:
Combining certain drugs may alter their action or produce unwanted side effects. Tell your healthcare provider or pharmacist about all other drugs you're taking, including non-prescription medicines, herbal products, and nutritional supplements; if you are a frequent user of drinks with caffeine or alcohol; if you smoke; or if you use illegal drugs. Check before stopping or starting any of your medications.

Things to watch for while taking Fuzeon®:
• Fuzeon® can cause injection site reactions. Call your healthcare provider right away if there are signs of infection at the injection site such as oozing, increasing heat, swelling, redness, or pain.
• Do not throw away used needles and syringes in the trash. Ask your healthcare provider for a sharps container for needle and syringe disposal.

Storage Conditions:
Store at room temperature between 15–30°C (59 86°F). Reconstituted solution should be stored under refrigeration at 2–8°C (36°–46°F) and used within 24 hours.

If you have any questions, please don't be afraid to ask your healthcare provider, pharmacist, or nurse for help

PATIENT MEDICATION INFORMATION

Invirase®
(Saquinavir — hard gel capsules, HGC, or tablets, SQV)

Invirase® is a type of anti-HIV drug called a Protease Inhibitor ("PI"). When taken with other anti-HIV drugs it can lower the amount of HIV in the blood (called "viral load") and increase the number of CD4 cells (a type of immune cell in the blood). Therefore, it can slow the damage to the immune system caused by HIV and delay symptoms of advanced HIV infection/AIDS.

You should always use anti-HIV drugs in combination with one another as a "cocktail." If you are starting a new regimen, do not start the meds until you receive all of them from the pharmacy.

Remember to call your pharmacy 5 days ahead for refills so that the pharmacist can order the medications for you!

How to take Invirase®:
Invirase® should always be used in combination with other PIs (e.g., Norvir® or Kaletra®). Take Invirase® together with other PI and with food if possible to decrease stomach upset.

Your healthcare professional should know if you have any of the following conditions before prescribing Invirase®:
- liver or kidney disease (including Hepatitis B or C infection)
- diabetes
- high cholesterol
- pregnant or trying to be pregnant
- breastfeeding
- hemophilia

Side effects:
Serious side effects include:
- increased blood sugar (thirst, frequent urination, increased appetite)
Call your healthcare provider immediately if you get any of these side effects.

Minor/moderate side effects include:
- diarrhea, gas, nausea
- increased cholesterol
- headache
- changes in fat distribution
Let your healthcare provider know about these side effects if they do not go away or if they bother you.

Drug Interactions:
Combining certain drugs may alter their action or produce unwanted side effects. Tell your healthcare provider or pharmacist about all other drugs you're taking, including non-prescription medicines, herbal products, and nutritional supplements; if you are a frequent user of drinks with caffeine or alcohol; if you smoke; or if you use illegal drugs. Check with your healthcare provider or pharmacist before stopping or starting any of your medications.

Things to watch for while taking Invirase®:
- Similar to all PIs, Invirase® can cause an increase in blood sugar (increased thirst, frequent urination, increased appetite). You should notify your healthcare provider if you develop these symptoms.

Storage Conditions:
Store at controlled room temperature between 20–25°C (68–77°F). Excursions permitted to between 15–30°C (59–86°F). Avoid leaving medications in damp and/or hot environments such as the bathroom or hot car.

If you have any questions, please don't be afraid to ask your healthcare provider, pharmacist, or nurse for help.

PATIENT MEDICATION INFORMATION

Kaletra®
(Lopinavir+ Ritonavir, KAL)

Kaletra® is a type of anti-HIV drug called a Protease Inhibitor ("PI"). When taken with other anti-HIV drugs it can lower the amount of HIV in the blood (called "viral load") and increase the number of CD4 cells (a type of immune cell in the blood). Therefore, it can slow the damage to the immune system caused by HIV and delay symptoms of advanced HIV infection/AIDS.

You should always use anti-HIV drugs in combination with one another as a "cocktail." If you are starting a new regimen, do not start the meds until you receive all of them from the pharmacy.

Remember to call your pharmacy 5 days ahead for refills so that the pharmacist can order the medications for you!

How to take Kaletra®:
Kaletra® tablets can be taken with or without food. If it upsets your stomach, take with food. Kaletra® solution should be taken with food to increase the amount that gets into your system and decrease the chance for upset stomach.

Your healthcare professional should know if you have any of the following conditions before prescribing Kaletra®:

- kidney or liver disease (including Hepatitis B or C infection)
- diabetes
- high cholesterol
- pregnant or trying to be pregnant
- breastfeeding
- pancreatitis
- hemophilia

Side effects:
Serious side effects include:
- severe nausea, vomiting, stomach pain (signs of inflamed pancreas)
- increased blood sugar (thirst, frequent urination, increased appetite)

Call your healthcare provider immediately if you get any of these side effects.

Minor/moderate side effects include:
- change in taste, loss of appetite
- nausea, vomiting, diarrhea, heartburn
- changes in fat distribution
- increased cholesterol
- hair loss

Let your healthcare provider know about these side effects if they do not go away or if they bother you.

Drug Interactions:
Combining certain drugs may alter their action or produce unwanted side effects. Tell your healthcare provider or pharmacist about all other drugs you are taking, including non-prescription medicines, herbal products, and nutritional supplements; if you are a frequent user of drinks with caffeine or alcohol; if you smoke; or if you use illegal drugs. Check with your healthcare provider or pharmacist before stopping or starting any of your medications.

Things to watch for while taking Kaletra®:

- Alcohol can increase the risk of developing stomach pain, nausea, vomiting, which can indicate an inflamed pancreas, a severe side effect. Avoid alcoholic drinks while you are taking Kaletra®. Do not treat yourself for nausea, vomiting, or stomach pain – call your healthcare provider for advice.
- Kaletra® can decrease the effectiveness of oral birth control pills and other hormonal methods of birth control. Use alternate/additional forms of birth control methods.
- Similar to all PIs, Kaletra® can cause an increase in blood sugar (increased thirst, frequent urination, increased appetite, or hunger). You should notify your healthcare provider if you develop these symptoms.

Storage Conditions:

Kaletra® tablets can be stored at controlled room temperature between 20–25°C (68–77°F). Excursions permitted to between 15–30°C/59–86°F.
Kaletra® oral solution should be kept in the refrigerator between 2–8°C (36–46°F) if possible but can be stored outside of the refrigerator between 15–30°C (59–86°F) for up to 60 days. Avoid leaving medications in damp and/or hot environments such as the bathroom or hot car.

If you have any questions, please don't be afraid to ask your healthcare provider, pharmacist, or nurse for help.

PATIENT MEDICATION INFORMATION

Lexiva®
(Fosamprenavir, fos-APV)

Lexiva® is a type of anti-HIV drug called a Protease Inhibitor ("PI"). When taken with other anti-HIV drugs it can lower the amount of HIV in the blood (called "viral load") and increase the number of CD4 cells (a type of immune cell in the blood). Therefore, it can slow the damage to the immune system caused by HIV and delay symptoms of advanced HIV infection/AIDS. Lexiva® is a prodrug of Agenerase® and is converted to amprenavir in the body.

You should always use anti-HIV drugs in combination with one another as a "cocktail." If you are starting a new regimen, do not start the meds until you receive all of them from the pharmacy.

Remember to call your pharmacy 5 days ahead for refills so that the pharmacist can order the medications for you!

How to take Lexiva®:
Lexiva® is usually combined with another PI (e.g., Norvir®) to decrease the number of pills you are required to take. Lexiva® can be taken with or without food.

Your healthcare professional should know if you have any of the following conditions before prescribing Lexiva®:
- liver or kidney disease (including Hepatitis B or C infection)
- diabetes
- high cholesterol
- pregnant or trying to be pregnant
- breastfeeding
- hemophilia

Side effects:
Serious side effects include:
- severe rash or rash accompanied with fever, blistering, oral lesions, swelling of eyelids, muscle or joint pain
- increased blood sugar (thirst, frequent urination, increased appetite)
Call your healthcare provider immediately if you get any of these side effects.

Minor side effects include:
- nausea, vomiting, diarrhea
- increased cholesterol
- tingling sensation around mouth
- changes in fat distribution
- minor rash or itching
Let your healthcare provider know about these side effects if they do not go away or if they bother you.

Drug Interactions:
Combining certain drugs may alter their action or produce unwanted side effects. Tell your healthcare provider or pharmacist about all other drugs you're taking, including non-prescription medicines, herbal products, and nutritional supplements; if you are a frequent user of drinks with caffeine or alcohol; if you smoke; or if you use illegal drugs. Check with your healthcare provider or pharmacist before stopping or starting any of your medications.

Things to watch for while taking Lexiva®:
- Similar to all PIs, Lexiva® can cause an increase in blood sugar (increased thirst, frequent urination, increased appetite, or hunger). You should notify your healthcare provider if you develop these symptoms.

Storage Conditions:
Store at controlled room temperature between 20–25°C (68–77°F). Excursions permitted to between 15–30°C (59–86°F). Avoid leaving medications in damp and/or hot environments such as the bathroom or hot car.

If you have any questions, please don't be afraid to ask your healthcare provider, pharmacist, or nurse for help.

PATIENT MEDICATION INFORMATION
Norvir®
(Ritonavir, RTV)

Norvir® is a type of anti-HIV drug called a Protease Inhibitor ("PI"). When taken with other anti-HIV drugs it can lower the amount of HIV in the blood (called "viral load") and increase the number of CD4 cells (a type of immune cell in the blood). Therefore, it can slow the damage to the immune system caused by HIV and delay symptoms of advanced HIV infection/AIDS. Norvir® is often combined with other PIs (i.e., Agenerase,® Crixivan,® Fortovase,® Invirase,® Reyataz®) to decrease the number of pills that need to be taken. This is often called "boosting."

You should always use anti-HIV drugs in combination with one another as a "cocktail." If you are starting a new regimen, do not start the meds until you receive all of them from the pharmacy.

Remember to call your pharmacy 5 days ahead for refills so that the pharmacist can order the medications for you!

How to take Norvir®:
Norvir® should be taken with food, either a meal or snack. May not be required when taken with other PIs; follow the instructions of your healthcare provider.

Your healthcare professional should know if you have any of the following conditions before prescribing Norvir®:
• liver or kidney disease (including Hepatitis B or C infection)
• diabetes
• high cholesterol
• pregnant or trying to be pregnant
• breastfeeding
• hemophilia

Side effects (Note: side effects appear to be less common and less severe when Norvir® is used in low doses for "boosting"):
Serious side effects include:
• increased blood sugar (thirst, frequent urination, increased appetite)
Call your healthcare provider immediately if you get any of these side effects.

Minor/moderate side effects include:
• change in taste, loss of appetite
• nausea, vomiting, diarrhea, heartburn
• tingling sensation around the mouth
• increased cholesterol (less common when used in low doses with Reyataz®)
• changes in fat distribution
Let your healthcare provider know about these side effects if they do not go away or if they bother you.

Drug Interactions:
Combining certain drugs may alter their action or produce unwanted side effects. Tell your healthcare provider or pharmacist about all other drugs you're taking, including non-prescription medicines, herbal products, and nutritional supplements; if you are a frequent user of drinks with caffeine or alcohol; if you smoke; or if you use illegal drugs. Check with your healthcare provider or pharmacist before stopping or starting any of your medications.

Things to watch for while taking Norvir®:
• Norvir® can decrease the effectiveness of oral birth control pills and other hormonal methods of birth control. Use alternate/additional form of birth control methods.
• Similar to all PIs, Norvir® can cause an increase in blood sugar (increased thirst, frequent urination, increased appetite). You should notify your healthcare provider if you develop these symptoms.

Storage Conditions:
Capsules should be kept in refrigerator between 2–8°C (36–46°F) if possible, but can be stored outside of the refrigerator for up to 30 days. Never keep your medicines in your car. If you live in a hot climate or your home is hot in the summer, you should keep Norvir® refrigerated.
Oral solution should be stored at room temperature between 20–25°C (68–77°F). Do not refrigerate. Avoid leaving medications in damp and/or hot environments such as the bathroom or hot car.

If you have any questions, please don't be afraid to ask your healthcare provider, pharmacist, or nurse for help.

PATIENT MEDICATION INFORMATION

Rescriptor®
(Delavirdine, DLV)

Rescriptor® is a type of anti-HIV drug called a Non-nucleoside Reverse Transcriptase Inhibitor (NNRTI or "Non-"Nuke"). When taken with other anti-HIV drugs it can lower the amount of HIV in the blood (called "viral load") and increase the number of CD4 cells (a type of immune cell in the blood). Therefore, it can slow the damage to the immune system caused by HIV and delay symptoms of advanced HIV infection/AIDS.

You should always use anti-HIV drugs in combination with one another as a "cocktail." If you are starting a new regimen, do not start the meds until you receive all of them from the pharmacy.

Remember to call your pharmacy 5 days ahead for refills so that the pharmacist can order the medications for you!

How to take Rescriptor®:

Rescriptor® can be taken with or without food. If it upsets your stomach, take it with food. Tablets may be dispersed in 3 ounces of water prior to consumption for better taste. Antacids, if taken, should be separated by at least 1 hour from Rescriptor®.

Your healthcare professional should know if you have any of the following conditions before prescribing Rescriptor®:
* liver or kidney disease (including Hepatitis B or C infection)
* pregnant or trying to be pregnant
* breastfeeding

Side effects:
Serious side effects include:
* moderate/severe rash or rash accompanied with fever, blistering, oral lesions, swelling of eyelids, muscle or joint pain
Call your healthcare provider immediately if you get any of these side effects.

Minor/moderate side effects include:
* headache
* minor skin rash, itching
* nausea, vomiting, diarrhea
Let your healthcare provider know about these side effects if they do not go away or if they bother you.

Drug Interactions:
Combining certain drugs may alter their action or produce unwanted side effects. Tell your healthcare provider or pharmacist about all other drugs you're taking, including non-prescription medicines, herbal products, and nutritional supplements; if you are a frequent user of drinks with caffeine or alcohol; if you smoke; or if you use illegal drugs. Check with your healthcare provider or pharmacist before stopping or starting any of your medications.

Things to watch for while taking Rescriptor®:
The major toxicity of Rescriptor® is rash. The majority of rashes associated with Rescriptor® occur within 1 to 3 weeks after initiating treatment. The rash usually resolves in 3 to 14 days while the therapy is still continued. You should promptly notify your healthcare provider if you develop a rash.

Storage Conditions:
Store at room temperature between 20–25°C (68–77°F). Protect from high humidity. Avoid leaving medications in damp and/or hot environments such as the bathroom or hot car.

If you have any questions, please don't be afraid to ask your healthcare provider, pharmacist, or nurse for help.

PATIENT MEDICATION INFORMATION

Retrovir®
(Zidovudine, AZT, ZDV)

Retrovir® is a type of anti-HIV drug called a Nucleoside Reverse Transcriptase Inhibitor (NRTI or "Nuke"). When taken with other anti-HIV drugs it can lower the amount of HIV in the blood (called "viral load") and increase the number of CD4 cells (a type of immune cell in the blood). Therefore, it can slow the damage to the immune system caused by HIV and delay symptoms of advanced HIV infection/AIDS.

You should always use anti-HIV drugs in combination with one another as a "cocktail." If you are starting a new regimen, do not start the meds until you receive all of them from the pharmacy.

Remember to call your pharmacy 5 days ahead for refills so that the pharmacist can order the medications for you!

How to take Retrovir®:
Retrovir® can be taken with or without food. If it upsets your stomach, take it with food.

Your healthcare professional should know if you have any of the following conditions before prescribing Retrovir®:
- anemia
- dental disease
- liver or kidney disease (including Hepatitis B or C infection)
- recent radiation therapy
- vitamin B12 or folic acid deficiency
- pregnant or trying to be pregnant
- breastfeeding

Side effects:
Serious side effects include:
- unusual weakness, fatigue, pale skin
- fever or chills, sore throat
- abnormal bleeding
- muscle pain
- persistent nausea, vomiting, stomach discomfort, decreased appetite, tiredness, weakness, shortness of breath (signs of lactic acidosis)

Call your healthcare provider immediately if you get any of these side effects.

Minor/moderate side effects include:
- nausea, diarrhea
- headache
- nail or skin discoloration

Let your healthcare provider know about these side effects if they do not go away or if they bother you.

Drug Interactions:
Combining certain drugs may alter their action or produce unwanted side effects. Tell your healthcare provider or pharmacist about all other drugs you're taking, including non-prescription medicines, herbal products, and nutritional supplements; if you are a frequent user of drinks with caffeine or alcohol; if you smoke; or if you use illegal drugs. Check with your healthcare provider or pharmacist before stopping or starting any of your medications.

Storage Conditions:
Store between 15–25°C (59–77°F). Avoid leaving medications in damp and/or hot environments such as the bathroom or hot car.

If you have any questions, please don't be afraid to ask your healthcare provider, pharmacist, or nurse for help.

PATIENT MEDICATION INFORMATION
Reyataz®
(Atazanavir, ATV)

Reyataz® is a type of anti-HIV drug called a Protease Inhibitor (PI). It interferes with the replication of the human immunodeficiency virus (HIV), the virus that causes AIDS. When taken with other anti-HIV drugs it can lower the amount of HIV in the blood (called "viral load") and increase the number of CD4 cells (a type of immune cell in the blood). Therefore, it can slow damage to the immune system caused by HIV and delay symptoms of advanced HIV infection/AIDS. Reyataz® is different from other PIs because it does not increase cholesterol or triglycerides.

You should always use anti-HIV drugs in combination with one another as a "cocktail." If you are starting a new regimen, do not start the meds until you receive all of them from the pharmacy.

Remember to call your pharmacy 5 days ahead for refills so that the pharmacist may order the medications for you!

How to take Reyataz®:
Take with food to increase the amount of Reyataz® that enters your bloodstream. Take 2 capsules one time daily with food. Separate dosing by 2 hours from antacids (e.g., Tums®), 12 hours from H-2 blockers (e.g., Pepcid®) and do not take with proton pump inhibitors (e.g., Prilosec®, Prevacid®, or Protonix®).

Your healthcare professional should know if you have any of the following conditions before prescribing Reyataz®:
• liver or kidney disease (including Hepatitis B or C infection)
• diabetes
• pregnant or trying to be pregnant
• breastfeeding
• hemophilia

Side effects:
Serious side effects include:
• changes in heartbeat, dizziness, or lightheadedness
• increased blood sugar (thirst, frequent urination, increased appetite
Call your healthcare provider immediately if you get any of these side effects.

Minor side effects include:
• nausea/vomiting
• yellowing of eyes or skin
• rash
• changes in fat distribution
Let your healthcare provider know about these side effects if they do not go away or if they bother you.

Drug Interactions:
Combining certain drugs may alter their action or produce unwanted side effects. Tell your healthcare provider or pharmacist about all other drugs you're taking, including non-prescription medicines, herbal products, and nutritional supplements; if you are a frequent user of drinks with caffeine or alcohol; if you smoke; or if you use illegal drugs. Check with your healthcare provider or pharmacist before stopping or starting any of your medications. Reyataz® interacts with over-the-counter and prescription drugs used to treat stomach acid. Talk to your healthcare provider or pharmacist if you are taking antacids (e.g., Tums®), an "H-2 blocker" (e.g., Pepcid®, Axid®, Zantac®), or a proton pump inhibitor (e.g., Prevacid®, Protonix®, Prilosec®).

Things to watch for while taking Reyataz®:
• Reyataz® can cause yellowing of skin and eyes in some patients. This is called jaundice but is not related to liver damage. Notify your healthcare provider if you develop noticeable yellowing of eyes or skin.
• Similar to all PIs, Reyataz® can cause an increase in blood sugar (increased thirst, frequent urination, increased appetite or hunger). You should notify your healthcare provider if you develop these symptoms.

Storage Conditions:
Store at controlled room temperature between 20–25ºC (68–77ºF). Excursions permitted to between 15–30ºC (59–86ºF). Avoid leaving medications in damp and/or hot environments such as the bathroom or hot car.

If you have any questions, please don't be afraid to ask your healthcare provider, pharmacist, or nurse for help.

PATIENT MEDICATION INFORMATION

Sustiva®
(Efavirenz, EFV)

Sustiva® is a type of anti-HIV drug called a Non-nucleoside Reverse Transcriptase Inhibitor (NNRTI or "Non-Nuke"). When taken with other anti-HIV drugs it can lower the amount of HIV in the blood (called "viral load") and increase the number of CD4 cells (a type of immune cell in the blood). Therefore, it can slow the damage to the immune system caused by HIV and delay symptoms of advanced HIV infection/AIDS.

You should always use anti-HIV drugs in combination with one another as a "cocktail." If you are starting a new regimen, do not start the meds until you receive all of them from the pharmacy.

Remember to call your pharmacy 5 days ahead for refills so that the pharmacist can order the medications for you!

How to take Sustiva®:
Sustiva® capsules can be taken with or without food (avoid taking with high fat meal). Tablets should ideally be taken on an empty stomach. Take at bedtime.
Your healthcare professional should know if you have any of the following conditions before prescribing Sustiva®:
* liver or kidney disease (including Hepatitis B or C infection)
* pregnant or trying to be pregnant
* breastfeeding

Side effects:
Serious side effects include:
* severe rash or rash accompanied with fever, blistering, oral lesions, swelling of eyelids, muscle or joint pain
* depression, anxiety
* hallucinations
Call your healthcare provider immediately if you get any of these side effects.

Minor side effects include:
* dizziness
* drowsiness
* vivid dreams
* impaired cognition
* insomnia
* headache
* minor skin rash, itching
* nausea, vomiting, diarrhea

Let your healthcare provider know about these side effects if they do not go away or if they bother you.

Drug Interactions:
Combining certain drugs may alter their action or produce unwanted side effects. Tell your healthcare provider or pharmacist about all other drugs you're taking, including non-prescription medicines, herbal products, and nutritional supplements; if you are a frequent user of drinks with caffeine or alcohol; if you smoke; or if you use illegal drugs. Check with your healthcare provider or pharmacist before stopping or starting any of your medications.

Things to watch for while taking Sustiva®:
The major side effects of Sustiva® are dizziness and vivid dreams. These adverse effects usually improve after the first month of therapy. If you have difficulty sleeping, contact your healthcare provider. The majority of rashes associated with Sustiva® occur within 1 to 3 weeks after initiating treatment. The rash usually resolves in 3 to 14 days while the therapy is still continued. You should promptly notify your healthcare provider of any severe rash or rash accompanied with fever, blistering, oral lesions, swelling of eyelids, face or hands, muscle or joint pain.
Sustiva® can be harmful to your fetus if you become pregnant — let your healthcare provider know if you are trying to get pregnant or do not use a regular form of contraception.

Storage Conditions:
Store at controlled room temperature between 20–25°C (68–77°F). Excursions permitted to between 15–30°C (59–86°F). Avoid leaving medications in damp and/or hot environments such as the bathroom or hot car.

If you have any questions, please don't be afraid to ask your healthcare provider, pharmacist, or nurse for help.

PATIENT MEDICATION INFORMATION

Trizivir®
(Lamivudine, 3TC + Zidovudine, AZT, Abacavir, ABC)

Trizivir® is a combination of three anti-HIV drugs called Epivir® (lamivudine), Retovir® (zidovudine) and Ziagen® (abacavir). These are a type of anti-HIV drug called a Nucleoside Reverse Transcriptase Inhibitors (NRTIs or "Nukes"). When taken with other anti-HIV drugs it can lower the amount of HIV in the blood (called "viral load") and increase the number of CD4 cells (a type of immune cell in the blood). Therefore, it can slow the damage to the immune system caused by HIV and delay symptoms of advanced HIV infection/AIDS.

Remember to call your pharmacy 5 days ahead for refills so that the pharmacist can order the medications for you!
How to take Trizivir®:
Trizivir® can be taken with or without food. If it upsets your stomach, take it with food.

Your healthcare professional should know if you have any of the following conditions before prescribing Trizivir®:

- anemia
- dental disease
- liver or kidney disease
- recent radiation therapy
- vitamin B12 or folic acid deficiency

- pregnant or trying to be pregnant
- breastfeeding
- history of abacavir (Ziagen®) hypersensitivity reaction/allergy

Side effects:
Serious side effects include:
- unusual weakness, fatigue, pale skin
- abnormal bleeding
- muscle pain
- persistent nausea, vomiting, stomach discomfort, decreased appetite, tiredness, weakness, shortness of breath (signs of lactic acidosis-a rare, but serious potential adverse effect of all Nukes)
- **hypersensitivity reaction**

You may be having this reaction if: 1) you get a skin rash or 2) you get 1 or more symptoms from at least 2 of the following groups: 1-fever; 2-nausea, vomiting, diarrhea, stomach pain; 3-extreme tiredness, achiness, general ill feeling; 4-sore throat, shortness of breath, cough
It is important to stop taking Trizivir® and call your healthcare provider immediately if you experience these side effects. If you must stop treatment with Trizivir® because you have had this serious reaction, NEVER TAKE TRIZIVIR® OR ZIAGEN® OR EPZICOM® AGAIN.

Note: Lamivudine (a component of Trizivir®) is also used in the treatment of hepatitis B infection; severe acute exacerbations of hepatitis B can be seen when lamivudine is discontinued in HIV/hepatitis B co-infected patients; liver function must be monitored closely for several months after discontinuation of lamivudine if you are co-infected with hepatitis B.
Call your healthcare provider immediately if you get any of these side effects.

Minor/moderate side effects include:
- nausea, diarrhea
- headache
- nail or skin discoloration
Let your healthcare provider know about these side effects if they do not go away or if they bother you.

Drug Interactions:
Combining certain drugs may alter their action or produce unwanted side effects. Tell your healthcare provider or pharmacist about all other drugs you're taking, including non-prescription medicines, herbal products, and nutritional supplements; if you are a frequent user of drinks with caffeine or alcohol; if you smoke; or if you use illegal drugs. Check with your healthcare provider or pharmacist before stopping or starting any of your medications.
Things to watch for while taking Trizivir®:
- Trizivir® can cause a serious allergic reaction in some patients. You must be familiar with the possible side effects above and immediately call your healthcare provider if they occur.

Storage Conditions:
Store at controlled room temperature between 20–25ºC (68–77ºF). Excursions permitted to between 15–30°C (59–86° F). Avoid leaving medications in damp and/or hot environments such as the bathroom or hot car.

If you have any questions, please don't be afraid to ask your healthcare provider, pharmacist, or nurse for help.

PATIENT MEDICATION INFORMATION

Truvada®
(Emtricitabine, FTC + Tenofovir, TDF)

Truvada® is a combination of two anti-HIV drugs called Emtriva® (emtricitabine) and Viread® (tenofovir). These are a type of anti-HIV drug called a Nucleoside/Nucleotide Reverse Transcriptase Inhibitors (NRTIs or "Nukes"). When taken with other anti-HIV drugs it can lower the amount of HIV in the blood (called "viral load") and increase the number of CD4 cells (a type of immune cell in the blood). Therefore, it can slow the damage to the immune system caused by HIV and delay symptoms of advanced HIV infection/AIDS. Truvada® contains Emtriva® which is similar to Epivir® (lamivudine) and shares resistance patterns with Epivir®.

You should always use anti-HIV drugs in combination with one another as a "cocktail." If you are starting a new regimen, do not start the meds until you receive all of them from the pharmacy.

Remember to call your pharmacy 5 days ahead for refills so that the pharmacist may order the medications for you!

How to take Truvada®:
Take 1 tablet once daily.
Can be taken with or without food. If it upsets your stomach, take it with food. If taking Videx®/Videx EC® (didanosine) with Truvada®, a reduced dose of Videx®/Videx EC® is needed.

Your healthcare professional should know if you have any of the following conditions before prescribing Truvada®:
• breastfeeding
• liver or kidney disease (including Hepatitis B or C infection)
• pregnant or trying to be pregnant
• osteoporosis or other bone problems

Side effects:
Serious side effects include:
• persistent nausea, vomiting, stomach discomfort, decreased appetite, tiredness, weakness, shortness of breath (signs of lactic acidosis rare, but serious potential adverse effect of all Nukes)
• decrease in kidney function (your doctor will monitor labs to check for this side effect; notify your healthcare provider immediately if you develop difficulty passing urine)

Note: Tenofovir and emtricitabine (components Truvada®) also have activity against Hepatitis B; severe acute exacerbations of Hepatitis B can be seen when tenofovir/emtricitabine are discontinued in HIV/Hepatitis B co-infected patients; liver function must be monitored closely for several months after discontinuation of tenofovir/emtricitabine if you are co-infected with Hepatitis B.
Call your healthcare provider immediately if you get any of these side effects.

Minor side effects include:
Truvada® is generally well tolerated.
• mild to moderate headache
• nausea/vomiting/diarrhea (usually mild)
• flatulence (intestinal gas)
• hyperpigmentation or darkening of the skin on the palms or soles (more common in African American and Hispanic patients)
Let your healthcare provider know about these side effects if they do not go away or if they bother you

Drug Interactions:
Combining certain drugs may alter their action or produce unwanted side effects. Tell your healthcare provider or pharmacist about all other drugs you're taking, including non-prescription medicines, herbal products, and nutritional supplements; if you are a frequent user of drinks with caffeine or alcohol; if you smoke; or if you use illegal drugs. Truvada® can increase levels of Videx®/Videx EC® – you may require a reduced dose of Videx®/Videx EC® when used with Truvada®. Check with your healthcare provider or pharmacist before stopping or starting any of your medications.

Storage Conditions:
Store at controlled room temperature between 20–25ºC (68–77ºF). Excursions permitted to between 15–30ºC (59–86º F). Avoid leaving medications in damp and/or hot environments such as the bathroom or hot car.

If you have any questions, please don't be afraid to ask your healthcare provider, pharmacist, or nurse for help.

PATIENT MEDICATION INFORMATION

Videx®
(Didanosine, ddl)

Videx® is a type of anti-HIV drug called a Nucleoside Reverse Transcriptase Inhibitor (NRTI or "Nuke"). When taken with other anti-HIV drugs it can lower the amount of HIV in the blood (called "viral load") and increase the number of CD4 cells (a type of immune cell in the blood). Therefore, it can slow the damage to the immune system caused by HIV and delay symptoms of advanced HIV infection/AIDS.

You should always use anti-HIV drugs in combination with one another as a "cocktail." If you are starting a new regimen, do not start the meds until you receive all of them from the pharmacy.

Remember to call your pharmacy 5 days ahead for refills so that the pharmacist may order the medications for you!

How to take Videx®:
You must take 2 tablets for each dose; chew tablets thoroughly.
Must be taken on an <u>empty stomach</u>, at least 30 minutes before or 2 hours after a meal (can be taken with or without food when given with Viread® or Truvada®).
If taking Videx/Videx EC® with Viread® or Truvada®, a reduced dose of Videx/Videx EC® is needed.

Your healthcare professional should know if you have any of the following conditions before prescribing Videx®:
• pancreatitis (inflamed pancreas)
• liver or kidney problems (including Hepatitis B or C infection)
• alcoholism
• gout
• tingling or numbness in the hands or feet
• pregnant or trying to be pregnant
• breastfeeding

Side effects:
Serious side effects include:
• persistent nausea, vomiting, stomach discomfort, decreased appetite, tiredness, weakness, shortness of breath (signs of lactic acidosis-a rare, but serious potential adverse effect of all Nukes)
• severe nausea, vomiting, stomach pain (signs of inflamed pancreas)
• vision changes (seeing colors or blurred vision)
• muscle pain
Call your healthcare provider immediately if you get any of these side effects.

Minor/moderate side effects include:
• nausea, diarrhea (more common with chewable tablets)
• tingling, pain or numbness in the hands or feet
Let your healthcare provider know about these side effects if they do not go away or if they bother you.

Drug Interactions:
Combining certain drugs may alter their action or produce unwanted side effects. Tell your healthcare provider or pharmacist about all other drugs you're taking, including non-prescription medicines, herbal products, and nutritional supplements; if you are a frequent user of drinks with caffeine or alcohol; if you smoke; or if you use illegal drugs. Check with your healthcare provider or pharmacist before stopping or starting any of your medications. Videx® contains a magnesium buffer that can affect the absorption of other medications; ask your healthcare provider or pharmacist if you are not sure if you are taking a medication that may interact with Videx®.

Things to watch for while taking Videx®:
• Alcohol can increase the risk of developing stomach pain, nausea, vomiting, which can indicate inflamed pancreas, a severe side effect. Do not treat yourself for these symptoms — call your healthcare provider for advice.

Storage Conditions:
Store tablets between 15–30°C (59–86° F). After reconstitution of powder at pharmacy, refrigerate oral solution at 2–8°C (36–46°F). Avoid leaving medications in damp and/or hot environments such as the bathroom or hot car.

If you have any questions, please don't be afraid to ask your healthcare provider, pharmacist, or nurse for help.

PATIENT MEDICATION INFORMATION
Videx EC ®
(Didanosine enteric coated, ddI)

Videx EC® is a type of anti-HIV drug called a Nucleoside Reverse Transcriptase Inhibitor (NRTI or "Nuke"). When taken with other anti-HIV drugs it can lower the amount of HIV in the blood (called "viral load") and increase the number of CD4 cells (a type of immune cell in the blood). Therefore, it can slow the damage to the immune system caused by HIV and delay symptoms of advanced HIV infection/AIDS.

You should always use anti-HIV drugs in combination with one another as a "cocktail." If you are starting a new regimen, do not start the meds until you receive all of them from the pharmacy.

Remember to call your pharmacy 5 days ahead for refills so that the pharmacist may order the medications for you!

How to take Videx EC®:
Must be taken on an empty stomach, at least 30 minutes before or 2 hours after a meal (can be taken with food when given with Viread®).
Swallow capsules whole, do not chew or break open. If taking Videx/Videx EC® with Viread®, a reduced dose of Videx/Videx EC® is needed.

Your healthcare professional should know if you have any of the following conditions before prescribing Videx EC®:
- pancreatitis (inflamed pancreas)
- liver or kidney problems (including Hepatitis B or C infection)
- alcoholism
- gout
- tingling or numbness in the hands or feet
- pregnant or trying to be pregnant
- breastfeeding

Side effects:
Serious side effects include:
- persistent nausea, vomiting, stomach discomfort, decreased appetite, tiredness, weakness, shortness of breath (signs of lactic acidosis rare, but serious potential adverse effect of all Nukes)
- severe nausea, vomiting, stomach pain (signs of inflamed pancreas)
- vision changes (seeing colors or blurred vision)
- muscle pain

Call your healthcare provider immediately if you get any of these side effects.

Minor/moderate side effects include:
- nausea, diarrhea (more common with non-enteric coated tablets)
- tingling, pain or numbness in the hands or feet

Let your healthcare provider know about these side effects if they do not go away or if they bother you.

Drug Interactions:
Combining certain drugs may alter their action or produce unwanted side effects. Tell your healthcare provider or pharmacist about all other drugs you're taking, including non-prescription medicines, herbal products, and nutritional supplements; if you are a frequent user of drinks with caffeine or alcohol; if you smoke; or if you use illegal drugs. Videx EC® interacts with Viread® and Truvada® - you may require a reduced dose of Videx EC® if you are taking it with Viread® or Truvada®. Check with your healthcare provider or pharmacist before stopping or starting any of your medications.

Things to watch for while taking Videx EC®:
- Alcohol can increase the risk of developing stomach pain, nausea, vomiting, which can indicate inflamed pancreas, a severe side effect. Do not treat yourself for these symptoms — call your healthcare provider for advice.

Storage Conditions:
Store at controlled room temperature between 20-25ºC (68-77ºF). Excursions permitted to 15 and 30° C (59 and 86° F). Avoid leaving medications in damp and/or hot environments such as the bathroom or hot car.

If you have any questions, please don't be afraid to ask your healthcare provider, pharmacist, or nurse for help.

PATIENT MEDICATION INFORMATION

Viracept®
(Nelfinavir, NFV)

Viracept® is a type of anti-HIV drug called a Protease Inhibitor ("PI"). When taken with other anti-HIV drugs it can lower the amount of HIV in the blood (called "viral load") and increase the number of CD4 cells (a type of immune cell in the blood). Therefore, it can slow the damage to the immune system caused by HIV and delay symptoms of advanced HIV infection/AIDS.

You should always use anti-HIV drugs in combination with one another as a "cocktail." If you are starting a new regimen, do not start the meds until you receive all of them from the pharmacy.

Remember to call your pharmacy 5 days ahead for refills so that the pharmacist can order the medications for you!

How to take Viracept®:
Viracept® is to be taken with food, either a meal or snack.

Your healthcare professional should know if you have any of the following conditions before prescribing Viracept®:
- liver or kidney disease
- diabetes
- high cholesterol
- pregnant or trying to be pregnant
- breastfeeding
- hemophilia

Side effects:
Serious side effects include:
- increased blood sugar (thirst, frequent urination, increased appetite)

Call your healthcare provider immediately if you get any of these side effects.

Minor/moderate side effects include:
- diarrhea or gas
- headache
- increased cholesterol
- changes in fat distribution

Let your healthcare provider know about these side effects if they do not go away or if they bother you.

Drug Interactions:
Combining certain drugs may alter their action or produce unwanted side effects. Tell your healthcare provider or pharmacist about all other drugs you're taking, including non-prescription medicines, herbal products, and nutritional supplements; if you are a frequent user of drinks with caffeine or alcohol; if you smoke; or if you use illegal drugs. Check with your healthcare provider or pharmacist before stopping or starting any of your medications.

Things to watch for while taking Viracept®:
- The most common side effect of Viracept® is diarrhea. This can usually be controlled with non-prescription drugs, such as Imodium ®(loperamide).
- Viracept® can decrease the effectiveness of oral birth control pills and other hormonal methods of birth control. Use alternate/additional form of birth control methods.
- Similar to all PIs, Viracept® can cause an increase in blood sugar (increased thirst, frequent urination, increased appetite, or hunger). You should notify your healthcare provider if you develop these symptoms.

Storage Conditions:
Store at room temperature between 15–30°C (59–86°F). Avoid leaving medications in damp and/or hot environments such as the bathroom or hot car.

If you have any questions, please don't be afraid to ask your healthcare provider, pharmacist, or nurse for help.

PATIENT MEDICATION INFORMATION

Viramune®
(Nevirapine, NVP)

Viramune® is a type of anti-HIV drug called a Non-nucleoside Reverse Transcriptase Inhibitor (NNRTI or "Non-Nuke"). When taken with other anti-HIV drugs it can lower the amount of HIV in the blood (called "viral load") and increase the number of CD4 cells (a type of immune cell in the blood). Therefore, it can slow the damage to the immune system caused by HIV and delay symptoms of advanced HIV infection/AIDS.

You should always use anti-HIV drugs in combination with one another as a "cocktail." If you are starting a new regimen, do not start the meds until you receive all of them from the pharmacy.

Remember to call your pharmacy 5 days ahead for refills so that the pharmacist can order the medications for you!

How to take Viramune®:
Viramune® can be taken with or without food. If it upsets your stomach, take with food. For the first 2 weeks of therapy, you will need to take a lower dose of Viramune®. Do not increase your dose of Viramune® if you experience rash during that time. Contact your healthcare provider immediately.

Your healthcare professional should know if you have any of the following conditions before prescribing Viramune®:
• kidney or liver disease (including Hepatitis B or C infection)
• pregnant or trying to be pregnant
• breastfeeding

Side effects:
Serious side effects include:
• severe rash or rash accompanied with fever, blistering, oral lesions, swelling of eyelids, muscle or joint pain
• abdominal pain
• yellowing of skin/eyes
Call your healthcare provider immediately if you develop a rash or any of the side effects listed above.

Minor/moderate side effects include:
• headache
• nausea, vomiting
Let your healthcare provider know about these side effects if they do not go away or if they bother you.

Drug Interactions:
Combining certain drugs may alter their action or produce unwanted side effects. Tell your healthcare provider or pharmacist about all other drugs you're taking, including non-prescription medicines, herbal products, and nutritional supplements; if you are a frequent user of drinks with caffeine or alcohol; if you smoke; or if you use illegal drugs. Check with your healthcare provider or pharmacist before stopping or starting any of your medications.

Things to watch for while taking Viramune®:
•   The major toxicities of Viramune® are rash and liver toxicity. You should promptly notify your healthcare provider if you develop a rash. Your healthcare provider will monitor your liver function closely while on Viramune®. You should not increase your Viramune® dose if you develop rash during the first 2 weeks of therapy — call your healthcare provider.
•   Viramune® can decrease the effectiveness of oral birth control pills and other hormonal methods of birth control. Use alternate/additional form of birth control methods.

Storage Conditions:
Store at controlled room temperature between 20–25°C (68–77°F). Excursions permitted to between 15–30°C (59–86°F). Avoid leaving medications in damp and/or hot environments such as the bathroom or hot car.

If you have any questions, please don't be afraid to ask your healthcare provider, pharmacist, or nurse for help.

PATIENT MEDICATION INFORMATION

Viread®
(Tenofovir, TDF)

Viread® is a type of anti-HIV drug called a Nucleo*tide* Reverse Transcriptase Inhibitor. It works similarly to the Nucleoside Reverse Transcriptase Inhibitors (NRTI or "Nuke"). When taken with other anti-HIV drugs it can lower the amount of HIV in the blood (called "viral load") and increase the number of CD4 cells (a type of immune cell in the blood). Therefore, it can slow the damage to the immune system caused by HIV and delay symptoms of advanced HIV infection/AIDS.

You should always use anti-HIV drugs in combination with one another as a "cocktail." If you are starting a new regimen, do not start the meds until you receive all of them from the pharmacy.

Remember to call your pharmacy 5 days ahead for refills so that the pharmacist can order the medications for you!

How to take Viread®:
Viread® should be taken once a day with or without food. If taking Videx®/Videx EC® (didanosine) with Viread®, a reduced dose of Videx®/Videx EC® is needed.

Your healthcare professional should know if you have any of the following conditions before prescribing Viread®:
- **liver or kidney disease (including Hepatitis B or C infection)**
- **pregnant or trying to be pregnant**
- **breastfeeding**
- **osteoporosis or other bone problems**

Side effects:
Serious side effects include:
- decrease in kidney function (your doctor will monitor labs to check for this side effect; notify your healthcare provider immediately if you develop difficulty passing urine)
- persistent nausea, vomiting, stomach discomfort, decreased appetite, tiredness, weakness, shortness of breath (signs of lactic acidosis rare, but serious potential adverse effect of all Nukes)

Note: Tenofovir also has activity against Hepatitis B; severe acute exacerbations of Hepatitis B can be seen when tenofovir is discontinued in HIV/Hepatitis B co-infected patients; liver function must be monitored closely for several months after discontinuation of tenofovir if you are co-infected with Hepatitis B.
Call your healthcare provider immediately if you get any of these side effects.

Minor/moderate side effects include:
- diarrhea, nausea, vomiting
- flatulence (gas)
Let your healthcare provider know about these side effects if they do not go away or if they bother you.

Drug Interactions:
Combining certain drugs may alter their action or produce unwanted side effects. Tell your healthcare provider or pharmacist about all other drugs you're taking, including non-prescription medicines, herbal products, and nutritional supplements; if you are a frequent user of drinks with caffeine or alcohol; if you smoke; or if you use illegal drugs. Check with your healthcare provider or pharmacist before starting or stopping any of your medications. Viread® and Truvada® interact with Videx®/Videx EC® – you may require a reduced dose of Videx®/Videx EC® if you are taking it with Viread® or Truvada®.

Storage Conditions:
Store at controlled room temperature between 20–25°C (68–77°F). Excursions permitted to between 15–30°C (59–86°F). Avoid leaving medications in damp and/or hot environments such as the bathroom or hot car.

If you have any questions, please don't be afraid to ask your healthcare provider, pharmacist, or nurse for help.

PATIENT MEDICATION INFORMATION

Zerit®
(Stavudine, d4T)

Zerit® is a type of anti-HIV drug called a Nucleoside Reverse Transcriptase Inhibitor (NRTI or "Nuke"). When taken with other anti-HIV drugs it can lower the amount of HIV in the blood (called "viral load") and increase the number of CD4 cells (a type of immune cell in the blood). Therefore, it can slow the damage to the immune system caused by HIV and delay symptoms of advanced HIV infection/AIDS.

You should always use anti-HIV drugs in combination with one another as a "cocktail." If you are starting a new regimen, do not start the meds until you receive all of them from the pharmacy.

Remember to call your pharmacy 5 days ahead for refills so that the pharmacist can order the medications for you!

How to take Zerit®:

Zerit® can be taken with or without food. If it upsets your stomach, take it with food.

Your healthcare professional should know if you have any of the following conditions before prescribing Zerit®:
- pancreatitis (inflamed pancreas)
- liver or kidney problems (including hepatitis B or C infection)
- alcoholism
- tingling or numbness in the hands or feet
- pregnant or trying to be pregnant
- breastfeeding

Side effects:
Serious side effects include:
- tingling, pain, or numbness in the hands or feet
- muscle pain
- severe nausea, vomiting, stomach pain (signs of inflamed pancreas)
- persistent nausea, vomiting, stomach discomfort, decreased appetite, tiredness, weakness, shortness of breath are signs of lactic acidosis rare, but serious potential adverse effect of all Nukes.

Call your healthcare provider immediately if you get any of these side effects.

Minor side effects include:
- stomach upset, diarrhea
- difficulty sleeping
- headache
- lipoatrophy (loss of fat in face, buttocks, extremities)

Let your healthcare provider know about these side effects if they do not go away or if they bother you.

Drug Interactions:
ombining certain drugs may alter their action or produce unwanted side effects. Tell your healthcare provider or pharmacist about all other drugs you're taking, including non-prescription medicines, herbal products, and nutritional supplements; if you are a frequent user of drinks with caffeine or alcohol; if you smoke; or if you use illegal drugs. Check before stopping or starting any of your medications.

Things to watch for while taking Zerit®:
- Alcohol can increase the risk of developing stomach pain, nausea, vomiting, which can indicate inflamed pancreas, a severe side effect. Avoid alcoholic drinks while you are taking Zerit®. Do not treat yourself for these symptoms-call your healthcare provider for advice.

Storage Conditions:
Store capsules at controlled room temperature between 20–25ºC (68–77ºF). Excursions permitted to 15 and 30° C (59 and 86° F). After reconstitution of powder at pharmacy, store solution in refrigerator (2–8ºC/36–46ºF) and discard any unused portion after 30 days. Avoid leaving medications in damp and/or hot environments such as the bathroom or hot car.

If you have any questions, please don't be afraid to ask your healthcare provider, pharmacist, or nurse for help.

PATIENT MEDICATION INFORMATION

Ziagen®
(Abacavir, ABC)

Ziagen® is a type of anti-HIV drug called a Nucleoside Reverse Transcriptase Inhibitor (NRTI or "Nuke"). When taken with other anti-HIV drugs it can lower the amount of HIV in the blood (called "viral load") and increase the number of CD4 cells (a type of immune cell in the blood). Therefore, it can slow the damage to the immune system caused by HIV and delay symptoms of advanced HIV infection/AIDS.

You should always use anti-HIV drugs in combination with one another as a "cocktail." If you are starting a new regimen, do not start the meds until you receive all of them from the pharmacy.

Remember to call your pharmacy 5 days ahead for refills so that the pharmacist can order the medications for you!

How to take Ziagen®:
Ziagen® can be taken with or without food. If it upsets your stomach, take it with food.

Your healthcare professional should know if you have any of the following conditions before prescribing Ziagen®:
*   anemia
*   liver or kidney disease
*   pregnant or trying to be pregnant
*   breastfeeding
*   history of abacavir (Ziagen®) hypersensitivity reaction/allergy

Side effects:
Serious side effects include:
*   persistent nausea, vomiting, stomach discomfort, decreased appetite, tiredness, weakness, shortness of breath are signs of lactic acidosis rare, but serious potential adverse effect of all Nukes.
* hypersensitivity reaction
You may be having this reaction if: 1) you get a skin rash or 2) you get 1 or more symptoms from at least 2 of the following groups: 1-fever; 2-nausea, vomiting, diarrhea, stomach pain; 3-extreme tiredness, achiness, general ill feeling; 4-sore throat, shortness of breath, cough
It is important to stop taking Ziagen® and call your healthcare provider immediately if you experience these side effects. If you must stop treatment with Ziagen® because you have had a hypersensitivity reaction, NEVER TAKE ZIAGEN® or TRIZIVIR® AGAIN.

Drug Interactions:
Combining certain drugs may alter their action or produce unwanted side effects. Tell your healthcare provider or pharmacist about all other drugs you're taking, including non-prescription medicines, herbal products, and nutritional supplements; if you are a frequent user of drinks with caffeine or alcohol; if you smoke; or if you use illegal drugs. Check with your healthcare provider or pharmacist before stopping or starting any of your medications.

Things to watch for while taking Ziagen®:
*   Ziagen® can cause a serious hypersensitivity (allergic) reaction in some patients. You must be familiar with the possible side effects above and immediately call you healthcare provider if they occur.

Storage Conditions:
Store at controlled room temperature between 20–25ºC (68–77ºF). Excursions permitted to between 15–30ºC (59–86ºF). Solution may be refrigerated but do not freeze. Avoid leaving medications in damp and/or hot environments such as the bathroom or hot car.

If you have any questions, please don't be afraid to ask your healthcare provider, pharmacist, or nurse for help.

6

Antiretroviral Drug Interactions

Michael Thompson PharmD, BCNSP
Professor of Pharmacy Practice
College of Pharmacy and Pharmaceutical Sciences
Florida A&M University
Faculty, Florida/Caribbean AIDS Education and Training Center

Introduction

Clinicians responsible for prescribing, dispensing and/or monitoring antiretroviral drug therapy must thoroughly understand the role of drug-drug interactions involving these agents. Because of their unique metabolism and physical characteristics, antiretroviral agents can negatively interact with a wide host of pharmacologic agents. In order to avoid adverse consequences, those providing care for these patients should become familiar with these drug interactions in order to achieve and maintain therapeutic success. The purpose of this chapter is:

- To identify and discuss important factors to consider in order to successfully identify, predict and manage drug interactions
- To discuss the mechanisms of drug interactions and
- To provide a detailed summary of various interactions with specific emphasis on patient management issues to avoid or manage potential interactions

Drug Interactions: Patient Considerations

Antiretroviral agents have the potential to interact with a wide variety of prescription and nonprescription medications. A thorough medication history **must** be obtained in order to identify potential interactions so that decisions can be made concerning current drug therapy. When determining if an antiretroviral agent will interact adversely with medications that a patient is taking, the clinician should:

- Obtain a thorough history of all medications being consumed including all nonprescription products (OTC), prescription drugs and dietary/herbal supplements
- Determine which interactions have potential clinical significance by consulting appropriate primary literature sources and textbooks when appropriate

- Develop an understanding of the mechanisms that cause drug interactions with antiretrovirals to enable in order to predict the potential for their occurrence
- Recommend changes in therapy to avoid negative interactions
- Discuss the positive drug interactions that are desirable in order to improve therapeutic success with antiretroviral regimens
- Base decisions on sound information obtained from primary care provider

Drug Interactions: Understanding the Mechanisms Involved

Although research in the area of drug interactions with antiretroviral drugs has increased in recent years, gaps still exist in knowledge relative to many of these interactions. The clinician must be careful to derive sound decisions based upon the source of information balanced against the clinical situation of the patient. To this end, controlled trials utilizing large numbers of patients are always preferable to case reports with small numbers of patients involved. A brief review of major mechanisms involved in drug interactions is provided.

DRUG ABSORPTION

Drug-Food Interactions Involving Absorption

Clinicians often overlook the importance between drugs and food. This phenomenon is incredibly important since concomitant administration of some medications with food can result in decreased absorption of the antiretroviral. In contrast, some medications should be taken with food to improve bioavailability. A summary of antiretroviral-food interactions is provided in Table 1.

Table 1. Summary of Antiretrovirals (ARVs) and Food Interactions

No Effect	Food decreases ARV levels	Food Increases ARV levels
Abacavir	Didanosine	Atazanvir
Delavirdine	Amprenavir[1]	Lopinavir/ritonavir
Emtricitabine	Indinavir (unboosted)	Nelfinavir
Fosamprenavir		Ritonavir[2]
Indinavir (boosted)		Saquinavir (soft gel caps)
Lamivudine		Efavirenz[3]
Nevirapine		
Stavudine		
Tenofovir		
Zalcitabine		
Zidovudine		

1. High fat meal may decrease blood concentration
2. Food intake can increase bioavailability but also improves tolerability
3. Take on an empty stomach. High fat/high caloric meals may increase plasma concentrations by 39% or higher·

Understanding the importance of the interaction with food is important in order to assure adequate adherence to prescribed regimens. Thus, clinicians must be sure to properly educate patients as to the best time to administer their medications to avoid problems with absorption.

Drug-Drug Interactions Involving Absorption
Antacids, Proton Pump Inhibitors and H$_2$Antagonist Blockers

- Drugs affecting the gastric acidity can have a profound effect on absorption. Two main antiretrovirals to consider include atazanavir and didanosine.
  — Atazanivir (Reyataz®) should not be administered with medications that reduce gastric acidity because its gastric absorption is decreased. Using ritonavir to boost atazanvir concentrations in patients receiving antacids, proton pump inhibitors or H2-antagonists is not recommended.
  — Didanosine (Videx®) contains buffering agents that can affect the absorption of other medications including atazanavir, tetracyclines, quinolones, and itraconazole.

INTERACTIONS INVOLVING DRUG METABOLISM

The protease inhibitors and the non-nucleoside reverse transcriptase inhibitors (NNRTIs) are primarily metabolized through the cytochrome P-450 family of enzymes. These enzymes are present in the highest concentration in the liver, but are also present in the apical enterocytes of the gastrointestinal tract. There are multiple metabolic pathways by which these drugs are metabolized, with the most significant being CYP3A4.[1]

Inhibition of CYP450 enzymes can lead to increases in drug levels of agents that are normally metabolized through CYP450 and can occur after the first dose of an enzyme inhibitor. In contrast, CYP450 enzyme induction leads to a decrease in serum concentrations in drug levels with the time frame for maximal induction being about 2 weeks. In vitro studies have indicated that inhibition of metabolism is most potent with ritonavir, followed by saquinavir, lopinavir, and indinavir, which in turn are more potent inhibitors than amprenavir.[1]

Clinically, ritonavir is used to inhibit hepatic metabolism in order to increase the serum concentration of other protease inhibitors. Unfortunately, all of these medications can affect the serum concentration of *any drugs* metabolized via cytochrome P-45 pathways.

Antiretroviral-Antiretroviral Interactions Involving Metabolism

There are several clinically significant drug-drug interactions between various antiretrovirals that are summarized as follows:

Atazanivir with efavirenz or nevirapine
  — Atazanavir serum concentrations have been shown to decrease when given concurrently with efavirenz.[2] Studies have demonstrated that concurrent boosting with ritonavir can increase the serum concentration to acceptable levels. Specific studies with nevirapine have not been conducted and concurrent use is not recommended by the manufacturer.[2]

Atazanavir with didanosine
  — Co-administration of atazanavir with buffered formulations of didanosine will result in reduced absorption of atazanavir. Buffering agents formulated in didanosine increase the pH of gastric contents resulting in reduced solubility of the drug in the stomach which reduces absorption. Atazanavir should be given with meals two (2) hours before one (1) hour after didanosine buffered formulations.[2] Because didanosine EC capsules are to be given on an empty stomach and atazanavir is to be given with food, patients must be informed to administer these medications at these different times to avoid reduced absorption.

Tenofovir and Didanosine

— When tenofovir and didanosine are administered concurrently, concentrations of didanosine may increase significantly leading to adverse effects. The mechanism of action of this interaction is unknown. In patients weighing >60kg, the dosage of didanosine is reduced to 250 mg daily. For patients weighing less than 60kg, the dosage of didanosine is reduced to 200 mg daily.

— Tenofovir is eliminated via renal excretion and drugs that reduce renal function or compete for active tubular secretion may increase serum levels of this medication. Patients receiving drugs that fall into these categories should be monitored for potential tenofovir–associated adverse effects.

Herbal and Dietary Products

Herbal products have gained wide acceptance and are frequently used in the HIV-infected population. Although many of the claims promoted by the manufacturers of these products have not been substantiated through clinical trials, patients continue to use them. Unfortunately, some of these products have the potential to interfere with antiretroviral therapy and the clinician should be aware of the potential interferences. Examples include **St. John's Wort** (stimulates hepatic metabolism of protease inhibitors, induces gut p-glycoprotein resulting in decreased concentrations of indinavir and others), **kava** (metabolites can inhibit cytochrome P450 enzymes and elevate liver function tests as well as causing CNS depression), **garlic** (may reduce serum concentrations of certain protease inhibitors), **grapefruit juice** (inhibits gut cytochrome P450 and can increase levels of concurrently administered antiretrovirals) and others. Many of these interactions have been included in the tables that follow.

The following tables provided by the University of California illustrate potential drug interactions.(Database of Antiretroviral Drug Interactions; *HIV InSite,* University of California, 2006. Available at http://hivinsite.ucsf.edu/InSite?page=ar-00-02).

It is important for the reader to consult to use sound clinical judgment since many interactions have not been studied. Understanding the potential mechanisms discussed in this chapter should assist the practitioner, but keeping abreast of the latest changes in the literature and understanding the unique needs of each patient is of paramount importance.

References

1. Preston SL, Piliero PJ, Drusano GL. Pharmacodynamics and clinical use of anti HIV drugs. *Infectious Disease Clinics of North America* (September 2003); 17(3):651–74.
2. Product Information. Aptivus® (tipranavir). Ridgefield, CT: Boehringer Ingelheim. 2005.
3. Product Information. Reyataz® (atazanavir). Princeton, NJ: Bristol-Myers Squibb. 2005.
4. Product Information. Viread® (tenofovir). Foster City, CA. Gilead Sciences, Inc. 2005.
5. Drug Interaction Databases. University of California in San Francisco. Available at: http://hivinsite.ucsf.edu/arvdb?page=ar-00-02.
6. Lesho EP, Gey DC. Managing issues related to antiretroviral therapy. *Am Fam Physician.* (August 15, 2003); 68(4):675–686.
7. Ahmad K. Herbal treatment for HIV/AIDS is not recommended. *Lancet* (September 2005); 5(9):537.
8. Bailey DG. Natural products and adverse drug interactions. *Can Med Assoc Journal (CMAJ).* (May 2004);170(10);1531–1532.

Interactions with Abacavir (Ziagen)

Coadministered Drug	Dose of Drug	Dose of Abacavir	Effect on Coadministered Drug Levels	Effect on Abacavir Levels	Potential Clinical Effects	Mechanism of Interaction	Management	Suggested Alternative Agent(s)
Alcohol (ethanol, wine, liquor, beer, spirits)	0.7 g/kg body weight	600 mg QD	No significant change	Abacavir AUC: increased 41%; half-life: increased 26%	-	Decreased abacavir metabolism by alcohol dehydrogenase	No dose adjustment necessary	-
Methadone (Dolophine)	40 mg QD, 90 mg QD	600 mg BID	Methadone clearance: increased 22%	No significant change	Decreased methadone effects (eg, withdrawal)		Monitor for signs and symptoms of methadone withdrawal; some patients may need an increase in the methadone dose	-
Coadministered Drug	Dose of Drug	Dose of Abacavir	Effect on Coadministered Drug Levels	Effect on Abacavir Levels	Potential Clinical Effects	Mechanism of Interaction	Management	Suggested Alternative Agent(s)
Tenofovir (Viread)	300 mg QD x 13 days	300 mg BID	No significant change	No significant change			No dose adjustment necessary	-
Tipranavir (Aptivus)	1250 mg BID with 100 mg ritonavir BID x 42 doses	300 mg BID x 43 doses	-	Abacavir AUC: decreased 35%; Cmax: decreased 52%		-	No dose adjustment necessary	-
Tipranavir (Aptivus)	250 mg BID with 200 mg ritonavir BID	300 mg BID x 43 doses	-	Abacavir AUC: decreased 44%; Cmax: decreased 44%		-	No dose adjustment necessary	-
Tipranavir (Aptivus)	750 mg BID with 100 mg ritonavir BID	300 mg BID x 43 doses	-	Abacavir AUC: decreased 36%; Cmax: decreased 46%		-	No dose adjustment necessary	-
Zidovudine (Retrovir)	200 mg TID, 300 mg BID	200 mg TID, 400 mg TID, 600 mg TID, 300 mg BID	Not studied	Inconsistent effect across all dosing regimens		-	No dose adjustment necessary	-
Zidovudine (Retrovir)	300 mg x 1 dose	600 mg x 1 dose	Zidovudine Cmax: decreased 20%; AUC: no significant change	No significant change	-	Delayed zidovudine absorption	No dose adjustment necessary	-

Interactions with Amprenavir (Agenerase)

Coadministered Drug	Dose of Drug	Dose of Amprenavir	Effect on Coadministered Drug Levels	Effect on Amprenavir Levels	Potential Clinical Effects	Mechanism of Interaction	Management	Suggested Alternative Agent(s)
Abacavir (Ziagen)	300 mg BID x 3 weeks	900 mg BID x 3 weeks	Not studied	Amprenavir Cmax: increased 47%; AUC: increased 29%; Cmin: increased 27%	-	-	Dose adjustment not established	-
Alprazolam (Xanax)	-	-	Not studied; may increase alprazolam levels		Increased alprazolam effects (eg, increased sedation, confusion, respiratory depression)	Inhibition of CYP450 3A4 by amprenavir	Avoid combination; consider alternative agents	Lorazepam
Antacids (Maalox, Mylanta, Riopan, Milk of Magnesia, others)	-	-	-	Decreased amprenavir levels	-	Decreased amprenavir bioavailability	Separate dosing by at least 1 hour	-
Atorvastatin (Lipitor)	-	-	Not studied; may increase atorvastatin levels		Increased atorvastatin effects (eg, myopathy, rhabdomyolysis)	Inhibition of CYP450 3A4 by amprenavir	Avoid combination if possible; may consider low dose atorvastatin or alternative agents; monitor for myopathy	Pravastatin
Clarithromycin (Biaxin)	500 mg BID x 7 doses	1200 mg BID x 7 doses	Clarithromycin Cmax: no significant change; AUC: no significant change; 14-hydroxy clarithromycin Cmax: decreased 32%; AUC: decreased 35%	Amprenavir Cmax: increased 15%; AUC: increased 18%; Cmin: increased 39%	-	Inhibition of CYP450 3A4 by amprenavir	No dose adjustment necessary	-
Delavirdine (Rescriptor)	1000 mg BID x 10 days	450 mg BID x 10 days	Delavirdine AUC: increased 126%; Cmin: increased 372%; Cmax: increased 115%(compared to amprenavir 600 mg and delavirdine 600 mg BID)	Amprenavir AUC: increased 20%	Increased delavirdine effects	Inhibition of CYP450 3A4 by amprenavir	Dose adjustment not established	-

Coadministered Drug	Dose of Drug	Dose of Amprenavir	Effect on Coadministered Drug Levels	Effect on Amprenavir Levels	Potential Clinical Effects	Mechanism of Interaction	Management	Suggested Alternative Agent(s)
Delavirdine (Rescriptor)	600 mg BID	600 mg BID	Delavirdine AUC: decreased 61%; Cmax: decreased 47%; Cmin: decreased 88%	Amprenavir AUC: increased 130%; Cmax: increased 40%; Cmin: increased 125%	Decreased delavirdine and increased amprenavir effects	Induction of CYP450 3A4 by amprenavir and inhibition of CYP450 3A4 by delavirdine	Do not coadminister	-
Delavirdine (Rescriptor)	600 mg BID	600 mg BID	Delavirdine AUC: decreased 50%; Cmax: decreased 30%; Cmin: decreased 70%	Amprenavir AUC: increased 30%; Cmax: increased 18%; Cmin: increased 90%	Decreased delavirdine and increased amprenavir effects	Induction of CYP450 3A4 by amprenavir and inhibition of CYP450 3A4 by delavirdine	Do not coadminister	-
Didanosine (Videx)	-	-		May decrease amprenavir bioavailability	Decreased amprenavir effects	Decreased amprenavir absorption	Separate didanosine and amprenavir doses by at least 1 hour	-
Didanosine (Videx)	2-200 mg (buffered tabs) QD	600 mg BID on days 1-4 and 15-18	Not studied	No significant change	-	-	No dose adjustment necessary	-
Didanosine (Videx)	400 mg enteric coated capsule QD	600 mg BID on days 1-4 and 15-18	Not studied	No significant change	-	-	No dose adjustment necessary	-

Coadministered Drug	Dose of Drug	Dose of Amprenavir	Effect on Coadministered Drug Levels	Effect on Amprenavir Levels	Potential Clinical Effects	Mechanism of Interaction	Management	Suggested Alternative Agent(s)

Coadministered Drug	Dose of Drug	Dose of Amprenavir	Effect on Coadministered Drug Levels	Effect on Amprenavir Levels	Potential Clinical Effects	Mechanism of Interaction	Management	Suggested Alternative Agent(s)
Didanosine (Videx)	400 mg QD (buffered and enteric coated) x 4 days	600 mg BID x 4 days	Not studied	No significant effect (with either didanosine formulation)	-	-	No dose adjustment necessary	-
Diltiazem (Cardizem, Tiazac, Dilacor, others)		-	May increase diltiazem levels		Increased diltiazem effects (eg, hypotension, heart block)	Inhibition of CYP450 3A4 by amprenavir	Monitor and adjust diltiazem as indicated	
Disulfiram (Antabuse)	-	Oral solution (contains propylene glycol)			Propylene glycol toxicity (acidosis, CNS depression)	Inhibition of aldehyde dehydrogenase by disulfiram	Do not coadminister disulfiram with amprenavir oral solution	Amprenavir capsules
Efavirenz (Sustiva)	-	-	Not studied	Amprenavir AUC: decreased 24%; Cmax: decreased 33%; Cmin: decreased 43%	Decreased amprenavir effects	Induction of CYP450 3A4 by efavirenz	Dose adjustment not established	-
Efavirenz (Sustiva)	600 mg QD	1200 mg BID	Not studied	Amprenavir AUC: decreased 24%; Cmax: decreased 33%; Cmin: decreased 43%	Decreased amprenavir effects	Induction of CYP450 3A4 by efavirenz	Increase amprenavir dose to 1200 mg TID when used as single PI; use combination amprenavir 1200 mg BID with ritonavir 200 mg BID	-

Coadministered Drug	Dose of Drug	Dose of Amprenavir	Effect on Coadministered Drug Levels	Effect on Amprenavir Levels	Potential Clinical Effects	Mechanism of Interaction	Management	Suggested Alternative Agent(s)
Efavirenz (Sustiva)	600 mg QD	1200 mg BID	Not studied	Decreased mean amprenavir levels	Decreased amprenavir effects	Induction of CYP450 3A4 by efavirenz	May consider adding ritonavir or nelfinavir	-
Efavirenz (Sustiva)	600 mg QD	1200 mg BID	Not studied	AUC: decreased 24%, Cmax: decreased 33%; Cmin: decreased 43%	Decreased amprenavir effects	Induction of CYP450 3A4 by efavirenz	Dose adjustment not established	-
Efavirenz (Sustiva)	600 mg QD added to stable amprenavir/ritonavir regimen	600 mg BID with ritonavir 100 mg BID	Not studied	Amprenavir AUC: decreased 40%; Cmax: decreased 42%; Cmin: decreased 29%; Ritonavir AUC: decreased 58%; Cmax: decreased 57%; Cmin: decreased 47% (compared to amprenavir 600 mb BID and ritonavir 100 mg BID)	When amprenavir and ritonavir are used with efavirenz, ritonavir is able to overcome the efavirenz induction so amprenavir levels are well above those of amprenavir alone	Induction of CYP450 3A4 by efavirenz	No dose adjustment necessary	-
Efavirenz (Sustiva)	600 mg QD on days 2-15	1200 mg QD with 200 mg ritonavir QD on day 1, then 300 mg ritonavir on days 2-15	Not studied	No significant change	-	Inhibition of CYP450 3A4 by ritonavir	No dose adjustment necessary	-
Coadministered Drug	Dose of Drug	Dose of Amprenavir	Effect on Coadministered Drug Levels	Effect on Amprenavir Levels	Potential Clinical Effects	Mechanism of Interaction	Management	Suggested Alternative Agent(s)
Ethinyl estradiol/norethindrone acetate (Ortho-Novum, others)	0.035 mg ethinyl estradiol/1 mg norethindrone x 1 cycle	1200 mg BID x 28 days	Ethinyl estradiol Cmin: increased 32%; Norethindrone AUC: increased 18%; Cmin: increased 45%	Amprenavir AUC: decreased 22%; Cmin: decreased 20%	Unknown effect on birth control	Not established	Dose adjustment not established; may need to use alternative method of birth control	Barrier devices, condoms
Indinavir (Crixivan)	1200 mg BID	1200 mg BID with efavirenz 600 mg QD	Not studied	Amprenavir clearance: decreased 54%	-	Induction of CYP450 3A4 by amprenavir or efavirenz	Dose adjustment not established	-
Indinavir (Crixivan)	750 mg or 800 mg TID x 2 weeks (fasted)	800 mg TID x 2 weeks (fasted)	Indinavir AUC: decreased 38%; Cmax: decreased 22%; Cmin: decreased 27%	Amprenavir AUC: increased 33%; Cmax: increased 18%; Cmin: increased 25%	-	Inhibition of CYP450 3A4 by indinavir; induction of CYP450 3A4 by amprenavir	No dose adjustment necessary	-
Indinavir (Crixivan)	800 mg TID (fasted)	750 mg or 800 mg TID (fasted)	Indinavir Cmax: decreased 22%; AUC: decreased 38%; Cmin: decreased 27%	Amprenavir Cmax: increased 18%; AUC: increased 33%; Cmin: increased 25%	-	Inhibition of CYP450 3A4 by indinavir	No dose adjustment necessary	-

Coadministered Drug	Dose of Drug	Dose of Amprenavir	Effect on Coadministered Drug Levels	Effect on Amprenavir Levels	Potential Clinical Effects	Mechanism of Interaction	Management	Suggested Alternative Agent(s)
Ketoconazole (Nizoral)	400 mg x 1 dose	1200 mg x 1 dose	Ketoconazole AUC: increased 44%; Cmax: increased 19%	Amprenavir AUC: increased 31%; Cmax: decreased 16%	No significant change	Inhibition of gastrointestinal and hepatic CYP450 3A4 by amprenavir; inhibition of P-glycoprotein by amprenavir; inhibition of CYP 3A4 by ketoconazole	Dose adjustment not established	-
Lamivudine (Epivir)	150 mg x 1 dose	150 mg x 1 dose	No significant change	No significant change	-	-	No dose adjustment necessary	-
Lopinavir/ritonavir (Kaletra)	400/100 mg BID	600 mg BID	Not studied	Amprenavir Cmin: decreased 37% (when compared to standard curve obtained from amprenavir and ritonavir at same doses)	Decreased amprenavir levels	Not established	Dose adjustment not established	-
Lopinavir/ritonavir (Kaletra)	400/100 mg BID x 22 days	450 mg BID x 5 days, 750 mg BID x 5 days	Lopinavir AUC: decreased 15%; lopinavir Cmax: no significant change; Cmin: decreased 19%	No significant change	-	-	No dose adjustment necessary	-
Coadministered Drug	Dose of Drug	Dose of Amprenavir	Effect on Coadministered Drug Levels	Effect on Amprenavir Levels	Potential Clinical Effects	Mechanism of Interaction	Management	Suggested Alternative Agent(s)
Lopinavir/ritonavir (Kaletra)	400/100 mg BID x weeks 2-26	Group 2: 1200 mg amprenavir/200 mg ritonavir BID; Group 4: 1200 mg amprenavir/400 mg ritonavir BID x weeks 1-26	Not studied	Amprenavir Cmin: decreased 42% (in Group 2); Cmin decreased 69% (in Group 4)	Decreased amprenavir levels	-	Dose adjustment not established	-
Lopinavir/ritonavir (Kaletra)	533mg/133 mg BID with and without efavirenz 600 mg QHS	750 mg BID	Lopinavir AUC: no significant change; Cmax: no significant change; Cmin: no significant change; half-life: decreased 32% (when compared to amprenavir, lopinavir/ritonavir with efavirenz)	Amprenavir AUC: no significant change; Cmax: decreased 34%; Cmin: increased 22% (when compared to amprenavir, lopinavir/ritonavir with efavirenz)	-	-	No dose adjustment necessary	-
Methadone (Dolophine)	-	1200 mg BID	Methadone concentration: decreased 35%	-	Decreased methadone effects (eg. withdrawal)	Possible induction of CYP450 3A4 by amprenavir	Monitor for signs and symptoms of methadone withdrawal; Some patients may need an increase in the methadone dose	-

Coadministered Drug	Dose of Drug	Dose of Amprenavir	Effect on Coadministered Drug Levels	Effect on Amprenavir Levels	Potential Clinical Effects	Mechanism of Interaction	Management	Suggested Alternative Agent(s)
Methadone (Dolophine)	44-100 mg QD for more than 30 days	1200 mg BID x 10 days	R-methadone AUC: no significant change; Cmax: decreased 25%; Cmin: decreased 21%; S-methadone AUC: decreased 40%; Cmax: decreased 48%; Cmin: decreased 53%		Decreased methadone effects (eg, withdrawal)	Induction of CYP450 3A4 by amprenavir	Monitor for signs and symptoms of methadone withdrawal; some patients may need an increase in the methadone dose	-
Methadone (Dolophine)	stable daily dose	1200 mg BID	R-methadone AUC: no significant change; Cmax: decreased 25%; Cmin: decreased 21%; S-methadone AUC: decreased 40%; Cmax: decreased 48%; Cmin: decreased 53%	-	-	-	No dose adjustment necessary	-
Methadone (Dolophine)	stable dose	1200 mg BID x 10 days	R-methadone AUC: no significant change; Cmax: decreased 25%; Cmin: decreased 21%; S-methadone AUC: decreased 40%; Cmax: decreased 48%; Cmin: decreased 52%		Decreased methadone effects (eg, withdrawal)	Possible induction of CYP450 3A4 by amprenavir	Monitor for signs and symptoms of methadone withdrawal; some patients may need an increase in the methadone dose	-
Nelfinavir (Viracept)	1250 mg BID	1200 mg BID with efavirenz 600 mg QD	Not studied	Amprenavir clearance: decreased 41%	-	Induction of CYP450 3A4 by amprenavir or efavirenz	Dose adjustment not established	-
Nelfinavir (Viracept)	750 mg TID x 2 weeks (fed)	750 mg or 800 mg TID x 2 weeks (fed)	Nelfinavir AUC: increased 15%; Cmax: no significant change	No significant change			No dose adjustment necessary	-
Nelfinavir (Viracept)	750 mg TID x 2 weeks (fed)	750 mg or 800 mg TID x 2 weeks (fed)	Nelfinavir AUC: increased 15%; Cmax: no significant change; Cmin: no significant change	Amprenavir AUC: no significant change. Cmax: no significant change. Cmin: increased 189%	Increased amprenavir effects	Inhibition of CYP450 3A4 by both drugs	No dose adjustment necessary	-
Nevirapine (Viramune)	-	-	-	May decrease amprenavir levels	Decreased amprenavir effects	Induction of CYP450 3A4 by nevirapine	Dose adjustment not established	-
Rifabutin (Mycobutin)	300 mg QD x 10 days	1200 mg BID x 10 days	Rifabutin AUC: increased 193%; Cmax: increased 119%; Cmin: increased 271%	Amprenavir AUC: decreased 15%; Cmax: no significant change; Cmin: decreased 15%	Increased rifabutin effects (eg, uveitis)	Inhibition of CYP450 3A4 by amprenavir	Decrease rifabutin to 150 mg QD or 300 mg 3 times/week	-
Rifabutin (Mycobutin)	300 mg QD x 14 days	1200 mg BID	Rifabutin AUC: increased 193%; Cmax: increased 119%; 25-O-desacetylrifabutin AUC: increased 1230%; clearance: decreased 66%	No significant change	Increased rifabutin effects (eg, uveitis)	Inhibition of CYP450 3A4 by amprenavir	Decrease rifabutin to 150 mg QD or 300 mg 3 times/week	-

Coadministered Drug	Dose of Drug	Dose of Amprenavir	Effect on Coadministered Drug Levels	Effect on Amprenavir Levels	Potential Clinical Effects	Mechanism of Interaction	Management	Suggested Alternative Agent(s)
Rifampin (Rifadin)	300 mg QD x 4 days	1200 mg BID x 4 days	No significant change	Amprenavir AUC: decreased 82%; Cmax: decreased 70%; Cmin: decreased 92%	Decreased amprenavir effects	Induction of CYP450 3A4 by rifampin	Do not coadminister	Rifabutin
Rifampin (Rifadin)	600 mg QD x 14 days	1200 mg BID	No significant change	AUC: decreased 82%	Decreased amprenavir effects	Induction of CYP450 3A4 by rifampin	Do not coadminister	Rifabutin
Coadministered Drug	**Dose of Drug**	**Dose of Amprenavir**	**Effect on Coadministered Drug Levels**	**Effect on Amprenavir Levels**	**Potential Clinical Effects**	**Mechanism of Interaction**	**Management**	**Suggested Alternative Agent(s)**
Ritonavir (Norvir)	-	-	Not studied	Increased amprenavir levels	Increased amprenavir effects	Inhibition of CYP450 3A4 by ritonavir	Dose adjustment not established	-
Ritonavir (Norvir)	100 mg BID x 2-4 weeks	600 mg BID	Not studied	Amprenavir AUC: increased 64%; Cmax: decreased 30%; Cmin: increased 508%	Increased amprenavir effects	Inhibition of CYP450 3A4 by ritonavir		
Ritonavir (Norvir)	100 mg on days 8-14, 200 mg QD on days 15-21	1200 mg QD on days 1-7	Not studied	AUC: increased 119%; Cmax: no significant change; Cmin: increased 840% (with 100 mg ritonavir); no significant change with 200 mg ritonavir	Increased amprenavir effects	Inhibition of CYP450 3A4 by ritonavir		
Ritonavir (Norvir)	100 mg Q12H	900 mg Q12H	Ritonavir AUC: decreased 64%; Cmax: decreased 32%; Cmin: decreased 65%	Amprenavir AUC: increased 109%; Cmax: no significant change; Cmin: increased 585%	Increased amprenavir effects	Inhibition of CYP450 3A4 by ritonavir and induction of CYP450 3A4 by amprenavir	Dose adjustment not established	-
Ritonavir (Norvir)	200 mg BID	1200 mg BID	Not studied	Amprenavir AUC: increased 127%; Cmin: increased 395%	Increased amprenavir effects	Inhibition of CYP450 3A4 by ritonavir	No dose adjustment necessary	-
Ritonavir (Norvir)	200 mg BID	1200 mg BID with efavirenz 600 mg QD	Not studied	No significant change	-	Inhibition of CYP450 3A4 by ritonavir and induction of CYP450 3A4 by efavirenz	No dose adjustment necessary	-
Coadministered Drug	**Dose of Drug**	**Dose of Amprenavir**	**Effect on Coadministered Drug Levels**	**Effect on Amprenavir Levels**	**Potential Clinical Effects**	**Mechanism of Interaction**	**Management**	**Suggested Alternative Agent(s)**
Ritonavir (Norvir)	200 mg BID x 2-4 weeks	1200 mg QD	Not studied	Amprenavir AUC: increased 62%; Cmin: increased 319%	Increased amprenavir effects	Inhibition of CYP450 3A4 by ritonavir	Dose adjustment not established	-
Ritonavir (Norvir)	500 mg BID	1200 mg BID	Not studied	Amprenavir AUC: increased 143%; Cmin: increased 576%	Increased amprenavir effects	Inhibition of CYP450 3A4 by ritonavir	Dose adjustment not established	-

Coadministered Drug	Dose of Drug	Dose of Amprenavir	Effect on Coadministered Drug Levels	Effect on Amprenavir Levels	Potential Clinical Effects	Mechanism of Interaction	Management	Suggested Alternative Agent(s)
Saquinavir (Invirase, Fortovase)	1600 mg BID (soft gel caps)	1200 mg BID with efavirenz 600 mg QD	Not studied	Amprenavir clearance; no significant change	-	-	No dose adjustment necessary	
Saquinavir (Invirase, Fortovase)	800 mg TID x 2 weeks (fed)	750 mg or 800 mg TID x 2 weeks (fed)	Saquinavir AUC: decreased 19%; Cmax: increased 21%; Cmin: decreased 48%	Amprenavir AUC: decreased 32%; Cmax: decreased 37%; Cmin: no significant change	Decreased amprenavir effects	Induction of CYP450 3A4 by either drug	No dose adjustment necessary	
Simvastatin (Zocor)	-	-	Not studied; may increase simvastatin levels		Increased simvastatin effects (eg, myopathy, rhabdomyolysis)	Inhibition of CYP450 3A4 by amprenavir	Do not coadminister	Atorvastatin Pravastatin
St. John's Wort (Hypericum perforatum, hypericin, hyperforin)	-	-	Not studied	Not studied; may decrease amprenavir levels	May decrease amprenavir effects	Induction of CYP450 3A4 by St. John's Wort	Do not coadminister	-
Tipranavir (Aptivus)	500 mg BID with 200 mg ritonavir BID x 28 doses	600 mg BID with 100 mg ritonavir BID x 27 doses	-	Amprenavir AUC: decreased 44%; Cmax: decreased 39%; Cmin: decreased 56%	Decreased amprenavir effects	Possible induction of CYP450 3A4 by tipranavir/ritonavir	Do not coadminister	
Triazolam (Halcion)	-	-	Not studied; may increase triazolam levels		Increased triazolam effects (eg, increased sedation, confusion, respiratory depression)	Inhibition of CYP450 3A4 by amprenavir	Avoid combination; consider alternative agents	Lorazepam Oxazepam Temazepam Trazodone
Warfarin (Coumadin)	-	-	Not studied; may increase warfarin effects	-	Increased warfarin effects (eg, increased INR, increased risk of bleeding)	Inhibition of CYP450 3A4 by amprenavir	Monitor INR and adjust warfarin as indicated	
Zidovudine (Retrovir)	300 mg x 1 dose	600 mg x 1 dose	Zidovudine AUC: increased 31%; Cmax: increased 40%	No significant change	-	-	No dose adjustment necessary	-

All Interactions with Delavirdine (Rescriptor)

Coadministered Drug	Dose of Drug	Dose of Delavirdine	Effect on Coadministered Drug Levels	Effect on Delavirdine Levels	Potential Clinical Effects	Mechanism of Interaction	Management	Suggested Alternative Agent(s)
Amprenavir (Agenerase)	450 mg BID x 10 days	1000 mg BID x 10 days	Amprenavir AUC: increased 20%	Delavirdine AUC: increased 126%; Cmin: increased 372%; Cmax: increased 115% (compared to amprenavir 600 mg and delavirdine 600 mg BID)	Increased delavirdine effects	Inhibition of CYP450 3A4 by amprenavir	Dose adjustment not established	-
Amprenavir (Agenerase)	600 mg BID	600 mg BID	Amprenavir AUC: increased 130%, Cmax: increased 40%; Cmin: increased 125%	Delavirdine AUC: decreased 61%; Cmax: decreased 47%; Cmin: decreased 88%	Decreased delavirdine and increased amprenavir effects	Induction of CYP450 3A4 by amprenavir and inhibition of CYP450 3A4 by delavirdine	Do not coadminister	-
Amprenavir (Agenerase)	600 mg BID	600 mg BID	Amprenavir AUC: increased 30%; Cmax: increased 18%; Cmin: increased 90%	Delavirdine AUC: decreased 50%; Cmax: decreased 30%; Cmin: decreased 70%	Decreased delavirdine and increased amprenavir effects	Induction of CYP450 3A4 by amprenavir and inhibition of CYP450 3A4 by delavirdine	Do not coadminister	-
Coadministered Drug	**Dose of Drug**	**Dose of Delavirdine**	**Effect on Coadministered Drug Levels**	**Effect on Delavirdine Levels**	**Potential Clinical Effects**	**Mechanism of Interaction**	**Management**	**Suggested Alternative Agent(s)**
Carbamazepine (Tegretol)	-	-	-	Delavirdine Cmin: decreased	Decreased delavirdine effects	Induction of CYP450 3A4 by carbamazepine	Avoid combination if possible; consider alternative agents; monitor carbamazepine levels and adjust as indicated	Gabapentin Lamotrigine Tiagabine Topiramate
Clarithromycin (Biaxin)	500 mg BID	300 mg TID	Clarithromycin AUC: increased 100%; 14-hydroxy clarithromycin AUC: decreased 75%	Delavirdine AUC: increased 44%	Not studied	Inhibition of CYP450 3A4 and 2C9 by delavirdine	-	-
Coadministered Drug	**Dose of Drug**	**Dose of Delavirdine**	**Effect on Coadministered Drug Levels**	**Effect on Delavirdine Levels**	**Potential Clinical Effects**	**Mechanism of Interaction**	**Management**	**Suggested Alternative Agent(s)**
Cotrimoxazole (TMP/SMX) (Trimethoprim/Sulfamethoxazole, Septra, Bactrim)	-	-	-	No significant change	-	-	No dose adjustment necessary	-
Dapsone (Avlosulfon, others)	-	-	Not studied; may increase dapsone levels	-	Increased dapsone effects		No dose adjustment necessary	-
Didanosine (Videx)	-	-	Not studied	Delavirdine AUC: decreased 20%	Decreased delavirdine effects		Consider didanosine EC or administer delavirdine at least 1 hour prior to didanosine tablets/suspension	-
Didanosine (Videx)	125 or 200 mg (buffered formulation)	400 mg x 1 dose	Not studied	Delavirdine AUC: decreased 32%; Cmax: decreased 53%	-	-	Dose adjustment not established	-

Coadministered Drug	Dose of Drug	Dose of Delavirdine	Effect on Coadministered Drug Levels	Effect on Delavirdine Levels	Potential Clinical Effects	Mechanism of Interaction	Management	Suggested Alternative Agent(s)
Didanosine (Videx)	125 or 200 mg (buffered formulation) Q12H	400 mg x 1 dose (administered 1 hr before didanosine)	Not studied	Delavirdine AUC: increased 20%; Cmax: increased 18%	-	-	No dose adjustment necessary	-
Didanosine (Videx)	125 or 250 mg BID x 28 days	400 mg TID x 28 days	Didanosine AUC: decreased 21%, Cmax: decreased 20%	Delavirdine AUC: decreased 19%; Cmax: decreased 32%		Decreased didanosine and delavirdine absorption	Separate didanosine and delavirdine doses by at least 1 hour	-
Fluconazole (Diflucan)	400 mg x 1 dose	300 mg TID	No significant change	No significant change	Not studied		No dose adjustment necessary	-
Fluoxetine (Prozac, Sarafem, others)	-	-		Delavirdine Cmin: increased 50%	Increased delavirdine effects	Inhibition of CYP450 3A4 by fluoxetine	No dose adjustment necessary	-
Indinavir (Crixivan)	400 mg TID x 7 days	400 mg TID	Indinavir AUC: no significant change; Cmax: decreased 36%; Cmin: increased 118%	No significant change		Inhibition of CYP450 3A4 by delavirdine	Decrease indinavir to 600 mg Q8H	-
Indinavir (Crixivan)	400 mg x 1 dose	400 mg TID	Indinavir AUC: increased 40%	Not studied	Increased indinavir effects	Inhibition of CYP450 3A4 by delavirdine	Decrease indinavir to 600 mg Q8H	-
Indinavir (Crixivan)	600 mg TID x 7 days	400 mg TID	Indinavir AUC: increased 53%; Cmax: no significant change; Cmin: increased 298%	No significant change	Increased indinavir effects	Inhibition of CYP450 3A4 by delavirdine	Decrease indinavir to 600 mg Q8H	-
Indinavir (Crixivan)	600 mg x 1 dose	400 mg TID	Indinavir AUC: increased 44% (compared to 800 mg dose)	No significant change	Increased indinavir effects	Inhibition of CYP450 3A4 by delavirdine	Decrease indinavir to 600 mg Q8H	-
Ketoconazole (Nizoral)	-	-		Delavirdine Cmin: increased 50%	Increased delavirdine effects	Inhibition of CYP450 3A4 by ketoconazole	No dose adjustment necessary	-
Lopinavir/ritonavir (Kaletra)	-	-	Not studied; may increase lopinavir/ritonavir levels	-	Increased lopinavir/ritonavir effects		Dose adjustment not established	-
Methadone (Dolophine)	40-120 mg QD	600 mg BID x 5 days	No significant change	No significant change	-		No dose adjustment necessary	

Coadministered Drug	Dose of Drug	Dose of Delavirdine	Effect on Coadministered Drug Levels	Effect on Delavirdine Levels	Potential Clinical Effects	Mechanism of Interaction	Management	Suggested Alternative Agent(s)
Nelfinavir (Viracept)	750 mg TID	400 mg TID	Nelfinavir AUC: increased 72%	Delavirdine AUC: decreased 42%; Cmin: decreased 52%	Increased nelfinavir effects	Inhibition of CYP450 3A4 by delavirdine	Dose adjustment not established	-
Phenobarbital (Luminal, others)	-	-	-	Delavirdine Cmin: decreased	Decreased delavirdine effects	Induction of CYP450 3A4 by phenobarbital	Avoid combination if possible; consider alternative agents; monitor phenobarbital levels and adjust as indicated	Gabapentin Lamotrigine Tiagabine Topiramate
Phenytoin (Dilantin)	-			Delavirdine Cmin: decreased	Decreased delavirdine effects	Induction of CYP450 3A4 by phenytoin	Avoid combination if possible; consider alternative agents; monitor phenytoin levels and adjust as indicated	Gabapentin Lamotrigine Tiagabine Topiramate
Coadministered Drug	Dose of Drug	Dose of Delavirdine	Effect on Coadministered Drug Levels	Effect on Delavirdine Levels	Potential Clinical Effects	Mechanism of Interaction	Management	Suggested Alternative Agent(s)
Rifabutin (Mycobutin)	300 mg QD	400 mg TID	Rifabutin AUC: increased 100%	Delavirdine AUC: decreased 80%	Decreased delavirdine effects; increased rifabutin effects (eg, uveitis)	Induction of CYP450 3A4 by rifabutin; inhibition of CYP450 3A4 by delavirdine	Do not coadminister	-
Rifampin (Rifadin)	600 mg QD	400 mg TID	Not studied	Delavirdine AUC: decreased 96%	Decreased delavirdine effects	Induction of CYP450 3A4 by rifampin	Do not coadminister	Rifabutin
Ritonavir (Norvir)	100 mg BID x 10 days	600 mg BID x 10 days	Ritonavir AUC: increased 81%; Cmax: increased 50%; Cmin: increased 113%	No significant change	Increased ritonavir effects	Inhibition of CYP450 3A4 by delavirdine	No dose adjustment necessary	-
Ritonavir (Norvir)	300 mg BID	400 or 600 mg BID	No significant change	No significant change	-	-	No dose adjustment necessary	-
Saquinavir (Invirase, Fortovase)	600 mg TID	400 mg TID	Saquinavir AUC: increased 500%	Delavirdine AUC: decreased 15%	-	Increased saquinavir effects	-	-
Coadministered Drug	Dose of Drug	Dose of Delavirdine	Effect on Coadministered Drug Levels	Effect on Delavirdine Levels	Potential Clinical Effects	Mechanism of Interaction	Management	Suggested Alternative Agent(s)
Saquinavir (Invirase, Fortovase)	600 mg TID (hard gel caps) x 21 days	400 mg TID x 14 days	Saquinavir AUC: increased 500%	No significant change	Increased saquinavir effects	Inhibition of CYP450 3A4 by delavirdine	Dose adjustment not established	-
Triazolam (Halcion)	-		Not studied; may increase triazolam levels		Increased triazolam effects (eg, increased sedation, confusion, respiratory depression)	Inhibition of CYP450 3A4 and 2C9 by delavirdine	Avoid combination; consider alternative agents	Lorazepam Oxazepam Temazepam Trazodone
Zidovudine (Retrovir)	-	-	No significant change	No significant change	-	-	No dose adjustment necessary	-

All Interactions with Didanosine (Videx)

Coadministered Drug	Dose of Drug	Dose of Didanosine	Effect on Coadministered Drug Levels	Effect on Didanosine Levels	Potential Clinical Effects	Mechanism of Interaction	Management	Suggested Alternative Agent(s)
Allopurinol (Zyloprim)	300 mg QD x 7 days	400 mg (buffered formulation) x 1 dose	Not studied	Didanosine AUC: increased 113-122%; Cmax: increased 69-116%	Increased didanosine effects (pancreatitis, neuropathy)	Inhibition of presystemic metabolism by allopurinol	Consider reducing didanosine dose by 50%	-
Amprenavir (Agenerase)	-	-	May decrease amprenavir bioavailability		Decreased amprenavir effects	Decreased amprenavir absorption	Separate didanosine and amprenavir doses by at least 1 hour	-
Amprenavir (Agenerase)	600 mg BID on days 14 and 15-18	2-200 mg (tablets) QD	No significant change	Not studied	-	-	No dose adjustment necessary	-
Amprenavir (Agenerase)	600 mg BID on days 14 and 15-18	400 mg (enteric coated capsules) QD	No significant change	Not studied	-	-	No dose adjustment necessary	-
Amprenavir (Agenerase)	600 mg BID x 4 days	400 mg QD (buffered and enteric coated) x 4 days	No significant effect (with either didanosine formulation)	Not studied	-		No dose adjustment necessary	-
Coadministered Drug	Dose of Drug	Dose of Didanosine	Effect on Coadministered Drug Levels	Effect on Didanosine Levels	Potential Clinical Effects	Mechanism of Interaction	Management	Suggested Alternative Agent(s)
Atazanavir (Reyataz)	300 mg with ritonavir 100 mg QD	400 mg (enteric coated capsule) QD with food	Atazanavir AUC: no significant change; Cmax: no significant change; Ritonavir AUC: no significant change; Cmax: no significant change	Didanosine AUC: decreased 34%; Cmax: decreased 38%	Decreased didanosine effects	Reduced didanosine absorption due to presence of food	Administer didanosine EC at least 1 hour prior to or 2 hours after any food	-
Atazanavir (Reyataz)	400 mg QD with food	250 mg EC x 1 dose	Atazanavir AUC: decreased 26%; Cmax: decreased 24%	Didanosine AUC: no significant change (AUC comparable to that of didanosine 400 mg QD without tenofovir)	-		No dose adjustment necessary	-
Atazanavir (Reyataz)	400 mg QD with food	400 mg (enteric coated capsule) QD with food	No significant change	Didanosine AUC: decreased 34%; Cmax: decreased 36%	Decreased didanosine effects	Reduced didanosine absorption due to presence of food	Administer didanosine EC at least 1 hour prior to or 2 hours after any food	-
Atazanavir (Reyataz)	400 mg QD x 1 (given 1 hour after stavudine and didanosine)	200 mg (buffered tabs) x 1 dose	No significant change	Not studied	-		No dose adjustment necessary	-
Atazanavir (Reyataz)	400 mg x 1 dose	Also dosed with stavudine	Atazanavir Cmax: decreased 89%; AUC: decreased 87%	Not studied	Decreased atazanavir effects		Dose adjustment not established	-
Atazanavir (Reyataz)	400 mg x 1 dose (given simultaneously with stavudine and didanosine)	200 mg (buffered tabs) x 1 dose	Atazanavir AUC: decreased 87%; Cmin: decreased 84%; Cmax: decreased 89%	No significant change	Decreased atazanavir effects	Altered gastric pH decreasing atazanavir absorption	Administer didanosine tablets on an empty stomach and 2 hours before or 1 hour after food or atazanavir	-

Coadministered Drug	Dose of Drug	Dose of Didanosine	Effect on Coadministered Drug Levels	Effect on Didanosine Levels	Potential Clinical Effects	Mechanism of Interaction	Management	Suggested Alternative Agent(s)
Ciprofloxacin (Cipro)	750 mg Q12H x 3 days	200 mg (buffered formulation) Q12H x 3 days	Ciprofloxacin AUC: decreased 26% when ciprofloxacin is dosed 2 hours before or 6 hours after didanosine tablets. Ciprofloxacin AUC: decreased 15-fold (with simultaneous didanosine dosing)	Didanosine AUC: decreased 16%; Cmax: decreased 28%	Decreased ciprofloxacin effects	Chelation and adsorption of ciprofloxacin by divalent/trivalent cations contained in didanosine buffer	Consider didanosine EC or administer didanosine tablets/suspension 6 hours prior to or 2 hours after ciprofloxacin administration	-
Dapsone (Avlosulfon, others)	100 mg x 1 dose	200 mg (buffered formulation) Q12H x 14 days	No significant change	No significant change	-	-	No dose adjustment necessary	-
Coadministered Drug	**Dose of Drug**	**Dose of Didanosine**	**Effect on Coadministered Drug Levels**	**Effect on Didanosine Levels**	**Potential Clinical Effects**	**Mechanism of Interaction**	**Management**	**Suggested Alternative Agent(s)**
Delavirdine (Rescriptor)	400 mg TID x 28 days	125 or 250 mg BID x 28 days	Delavirdine AUC: decreased 19%; Cmax: decreased 32%	Didanosine AUC: decreased 21%; Cmax: decreased 20%	-	Decreased didanosine and delavirdine absorption	Separate didanosine and delavirdine doses by at least 1 hour	-
Delavirdine (Rescriptor)	400 mg x 1 dose	125 or 200 mg (buffered formulation) Q12H	Delavirdine AUC: decreased 32%; Cmax: decreased 53%	Not studied	-		Dose adjustment not established	-
Delavirdine (Rescriptor)	400 mg x 1 dose (administered 1 hr before didanosine)	125 or 200 mg (buffered formulation) Q12H	Delavirdine AUC: increased 20%; Cmax: increased 18%	Not studied	-		No dose adjustment necessary	-
Efavirenz (Sustiva)	-		-		Potential early virologic failure	-	Use caution when coadministering tenofovir, didanosine and either efavirenz or nevirapine in treatment-naive patients	
Food	High-fat meal, light meal, yogurt or apple sauce	400 mg (enteric coated capsule) x 1 dose	-	Didanosine AUC(with high-fat meal): decreased 19%; AUC(with light meal): decreased 27%; AUC(with yogurt): decreased 20%; AUC(with applesauce): decreased 18%; AUC(1 hour before meal): decreased 24%; AUC (2 hours after meal): no significant change	Decreased didanosine EC effects(reduction in bioavailability by 20-25% when given with any food)	Possible increase in gastric acidity affecting didanosine EC bioavailability	Administer didanosine EC at least 1 hour prior to or 2 hours after any food	
Ganciclovir (Cytovene)	1000 mg PO Q8H	200 mg (buffered formulation) Q12H	Ganciclovir AUC: decreased 21%	Didanosine AUC: increased 111%	Decreased ganciclovir effects; increased didanosine effects	Decreased oral ganciclovir absorption due to decreased gastric acidity resulting from antacid buffer contained within didanosine tablets/suspension	Consider didanosine EC or do not give didanosine tablets/suspension concurrently or within 2 hours of oral ganciclovir administration	-

Coadministered Drug	Dose of Drug	Dose of Didanosine	Effect on Coadministered Drug Levels	Effect on Didanosine Levels	Potential Clinical Effects	Mechanism of Interaction	Management	Suggested Alternative Agent(s)
Ganciclovir (Cytovene)	1000 mg PO Q8H	buffered formulation	Ganciclovir AUC: increased 115%; Cmax: incrased 116% (when separated by 2 hours); Ganciclovir AUC: increased 107%; Cmax: increased 108% (when taken simultaneously)	Not studied	Increased ganciclovir effects		No dose adjustment necessary	-
Indinavir (Crixivan)	-	Buffered formulation	Indinavir AUC: decreased 84%	Not studied	Decreased indinavir effects	Decreased indinavir absorption	Take drugs at least one hour apart	Didanosine enteric coated
Indinavir (Crixivan)	-	Buffered formulation	Indinavir AUC: decreased 84%	Not studied	Decreased indinavir effects	Decreased indinavir absorption due to decreased gastric acidity resulting from antacid buffer contained within didanosine tablets/suspension	Consider didanosine EC or administer indinavir at least 1 hour prior to didanosine tablets/suspension	-
Indinavir (Crixivan)	800 mg x 1 dose	400 mg (enteric coated capsule) x 1 dose	No significant change	Not studied	-	-	No dose adjustment necessary	-
Indinavir (Crixivan)	800 mg x 1 dose	200 mg (buffered formulation) x 1 dose	Not studied	No significant charge			No dose adjustment necessary	-
Indinavir (Crixivan)	800 mg x 1 dose (administered 1 hour before didanosine)	200 mg (buffered formulation) x 1 dose	Not studied	Didanosine AUC: decreased 17%; Cmax: no significant change	-	-	No dose adjustment necessary	-
Coadministered Drug	Dose of Drug	Dose of Didanosine	Effect on Coadministered Drug Levels	Effect on Didanosine Levels	Potential Clinical Effects	Mechanism of Interaction	Management	Suggested Alternative Agent(s)
Itraconazole (Sporanox)	200 mg (capsule) x 1 dose	300 mg (buffered formulation) x 1 dose	Itraconaxole Cmax: undetectable	Not studied	Decreased itraconazole effects	Decreased itraconazole absorption due to decreased gastric acidity resulting from antacid buffer contained within didanosine tablets/suspension	Administer itraconazole capsules at least 2 hours after didanosine tablets/suspension	Itraconazole solution
Ketoconazole (Nizoral)	200 mg QD x 4 days	375 mg (buffered formulation) BID x 4 days	No significant change	No significant change	Possibly decreased didanosine effects	Decreased ketoconazole absorption due to decreased gastric acidity resulting from antacid buffer contained within didanosine tablets/suspension	Consider didanosine EC or administer ketoconazole at least 2 hours prior to didanosine tablets/suspension	-
Ketoconazole (Nizoral)	200 mg x 1 dose	400 mg (enteric coated capsule) x 1 dose	No significant change	Not studied	-		No dose adjustment necessary	-

Coadministered Drug	Dose of Drug	Effect on Coadministered Drug Levels	Dose of Didanosine	Effect on Didanosine Levels	Potential Clinical Effects	Mechanism of Interaction	Management	Suggested Alternative Agent(s)
Loperamide (Imodium, Imodium A-D)	4 mg Q6H x 1 day	Not studied	300 mg (buffered formulation) x 1 dose	Didanosine AUC: no significant change; Cmax: decreased 23%	-	-	No dose adjustment necessary	-
Lopinavir/ritonavir (Kaletra)	-	-	-	-	-	Decreased lopinavir/ritonavir absorption	Take didanosine 1 hour before or 2 hours after lopinavir/ritonavir	-
Methadone (Dolophine)	-	Not studied	200 mg (buffered formulation) BID	Didanosine AUC: decreased 57%; Cmax: decreased 44%	Decreased didanosine effects	Decreased didanosine bioavailability by methadone	Dose adjustment not established	-
Coadministered Drug	**Dose of Drug**	**Effect on Coadministered Drug Levels**	**Dose of Didanosine**	**Effect on Didanosine Levels**	**Potential Clinical Effects**	**Mechanism of Interaction**	**Management**	**Suggested Alternative Agent(s)**
Methadone (Dolophine)	stable	Not studied	200 mg (buffered formulation) x 1 dose	Didanosine AUC: decreased 41%; Cmax: decreased 59%	Decreased didanosine effects	Decreased didanosine bioavailability by methadone	Dose adjustment not established	-
Nelfinavir (Viracept)	750 mg x 1 dose	No significant change	200 mg x 1 dose	Not studied	-	-	No dose adjustment necessary	-
Nelfinavir (Viracept)	750 mg x 1 dose	No significant change	200 mg (buffered formulation) x 1 dose	Not studied	-	-	No dose adjustment necessary	-
Nevirapine (Viramune)	-	No significant change	-	Not studied	-	-	No dose adjustment necessary	-
Nevirapine (Viramune)	-	-	-	-	Potential early virologic failure	-	Use caution when coadministering tenofovir, didanosine and either efavirenz or nevirapine in treatment-naive patients	-
Coadministered Drug	**Dose of Drug**	**Effect on Coadministered Drug Levels**	**Dose of Didanosine**	**Effect on Didanosine Levels**	**Potential Clinical Effects**	**Mechanism of Interaction**	**Management**	**Suggested Alternative Agent(s)**
Ranitidine (Zantac)	150 mg x 1 dose	Ranitidine AUC: decreased 16%; Cmax: no significant change	375 mg (sachet) x 1 dose	No significant change	-	Inhibition of gastric acid slightly enhancing didanosine bioavailability by reducing acid degradation	No dose adjustment necessary	-
Ribavirin (Rebetol, Virazole)	600 mg QD x 8 weeks	No significant change	200 mg (tablets) BID x 12 weeks	No significant change	Increased risk of mitochondrial toxicity	Ribavirin has been shown in vitro to increase intracellular triphosphate levels of didanosine.	Information from a case series suggests that combining didanosine and ribavirin increases mitochondrial toxicity by five fold. Avoid combination if possible. Monitor closely and discontinue if signs of mitochondrial toxicity develop.	
Rifabutin (Mycobutin)	300 mg or 600 mg QD x 12 days	Not studied	167 mg or 250 mg (buffered formulation) Q12H x 12 days	Didanosine AUC: no significant change; Cmax: increased 17%	-	-	No dose adjustment necessary	-
Ritonavir (Norvir)	600 mg BID	Not studied	200 mg (tablets) BID	Didanosine AUC: decreased 15%; Cmax: decreased 15%	Decreased didanosine effects	Formulation incompatibility	Separate didanosine and ritonavir administration by at least 2.5 hours	-

Coadministered Drug	Dose of Drug	Dose of Didanosine	Effect on Coadministered Drug Levels	Effect on Didanosine Levels	Potential Clinical Effects	Mechanism of Interaction	Management	Suggested Alternative Agent(s)
Ritonavir (Norvir)	600 mg Q12H x 4 days	200 mg (buffered formulation) Q12H x 4 days	No significant change	Didanosine AUC: no significant change; Cmax: decreased 16%	-	-	No dose adjustment necessary	-
Stavudine (Zerit)	40 mg Q12H x 4 days	100 mg (buffered formulation) x 4 days	Stavudine AUC: no significant change; Cmax: increased 17%	No significant change	-	-	No dose adjustment necessary	-
Stavudine (Zerit)	40 mg Q12H x 9 doses	100 mg Q12H x 9 doses	No significant change	No significant change	-	-	No dose adjustment necessary	-
Sulfamethoxazole	1000 mg x 1 dose	200 mg (buffered formulation) x 1 dose	No significant change	No significant change	-	-	No dose adjustment necessary	-
Tenofovir (Viread)	-	-			Potential early virologic failure		Use caution when coadministering tenofovir, didanosine and either efavirenz or nevirapine in treatment-naive patients	-
Tenofovir (Viread)	300 mg QD	400 mg (enteric coated capsule) x 1 dose	No significant change	Didanosine AUC: increased 48% (fasted); Cmax: increased 48% (fasted) Didanosine AUC: increased 60% (fed); Cmax: increased 64% (fed)	Increased didanosine effects	Possible shared elimination pathway	Reduce didanosine dose to 250 mg QD when used with tenofovir	-
Tenofovir (Viread)	300 mg QD	250 mg or 400 mg (buffered formulation) QD x 7 days	No significant change	Didanosine AUC: increased 44%; Cmax: increased 28%	Increased didanosine effects	Possible shared elimination pathway	Reduce didanosine dose to 250 mg QD when used with tenofovir	-
Tenofovir (Viread)	300 mg QD x 7 days	400 mg (buffered formulation) QD x 7 days	No significant change	Didanosine AUC: increased 44%; Cmax: increased 28%	Increased didanosine effects	Possible shared elimination pathway	Reduce didanosine dose to 250 mg QD when used with tenofovir	-

Coadministered Drug	Dose of Drug	Dose of Didanosine	Effect on Coadministered Drug Levels	Effect on Didanosine Levels	Potential Clinical Effects	Mechanism of Interaction	Management	Suggested Alternative Agent(s)
Tenofovir (Viread)	300 mg QD x 9 days	250 mg QD (enteric coated) x 1 (given with food, without food and staggered by 2 hours)	No significant change	Didanosine AUC: no significant change (fed); Cmax: no significant change; Didanosine AUC: no significant change (staggered); Cmax: no significant change (staggered); Didanosine AUC: no significant change (fed); Cmax: decreased 29% (fed) All values compared to 400 mg QD (enteric coated) reference dose.		Possible shared elimination pathway	Reduce didanosine dose to 250 mg QD when used with tenofovir	-
Tipranavir (Aptivus)	1250 mg BID with 100 mg ritonavir BID x 42 doses	125 mg BID x 43 doses	-	Didanosine AUC: no significant change; Cmax: decreased 23%	-	-	No dose adjustment necessary; separate didanosine formulations from tipranavir by 2 hours	-
Tipranavir (Aptivus)	250 mg BID with 200 mg ritonavir BID	200 mg BID	-	Didanosine AUC: decreased 33%; Cmax: decreased 43%	-	-	No dose adjustment necessary; separate didanosine formulations away from tipranavir by 2 hours	-
Tipranavir (Aptivus)	500 mg BID with 100 mg ritonavir BID x 27 doses	400 mg x 1	Tipranavir AUC: no significant change; Cmax: increased 32%; Cmin: decreased 34%	Didanosine AUC: no significant change; Cmax: decreased 20%; Cmin: no significant change	-	-	No dose adjustment necessary	-
Tipranavir (Aptivus)	750 mg BID with 100 mg ritonavir BID	200 mg BID	-	Didanosine AUC: no significant change; Cmax: decreased 24%	-	-	No dose adjustment necessary; separate didanosine formulations from tipranavir by 2 hours	-
Trimethoprim (Trimpex)	200 mg x 1 dose	200 mg (buffered formulation) x 1 dose	Trimethoprim AUC: no significant change; Cmax: decreased 22%	Didanosine AUC: no significant change; Cmax: increased 17%	-	-	No dose adjustment necessary	-
Zidovudine (Retrovir)	200 mg Q8H x 3 days	200 mg (buffered formulation) Q12H x 3 days	Zidovudine AUC: no significant change; Cmax: decreased 16.5%	No significant change	-	-	No dose adjustment necessary	-

All Interactions with Efavirenz (Sustiva)

Coadministered Drug	Dose of Drug	Dose of Efavirenz	Effect on Coadministered Drug Levels	Effect on Efavirenz Levels	Potential Clinical Effects	Mechanism of Interaction	Management	Suggested Alternative Agent(s)
Amprenavir (Agenerase)	-	-	Amprenavir AUC: decreased 24%; Cmax: decreased 33%; Cmin: decreased 43%	Not studied	Decreased amprenavir effects	Induction of CYP450 3A4 by efavirenz	Dose adjustment not established	-
Amprenavir (Agenerase)	1200 mg BID	600 mg QD	Amprenavir AUC: decreased 24%, Cmax: decreased 33%; Cmin: decreased 43%	Not studied	Decreased amprenavir effects	Induction of CYP450 3A4 by efavirenz	Increase amprenavir dose to 1200 mg TID when used as single PI; use combination amprenavir 1200 mg BID with ritonavir 200 mg BID	-
Amprenavir (Agenerase)	1200 mg BID	600 mg QD	Decreased mean amprenavir levels	Not studied	Decreased amprenavir effects	Induction of CYP450 3A4 by efavirenz	May consider adding ritonavir or nelfinavir	-
Amprenavir (Agenerase)	1200 mg BID	600 mg QD	AUC: decreased 24%, Cmax: decreased 33%; Cmin: decreased 43%	Not studied	Decreased amprenavir effects	Induction of CYP450 3A4 by efavirenz	Dose adjustment not established	-
Amprenavir (Agenerase)	1200 mg QD with 200 mg ritonavir QD on day 1, then 300 mg ritonavir on days 2-15	600 mg QD on days 2-15	No significant change	Not studied	-	Inhibition of CYP450 3A4 by ritonavir	No dose adjustment necessary	-
Coadministered Drug	Dose of Drug	Dose of Efavirenz	Effect on Coadministered Drug Levels	Effect on Efavirenz Levels	Potential Clinical Effects	Mechanism of Interaction	Management	Suggested Alternative Agent(s)
Amprenavir (Agenerase)	600 mg BID with ritonavir 100 mg BID	600 mg QD added to stable amprenavir/ritonavir regimen	Amprenavir AUC: decreased 40%; Cmax: decreased 42%; Cmin: decreased 29%; Ritonavir AUC: decreased 58%; Cmax: decreased 57%; Cmin: decreased 47% (compared to amprenavir 600 mb BID and ritonavir 100 mg BID)	Not studied	When amprenavir and ritonavir are used with efavirenz, ritonavir is able to overcome the efavirenz induction so amprenavir levels are well above those of amprenavir alone	Induction of CYP450 3A4 by efavirenz	No dose adjustment necessary	-
Antacids (Maalox, Mylanta, Riopan, Milk of Magnesia, others)	30 mL x 1 dose	400 mg x 1 dose	-	No significant change	-	-	No dose adjustment necessary	-
Atazanavir (Reyataz)	-	-	-	-	Decreased atazanavir effects	Induction of CYP450 3A4 by efavirenz	Increase dose to 300 mg atazanavir with 100 mg ritonavir taken at the same time (boosted atazanavir). Dose adjustments not established for treatment experienced patients.	-
Atazanavir (Reyataz)	400 mg QD on days 1-20	600 mg QD on days 7-20	Atazanavir AUC: decreased 74%; Cmax: decreased 59%; Cmin: decreased 93%; half-life: decreased 27%	Not studied	Decreased atazanavir effects	Induction of CYP450 3A4 by efavirenz	Dose adjustment not established	-

Coadministered Drug	Dose of Drug	Dose of Efavirenz	Effect on Coadministered Drug Levels	Effect on Efavirenz Levels	Potential Clinical Effects	Mechanism of Interaction	Management	Suggested Alternative Agent(s)
Atazanavir (Reyataz)	400 mg QD on days 1-28	600 mg QD with ritonavir 200 mg on days 15-28	Atazanavir AUC: increased 241%; Cmax: increased 124%; Cmin: increased 671%; half-life: increased 79%	Not studied	Increased atazanavir effects	Inhibition of CYP450 3A4 by ritonavir	Dose adjustment not established	-
Atazanavir (Reyataz)	400 mg QD on days 1-6 then 300 mg with ritonavir 100 mg QD on days 7-20	600 mg QD x days 7-20	Atazanavir (all values compared to atazanavir 400 mg QD) AUC: increased 39%; Cmax: no significant change; Cmin: increased 48%	Not studied	Increased atazanavir effects	Inhibition of P450 3A4 by ritonavir	No dose adjustment necessary	
Atazanavir (Reyataz)	600 mg QD on days 7-20	600 mg QD on days 7-20	Atazanavir (all values compared to atazanavir 400 mg QD) AUC: decreased 21%; Cmax: no significant charge; Cmin: decreased 59%	Not studied	Decreased atazanavir effects	Induction of P450 3A4 by efavirenz	Dose adjustment not established	-
Atorvastatin (Lipitor)	10 mg QD	600 mg QD x 14 days	Atorvastatin AUC: decreased 48%	No significant change	Decreased lipid effects	Induction of CYP450 3A4 by efavirenz	May need to increase atorvastatin dose	-
Azithromycin (Zithromax)	600 mg x 1 dose	400 mg x 7 days	Azithromycin AUC: no significant change; Cmax: increased 22%	No significant change	-	-	No dose adjustment necessary	-
Carbamazepine (Tegretol)	-	-	Not studied; may decrease carbamazepine levels	Not studied; may decrease efavirenz levels	Decreased efavirenz and carbamazepine effects	Induction of CYP450 3A4 by both drugs	Avoid combination if possible, consider alternative agents; monitor carbamazepine levels and adjust as indicated	Gabapentin Lamotrigine Tiagabine Topiramate
Clarithromycin (Biaxin)	500 mg Q12H x 7 days	400 mg x 7 days	Clarithromycin AUC: decreased 39%; Cmax: decreased 26%; 14-hydroxy clarithromycin AUC: increased 34%; Cmax: increased 49%	No significant change		Inhibition of CYP450 3A4 by efavirenz	Dose adjustment not established	-
Didanosine (Videx)	-	-	-	-	Potential early virologic failure		Use caution when coadministering tenofovir, didanosine and either efavirenz or nevirapine in treatment-naive patients	-
Ergotamine (Cafergot, ergot derivatives)	-	-	Not studied; may increase ergotamine levels	-	Increased ergotamine effects (eg, ergotism)	Inhibition of CYP450 3A4 by efavirenz	Do not coadminister	5-HT agonists ("triptans")
Ethinyl estradiol/norethindrone acetate (Ortho-Novum, others)	Ethinyl estradiol 50 mcg x 1 dose	400 mg x 10 days	Ethinyl estradiol AUC: increased 37%; Cmax: no significant change	No significant change	-	-	No dose adjustment necessary	-

Coadministered Drug	Dose of Drug	Dose of Efavirenz	Effect on Coadministered Drug Levels	Effect on Efavirenz Levels	Potential Clinical Effects	Mechanism of Interaction	Management	Suggested Alternative Agent(s)
Famotidine (Pepcid)	40 mg x 1 dose	400 mg x 1 dose	-	No significant change	-	-	No dose adjustment necessary	-
Fluconazole (Diflucan)	200 mg x 7 days	400 mg x 7 days	No significant change	AUC: increased 16%; Cmax: no significant change		Inhibition of CYP450 3A4 by fluconazole	No dose adjustment necessary	-
Fosamprenavir (Lexiva)	1400 mg QD with 300 mg ritonavir x 2 weeks	600 mg QD x 2 weeks	No significant change	Not studied		Inhibition of CYP450 3A4 by ritonavir compensating for CYP450 3A4 induction by efavirenz	No dose adjustment necessary	-
Fosamprenavir (Lexiva)	1400 mg QD with ritonavir 200 mg QD x 2 weeks	600 mg QD x 2 weeks	Amprenavir Cmin: decreased 36%; Ritonavir AUC: decreased 31%; Cmin: decreased 40%	Not studied	Decreased amprenavir effects	Induction of CYP450 3A4 by efavirenz	Increase ritonavir dose to 300 mg when administered with fosamprenavir and efavirenz once daily	-
Fosamprenavir (Lexiva)	700 mg BID with ritonavir 100 mg BID x 28 days	600 mg QD x 14 days	No significant change	Not studied			No dose adjustment necessary	-
Fosamprenavir (Lexiva)	700 mg BID with ritonavir 100 mg BID x 2 weeks	600 mg QD x 2 weeks	No significant change	Not studied			No dose adjustment necessary	-
Coadministered Drug	Dose of Drug	Dose of Efavirenz	Effect on Coadministered Drug Levels	Effect on Efavirenz Levels	Potential Clinical Effects	Mechanism of Interaction	Management	Suggested Alternative Agent(s)
Fosamprenavir (Lexiva)	700 mg BID with ritonavir 200 mg BID x 28 days	600 mg QD x 14 days	No significant change	Not studied			No dose adjustment necessary	-
Indinavir (Crixivan)	1000 mg TID x 10 days	600 mg QD x 10 days	Indinavir AUC: decreased 33-46%; Cmax: decreased 29%; Cmin: decreased 39-57%	Not studied	Decreased indinavir effects	Induction of CYP450 3A4 by efavirenz	Do not coadminister. Increasing indinavir dose to 1000 mg Q8H may not be sufficient to compensate for interaction.	-
Indinavir (Crixivan)	800 mg indinavir/100 mg ritonavir Q12H x 29 days	600 mg QD x 14 days	Indinavir AUC: decreased 19%; Cmin: decreased 48%; Cmax: decreased 13%	No significant change	Decreased indinavir effects	Induction of CYP450 3A4 by efavirenz	Increase indinavir to 1000 mg Q12H if dosed with ritonavir 100 mg Q12H	-
Indinavir (Crixivan)	800 mg Q8H x 14 days	200 mg QD x 14 days	Indinavir AUC: decreased 31-35%; Cmax: decreased 16%	No significant change	Decreased indinavir effects	Induction of CYP450 3A4 by efavirenz	Do not coadminister. Increasing indinavir dose to 1000 mg Q8H may not be sufficient to compensate for interaction.	-

Coadministered Drug	Dose of Drug	Dose of Efavirenz	Effect on Coadministered Drug Levels	Effect on Efavirenz Levels	Potential Clinical Effects	Mechanism of Interaction	Management	Suggested Alternative Agent(s)
Indinavir (Crixivan)	800 mg Q8H x 14 days	200 mg x 14 days	Indinavir AUC: decreased 31%; Cmax: decreased 16%	No significant change	Decreased indinavir effects	Induction of CYP450 3A4 by efavirenz	Do not coadminister. Increasing indinavir dose to 1000 mg Q8H may not be sufficient to compensate for interaction.	-
Itraconazole (Sporanox)	-	-	Not studied; may decrease itraconazole levels	-	Decreased itraconazole effects	Induction of CYP450 3A4 by efavirenz	Do not coadminister	-
Coadministered Drug	Dose of Drug	Dose of Efavirenz	Effect on Coadministered Drug Levels	Effect on Efavirenz Levels	Potential Clinical Effects	Mechanism of Interaction	Management	Suggested Alternative Agent(s)
Ketoconazole (Nizoral)			Not studied; may decrease ketoconazole levels		Decreased ketoconazole effects	Induction of CYP450 3A4 by efavirenz	Do not coadminister	-
Lamivudine (Epivir)	150 mg Q12H x 14 days	600 mg x 14 days	No significant change	Not studied			No dose adjustment necessary	-
Lopinavir/ritonavir (Kaletra)	400/100 mg BID on days 1-14, then increased to 533/133 mg BID on 15-35	600 mg QD on days 1-35	Lopinavir AUC: increased 46%, Cmax: increased 33%; Cmin: increased 141%; Ritonavir AUC: increased 48%; Cmax: increased 46%; Cmin: increased 63% (compared to lopinavir/ritonavir 400/100 mg BID)	Not studied	Increased lopinavir/ritonavir effects	Inhibition of CYP450 3A4 by lopinavir/ritonavir	Increase lopinavir/ritonavir to 533/133 mg BID when used with efavirenz	-
Lopinavir/ritonavir (Kaletra)	400/100 mg BID	-	Lopinavir AUC: decreased 20-25%; Cmin: decreased 40-45%	No significant change			Increase dose of lopinavir/ritonavir to 533 mg/133 mg (4 capsules) BID with food	-
Lopinavir/ritonavir (Kaletra)	400 mg/100 mg BID x 9 days	600 mg QHS x 9 days	Lopinavir AUC: decreased 19%; Cmax: no significant change; Cmin: decreased 39%; Ritonavir AUC: no significant change; Cmax: no significant change	Efavirenz AUC: decreased 16%; Cmax: no significant change; Cmin: decreased 16%	Decreased lopinavir effects	Induction of CYP450 3A4 by efavirenz	Increase dose of lopinavir/ritonavir to 533 mg/133 mg (4 capsules) BID with food	-
Lorazepam (Ativan, others)	2 mg x 1 dose	600 mg x 10 days	Lorazepam AUC: no significant change; Cmax: increased 16%	-			No dose adjustment necessary	-
Coadministered Drug	Dose of Drug	Dose of Efavirenz	Effect on Coadministered Drug Levels	Effect on Efavirenz Levels	Potential Clinical Effects	Mechanism of Interaction	Management	Suggested Alternative Agent(s)
Medroxyprogesterone acetate (Depo-Provera)	150 mg	-	Progesterone levels: no significant change	Efavirenz AUC: no significant change			No dose adjustment necessary	-
Methadone (Dolophine)	-	600 mg QD x 14 days	Methadone AUC: decreased 57%; Cmax: decreased 48%	Not studied	Decreased methadone effects (eg, withdrawal)	Induction of CYP450 3A4 by efavirenz	Monitor for signs and symptoms of methadone withdrawal; some patients may need an increase in the methadone dose	-
Methadone (Dolophine)	35-100 mg QD	600 mg x 14-21 days	Methadone AUC: decreased 52%; Cmax: decreased 45%		Decreased methadone effects (eg, withdrawal)	Induction of CYP450 3A4 by efavirenz	Monitor for signs and symptoms of methadone withdrawal; some patients may need an	-

Coadministered Drug	Dose of Drug	Dose of Efavirenz	Effect on Coadministered Drug Levels	Effect on Efavirenz Levels	Potential Clinical Effects	Mechanism of Interaction	Management	Suggested Alternative Agent(s)
Methadone (Dolophine)	stable dose over period of 60 weeks	600 mg QD over period of 60 weeks	Methadone AUC: decreased 39%; Cmax: decreased 33%; Cmin: decreased 44% EDDP (methadone metabolite) AUC: decreased 14.5%; Cmax: no significant change; Cmin: no significant change		Decreased methadone effects (eg, withdrawal)	Induction of methadone metabolism by efavirenz	Study patients required mean dose increase of 30% over period of 60 weeks	
Midazolam (Versed)	-	-	Not studied; may increase midazolam levels		Increased midazolam effects (eg, sedation, confusion, respiratory depression)	Inhibition of CYP450 3A4 by efavirenz	Single dose intravenous midazolam may be used; chronic midazolam administration (oral or intravenous) should be avoided	Lorazepam
Nelfinavir (Viracept)	750 mg Q8H x 7 days	600 mg QD x 7 days	Nelfinavir AUC: increased 20%; Cmax: increased 21%. M8 AUC: decreased 37%; Cmax: decreased 40%	No significant change	-		No dose adjustment necessary	-
Nelfinavir (Viracept)	750 mg TID	600 mg QHS	Nelfinavir clearance: no significant change M8 clearance: increased 43%	-	-	-	No dose adjustment necessary	
Nevirapine (Viramune)	200 mg QD x 2 weeks, then 400 mg QD	600 mg QD	No significant change	Efavirenz AUC: decreased 22%; Cmin: decreased 36%	Decreased efavirenz effects	Induction of CYP450 3A4 by nevirapine	Monitor and adjust therapy as indicated; may consider increasing efavirenz to 800 mg QD	
Phenobarbital (Luminal, others)	-			Not studied; may decrease levels	Decreased efavirenz effects	Induction of CYP450 3A4 by phenobarbital	Avoid combination if possible; consider alternative agents; monitor phenobarbital levels and adjust as indicated	Gabapentin Lamotrigine Tiagabine Topiramate
Phenytoin (Dilantin)	-		Not studied; may decrease phenytoin levels	Not studied; may decrease efavirenz levels	Decreased efavirenz and phenytoin effects	Induction of CYP450 3A4 by both drugs	Avoid combination if possible; consider alternative agents; monitor phenytoin levels and adjust as indicated	Gabapentin Lamotrigine Tiagabine Topiramate
Rifabutin (Mycobutin)	300 mg or 450 mg twice weekly	600 mg QD	On 300 mg rifabutin twice weekly, rifabutin level 2 hours after dose: no significant change; rifabutin level 6 hours post dose: decreased 27%; on 450 mg twice weekly, rifabutin level 2 hours post dose: no significant change; rifabutin level 6 hours post dose: decreased 58% (all values compared to rifabutin alone)	Not studied	Possibly decreased rifabutin effects	Induction of CYP450 3A4 by efavirenz	Increase rifabutin to 450-600 mg QD	
Rifabutin (Mycobutin)	300 mg QD x 14 days	600 mg x 14 days	Rifabutin AUC: decreased 38%; Cmax: decreased 32%	No significant change	Decreased rifabutin effects	Induction of CYP450 3A4 by efavirenz	Increase rifabutin to 450-600 mg QD	-

Coadministered Drug	Dose of Drug	Dose of Efavirenz	Effect on Coadministered Drug Levels	Effect on Efavirenz Levels	Potential Clinical Effects	Mechanism of Interaction	Management	Suggested Alternative Agent(s)
Rifabutin (Mycobutin)	600 mg twice weekly	600 mg QD	Rifabutin AUC: no significant change; Cmax: no significant change (when compared to rifabutin 300 mg twice weekly without efavirenz)	Not studied	-	-	No dose adjustment necessary	-
Rifampin (Rifadin)	600 mg QD x 14 days	600 mg QD x 14 days	No significant change	Efavirenz AUC: decreased 22%; Cmax: decreased 24%; Cmin: decreased 25%	Decreased efavirenz effects	Induction of CYP450 3A4 by rifampin	Dose adjustment not established; may consider increasing efavirenz to 800 mg QD when used with rifampin	Rifabutin
Rifampin (Rifadin)	600 mg x 7 days	600 mg x 7 days	-	Efavirenz AUC: decreased 26%; Cmax: decreased 20%	Decreased efavirenz effects	Induction of CYP450 3A4 by rifampin	Dose adjustment not established; may consider increasing efavirenz to 800 mg QD when used with rifampin	Rifabutin
Ritonavir (Norvir)	500 mg Q12H x 8 days	600 mg x 10 days	Ritonavir AUC: increased 18% after AM dose; Cmax: increased 24% after AM dose; AUC: no significant change after PM dose; Cmax: no significant change after PM dose	Efavirenz AUC: increased 21%; Cmax: no significant change	Increased efavirenz and ritonavir effects	Inhibition of CYP450 3A4 by both drugs	No dose adjustment necessary	-
Ritonavir (Norvir)	Day 1: 300 mg Q12H; Day 2: 400mg Q12H; Days 3-10: 500 mg Q12H	600 mg QD	Ritonavir AUC: increased 18%	Efavirenz AUC: increased 21%	Possible increased effects of both drugs	Inhibition of CYP450 3A4 by both drugs	May dose ritonavir at 500 mg BID when given with efavirenz; no dose adjustment required for efavirenz	-
Saquinavir (Invirase, Fortovase)	1200 mg (soft gel caps) Q8H x 10 days	600 mg x 10 days	Saquinavir AUC: decreased 62%; Cmax: decreased 50%	No significant change	Decreased saquinavir effects	Induction of CYP450 3A4 by efavirenz	Consider adding ritonavir to saquinavir containing regimen	-
Coadministered Drug	Dose of Drug	Dose of Efavirenz	Effect on Coadministered Drug Levels	Effect on Efavirenz Levels	Potential Clinical Effects	Mechanism of Interaction	Management	Suggested Alternative Agent(s)
Saquinavir (Invirase, Fortovase)	400 mg (soft gel caps) BID with ritonavir 400 mg BID on day 1-10	600 mg QHS on day 10-24	Saquinavir Cmin: decreased 10%; ritonavir Cmin: no significant change	No significant change	Not clinically significant	Induction of CYP450 3A4 by efavirenz	No dose adjustment necessary	
Simvastatin (Zocor)	40 mg QD	600 mg QD x 14 days	Simvastatin AUC: decreased 58%	No significant change	Decreased lipid effects	Induction of CYP450 3A4 by efavirenz	May need to increase simvastatin dose	-
St. John's Wort (Hypericum perforatum, hypericin, hyperforin)	-			Not studied, may decrease efavirenz levels		Induction of CYP450 3A4 by St. John's Wort	Do not coadminister	-
Tenofovir (Viread)	-	-	-	-	Potential early virologic failure		Use caution when coadministering tenofovir, didanosine and either efavirenz or nevirapine in treatment-naive patients	
Tenofovir (Viread)	300 mg QD x 7 days	600 mg QD x 14 days	No significant change	No significant change	-	-	No dose adjustment necessary	-

Coadministered Drug	Dose of Drug	Dose of Efavirenz	Effect on Coadministered Drug Levels	Effect on Efavirenz Levels	Potential Clinical Effects	Mechanism of Interaction	Management	Suggested Alternative Agent(s)
Tipranavir (Aptivus)	500 mg BID with 100 mg ritonavir BID	600 mg QD	Tipranavir AUC: decreased 71%; Cmax: decreased 21%; Cmin: decreased 42%	No significant change	Decreased tipranavir effects	Induction of CYP450 3A4 by efavirenz	-	-
Tipranavir (Aptivus)	750 mg BID with 200 mg ritonavir BID	600 mg QD x 8 doses	No significant change	No significant change	-	-	No dose adjustment necessary	-
Valproic Acid (Depakote, Depakene, Depacon)	250 mg BID x 7 days	600 mg QD	No significant change	Efavirenz Cmin: no significant change; Cmax: no significant change; AUC: no significant change; half-life: decreased 22%	-	-	No dose adjustment necessary	-
Voriconazole (VFend)	400 mg PO Q12H on day 1, then 200 mg Q12H on days 2-8	400 mg QD x 9 days	Voriconazole AUC: decreased 77%; Cmax: decreased 61%	Efavirenz AUC: increased 44%; Cmax: increased 38%	Increased efavirenz effects and decreased voriconazole effects	Inhibition of CYP450 3A4 by voriconazole and induction of CYP450 3A4 by efavirenz	Do not coadminister	-
Voriconazole (VFend)	400 mg Q12H x 1 day then 200 mg Q12H x 8 days	400 mg QD x 9 days	Voriconazole AUC: decreased 77%; Cmax: decreased 61%	Efavirenz AUC: increased 44%; Cmax: increased 38%	Decreased voriconazole effects; increased efavirenz effects	Induction of CYP450 3A4 by efavirenz; possible inhibition of CYP450 by voriconazole	Do not coadminister	-
Zidovudine (Retrovir)	300 mg Q12h x 14 days	600 mg QD x 14 days		No significant change			No dose adjustment necessary	-

All Interactions with Emtricitabine (Emtriva)

Coadministered Drug	Dose of Drug	Dose of Emtricitabine	Effect on Coadministered Drug Levels	Effect on Emtricitabine Levels	Potential Clinical Effects	Mechanism of Interaction	Management	Suggested Alternative Agent(s)
Famciclovir (Famvir)	500 mg x 1 dose	200 mg x 1 dose	No significant change	No significant change	-	-	No dose adjustment necessary	-
Indinavir (Crixivan)	800 mg x 1 dose	200 mg x 1 dose	No significant change	No significant change	-	-	No dose adjustment necessary	-
Stavudine (Zerit)	40 mg x 1 dose	200 mg x 1 dose	No significant change	No significant change	-	-	No dose adjustment necessary	-
Tenofovir (Viread)	300 mg QD	200 mg QD x 7 days	No significant change	No significant change	-	-	No dose adjustment necessary	-
Tenofovir (Viread)	300 mg QD x 7 days	200 mg QD x 7 days	No significant change	No significant change	-	-	No dose adjustment necessary	-

| Zidovudine (Retrovir) | 300 mg BID x 7 days | 200 mg QD x 7 days | No significant change | No significant change | - | - | No dose adjustment necessary | - |

All Interactions with Enfuvirtide (Fuzeon)

Coadministered Drug	Dose of Drug	Dose of Enfuvirtide	Effect on Coadministered Drug Levels	Effect on Enfuvirtide Levels	Potential Clinical Effects	Mechanism of Interaction	Management	Suggested Alternative Agent(s)
Rifampin (Rifadin)	600 mg QD x 10 days	90 mg SQ BID	No significant change	No significant change	-	-	No dose adjustment necessary	-
Ritonavir (Norvir)	200 mg BID on days 4-7	90 mg SQ BID on days 1-7	No significant change	Enfuvirtide Cmax: increased 24%; Cmin: no significant change; AUC: increased 22%	-	-	No dose adjustment necessary	-
Saquinavir (Invirase, Fortovase)	1000 mg BID with ritonavir 100 mg BID on days 4-7	90 mg SQ BID on days 1-7	No significant change	Enfuvirtide Cmax: no significant change; Cmin: increased 26%; AUC: no significant change	-	-	No dose adjustment necessary	-

All Interactions with Fosamprenavir (Lexiva)
See also interactions for Amprenavir.

Coadministered Drug	Dose of Drug	Dose of Fosamprenavir	Effect on Coadministered Drug Levels	Effect on Fosamprenavir Levels	Potential Clinical Effects	Mechanism of Interaction	Management	Suggested Alternative Agent(s)
Antacids (Maalox, Mylanta, Riopan, Milk of Magnesia, others)	30 mL x 1 dose	1400 mg x 1 dose	Not studied	Amprenavir Cmax: decreased 35%; AUC: decreased 18%; Cmin: no significant change	-	-	Dose adjustment not established; may consider separating antacid 2 hours away from fosamprenavir	-
Atorvastatin (Lipitor)	10 mg QD	1400 mg BID or 700 mg fosamprenavir with 100 mg ritonavir BID x 14 days	Atorvastatin AUC: increased 130% (on 1400 mg BID); Cmax: increased 304% (on 1400 mg BID); AUC: increased 153% (on 700/100 mg BID); Cmax: increased 184% (on 700/100 mg BID)	Amprenavir AUC: decreased 27% (on 1400 mg BID); Cmax: decreased 18% (on 1400 mg BID)	Increased atorvastatin effects	Inhibition of CYP450 3A4 by amprenavir	Avoid combination if possible; may consider low dose atorvastatin or alternative agents; monitor for myopathy	-
Atorvastatin (Lipitor)	10 mg QD x 4 days	1400 mg BID x 2 weeks	Atorvastatin Cmax: increased 304%; AUC: increased 130%; Cmin: no significant change	Amprenavir Cmax: decreased 18%; AUC: decreased 27%; Cmin: no significant change	Increased atorvastatin effects (eg, myopathy, rhabdomyolysis)	Inhibition of CYP450 3A4 by fosamprenavir	Avoid combination if possible; may consider low dose atorvastatin or alternative agents; monitor for myopathy	-
Atorvastatin (Lipitor)	10 mg QD x 4 days	700 mg BID with ritonavir 100 mg BID x 2 weeks	Atorvastatin Cmax: increased 184%; AUC: increased 153%; Cmin: increased 73%	No significant change	Increased atorvastatin effects (eg, myopathy, rhabdomyolysis)	Inhibition of CYP450 3A4 by fosamprenavir	Avoid combination if possible; may consider low dose atorvastatin or alternative agents; monitor for myopathy	Pravastatin
Efavirenz (Sustiva)	600 mg QD x 14 days	700 mg BID with ritonavir 100 mg BID x 28 days	Not studied	No significant change	-	-	No dose adjustment necessary	-

Coadministered Drug	Dose of Drug	Dose of Fosamprenavir	Effect on Coadministered Drug Levels	Effect on Fosamprenavir Levels	Potential Clinical Effects	Mechanism of Interaction	Management	Suggested Alternative Agent(s)
Efavirenz (Sustiva)	600 mg QD x 14 days	700 mg BID with ritonavir 200 mg BID x 28 days	Not studied	No significant change	-		No dose adjustment necessary	-
Efavirenz (Sustiva)	600 mg QD x 2 weeks	700 mg BID with ritonavir 100 mg BID x 2 weeks	Not studied	No significant change	-		No dose adjustment necessary	-
Efavirenz (Sustiva)	600 mg QD x 2 weeks	1400 mg QD with ritonavir 200 mg QD x 2 weeks	Not studied	Amprenavir Cmin: decreased 36%; Ritonavir AUC: decreased 31%; Cmin: decreased 40%	Decreased amprenavir effects	Induction of CYP450 3A4 by efavirenz	Increase ritonavir dose to 300 mg when administered with fosamprenavir and efavirenz once daily	-
Efavirenz (Sustiva)	600 mg QD x 2 weeks	1400 mg QD with 300 mg ritonavir x 2 weeks	Not studied	No significant change	-	Inhibition of CYP450 3A4 by ritonavir compensating for CYP450 3A4 induction by efavirenz	No dose adjustment necessary	-
Esomeprazole (Nexium)	20 mg QD x 21 days	1400 mg BID x 14 days	Esomeprazole AUC: increased 55%; Cmax: no significant change	No significant change	-		No dose adjustment necessary	-
Esomeprazole (Nexium)	20 mg QD x 21 days	700 mg BID with 100 mg ritonavir BID x 14 days	No significant change	No significant change	-		No dose adjustment necessary	-
Coadministered Drug	Dose of Drug	Dose of Fosamprenavir	Effect on Coadministered Drug Levels	Effect on Fosamprenavir Levels	Potential Clinical Effects	Mechanism of Interaction	Management	Suggested Alternative Agent(s)
Lopinavir/ritonavir (Kaletra)	400/100 mg BID	700 mg BID with 100 mg ritonavir BID x 2-4 weeks	Lopinavir AUC: decreased 48%; Cmax: decreased 61%; Cmin: decreased 69%	Amprenavir AUC: decreased 64%; Cmin: decreased 69%	Decreased lopinavir and amprenavir effects	Induction of CYP450 3A4 by lopinavir and amprenavir	Do not coadminister	-
Lopinavir/ritonavir (Kaletra)	400/100 mg BID x 10 days	700 mg BID x 10 days taken simultaneously, 4 hours or 12 hours away from lopinavir/ritonavir dose	Lopinavir AUC (12 hours apart and compared to simultaneous dosing): increased 187%; Cmax: increased 53%; Cmin: increased 69%; Amprenavir AUC: increased 53%; Cmax: increased 56%; Cmin: decreased 71%	Not studied	Decreased amprenavir and increased lopinavir effects	Induction of CYP450 3A4 by lopinavir and amprenavir	Avoid coadministration; Despite separating doses by 12 hours, significant induction still exists when amprenavir and lopinavir levels are compared to historical controls	
Lopinavir/ritonavir (Kaletra)	400/100 mg BID x 14 days	700 mg BID with ritonavir 100 mg BID x 14 days	Lopinavir AUC: increased 37%; Cmax: increased 30%; Cmin: increased 52%	Amprenavir AUC: decreased 63%; Cmax: decreased 58%; Cmin: decreased 65%	Decreased amprenavir effects; increased lopinavir effects	Induction of CYP450 3A4 by lopinavir/ritonavir and inhibition of CYP450 3A4 by amprenavir/ritonavir	Avoid coadministration	-
Lopinavir/ritonavir (Kaletra)	533/133 mg BID x 14 days	1400 mg BID x 14 days	No significant change	Amprenavir AUC: decreased 26%; Cmax: no significant change; Cmin: decreased 42%	Decreased amprenavir effects	Induction of CYP450 3A4 by lopinavir/ritonavir	Avoid coadministration	-
Nevirapine (Viramune)	200 mg BID	700 mg fosamprenavir BID with 100 mg ritonavir BID	Nevirapine Cmin: increased 22%	No significant change		Induction of CYP450 3A4 by nevirapine; inhibition of CYP450 3A4 by ritonavir	No dose adjustment necessary	-

Coadministered Drug	Dose of Drug	Dose of Fosamprenavir	Effect on Coadministered Drug Levels	Effect on Fosamprenavir Levels	Potential Clinical Effects	Mechanism of Interaction	Management	Suggested Alternative Agent(s)
Nevirapine (Viramune)	200 mg BID	1400 mg BID	Nevirapine AUC: increased 29%; Cmax: increased 25%; Cmin: increased 34%	Fosamprenavir AUC: decreased 33%; Cmax: decreased 25%; Cmin: decreased 35%	Decreased fosamprenavir effects	Induction of CYP450 3A4 by nevirapine	Do not coadminister	Consider ritonavir-boosted fosamprenavir
Paroxetine (Paxil)	20 mg QD x 10 days	700 mg BID with 100 mg ritonavir BID	Paroxetine AUC: decreased 58%; Cmax: decreased 60%; half-life decreased 25%	Amprenavir: no significant change; Ritonavir: no significant change	Decreased paroxetine effects	-	Titrate paroxetine to effect	-
Ranitidine (Zantac)	300 mg x 1 dose	1400 mg x 1 dose	Not studied	Amprenavir AUC: decreased 30%; Cmax: decreased 51%; Cmin: no significant change	Decreased amprenavir effects	-	Dose adjustment not established	-
Ritonavir (Norvir)	300 mg QD	1400 mg QD with efavirenz 600 mg QD	Not studied	Amprenavir AUC: no significant change; Cmax: increased 18%; Cmin: no significant change	-	Inhibition of CYP450 3A4 by ritonavir	No dose adjustment necessary	-
Saquinavir (Invirase, Fortovase)	1000 mg BID with ritonavir 100 mg BID on days 1-11	700 mg BID on days 2-22	Saquinavir AUC (with ritonavir 100 mg BID); AUC: no significant change; Cmax: no significant change; Cmin: decreased 24%	Not studied	-	-	No dose adjustment necessary	-
Saquinavir (Invirase, Fortovase)	1000 mg BID with ritonavir 200 mg BID on days 12-22	700 mg BID on days 2-22	Saquinavir AUC (with ritonavir 200 mg BID): no significant change; Cmax: no significant change; Cmin: increased 2C%	Not studied	-	-	No dose adjustment necessary	-
Tenofovir (Viread)	300 mg QD	1400 mg with 100 mg ritonavir QD x 14 days	No significant change	Amprenavir AUC: no significant change; Cmax: no significant change; Cmin: increased 24%	-	-	No dose adjustment necessary	-
Tenofovir (Viread)	300 mg QD	1400 mg with 200 mg ritonavir QD x 14 days	No significant change	No significant change	-	-	No dose adjustment necessary	-

All Interactions with Indinavir (Crixivan)

Coadministered Drug	Dose of Drug	Dose of Indinavir	Effect on Coadministered Drug Levels	Effect on Indinavir Levels	Potential Clinical Effects	Mechanism of Interaction	Management	Suggested Alternative Agent(s)
Adefovir dipivoxil (Hepsera)	-	-	No significant change	No significant change	-	-	No dose adjustment necessary	-
Amprenavir (Agenerase)	1200 mg BID with efavirenz 600 mg QD	1200 mg BID	Amprenavir clearance: decreased 54%	Not studied	-	Induction of CYP450 3A4 by amprenavir or efavirenz	Dose adjustment not established	-
Amprenavir (Agenerase)	750 mg or 800 mg TID (fasted)	800 mg TID (fasted)	Amprenavir Cmax: increased 18%; AUC: increased 33%; Cmin: increased 25%	Indinavir Cmax: decreased 22%; AUC: decreased 38%; Cmin: decreased 27%		Inhibition of CYP450 3A4 by indinavir	No dose adjustment necessary	-
Amprenavir (Agenerase)	800 mg TID x 2 weeks (fasted)	750 mg or 800 mg TID x 2 weeks (fasted)	Amprenavir AUC: increased 33%; Cmax: increased 18%; Cmin: increased 25%	Indinavir AUC: decreased 38%; Cmax: decreased 22%; Cmin: decreased 27%	-	Inhibition of CYP450 3A4 by indinavir; induction of CYP450 3A4 by amprenavir	No dose adjustment necessary	
Coadministered Drug	**Dose of Indinavir**		**Effect on Coadministered Drug Levels**	**Effect on Indinavir Levels**	**Potential Clinical Effects**	**Mechanism of Interaction**	**Management**	**Suggested Alternative Agent(s)**
Atorvastatin (Lipitor)			Not studied; may increase atorvastatin levels	-	Increased atorvastatin effects (eg, myopathy, rhabdomyolysis)	Inhibition of CYP450 3A4 by indinavir	Avoid combination if possible; may consider low dose atorvastatin or alternative agents; monitor for myopathy	Pravastatin
Atovaquone (Mepron)	750 mg BID (with food)	800 mg TID (fasted)	Atovaquone Cmax: increased 16%; AUC: increased 13%	Indinavir Cmax: increased 7%; AUC: decreased 5%	-		No dose adjustment necessary	-
Azithromycin (Zithromax)	1200 mg x 1 dose	800 mg TID	-	No significant change			No dose adjustment necessary	-
Carbamazepine (Tegretol)	200 mg QD	800 mg Q8H		Indinavir levels: decreased 4-25% of mean population values	Decreased indinavir effects	Induction of CYP450 3A4 by carbamazepine	Avoid combination if possible; consider alternative agents; monitor carbamazepine levels and adjust as indicated	Gabapentin Lamotrigine Tiagabine Topiramate
Coadministered Drug	**Dose of Drug**	**Dose of Indinavir**	**Effect on Coadministered Drug Levels**	**Effect on Indinavir Levels**	**Potential Clinical Effects**	**Mechanism of Interaction**	**Management**	**Suggested Alternative Agent(s)**
Cimetidine (Tagamet)	600 mg Q12	400 mg x 1 dose	-	No significant change	-	-	No dose adjustment necessary	-
Cisapride (Propulsid)	-	-	Not studied; may increase cisapride levels		Increased cisapride effects (eg, cardiac arrhythmias)	Inhibition of CYP450 3A4 by indinavir	Do not coadminister	Metoclopramide
Clarithromycin (Biaxin)	500 mg Q12H x 1 week	800 mg Q8H x 1 week	Clarithromycin AUC: increased 47%; Cmax: increased 20%; 14-hydroxyclarithromycin AUC: decreased 49%; Cmax: decreased 49%	Indinavir AUC: increased 19%; Cmax: no significant change; Cmin: increased 52%	Increased indinavir effects	Inhibition of CYP450 3A4 by both drugs	No dose adjustment necessary	

Coadministered Drug	Dose of Drug	Dose of Indinavir	Effect on Coadministered Drug Levels	Effect on Indinavir Levels	Potential Clinical Effects	Mechanism of Interaction	Management	Suggested Alternative Agent(s)
Clarithromycin (Biaxin)	500 mg Q12H x 1 week	800 mg Q8H x 1 week	Clarithromycin AUC: increased 53%	Indinavir AUC: increased 29%	-	Inhibition of CYP450 3A4 by both drugs	No dose adjustment necessary	-
Cotrimoxazole (TMP/SMX) (Trimethoprim/Sulfamethoxazole, Septra, Bactrim)	160 mg/800 mg Q12H x 1 week	400 mg Q6H x 1 week	Trimethoprim AUC: increased 19%; sulfamethoxazole AUC: no significant change	No significant change	-	-	No dose adjustment necessary	-
Coadministered Drug	**Dose of Drug**	**Dose of Indinavir**	**Effect on Coadministered Drug Levels**	**Effect on Indinavir Levels**	**Potential Clinical Effects**	**Mechanism of Interaction**	**Management**	**Suggested Alternative Agent(s)**
Delavirdine (Rescriptor)	400 mg TID	600 mg x 1 dose	No significant change	Indinavir AUC: increased 44% (compared to 800 mg dose)	Increased indinavir effects	Inhibition of CYP450 3A4 by delavirdine	Decrease indinavir to 600 mg Q8H	-
Delavirdine (Rescriptor)	400 mg TID	400 mg x 1 dose	Not studied	Indinavir AUC: increased 40%	Increased indinavir effects	Inhibition of CYP450 3A4 by delavirdine	Decrease indinavir to 600 mg Q8H	-
Delavirdine (Rescriptor)	400 mg TID	400 mg TID x 7 days	No significant change	Indinavir AUC: no significant change; Cmax: decreased 36%; Cmin: increased 118%	-	Inhibition of CYP450 3A4 by delavirdine	Decrease indinavir to 600 mg Q8H	-
Delavirdine (Rescriptor)	400 mg TID	600 mg TID x 7 days	No significant change	Indinavir AUC: increased 53%; Cmax: no significant change; Cmin: increased 298%	Increased indinavir effects	Inhibition of CYP450 3A4 by delavirdine	Decrease indinavir to 600 mg Q8H	-
Didanosine (Videx)	200 mg (buffered formulation) x 1 dose	800 mg x 1 dose	No significant change	Not studied	-	-	No dose adjustment necessary	-
Coadministered Drug	**Dose of Drug**	**Dose of Indinavir**	**Effect on Coadministered Drug Levels**	**Effect on Indinavir Levels**	**Potential Clinical Effects**	**Mechanism of Interaction**	**Management**	**Suggested Alternative Agent(s)**
Didanosine (Videx)	200 mg (buffered formulation) x 1 dose	800 mg x 1 dose (administered 1 hour before didanosine)	Didanosine AUC: decreased 17%; Cmax: no significant change	Not studied	-	-	No dose adjustment necessary	-
Didanosine (Videx)	400 mg (enteric coated capsule) x 1 dose	800 mg x 1 dose	Not studied	No significant change	-	-	No dose adjustment necessary	-
Didanosine (Videx)	Buffered formulation	-	Not studied	Indinavir AUC: decreased 84%	Decreased indinavir effects	Decreased indinavir absorption	Take drugs at least one hour apart	Didanosine enteric coated
Didanosine (Videx)	Buffered formulation	-	Not studied	Indinavir AUC: decreased 84%	Decreased indinavir effects	Decreased indinavir absorption due to decreased gastric acidity resulting from antacid buffer contained within didanosine tablets/suspension	Consider didanosine EC or administer indinavir at least 1 hour prior to didanosine tablets/suspension	-

Coadministered Drug	Dose of Drug	Dose of Indinavir	Effect on Coadministered Drug Levels	Effect on Indinavir Levels	Potential Clinical Effects	Mechanism of Interaction	Management	Suggested Alternative Agent(s)
Dronabinol (Marinol)	2.5 mg TID	800 mg Q8H x 21 days (PK measured at day 14)	-	No significant change	-		No dose adjustment necessary	-
Efavirenz (Sustiva)	200 mg QD x 14 days	800 mg Q8H x 14 days	No significant change	Indinavir AUC: decreased 31-35%; Cmax: decreased 16%	Decreased indinavir effects	Induction of CYP450 3A4 by efavirenz	Do not coadminister. Increasing indinavir dose to 1000 mg Q8H may not be sufficient to compensate for interaction.	-
Efavirenz (Sustiva)	200 mg x 14 days	800 mg Q8H x 14 days	No significant change	Indinavir AUC: decreased 31%; Cmax: decreased 16%	Decreased indinavir effects	Induction of CYP450 3A4 by efavirenz	Do not coadminister. Increasing indinavir dose to 1000 mg Q8H may not be sufficient to compensate for interaction.	-
Efavirenz (Sustiva)	600 mg QD x 10 days	1000 mg TID x 10 days	Not studied	Indinavir AUC: decreased 33-46%; Cmax: decreased 29%; Cmin: decreased 39-57%	Decreased indinavir effects	Induction of CYP450 3A4 by efavirenz	Do not coadminister. Increasing indinavir dose to 1000 mg Q8H may not be sufficient to compensate for interaction.	-
Efavirenz (Sustiva)	600 mg QD x 14 days	800 mg indinavir/100 mg ritonavir Q12H x 29 days	No significant change	Indinavir AUC: decreased 19%; Cmin: decreased 48%; Cmax: decreased 13%	Decreased indinavir effects	Induction of CYP450 3A4 by efavirenz	Increase indinavir to 1000 mg Q12H if dosed with ritonavir 100 mg Q12H	-
Coadministered Drug	**Dose of Drug**	**Dose of Indinavir**	**Effect on Coadministered Drug Levels**	**Effect on Indinavir Levels**	**Potential Clinical Effects**	**Mechanism of Interaction**	**Management**	**Suggested Alternative Agent(s)**
Emtricitabine (Emtriva)	200 mg x 1 dose	800 mg x 1 dose	No significant change	No significant change	-		No dose adjustment necessary	-
Ergotamine (Cafergot, ergot derivatives)	-	-	Not studied; may increase ergotamine levels		Increased ergotamin effects (eg, ergotism)		Do not coadminister	5-HT agonists ("triptans")
Ethinyl estradiol/norethindrone acetate (Ortho-Novum, others)	0.035 mcg ethinyl estradiol/1 mg norethindrone QD x 1 week	800 mg Q8H x 1 week	Ethinyl estradiol AUC: increased 24%; norethindrone AUC: increased 26%	Not studied		Inhibition of CYP450 3A4 by indinavir	No dose adjustment necessary	-
Fluconazole (Diflucan)	400 mg QD	1000 mg Q8H	No significant change	Indinavir AUC: decreased 19-24%; Cmax: no significant change; Cmin: no significant change	-		No dose adjustment necessary	-
Fosphenytoin (Cerebyx)	-	-	-	Not studied, may decrease indinavir levels	Decreased indinavir effects	Induction of CYP450 3A4 by phenytoin	Dose adjustment not established	-
Grapefruit Juice	6 ounces double strength	800 mg x 1	-	No significant change	-		No dose adjustment necessary	-

Coadministered Drug	Dose of Drug	Dose of Indinavir	Effect on Coadministered Drug Levels	Effect on Indinavir Levels	Potential Clinical Effects	Mechanism of Interaction	Management	Suggested Alternative Agent(s)
Grapefruit Juice	8 oz grapefruit juice	400 mg x 1 dose	Not studied	Indinavir AUC: decreased 26%	Decreased indinavir effects	Increased gastric acidity reduced indinavir absorption	Consider separating grapefruit juice and indinavir by at least 2 hours	-
Grapefruit Juice	Single strength	800 mg Q8H x 4 doses		No significant change	-	Inhibition of CYP450 3A4 by Seville orange juice or grapefruit juice was not observed in this study	No dose adjustment necessary	-
Interleukin-2 (IL-2) (Aldesleukin)	Continuous Infusion x 5 days	800 mg Q8H	-	AUC: increased 88%	-	Possible inhibition of CYP450 3A4 by IL-6 triggered by IL-2	No dose adjustment established	-
Isoniazid (Laniazid, others)	300 mg QD x 1 week	800 mg Q8H x 1 week	No significant change	No significant change	-	-	No dose adjustment necessary	-
Itraconazole (Sporanox)	200 mg BID (fasted)	600 mg Q8H		Indinavir AUC: similar to AUC of 800 mg Q8H alone	Increased indinavir effects	Inhibition of CYP450 3A4 by itraconazole	Decrease indinavir to 600 mg Q8H	-
Ketoconazole (Nizoral)	400 mg QD	600 mg Q8H	-	Indinavir AUC: decreased 18%	Decreased indinavir effects	-	Dose adjustment not established	-
Coadministered Drug	**Dose of Drug**	**Dose of Indinavir**	**Effect on Coadministered Drug Levels**	**Effect on Indinavir Levels**	**Potential Clinical Effects**	**Mechanism of Interaction**	**Management**	**Suggested Alternative Agent(s)**
Ketoconazole (Nizoral)	400 mg x 1 dose	400 mg x 1 dose	-	Indinavir AUC: increased 68%	Increased indinavir effects	Inhibition of CYP450 3A4 by ketoconazole	May consider decreasing indinavir to 600 mg Q8H	-
Lamivudine (Epivir)	150 mg BID x 1 week	800 mg Q8H x 1 week	No significant change	No significant change	-	-	No dose adjustment necessary	-
Levodopa (Larodopa)	700-750 mg per day	2400 mg per day			Increased levodopa effects (eg, gastrointestinal distress, dystonia, confusion)	Inhibition of CYP450 3A4 by indinavir	Decrease levodopa dose as tolerated	-
Lopinavir/ritonavir (Kaletra)	400/100 mg BID	400 mg BID x 14 days	No significant change	Indinavir Cmax: no significant change; Cmin: increased 46%; AUC: increased 20%	-	Inhibition of P450 3A4 by lopinavir/ritonavir	Dose adjustment not necessary	-
Lopinavir/ritonavir (Kaletra)	400/100 mg BID on days 6-15	800 mg TID on days 1-5, 600 mg BID on days 6-15	No significant change	Indinavir AUC: no significant change; Cmax: decreased 29%; Cmin: increased 247%	-	Inhibition of CYP450 3A4 by lopinavir/ritonavir	No dose adjustment necessary	-
Lopinavir/ritonavir (Kaletra)	400 mg/100 mg BID x 10 days	600 mg x 1 dose	Not studied	Indinavir AUC: no significant change; Cmax: decreased; Cmin: increased	No significant change	-	Dose adjustment not established	-

Coadministered Drug	Dose of Drug	Dose of Indinavir	Effect on Coadministered Drug Levels	Effect on Indinavir Levels	Potential Clinical Effects	Mechanism of Interaction	Management	Suggested Alternative Agent(s)
Marijuana (THC)	4% THC cigarettes	800 mg Q8H x 21 days (PK measured at 14 days)	Not studied	Indinavir AUC: no significant change; Cmax: no significant change; Cmin: decreased 34%	-	Possible induction of CYP450 3A4 by cannabinoids	No dose adjustment necessary	-
Methadone (Dolophine)	20-60 mg QD x 1 week	800 mg Q8H x 1 week	No significant change	No significant change	-		No dose adjustment necessary	-
Midazolam (Versed)	-	-	No significant change in procedure time or oxygenation	-	Increased midazolam effects (eg, increased sedation, confusion, respiratory depression)	Inhibition of CYP450 3A4 by indinavir	Single dose intravenous midazolam may be used; chronic midazolam administration (oral or intravenous) should be avoided	Lorazepam
Milk thistle	160 mg TID on days 3-17	800 mg TID x 4 doses on days 1, 2 and days 16 and 17	Not studied	No significant effect	-		No dose adjustment necessary	-
Milk thistle	175 mg TID x 3 weeks	800 mg Q8H	-	Indinavir AUC: no significant change; Cmin: decreased 25%	-	Unknown	No dose adjustment necessary	-
Coadministered Drug	Dose of Drug	Dose of Indinavir	Effect on Coadministered Drug Levels	Effect on Indinavir Levels	Potential Clinical Effects	Mechanism of Interaction	Management	Suggested Alternative Agent(s)
Milk thistle	450 mg TID on days 2-30	800 mg Q8H on days 1-30	-	No significant change	-	-	No dose adjustment necessary	-
Mycophenolate (CellCept)	500 mg BID x 8 weeks	800 mg BID	Not studied	No significant change	-	-	No dose adjustment necessary	-
Nelfinavir (Viracept)	1250 mg Q12H	1200 mg Q12H	No significant change	Indinavir AUC: no significant change (similar to indinavir 800 mg Q8H); indinavir Cmax: no significant change	-	-	Indinavir 1200 mg Q12H and nelfinavir 1250 mg Q12H	-
Nelfinavir (Viracept)	750 mg Q8H x 7 days	800 mg x 1 dose	Nelfinavir AUC: increased 83%; Cmax: increased 31%	Indinavir AUC: increased 51%; AUC of 1000 mg Q12H with nelfinavir was similar to AUC of 800 mg Q8H without nelfinavir	Increased nelfinavir and indinavir effects	Inhibition of CYP450 3A4 by both drugs	Dose adjustment not established; may consider indinavir 1000-1200 mg Q12H when coadministered with nelfinavir 1000-1250 mg Q12H	-
Nelfinavir (Viracept)	750 mg x 1 dose	800 mg Q8H x 7 days	Nelfinavir AUC: increased 83%; Cmax: increased 31%	Not studied	Increased nelfinavir effects	Inhibition of CYP450 3A4 by indinavir	Indinavir 1200 mg Q12H and nelfinavir 1250 mg Q12H	-

Coadministered Drug	Dose of Drug	Dose of Indinavir	Effect on Coadministered Drug Levels	Effect on Indinavir Levels	Potential Clinical Effects	Mechanism of Interaction	Management	Suggested Alternative Agent(s)
Nelfinavir (Viracept)	750 mg x 7 days	800 mg x 1 dose	Not studied	Indinavir AUC: increased 51%; Cmax: no significant change	Increased indinavir effects	Inhibition of CYP450 3A4 by nelfinavir	Indinavir 1200 mg Q12H and nelfinavir 1250 mg Q12H	-
Coadministered Drug	Dose of Drug	Dose of Indinavir	Effect on Coadministered Drug Levels	Effect on Indinavir Levels	Potential Clinical Effects	Mechanism of Interaction	Management	Suggested Alternative Agent(s)
Nevirapine (Viramune)	200 mg BID	800 mg Q8H	No significant change	Indinavir AUC: decreased 28%; Cmax: decreased 11%	Decreased indinavir effects	Induction of CYP450 3A4 by nevirapine	Increase indinavir to 1000 mg Q8H	-
Nevirapine (Viramune)	200 mg QD x 2 weeks, 200 mg BID x 28 days	800 mg Q8H	Not studied	Indinavir AUC: decreased 28%; Cmax: no significant change	Decreased indinavir effects	Induction of CYP450 3A4 by nevirapine	Increase incinavir to 1000 mg Q8H	-
Omeprazole (Prilosec)	20-40 mg QD	800 mg TID	-	Indinavir AUC: decreased 25%	Decreased indinavir effects	Decreased gastric acidity may affect indinavir solubility and absorption	No dose adjustment necessary	-
Omeprazole (Prilosec)	20 mg or 40 mg x 7 days	800 mg or 800 mg with 200 mg ritonavir	Not studied	Indinavir AUC: decreased 47%; Cmin: decreased 55%	Decreased indinavir effects	-	No dose adjustment necessary	-
Coadministered Drug	Dose of Drug	Dose of Indinavir	Effect on Ccadministered Drug Levels	Effect on Indinavir Levels	Potential Clinical Effects	Mechanism of Interaction	Management	Suggested Alternative Agent(s)
Quinidine (Quindex, others)	200 mg x 1 dose	400 mg x 1 dose	Not studied	AUC: increased 10%	-	-	No dose adjustment necessary	-
Rifabutin (Mycobutin)	150 mg QD	800 mg Q8H x 1 week	Rifabutin AUC: increased 60%	Indinavir AUC: decreased 31%; AUC of indinavir 800 mg Q8H is comparable to that of 1000 mg Q8H if given with rifabutin	Increased rifabutin effects (eg, uveitis); decreased indinavir effects	Inhibition of CYP450 3A4 by indinavir; induction of CYP450 3A4 by rifabutin	Decrease rifabutin to 150 mg QD or 300 mg 3 times/week and increase indinavir to 1000 mg Q8H	-
Coadministered Drug	Dose of Drug	Dose of Indinavir	Effect on Coadministered Drug Levels	Effect on Indinavir Levels	Potential Clinical Effects	Mechanism of Interaction	Management	Suggested Alternative Agent(s)
Rifabutin (Mycobutin)	150 mg QD x 10 days	800 mg Q8H x 10 days	Rifabutin AUC: increased 54% (compared to 300 mg rifabutin)	Indinavir AUC: decreased 32%	Increased rifabutin effects (eg, uveitis); decreased indinavir effects	Inhibition of CYP450 3A4 by indinavir	Decrease rifabutin to 150 mg QD or 300 mg 3 times/week and increase indinavir to 1000 mg Q8H	-
Rifabutin (Mycobutin)	150 mg QD x 14 days	1000 mg Q8H	Rifabutin AUC: increased 60% (when compared to rifabutin 300 mg QD monotherapy); 25-desacetyl rifabutin AUC: increased 125% (when compared to 25-desacetyl rifabutin from rifabutin 300 mg QD monotherapy)	Indinavir AUC: increased 15%	Increased rifabutin effects (eg, uveitis)	Induction of CYP450 3A4 by rifabutin	Decrease rifabutin to 150 mg QD or 300 mg 3 times/week and increase indinavir to 1000 mg Q8H	-

Coadministered Drug	Dose of Drug	Dose of Indinavir	Effect on Coadministered Drug Levels	Effect on Indinavir Levels	Potential Clinical Effects	Mechanism of Interaction	Management	Suggested Alternative Agent(s)
Rifabutin (Mycobutin)	300 mg QD	800 mg Q8H	Rifabutin AUC: increased 204%	Indinavir AUC: decreased 32%	Increased rifabutin effects (eg, uveitis); decreased indinavir effects	Inhibition of CYP450 3A4 by indinavir; induction of CYP450 3A4 by rifabutin	Decrease rifabutin to 150 mg QD or 300 mg 3 times/week and increase indinavir to 1000 mg Q8H	-
Rifabutin (Mycobutin)	300 mg QD x 10 days	800 mg Q8H x 10 days	Rifabutin AUC: increased 173%	Indinavir AUC: decreased 34%	Increased rifabutin effects (eg, uveitis); decreased indinavir effects	Inhibition of CYP450 3A4 by indinavir	Decrease rifabutin to 150 mg QD or 300 mg 3 times/week and increase indinavir to 1000 mg Q8H	-
Rifampin (Rifadin)	-	800 mg with ritonavir 100 mg BID x 1, administered with food	Rifampin AUC: increased 25%; desacetylrifampin AUC: increased 63%	Indinavir AUC: decreased 81%; ritonavir AUC: decreased 89%	Increased rifampin effects; decreased indinavir and ritonavir effects	Induction of CYP450 3A4 by rifampin; inhibition of CYP450 3A4 by indinavir/ritonavir	Do not coadminister	Rifabutin
Rifampin (Rifadin)	300 mg QD x 4 days	800 mg with ritonavir 100 mg BID	Not studied	Indinavir Cmin: decreased 87%; Cmax: no significant change; half-life: decreased 39%; Ritonavir Cmin: decreased 94%; Cmax: decreased 38%; half-life: decreased 53%	Decreased indinavir and ritonavir effects	Induction of P450 3A4 by rifampin	Do not coadminister	Rifabutin
Coadministered Drug	Dose of Drug	Dose of Indinavir	Effect on Coadministered Drug Levels	Effect on Indinavir Levels	Potential Clinical Effects	Mechanism of Interaction	Management	Suggested Alternative Agent(s)
Rifampin (Rifadin)	600 mg QD x 1 week	800 mg Q8H x 1 week	-	Indinavir AUC: decreased 89%	Decreased indinavir effects	Induction of CYP450 3A4 by rifampin	Do not coadminister	Rifabutin
Rifapentine (Priftin)	600 mg twice a week x 14 days	800 mg TID x 14 days	No significant change	Indinavir AUC: decreased 70%; Cmax: decreased 55%	Decreased indinavir effects	Induction of CYP450 3A4 by rifapentine	Dosage adjustment not established	Rifabutin
Ritonavir (Norvir)	100 mg BID x 14 days	800 mg BID x 14 days	Not studied	Indinavir AUC: increased 170%; Cmax: increased 60%; Cmin: increased 1000% (compared to indinavir 800 mg Q8H)	Increased indinavir effects	Inhibition of CYP450 3A4 by ritonavir	No dose adjustment necessary	-
Ritonavir (Norvir)	200 mg BID x 14 days	800 mg BID x 14 days	Not studied	Indinavir AUC: increased 254%; Cmax: increased 77%; Cmin: increased 2356% (compared to indinavir 800 mg Q8H)	Increased indinavir effects	Inhibition of CYP450 3A4 by ritonavir	No dose adjustment necessary	-
Ritonavir (Norvir)	400 mg BID x 14 days	800 mg BID x 14 days	Not studied	Indinavir AUC: increased 209%; Cmax: increased 49%; Cmin: increased 2344% (compared to indinavir 800 mg Q8H)	Increased indinavir effects	Inhibition of CYP450 3A4 by ritonavir	No dose adjustment necessary	-

Coadministered Drug	Dose of Drug	Dose of Indinavir	Effect on Coadministered Drug Levels	Effect on Indinavir Levels	Potential Clinical Effects	Mechanism of Interaction	Management	Suggested Alternative Agent(s)
Ritonavir (Norvir)	400 mg BID x 14 days	400 mg BID x 14 days	Not studied	Indinavir AUC: increased 62%; Cmax: no significant change; Cmin: increased 929% (compared to indinavir 800 mg Q8H)	Increased indinavir effects	Inhibition of CYP450 3A4 by ritonavir	No dose adjustment necessary	-
Coadministered Drug	**Dose of Drug**	**Dose of Indinavir**	**Effect on Coadministered Drug Levels**	**Effect on Indinavir Levels**	**Potential Clinical Effects**	**Mechanism of Interaction**	**Management**	**Suggested Alternative Agent(s)**
Ritonavir (Norvir)	400 mg Q12H x 15 days	400 mg Q12H x 15 days	Not studied	Indinavir Cmin: increased 400%	-	Inhibition of CYP450 3A4 by ritonavir	May consider indinavir/ritonavir combination as follows (BID dosing): 800/100; 800/200; 400/400	-
Saquinavir (Invirase, Fortovase)	1200 mg x 1 dose	800 mg Q8H x 2 days	Saquinavir AUC: increased 364%; Cmax: increased 299%	Indinavir concentration: increased	Increased saquinavir effects	Inhibition of CYP450 3A4 by indinavir	Dose adjustment not established	-
Saquinavir (Invirase, Fortovase)	Saquinavir soft gel cap 800 mg or 1200 mg x 1 dose	800 mg Q8H x 2 days	Saquinavir 800 mg AUC: increased 620%; Cmax: increased 551%; saquinavir 1200mg AUC: increased 364%; Cmax: increased 299%	Not studied	Increased saquinavir effects	Inhibition of CYP450 3A4 by indinavir	Dose adjustment not established	-
Sildenafil (Viagra)	25 mg x 1 dose	800 mg TID	Sildenafil AUC: increased 343%; Cmax: increased 300% (Levels exceeded those achieved by a 100 mg single dose)	Indinavir AUC: increased 11%; Cmax: increased 48%	Increased sildenafil effects (eg, hypotension, priapism)	Inhibition of CYP450 3A4 by indinavir	Initiate sildenafil at 25 mg QOD-QD; adjust dose as indicated; not recommended to exceed 25 mg in a 48 hour period	-
Simvastatin (Zocor)	-	-	Increased simvastatin levels		Increased simvastatin effects (eg, myopathy, rhabdomyolysis)	Inhibition of CYP450 3A4 by indinavir	Do not coadminister	Atorvastatin Pravastatin
Coadministered Drug	**Dose of Drug**	**Dose of Indinavir**	**Effect on Coadministered Drug Levels**	**Effect on Indinavir Levels**	**Potential Clinical Effects**	**Mechanism of Interaction**	**Management**	**Suggested Alternative Agent(s)**
Sirolimus (Rapamune)	-		May increase sirolimus levels	-	Increased sirolimus effects (eg, excessive immunosuppression)	Inhibition of CYP450 3A4 by indinavir	Dose adjustment not established; monitor and adjust sirolimus as indicated	-
St. John's Wort (Hypericum perforatum, hypericin, hyperforin)	300 mg TID (with meals)	800 mg Q8H	Not studied	Indinavir AUC: decrease 57+/-19%	May decrease effect of indinavir; indinavir resistance	Possible induction of CYP450 3A4 by St. John's wort	Do not coadminister; active ingredient/quantity of hypericum varies between products and among individual tablets or capsules within the same product	-
Stavudine (Zerit)	40 mg BID	800 mg on days 1 and 2, 800 mg indinavir with 200 mg ritonavir BID on days 3-17	Stavudine AUC: increased 24% (with indinavir and ritonavir); AUC: increased 14% (with indinavir alone); Cmax: no significant effect	Not studied	-		No dose adjustment necessary	-

Coadministered Drug	Dose of Drug	Dose of Indinavir	Effect on Coadministered Drug Levels	Effect on Indinavir Levels	Potential Clinical Effects	Mechanism of Interaction	Management	Suggested Alternative Agent(s)
Stavudine (Zerit)	40 mg Q12H x 1 week	800 mg Q8H x 1 week	Stavudine AUC: increased 25%	No significant change	-	-	No dose adjustment necessary	-
Tenofovir (Viread)	300 mg QD x 7 days	800 mg TID x 7 days	No significant change	No significant change	-	-	No dose adjustment necessary	-
Coadministered Drug	**Dose of Drug**	**Dose of Indinavir**	**Effect on Coadministered Drug Levels**	**Effect on Indinavir Levels**	**Potential Clinical Effects**	**Mechanism of Interaction**	**Management**	**Suggested Alternative Agent(s)**
Theophylline (Theo-Dur, Slo-Phyllin, Theo-24, Aminophyllin)	250 mg x 1 dose	800 mg Q8H x 6 days	Theophylline AUC: increased 18%; theophylline Cmax: within 8% of that when given alone	Not studied	-	Inhibition of P450 3A4 by indinavir	No dose adjustment necessary	-
Trazodone (Desyrel)	-	-	-		Increased trazodone effects (eg, nausea, dizziness, hypotension, syncope)	Inibition of CYP450 3A4 by indinavir	Decrease trazodone dose or start low and titrate to effect	-
Triazolam (Halcion)	-	-	Not studied; may increase trazolam levels		Increased triazolam effects (eg, increased sedation, confusion, respiratory depression)	Inhibition of CYP450 3A4 by indinavir	Avoid combination; consider alternative agents	Lorazepam Oxazepam Temazepam Trazodone
Vardenafil (Levitra)	10 mg x 1 dose	800 mg Q8H	Vardenafil AUC: increased 16-fold; Cmax: increased 7-fold; half-life: increased 2-fold	Not studied	Increased vardenafil effects (eg, hypotension, nausea, priapism, syncope)	Inhibition of CYP450 3A4 by indinavir	Consider initiating vardenafil at lower dose and titrate to effect. Dose should not exceed 2.5 mg in any 24 hour period.	-
Coadministered Drug	**Dose of Drug**	**Dose of Indinavir**	**Effect on Coadministered Drug Levels**	**Effect on Indinavir Levels**	**Potential Clinical Effects**	**Mechanism of Interaction**	**Management**	**Suggested Alternative Agent(s)**
Vitamin C	1 g QD x 7 days	800 mg Q8H x 4 doses	-	Indinavir AUC: no significant change; Cmin: decreased 32%; Cmax: decreased 20%	-	-	No dose adjustment necessary	-
Voriconazole (VFend)	200 mg Q12H x 7 days	800 mg TID x 10 days	No significant effect	No significant effect	-	-	No dose adjustment necessary	-
Warfarin (Coumadin)	5 mg QD	800 mg Q8H x 12 days	Prothrombin complex activity increased from 25-35% to 53 and 43% at 10 and 25 days after indinavir discontinued in one patient	-	Increased warfarin effects (eg, increased INR, risk of bleeding)	Inhibition of CYP450 by indinavir	Monitor INR and adjust warfarin as indicated	-
Zidovudine (Retrovir)	200 mg Q8H x 1 week	1000 mg Q8H x 1 week	Zidovudine AUC: increased 17-36%	No significant change	-	-	No dose adjustment necessary	-

All Interactions with Lamivudine (Epivir)

Coadministered Drug	Dose of Drug	Dose of Lamivudine	Effect on Coadministered Drug Levels	Effect on Lamivudine Levels	Potential Clinical Effects	Mechanism of Interaction	Management	Suggested Alternative Agent(s)
Abacavir (Ziagen)	600 mg x 1 dose	150 mg x 1 dose	No significant change	Lamivudine Cmax: decreased 35%; AUC: decreased 15%	-	Delayed lamivudine absorption	No dose adjustment necessary	-
Adefovir dipivoxil (Hepsera)	10 mg QD	-	No significant change				No dose adjustment necessary	-
Amprenavir (Agenerase)	150 mg x 1 dose	150 mg x 1 dose	No significant change	No significant change	-		No dose adjustment necessary	-
Atazanavir (Reyataz)	400 mg QD x 6 days	150 mg BID with zidovudine 300 mg BID x 6 days	Not studied	No significant change	-		No dose adjustment necessary	-
Cotrimoxazole (TMP/SMX) (Trimethoprim/Sulfamethoxazole, Septra, Bactrim)	160 mg/800 mg QD x 5 days	300 mg QD x 1dose	Not studied	Lamivudine AUC: increased 44%	Increased lamivudine effects	-	No dose adjustment necessary	-
Coadministered Drug	Dose of Drug	Dose of Lamivudine	Effect on Coadministered Drug Levels	Effect on Lamivudine Levels	Potential Clinical Effects	Mechanism of Interaction	Management	Suggested Alternative Agent(s)
Efavirenz (Sustiva)	600 mg x 14 days	150 mg Q12H x 14 days	Not studied	No significant change	-	-	No dose adjustment necessary	-
Indinavir (Crixivan)	800 mg Q8H x 1 week	150 mg BID x 1 week	No significant change	No significant change	-	-	No dose adjustment necessary	-
Methadone (Dolophine)	-	150 mg lamivudine/300 mg zidovudine (combination tablet)	No significant effect	Not studied	-		No dose adjustment necessary	-
Nelfinavir (Viracept)	750 mg Q8h x 7-10 days	150 mg x 1 dose	Not studied	Lamivudine AUC: no significant change; Cmax: increased 31%	Increased lamivudine effects		No dose adjustment necessary	-
Ribavirin (Rebetol, Virazole)	800 mg QD	150 mg BID	-	No significant change	-		No dose adjustment necessary	-
Coadministered Drug	Dose of Drug	Dose of Lamivudine	Effect on Coadministered Drug Levels	Effect on Lamivudine Levels	Potential Clinical Effects	Mechanism of Interaction	Management	Suggested Alternative Agent(s)
Stavudine (Zerit)	-	-	No significant change	No significant change	-		No dose adjustment necessary	-
Tenofovir (Viread)	300 mg QD x 7 days	150 mg BID x 7 days	No significant change	Lamivudine Cmax: decreased 24%	-	-	No dose adjustment necessary	-
Tipranavir (Aptivus)	1250 mg BID with 100 mg ritonavir BID x 42 doses	150 mg BID x 43 doses	-	Lamivudine Cmax: decreased 29%	-		No dose adjustment necessary	-

Coadministered Drug	Dose of Drug	Dose of Lopinavir/ritonavir	Effect on Coadministered Drug Levels	Effect on Lopinavir/ritonavir Levels	Potential Clinical Effects	Mechanism of Interaction	Management	Suggested Alternative Agent(s)
Tipranavir (Aptivus)	250 mg BID with 200 mg ritonavir BID	150 mg BID x 43 doses	-	No significant change			No dose adjustment necessary	-
Tipranavir (Aptivus)	750 mg BID with 100 mg ritonavir BID x 42 doses	150 mg BID x 43 doses	-	No significant change			No dose adjustment necessary	-
Zidovudine (Retrovir)	-	-	Zidovudine Cmax: increased 39%	No significant change	Increased zidovudine effects		No dose adjustment necessary	-

All Interactions with Lopinavir/ritonavir (Kaletra)

Coadministered Drug	Dose of Drug	Dose of Lopinavir/ritonavir	Effect on Coadministered Drug Levels	Effect on Lopinavir/ritonavir Levels	Potential Clinical Effects	Mechanism of Interaction	Management	Suggested Alternative Agent(s)
Amprenavir (Agenerase)	450 mg BID x 5 days, 750 mg BID x 5 days	400 mg/100 mg BID x 22 days	No significant change	Lopinavir AUC: decreased 15%, lopinavir Cmax: no significant change; Cmin: decreased 19%	-	-	No dose adjustment necessary	-
Amprenavir (Agenerase)	600 mg BID	400 mg/100 mg BID	Amprenavir Cmin: decreased 37% (when compared to standard curve obtained from amprenavir and ritonavir at same doses)	Not studied	Decreased amprenavir levels	Not established	Dose adjustment not established	
Amprenavir (Agenerase)	750 mg BID	533mg/133 mg BID with and without efavirenz 600 mg QHS	Amprenavir AUC: no significant change; Cmax: decreased 34%; Cmin: increased 22% (when compared to amprenavir, lopinavir/ritonavir with efavirenz)	Lopinavir AUC: no significant change, Cmax: no significant change; Cmin: no significant change: half-life: decreased 32% (when compared to amprenavir, lopinavir/ritonavir with efavirenz)		-	No dose adjustment necessary	-
Amprenavir (Agenerase)	Group 2: 1200 mg amprenavir/200 mg ritonavir BID; Group 4: 1200 mg amprenavir/400 mg ritonavir BID x weeks 1-26	400 mg/100 mg BID x weeks 2-26	Amprenavir Cmin: decreased 42% (in Group 2); Cmin decreased 69% (in Group 4)	Not studied	Decreased amprenavir levels	-	Dose adjustment not established	-
Coadministered Drug	Dose of Drug	Dose of Lopinavir/ritonavir	Effect on Coadministered Drug Levels	Effect on Lopinavir/ritonavir Levels	Potential Clinical Effects	Mechanism of Interaction	Management	Suggested Alternative Agent(s)
Atorvastatin (Lipitor)	20 mg QD x 4 days	400 mg/100 mg BID x 14 days	Atorvastatin AUC: increased 488%; Cmax: increased 367%; Cmin: increased 128%	No significant change	Increased atorvastatin effects (eg, myopathy, rhabdomyolysis)	Inhibition of CYP450 3A4 by lopinavir/ritonavir	Avoid combination if possible; may consider low dose atorvastatin or alternative agents; monitor for myopathy	Pravastatin
Atovaquone (Mepron)	-	-	May decrease atovaquone levels	-	Decreased atovaquone effects		No dose adjustment necessary	-
Carbamazepine (Tegretol)	-	-	-	Not studied; may decrease lopinavir levels	Decreased lopinavir/ritonavir effects		Avoid combination if possible; consider alternative agents,	Gabapentin Lamotrigine Tiagabine Topiramate

monitor carbamazepine levels and adjust as indicated

Coadministered Drug	Dose of Drug	Dose of Lopinavir/ritonavir	Effect on Coadministered Drug Levels	Effect on Lopinavir/ritonavir Levels	Potential Clinical Effects	Mechanism of Interaction	Management	Suggested Alternative Agent(s)
Clarithromycin (Biaxin)	-	-	May increase clarithromycin levels	-	Increased clarithromycin effects	Inhibition of CYP450 3A4 by lopinavir/ritonavir	No dose adjustment necessary	-
Cyclosporine (Sandimmune, Neoral)	-	-	May increase cyclosporine levels	-	Increased cyclosporine effects (increased immunosuppression, renal toxicity)	Inhibition of CYP450 3A4 by lopinavir/ritonavir	Monitor and adjust cyclosporine as indicated	-
Delavirdine (Rescriptor)	-	-	-	Not studied; may increase lopinavir/ritonavir levels	Increased lopinavir/ritonavir effects	-	Dose adjustment not established	-
Didanosine (Videx)	-	-	-	-	-	Decreased lopinavir/ritonavir absorption	Take didanosine 1 hour before or 2 hours after lopinavir/ritonavir	-
Coadministered Drug	Dose of Drug	Dose of Lopinavir/ritonavir	Effect on Coadministered Drug Levels	Effect on Lopinavir/ritonavir Levels	Potential Clinical Effects	Mechanism of Interaction	Management	Suggested Alternative Agent(s)
Disulfiram (Antabuse)	-	Oral solution (contains alcohol)	-	-	Disulfiram reaction (eg, nausea, vomiting, hypotension, headache)	Inhibition of alcohol and aldehyde dehydrogenase by disulfiram	Do not coadminister; consider lopinavir/ritonavir capsules	-
Efavirenz (Sustiva)	-	400 mg/100 mg BID	No significant change	Lopinavir AUC: decreased 20-25%; Cmin: decreased 40-45%	-	-	Increase dose of lopinavir/ritonavir to 533 mg/133 mg (4 capsules) BID with food	-
Efavirenz (Sustiva)	600 mg QD on days 1-35	400/100 mg BID on days 1-14, then increased to 533/133 mg BID on 15-35	-	Lopinavir AUC: increased 46%; Cmax: increased 33%, Cmin: increased 141%; Ritonavir AUC: increased 48%; Cmax: increased 46%; Cmin: increased 63% (compared to lopinavir/ritonavir 400/100 mg BID)	Increased lopinavir/ritonavir effects	Inhibition of CYP450 3A4 by lopinavir/ritonavir	Increase lopinavir/ritonavir to 533/133 mg BID when used with efavirenz	-
Efavirenz (Sustiva)	600 mg QHS x 9 days	400 mg/100 mg BID x 9 days	Efavirenz AUC: decreased 16%; Cmax: no significant change; Cmin: decreased 16%	Lopinavir AUC: decreased 19%; Cmax: no significant change; Cmin: decreased 39%; Ritonavir AUC: no significant change; Cmax: no significant change	Decreased lopinavir effects	Induction of CYP450 3A4 by efavirenz	Increase dose of lopinavir/ritonavir to 533 mg/133 mg (4 capsules) BID with food	-

Coadministered Drug	Dose of Drug	Dose of Lopinavir/ritonavir	Effect on Coadministered Drug Levels	Effect on Lopinavir/ritonavir Levels	Potential Clinical Effects	Mechanism of Interaction	Management	Suggested Alternative Agent(s)
Ethinyl estradiol/norethindrone acetate (Ortho-Novum, others)	Norethindrone 1 mg QD x 21 days	400 mg/100 mg BID x 14 days	Norethindrone AUC: decreased 17%; Cmax: decreased 16%; Cmin: decreased 32%	-	Decreased norethindrone effects (eg, contraceptive failure)	Induction of CYP450 3A4 by ritonavir	Use alternative contraceptive method	Barrier devices Condoms
Flecainide (Tambocor)	-	-	Not studied: may increase flecainide levels	-	Increased flecainide effects (eg, cardiac arrhythmias)	Inhibition of CYP450 3A4 by lopinavir/ritonavir	Do not coadminister	-
Fosamprenavir (Lexiva)	1400 mg BID x 14 days	533/133 mg BID x 14 days	Amprenavir AUC: decreased 26%; Cmax: no significant change; Cmin: decreased 42%	No significant change	Decreased amprenavir effects	Induction of CYP450 3A4 by lopinavir/ritonavir	Avoid coadministration	-
Fosamprenavir (Lexiva)	700 mg BID with 100 mg ritonavir BID x 2-4 weeks	400/100 mg BID	Amprenavir AUC: decreased 64%; Cmin: decreased 69%	Lopinavir AUC: decreased 48%; Cmin: decreased 61%	Decreased lopinavir and amprenavir effects	Induction of CYP450 3A4 by lopinavir and amprenavir	Do not coadminister	-

Coadministered Drug	Dose of Drug	Dose of Lopinavir/ritonavir	Effect on Coadministered Drug Levels	Effect on Lopinavir/ritonavir Levels	Potential Clinical Effects	Mechanism of Interaction	Management	Suggested Alternative Agent(s)
Fosamprenavir (Lexiva)	700 mg BID with ritonavir 100 mg BID x 14 days	400/100 mg BID x 14 days	Amprenavir AUC: decreased 63%; Cmax: decreased 58%; Cmin: decreased 65%	Lopinavir AUC: increased 37%; Cmax: increased 30%; Cmin: increased 52%	Decreased amprenavir effects; increased lopinavir effects	Induction of CYP450 3A4 by lopinavir/ritonavir and inhibition of CYP450 3A4 by amprenavir/ritonavir	Avoid coadministration	-
Fosamprenavir (Lexiva)	700 mg BID x 10 days taken simultaneously, 4 hours or 12 hours away from lopinavir/ritonavir dose	400/100 mg BID x 10 days	Not studied	Lopinavir AUC (12 hours apart and compared to simultaneous dosing): increased 187%; Cmax: increased 53%; Cmin: increased 69%; Amprenavir AUC: increased 53%; Cmax: increased 56%; Cmin: decreased 71%	Decreased amprenavir and increased lopinavir effects	Induction of CYP450 3A4 by lopinavir and amprenavir	Avoid coadministration; Despite separating doses by 12 hours, significant induction still exists when amprenavir and lopinavir levels are compared to historical controls	-
Indinavir (Crixivan)	400 mg BID x 14 days	400/100 mg BID	Indinavir Cmax: no significant change; Cmin: increased 46%; AUC: increased 20%	No significant change		Inhibition of P450 3A4 by lopinavir/ritonavir	Dose adjustment not necessary	-
Indinavir (Crixivan)	600 mg x 1 dose	400 mg/100 mg BID x 10 days	Indinavir AUC: no significant change; Cmax: decreased; Cmin: increased	Not studied	No significant change	-	Dose adjustment not established	-
Indinavir (Crixivan)	800 mg TID on days 1-5, 600 mg BID on days 6-15	400/100 mg BID on days 6-15	Indinavir AUC: no significant change; Cmax: decreased 29%; Cmin: increased 247%	No significant change	-	Inhibition of CYP450 3A4 by lopinavir/ritonavir	No dose adjustment necessary	-

Coadministered Drug	Dose of Drug	Dose of Lopinavir/ritonavir	Effect on Coadministered Drug Levels	Effect on Lopinavir/ritonavir Levels	Potential Clinical Effects	Mechanism of Interaction	Management	Suggested Alternative Agent(s)
Ketoconazole (Nizoral)	200 mg x 1 dose	400 mg/100 mg BID x 16 days	Ketoconazole AUC: increased 204%; Cmax: no significant change	Lopinavir AUC: no significant change; Cmax: no significant change; Cmin: decreased 25%	Increased ketoconazole effects; decreased lopinavir/ritonavir effects	-	Manufacturer recommends against using high doses of ketoconazole(>200 mg daily)	Fluconazole
Lamotrigine (Lamictal)	50 mg QD on days 1 and 2, then 100 mg BID on days 3-20	400/100 mg BID on days 11-20	Lamotrigine AUC: decreased 50%; Cmax: decreased 46%; Cmin: decreased 56%; half-life: decreased 46%	No significant change	Decreased lamotrigine effects	-	Titrate to effect but may need to increase dose to 200 mg BID while patient is receiving lopinavir/ritonavir	-
Methadone (Dolophine)	-	400/100 mg BID x 14 days	Methadone AUC: decreased 36%; Cmax: decreased 44%	Not studied	Decreased methadone effects (eg, withdrawal)	-	Monitor and adjust methadone as indicated	-
Methadone (Dolophine)	5 mg x 1 dose	400 mg/100 mg BID x 10 days	Methadone AUC: decreased 53%; Cmax: decreased 45%	-	Decreased methadone effects (eg, withdrawal)	Possible induction of CYP450 3A4 by lopinavir/ritonavir	Monitor and adjust methadone as indicated	-
Coadministered Drug	Dose of Drug	Dose of Lopinavir/ritonavir	Effect on Coadministered Drug Levels	Effect on Lopinavir/ritonavir Levels	Potential Clinical Effects	Mechanism of Interaction	Management	Suggested Alternative Agent(s)
Methadone (Dolophine)	Stable methadone dose	400/100 mg BID x 7 days	Methadone AUC: decreased 26%; Cmax: decreased 28%; Cmin: decreased 28%	-	Decreased methadone effects (eg, withdrawal)	Possible induction of methadone metabolism by lopinavir/ritonavir	Monitor for signs and symptoms of methadone withdrawal; some patients may need an increase in the methadone dose	-
Nelfinavir (Viracept)	1250 mg BID	400/100 mg BID	Nelfinavir Cmax: no significant change; AUC: no significant change; Cmin: increased 113%	Lopinavir Cmax: decreased 21%; AUC: decreased 27%; Cmin: decreased 33% Ritonavir Cmax: decreased 26%; AUC: decreased 24%; Cmin: decreased 29%	Decreased lopinavir/ritonavir effects	Induction of P450 3A4 by lopinavir/ritonavir and nelfinavir	Dose adjustment not established	-
Nevirapine (Viramune)	200 mg QD x 14 days, 200 mg BID x 6 days	400 mg/100 mg BID x 20 days	Nevirapine AUC: no significant change; Cmax: no significant change; Cmin: increased 15%	Lopinavir: no significant change	Though study does not suggest need to increase lopinavir/ritonavir dose, other evidence indicated decreased lopinavir/ritonavir effects	Induction of CYP450 3A4 by nevirapine	Increase dose of lopinavir/ritonavir to 533 mg/133 mg (4 capsules) BID with food	-
Nevirapine (Viramune)	7 mg/kg or 4 mg/kg QD x 2 weeks; BID x 1 week	300 mg/75 mg/square meter BID x 3 weeks	-	Lopinavir AUC: decreased 22%; Cmax: no significant change; Cmin: decreased 55%	Decreased lopinavir/ritonavir effects	Induction of CYP450 3A4 by nevirapine	Increase dose of lopinavir/ritonavir to 6.5 mL BID with food	-

Coadministered Drug	Dose of Drug	Dose of Lopinavir/ritonavir	Effect on Coadministered Drug Levels	Effect on Lopinavir/ritonavir Levels	Potential Clinical Effects	Mechanism of Interaction	Management	Suggested Alternative Agent(s)
Phenytoin (Dilantin)	300 mg QHS for 10 days	400/100 mg BID on days 1-22	Phenytoin AUC: decreased 31%; Cmax: decreased 28%; Cmin: decreased 34%; half-life: decreased 38%	Lopinavir AUC: decreased 33%, Cmax: decreased 24%, Cmin: decreased 46%, half-life: decreased 51%. Ritonavir AUC: decreased 28%; Cmax: decreased 20%; Cmin: decreased 47%; half-life: decreased 38%	Decreased lopinavir/ritonavir and phenytoin effects	Induction of CYP450 3A4 by phenytoin; possible induction of CYP450 2C9 by lopinavir	Avoid combination if possible; consider alternative agents; monitor phenytoin levels and adjust as indicated; if combination cannot be avoided, possible options include increasing LPV/r to 4 caps BID or adding ritonavir 100 mg BID to regimen and monitoring levels. Neither option currently has any data.	Gabapentin Lamotrigine Tiagabine Topiramate
Coadministered Drug	Dose of Drug	Dose of Lopinavir/ritonavir	Effect on Coadministered Drug Levels	Effect on Lopinavir/ritonavir Levels	Potential Clinical Effects	Mechanism of Interaction	Management	Suggested Alternative Agent(s)
Pravastatin (Pravachol)	20 mg QD x 4 days	400 mg/100 mg BID x 14 days	Pravastatin AUC: increased 33%; Cmax: increased 26%	No significant change	-	Unknown	No dose adjustment necessary	-
Rifabutin (Mycobutin)	150 mg QD x 10 days	400 mg/100 mg BID x 20 days	-	Lopinavir AUC: increased 17%; Cmax: no significant change; Cmin: increased 20%	Increased lopinavir/ritonavir effects	-	No dose adjustment necessary	-
Rifabutin (Mycobutin)	300 mg QD x 10 days, 150 mg QD x 10 days	400 mg/100 mg BID x 10 days	Rifabutin AUC: increased 203%; Cmax: increased 112%; Cmin: increased 390%, 25-O-desacetyl rifabutin AUC: increased 4650%; Cmax: increased 2260%; Cmin: increased 9390%	-	Increased rifabutin effects (eg, uveitis)	Inhibition of CYP450 3A4 by lopinavir/ritonavir	Decrease rifabutin to 150 mg QOD	-

Coadministered Drug	Dose of Drug	Dose of Lopinavir/ritonavir	Effect on Coadministered Drug Levels	Effect on Lopinavir/ritonavir Levels	Potential Clinical Effects	Mechanism of Interaction	Management	Suggested Alternative Agent(s)
Rifampin (Rifadin)	600 mg QD on days 11-24	400/100 mg BID on days 1-15, then 800/200 mg BID or 400/400 mg BID on days 16-24	Not studied	Lopinavir AUC: decreased 16% (in 800/200 mg BID group when compared to 400/100 mg BID); Cmax: decreased 57%; Cmin: no significant change. Ritonavir AUC: increased 42%, Cmax: increased 75%, Cmin: no significant change. Lopinavir pharmacokinetics: No significant change (in 400/400 mg BID group) Ritonavir AUC: increased 612%, Cmax: increased 738%; Cmin: increased 389% (in 400 mg/400 mg BID group)	Decreased lopinavir effects	Inhibition of CYP450 3A4 by ritonavir; Induction of CYP450 3A4 by rifampin	Consider using lopinavir/ritonavir 400 mg BID with ritonavir 400 mg BID when combined with rifampin	-
Rifampin (Rifadin)	600 mg QD x 10 days	400 mg/100 mg BID x 20 days	-	Lopinavir AUC: decreased 75%; Cmax: decreased 55%; Cmin: decreased 99%	Decreased lopinavir/ritonavir effects	Induction of CYP450 3A4 by rifampin	Do not coadminister	Rifabutin
Ritonavir (Norvir)	100 mg BID x 3-4 weeks	400 mg/100 mg BID x 3-4 weeks	-	Lopinavir AUC: increased 46%; Cmax: increased 28%; Cmin: increased 116%	Increased lopinavir/ritonavir effects	Inhibition of CYP450 3A4 by ritonavir	Dose adjustment not established	-
Saquinavir (Invirase, Fortovase)	1000 mg (soft gel caps) BID	400/100 mg BID	Saquinavir AUC: no significant change; Cmax: no significant change; Cmin: increased 27% (compared to saquinavir/ritonavir control) Ritonavir AUC: decreased 54%; Cmax: decreased 37%; Cmin: decreased 60%; Clearance total: increased 107%(compared to saquinavir/ritonavir control)	Lopinavir AUC: no significant change, Cmax: no significant change; Cmin: no significant change; (compared to historical control)		Possibly increased clearance resulting in decreased ritonavir levels	No dose adjustment necessary	-
Saquinavir (Invirase, Fortovase)	1200 mg TID on days 1-5, 800 mg BID on days 6-15	400/100 mg BID on days 6-20	Saquinavir AUC: increased 838%; Cmax: increased 517%; Cmin: increased 1700%	No significant change	Increased saquinavir effects	Inhibition of CYP450 3A4 by lopinavir/ritonavir	Dose adjustment not established	-
Saquinavir (Invirase, Fortovase)	800 mg BID	400 mg/100 mg BID x 10 days	Saquinavir AUC: no significant change; Cmin: increased	-	Increased saquinavir effects	Inhibition of CYP450 3A4 by lopinavir/ritonavir	Dose adjustment not established	-

Coadministered Drug	Dose of Drug	Dose of Lopinavir/ritonavir	Effect on Coadministered Drug Levels	Effect on Lopinavir/ritonavir Levels	Potential Clinical Effects	Mechanism of Interaction	Management	Suggested Alternative Agent(s)
Tenofovir (Viread)	300 mg QD	400 mg/100 mg BID x 14 days	Tenofovir AUC: increased 34%; Cmax: increased 31%; Cmin: increased 29%	Lopinavir AUC: decreased 15%; Cmax: decreased 15%; Cmin: no significant change; Ritonavir AUC: decreased 24%; Cmax: decreased 28%; Cmin: no significant change	Increased tenofovir effects	-	No dose adjustment necessary	-

Coadministered Drug	Dose of Drug	Dose of Lopinavir/ritonavir	Effect on Coadministered Drug Levels	Effect on Lopinavir/ritonavir Levels	Potential Clinical Effects	Mechanism of Interaction	Management	Suggested Alternative Agent(s)
Tenofovir (Viread)	300 mg QD	400/100 mg BID	Not studied	Lopinavir: no significant change. Ritonavir: no significant change	-	-	No dose adjustment necessary	-
Tenofovir (Viread)	300 mg QD	400/100 mg BID	Tenofovir AUC: increased 32%; Cmin: increased 51%; half-life: no significant change	No significant change	Possibly increased tenofovir effects	-	No dose adjustment necessary	-
Trazodone (Desyrel)	-	-	Increased trazodone concentrations	-	Increased trazodone effects (eg, nausea, dizziness, hypotension, syncope)	Possible inhibition of trazodone metabolism	Use with caution; if benefit outweighs risk, initiate trazodone at lower dose	

Coadministered Drug	Dose of Drug	Dose of Lopinavir/ritonavir	Effect on Coadministered Drug Levels	Effect on Lopinavir/ritonavir Levels	Potential Clinical Effects	Mechanism of Interaction	Management	Suggested Alternative Agent(s)
Valproic Acid (Depakote, Depakene, Depacon)	250 mg BID x 7 days	400/100 mg BID	No significant change	Lopinavir Cmax: increased 33%; Cmin: increased 57%; AUC: increased 75%; half-life: no significant change	Increased lopinavir effects	Possible inhibition of UGT-mediated metabolism of lopinavir	Dose adjustment not established	

All Interactions with Nelfinavir (Viracept)

Coadministered Drug	Dose of Drug	Dose of Nelfinavir	Effect on Coadministered Drug Levels	Effect on Nelfinavir Levels	Potential Clinical Effects	Mechanism of Interaction	Management	Suggested Alternative Agent(s)
Amiodarone (Cordarone)	-	-	Not studied; may increase amiodarone levels		Increased amiodarone effects (eg, hypotension, bradycardia, cardiac arrhythmias)	Inhibition of CYP450 3A4 by nelfinavir	Monitor and adjust amiodarone as indicated	-
Amprenavir (Agenerase)	1200 mg BID with efavirenz 600 mg QD	1250 mg BID	Amprenavir clearance: decreased 41%	Not studied		Induction of CYP450 3A4 by amprenavir or efavirenz	Dose adjustment not established	-
Amprenavir (Agenerase)	750 mg or 800 mg TID x 2 weeks (fed)	750 mg TID x 2 weeks (fed)	No significant change	Nelfinavir AUC: increased 15%; Cmax: no significant change	-	-	No dose adjustment necessary	-
Amprenavir (Agenerase)	750 mg or 800 mg TID x 2 weeks (fed)	750 mg TID x 2 weeks (fed)	Amprenavir AUC: no significant change; Cmax: no significant change; Cmin: increased 189%	Nelfinavir AUC: increased 15%; Cmax: no significant change; Cmin: no significant change	Increased amprenavir effects	Inhibition of CYP450 3A4 by both drugs	No dose adjustment necessary	-

Coadministered Drug	Dose of Drug	Dose of Nelfinavir	Effect on Coadministered Drug Levels	Effect on Nelfinavir Levels	Potential Clinical Effects	Mechanism of Interaction	Management	Suggested Alternative Agent(s)
Ethinyl estradiol/norethindrone acetate (Ortho-Novum, others)	Ethinyl estradiol (EE) 35 mcg/Norethindrone (N) 0.4 mg QD x 15 days	750 mg Q8H x 7 days	Ethinyl estradiol AUC: decreased 47%; Cmax: decreased 28%; Norethindrone AUC: decreased 18%; Cmax: no significant change	-	Contraceptive failure	Induction of glucuronyl transferase by nelfinavir; inhibition of CYP450 3A4 by nelfinavir	Use alternative method of birth control	Condoms; barrier methods
Indinavir (Crixivan)	1200 mg Q12H	1250 mg Q12H	Indinavir AUC: no significant change (similar to indinavir 800 mg Q8H); indinavir Cmax: no significant change	No significant change	-	-	Indinavir 1200 mg Q12H and nelfinavir 1250 mg Q12H	-
Indinavir (Crixivan)	800 mg Q8H x 7 days	750 mg x 1 dose	Not studied	Nelfinavir AUC: increased 83%; Cmax: increased 31%	Increased nelfinavir effects	Inhibition of CYP450 3A4 by indinavir	Indinavir 1200 mg Q12H and nelfinavir 1250 mg Q12H	-
Indinavir (Crixivan)	800 mg x 1 dose	750 mg Q8H x 7 days	Indinavir AUC: increased 51%; AUC of 1000 mg Q12H with nelfinavir was similar to AUC of 800 mg Q8H without nelfinavir	Nelfinavir AUC: increased 83%; Cmax: increased 31%	Increased nelfinavir and indinavir effects	Inhibition of CYP450 3A4 by both drugs	Dose adjustment not established; may consider indinavir 1000-1200 mg Q12H when coadministered with nelfinavir 1000-1250 mg Q12H	-
Indinavir (Crixivan)	800 mg x 1 dose	750 mg x 7 days	Indinavir AUC: increased 51%; Cmax: no significant change	Not studied	Increased indinavir effects	Inhibition of CYP450 3A4 by nelfinavir	Indinavir 1200 mg Q12H and nelfinavir 1250 mg Q12H	-
Ketoconazole (Nizoral)	400 mg QD x 7 days	500 mg Q8H x 5-6 days		AUC: increased 35%; Cmax: increased 25%	Increased nelfinavir effects	Inhibition of CYP450 3A4 by ketoconazole	No dose adjustment necessary	-
Lamivudine (Epivir)	150 mg x 1 dose	750 mg Q8H x 7-10 days	Lamivudine AUC: no significant change; Cmax: increased 31%	Not studied	Increased lamivudine effects		No dose adjustment necessary	
Coadministered Drug	Dose of Drug	Dose of Nelfinavir	Effect on Coadministered Drug Levels	Effect on Nelfinavir Levels	Potential Clinical Effects	Mechanism of Interaction	Management	Suggested Alternative Agent(s)
Lopinavir/ritonavir (Kaletra)	400/100 mg BID	1250 mg BID	Lopinavir Cmax: decreased 21%; AUC: decreased 27%; Cmin: decreased 33%. Ritonavir Cmax: decreased 26%; AUC: decreased 24%; Cmin: decreased 29%	Nelfinavir Cmax: no significant change; AUC: no significant change; Cmin: increased 113%	Decreased lopinavir/ritonavir effects	Induction of P450 3A4 by lopinavir/ritonavir and nelfinavir	Dose adjustment not established	-
Lovastatin (Mevacor)	-	-	Not studied; may increase lovastatin levels	-	Increased lovastatin effects (eg, myopathy, rhabdomyolysis)	Inhibition of CYP450 3A4 by nelfinavir	Do not coadminister	Atorvastatin Pravastatin
Marijuana (THC)	4% THC cigarettes or 2.5 mg dronabinol TID	750 mg TID		Nelfinavir AUC: no significant change; Cmax: decreased 17%; Cmin: no significant change		Possible induction of CYP450 3A4 by cannabinoids	No dose adjustment necessary	
Medroxyprogesterone acetate (Depo-Provera)	150 mg	-	Progesterone levels: no significant change	Nelfinavir AUC: no significant change; M8 AUC: no significant change		-	No dose adjustment necessary	-

Coadministered Drug	Dose of Drug	Dose of Nelfinavir	Effect on Coadministered Drug Levels	Effect on Nelfinavir Levels	Potential Clinical Effects	Mechanism of Interaction	Management	Suggested Alternative Agent(s)
Ethinyl estradiol/norethindrone acetate (Ortho-Novum, others)	Ethinyl estradiol (EE) 35 mcg/ Norethindrone (N) 0.4 mg QD x 15 days	750 mg Q8H x 7 days	Ethinyl estradiol AUC: decreased 47%; Cmax: decreased 28%; Norethindrone AUC: decreased 18%; Cmax: no significant change	-	Contraceptive failure	Induction of glucuronyl transferase by nelfinavir; inhibition of CYP450 3A4 by nelfinavir	Use alternative method of birth control	Condoms; barrier methods
Indinavir (Crixivan)	1200 mg Q12H	1250 mg Q12H	Indinavir AUC: no significant change (similar to indinavir 800 mg Q8H); indinavir Cmax: no significant change	No significant change	-		Indinavir 1200 mg Q12H and nelfinavir 1250 mg Q12H	-
Indinavir (Crixivan)	800 mg Q8H x 7 days	750 mg x 1 dose	Not studied	Nelfinavir AUC: increased 83%; Cmax: increased 31%	Increased nelfinavir effects	Inhibition of CYP450 3A4 by indinavir	Indinavir 1200 mg Q12H and nelfinavir 1250 mg Q12H	-
Indinavir (Crixivan)	800 mg x 1 dose	750 mg Q8H x 7 days	Indinavir AUC: increased 51%; AUC of 1000 mg Q12H with nelfinavir was similar to AUC of 800 mg Q8H without nelfinavir	Nelfinavir AUC: increased 83%; Cmax: increased 31%	Increased nelfinavir and indinavir effects	Inhibition of CYP450 3A4 by both drugs	Dose adjustment not established; may consider indinavir 1000-1200 mg Q12H when coadministered with nelfinavir 1000-1250 mg Q12H	-
Indinavir (Crixivan)	800 mg x 1 dose	750 mg x 7 days	Indinavir AUC: increased 51%; Cmax: no significant change	Not studied	Increased indinavir effects	Inhibition of CYP450 3A4 by nelfinavir	Indinavir 1200 mg Q12H and nelfinavir 1250 mg Q12H	-
Ketoconazole (Nizoral)	400 mg QD x 7 days	500 mg Q8H x 5-6 days		AUC: increased 35%; Cmax: increased 25%	Increased nelfinavir effects	Inhibition of CYP450 3A4 by ketoconazole	No dose adjustment necessary	-
Lamivudine (Epivir)	150 mg x 1 dose	750 mg Q8H x 7-10 days	Lamivudine AUC: no significant change; Cmax: increased 31%	Not studied	Increased lamivudine effects		No dose adjustment necessary	-
Coadministered Drug	Dose of Drug	Dose of Nelfinavir	Effect on Coadministered Drug Levels	Effect on Nelfinavir Levels	Potential Clinical Effects	Mechanism of Interaction	Management	Suggested Alternative Agent(s)
Lopinavir/ritonavir (Kaletra)	400/100 mg BID	1250 mg BID	Lopinavir Cmax: decreased 21%; AUC: decreased 27%; Cmin: decreased 33%. Ritonavir Cmax: decreased 26%; AUC: decreased 24%; Cmin: decreased 29%	Nelfinavir Cmax: no significant change; AUC: no significant change; Cmin: increased 113%	Decreased lopinavir/ritonavir effects	Induction of P450 3A4 by lopinavir/ritonavir and nelfinavir	Dose adjustment not established	-
Lovastatin (Mevacor)	-	-	Not studied; may increase lovastatin levels	-	Increased lovastatin effects (eg, myopathy, rhabdomyolysis)	Inhibition of CYP450 3A4 by nelfinavir	Do not coadminister	Atorvastatin Pravastatin
Marijuana (THC)	4% THC cigarettes or 2.5 mg dronabinol TID	750 mg TID	-	Nelfinavir AUC: no significant change; Cmax: decreased 17%; Cmin: no significant change		Possible induction of CYP450 3A4 by cannabinoids	No dose adjustment necessary	-
Medroxyprogesterone acetate (Depo-Provera)	150 mg	-	Progesterone levels: no significant change	Nelfinavir AUC: no significant change; M8 AUC: no significant change	-		No dose adjustment necessary	-

Coadministered Drug	Dose of Drug	Dose of Nelfinavir	Effect on Coadministered Drug Levels	Effect on Nelfinavir Levels	Potential Clinical Effects	Mechanism of Interaction	Management	Suggested Alternative Agent(s)
Methadone (Dolophine)	10 to 40 mg QD x 1 month	1250 mg BID x 8 days	Decreased methadone and methadone metabolite exposure	-	Withdrawal symptoms not observed	Induction of CYP450 3A4 by nelfinavir	Monitor and adjust methadone as indicated	-
Methadone (Dolophine)	40-120 mg QD x 4 weeks	1250 mg BID x 5 days	-	Cmin: increased 300%	Not clinically significant	Inhibition of nelfinavir metabolism by methadone	No dose adjustment necessary	-
Coadministered Drug	**Dose of Drug**	**Dose of Nelfinavir**	**Effect on Coadministered Drug Levels**	**Effect on Nelfinavir Levels**	**Potential Clinical Effects**	**Mechanism of Interaction**	**Management**	**Suggested Alternative Agent(s)**
Nevirapine (Viramune)	200 mg QD x 14 days, 200 mg BID x 14 days	750 mg TID x 36 days	Not studied	No significant change	-	-	No dose adjustment necessary	-
Phenytoin (Dilantin)	300 mg QAM	1250 mg BID	Phenytoin Cmax: decreased 21%; AUC: decreased 30%; Cmin: decreased 39%	Nelfinavir: no significant change; M8 levels: decreased 20-30%	Decreased phenytoin effects	Induction of CYP450 3A4 by phenytoin	Avoid combination if possible; consider alternative agents; monitor phenytoin levels and adjust as indicated	Gabapentin Lamotrigine Tiagabine Topiramate
Pravastatin (Pravachol)	40 mg QD on days 15-18	1250 mg BID on days 1-18	Not studied	Nelfinavir AUC: no significant change; Cmin: increased 61%; M8 AUC: no significant change; M8 Cmin: increased 31%	-	Unknown	No dose adjustment necessary	-
Coadministered Drug	**Dose of Drug**	**Dose of Nelfinavir**	**Effect on Coadministered Drug Levels**	**Effect on Nelfinavir Levels**	**Potential Clinical Effects**	**Mechanism of Interaction**	**Management**	**Suggested Alternative Agent(s)**
Quinidine (Quindex, others)	-	-	May increase quinidine levels	-	Increased quinidine effects (eg, cardiac arrhythmias)	Inhibition of CYP450 3A4 by nelfinavir	Do not coadminister	-
Rifabutin (Mycobutin)	150 mg QD x 8 days	1250 mg Q12H x 7-8 days		No significant change	-		Decrease rifabutin to 150 mg QD or 300 mg 2 to 3 times/week and increase nelfinavir to 1000 mg TID	
Rifabutin (Mycobutin)	150 mg QD x 8 days	750 mg Q8H x 7-8 days	Rifabutin AUC: increased 83%; Cmax: increased 19%	Nelfinavir AUC: decreased 23%; Cmax: decreased 18%	Increased rifabutin effects (eg, uveitis); decreased nelfinavir effects	Inhibition of CYP450 3A4 by nelfinavir; induction of CYP450 3A4 by rifabutin	Decrease rifabutin to 150 mg QD or 300 mg 2 to 3 times/week and increase nelfinavir to 1000 mg TID	
Rifabutin (Mycobutin)	300 mg QD x 8 days	750 mg Q8H x 7-8 days	Rifabutin AUC: increased 207%; Cmax: increased 146%	Nelfinavir AUC: decreased 32%; Cmax: decreased 25%	Increased rifabutin effects (eg, uveitis); decreased nelfinavir effects	Inhibition of CYP450 3A4 by nelfinavir; induction of CYP450 3A4 by rifabutin	Decrease rifabutin to 150 mg QD or 300 mg 2 to 3 times/week and increase nelfinavir to 1000 mg TID	-
Rifampin (Rifadin)	600 mg QD x days	750 mg Q8H x 5-6 days	-	Nelfinavir AUC: decreased 82%; Cmax: decreased 76%	Decreased nelfinavir effects	Induction of CYP450 3A4 by rifampin	Do not coadminister	Rifabutin
Coadministered Drug	**Dose of Drug**	**Dose of Nelfinavir**	**Effect on Coadministered Drug Levels**	**Effect on Nelfinavir Levels**	**Potential Clinical Effects**	**Mechanism of Interaction**	**Management**	**Suggested Alternative Agent(s)**
Rifapentine (Priftin)	-	-	-	Not studied; may decrease nelfinavir levels	Decreased nelfinavir effects	Induction of CYP450 3A4 by rifapentine	Do not coadminister	Rifabutin

Coadministered Drug	Dose of Drug	Dose of Nelfinavir	Effect on Coadministered Drug Levels	Effect on Nelfinavir Levels	Potential Clinical Effects	Mechanism of Interaction	Management	Suggested Alternative Agent(s)
Ritonavir (Norvir)	100 mg or 200 mg BID on days 15-31	1250 mg BID on days 1-31	Not studied	Nelfinavir AUC: increased 17-27% (on ritonavir 100 mg BID; M8 AUC: increased 100 mg BID): nelfinavir AUC: increased 20-53% (on ritonavir 200 mg BID); M8 AUC: increased 69-87% (on ritonavir 200 mg BID)		Inhibition of CYP450 3A4 by both ritonavir and nelfinavir	Dose adjustment not established	-
Ritonavir (Norvir)	200 mg or 400 mg QD with food x 15 days	2000 mg/ritonavir 200 mg, 2000 mg/ritonavir 400 mg, or 2500 mg/200 mg QD with food x 15 days	-	Nelfinavir 2000 mg/ritonavir 200 mg AUC: increased 100%; Cmax: increased 95%; Cmin: increased 92% (all values are compared to nelfinavir 1250 mg BID)		Inhibition of CYP450 3A4 by ritonavir	Using nelfinavir 2000 mg/ritonavir 200 mg QD with food may allow for QD dosing	-
Ritonavir (Norvir)	500 mg Q12H x 3 doses	750 mg x 1 dose	Not studied	Nelfinavir AUC: increased 152%; Cmax: increased 44%	Increased nelfinavir effects	Inhibition of CYP450 3A4 by ritonavir	No dose adjustment necessary	-
Ritonavir (Norvir)	500 mg x 1 dose	750 mg Q8H x 5 dose	No significant change	-	-		No dose adjustment necessary	-
Saquinavir (Invirase, Fortovase)	1000 mg saquinavir BID with 100 mg ritonavir BID on days 1-14	1250 mg BID on days 16-21	Saquinavir Cmax: increased 172%	Nelfinavir Cmax: increased 55%; M8 AUC: increased 622%; Cmax: increased 94%; Cmin: increased 179%		Inhibition of CYP450 3A4 by saquinavir/ritonavir	No dose adjustment necessary	-
Saquinavir (Invirase, Fortovase)	1200 mg (soft gel cap) x 1 dose	750 mg TID x 4 days	Saquinavir AUC: increased 392%; Cmax: increased 179%		Increased saquinavir effects	Inhibition of CYP450 3A4 by nelfinavir	May consider saquinavir 800 mg TID with nelfinavir 750 mg TID or saquinavir 1200 mg BID with nelfinavir 1250 mg BID	
Saquinavir (Invirase, Fortovase)	1200 mg (soft gel caps) TID x 4 days	750 mg x 1 dose	Not studied	Nelfinavir AUC: increased 18%; Cmax: no change	-	Inhibition of CYP450 3A4 by nelfinavir	No dose adjustment necessary	-
Saquinavir (Invirase, Fortovase)	1200 mg TID x 4 days (1200 mg single dose)	750 mg (single dose) x 4 days	Saquinavir AUC: increased 392%	Nelfinavir AUC: increased 18%		Inhibition of CYP450 3A4 by both drugs	Decrease saquinavir to 800 mg TID or 1200 mg BID; no change in nelfinavir dose necessary	
Sildenafil (Viagra)			Not studied; may increase sildenafil levels	-	Increased silfenafil effects (eg, hypotension, priapism)	Inhibition of CYP450 3A4 by nelfinavir	Initiate sildenafil at 25 mg QOD-QD; adjust dose as indicated; not recommended to exceed 25 mg in a 48 hour period	
Sildenafil (Viagra)	25 mg x 1	1250 mg Q12H	No significant change	Not studied	-		No dose adjustment necessary	-
Simvastatin (Zocor)	-	-	Simvastatin AUC: increased 506%; Cmax: increased 517%	No significant change	Increased simvastatin effects (eg, myopathy, rhabdomyolysis)	Inhibition of CYP450 3A4 by nelfinavir	Do not coadminister	Atorvastatin Pravastatin

Coadministered Drug	Dose of Drug	Dose of Nelfinavir	Effect on Coadministered Drug Levels	Effect on Nelfinavir Levels	Potential Clinical Effects	Mechanism of Interaction	Management	Suggested Alternative Agent(s)
St. John's Wort (Hypericum perforatum, hypericin, hyperforin)	-	-		May decrease nelfinavir levels	Decreased nelfinavir effects	Induction of CYP450 3A4 by St. John's wort	Do not coadminister	-
Stavudine (Zerit)	-	-					No dose adjustment necessary	-
Stavudine (Zerit)	30 mg to 40 mg BID x 56 days	750 mg TID x 56 days	No significant change	Not studied	-		No dose adjustment necessary	-
Terfenadine (Seldane)	-	-	Not studied; may increase terfenadine levels		Increased terfenadine effects (eg, cardiac arrhythmias)	Inhibition of CYP450 3A4 by nelfinavir	Do not coadminister	Cetirizine Fexofenadine Loratadine
Triazolam (Halcion)	-	-	Not studied; may increase triazolam levels	-	Increased triazolam effects (increased sedation, confusion, respiratory depression)	Inhibition of CYP450 3A4 by nelfinavir	Avoid combination; consider alternative agents	Lorazepam Oxazepam Temazepam Trazodone
Zidovudine (Retrovir)	200 mg x 1 dose	750 mg Q8H x 7-10 days	Zidovudine AUC: decreased 35%; Cmax: decreased 31%	Not studied			No dose adjustment necessary	-

All Interactions with Nevirapine (Viramune)

Coadministered Drug	Dose of Drug	Dose of Nevirapine	Effect on Coadministered Drug Levels	Effect on Nevirapine Levels	Potential Clinical Effects	Mechanism of Interaction	Management	Suggested Alternative Agent(s)
Amprenavir (Agenerase)	-	-	May decrease amprenavir levels	-	Decreased amprenavir effects	Induction of CYP450 3A4 by nevirapine	Dose adjustment not established	-
Cimetidine (Tagamet)	-	-		Cmin: increased 21%	-	Inhibition of CYP450 3A4 by cimetidine	No dose adjustment necessary	-
Clarithromycin (Biaxin)	500 mg BID	200 mg QD x 2 weeks then 200 BID	Clarithromycin AUC: decreased 29%; Cmax: decreased 20%; Cmin: decreased 46%; 14-hydroxy clarithromycin AUC: increased 27%	Nevirapine Cmin: no significant change			No dose adjustment necessary	-
Didanosine (Videx)	-	-	Not studied	No significant change	-		No dose adjustment necessary	-
Didanosine (Videx)	-	-	-		Potential early virologic failure		Use caution when coadministering tenofovir, didanosine and either efavirenz or nevirapine in treatment-naive patients	-
Coadministered Drug	Dose of Drug	Dose of Nevirapine	Effect on Coadministered Drug Levels	Effect on Nevirapine Levels	Potential Clinical Effects	Mechanism of Interaction	Management	Suggested Alternative Agent(s)
Efavirenz (Sustiva)	600 mg QD	200 mg QD x 2 weeks, then 400 mg QD	Efavirenz AUC: decreased 22%; Cmin: decreased 36%	No significant change	Decreased efavirenz effects	Induction of CYP450 3A4 by nevirapine	Monitor and adjust therapy as indicated; may consider increasing efavirenz to 800 mg QD	-

Coadministered Drug	Dose of Drug	Dose of Nevirapine	Effect on Coadministered Drug Levels	Effect on Nevirapine Levels	Potential Clinical Effects	Mechanism of Interaction	Management	Suggested Alternative Agent(s)
Ethinyl estradiol/norethindrone acetate (Ortho-Novum, others)	Ethinyl estradiol 0.035 mg/Norethindrone 1 mg QD x 30 days	200 mg BID x 30 days	Ethinyl estradiol: AUC decreased 23%; half-life: decreased 44%; Norethindrone: AUC decreased 18%; half-life: decreased 15%	No significant change	Possible contraceptive failure	Induction of CYP450 3A4 by nevirapine	Avoid coadministration; additional contraceptive measures may be needed	Barrier devices; Condoms
Ethinyl estradiol/norethindrone acetate (Ortho-Novum, others)	Ethinyl estradiol 0.035 mg/Norethindrone 1 mg x 1 dose	200 mg QD x 2 weeks then 200 mg BID	Ethinyl estradiol AUC: decreased 19%; Cmax: no significant change Norethindrone AUC: decreased 18%	No significant change	Possible contraceptive failure	Induction of CYP450 3A4 by nevirapine	Use alternative contraceptive method	
Fluconazole (Diflucan)	200 mg QD x 40 days	200 mg QD x 14 days then 200 mg BID	No significant change	Nevirapine AUC: increased 110%; Cmax: increased 115%; Cmin: increased 135%; half-live: decreased 52% (data compared to historical controls)	Increased nevirapine effects	Possible inhibition of CYP450 3A4 by fluconazole	Dose adjustment not established	
Fosamprenavir (Lexiva)	1400 mg BID	200 mg BID	Fosamprenavir AUC: decreased 33%; Cmax decreased 25%; Cmin: decreased 35%	Nevirapine AUC: increased 29%; Cmax: increased 25%; Cmin: increased 34%	Decreased fosamprenavir effects	Induction of CYP450 3A4 by nevirapine	Do not coadminister	Consider ritonavir-boosted fosamprenavir
Fosamprenavir (Lexiva)	700 mg fosamprenavir BID with 100 mg ritonavir BID	200 mg BID	No significant change	Nevirapine Cmin: increased 22%	-	Induction of CYP450 3A4 by nevirapine; inhibition of CYP450 3A4 by ritonavir	No dose adjustment necessary	-
Coadministered Drug	Dose of Drug	Dose of Nevirapine	Effect on Coadministered Drug Levels	Effect on Nevirapine Levels	Potential Clinical Effects	Mechanism of Interaction	Management	Suggested Alternative Agent(s)
Indinavir (Crixivan)	800 mg Q8H	200 mg BID	Indinavir AUC: decreased 28%; Cmax: decreased 11%	No significant change	Decreased indinavir effects	Induction of CYP450 3A4 by nevirapine	Increase indinavir to 1000 mg Q8H	-
Indinavir (Crixivan)	800 mg Q8H	200 mg QD x 2 weeks, 200 mg BID x 28 days	Indinavir AUC: decreased 28%; Cmax: no significant change	Not studied	Decreased indinavir effects	Induction of CYP450 3A4 by nevirapine	Increase indinavir to 1000 mg Q8H	
Ketoconazole (Nizoral)	400 mg QD x 2 weeks	200 mg QD x 2 weeks then 200 mg BID x 2 weeks	Ketoconazole AUC: decreased 63%; Cmax: decreased 40%	Levels: increased 15-30%	Decreased ketoconazole effects	Induction of CYP450 3A4 by nevirapine	Do not coadminister	-
Lopinavir/ritonavir (Kaletra)	300 mg/75 mg/square meter BID x 3 weeks	7 mg/kg or 4 mg/kg QD x 2 weeks; BID x 1 week	Lopinavir AUC: decreased 22%; Cmax: no significant change; Cmin: decreased 55%	-	Decreased lopinavir/ritonavir effects	Induction of CYP450 3A4 by nevirapine	Increase dose of lopinavir/ritonavir to 6.5 mL BID with food	
Lopinavir/ritonavir (Kaletra)	400 mg/100 mg BID x 20 days	200 mg QD x 14 days, 200 mg BID x 6 days	Lopinavir: no significant change	Nevirapine AUC: no significant change; Cmax: no significant change; Cmin: increased 15%	Though study does not suggest need to increase lopinavir/ritonavir dose, other evidence indicated decreased lopinavir/ritonavir effects	Induction of CYP450 3A4 by nevirapine	Increase dose of lopinavir/ritonavir to 533 mg/133 mg (4 capsules) BID with food	
Medroxyprogesterone acetate (Depo-Provera)	150 mg	-	Progesterone levels: no significant change	Nevirapine AUC: no significant change	-		No dose adjustment necessary	-

Coadministered Drug	Dose of Drug	Dose of Nevirapine	Effect on Coadministered Drug Levels	Effect on Nevirapine Levels	Potential Clinical Effects	Mechanism of Interaction	Management	Suggested Alternative Agent(s)
Methadone (Dolophine)	stable dose: racemic methadone 35-220 mg daily; (R)-methadone 45-115 mg daily	200 mg QD x 14 days, then 200 mg BID thereafter	racemic methadone AUC: decreased 37%; (R)-methadone AUC: decreased 44%	-	Decreased methadone effects (eg, withdrawal)	Possible induction of CYP450 2B6 by nevirapine	Monitor for signs and symptoms of methadone withdrawal; some patients may need an increase in the methadone dose	-
Methadone (Dolophine)	Stable methadone dose	200 mg QD x 14 days	Methadone AUC: decreased 51%; Cmax: decreased 36%	Not studied	Decreased methadone effects (eg, methadone withdrawal)	Induction of CYP450 3A4 by nevirapine	Monitor for signs and symptoms of methadone withdrawal; some patients may need an increase in the methadone dose	-
Methadone (Dolophine)	Stable methadone maintenance	200-400 mg QD	Methadone AUC: decreased 46%	Not studied	Decreased methadone effects (eg, methadone withdrawal; interaction observed one week into therapy	Induction of CYP450 3A4 by nevirapine	Monitor for signs and symptoms of methadone withdrawal; some patients may need an increase in the methadone dose	-
Mycophenolate (CellCept)	500 mg BID x 8 weeks	200 mg BID	Not studied	Clearance: increased 27%	-	-	Dose adjustment not established	-
Nelfinavir (Viracept)	750 mg TID x 36 days	200 mg QD x 14 days, 200 mg BID x 14 days	No significant change	Not studied		-	No dose adjustment necessary	-
Coadministered Drug	**Dose of Drug**	**Dose of Nevirapine**	**Effect on Coadministered Drug Levels**	**Effect on Nevirapine Levels**	**Potential Clinical Effects**	**Mechanism of Interaction**	**Management**	**Suggested Alternative Agent(s)**
Paclitaxel (Taxol)	100 mg/square meter infusion over 3 hours	200 mg BID	Not studied	No significant change	-		No dose adjustment necessary	-
Rifampin (Rifadin)	600 mg QD	200 mg BID	No significant change	Nevirapine AUC: decreased 31%; Cmax: decreased 36%; Cmin: decreased 21%	Decreased nevirapine effects	Induction of CYP450 by rifampin	Avoid if possible	Rifabutin
Ritonavir (Norvir)	600 mg BID	200 mg BID	No significant change	No significant change	-		No dose adjustment necessary	-
Saquinavir (Invirase, Fortovase)	600 mg (hard gel caps) TID	200 mg QD x 2 weeks then 200 mg BID x 28 days	Saquinavir AUC: decreased 24%; Cmax: decreased 28%	No significant change	Decreased saquinavir effects	Induction of CYP450 3A4 by nevirapine	Dose adjustment not established	-
Coadministered Drug	**Dose of Drug**	**Dose of Nevirapine**	**Effect on Coadministered Drug Levels**	**Effect on Nevirapine Levels**	**Potential Clinical Effects**	**Mechanism of Interaction**	**Management**	**Suggested Alternative Agent(s)**
Saquinavir (Invirase, Fortovase)	600 mg (hard gel caps) TID x 7 days	200 mg BID x 21 days	Saquinavir AUC: decreased 24%; Cmax: decreased 28%	No significant change	May decrease saquinavir effects	Induction of CYP450 by nevirapine	Dose adjustment not established	-

Coadministered Drug	Dose of Drug	Dose of Nevirapine	Effect on Coadministered Drug Levels	Effect on Nevirapine Levels	Potential Clinical Effects	Mechanism of Interaction	Management	Suggested Alternative Agent(s)
St. John's Wort (Hypericum perforatum, hypericin, hyperforin)	-	200 mg BID	-	Clearance: increased 35%	Decreased nevirapine effects	Induction of CYP450 3A4 by St. John's Wort	Do not coadminister	-
Tenofovir (Viread)			-	-	Potential early virologic failure	-	Use caution when coadministering tenofovir, didanosine and either efavirenz or nevirapine in treatment naïve patients	-
Tipranavir (Aptivus)	1250 mg BID with 100 mg ritonavir BID x 42 doses	200 mg BID x 43 doses	-	Nevirapine AUC: decreased 24%; Cmax: decreased 29%; Cmin: decreased 23%	Possible decreased nevirapine effects	Possible induction of CYP450 3A4 by tipranavir/ritonavir	Dose adjustment not established	-
Tipranavir (Aptivus)	250 mg BID with 200 mg ritonavir BID	200 mg BID x 43 doses	-	No significant change	-	-	No dose adjustment necessary	-
Tipranavir (Aptivus)	750 mg BID with 100 mg ritonavir BID	200 mg BID x 43 doses	-	No significant change	-	-	No dose adjustment necessary	-
Warfarin (Coumadin)			-		Possibly decreased warfarin effects (eg, altered INR, increased risk of clotting)		Monitor INR and adjust warfarin as indicated	-
Zalcitabine (Hivid)	-	-	Not studied	No significant change	-	-	No dose adjustment necessary	-
Zidovudine (Retrovir)	-	-	-	No significant change	-	-	No dose adjustment necessary	-

All Interactions with Ritonavir (Norvir)

Coadministered Drug	Dose of Drug	Dose of Ritonavir	Effect on Coadministered Drug Levels	Effect on Ritonavir Levels	Potential Clinical Effects	Mechanism of Interaction	Management	Suggested Alternative Agent(s)
Alprazolam (Xanax)	1 mg x 1 dose	200 mg QID	Alprazolam clearance: decreased 59%; half-life: increased 200%		Increased alprazolam effects (eg, increased sedation, confusion, respiratory depression)	Inhibition of CYP450 3A4 by ritonavir	Avoid combination; consider alternative agents	Lorazepam
Amitriptyline (Elavil)	-	-	Increased amitriptyline levels		Increased amitriptyline effects (eg, dry mouth, hypotension, confusion)	Inhibition of CYP450 3A4 and 2D6 by ritonavir	Monitor and adjust amitriptyline as indicated	-
Amprenavir (Agenerase)	-	-	Increased amprenavir levels	Not studied	Increased amprenavir effects	Inhibition of CYP450 3A4 by ritonavir	Dose adjustment not established	-
Coadministered Drug	Dose of Drug	Dose of Ritonavir	Effect on Coadministered Drug Levels	Effect on Ritonavir Levels	Potential Clinical Effects	Mechanism of Interaction	Management	Suggested Alternative Agent(s)
Amprenavir (Agenerase)	1200 mg BID	200 mg BID	Amprenavir AUC: increased 127%; Cmin: increased 395%;	Not studied	Increased amprenavir effects	Inhibition of CYP450 3A4 by ritonavir	No dose adjustment necessary	-
Amprenavir (Agenerase)	1200 mg BID	500 mg BID	Amprenavir AUC: increased 143%; Cmin: increased 576%	Not studied	Increased amprenavir effects	Inhibition of CYP450 3A4 by ritonavir	Dose adjustment not established	-

Coadministered Drug	Dose of Drug	Dose of Ritonavir	Effect on Coadministered Drug Levels	Effect on Ritonavir Levels	Potential Clinical Effects	Mechanism of Interaction	Management	Suggested Alternative Agent(s)
Amprenavir (Agenerase)	1200 mg BID with efavirenz 600 mg QD	200 mg BID	No significant change	Not studied	-	Inhibition of CYP450 3A4 by ritonavir and induction of CYP450 3A4 by efavirenz	No dose adjustment necessary	-
Amprenavir (Agenerase)	1200 mg QD	200 mg BID x 2-4 weeks	Amprenavir AUC: increased 62%; Cmin: increased 319%	Not studied	Increased amprenavir effects	Inhibition of CYP450 3A4 by ritonavir	Dose adjustment not established	-
Amprenavir (Agenerase)	1200 mg QD on days 1-7	100 mg on days 8-14, 200 mg QD on days 15-21	Amprenavir AUC: increased 119%, Cmax: no significant change; Cmin: increased 840% (with 100 mg ritonavir); no significant change with 200 mg ritonavir	Not studied	Increased amprenavir effects	Inhibition of CYP450 3A4 by ritonavir	Dose adjustment not established	-
Amprenavir (Agenerase)	600 mg BID	100 mg BID x 2-4 weeks	Amprenavir AUC: increased 64%; Cmax: decreased 30%; Cmin: increased 508%	Not studied	Increased amprenavir effects	Inhibition of CYP450 3A4 by ritonavir	-	-
Coadministered Drug	**Dose of Drug**	**Dose of Ritonavir**	**Effect on Coadministered Drug Levels**	**Effect on Ritonavir Levels**	**Potential Clinical Effects**	**Mechanism of Interaction**	**Management**	**Suggested Alternative Agent(s)**
Amprenavir (Agenerase)	900 mg Q12H	100 mg Q12H	Amprenavir AUC: increased 109%; Cmax: no significant change; Cmin: increased 585%	Ritonavir AUC: decreased 64%; Cmax decreased 32%; Cmin: decreased 65%	Increased amprenavir effects	Inhibition of CYP450 3A4 by ritonavir and induction of CYP450 3A4 by amprenavir	Dose adjustment not established	-
Atazanavir (Reyataz)	300 mg QD on days 1-20	100 mg QD on days 11-20	Atazanavir AUC: increased 238%; Cmax: increased 86%; Cmin: increased 1089%	Not studied	Increased atazanavir effects	Inhibition of CYP450 3A4 by ritonavir	Dose adjustment not established	-
Carbamazepine (Tegretol)	350 mg BID	200 mg QD-TID	Not studied; May increase carbamazepine levels	Decreased ritonavir levels	Increased carbamazepine effects; decreased ritonavir effects	Induction of CYP450 2C and 3A4	Avoid combination if possible; consider alternative agents; monitor carbamazepine levels and adjust as indicated	Gabapentin Lamotrigine Tiagabine Topiramate
Coadministered Drug	**Dose of Drug**	**Dose of Ritonavir**	**Effect on Coadministered Drug Levels**	**Effect on Ritonavir Levels**	**Potential Clinical Effects**	**Mechanism of Interaction**	**Management**	**Suggested Alternative Agent(s)**
Clarithromycin (Biaxin)	500 mg BID	200 mg TID	Clarithromycin AUC: increased 77%; Cmax: increased 31%; Cmin: increased 182%	AUC: no significant change; Cmax: increased 15%	Increased clarithromycin effects	Inhibition of CYP450 3A4 by ritonavir	No dose adjustment necessary	-
Cotrimoxazole (TMP/SMX) (Trimethoprim/Sulfamethoxazole, Septra, Bactrim)	160 mg/800 mg x 1 dose	500 mg Q12H x 12 days	Sulfamethoxazole AUC: decreased 20%; trimethoprim AUC: increased 20%	-	-	Induction of CYP450 3A4 by ritonavir	No dose adjustment necessary	-
Delavirdine (Rescriptor)	400 or 600 mg BID	300 mg BID	No significant change	No significant change	-	-	No dose adjustment necessary	-
Delavirdine (Rescriptor)	600 mg BID x 10 days	100 mg BID x 10 days	No significant change	Ritonavir AUC: increased 81%; Cmax: increased 50%; Cmin: increased 113%	Increased ritonavir effects	Inhibition of CYP450 3A4 by delavirdine	No dose adjustment necessary	-

Coadministered Drug	Dose of Drug	Dose of Ritonavir	Effect on Coadministered Drug Levels	Effect on Ritonavir Levels	Potential Clinical Effects	Mechanism of Interaction	Management	Suggested Alternative Agent(s)
Desipramine (Norpramin)	-	-	Desipramine clearance: decreased 59%	-	Increased desipramine effects (eg, dry mouth, dizziness, urinary retention)	Inhibition of CYP450 2D6 by ritonavir	Monitor and adjust desipramine as indicated	-
Diazepam (Valium)	-	-	Increased diazepam levels	-	Increased diazepam effects (eg, increased sedation, confusion, respiratory depression)	Inhibition of CYP450 3A by ritonavir	Do not coadminister	Lorazepam Oxazepam Temazepam
Didanosine (Videx)	200 mg (buffered formulation) Q12H x 4 days	600 mg Q12H x 4 days	Didanosine AUC: no significant change; Cmax: decreased 16%	No significant change	-	-	No dose adjustment necessary	-
Didanosine (Videx)	200 mg (tablets) BID	600 mg BID	Didanosine AUC: decreased 15%; Cmax: decreased 15%	Not studied	Decreased didanosine effects	Formulation incompatibility	Separate didanosine and ritonavir administration by at least 2.5 hours	
Digoxin (Lanoxin, others)	0.4 mg x 1 dose	200 mg BID x 15 days	Digoxin AUC (0-8 hr): increased 29%; AUC (0-72 hr): increased 22%; clearance: decreased 30%; half-life: increased 43%	Not studied	Increased digoxin effects	Possible inhibition of P-gp by ritonavir	Monitor digoxin concentrations closely	
Disulfiram (Antabuse)	-	-	Oral solution (contains alcohol) and capsules		Disulfiram reaction (eg, headache, hypotension, flushing, vomiting)	Inhibition of aldehyde dehydrogenase by disulfiram	Do not coadminister	
Efavirenz (Sustiva)	600 mg QD	Day 1: 300 mg Q12H; Day 2: 400mg Q12H; Days 3-10: 500 mg Q12H	Efavirenz AUC: increased 21%	Ritonavir AUC: increased 18%	Possible increased effects of both drugs	Inhibition of CYP450 3A4 by both drugs	May dose ritonavir at 500 mg BID when given with efavirenz; no dose adjustment required for efavirenz	

Coadministered Drug	Dose of Drug	Dose of Ritonavir	Effect on Coadministered Drug Levels	Effect on Ritonavir Levels	Potential Clinical Effects	Mechanism of Interaction	Management	Suggested Alternative Agent(s)
Efavirenz (Sustiva)	600 mg x 10 days	500 mg Q12H x 8 days	Efavirenz AUC: increased 21%; Cmax: no significant change	Ritonavir AUC: increased 18% after AM dose; Cmax: increased 24% after AM dose; AUC: no significant change after PM dose; Cmax: no significant change after PM dose	Increased efavirenz and ritonavir effects	Inhibition of CYP450 3A4 by both drugs	No dose adjustment necessary	
Enfuvirtide (Fuzeon)	90 mg SQ BID on days 1-7	200 mg BID on days 4-7	Enfuvirtide Cmax: increased 24%, Cmin: no significant change; AUC: increased 22%	No significant change			No dose adjustment necessary	
Ergotamine (Cafergot, ergot derivatives)	-		Not studied; may increase ergotamine levels		Increased ergotamine effects (eg, ergotism)	Inhibition of CYP450 3A4 by ritonavir	Do not coadminister	5-HT agonists ("triptans")

Coadministered Drug	Dose of Drug	Dose of Ritonavir	Effect on Coadministered Drug Levels	Effect on Ritonavir Levels	Potential Clinical Effects	Mechanism of Interaction	Management	Suggested Alternative Agent(s)
Escitalopram (Lexapro)	20 mg x 1 dose	600 mg x 1 dose	No significant change	No significant change	-	-	No dose adjustment necessary	-
Ethinyl estradiol/norethindrone acetate (Ortho-Novum, others)	50 mcg x 2 doses	500 mg Q12H	Ethinyl estradiol Cmax: decreased 32%, AUC: decreased 41%	-	Decreased oral contraceptive effectiveness	Induction CYP450 3A4 by ritonavir	Use alternative contraceptive method	Barrier devices; Condoms
Fentanyl (Duragesic, Various)	5 mcg/kg	Day 1: 200 mg TID; Day 2: 300 mg TID; Day 3: 300 mg QAM	Fentanyl clearance: decreased 67%	-	Increased fentanyl effects (eg, increased sedation, confusion, respiratory depression)	Inhibition of CYP450 3A4 by ritonavir	Monitor closely when using together; start with low dose and titrate to pain response as indicated	-
Coadministered Drug	**Dose of Drug**	**Dose of Ritonavir**	**Effect on Coadministered Drug Levels**	**Effect on Ritonavir Levels**	**Potential Clinical Effects**	**Mechanism of Interaction**	**Management**	**Suggested Alternative Agent(s)**
Fluconazole (Diflucan)	400 mg x 1 day, then 200 mg days 2-5	200 mg Q6H x 4 days		Cmax: increased 14.5%; AUC: increased 12%; Cmin: increased 14%	-	Inhibition of CYP450 3A4 by fluconazole	No dose adjustment necessary	-
Fluoxetine (Prozac, Sarafem, others)	30 mg Q12H	600 mg x 1 dose days 1 and 10	-	AUC: increased 19%; Cmax: no significant change	Increased ritonavir effects; possibly increased fluoxetine effects	Inhibition of CYP450 2D6 by both drugs	No dose adjustment necessary	-
Fluticasone (Flonase, Aerobid)	-	-	Fluticasone AUC: increased 350-fold; Cmax: increased 25-fold		Decreased plasma cortisol concentrations (eg, Cushing's syndrome, adrenal suppression)	-	Avoid if possible	-
Fosamprenavir (Lexiva)	1400 mg QD with efavirenz 600 mg QD	300 mg QD	Amprenavir AUC: no significant change; Cmax: increased 18%; Cmin: no significant change	Not studied	-	Inhibition of CYP450 3A4 by ritonavir	No dose adjustment necessary	-
Indinavir (Crixivan)	400 mg BID x 14 days	400 mg BID x 14 days	Indinavir AUC: increased 62%; Cmax: no significant change; Cmin: increased 929% (compared to indinavir 800 mg Q8H)	Not studied	Increased indinavir effects	Inhibition of CYP450 3A4 by ritonavir	No dose adjustment necessary	-
Coadministered Drug	**Dose of Drug**	**Dose of Ritonavir**	**Effect on Coadministered Drug Levels**	**Effect on Ritonavir Levels**	**Potential Clinical Effects**	**Mechanism of Interaction**	**Management**	**Suggested Alternative Agent(s)**
Indinavir (Crixivan)	400 mg Q12H x 15 days	400 mg Q12H x 15 days	Indinavir Cmin: increased 400%	Not studied		Inhibition of CYP450 3A4 by ritonavir	May consider indinavir/ritonavir combination as follows (BID dosing): 800/100; 800/200; 400/400	-
Indinavir (Crixivan)	800 mg BID x 14 days	100 mg BID x 14 days	Indinavir AUC: increased ~70%; Cmax: increased 60%; Cmin: increased ~000% (compared to indinavir 800 mg Q8H)	Not studied	Increased indinavir effects	Inhibition of CYP450 3A4 by ritonavir	No dose adjustment necessary	-
Indinavir (Crixivan)	800 mg BID x 14 days	200 mg BID x 14 days	Indinavir AUC: increased 254%; Cmax: increased 77%; Cmin: increased 2356% (compared to indinavir 800 mg Q8H)	Not studied	Increased indinavir effects	Inhibition of CYP450 3A4 by ritonavir	No dose adjustment necessary	-

Coadministered Drug	Dose of Drug	Dose of Ritonavir	Effect on Coadministered Drug Levels	Effect on Ritonavir Levels	Potential Clinical Effects	Mechanism of Interaction	Management	Suggested Alternative Agent(s)
Indinavir (Crixivan)	800 mg BID x 14 days	400 mg BID x 14 days	Indinavir AUC: increased 209%; Cmax: increased 49%; Cmin: increased 2344% (compared to indinavir 800 mg Q8H)	Not studied	Increased indinavir effects	Inhibition of CYP450 3A4 by ritonavir	No dose adjustment necessary	-
Itraconazole (Sporanox)	-	-	-	Increased ritonavir levels	Increased ritonavir effects	Inhibition of CYP450 3A4 by itraconazole	Dose adjustment not established	-
Ketoconazole (Nizoral)	-	-	-	Increased ritonavir levels	Increased ritonavir effects	Inhibition of CYP450 3A4 by ketoconazole	Dose adjustment not established	-
Coadministered Drug	Dose of Drug	Dose of Ritonavir	Effect on Coadministered Drug Levels	Effect on Ritonavir Levels	Potential Clinical Effects	Mechanism of Interaction	Management	Suggested Alternative Agent(s)
Levothyroxine (Synthroid, Levoxyl)	0.125 mg	600 mg BID	-		Increased TSH levels (eg, Signs and symptoms of hypothyroidism)	Induction of glucuronosyl transferases by ritonavir	Monitor and adjust levothyroxine as indicated	-
Lopinavir/ritonavir (Kaletra)	400 mg/100 mg BID x 3-4 weeks	100 mg BID x 3-4 weeks	Lopinavir AUC: increased 46%; Cmax increased 28%; Cmin: increased 116%		Increased lopinavir/ritonavir effects	Inhibition of CYP450 3A4 by ritonavir	Dose adjustment not established	-
Mefloquine (Larium)	250 mg QD x 3 days, then once weekly for 3 weeks	200 mg BID x 7 days	No significant change	AUC: decreased 31%; Cmax: increased 36%; Cmin: decreased 43%	-	Unknown	Dose adjustment not established	-
Meperidine (Demerol)	50 mg PO x 1 dose	500 mg BID x 10 days	Meperidine AUC: decreased 67%; normeperidine AUC: increased 47%		Increased normeperidine effects	Induction of CYP450 1A2 by ritonavir; inhibition of p-glycoprotein reducing first-pass metabolism of meperidine	Avoid combination	Morphine
Methadone (Dolophine)		400 mg BID combined with 400 mg BID saquinavir	S-methadone AUC: decreased 25%; R-methadone AUC: decreased 20%		Not clinically significant	Induction of CYP450 by ritonavir and saquinavir	Monitor and adjust methadone as indicated	-
Methadone (Dolophine)	90 mg QD x 2 years	400 mg BID x 7 days	Methadone AUC: decreased		Decreased methadone effects (eg, methadone withdrawal)	Possible induction of CYP450 2C9, 3A4 and 2D6 by ritonavir	Monitor and adjust methadone as Indicated	-
Coadministered Drug	Dose of Drug	Dose of Ritonavir	Effect on Coadministered Drug Levels	Effect on Ritonavir Levels	Potential Clinical Effects	Mechanism of Interaction	Management	Suggested Alternative Agent(s)
Methadone (Dolophine)	Stable methadone dose	100 mg BID x 7 days	No significant effect				Monitor and adjust methadone as indicated	-
Metronidazole (Flagyl)	Oral solution (contains alcohol) and capsules	-			Disulfiram-like reaction (eg, headache, hypotension, flushing, vomiting)	Inhibition of alcohol and aldehyde dehydrogenase by metronidazole	Do not coadminister	-

Coadministered Drug	Dose of Drug	Dose of Ritonavir	Effect on Coadministered Drug Levels	Effect on Ritonavir Levels	Potential Clinical Effects	Mechanism of Interaction	Management	Suggested Alternative Agent(s)
Rifabutin (Mycobutin)	150 mg QD x 24 days	300 mg on day 15; 400 mg on day 16; 500 mg on days 17-24	Rifabutin AUC: increased 400%; Cmax: increased 250%	-	Increased rifabutin effects (eg, uveitis)	Inhibition of CYP450 3A4 by ritonavir	Decrease rifabutin to 150 mg QOD or 300 mg 3 times/week	-
Rifampin (Rifadin)	300 or 600 mg x 10 days	500 mg Q12H x 20 days	-	Ritonavir AUC: decreased 35%; Cmax: decreased 25%	Decreased ritonavir effects	Induction of CYP450 3A4 by rifampin	Do not coadminister	Rifabutin
Saquinavir (Invirase, Fortovase)	1600 mg QD x 13 days	100 mg QD	Saquinavir AUC: increased 592%; Cmax: increased 566%; Cmin: increased 424% (compared to saquinavir 1200 mg TID)	-	Increased saquinavir effects	Inhibition of CYP450 3A4 by ritonavir	-	-
Saquinavir (Invirase, Fortovase)	400 mg (hard gel caps) BID at steady state	400 mg BID at steady state	Saquinavir AUC: increased 1587%; Cmax: increased 1277%	Not studied	Increased saquinavir effects	Inhibition of CYP450 3A4 by ritonavir	Consider ritonavir-boosted saquinavir	-
Coadministered Drug	Dose of Drug	Dose of Ritonavir	Effect on Coadministered Drug Levels	Effect on Ritonavir Levels	Potential Clinical Effects	Mechanism of Interaction	Management	Suggested Alternative Agent(s)
Saquinavir (Invirase, Fortovase)	400 mg (soft gel caps) BID x 14 days	400 mg BID x 14 days	Saquinavir AUC: increased by 121%; Cmax: increased by 64%	Not studied	Increased saquinavir effects	Inhibition of CYP450 3A4 by ritonavir	Consider ritonavir-boosted saquinavir	-
Saquinavir (Invirase, Fortovase)	Multiple saquinavir hard gel caps doses studied: 200 mg, 400 mg, 600 mg	Multiple doses studied; 200 mg, 300 mg, 600 mg	Saquinavir AUC: increased 5000%; Cmax: increased 2100%	Ritonavir AUC: no significant change	Increased saquinavir effects	Inhibition of CYP450 3A4 by ritonavir	Consider ritonavir-boosted saquinavir	-
Saquinavir (Invirase, Fortovase)	Saquinavir soft gel caps 1000 mg/ritonavir 100 mg BID or saquinavir hard gel caps 1000 mg/ritonavir 100 mg BID, administered with food for at least 3 weeks	100 mg BID	Saquinavir soft gel caps AUC: increased 30% (compared to hard gel caps/ritonavir AUC); Cmin: increased 17% (when compared to hard gel caps/ritonavir regimen Cmin)	Not studied	Increased saquinavir effects (AUC achieved with hard gel caps/ritonavir regimen is comparable, but not equivalent to, soft gel caps/ritonavir AUC)	Inhibition of CYP450 3A4 by ritonavir	Consider ritonavir-boosted saquinavir	-
Sildenafil (Viagra)	100 mg x 1 dose	300 mg, 400 mg and 500 mg BID on days 2, 3 and 4-8	Sildenafil AUC: increased 1000%; Cmax: increased 290%; Tmax: delayed 3 hours		Increased sildenafil effects (eg, hypotension, priapism)	Inhibition of CYP450 3A4 by ritonavir	Initiate therapy at 25 mg dose; do not exceed 25 mg in 48 hour period	-
St. John's Wort (Hypericum perforatum, hypericin, hyperforin)	-	-	-	Not studied; may decrease ritonavir levels	Decreased ritonavir effects	Induction of CYP450 3A4 by St John's Wort	Do not coadminister	-
Tacrolimus (Prograf)	4 mg BID	-	-	-	Increased tacrolimus effects (eg, bone marrow suppression)	Inhibition of CYP450 3A4 by ritonavir	Monitor and adjust tacrolimus as indicated	-

Coadministered Drug	Dose of Drug	Dose of Ritonavir	Effect on Coadministered Drug Levels	Effect on Ritonavir Levels	Potential Clinical Effects	Mechanism of Interaction	Management	Suggested Alternative Agent(s)
Rifabutin (Mycobutin)	150 mg QD x 24 days	300 mg on day 15; 400 mg on day 16; 500 mg on days 17-24	Rifabutin AUC: increased 400%; Cmax: increased 250%	-	Increased rifabutin effects (eg, uveitis)	Inhibition of CYP450 3A4 by ritonavir	Decrease rifabutin to 150 mg QOD or 300 mg 3 times/week	-
Rifampin (Rifacin)	300 or 600 mg x 10 days	500 mg Q12H x 20 days		Ritonavir AUC: decreased 35%; Cmax: decreased 25%	Decreased ritonavir effects	Induction of CYP450 3A4 by rifampin	Do not coadminister	Rifabutin
Saquinavir (Invirase, Fortovase)	1600 mg QD x 13 days	100 mg QD	Saquinavir AUC: increased 592%; Cmax: increased 566%; Cmin: increased 424% (compared to saquinavir 1200 mg TID)		Increased saquinavir effects	Inhibition of CYP450 3A4 by ritonavir	-	-
Saquinavir (Invirase, Fortovase)	400 mg (hard gel caps) BID at steady state	400 mg BID at steady state	Saquinavir AUC: increased 1587%; Cmax: increased 1277%	Not studied	Increased saquinavir effects	Inhibition of CYP450 3A4 by ritonavir	Consider ritonavir-boosted saquinavir	-

Coadministered Drug	Dose of Drug	Dose of Ritonavir	Effect on Coadministered Drug Levels	Effect on Ritonavir Levels	Potential Clinical Effects	Mechanism of Interaction	Management	Suggested Alternative Agent(s)
Saquinavir (Invirase, Fortovase)	400 mg (soft gel caps) BID x 14 days	400 mg BID x 14 days	Saquinavir AUC: increased by 121%; Cmax: increased by 64%	Not studied	Increased saquinavir effects	Inhibition of CYP450 3A4 by ritonavir	Consider ritonavir-boosted saquinavir	-
Saquinavir (Invirase, Fortovase)	Multiple saquinavir hard gel caps doses studied; 200 mg, 400 mg, 600 mg	Multiple doses studied: 200 mg, 300 mg, 600 mg	Saquinavir AUC: increased 5000%; Cmax: increased 2100%	Ritonavir AUC: no significant change	Increased saquinavir effects	Inhibition of CYP450 3A4 by ritonavir	Consider ritonavir-boosted saquinavir	-
Saquinavir (Invirase, Fortovase)	Saquinavir soft gel caps 1000 mg/ritonavir 100 mg BID or saquinavir hard gel caps 1000 mg/ritonavir 100 mg BID, administered with food for at least 3 weeks	100 mg BID	Saquinavir soft gel caps AUC: increased 30% (compared to hard gel caps/ritonavir AUC); Cmin: increased 17% (when compared to hard gel caps/ritonavir regimen Cmin)	Not studied	Increased saquinavir effects (AUC achieved with hard gel caps/ritonavir regimen is comparable, but not equivalent to, soft gel caps/ritonavir AUC)	Inhibition of CYP450 3A4 by ritonavir	Consider ritonavir-boosted saquinavir	-
Sildenafil (Viagra)	100 mg x 1 dose	300 mg, 400 mg and 500 mg BID on days 2, 3 and 4-8	Sildenafil AUC: increased 1000%; Cmax: increased 290%; Tmax: delayed 3 hours	-	Increased sildenafil effects (eg, hypotension, priapism)	Inhibition of CYP450 3A4 by ritonavir	Initiate therapy at 25 mg dose; do not exceed 25 mg in 48 hour period	-
St. John's Wort (Hypericum perforatum, hypericin, hyperforin)	-	-		Not studied; may decrease ritonavir levels	Decreased ritonavir effects	Induction of CYP450 3A4 by St. John's Wort	Do not coadminister	-
Tacrolimus (Prograf)	4 mg BID	-		-	Increased tacrolimus effects (eg, bone marrow suppression)	Inhibition of CYP450 3A4 by ritonavir	Monitor and adjust tacrolimus as indicated	-

Coadministered Drug	Dose of Drug	Dose of Ritonavir	Effect on Coadministered Drug Levels	Effect on Ritonavir Levels	Potential Clinical Effects	Mechanism of Interaction	Management	Suggested Alternative Agent(s)
Tadalafil (Cialis)	20 mg x 1	200 mg BID	-	Ritonavir AUC: increased 124%; Cmax: no significant change	Increased tadalafil effects	Inhibition of CYP450 3A4 by ritonavir	Do not exceed 10 mg tadalafil every 72 hours	-
Theophylline (Theo-Dur, Slo-Phyllin, Theo-24, Aminophyllin)	3 mg/kg Q8H	Days 1-5 none; day 6 300 mg Q12H; day 7 400 mg Q12H; days 8-15 500 mg Q12H	Theophylline AUC: decreased 43%; Cmax: decreased 32%; Cmin: decreased 57%; half-life: decreased 57%		Decreased theophylline effects	Possible induction of CYP450 1A2 by ritonavir	Monitor and adjust theophylline as indicated	-
Trazodone (Desyrel)	-	-	Trazodone AUC: increased 2.4-fold; Cmax: increased 34%	-	Increased trazodone effects (eg, nausea, dizziness, hypotension, syncope)	Possible inhibition of trazodone metabolism	Use with caution; if benefits outweigh risk, initiate trazodone at lower dose	-
Trazodone (Desyrel)	50 mg x 1 dose	200 mg BID for 2 days	Trazodone AUC: increased 240%; Cmax: increased 34%; half-life: increased 220%	Not studied	Increased trazodone effects (eg, nausea, hypotension, syncope)	Inhibition of CYP450 3A4 by ritonavir	Decrease trazodone dose or start low and titrate to effect	-
Coadministered Drug	Dose of Drug	Dose of Ritonavir	Effect on Coadministered Drug Levels	Effect on Ritonavir Levels	Potential Clinical Effects	Mechanism of Interaction	Management	Suggested Alternative Agent(s)
Triazolam (Halcion)	0.125 mg x 1 dose	200 mg BID x 2 days	Triazolam AUC: increased 20%; half-life: increased 1200%		Increased triazolam effects (eg, increased confusion, sedation, respiratory depression)	Inhibition of CYP450 3A4 by ritonavir	Avoid combination; consider alternative agents	Lorazepam Oxazepam Temazepam Trazodone
Voriconazole (VFend)	400 mg Q12H on day 1, then 200 mg Q12H on days 2-9	400 mg Q12H x 9 days	Voriconazole AUC: decreased 82%; Cmax: decreased 66%	No significant change	Decreased voriconazole effects	Induction of CYP450 3A4 by ritonavir	Do not coadminister	-
Warfarin (Coumadin)	12.5 mg QD	400 mg BID	INR: decreased		Decreased warfarin effects (eg, decreased INR, increased risk of clotting)	Possible inhibition of CYP450 3A4, 2C9 and 1A2 by ritonavir	Monitor INR and adjust warfarin as indicated	-
Zidovudine (Retrovir)	200 mg Q8H	300 mg Q6H	Zidovudine Cmax: decreased 27%; AUC: decreased 26%	No significant change	Decreased zidovudine effects	Unknown	No dose adjustment necessary	-
Zolpidem (Ambien)	5 mg x 1 dose	200 mg BID x 2 days	Zolpidem AUC: increased 27%		Increased zolpidem effects (eg, increased sedation, confusion)	Inhibition of CYP450 3A4 by ritonavir	No dose adjustment necessary	-

All Interactions with Saquinavir (Invirase, Fortovase)

Coadministered Drug	Dose of Drug	Dose of Saquinavir	Effect on Coadministered Drug Levels	Effect on Saquinavir Levels	Potential Clinical Effects	Mechanism of Interaction	Management	Suggested Alternative Agent(s)
Adefovir dipivoxil (Hepsera)	-		No significant change	No significant change	-	-	No dose adjustment necessary	-
Amprenavir (Agenerase)	1200 mg BID with efavirenz 600 mg QD	1600 mg BID (soft gel caps)	Amprenavir clearance: no significant change	Not studied			No dose adjustment necessary	-
Amprenavir (Agenerase)	750 mg or 800 mg TID x 2 weeks (fed)	800 mg TID x 2 weeks (fed)	Amprenavir AUC: decreased 32%; Cmax: decreased 37%; Cmin: no significant change	Saquinavir AUC: decreased 19%; Cmax: increased 21%; Cmin: decreased 48%	Decreased amprenavir effects	Induction of CYP450 3A4 by either drug	No dose adjustment necessary	-
Atazanavir (Reyataz)	300 mg QD x 30 days	1600 mg QD with ritonavir 100 mg QD x 30 days	Not studied	Saquinavir AUC: increased 61%; Cmax: increased 42%; Cmin: increased 112%; Ritonavir AUC: increased 41%; Cmax: increased 58%; Cmin: decreased 27%	Increased saquinavir effects	Inhibition of CYP450 3A4 by atazanavir and ritonavir	Dose adjustment not established	-
Coadministered Drug	Dose of Drug	Dose of Saquinavir	Effect on Coadministered Drug Levels	Effect on Saquinavir Levels	Potential Clinical Effects	Mechanism of Interaction	Management	Suggested Alternative Agent(s)
Atazanavir (Reyataz)	400 mg QD on days 7-13	1200 mg (soft gel caps) QD on days 1-13	Not studied	Saquinavir AUC: increased 449%; Cmax: increased 339%; Cmin: increased 586%	Increased saquinavir effects	Inhibition of CYP450 3A4 by atazanavir	Dose adjustment not established	-
Atazanavir (Reyataz)	400 mg x 7 days	800 mg, 1200 mg, 1600 mg QD	No significant change	Saquinavir AUC: increased 440-610%; Cmin: increased 560-1660%	Increased saquinavir effects	Inhibition of CYP450 3A4 by atazanavir	Dose adjustment not established	-
Atorvastatin (Lipitor)	40 mg QD on days 1-4 and 15-18	400 mg BID with ritonavir 400 mg BID on days 4-18	Atorvastatin AUC: increased 79%; Cmax: increased 330%	Not studied	Increased atorvastatin effects (eg, myopathy, rhabdomyolysis)	Inhibition of CYP450 3A4 by saquinavir and ritonavir	Avoid combination if possible; may consider low dose atorvastatin or alternative agents; monitor for myopathy	Pravastatin
Carbamazepine (Tegretol)			-	May decrease saquinavir levels	Decreased saquinavir effects	Induction of CYP450 3A4 by carbamazepine	Avoid combination if possible; consider alternative agents; monitor carbamazepine levels and adjust as indicated	Gabapentin Lamotrigine Tiagabine Topiramate
Clarithromycin (Biaxin)	500 mg BID x 7 days	1200 mg TID x 7 days	Clarithromycin AUC: increased 45%	Saquinavir soft gel caps AUC: increased 177%; saquinavir hard gel caps AUC: increased 500%		Inhibition of CYP450 3A4 by clarithromycin	Dose adjustment not established	-

Coadministered Drug	Dose of Drug	Dose of Saquinavir	Effect on Coadministered Drug Levels	Effect on Saquinavir Levels	Potential Clinical Effects	Mechanism of Interaction	Management	Suggested Alternative Agent(s)
Cyclosporine (Sandimmune, Neoral)	150 mg BID	1200 mg TID	Cyclosporine Cmin: increased 300%	-	Increased cyclosporine effects (eg, excessive bone marrow suppression, nephrotoxicity)	Inhibition of CYP450 3A4 by saquinavir; competitive binding to P-glycoprotein	Monitor and adjust cyclosporine as indicated	-
Delavirdine (Rescriptor)	400 mg TID	600 mg TID	Delavirdine AUC: decreased 15%	Saquinavir AUC: increased 500%	-	Increased saquinavir effects	-	-
Delavirdine (Rescriptor)	400 mg TID x 14 days	600 mg TID (hard gel caps) x 21 days	No significant change	Saquinavir AUC: increased 500%	Increased saquinavir effects	Inhibition of CYP450 3A4 by delavirdine	Dose adjustment not established	-
Efavirenz (Sustiva)	600 mg QHS on day 10-24	400 mg (soft gel caps) BID with ritonavir 400 mg BID on day 1-10	No significant change	Saquinavir Cmin: decreased 10%; ritonavir Cmin: no significant change	Not clinically significant	Induction of CYP450 3A4 by efavirenz	No dose adjustment necessary	-

Coadministered Drug	Dose of Drug	Dose of Saquinavir	Effect on Coacministered Drug Levels	Effect on Saquinavir Levels	Potential Clinical Effects	Mechanism of Interaction	Management	Suggested Alternative Agent(s)
Efavirenz (Sustiva)	600 mg x 10 days	1200 mg (soft gel caps) Q8H x 10 days	No significant change	Saquinavir AUC: decreased 62%; Cmax: decreased 50%	Decreased saquinavir effects	Induction of CYP450 3A4 by efavirenz	Consider adding ritonavir to saquinavir containing regimen	-
Enfuvirtide (Fuzeon)	90 mg SQ BID on days 1-7	1000 mg BID with ritonavir 100 mg BID on days 4-7	Enfuvirtide Cmax: no significant change; Cmin: increased 26%; AUC: no significant change	No significant change	-	-	No dose adjustment necessary	-
Erythromycin (E-Base, Ilosone, E-Mycin, Eryc, Ery-Tab)	250 mg QID x 7 days	1200 mg TID	-	Saquinavir AUC: increased 99%; Cmax: increased 106% when studied in HIV-infected patients	Increased saquinavir effects	Inhibition of CYP450 3A4 by erythromycin	Dose adjustment not established	-
Ethinyl estradiol/norethindrone acetate (Ortho-Novum, others)	0.03 mg ethinyl estradiol/0.075 mg gestodene QD on days 4-22	600 mg saquinavir hard gel caps on days 1 and 22	No significant change	No significant change	-	-	No dose adjustment necessary	-
Fluconazole (Diflucan)	400 mg QD on day 2, then 200 mg QD on days 3-8	1200 mg TID	Not reported	Saquinavir AUC: increased 50%; Cmax: increased 56%	Increased saquinavir effects	Inhibition of CYP450 3A4 by fluconazole	Dose adjustment not established	-
Fosamprenavir (Lexiva)	700 mg BID on days 2-22	1000 mg BID with ritonavir 100 mg BID on days 1-11	Not studied	Saquinavir AUC (with ritonavir 100 mg BID): no significant change; Cmax: no significant change; Cmin: decreased 24%	-	-	No dose adjustment necessary	-

Coadministered Drug	Dose of Drug	Dose of Saquinavir	Effect on Coadministered Drug Levels	Effect on Saquinavir Levels	Potential Clinical Effects	Mechanism of Interaction	Management	Suggested Alternative Agent(s)
Fosamprenavir (Lexiva)	700 mg BID on days 2-22	1000 mg BID with ritonavir 200 mg BID on days 12-22	Not studied	Saquinavir AUC (with ritonavir 200 mg BID): no significant change; Cmax: no significant change; Cmin: increased 20%		-	No dose adjustment necessary	-
Garlic (Allium sativum)	Garlic capsules (3.6 mg/caplet) BID on days 5-24	1200 mg (soft gel caps) TID with food x 4 days	Not studied	Saquinavir AUC: decreased 51%; Cmax: decreased 54%; Cmin: decreased 49% After a 10 day garlic washout period, pharmacokinetic values returned to only 60-70% of baseline	Decreased saquinavir effects	Possible induction of gut mucosal CYP450 3A4 by garlic; P-glycoprotein effects are also possible	Avoid garlic supplements when saquinavir is used as the sole protease inhibitor	
Grapefruit Juice	200 mL single strength (grapefruit juice from concentrate)	600 mg (hard gel cap) x 1 dose	-	AUC: increased 50% Oral bioavailability: increased 100%	Increased saquinavir effects	Inhibition of gastrointestinal CYP450 3A4 by grapefruit juice	Separate grapefruit juice from saquinavir dose by at least 2 hours	-
Indinavir (Crixivan)	800 mg Q8H x 2 days	Saquinavir soft gel cap 800 mg or 1200 mg x 1 dose	Not studied	Saquinavir 800 mg AUC: increased 620%; Cmax: increased 551%; saquinavir 1200mg AUC: increased 364%; Cmax: increased 299%	Increased saquinavir effects	Inhibition of CYP450 3A4 by indinavir	Dose adjustment not established	-
Indinavir (Crixivan)	800 mg Q8H x 2 days	1200 mg x 1 dose	Indinavir concentration: increased	Saquinavir AUC: increased 364%; Cmax: increased 299%	Increased saquinavir effects	Inhibition of CYP450 3A4 by indinavir	Dose adjustment not established	-
Itraconazole (Sporanox)	100 mg QD x 14 days	800 mg or 1200 mg saquinavir soft gel caps BID with 100 mg itraconazole QD x 14 days	Not studied	No significant changes (compared to 1400 mg saquinavir soft gel caps BID with no itraconazole)		Inhibition of CYP450 3A4 by itraconazole	No dose adjustment necessary	

| Coadministered Drug | Dose of Drug | Dose of Saquinavir | Effect on Coadministered Drug Levels | Effect on Saquinavir Levels | Potential Clinical Effects | Mechanism of Interaction | Management | Suggested Alternative Agent(s) |

Coadministered Drug	Dose of Drug	Dose of Saquinavir	Effect on Coadministered Drug Levels	Effect on Saquinavir Levels	Potential Clinical Effects	Mechanism of Interaction	Management	Suggested Alternative Agent(s)
Itraconazole (Sporanox)	200 mg BID	400 mg BID (with ritonavir 600 mg BID)	Itraconazole half-life: increased 414%	-	Increased itraconazole effects; increased saquinavir effects	Inhibition of CYP450 3A4 by itraconazole and saquinavir and ritonavir	Consider reducing itraconazole to 100 mg BID	-
Ketoconazole (Nizoral)	200 mg QD	1200 mg TID	No significant change	Saquinavir AUC: increased 69%; Cmax: increased 36% when studied in HIV-infected patients	Increased saquinavir effects	Inhibition of CYP450 3A4 by ketoconazole	Dose adjustment not established	-
Ketoconazole (Nizoral)	200 mg QD x 6 days	600 mg TID (hard gel caps) x 6 days	-	AUC: increased 130%; Cmax: increased 147%	Increased saquinavir effects	Inhibition of CYP450 3A4 by ketoconazole	-	-
Ketoconazole (Nizoral)	400 mg QD x 14 days	2000 mg x 14 days	-	Saquinavir AUC: decreased 78%; Cmax: decreased 76%; Cmin: decreased 87% (compared to saquinavir/ritonavir 2000 mg/100 mg QD)	Decreased saquinavir effects	Inadequate boosting due to ketoconazole	Do not use ketoconazole as a pharmacokinetic "booster" with saquinavir	-

Coadministered Drug	Dose of Drug	Dose of Saquinavir	Effect on Coadministered Drug Levels	Effect on Saquinavir Levels	Potential Clinical Effects	Mechanism of Interaction	Management	Suggested Alternative Agent(s)
Ketoconazole (Nizoral)	400 mg QD x 7 days	1200 mg TID	No significant change	Saquinavir AUC: increased 190%; Cmax: increased 171%	Increased saquinavir effects	Inhibition of CYP450 3A4 by ketoconazole	Dose adjustment not established	-
Lopinavir/ritonavir (Kaletra)	400/100 mg BID	1000 mg (soft gel caps) BID	Lopinavir AUC: no significant change; Cmax: no significant change; Cmin: no significant change; (compared to historical control)	Saquinavir AUC: no significant change; Cmax: no significant change; Cmin: increased 27% (compared to saquinavir/ritonavir control) Ritonavir AUC: decreased 54%; Cmax: decreased 37%; Cmin: decreased 60%; Clearance total increased 107%(compared to saquinavir/ritonavir control)	-	Possibly increased clearance resulting in decreased ritonavir levels	No dose adjustment necessary	-
Coadministered Drug	Dose of Drug	Dose of Saquinavir	Effect on Coadministered Drug Levels	Effect on Saquinavir Levels	Potential Clinical Effects	Mechanism of Interaction	Management	Suggested Alternative Agent(s)
Lopinavir/ritonavir (Kaletra)	400/100 mg BID on days 6-20	1200 mg TID on days 1-5, 800 mg BID on days 6-15	No significant change	Saquinavir AUC: increased 836%; Cmax: increased 517%; Cmin: increased 1700%	Increased saquinavir effects	Inhibition of CYP450 3A4 by lopinavir/ritonavir	Dose adjustment not established	-
Lopinavir/ritonavir (Kaletra)	400 mg/100 mg BID x 10 days	800 mg BID		Saquinavir AUC: no significant change; Cmin: increased	Increased saquinavir effects	Inhibition of CYP450 3A4 by lopinavir/ritonavir	Dose adjustment not established	-
Lovastatin (Mevacor)	-	-	Increased lovastatin levels	-	Increased lovastatin effects (eg, myopathy, rhabdomyolysis)	Inhibition of CYP450 3A4 by saquinavir	Do not coadminister	Atorvastatin Pravastatin
Methadone (Dolophine)	-	400 mg BID combined with 400 mg BID ritonavir	S-methadone AUC: decreased 25%; R-methadone AUC: decreased 20%	Not studied	Not clinically significant	Induction of CYP450 by saquinavir/ritonavir	Monitor and adjust methadone as indicated	-
Methadone (Dolophine)	35-100 mg QD x 14 days	1600 mg (soft gel caps) QD with ritonavir 100 mg QD x 14 days	Unbound R-methadone GMR: decreased 8%; alpha-1-acid glycoprotein GMR: increased 14%	No significant change		Reduction in unbound R-methadone mediated by increased alpha1-acid glycoprotein	No dose adjustment necessary	-
Midazolam (Versed)	5 mg IV x 1 dose	600 mg TID x 8 weeks	Increased midazolam levels	-	Increased midazolam effects (eg, increased sedation, confusion, respiratory depression)	Inhibition of CYP450 3A4 by saquinavir	Single dose intravenous midazolam may be used; chronic midazolam administration (oral or intravenous) should be avoided	Lorazepam

Coadministered Drug	Dose of Drug	Dose of Saquinavir	Effect on Coadministered Drug Levels	Effect on Saquinavir Levels	Potential Clinical Effects	Mechanism of Interaction	Management	Suggested Alternative Agent(s)
Nelfinavir (Viracept)	1250 mg BID on days 16-21	1000 mg saquinavir BID with 100 mg ritonavir BID on days 1-14	Nelfinavir Cmax: increased 55%, M8 AUC: increased 622%; Cmax: increased 94%; Cmin: increased 179%	Saquinavir Cmax: increased 172%	-	Inhibition of CYP450 3A4 by saquinavir/ritonavir	No dose adjustment necessary	-
Nelfinavir (Viracept)	750 mg (single dose) x 4 days	1200 mg TID x 4 days (1200 mg single dose)	Nelfinavir AUC: increased 18%	Saquinavir AUC: increased 392%	-	Inhibition of CYP450 3A4 by both drugs	Decrease saquinavir to 800 mg TID or 1200 mg BID; no change in nelfinavir cose necessary	-
Nelfinavir (Viracept)	750 mg TID x 4 days	1200 mg (soft gel cap) x 1 dose		Saquinavir AUC: increased 392%; Cmax: increased 179%	Increased saquinavir effects	Inhibition of CYP450 3A4 by nelfinavir	May consider saquinavir 800 mg TID with nelfinavir 750 mg TID or saquinavir 1200 mg BID with nelfinavir 1250 mg BID	-
Nelfinavir (Viracept)	750 mg x 1 dose	1200 mg (soft gel caps) TID x 4 days	Nelfinavir AUC: increased 18%, Cmax: no change	Not studied	-	-	No dose adjustment necessary	-
Nevirapine (Viramune)	200 mg BID x 21 days	600 mg (hard gel caps) TID x 7 days	No significant change	Saquinavir AUC: decreased 24%, Cmax: decreased 28%	May decrease saquinavir effects	Induction of CYP450 3A4 by nevirapine	Dose adjustment not established	-
Nevirapine (Viramune)	200 mg QD x 2 weeks then 200 mg BID x 28 days	600 mg (hard gel caps) TID	No significant change	Saquinavir AUC: decreased 24%, Cmax: decreased 28%	Decreased saquinavir effects	Induction of CYP450 3A4 by nevirapine	Dose adjustment not established	-
Coadministered Drug	**Dose of Drug**	**Dose of Saquinavir**	**Effect on Coadministered Drug Levels**	**Effect on Saquinavir Levels**	**Potential Clinical Effects**	**Mechanism of Interaction**	**Management**	**Suggested Alternative Agent(s)**
Phenobarbital (Luminal, others)	-		-	May decrease saquinavir levels	May decrease saquinavir effects	Induction of CYP450 3A4 by phenobarbital	Avoid combination if possible; consider alternative agents; monitor phenobarbital levels and adjust as indicated	Gabapentin Lamotrigine Tiagabine Topiramate
Phenytoin (Dilantin)	-		-	May decrease saquinavir levels	May decrease saquinavir effects	Induction of CYP450 3A4 by phenytoin	Avoid combination if possible; consider alternative agents; monitor phenytoin levels and adjust as indicated	Gabapentin Lamotrigine Tiagabine Topiramate
Pravastatin (Pravachol)	40 mg QD on days 1-4 and 15-18	400 mg BID with ritonavir 400 mg BID on days 4-18	Pravastatin AUC: decreased 50%; Cmax: decreased 42%	Not studied	Decreased pravastatin effects	Induction of glucuronidation by ritonavir	No dose adjustment necessary	-
Ranitidine (Zantac)	150 mg x 2 doses	600 mg x 1 dose		AUC: increased 67%; Cmax: increased 74%	-	Inhibition of CYP450 3A4 by ranitidine	No dose adjustment necessary	-
Rifabutin (Mycobutin)	150 mg Q3D or 300 mg Q7D	400 mg with ritonavir 400 mg BID	Rifabutin weekly AUC: no significant difference between dosing regimens	-	Avoidance of increased rifabutin effects	Inhibition of CYP450 3A4 by both ritonavir and saquinavir	Decrease rifabutin to 150 mg 2 to 3 times/week	-

Coadministered Drug	Dose of Drug	Dose of Saquinavir	Effect on Coadministered Drug Levels	Effect on Saquinavir Levels	Potential Clinical Effects	Mechanism of Interaction	Management	Suggested Alternative Agent(s)
Rifabutin (Mycobutin)	300 mg QD x 14 days	600 mg (hard gel caps) TID x 14 days	-	AUC: decreased 43%; Cmax: decreased 30%	Decreased saquinavir effects	Induction of CYP450 3A4 by rifabutin	No dose adjustment necessary	-
Rifampin (Rifadin)	600 mg QD x 14 days	1200 mg TID	-	Saquinavir AUC: decreased 70%; Cmax: decreased 65%	Decreased saquinavir effects	Induction of CYP450 3A4 by rifampin	Do not coadminister	-
Rifampin (Rifadin)	600 mg QD x 14 days	1200 mg TID	-	Saquinavir AUC: decreased 46%; Cmax: decreased 43% when studied in HIV-infected patients	Decreased saquinavir effects	Induction of CYP450 3A4 by rifampin	Do not coadminister	-
Rifampin (Rifadin)	600 mg QD x 7 days	600 mg (hard gel caps) TID x 14 days	-	AUC: decreased 84%; Cmax: decreased 79%	Decreased saquinavir effects	Induction of CYP450 3A4 by rifampin	Avoid if possible; may consider saquinavir 400 mg BID with ritonavir 400 mg BID	Rifabutin
Ritonavir (Norvir)	100 mg BID	Saquinavir soft gel caps 1000 mg/ritonavir 100 mg BID or saquinavir hard gel caps 1000 mg/ritonavir 100 mg BID, administered with food for at least 3 weeks	Not studied	Saquinavir soft gel caps AUC: increased 30% (compared to hard gel caps/ritonavir AUC); Cmin: increased 17% (when compared to hard gel caps/ritonavir regimen Cmin)	Increased saquinavir effects (AUC achieved with hard gel caps/ritonavir regimen is comparable, but not equivalent to, soft gel caps/ritonavir AUC)	Inhibition of CYP450 3A4 by ritonavir	Consider ritonavir-boosted saquinavir	-
Ritonavir (Norvir)	100 mg QD	1600 mg QD x 13 days	-	Saquinavir AUC: increased 592%; Cmax: increased 566%; Cmin: increased 424% (compared to saquinavir 1200 mg TID)	Increased saquinavir effects	Inhibition of CYP450 3A4 by ritonavir	-	-
Coadministered Drug	Dose of Drug	Dose of Saquinavir	Effect on Coadministered Drug Levels	Effect on Saquinavir Levels	Potential Clinical Effects	Mechanism of Interaction	Management	Suggested Alternative Agent(s)
Ritonavir (Norvir)	400 mg BID at steady state	400 mg (hard gel caps) BID at steady state	Not studied	Saquinavir AUC: increased 1587%; Cmax: increased 1277%	Increased saquinavir effects	Inhibition of CYP450 3A4 by ritonavir	Consider ritonavir-boosted saquinavir	-
Ritonavir (Norvir)	400 mg BID x 14 days	400 mg (soft gel caps) BID x 14 days	Not studied	Saquinavir AUC: increased by 121%; Cmax: increased by 64%	Increased saquinavir effects	Inhibition of CYP450 3A4 by ritonavir	Consider ritonavir-boosted saquinavir	-
Ritonavir (Norvir)	Multiple doses studied; 200 mg, 300 mg, 600 mg	Multiple saquinavir hard gel caps doses studied; 200 mg, 400 mg, 600 mg	Ritonavir AUC: no significant change	Saquinavir AUC: increased 5000%; Cmax: increased 2100%	Increased saquinavir effects	Inhibition of CYP450 3A4 by ritonavir	Consider ritonavir-boosted saquinavir	-
Sildenafil (Viagra)	-	-	Sildenafil AUC: increased 200-1100%	-	Increased sildenafil effects (eg, headache, flushing, priapism)	Inhibition of CYP450 3A4 by saquinavir	Initiate sildenafil at 25 mg QOD-QD; adjust dose as indicated; not recommended to exceed 25 mg in a 48 hour period	-

Coadministered Drug	Dose of Drug	Dose of Saquinavir	Effect on Coadministered Drug Levels	Effect on Saquinavir Levels	Potential Clinical Effects	Mechanism of Interaction	Management	Suggested Alternative Agent(s)
Simvastatin (Zocor)	-	-	Increased simvastatin levels	-	Increased simvastatin effects (eg, myopathy, rhabdomyolysis)	Inhibition of CYP450 3A4 by saquinavir	Do not coadminister	Atorvastatin Pravastatin
Simvastatin (Zocor)	40 mg QD on days 1-4 and 15-18	400 mg BID with ritonavir 400 mg BID on days 4-18	Simvastatin AUC: increased 3059%; Cmax: increased 3000%		Increased simvastatin effects	Inhibition of CYP450 3A4 by saquinavir and ritonavir	Do not coadminister	Atorvastatin Pravastatin
St. John's Wort (Hypericum perforatum, hypericin, hyperforin)	-	-	-	May decrease saquinavir levels	Decreased saquinavir effects	Possible induction of CYP450 3A4 by St. John's Wort	Avoid combination	
Tenofovir (Viread)	300 mg QD	1000 mg saquinavir BID with 100 mg ritonavir BID	Tenofovir Cmin: increased 23%	Saquinavir AUC: increased 29%; Cmax: increased 22%; Cmin: increased 47%	-		No dose adjustment necessary	-
Tenofovir (Viread)	300 mg QD on days 2-14	1000 mg BID with 100 mg ritonavir on days 1-14	No significant change	No significant change either for saquinavir or ritonavir			No dose adjustment necessary	-
Tenofovir (Viread)	300 mg QD on days 3-14	1000 mg (hard gel caps) with ritonavir 100 mg BID on days 1-14	Not studied	Saquinavir AUC: no significant change; Cmax: no significant change; Cmin: no significant change; Ritonavir AUC: no significant change; Cmax: no significant change; Cmin: increased 27%			No dose adjustment necessary	
Terfenadine (Seldane)	60 mg BID x 11 days	1200 mg TID x 4 days	Terfenadine AUC: increased 368%; Cmax: increased 253%	-	Increased terfenadine effects (eg, cardiac arrhythmias)	Inhibition of CYP450 3A4 by saquinavir	Do not coadminister	Cetirizine Fexofenadine Loratadine
Tipranavir (Aptivus)	500 mg BID with 200 mg ritonavir BID x 28 doses	600 mg BID with 100 mg ritonavir BID x 27 doses		Saquinavir AUC: decreased 76%; Cmax: decreased 70%; Cmin: decreased 82%	Decreased saquinavir effects	Possible induction of CYP450 3A4 by tipranavir/ritonavir	Do not coadminister	-
Triazolam (Halcion)			Not studied; may increase triazolam levels		Increased triazolam effects (eg, increased sedation, confusion, respiratory depression)	Inhibition of CYP450 3A4 by saquinavir	Avoid combination; consider alternative agents	Lorazepam Oxazepam Temazepam Trazodone
Warfarin (Coumadin)		600 mg TID x 8 weeks	Increased warfarin levels (INR increased from 2.1 to 4.24)	-	Increased warfarin effects (eg, increased INR and risk of bleeding)	Possible inhibition of CYP450 by saquinavir	Monitor INR and adjust warfarin as indicated	
Zalcitabine (Hivid)			No significant change	No significant change	-		No dose adjustment necessary	-

Drug Interactions with Stavudine (d4T)

Coadministered Drug	Dose of Drug	Dose of Stavudine	Effect on Coadministered Drug Levels	Effect on Stavudine Levels	Potential Clinical Effects	Mechanism of Interaction	Management	Suggested Alternative Agent(s)
Atazanavir (Reyataz)	400 mg x 1	also dosed with didanosine	Atazanavir AUC: decreased 87%; Cmax: decreased 89%	Not studied	Decreased atazanavir effects	-	Dose adjustment not established	-
Clarithromycin (Biaxin)	500 mg BID	40 mg BID	-	Stavudine AUC: no significant change; Cmax: decreased 15%; Cmin: decreased 41%	-	-	No dose adjustment necessary	-
Didanosine (Videx)	100 mg (buffered formulation) x 4 days	40 mg Q12H x 4 days	No significant change	Stavudine AUC: no significant change; Cmax: increased 17%	-	-	No dose adjustment necessary	-
Didanosine (Videx)	100 mg Q12H x 9 doses	40 mg Q12H x 9 doses	No significant change	No significant change	-	-	No dose adjustment necessary	-
Emtricitabine (Emtriva)	200 mg x 1 dose	40 mg x 1 dose	No significant change	No significant change	-	-	No dose adjustment necessary	-
Coadministered Drug	Dose of Drug	Dose of Stavudine	Effect on Coadministered Drug Levels	Effect on Stavudine Levels	Potential Clinical Effects	Mechanism of Interaction	Management	Suggested Alternative Agent(s)
Fluconazole (Diflucan)	200 mg QD	40 mg BID	-	Stavudine AUC: no significant change; Cmax: no significant change; Cmin: increased 25%	-	-	No dose adjustment necessary	-
Ganciclovir (Cytovene)	1000 mg Q8H (oral)	40 mg Q12H	No significant change	No significant change	-	-	No dose adjustment necessary	-
Indinavir (Crixivan)	800 mg on days 1 and 2, 800 mg indinavir with 200 mg ritonavir BID on days 3-17	40 mg BID	Not studied	Stavudine AUC: increased 24% (with indinavir and ritonavir); AUC: increased 14% (with indinavir alone); Cmax: no significant effect	-	-	No dose adjustment necessary	-
Indinavir (Crixivan)	800 mg Q8H x 1 week	40 mg Q12H x 1 week	No significant change	Stavudine AUC: increased 25%	-	-	No dose adjustment necessary	-
Methadone (Dolophine)	-	40 mg BID	-	Stavudine AUC: decreased 23%; Cmax: decreased 44%	-	Decreased stavudine bioavailability	No dose adjustment necessary	-
Coadministered Drug	Dose of Drug	Dose of Stavudine	Effect on Coadministered Drug Levels	Effect on Stavudine Levels	Potential Clinical Effects	Mechanism of Interaction	Management	Suggested Alternative Agent(s)
Rifabutin (Mycobutin)	300 mg QD	40 mg BID	-	Stavudine AUC: no significant change; Cmax: decreased 30%; Cmin: increased 105%	-	-	No dose adjustment necessary	-
Tenofovir (Viread)	300 mg QD on days 2-9	100 mg XR QD on days 1 and 9	No significant change	-	-	-	No dose adjustment necessary	-
Tenofovir (Viread)	300 mg QD x 7 days	100 mg extended release x 1 dose	Not studied	No significant change	-	-	No dose adjustment necessary	-

Coadministered Drug	Dose of Drug	Dose of Stavudine	Effect on Coadministered Drug Levels	Effect on Stavudine Levels	Potential Clinical Effects	Mechanism of Interaction	Management	Suggested Alternative Agent(s)
Tipranavir (Aptivus)	1250 mg BID with 200 mg ritonavir BID x 23 doses	30 mg BID x 43 doses	-	Stavudine Cmax: decreased 26%	-		No dose adjustment necessary	-
Tipranavir (Aptivus)	250 mg BID with 200 mg ritonavir BID	40 mg BID	-	No significant change	-	-	No dose adjustment necessary	
Tipranavir (Aptivus)	750 mg BID with 100 mg ritonavir BID	40 mg BID	-	Stavudine Cmax: decreased 24%	-	-	No dose adjustment necessary	
Zidovudine (Retrovir)	-	-	-	-	Decreased stavudine effects	Competitive inhibition of intracellular phosphorylation of stavudine	Do not coadminister	

All Interactions with Tenofovir (Viread)

Coadministered Drug	Dose of Drug	Dose of Tenofovir	Effect on Coadministered Drug Levels	Effect on Tenofovir Levels	Potential Clinical Effects	Mechanism of Interaction	Management	Suggested Alternative Agent(s)
Abacavir (Ziagen)	300 mg BID	300 mg QD x 13 days	No significant change	No significant change	-	-	No dose adjustment necessary	-
Adefovir dipivoxil (Hepsera)	10 mg QD	300 mg QD x 1 dose		No significant change	-	-	No dose adjustment necessary	-
Atazanavir (Reyataz)	300 mg QD with 100 mg ritonavir QD x 10 d	300 mg QD x 10 d, separated 12 hours away from atazanavir/ritonavir	Atazanavir Cmin: decreased 20%	Tenofovir AUC: increased 37%; Cmax: increased 34%; Cmin: increased 29%	Increased tenofovir effects	-	**Coadminister** atazanavir/ritonavir together with tenofovir	
Atazanavir (Reyataz)	300 mg QD with ritonavir 100 mg QD	300 mg QD	Atazanavir AUC: no significant change; Cmax: no significant change; Cmin: decreased 21% (compared to atazanavir 300 QD with ritonavir 100 mg QD) Ritonavir AUC: increased 20%; Cmax: no significant change; Cmin: no significant change			Unknown	No dose adjustment necessary	
Atazanavir (Reyataz)	300 mg QD with ritonavir 100 mg QD on days 1-42	300 mg QD on days 15-42	Atazanavir Cmax: decreased 28%; AUC: decreased 25%; Cmin: decreased 26%; Ritonavir Cmax: decreased 28%; AUC: decreased 25%; Cmin: no significant change	Not studied	Decreased atazanavir effects; increased tenofovir effects	-	Do not coadminister with unboosted atazanavir (400 mg); Administer 300 mg atazanavir with 100 mg ritonavir when used as part of a tenofovir containing regimen	-

Coadministered Drug	Dose of Drug	Dose of Tenofovir	Effect on Coadministered Drug Levels	Effect on Tenofovir Levels	Potential Clinical Effects	Mechanism of Interaction	Management	Suggested Alternative Agent(s)
Atazanavir (Reyataz)	400 mg QD with 100 mg ritonavir QD x 10 d	300 mg QD x 10 d	Atazanavir AUC: increased 38%; Cmax: increased 31%; Cmin: increased 33%	Tenofovir AUC: increased 55%; Cmax: increased 39%; Cmin: increased 70%	Increased atazanavir and tenofovir effects	-	Do not coadminister	-
Atazanavir (Reyataz)	400 mg QD with a light meal	300 mg QD with a light meal	Atazanavir AUC: decreased 26%; Cmax: decreased 24%; Cmin: decreased 40%	Tenofovir AUC: increased 25%; Cmax: no significant change	Decreased atazanavir effects; increased tenofovir effects	Unknown	Do not coadminister with unboosted atazanavir (400 mg); Administer 300 mg atazanavir with 100 mg ritonavir when used as part of a tenofovir containing regimen	
Didanosine (Videx)	-	-	-	-	Potential early virologic failure	-	Use caution when coadministering tenofovir, didanosine and either efavirenz or nevirapine in treatment-naive patients	
Didanosine (Videx)	250 mg or 400 mg QD (buffered formulation) x 7 days	300 mg QD	Didanosine AUC: increased 44%; Cmax: increased 28%	No significant change	Increased didanosine effects	Possible shared elimination pathway	Reduce didanosine dose to 250 mg QD when used with tenofovir	
Didanosine (Videx)	250 mg QD (enteric coated) x 1 (given with food, without food and staggered by 2 hours)	300 mg QD x 9 days	Didanosine AUC: no significant change (fed); Cmax: no significant change; Didanosine AUC: no significant change (staggered); Cmax: no significant change (staggered); Didanosine AUC: no significant change (fed); Cmax: decreased 29% (fed) All values compared to 400 mg QD (enteric coated) reference dose	No significant change		Possible shared elimination pathway	Reduce didanosine dose to 250 mg QD when used with tenofovir	
Didanosine (Videx)	400 mg QD (buffered formulation) x 7 days	300 mg QD x 7 days	Didanosine AUC: increased 44%; Cmax: increased 28%	No significant change	Increased didanosine effects	Possible shared elimination pathway	Reduce didanosine dose to 250 mg QD when used with tenofovir	-

Coadministered Drug	Dose of Drug	Dose of Tenofovir	Effect on Coadministered Drug Levels	Effect on Tenofovir Levels	Potential Clinical Effects	Mechanism of Interaction	Management	Suggested Alternative Agent(s)
Didanosine (Videx)	400 mg QD (enteric coated) x 1	300 mg QD	Didanosine AUC: increased 48% (fasted); Cmax: increased 48% (fasted) Didanosine AUC: increased 60% (fed); Cmax: increased 64% (fed)	No significant change	Increased didanosine effects	Possible shared elimination pathway	Reduce didanosine dose to 250 mg QD when used with tenofovir	-
Didanosine (Videx)	400 mg QD (enteric coated) x 7 days (given with food)	300 mg QD	-	-	Increased didanosine effects	Possible shared elimination pathway	Reduce didanosine dose to 250 mg QD when used with tenofovir	
Didanosine (Videx)	400 mg QD (enteric coated) x 7 days (given without food)	300 mg QD	Didanosine AUC: increased 48%, Cmax. increased 28%	Not studied	Increased didanosine effects	Possible shared elimination pathway	Reduce didanosine dose to 250 mg QD when used with tenofovir	-
Efavironz (Sustiva)	-	-	-	-	Potential early virologic failure	-	Use caution when coadministering tenofovir, didanosine and either efavirenz or nevirapine in treatment-naive patients	-
Efavironz (Sustiva)	600 mg QD x 14 days	300 mg QD x 7 days	No significant change	No significant change	-	-	No dose adjustment necessary	-
Emtricitabine (Emtriva)	200 mg QD x 7 days	300 mg QD x 7 days	No significant change	No significant change	-	-	No dose adjustment necessary	-
Coadministered Drug	**Dose of Drug**	**Dose of Tenofovir**	**Effect on Coadministered Drug Levels**	**Effect on Tenofovir Levels**	**Potential Clinical Effects**	**Mechanism of Interaction**	**Management**	**Suggested Alternative Agent(s)**
Emtricitabine (Emtriva)	200 mg QD x 7 days	300 mg QD	No significant change	No significant change	-	-	No dose adjustment necessary	-
Entecavir (Baraclude)	-	-	No significant change	No significant change	-	-	No dose adjustment necessary	-
Ethinyl estradiol/norethindrone acetate (Ortho-Novum, others)	1 tab QD	300 mg QD	No significant change	No significant change	-	-	No dose adjustment necessary	-
Fosamprenavir (Lexiva)	1400 mg with 100 mg ritonavir QD x 14 days	300 mg QD	Amprenavir AUC: no significant change; Cmax: no significant change; Cmin: increased 24%	No significant change	-	-	No dose adjustment necessary	-
Fosamprenavir (Lexiva)	1400 mg with 200 mg ritonavir QD x 14 days	300 mg QD	No significant change	No significant change	-	-	No dose adjustment necessary	-
Indinavir (Crixivan)	800 mg TID x 7 days	300 mg QD x 7 days	No significant change	No significant change	-	-	No dose adjustment necessary	-

Coadministered Drug	Dose of Drug	Dose of Tenofovir	Effect on Coadministered Drug Levels	Effect on Tenofovir Levels	Potential Clinical Effects	Mechanism of Interaction	Management	Suggested Alternative Agent(s)
Lamivudine (Epivir)	150 mg BID x 7 days	300 mg QD x 7 days	Lamivudine Cmax: decreased 24%	No significant change	-	-	No dose adjustment necessary	-
Lopinavir/ritonavir (Kaletra)	400/100 mg BID	300 mg QD	Lopinavir: no significant change. Ritonavir: no significant change	Not studied			No dose adjustment necessary	-
Lopinavir/ritonavir (Kaletra)	400/100 mg BID	300 mg QD	No significant change	Tenofovir AUC: increased 32%; half-life: no significant change	Possibly increased tenofovir effects		No dose adjustment necessary	-
Lopinavir/ritonavir (Kaletra)	400 mg/100 mg BID x 14 days	300 mg QD	Lopinavir AUC: decreased 15%; Cmax: decreased 15%; Cmin: no significant change. Ritonavir AUC: decreased 24%; Cmax: decreased 28%; Cmin: no significant change	Tenofovir AUC: increased 34%; Cmax: increased 31%; Cmin: increased 29%	Increased tenofovir effects		No dose adjustment necessary	-
Methadone (Dolophine)	40-110 mg/day	300 mg QD	No significant change	Not reported			No dose adjustment necessary	-
Methadone (Dolophine)	stable dose (range 45-130 mg) QD	300 mg QD on days 2-15	R-methadone: no significant change; S-methadone: no significant change; total methadone: no significant change	Not studied			No dose adjustment necessary	-
Coadministered Drug	**Dose of Drug**	**Dose of Tenofovir**	**Effect on Coadministered Drug Levels**	**Effect on Tenofovir Levels**	**Potential Clinical Effects**	**Mechanism of Interaction**	**Management**	**Suggested Alternative Agent(s)**
Nevirapine (Viramune)	-				Potential early virologic failure		Use caution when coadministering tenofovir, didanosine and either efavirenz or nevirapine in treatment naïve patients	-
Ribavirin (Rebetol, Virazole)	800 mg QD	300 mg QD x 1 dose		No significant change			No dose adjustment necessary	-
Rifampin (Rifadin)	600 mg QD on days 11-21	300 mg QD on days 1-20	No significant change	No significant change			No dose adjustment necessary	-
Saquinavir (Invirase, Fortovase)	1000 mg (hard gel caps) with ritonavir 100 mg BID on days 1-14	300 mg QD on days 3-14	Saquinavir AUC: no significant change; Cmax: no significant change; Cmin: no significant change Ritonavir AUC: no significant change; Cmax: no significant change; Cmin: increased 27%	Not studied			No dose adjustment necessary	-
Saquinavir (Invirase, Fortovase)	1000 mg BID with 100 mg ritonavir on days 1-14	300 mg QD on days 2-14	No significant change either for saquinavir or ritonavir	No significant change	-		No dose adjustment necessary	-

Coadministered Drug	Dose of Drug	Dose of Tenofovir	Effect on Coadministered Drug Levels	Effect on Tenofovir Levels	Potential Clinical Effects	Mechanism of Interaction	Management	Suggested Alternative Agent(s)
Saquinavir (Invirase, Fortovase)	1000 mg saquinavir BID with 100 mg ritonavir BID	300 mg QD	Saquinavir AUC: increased 29%; Cmax: increased 22%; Cmin: incresed 47%	Tenofovir Cmin: increased 23%	-	-	No dose adjustment necessary	-
Stavudine (Zerit)	100 mg extended release x 1 dose	300 mg QD x 7 days	No significant change	Not studied	-	-	No dose adjustment necessary	-
Stavudine (Zerit)	100 mg XR QD on days 1 and 9	300 mg QD on days 2-9	-	No significant change	-	-	No dose adjustment necessary	-
Tipranavir (Aptivus)	500 mg BID with 100 mg ritonavir BID	300 mg x 1 dose	Tipranavir Cmin: decreased 21%	Tenofovir Cmax: decreased 23%	-	-	No dose adjustment necessary	-
Tipranavir (Aptivus)	750 mg BID with 200 mg ritonavir BID x 23 doses	300 mg x 1 dose	No significant change	Tenofovir Cmax: decreased 38%	-	-	No dose adjustment necessary	-

7

Medication Adherence and Patient Education

Asim A. Jani, MD, MPH, FACP
Internal Medicine, Infectious Diseases and HIV Medicine
Assistant State Epidemiologist, Virginia Department of Health
Clinical Assistant Professor, Virginia Commonwealth University, Richmond, VA
Anne Stewart, PhD, ARNP
Immunology Clinic Manager
Faculty, Florida Southern College, Orlando
Robin D. Nolen, MSW
Adherence Facilitator & Health Educator
Lee Tavel, RPh
Pharmacist
Orange County Health Department, Florida Department of Health, Orlando

Introduction

Improvement in immune function, decreased opportunistic infections, and increased survival due to success of HAART is often achieved at the price of difficult and complex regimens leading to problems in *adherence*.

Three characteristics of currently available antiretroviral medications (ARVs) make the issue of non-adherence even more critical:

- ARVs lack pharmacologic forgiveness
    - In contrast to other chronic diseases, HIV requires continuous therapy and the medications over time, especially if not taken correctly can select for drug resistance
- The unfortunate long-term adverse complications (such as lipodystrophy) and the necessity for life-long treatment often present a real dilemma for long-term management with respect to risks and benefits
- Non-adherence, a determinant of the development of drug resistance, has been linked to population-based evidence of transmission of drug-resistant HIV.[1]

The patient's goals (or *existential* goals) may not be limited to an increase in months/years of functional life but may also include the discovery of the meaning of the patient's illness or treatment. Ability to retain a subjectively optimal quality of life before a presumed inevitable period of debilitation accompanying advanced HIV may involve decisions that could occasionally be part of *rational non-adherence*.

– A purposeful decision to follow a self-care plan different from the one prescribed.2 (Providers could be well served to recognize and accept this aspect of patient care without perceiving it as a problem.)

Decision-making ability may be affected by the disease, medication effects, or co-occurring psychiatric illness.

Summary

– The reality of high pill burden, side effects, and resistance undermine the capacity of people living with HIV to take these medicines for an extended, indeterminate period of time (possibly lifelong).

Collaborative Management Model of Chronic HIV Illness

Medication adherence must be ≥ 90–95% in order to obtain optimal suppression of HIV

Treatment issues:

• A *steep* drop in probability of sustaining a viral load below detection occurs as adherence rates drop from > 95% to < 70% (as defined by electronic MEMS caps data)[3]

• For every 10% decrease in adherence (see sections below for definition issues), there is a 16% increase in HIV-related mortality[4]

• Excellent rates of adherence in prison populations undergoing directly observed therapy (DOT) can be achieved but are impractical in the general population[5]

• It is critical that fundamental definition issues (discussed below) regarding *adherence* be clarified before any general statement regarding the effects of *nonadherence* on virologic control and drug resistance is made

• Strict adherence to salvage drug regimens in heavily treated patients may not lead to undetectable virus[6]

Achievement of excellent medication adherence is not an end in itself but perhaps the *means* to achieving the broader goal of collaborative patient and provider management

• *Collaborative management* is care that "strengthens and supports self-care in chronic illness while assuring that effective medical, preventive, and health maintenance interventions can take place"[6,7]

• The collaborative process is a dynamic, continuous process
– Begins with dialogue and mutual respect
– Does not end with regimen selection but progresses through stages in the direction of improving adherence, optimal health, and increased survival
– Starting point – the choice of desired and obtainable goals
♦ Goals and objectives provide direction but need not be so inflexible that care and communication are compromised

The **essential elements** of healthcare central to such collaborative management[8] are:

• Collaborative definition of problems
• Targeting, goal setting, and planning

- Creating a continuum of self-management training and support services
- Active, sustained follow-up
  - Though not originally applied to HIV medicine, these four elements provide a new paradigm shift in the approach to not only medication adherence issues but also to HIV medical care in general
    - Patients and providers define problems differently: patients may emphasize functionality, subjective complaints, and lifestyle choices whereas providers may emphasize disease prevention, therapy, non-adherence to recommendations, and risk factors related to prognosis
    - It is essential to have a mutual understanding of who sees which issues as *problems* and *harmonize the perspectives*[9]
  - Targeting a given problem allows the patient to focus on one thing at a time
  - Action plans conversely allow proactive identification of different options and potential barriers
- *Compliance* is traditionally defined as the entire spectrum of patient responses to both medical advice and pharmaceutical prescription[10]
  - Term assumes the patient is sufficiently informed and motivated to *do what the medical provider recommends*
  - Semantics have changed as there has been an evolution of scientific and societal perspectives on the patient/provider relationship and issues related to compliant behavior
- *Adherence* now largely replaces the term *compliance*
  - Definition of adherence reflects a paradigm shift about the interaction between patient and provider
  - Relationships primarily seen as a means to discover and apply approaches that assist the patient to adhere to those behavioral changes that will improve and maintain his/her health
  - *Adherence can be looked at as a collaborative process designed to optimize clinical outcomes*[11]
  - **Midwest AIDS Training Education Partnership** (MATEP: 1997–98) is a landmark initiative involving a multidisciplinary group
    - Findings:
    - MATEP reviewed the literature from several sources to provide a structured approach with practical suggestions to improve medication adherence
    - Adherence is the extent to which a client's behavior coincides with the healthcare regimen as determined through a shared decision-making process between the client and healthcare provider (Visit http://www.matep.org for additional information.)
  - Even when the definition supports a "cut off" threshold > 95% adherence (based largely on percentages of doses taken), adherence still seen to include many other factors:
    - Timing of doses
    - Frequency of doses
    - Food restrictions

- *Non-adherence* may have many different manifestations, none of which are mutually exclusive
  - Besides errors of missing doses, non-adherence includes:[12]
    - ◆ Taking doses at the wrong time
    - ◆ Incorrect dose
    - ◆ Not filling a prescription or filling it late
    - ◆ *Drug* holidays (multiple reasons)
    - ◆ Not adhering to certain food restrictions (timing/type of food)
    - ◆ Not following instructions regarding concomitant medications
    - ◆ Excess doses (to make up for missed doses)
    - ◆ Not completing the therapeutic course (relevant in opportunistic infection treatment)

    Complexity of medication adherence is the basis for patients and providers to *look at the bigger picture* (see Figure 1)
  - Address adherence issues in an upbeat, organized approach in order that the patient's life, medical, and virologic goals are optimized

Figure 1. Drug Failure

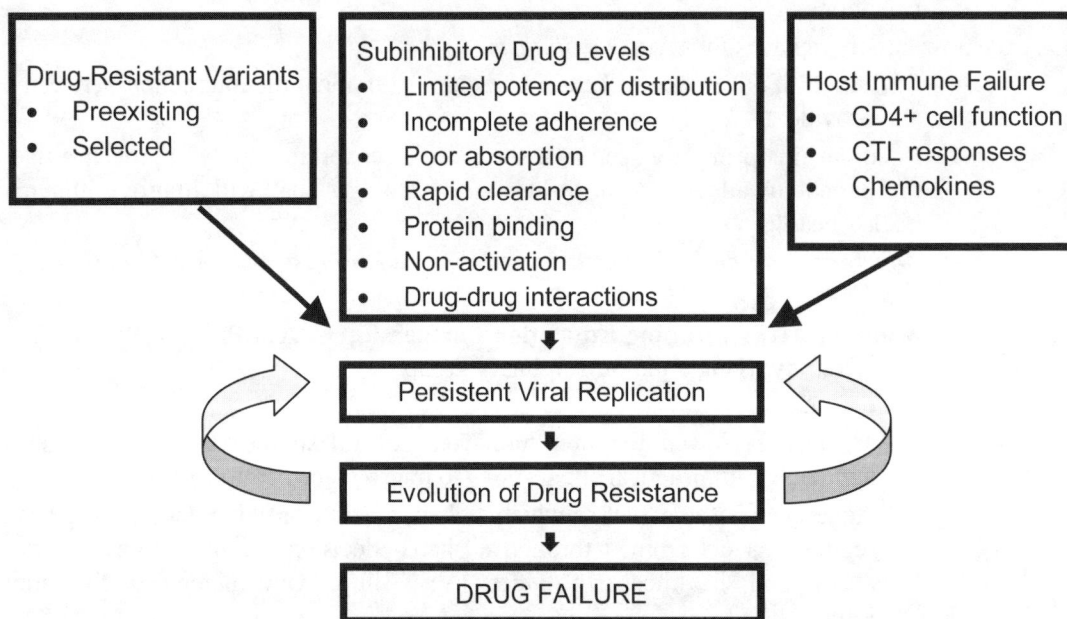

Adapted from Hirsch et al. *JAMA*. 1998; The International AIDS Society – USA

Practical Approach to Medication Adherence

- The **collaborative care model** of chronic HIV illness can be readily applied to medication adherence
- Key elements of this model reviewed earlier support a plan of care involving *a 4-step organized practical approach to HIV medication adherence* (listed below)

1. Assess clinical factors that may influence adherence
2. Create and maintain a therapeutic alliance between the patient and provider
3. Monitor the level of medication adherence
4. Identify strategies to improve medication adherence

- The approach incorporates principles of learning theory, the daily living challenges of the HIV-infected individual, and the complexity of medical and psychosocial factors specific to HIV practice
- The 4-step process outlined below is recommended because it is easy to implement in the clinical setting

STEP 1: ASSESS CLINICAL FACTORS THAT MAY INFLUENCE ADHERENCE

- A variety of factors can influence medication adherence; therefore, it is critical that clinical factors are assessed prior to initiation of therapy
- The two most important influential factors[13] are the *stage of treatment readiness*[14] and *the baseline self-efficacy for HIV disease management*. Of all the patient-based factors, these two aspects are inclusive of many of the other factors

  - *General health status*: medical history, nutritional assessment, opportunistic infections
  - *Life goals*: to understand deeper life issues such as what gives meaning to a patient's life, the context of illness and treatment in the patient's life, his/her definition of quality of life, and learning the patient's attitudes and motivations based on his/her self-perception
  - *Medication history*: past experience, current regimens, side-effect profile experienced on all medications
  - *Comorbidities*: psychiatric, substance abuse, medical illnesses (e.g., TB, STD, diabetes, liver disease, renal insufficiency, etc.)
  - *Social stability*: housing status, food resources, transportation needs, financial status, and insurance status
  - *Employment status*: type of job, constraints, on the job disclosure issues
  - *Health beliefs and cultural background*: language and perceptions towards illness, HIV disease, diagnosis, prognosis, role of medications, understanding of consequences of medication non-adherence, spiritual/religious orientation in reference to one's life and health goals
  - *Family and social support*: identification of personalized medication facilitator (buddy system) and network of social support
  - *Educational background*: educational level, literacy level, baseline knowledge regarding HIV, viral load, CD4+ cell count, medications, and significance of adherence

STEP 2: CREATE AND MAINTAIN A THERAPEUTIC ALLIANCE BETWEEN THE PATIENT AND PROVIDER

- **General**

  - Ensuring patient adherence to HIV medications involves *empowering* a patient to take an active role in his/her own healthcare
  - May be achieved by many means, central of which is to gain the *trust and respect* of the patient
  - Involves seeking to understand the values, health beliefs and goals of the patient first and foremost before attempting to *prescribe* a care plan or medication regimen. In fact, better adherence is likely to be achieved if and when the patient feels more *in control* of the illness, therapy choices, regimen efficacy, and clinical outcomes.

- **Communication process and informed consent**: Specific training and skills development for clinical interviewing is needed in order to establish a therapeutic alliance, keeping in mind the specific cultural and language background of the patient. A contractual agreement based on informed consent can assist in galvanizing the patient-provider rapport and commitment to medication adherence.

- **Individualized profile of pertinent factors**: This profile of pertinent factors that may influence issues regarding medication adherence should be created. These factors should be identified in the preliminary assessment.

- Identify barriers to reaching health goals: Potential and actual barriers to reaching health goals of the patient should be identified, including medication adherence. Conversely, it is important to identify special support systems that may be present and could be further strengthened.

- **Assess patient readiness**: Assess the stage of readiness for behavior change, including medication usage and adherence. This staging will assist the provider in the potential application of motivational interviewing to move the patient to the next level of readiness, if and when the patient is empowered to do so.

- **Determine medication regimen and implementation**: Establish definitions of success and failure in both the virologic and clinical arenas, drug sequencing, implications of resistance testing, tailored to daily lifestyle and potential utility of a pretreatment simulation trial.

  - Interventions may be misdirected if patient and provider perceptions about potential barriers to adherence are different. For example, barriers to adherence identified by patients included the following (ranked):[14]
    - Forgetting (more often the afternoon dose compared to morning/evening)
    - Inconvenient timing
    - Food restrictions
    - Adverse effects
    - Difficulty scheduling around sleeping
    - Size and number of medications and pills
    - Storage specifications
    - Hydration requirements with certain PIs (e.g., indinavir)
    - Disclosure issues (difficulty with discreet self-administration of medications)

STEP 3: MONITOR THE LEVEL OF MEDICATION ADHERENCE

- Medication adherence is considered as ongoing if virologic control is achieved but this is not necessarily true in all instances; adherence may be suboptimal and still result in virologic undetectability. Therefore adherence should be assessed and not assumed.

- Various strategies to measure adherence
  - Viral load measurements
  - Pill counts
  - Pharmacy tracking of medication pick ups
    - **Clinic visits**: for scheduled visits, processing of disability paperwork, patient education related activities and dietitian visits
    - **MEMS** bottle cap devices: if available
    - **Self-reports**: self-reporting tools and methods; both clinical care and epidemiological purposes; tends to underestimate levels of *non-adherence*
      - Decade-old Morisky four-question self-reporting tool has only limited supportive data for inclusion in the clinical encounter (Morisky Adherence Score – MAS).[15] Perhaps a more important purpose of using the scale is that the clinician can *uncover* non-adherence and promote further dialogue with the patient to better characterize the non-adherence, its frequency, and causation (see Table 1).

Table 1. MORISKY Simplified Self-Report Measure of Adherence

Yes = 1, No = 0
SCORING: 0 = HIGH ADHERENCE; 1-2 = MEDIUM ADHERENCE; 3-4 = LOW ADHERENCE

1. Do you ever forget to take your medicine?
2. Are you careless at times about taking your medicine?
3. When you feel better do you sometimes stop taking your medicine?
4. Sometimes if you feel worse when you take the medicine, do you stop taking it?

- Clinician assessment – commonly done but fraught with overestimation bias
  - **Reporting**: objective reports of patient taking medication provided by caregiver, medication facilitator, home nursing, outreach worker, peer educators, etc.
  - **Simulation trial results**: can clarify risk of missing doses; helps to prevent confusions regarding regimen
  - **Certain laboratory values**: i.e., MCV values that increase with the use of AZT
  - **Survey tools**: written forms of self-reporting, patient-centered group, or one-on-one sessions that facilitate open discussion and frank reporting of medication management and adherence

STEP 4: IDENTIFY STRATEGIES TO IMPROVE MEDICATION ADHERENCE

- Define the pattern(s) of non-adherence
- Identify specific barrier(s) that promote non-adherence and identify factors that can be modified that will enhance the patient's ability to adhere to the regimen
  - Establish a culturally sensitive therapeutic alliance and cooperative dialogue to implement solutions that improve adherence that in turn help patients realize their own health goals
  - Target solutions to match the specific barrier that impedes adherence and/or to facilitate the specific factor(s) in their lives that promote adherence
- Continuous communication with patient about patient perception of health goals, HIV disease, purpose of HAART medication, role of adherence, and consequence of non-adherence
- Specific strategies to improve medication adherence
- **Tailor the regimen** to fit lifestyle, job situation, and food habits

Table 2. Issues to Consider In Tailoring an Antiretroviral Regimen

Pill characteristics – size, taste, aftertaste concerns
Side effects – list and prioritize the ones of concern
Symptom relieving medications – availability
Toxicity concerns – short and long term
Timing and frequency of doses – once daily or twice daily associated with better adherence
Food restrictions – find out about dietary preferences in conjunction with pills (whether patient prefers pills with food or fasting issues required)
Baseline viral load and CD4+ cell count (the higher the baseline viral load, the more potent the regimen needed to reach *goal* levels of undetectability)
Treatment history – heavily experienced patients have more limited options; prior medications may have caused minor or major morbidity – should be avoided
Health status of the patient – more advanced patients have lower thresholds for toleration of side effects
Known or suspected viral resistance profiles (class specific) – genotype/phenotype may be needed
Existing comorbidities – may limit HAART options because of drug interactions and side effect profiles of concurrent medications, substances of abuse, and street drugs.
Domestic issues – (living situation/storage restrictions) – concern regarding stability and storage issues for medications
Employment disclosure issues – may need a regimen that can be taken outside of the work context or safely and discreetly within the work context
Polypharmacy concerns – HAART meds have multiple drug interactions that may limit options; adherence to polypharmacy, pill burden, and pill fatigue are real issues
Pill burden – desired versus tolerable

- Simplify the regimen by changing all or parts of the regimen to facilitate a better match of acceptable side effects, pill burden, dosing, and timing
- Management of side effects should include an assessment of their impact on the patient's life. Management of side effects should include changes in diet and alternatives such as acupuncture and herbal remedies where appropriate. It is proactive to give prescriptions for any medications that may assist the patient in side-effect management.
- Identify barriers to non-adherence focusing on prior/current causes of non-adherence so that subsequent new regimens are not likely to fail due to uncorrected problems
- Provide timely referrals and/or interventions for diagnosed comorbidities that may negatively influence adherence.
- Problem solve strategies to take medicines even if the patient does not want to stop using illicit drugs
- Take a *team* multidisciplinary approach where feasible to non-adherent patients who may require multiple sources of expertise and support (e.g., case management, nurse, social worker, medical provider, pharmacist, substance abuse and mental health counselors, health educators)
- Emphasize patient and provider education at every step
- Make available a range of reminder devices, such as pagers, watches, pillboxes with alarms and computerized supported devices. Assist patient in developing skills to incorporate treatment needs to their lifestyle, such as using cues from his/her daily routine to remember to take medicines.
- Minimizing inconvenience and unpleasant effects of medications and medication interactions is critical to successful adherence. Quality of life should be considered as important as numerical indicators of HIV status.

Role of the Pharmacist

- Pharmacists can play a vital role in development of action plans to increase adherence to HIV/AIDS treatment regimens (see Table 3)
    - Gather information, review data (prescription medication history and medical records when available), develop a pharmacy action plan, counsel patients, and monitor adherence to the plan and the medication regimen
    - Patient education is enhanced by involving pharmacists who are skilled in HIV disease management
    - May be considered a practical approach for pharmacists to use refill data to monitor adherence in addition to informal discussion regarding missed doses or dose taken incorrectly including the reasons why

Table 3. Pharmacists' Role in Medication Adherence

ON THE HEALTHCARE TEAM	WITH THE PATIENT	THE PATIENT'S MEDICATION REGIMEN
• Network with the healthcare team for a complete patient care plan • Provide medication history to healthcare team members • Assist in knowledge of cultural, language, or ethnic differences • Be aware of possible prescribing errors, or dispensing errors that may occur from *look-a-like names*, use of abbreviations, and suggest preventive measures to the clinician • Communicate to the healthcare team about the patient's general knowledge deficits — disease and therapy • Provide pill refill dates to the clinician or healthcare team • Provide information to case managers about pharmaceutical access or limitations to governmental programs like state ADAPs or Ryan White Titled programs	• Educate the patient about his/her medication, disease, and its treatment • Ensure the patient's lifestyle is considered when the treatment plan is developed • Provide complete and understandable information to the patient about medications. Provide drug information and prescription labels in the patient's own language • Monitor and consult team members of the patient's level of readiness. Use open-ended questions in counseling the patient to look for triggers that may indicate nonadherence. • Reinforce the need to stay adherent and not to embark on *drug holidays,* that have not been agreed upon • Provide information and/or tools that assist in improving adherence (pill boxes, medication calendars, diaries, MEMS containers, patient information handouts, audio/visual tapes, and access to Internet educational information if available)	Medication counseling should include the following: • Medication dose, route, indication • Adverse drug reactions • Possible drug interactions • Possible drug/food interactions • Missed dose information • Proper storage • Self-monitoring activities The pharmacist should also: • Reinforce the patient's understanding of his/her disease and the indications for medications • Insure the patient understands the consequence of nonadherence • Encourage the patient to stay adherent, and praise adherence • When adverse drug reactions occur, refer the patient to the primary HIV clinician • Monitor the viral load and CD4+ cell counts when provided (if not provided request that information from the primary HIV clinician) • Monitor for over and under drug utilization. This may indicate the patient does not understand the medication's directions.

Websites and Key Resources

HIGHLY RECOMMENDED READING

Shafer RW, Deresinski SC. Human immunodeficiency virus on the web: A guided tour. *Clinical Infectious Diseases* 2000; 31:568–577.

ADHERENCE GUIDELINES

- http://aidsinfo.nih.gov/ Living Document (*Guidelines for the Use of Antiretroviral Agents in HIV-Infected Adults and Adolescents*): March 23, 2004 – *has sections on adherence*)
- http://hivinsite.ucsf.edu/InSite?page=md-rr-04&doc=md-rr-04-07 (Miramontes, H., Frank, L. (1999) AIDS Education and Training Center Adherence Curriculum – University of California at San Francisco) – *This document is very helpful for provider training and covers a variety of adherence related topics*
- http://www.iasociety.org/search/search.asp?pageid=1110
- http://hivinsite.ucsf.edu/InSite?page=li-04-01 (this link also provides information on commercial products such as reminder tools, electronic devices, etc.)
- www.aidsinfonyc.org
- www.retroconference.org
- www.medscape.com
- www.iasusa.org/
- http://hab.hrsa.gov/womencare.htm
- www.nmac.org
- www.prn.org

References

1. Boden D, Hurley A, Zhang L, et al. HIV drug resistance in newly infected individuals. *JAMA*. 1999;282(12):1135–1141.

2. Chesney M. Quoted in: HAART adherence still an obstacle. *HIV Forefront*. 2000;2(4):15.

3. Paterson D, Swindells S, Mohr J, et al. How much adherence is enough? A prospective study of adherence to protease inhibitor therapy using MEMS caps. 6th Conference on Retroviruses and Opportunistic Infections,1999,Chicago, IL. Abstract 92.

4. Hogg RS, Yip B, Chan K, et al. Non-adherence to triple combination therapy is predictive of AIDS progression and death in HIV-positive men and women. Chicago, 7th Retrovirus Conference, 2000, Chicago, IL. Abstract 73.

5. Fischl M, Rodriguez A, Scerpella E, et al. Impact of directly observed therapy on outcomes in HIV clinical trials. 7th Retrovirus Conference, Chicago, IL, Abstract 71.

6. Kaplan A, Golin C, Beck K, et al. Adherence to protease inhibitor therapy and viral load. 6th Conference on Retroviruses and Opportunistic Infections, 1999, Chicago, IL. Abstract 96.

7. Von Korff M. Collaborative Management of Chronic Illnesses. *Ann Intern Med*. 1997;172:1097–1102.

8. Von Korff M. Collaborative Management of Chronic Illnesses. *Ann Intern Med*. 1997;172:1097–1102.

9. Von Korff M. Collaborative Management of Chronic Illnesses. *Ann Intern Med*. 1997;172:1097–1102.

10. Haynes RG. Determinants of compliance: The disease and the mechanics of treatment. *Compliance in Health Care*. Haynes RB, Taylor DW, Sackett DL, eds. Baltimore, MD: Johns Hopkins University Press, 1979, 49–62.

11. Waters M. *NYS DOH – Treatment Adherence Guidelines*. 1997.

12. Andrews L, Friedland G. Progress in HIV therapeutics and the challenges of adherence to antiretroviral therapy. Inf *Dis Clin N Amer*. December 2000; 14 (4):901–992.

13. Ostrop NJ, Hallett KA, Gill MJ. 2000. Long-term patient adherence to antiretroviral therapy. *Annals of Pharmacotherapy* 34(6):703–709.

14. Katzenstein DA, Lyons C, Molaghan JP, Ungvarski P, Wolfe GS, Williams A. HIV therapeutics: confronting adherence. *J Assoc Nurses AIDS Care*. 1997;8(Supp):46–58.

15. Morisky DE, Green LW, Levine DM. Concurrent and predictive validity of a self-reported measure of medication adherence. *Med Care*. 1986;24:67–74.

Antiretroviral Resistance Testing and Therapeutic Drug Monitoring

Jeffrey P. Nadler, MD, FACP
Professor of Medicine
University of South Florida, College of Medicine, Tampa

Introduction

Viral resistance testing has emerged as an important tool for helping clinicians select antiretroviral therapy. Issues of which test type to apply, when to use resistance testing, and how to interpret the results for the optimum care of patients infected with HIV, as well as reimbursement questions, still represent obstacles to the application of resistance testing. Some clinicians may be unfamiliar with the molecular information measured and presented by resistance testing laboratories.

There are two ways to assess the susceptibility of HIV isolates to antiviral drugs: genotyping and phenotyping. **Genotyping** is a method of amplifying the genetic sequence coding for the amino acids of a protein and noting any mutations, then assessing their possible contribution to resistance thus primarily measuring the likelihood of reduced susceptibility ("resistance"). **Phenotyping** amplifies the gene sequence in a recombinant viral system and assesses its ability to grow in lymphocyte culture in the presence of varying concentrations of antiviral drugs, and may be best thought of as indicating susceptibility to an antiviral drug.

Previously, the treatment paradigm had been to change the entire antiretroviral regimen upon confirmed virologic failure (in an adherent patient), if possible, since it would be difficult to predict which agent(s) in the regimen were not working. In the absence of resistance testing, it is difficult to determine whether the virologic failure represented failure due primarily to "pure" resistance or due to problems of adherence. This scenario could quickly lead to depletion of all reasonable therapeutic combinations. Furthermore, if adherence problems were due to the complexity of the antiretroviral regimen, newer regimens would often be *more* complex without the assistance of resistance testing. This situation would, indeed, result in a counter-productive change in therapy. Resistance testing, therefore, may permit more selective substitution of agents in a treatment regimen while preserving later treatment agents and options.

This chapter will discuss the indications and potential uses of antiretroviral resistance testing, introduce the methodologies that are currently most widely applied to perform the testing, and discuss some of the potential pitfalls of resistance testing. Studies in support of the clinical utility of resistance testing will be discussed briefly, as will tables of mutations used for genotypic test interpretation.

Why Does Resistance Develop?

Resistance may develop for a number of reasons. The mechanisms underlying the development of resistance are as follows: the rapid rate of HIV replication (approximately 10 billion viral particles/day), the spontaneous mutation rate in the typical HIV reproductive cycle (approximately one mutation/new copy),[1] and the absence in retroviruses (including HIV) of a repair mechanism for correcting transcriptional errors. These are natural processes. Applying the "selective pressure" of incompletely suppressive antiviral therapy enhances the process.

It is usually the case that the emergence of retroviral resistance is selected by lesser degrees of adherence to the prescribed regimen needed to maintain ongoing viral suppression. The use of regimens of inadequate potency to suppress the virus, regimens that may not adequately penetrate into reservoirs where there is viral replication, and host factors such as poor absorption or exceptional metabolic processing that result in sub-therapeutic drug levels may also predispose to the development of resistance.

How Is Resistance Testing Done?

There are two methods for testing viral isolates for susceptibility: **genotypic resistance testing** (GRT) and **phenotypic resistance testing** (PRT). GRT is a method of assaying for the presence of nucleotide base changes in the sequence of the gene segment being examined. It has the advantages of being more rapid, readily available, less technically demanding, less costly, and more commonly ordered than PRT. Mutations may be detected before they are *expressed* phenotypically as increased viral replication.

There are two methods currently used to genotype, *direct sequencing* and *hybridization* (gene chip arrays or line probe assays). Currently available hybridization assays may miss selected clinically significant amino acid insertions or be too limited in the portion of the genome examined; therefore, direct sequencing methods are more commonly used. Because current antiviral agents target the reverse transcriptase or protease enzyme of HIV, these gene segments are the targets of current genotyping assays. Assays for detection of key mutations associated with reduced susceptibility to the new fusion inhibitors are becoming more readily available.

Genotyping measures the nucleotide base "triplets" that code for the insertion of specific amino acids into the elongating protein chain of the reproducing virus that determines the viral growth characteristics. Genotyping permits a comparison of the patient's measured sequence to a consensus "normal" and mutant substitutions that are known to be associated with reduced susceptibility to a drug or drugs. The letter code assigned to the "normal" amino acid by consensus is given *before* its numerical position in the gene sequence. If a mutant substitute amino acid is detected, its code letter is given *after* its position. For example, methionine is normally found at position 184 of the reverse transcriptase (RT) sequence; replacement of one base pair that codes for valine to be inserted instead of methionine at this position would be reported as "M184V detected." The typical report includes a statement of which, if any, mutations were detected and an interpretation of their implications for reduced susceptibility. Thus, the report accompanying the M184V would note that this amino acid substitution is associated with significant reduced susceptibility to lamivudine and emtricitabine (some interpretive schemata may report that M184V may variably effect the activity of didanosine – not to a clinically significant degree — or zalcitabine, which is an example of how easily the reports can become confusing).

PRT is another way of assessing viral susceptibility. It is a more direct measure of susceptibility and somewhat more familiar conceptually to clinicians from bacterial susceptibility testing (MICs) than is GRT. Viral resistance phenotype refers to a comparison of the growth of the patient's viral isolate to that of a consensus normal isolate in the presence of varying concentrations of an antiviral drug. The tests express the result as the ratio ("fold change") of the drug concentration necessary to achieve 50% growth inhibition (the IC_{50}) of the patient isolate compared to the susceptibility control in the presence of typically achievable drug concentrations and extrapolated to indicate whether the drug is likely to be effective.

Two assay methods for phenotyping are currently employed. The traditional method involves the growth of the patient's entire virus in lymphocyte cultures with varying concentrations of antiviral drugs in the media. The other assay involves a recombinant technology: the patient's viral RT and protease gene sequences are transfected into a lab-adapted, standardized, rapid-growth variant of HIV whose corresponding genes were deleted. This procedure, therefore, "completes" the virus permitting its growth in culture. The viral products thus reflect the influence on growth of the patient's reverse transcriptase and protease genes. The advantages of this commercially available recombinant approach are the relative speed of achieving growth and the standardization permitting cross-isolate comparisons. The phenotype report gives an assessment of likely susceptibility based on the IC_{50} ratio with reference to antiviral drug concentrations felt to correlate with suppressive potential.

The **virtual phenotype** (VP) is a measured genotype, in which the sequence is compared to a large database of similar sequences for which the actual phenotype was measured, providing an extrapolation of what the actual phenotype would likely be if it was actually measured.

NOTE: The Editors would like to thank the International AIDS Society – USA (www.iasusa.org) for providing the following figures. Please visit their website to ensure you have the most up-to-date information.
Copyright International AIDS Society – USA. Reprinted with permission from: Johnson V, Brun-Vezinet F, Clotet B, et al. Drug Resistance Mutations in HIV-1:2005. *Topics in HIV Medicine*. 2005; 13:4.

Figure 1. Mutations Figures

MUTATIONS IN THE REVERSE TRANSCRIPTASE GENE ASSOCIATED WITH RESISTANCE TO REVERSE TRANSCRIPTASE INHIBITORS

Nucleoside and Nucleotide Reverse Transcriptase Inhibitors (nRTIs)[1]

Abacavir[2]		K 65 R	L 74 V			Y 115 F		M 184 V					
Didanosine[3,4]		K 65 R	L 74 V										
Emtricitabine[5]		K 65 R						M 184 V I					
Lamivudine		K 65 R						M 184 V I					
Stavudine[6,7,8]	M 41 L	E 44 D	K 65 R	D 67 N	K 70 R		V 118 I		L 210 W	T 215 Y F	K 219 Q E		
Tenofovir[9]			K 65 R										
Zidovudine[6,7,8]	M 41 L	E 44 D		D 67 N	K 70 R		V 118 I		L 210 W	T 215 Y F	K 219 Q E		

Multi-nRTI Resistance: Thymidine-associated Mutations[10] (TAMs; affect all nRTIs currently approved by the US FDA)

M 41 L		D 67 N	K 70 R		L 210 W	T 215 Y F	K 219 Q E

Multi-nRTI Resistance: 69 Insertion Complex[11] (affects all nRTIs currently approved by the US FDA)

M 41 L	A 62 V	▼ 69 Insert	K 70 R		L 210 W	T 215 Y F	K 219 Q E

Multi-nRTI Resistance: 151 Complex[12] (affects all nRTIs currently approved by the US FDA except tenofovir)

A 62 V	V 75 I	F 77 L		Q 116 Y	151 M

Nonnucleoside Reverse Transcriptase Inhibitors (NNRTIs)[1,13]

Drug							
Delavirdine		K 103 N	V 106 M		Y 181 C	Y 188 L	P 236 L
Efavirenz	L 100 I	K 103 N	V 106 M	V 108 I	Y 181 C I	Y 188 L	G 190 S A	P 225 H	
Nevirapine	L 100 I	K 103 N	V 106 A M	V 108 I	Y 181 C I	Y 188 C L H	G 190 A	

Multi-NNRTI Resistance[14] (affects all NNRTIs currently approved by the US FDA)

K 103 N	V 106 M	Y 188 L	

Multi-NNRTI Resistance: Accumulation of Mutations[15] (affects all NNRTIs currently approved by the US FDA)

L 100 I	V 106 A	Y 181 C I	G 190 S A	M 230 L

MUTATIONS IN THE PROTEASE GENE ASSOCIATED WITH RESISTANCE TO PROTEASE INHIBITORS [16,17]

Atazanavir[18] — positions (wild-type → substitutions):
- 10 L → I, F, V
- **16** G → E
- 20 K → R, M, I
- 24 L → I
- 32 V → I
- 33 L → I, F, V
- 36 M → I, L, V
- 46 M → I, L
- 48 G → V
- **50** I → L
- 54 I → L, V, M, T
- **60** D → E
- 62 I → V
- 71 A → V, I, T, L
- 73 G → C, S, T, A
- 82 V → A, T
- **84** I → V
- **85** I → V
- **88** N → S
- 90 L → M
- 93 I → L

(Fos) amprenavir — positions (wild-type → substitutions):
- 10 L → F, I, R, V
- 32 V → I
- 46 M → I, L
- 47 I → V
- **50** I → V
- 54 I → L, V, M
- 62 I → V
- 73 G → S
- 82 V → A, F, S, T
- **84** I → V
- 90 L → M

Indinavir — positions (wild-type → substitutions):
- 10 L → I, R, V
- 20 K → M, R
- 24 L → I
- **32** V → I
- 36 M → I
- **46** M → I, L
- 54 I → V
- 71 A → V, T
- 73 G → S, A
- 77 V → I
- **82** V → A, F, T
- 84 I → V
- 90 L → M

Lopinavir/ritonavir[19] — positions (wild-type → substitutions):
- 10 L → F, I, R, V
- 20 K → M, R
- 24 L → I
- **32** V → I
- 33 L → F
- 46 M → I, L
- **47** I → V, A
- 50 I → V
- 53 F → L
- 54 I → V, L, A, M, T, S
- 63 L → P
- 71 A → V, T
- 73 G → S
- 82 V → A, F, T, S
- **84** I → V
- 90 L → M

Nelfinavir[20] — positions (wild-type → substitutions):
- 10 L → F, I
- **30** D → N
- 36 M → I
- 46 M → I, L
- 71 A → V, T
- 77 V → I
- 82 V → A, F, T, S
- 84 I → A, V, D, S
- 88 N → D, S
- **90** L → M

Ritonavir — positions (wild-type → substitutions):
- 10 L → F, I, R, V
- 20 K → M, R
- 32 V → I
- 33 L → F
- 36 M → I
- 46 M → I, L
- 50 I → V
- 54 I → V, L
- 71 A → V, T
- 77 V → I, A, F, T, S
- **82** V → A, F
- **84** I → V
- 90 L → M

Saquinavir — positions (wild-type → substitutions):
- 10 L → I, R, V
- 48 G → V
- 54 I → L
- 71 A → V, T
- 73 G → S
- 77 V → I
- 82 V → A
- 84 I → V
- **90** L → M

Tipranavir/ritonavir[21] — positions (wild-type → substitutions):
- 10 L → V
- 13 I → V
- 20 K → M, R, V
- **33** L → F
- 35 E → G
- 36 M → I
- 43 K → T
- 46 M → L
- 47 I → V
- 54 I → A, M, V
- 58 Q → E
- 69 H → K
- 74 T → P
- **82** V → L, T
- **83** N → D
- 84 I → V
- 90 L → M

MUTATIONS IN THE GP41 ENVELOPE GENE ASSOCIATED WITH RESISTANCE TO ENTRY INHIBITORS

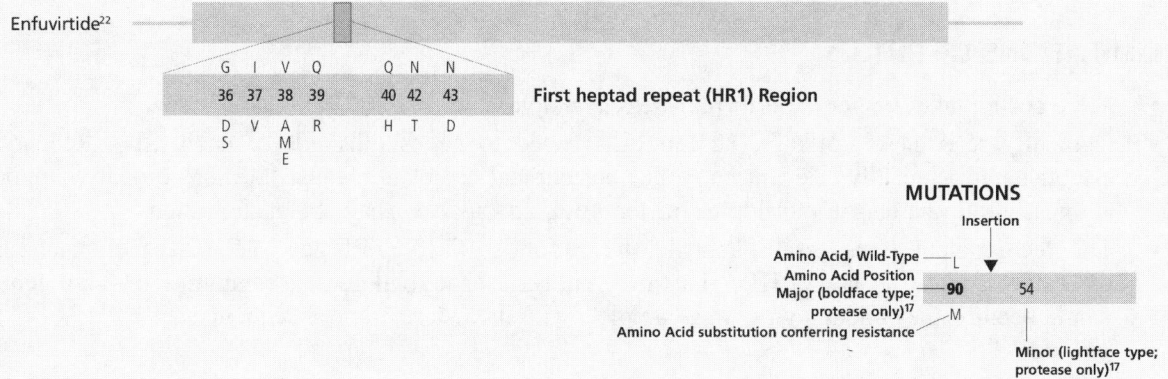

Enfuvirtide[22] — First heptad repeat (HR1) Region — positions (wild-type → substitutions):
- 36 G → D, S
- 37 I → V
- 38 V → A, M, E
- 39 Q → R
- 40 Q → H
- 42 N → T
- 43 N → D

MUTATIONS

- Insertion (↓)
- Amino Acid, Wild-Type — L
- Amino Acid Position — **90**, 54
- Major (boldface type; protease only)[17]
- Amino Acid substitution conferring resistance — M
- Minor (lightface type; protease only)[17]

What are the Pitfalls of Resistance Testing?

Resistance testing of viral isolates is an emerging field with many controversies and unanswered questions.

A **first principle** to remember is that "resistance" is what we're thinking but we measure *reduced susceptibility*, which is *relative to the usually achievable drug level*. If drug levels are either higher or lower than the average, the suppressive effect on the viral isolate in question may be greater or less than expected. There is considerable intrinsic variability from individual to individual of drug levels achieved *in vivo*. Drug levels in an individual may be affected significantly by the effect of concomitant medications and genetic variation on metabolic and clearance pathways and by varied tissue distribution or absorption due to pathophysiologic states (such as chronic diarrhea). The current DHHS treatment guidelines reflect this principal by endorsing the use of ritonavir-enhanced PI regimens. In these regimens, the effect of low-dose ritonavir on suppressing the cytochrome p450 and P-glycoprotein protease metabolic pathways is sufficiently profound to overcome reduced susceptibility to the usual levels of individual PIs. This "pharmacokinetic boosting" of PIs by ritonavir results in drug levels that exceed the phenotypic "resistance cut-off" levels reported for a particular drug. Thus, current resistance test standards may not be applicable to assessment of the use of ritonavir-enhanced drugs.

LIMITATIONS OF GRT

- Indirect measure of the likelihood of expressing reduced susceptibility, requires expert interpretation, and may not correlate with phenotype, especially since complex patterns of interacting mutations may be needed to compromise the activity of a drug or regimen.
- Result is dependent on the length and completeness of the RT fragment amplified (all commercial systems are generally capable of amplifying the critical portions of the 99 amino acid protease genome successfully). The RT genome consists of about 400 amino acids. Some vendors amplify shorter sequences within this genome potentially not identifying contributory mutations in other segments of the genome.
- Quality control — lack of specimen cross-contamination and reproducibility/reliability of results — is critical, and clinicians often are not aware of the applicable standards, if they exist.
- Interpretation of the result depends on how current and complete the interpretative algorithm is.
- Some labs may not distinguish *in vitro* from *in vivo* resistance patterns affecting resistance.

LIMITATIONS OF PRT

- More costly, takes longer to perform, is less available.
- Clinically relevant cut-offs for susceptibility need to be established for each drug. Recent data establishes biologically relevant cut-offs,[2] but clinical correlation must be more broadly supported. Clinically relevant cut-offs for lopinavir, tenofovir and abacavir have been suggested.[3]
- The recombinant virus assays analyze the patient's RT and PI gene sequences emplaced in a laboratory-adapted isolate of HIV. This may not reflect the total genetic regulation of these genes as would occur if the patient's virus was complete with its own regulatory sequences.

OTHER POTENTIAL PITFALLS IMPORTANT TO REMEMBER

- Technically, there must be a sufficient number of viral copies available (> 500-1000 copies/mL with current methodologies) to amplify sufficient product for resistance testing. Even with higher copy numbers, occasional isolates cannot be amplified for testing.
- Another consideration is that HIV evolves in an individual into a mixture of "quasispecies." Current methodologies are often unable to detect resistant quasispecies representing < 20–25% of a mixture.

Combined with low copy numbers, this could also potentially lead to measurement of a non-representative clone.

- Patients should be *on therapy* when resistance testing is performed. If the pressure of a drug is removed, the mixed viral population is likely to revert to the predominant "wild-type" virus that, by definition, is favored in its growth over mutated isolates in the mixture. Thus, resistant clones may not be expressed or measurable *off* therapy; indeed, they are genetically *archived* and can be rapidly reexpressed once therapy is reintroduced.
- The reporting formats may be confusing.
- We treat our patients with antiretroviral drugs in *combination*, but we assess reduced susceptibility to drugs *individually*.
- Resistance may not be purely due to genetic mutation. *Pharmacologic, pharmacokinetic, and pharmacogenomic* issues discussed above may be the major contributor to drug failure (as well as to the development of resistance). *Cellular* mechanisms may also contribute to resistance rather than intrinsically reduced drug susceptibility. For example, nucleoside RT inhibitors act via their tri-phosphorylated intracellular intermediates by competing for the binding site of natural substrate nucleoside triphosphates resulting in chain termination. Some cells have developed a compensatory mechanism restoring the advantage of the natural substrate.

In summary, there are many technical and practical considerations to keep in mind when performing and interpreting resistance testing. Properly applied, resistance testing can be an important patient management tool. Poorly applied or performed, resistance testing can be a waste of resources and a frustrating experience.

Studies in Support of the Clinical Utility of Resistance Testing

A large number of *retrospective* analyses of the utility of resistance testing in patient management have been presented. The past few years have seen an improvement in the technology and databases from which to predict susceptibility by testing viral isolates. Recent *prospective* trials applying resistance testing to clinical management have been presented, and generally suggest an improved virological outcome with the use of these tests, consistent with the conclusions of the prior retrospective studies.

A brief overview of the results of five trials is instructive. The GART[4] and Viradapt[5] studies were the first prospective trials to use genotypic testing in patient management. Both studies showed that resistance testing applied to patient management resulted in better short- to medium-term viral suppression than was achieved by expert advice alone. These results have been substantiated by two other studies, HAVANNA[6] and NARVAL[7], although the result in the latter study was less impressive. The VIRA 3001 trial[8] is the prototypical study demonstrating the utility of phenotypic testing in improving virologic outcomes. Remarkably, the quantitative benefit of all these studies is quite similar: about 0.5 $\log_{10}$ copies/ml greater viral suppression than is achieved without use of the test. While this may seem relatively small, we must remember that such relatively small reductions of viral load (typical of the activity of antiviral agents seen in the early days of NRTI monotherapy) are associated with clinically significant reductions in morbidity and mortality, clinically significant improvements in CD4+ cell count, and improved durability of the suppressive effects of the regimen. Furthermore, patients in both arms of the prospective trials were managed by highly experienced clinicians more likely to empirically select an active regimen for the comparator, non-resistance-tested arms of the studies. Thus, the study results likely minimized the perceived effect of resistance testing. An analysis of the HAVANNA trial results highlights this effect[9]. Clinical experience has often shown much more substantive improvement in viral suppression in individual patients having the results of resistance tests.

Another component of resistance testing is the perceived high cost. While the actual "up-front" dollar cost may seem high (~ \$300–400 for the genotype and ~ \$800–900 for the phenotype), the more relevant question is whether the expenditure will result in an improved outcome for the patient in a cost-effective manner: a reduction in clinical events that result from lesser degrees of viral suppression and a reduction in costs of ineffective medications. A recent publication by Weinstein, et al. addresses these issues and clearly suggests resistance testing is cost-effective.[10]

Several commercial labs are offering a **virtual phenotype** test. This modification of genotyping is based on interpreting a genotype to reflect the "typical" actually measured phenotype of isolates exhibiting the measured genotypic sequence. The technique utilizes a large database of genotypes and associated phenotypes. This is an attempt to provide a more directed, clinically useful resistance test result faster and for lower cost than a "true" phenotype. The major current limitations include the limited number of correlated phenotype and genotype pairs for some genotypic patterns measured, the number of mutations that are included in the relational database interpretive algorithm, and the fact that the virtual phenotype represents only a probability that the patient's isolate will behave identically. When the virtual phenotype interpretation does not reflect a large distinction between susceptible and resistant, the result is hard to apply. It is also necessary to recall that virtual phenotypes are derived from genotypes, and as such they are subject to all the limitations of genotyping previously noted. Nonetheless, the virtual phenotype is proving to be an extremely useful way of presenting the results of resistance testing to the clinician, especially those uncomfortable with interpretation of the genotype.

Interpreting Resistance Tests

The intuitive ease of reading and applying **phenotype test** results makes this an attractive test to order. The result is reported as "sensitive" if the isolate is not above a biologically or, ideally, clinically defined cut-off compared to a known susceptible isolate. If the reduction in susceptibility is > 10-fold for PIs or NNRTIs compared to a fully susceptible isolate, treatment with the agent is likely to fail. Lesser degrees of reduced susceptibility may be significant for some PIs, especially if they are not ritonavir boosted. For NRTIs, the cut-offs signifying likely failure are more varied and are still being evaluated. Whether resistance should be "called" at the fold change where drug activity begins to decline, or the point where it is totally unlikely to have clinical activity is one question. Another issue to be clarified is the limited dynamic range of fold change (relative to the reproducibility of the assay) between active and inactive. Regardless, it is important to keep in mind the pitfalls in testing noted above when applying the results of phenotypic testing.

Genotyping reports appear more complex in some respects to interpret and apply. The mutational patterns may be complicated and overlapping, and the reports may alternatively be misleadingly simple: the algorithmic interpretation of the implication of the detected mutations may be accepted blindly, without regard for the limitations noted above. Typical resistance patterns associated with the NRTIs, NNRTIs, and PIs are demonstrated in Figure 1. It is important to remember that new mutations and mutational patterns and associations are being recognized regularly. As examples, it is only recently appreciated that nucleoside analog mutations (NAMS), many of which were classically thought of solely as zidovudine resistance mutations, may also be selected for by stavudine, and can effect susceptibility to either or both NRTI, as well as abacavir and probably didanosine; newly described mutations at positions 44 and/or 118 may be associated with modest resistance to lamivudine and other nucleosides, and an 88 mutation is another associated with significant nelfinavir resistance. Remember, resistance mutations only indicate the *possibility* of expressing reduced susceptibility, not whether it is being expressed currently in the patient!

Indications and Potential Uses of Antiviral Resistance Tests

Resistance testing is usually advocated for patients who are **on a failing** antiretroviral regimen to help select a substitute regimen. Failure of a regimen in this context refers to *virologic* failure: either failure to suppress the virus to "undetectable" levels or a confirmed return towards pre-treatment viral load in a patient who had initially manifested virologic suppression on that HAART regimen. Because resistance testing is relatively expensive at the present time, it **should not be used** as a surrogate measure of adherence to a drug regimen.

The following outline of indications for resistance testing is derived by combining the recommendations of the IAS-USA expert panel[11] and those of the DHHS Guidelines[12] as modified by the author.

INDICATIONS

- To guide changes in therapy in patients currently failing or inadequately suppressed on their existing regimen:
    - May help select agent(s) more likely *not* to have compromised activity for the new regimen
    - May help preserve therapeutic options by suggesting which individual agent(s) likely contribute(s) to regimen failure, facilitating limited changes
    - May suggest an intensification strategy
    - May be a tool to direct adherence education
- In primary HIV infection to help optimize the chosen regimen:
    - Optimal viral suppression may permanently alter the natural history of infection in an individual.[13] Resistance may be transmitted in primary infection, and may be clinically significant, impeding adequate viral suppression.
- In selecting a regimen during pregnancy:
    - Because the extent of viral suppression in the HIV-infected pregnant woman correlates with reductions in perinatal transmission, optimized antiviral therapy is desirable
    - *Primary* resistance may be seen during HIV diagnosed in pregnancy, or *secondary* resistance may exist in a woman on therapy who becomes pregnant
- In patients whose history suggests an established but recent (<two years infection):
    - Recent infection is more likely to result from a source exposed previously to ART but carrying resistance that may be transmitted
    - Transmitted resistance may be durable for two years[14]
    - *Consider* resistance testing in selecting initial therapy in chronically infected patients (>two years or duration unknown) not an HAART
    - Presently the most controversial situation regarding resistance testing!
        - If "community" resistance is "frequent" prior to initiating therapy, resistance testing may be helpful
        - An important recent analysis[15] suggests it is possibly cost-effective even if resistance detection in this setting is uncommon
    - However, resistance may not be measurably expressed in mixtures with non-mutant, wild-type virus
- In research protocols:
    - May help define the limitations of new agents or regimens
    - Helps characterize the population under study
    - May be an endpoint or safety measure

- Although prospective trial data is lacking, similar indicators should apply in pediatric HIV care

Therapeutic Drug Monitoring (TDM)

The idea of measuring the individual patient's antiretroviral drug level is receiving increased attention. Plasma samples can be assayed by high-pressure liquid chromatography (HPLC) or mass spectroscopy to provide a quantitative measure of the amount of a specific drug present in the sample. The concept is to measure the peak level achieved, that may correlate with some side-effects, or, more commonly, the trough level (level at the end of the dosing interval). It is assumed that trough levels below the IC_{50} of the drug needed to suppress the virus will likely result in failure of the regimen or the development of resistance. In the Viradapt study referenced above, trough levels of indinavir were measured, and those patients having the best response were those with "optimal" levels, even if the genotype was available. Thus, having adequate drug levels is predictive of a better clinical response.

At the present time, a number of problems with therapeutic drug monitoring exist:
- Reliable commercial availability in the United States is limited
- The timing of obtaining the specimen is critical to accurate assessment of the result
- The IC_{50} of the patient's virus may differ from that of a standard reference isolate. Plasma levels may not reflect levels in other tissue compartments
- Nucleoside levels in plasma may not reflect those of the active, intracellular triphosphate metabolites
- Non-nucleoside levels may not be clinically relevant – these agents achieve such high levels and broad tissue penetration that it may not be relevant to measure their levels
- PI levels are best interpreted in the context of the susceptibility of the isolate
- Drug levels only reflect the last dose the patient took (they are not the equivalent of HgbA1c measurements reflecting long term control of diabetes) as a result, drug levels are not a measure of long-term adherence
- Intercellular nucleoside monitoring is complex and unavailable in the clinic, and plasma levels do not reflect active intracellular levels so nucleoside TDM is not currently useful to the clinician. Non-nucleoside levels are generally far in excess of those needed to suppress HIV, so these may only be useful if future studies show levels that may correlate with occurrence of a side-effect or toxicity. Once more data establishing clinical cut-off levels for boosted protease inhibitors is developed, this is likely to become the primary use of TDM (for reference, see the clinical fold-change cut-off for Kaletra phenotypic susceptibility).

Further investigation must be done to define the utility and appropriate application of therapeutic drug monitoring. This is a promising new technological approach to improve the dosing of antiretroviral therapy for individual patients

Conclusion

Antiretroviral resistance testing has become a critical tool for determining the patterns of resistance to therapy. The results of this information can be applied to enhance the management of individual patients, to help analyze developments in public health such as rates and patterns of viral transmission, to evaluate the characteristics of research populations, and determine the resistance patterns of new agents in development. Knowing when and how to do resistance testing is important for all HIV practitioners. Resistance testing will have an ongoing role in the laboratory management of HIV-infected patients alongside CD4 cell enumeration and viral load quantification. Improvements in the measurement of reduced susceptibility and improved reporting are likely to be available soon, with better clinical correlations. The possibility of combining resistance testing with therapeutic drug monitoring to facilitate individualized therapy selection may be the next arena to be explored in the clinical management of HIV-infected patients.

References

1. Coffin JM. HIV population dynamics *in vivo*: implications for genetic variation, pathogenesis, and therapy. *Science* January 27, 1995; 267(5197):483-489.

2. Harrigan PR, Hertog K, Larder, BA. Worldwide variation in antiretroviral phenotypic susceptibility in untreated individuals. 8th Conference on Retroviruses and Opportunistic Infections, February 4–8, 2001, Chicago, IL. Abstract 455.

3. Lanier ER, Hellman N, Scott J, Aitkhaled M, Melby T, Paxinos E, Werhane H, Petropoulos C, Kusaba E, St. Clair M, Smiley L. Determination of a clinically relevant phenotypic resistance "cutoff" for Abacavir using the PhenoSense assay. 8th Conference on Retroviruses and Opportunistic Infections, February 4–8, 2001, Chicago, IL. Abstract 254.

4. Baxter JD, Mayers DL, Wentworth DN, Neaton JD, Hoover ML, Winters MA, Mannheimer SB, Thompson MA, Abrams DI, Brizz BJ, Ioannidis JP, Merigan TC. A randomized study of antiretroviral management based on plasma genotypic antiretroviral resistance testing in patients failing therapy. CPCRA 046 Study Team for the Terry Beirn Community Programs for Clinical Research on AIDS. *AIDS* January 16, 2000; 14(9):F83-93.

5. Durant J, Clevenbergh P, Halfon P, Delgiudice P, Porsin S, Simonet P, Montagne N, Boucher CA, Schapiro JM, Dellamonica P. Drug-resistance genotyping in HIV-1 therapy: the VIRADAPT randomised controlled trial. *Lancet* January 26, 1999; 353(9171):2195–2199.

6. Tural C, Ojanguren I, Romeu J, Fuster D, Rovira C, Sirera G, Jimenez JA, Muga R, Rey-Joly C, Clotet B. Chronic hepatitis C in HIV-infected patients: effects of coinfection and HAART. 8th Conference on Retroviruses and Opportunistic Infections, February 4–8, 2001, Chicago, IL. Abstract 566.

7. Meynard JL, Vray M, Morand-Joubert L, et al. Impact of treatment guided by phenotypic or genotypic resistance tests on the response to antiretroviral therapy (ART): A randomised trial (NARVAL, ANRS 088). Program and abstracts of the 40th Interscience Conference on Antimicrobial Agents and Chemotherapy, September 17–20, 2000; Toronto, Ontario, Canada. Abstract 698.

8. Verbiest W, Brown S, Cohen C, Conant M, Henry K, Hunt S, Sension M, Stein A, Stryker R, Thompson M, Schel P, Van Den Broeck R, Bloor S, Alcorn T, Van Houtte M, Larder B, Hertogs K. Prevalence of HIV-1 drug resistance in antiretroviral-naive patients: a prospective study. *AIDS* March 30, 2001; 15(5):647–650.

9. Meynard JL, Vray M, Morand-Joubert L, et al. Impact of treatment guided by phenotypic or genotypic resistance tests on the response to antiretroviral therapy (ART): A randomised trial (NARVAL, ANRS 088). Program and abstracts of the 40th Interscience Conference on Antimicrobial Agents and Chemotherapy, September 17–20, 2000; Toronto, Ontario, Canada. Abstract 698.

10. Weinstein MC, Goldie SJ, Losina E, Cohen CJ, Baxter JD, Zhang H, Kimmel AD, Freedberg KA. Use of genotypic resistance testing to guide HIV therapy: clinical impact and cost-effectiveness. *Ann Intern Med* March 20, 2001; 134(6):440-450.

11. Hirsch MS, Richman DD. The role of genotypic resistance testing in selecting therapy for HIV. *JAMA* October 4, 2000; 284(13):1649–1650.

12. DHHS Guidelines for the use of antiretroviral agents in HIV-infected adults and adolescents. *The Living Document*.: March 23, 2004. Available at http://www.hivatis.org/guidelines/adult/AA_032304.html.

13. Tremblay C, Giguel F, Merrill D, Rosenberg E, Wong J, Davis B, Crumpacker C, Ives D, Kalams S, D'Aquila R, Walker BD, Hirsch MS. Longitudinal monitoring of chronically HIV-1-infected individuals for cell-associated virus and immune responses. 8th Conference on Retroviruses and Opportunistic Infections, February 4–8, 2001, Chicago, IL. Abstract 367.

14. Little SJ, Holte S, Routy JP, Daar ES, Markowitz M, Collier AC, Koup RA, Mellors JW, Connick E, Conway B, Kilby M, Wang L, Whitcomb JM, Hellmann NS. Antiretroviral drug resistance among patients recently infected with HIV. *NEJM* August 8, 2002; 347(6):385–394.

15. Little SJ, Holte S, Routy JP, Daar ES, Markowitz M, Collier AC, Koup RA, Mellors JW, Connick E, Conway B, Kilby M, Wang L, Whitcomb JM, Hellmann NS. Antiretroviral drug resistance among patients recently infected with HIV. *NEJM* August 8, 2002; 347(6):385–394.

9

Metabolic Complications of Highly Active Antiretroviral Therapy (HAART)

Asim A. Jani, MD, MPH, FACP
Internal Medicine, Infectious Diseases and HIV Medicine
Assistant State Epidemiologist, Virginia Department of Health
Clinical Assistant Professor, Virginia Commonwealth University, Richmond, VA

Editor's Note:

> *Our knowledge and understanding of the metabolic complications of HAART are changing at an extremely rapid pace. The information provided in this chapter is part of the attempt to hit a "moving target" as best as possible, i.e., to define syndromes and management based on the best currently available information. Please refer to the websites below and at the end of this chapter for the latest information.*

This updated chapter is based on the latest recommendations found in:

Guidelines for the Use of Antiretroviral Agents in HIV-1-Infected Adults and Adolescents (April 07, 2005) — Developed by the Panel on Clinical Practices for HIV Infection convened by the Department of Health and Human Services (DHHS). The panel regularly updates the guidelines, and the most recent information is available at: AIDSinfo website (http://AIDSinfo.nih.gov).

Based on the DHHS Guidelines (above), this chapter is organized into three sections:

1. Potentially life-threatening and serious adverse effects (including lactic acidosis)

2. Adverse effects associated with potential long-term (metabolic) complications

3. Adverse effects compromising quality of life* (including lipodystrophy)

Not all of the adverse events discussed in the above guidelines are presented here in detail. Those adverse events generally considered metabolic complications of HAART are emphasized in this chapter (lactic acidosis, cardiovascular effects, hyperlipidemia, insulin resistance/diabetes mellitus, osteonecrosis, lipodystrophy).

* It should be noted that any and all of the above three sets of side effects/adverse events may negatively influence the practice of medication adherence for chronic HIV management given the enormous impact of the medications on quality of life.

Introduction

- Highly Active Antiretroviral Therapy (HAART)
    - Convincingly demonstrated to decrease mortality
    - Reduce the incidence of opportunistic infections (Ois)
    - Return patients to functional status
- Cost-effectiveness of these drugs also has been demonstrated
- Several challenges remain
    - Tolerability issues
    - Complexity of regimens
    - Medication non adherence
    - Long-term toxicity of these agents
    - Development of drug resistance (genotypic and phenotypic)
    - Equitable distribution of HAART (resource-limited settings)
- New agents under investigation (for improved side-effect profiles, regimen simplicity, adherence, novel mechanisms)
- HIV medications have a number of side effects
    - Some anticipated, others unexpected
    - Easily referable to specific body systems and readily identified by providers – e.g., gastrointestinal, dermal, nervous system related, etc. (see Chapter 5, Antiretroviral Therapy)
- Numerous observations by patients and providers have pointed to multiple symptoms that appear to be either "connected" or overlapping with variable consistency

Pre-Treatment Decision Making

- Optimize the time prior to starting HAART by proactive patient education and assessment of goals (culturally sensitive and realistic care plan)
- Inform the patient not only about the probable but also possible long-term complications of therapy choice in addition to routine description of side-effect profiles and management (*informed* consent approach)
- Risk stratify the patient as best as possible prior to or while on HAART so appropriate patient selection and regimen choice can be made while balancing risks and benefits, always favoring the safest approach possible
- The process of communication about goal setting and action plan formulation is based on establishing a therapeutic alliance between the patient and the provider. This approach is especially necessary when dealing with the long-term duration and level of "risk" potentially caused by life-saving drugs in HAART. This is not only germane to the topic of complications of drug therapy but also to medication adherence (see Chapter 7, Medication Adherence and Patient Education).

SECTION I: Potentially life-threatening and serious adverse events

LACTIC ACIDOSIS

Features

- The prevalence of lactic acidemia (hyperlactatemia defined as > 2 mM)
  - Lactic acidemia (plus or minus mild symptoms) has ranged from 8–20% in many studies; although *symptomatic lactic acidosis is an overall uncommon event, it is significant for its toll of morbidity and risk of mortality* (up to 50–60%)
- **Risk factors** include use of prolonged nucleoside reverse transcriptase inhibitor (NRTI) agents, particularly stavudine (d4T) but may also occur with didanosine (ddI), zidovudine (AZT), abacavir (ABC), lamivudine (3TC). NRTI combinations such as ddI + d4T, ddI + hydroxyurea, or ddI + ribavirin; pregnancy (especially d4T + ddI contraindicated in pregnancy); female gender, obesity
- Key step in pathogenesis appears related to the NRTI induced inhibition of the mitochondrial DNA (mtDNA) polymerase enzyme
  - Results in abnormal pyruvate cellular metabolism and a shunting of pyruvate into lactate and gluceoneogenesis
  - Overproduction of acetyl CoA results in fat production and ketosis occurs leading to clinical manifestations of the syndrome – acidosis, ketosis, secondary hyperglycemia, **fatty liver**, and weight gain
- Non-nucleoside reverse transcriptase inhibitors (NNRTIs) do not have any affinity for the DNA polymerase enzyme
- Patients *may initially present with chronic nonspecific gastrointestinal symptoms* (nausea, anorexia, vomiting, abdominal pain, weight loss), fatigue, myalgias
- A specific "syndrome" may occur that is associated with progressive neuromuscular weakness consistent with *an ascending paralysis with rapidly progressive weakness* that may lead to respiratory failure (similar to the presentation of a patient with acute demyelinating neuropathy; Guillain-Barré syndrome). Besides laboratory findings discussed below, such patients may also have elevated creatine phospokinase – (CPK) levels.
- *Progressive symptoms may also occur including signs of respiratory or cardiovascular insufficiency* – increased heart rate, respiratory rate, respiratory distress, altered mental status; some individuals may not only present in an advanced stage but may progress to multi-system organ failure including pancreatitis, encephalopathy, renal and/or hepatic failure
- Laboratory findings may be sentinel "event" – such as increased anion gap, low bicarbonate, evidence of acidosis on arterial blood gas, elevated transaminase levels, low albumin. NB: increased lactate levels may be observed but attention to proper phlebotomy technique and processing 'on ice' may help to decrease falsely elevated lactate levels – see document: AACTG LACTIC ACIDOSIS GUIDELINES (see Table 1 for web address)
- **Lactate Level Specimen Collection Guidelines**
  - Venous lactate levels are highly dependent on collection techniques. If carefully collected, venous lactate level is equivalent to an arterial collection in most clinical situations. If the specimen cannot be collected without hand clenching or prolonged tourniquet time, an arterial lactate should be considered, as this will help exclude falsely elevated lactate levels.
  - Have subject sit, relaxed for 5 minutes prior to venipuncture
  - Instruct subject to not clench the fist before or during the procedure and to relax the hand as much as possible
  - If possible, do not use a tourniquet. If a tourniquet is necessary, then apply tourniquet lightly and draw lactate first before the other samples with the tourniquet still in place
  - Collect the blood in a chilled gray-top (sodium fluoride-potassium oxalate) tube
  - Place the specimen immediately on ice and send to the laboratory for immediate processing, preferably within 30 minutes of collection

 - If random lactate is elevated, then repeat as above with the following additional patient instructions: no alcohol within 24 hours, no exercise within 8 hours, and no food or drink except water within 4 hours of the draw.

Visit   http://aactg:cure@aactg.s-3.com/members/download/other/Metabolic/LacAcid.doc   for   more information.

Monitoring

- Lactic acid levels ought not to be *routinely* measured except when clinical suspicion arises
- Lactic acid levels should be checked if there is an elevated anion gap, low bicarbonate and/or if patient is "symptomatic" (see above)

Recommendations for Management

- Early recognition of the syndrome and **stop NRTIs immediately** when syndrome is suspected or diagnosed
- Supportive care is the primary intervention → may also require intensive care unit support in case of progressive disease (e.g., hemodialysis, intravenous bicarbonate infusions, mechanical ventilation)
- For serious NRTI-induced lactic acidosis, treatments such as intravenous thiamine and/or riboflavin have been tried (along with NRTI cessation)
- Interventions for syndrome associated with neuromuscular weakness include: early recognition of symptoms/etiologies, stopping NRTIs, supportive care (including ICU/mechanical ventilation when needed), plasmapheresis, intravenous immunoglobulin, carnitine, corticosteroids; it is very **important to NOT rechallenge the patient** with the NRTI at all. Once symptoms resolve and lactate level normalizes, can cautiously introduce a regimen containing NRTIs with less potential for mitochondrial toxicity (e.g., ABC, TDF, 3TC, FTC).
- Recovery overall may be prolonged with clinical improvements taking up to 28 weeks; the half-life of mitochondrial DNA is about 5 to 8 weeks

SECTION II: Adverse Events Associated with Potential Long-Term Complications

CARDIOVASCULAR DISEASE RISK

Features

- Onset of premature coronary artery disease (CAD) after a variable period of time (months to years) after HAART initiated
- **Risk Factors**: age, smoking, hypertension, hyperlipidemia, diabetes mellitus, history of prior cardiac disease and/or family history of premature CAD
- Association between insulin resistance and fat redistribution of significant concern regarding increased risk for the development of the CAD risk factor, diabetes mellitus (CROI 8)

Monitoring

- Evaluate risk factors for cardiac disease – resources available to help providers in the determination of CAD risks for their patients (this may help in risk/benefit analysis for starting or changing HAART regimens)

Recommendations for Management

- Secondary preventive measures include *early* diagnosis and treatment of cardiac risk factors as well as a complete assessment of baseline risks
- Emphasize interventions to reduce those modifiable risk factors as part of general health measures (e.g., dietary changes, smoking cessation, exercise)
- Make therapeutic decisions regarding use of HAART or change components of an ongoing regimen accordingly, possibly switching agents from a PI-based regimen and/or d4T to NNRTIs or atazanavir (a protease inhibitor not associated with significant hyperlipidemia). *Though there are data to suggest that use of combination HAART regimens may be independently associated with myocardial infarction, careful cardiovascular risk assessment of individuals who are starting on or currently on HAART is critical.*

HYPERLIPIDEMIA

Features

- Natural history of lipid changes in HIV: early in the course, HDL decreases followed by LDL **decreases;** with progression to AIDS, triglycerides and VLDL increase and later high VLDL triglyceride levels are noted along with further decreases in HDL and total cholesterol levels
- As few as 2 weeks of PI exposure (ritonavir) can induce abnormal lipid changes
- Increases in cholesterol have ranged from 30-77% with different PIs after a 6-month period
- Not only do PIs increase LDL, triglycerides, and total cholesterol but may also decrease HDL
- Risk factors for hypertriglyceridemia: male gender, age > 35, PI use/duration, and prior HAART

Monitoring

- Baseline assessment with **fasting (12 hours)** lipid profile – ideally; evaluation for baseline coronary artery disease risk factors (modifiable) and prognosis
- Follow-up **fasting** lipid profiles every 3 to 6 months – including total cholesterol, LDL and HDL, and triglycerides
- Referral to registered dietitian – baseline and follow-up care
- After either nonpharmacologic or drug therapy is started, it is reasonable to evaluate the lipid profile, especially LDL, at 4 to 6 weeks and again at 3 months
- When the desired level of LDL is reached, total cholesterol (fasting) may be measured every 3 to 4 months with LDL evaluation yearly
- Risk of myopathy ought to be tracked routinely when the patient is on a "statin" drug, especially if the combination of statin and fibrate is used – can be assessed by history, physical, and CPK (if symptomatic)

Recommendations for Management

- Discontinue PI therapy: this is a difficult decision especially in the virologically controlled patient; requires analysis of severity of lipid problems, patient's goals, quality of life, risk for CAD, stage of HIV disease, prior HAART experience, and future drug option(s)
- Multiple "switch" studies indicate improvement in lipid profiles by switching to agents that are less likely associated with inducing hyperlipidemia (overall, studies show an expected 16% reduction in cholesterol and 28% reduction in triglycerides on average 6 months after a switch to nevirapine or abacavir
- Follow **National Cholesterol Education Program (NCEP) Guidelines** (see Table 1 for web address)
- Diet and exercise are clearly underutilized measures

- First choice for drug therapy for isolated increased LDL should include HMG-CoA reductase inhibitor (statin) though limited choice with a number of agents not appropriate because of drug interactions/toxicity – PIs increase circulating statin levels
  - Pravastatin (Pravachol®) metabolized by non-CYP mechanisms and excreted primarily through kidney (no P450 enzyme interaction) – "safest statin" but less potent compared to atorvastatin
  - Use atorvastatin (Lipitor®) with caution (i.e., lower doses)
  - Lovastatin (Mevacor®) and simvastatin (Zocor®) **contraindicated**
- Non-drug approaches initially for isolated hypertriglyceridemia: aggressive dietary interventions, exercise, smoking cessation and decreased alcohol intake.
- Fibrate with subsequent combination use of statins often recommended for triglycerides over 1000 mg/dL – to reduce risk for pancreatitis; start with fibric acid derivatives gemfribozil or fenofibrate (latter with fewer adverse effects)
  - Recent study[9] demonstrated that gemfibrozil exerted a definite but limited (~125 mg/dl) reduction in TGs but no changes observed in total and HDL cholesterol, insulin C-peptide, free fatty acids or fasting glucose or insulin.
- **CAUTION** with the use of "statin" drugs along with fibric acid drugs: a risk exists for *rhabdomyolysis* especially in the setting of hepatic dysfunction, renal failure, concurrent NRTIs. Visit http://www.nlm.nih.gov/medlineplus/ency/article/000473.htm for more information on rhabdomyolysis.
- Niacin: effective but may cause insulin resistance
- *Make therapeutic decisions regarding use of HAART or change components of an ongoing regimen accordingly; as part of this strategy, switching agents from a PI-based regimen and/or d4T to NNRTIs or atazanavir (a protease inhibitor not associated with significant hyperlipidemia)*

INSULIN RESISTANCE/HYPERGLYCEMIA

Features

- Screen for symptoms of diabetes (e.g., dry mouth, polyuria, polydipsia, blurry vision, etc); additionally oral glucose tolerance tests useful to determine spectrum of insulin resistance syndrome
- In patients on PIs, abnormal glucose metabolism ~ 3–25% for hyperglycemia; 16–35% for abnormal glucose tolerance; 4–9% for frank diabetes mellitus
- Use of HAART may "uncover" propensity for hyperglycemic syndromes rather than be causative
- Insulin resistance can be induced *directly* by PI therapy
- Common to see concurrent lipid abnormalities in the patients with documented insulin resistance
- Hepatitis C may lead to Type 2 diabetes mellitus through chronic liver disease
  - Medication related risk for development of insulin resistance/diabetes mellitus may be amplified in these co-infected patients (see Mehta[2] et al)

Monitoring

- Hyperglycemia may occur as early as one month after starting PI
- Measure fasting serum glucose ≥ q 3 month intervals in patients after beginning HAART – especially in those with history of abnormal glucose tolerance and risks for Type 2 diabetes
- Periodic measurement of Hgb A1C in those individuals diagnosed with diabetes *(monitor generally 2 to 4 times/yr)*
- Consider glucose tolerance testing in normoglycemic patients
- If patient has frank diabetes, monitor as you would in an HIV (-) patient

Recommendations for Management

- Multiple "switch" studies indicate reversal of insulin resistance by switching to a "non-nucleoside" agent (NNRTI–e.g., nevirapine, efavirenz)
- Metformin has been shown to reduce insulin resistance by possibly preferentially reducing visceral adipose tissue, *although it should be generally avoided in patients with history of renal insufficiency, hyperlactatemia, transaminitis, or lipoatrophy*
- Diet modification, exercise and weight loss for obese individuals with hyperglycemia
- Treat diabetes as in HIV (-) patients
- Depending on severity of diabetes, insulin may be required and has no significant drug interactions
- Oral hypoglycemic agents to increase insulin sensitivity; possible use of thiazolidinediones; *recommend consultation with endocrinologists as indicated*
- Little data to treat primary insulin resistance in the absence of frank hyperglycemia

BONE DISORDERS

OSTEOPENIA / OSTEOPOROSIS

- Osteoporosis was identified to be a problem by "chance" observation when patients were being evaluated by DEXA scans for body composition
    - Prevalence rates of osteopenia ≤ 30% have been noted
    - *In vitro* studies show PIs can impair conversion of substrate to the active form of vitamin D
    - However, randomized studies evaluating effects of PIs previously suggested that osteopenia may not be related to PI use but rather to mitochondrial toxicity, lipoatrophy, or other cause(s)
    - More recent studies[3] evaluating scores from bone mineral densitometry exams suggest PI-experienced patients had bone demineralization **but** no correlation between such bone changes and lipodystrophy
- Risk factors derived from case-control studies include: prior PCP, possible prior corticosteroid use, a history of advanced HIV (i.e., having had a CD4 rise from a nadir of < 50 cells/mm^3) and presence of lipodystrophy, alcohol use, old age, hyperlipidemia; NB – overall role of antiretrovirals and incidence of osteonecrosis is still debatable (requiring further investigation)
- Avascular necrosis of the hip may be associated with hyperviscosity
- Avascular necrosis of the femoral head is the most common site; other sites include the humeral head, femoral condyle, proximal tibia and the small bones of the hand
- Diagnostic features – pain that is often disabling; CT or MRI scan most specific

Monitoring

- Routine screening for bone demineralization cannot be recommended at this time
- Age specific preventive measures – especially in selected populations (e.g., postmenopausal women who happen to be HIV-positive may benefit from greater scrutiny)

Recommendations for Management

- Medical therapy is often ineffective; analgesics as required; reducing/eliminating ongoing risk factors suggested; reduce weight bearing
- Surgery may be effective – including core decompression (with variable need for bone grafting) in earlier phase(s) of disease; progressive disease may warrant arthroplasty (joint replacement)
- Adequate intake of Vitamin D and calcium along with appropriate weight-bearing exercise should be done as primary prevention of bone demineralization

- If osteoporosis is discovered, then appropriate therapy with standard doses of e.g., *bisphosphonates may be used although the use of this class of drugs is under evaluation at present.* Visit http://www.emedicine.com/med/topic1693.htm#section~treatment for more information.

SECTION III: Adverse Effects Compromising Quality of Life

LIPODYSTROPHY

Definition

- No consensus exists; but understood as a syndrome with physical (body fat changes) and metabolic abnormalities
- Fat redistribution syndrome includes fat accumulation (visceral fat) along with peripheral fat loss (subcutaneous adipose tissue loss)
- Marrakech classification;[1] *newer data may influence both the presence and impact of defined risk factors*
    - **Type 1** – Fat loss "lipoatrophy" (primarily limbs, face and buttocks, vein prominence) – risk factors include treatment duration and age > 40 years; the male gender
    - **Type 2** – Fat accumulation "lipohypertrophy" (primarily buffalo hump, abdominal girth, breast enlargement and gynecomastia, symmetric lipomatosis) – risk factors include female gender, possible viral load <500 cells/mm^3, men > 40 years
    - **Type 3** – Combined forms "lipodystrophy" – risk factors include treatment duration, female gender, age and viral load below detection and metabolic changes
    - **Type 4** – Metabolic alterations without body shape changes – risk factors include male gender; weak association with treatment duration/HIV viral load status

Features

- Approximately 50% (< 40-61%) prevalence in unselected populations; manifestations may vary by gender and race
- Contributory roles for NRTIs (especially d4T: noted to be associated with lipoatrophy in a randomized trial comparing it with ZDV in combination regimens[24]
- Lipoatrophic changes may be due to mitochondrial toxicity especially associated with use of d4T
- Both *lipoatrophy* and *lipohypertrophy* associated with exposure to both NRTIs and PIs
- Normal cortisol levels – not associated with Cushing's syndrome
    - The lipodystrophy "syndrome" that includes the metabolic derangements (i.e., hyperlipidemia and insulin resistance) is also associated with "ectodermal dysplasia" – dry skin/lips, nail dystrophy and alopecia (indinavir, though other agents likely involved)
- HOPS data – showed that duration of antiretroviral therapy overall is correlated with the development of lipodystrophy

Monitoring

- **Early** identification of fat changes, especially lipoatrophy is warranted
- Subjective patient self-assessment, analysis – through questionnaire or numerical scale rating their body self-image
- Routine inquiry at regular medical visits – though imperfect measures of body fat changes, it is likely most practical to periodically assess waist size in men and bra and waist sizes in women. Serial fasting lipid and glucose and insulin levels are recommended. Fasting insulin or C-peptide levels are more sensitive compared to glucose or HbgA1C levels.
- Objective assessments (visit http://www.nhlbi.nih.gov/guidelines/obesity/prctgd_b.pdf for more information):
    - Hip-to-waist circumference ratios, CT/MRI scan of abdomen (at L4-5 levels)

- Serial photographs
- Anthropometric measurements (may necessitate a dietician or nurse)
- Serial BIA measurements – may be used follow body cell mass (BCM) and body fat percent although the results may be of limited use as a result of the influence of lipodystrophy
- Routinely assess psychosocial impact of the symptoms or signs; evaluate overall level of concern through open dialogue

Recommendations for Management

The following is derived from the Hopkins Guide (http://hopkins-hivguide.org/). If related insulin resistance is suspected or diagnosed, see above recommendations — e.g., initiation of metformin

- Resistance / aerobic training
- Recombinant Growth Hormone (rhGH): (exact dose not defined but range can be 3–6 mg qd to qod; max: 0.1 mg/kg/day or 6 mg/d); no evidence of insulin resistance and/or lipoatrophy should be present.
- Timely recognition of the changes is critical; this may prompt discontinuation and/or change in HAART therapies, i.e., if possible, may consider discontinuing PIs or changing to Atazanavir / FPV (if insulin resistance present)
- Cosmetic plastic surgical procedures (e.g., ultrasound guided liposuction for "buffalo hump"); fat reaccumulation may occur
- Rule out breast cancer and consider evaluation for hypogonadism if gynecomastia noted
- Timely recognition of the changes is critical; this may prompt discontinuation and/or change in ARTs (e.g., discontinue D4T before worsening; other options such as 3TC, FTC, ABC, TDF may be useful)
- Dermatologic/plastic surgical procedures may be helpful – i.e., cosmetically poor side effects may occur
- Dietary changes (low fat diet); RD evaluation
- Plastic surgery (not useful for visceral fat); injections with poly-L-lactic acid (Sculptra® recently approved by FDA but very expensive) for facial areas may be helpful
- Encouragement and optimism in patient encounters: more information and clarification likely to occur within the next year
- Patient perception of HAART and its relation to lipodystrophy-associated body habitus alterations can negatively impact quality of life and further treatment decisions including adherence

Conclusion

Finally, it should be recognized that there is a better understanding about the complexity of chronic care of the person living with HIV/AIDS as a result of the search to better define and manage complications of HAART:

- Goals involving patients with chronic HIV illness have to be initially defined and guide subsequent decision making.

- The greater role of a more formal informed consent approach about HAART – with adequate time spent and documentation supporting the risk/benefit discussion, given the overall impact of both mild and serious adverse events during the course of managing HIV illness.

- It is beneficial to have active participation of individuals living with HIV through greater involvement in their own care. Thus it is advisable to encourage patients to stay as informed about their medications, potential side effects and toxicities along with vigilance about reported symptoms as early as they occur.

- The patient and provider taking a very proactive approach to side effect management: up-front discussion, precautionary prescriptions (antiemetics, antidiarrheals, etc.), patient education literature (tailored to language and level of education), contact with a "medication" coach in the patient's life (if available), encouragement of early side-effect reporting and finally nonjudgmental responses to self-reported nonadherence

- Increasing awareness of the role of nutritional assessment, referral to registered dietitians and improving general health habits regardless of complications occurring

- Early detection and efficient management of comorbidities such as addiction disorders, cardiovascular risk modifications, diabetes management, chronic hepatitis, and psychiatric illness.

- Promotion of healthy diet intervention and maintenance along with the common sense benefits of regular exercise (prescription tailored to the patient's disease and CAD risk).

- Paramount attention to quality of life and psychosocial issues including ongoing inquiries into the patient's perception and health beliefs about the medications, HIV disease and the communication process.

Table 1. Key Websites

PROBLEM	RESOURCE
METABOLIC COMPLICATIONS	http://aactg.s-3.com/metabolic/default.htm — AIDS Clinical Trials Group Metabolic Complications guidelines
Lactic acidosis (diagnostic issues and specimen collection)	AACTG LACTIC ACIDOSIS GUIDELINES – available at: http://aactg:cure@aactg.s-3.com/members/download/other/Metabolic/LacAcid.doc
CVD risks	www.chd-taskforce.de/ coronary risk factor analysis (also done in Spanish) Risk Assessment Tool for Estimating 10-year Risk of Developing Hard CHD (Myocardial Infarction and Coronary Death) – available at: http://hin.nhlbi.nih.gov/atpiii/calculator.asp?usertype=prof
Hyperlipidemia in HIV (guidelines)	http://www.nhlbi.nih.gov/guidelines/cholesterol/ (NCEP Guidelines) http://www.aace.com/clin/guidelines/lipids.pdf (American Association for Clinical Endocrinologists – clinical practice guidelines – for dyslipidemia)
Diabetes management	http://www.aace.com/clin/guidelines/diabetes_2002.pdf (American Association for Clinical Endocrinologists – clinical practice guidelines – for diabetes)
Osteopenic syndromes	www.rad.washington.edu/mskbook/osteonecrosis.html (diagnosis/staging/tx)
Fat redistribution	http://aactg:cure@aactg.s-3.com/members/psmet.htm – assessment

References

1. Galli M, Veglia F, Angarano G, et al. Risk factors associated with types of metabolic and morphological alterations according to the Marrakech classification. 2nd International Workshop on Adverse Drug Reactions and Lipodystrophy in HIV, Toronto, Ontario, Canada, September 13–15, 2000; Abstract P61.

2. Mehta SH, Brancati FL, Sulkowski MS, Strathdee SA, Szklo M, Thomas DL. Prevalence of type 2 diabetes mellitus among persons with hepatitis C virus infection in the United States. *Annals of Internal Medicine*. October 17, 2000; 133(8):592–599.

3. Tebas P, Powderly WG, Claxton S, et al. Accelerated bone mineral loss in HIV-infected patients receiving potent antiretroviral therapy. *AIDS*. 2000; 14:F63–F67.

4. Tietz, N, ed. *Textbook of Clinical Chemistry*. Philadelphia, PA: W. B. Saunders, 1986. 817.

5. Guidelines for the use of antiretroviral agents in HIV-infected adults and adolescents — April 07, 2005; Panel on Clinical Practices for Treatment of HIV Infection (convened by DHHS). Available at: http://aidsinfo.nih.gov/guidelines/default_db2.asp?id=50.

6. Friis-Mýller N, Sabin CA, Weber R, et al, for the Data Collection on Adverse Events of Anti-HIV Drugs (DAD) Study Group. Combination antiretroviral therapy and the risk of myocardial infarction. *NEJM* 2003; 349:1993–2003.

7. Preliminary guidelines for the evaluation and management of dyslipidemia in adults infected with human immunodeficiency virus and receiving antiretroviral therapy: Recommendations of the Adult AIDS Clinical Trial Group Cardiovascular Disease Focus Group. Adult AIDS Clinical Trial Group Cardiovascular Disease Focus Group. *CID*. November 2000; 31(5):1216–1224.

8. Pasternak RC et al. ACC/AHA/NHLBI clinical advisory on statins. *JACC* (Vol. 40, No. 3). August 7, 2002:567–572.

9. Miller J, Carr A, Brown D, Cooper D. A randomised, double-blind study of gemfibrozil (GF) for the treatment of protease inhibitor-associated hypertriglyceridaemia. Available at: http://www.retroconference.org/2001/Abstracts/Abstracts/Abstracts/540.htm.

10. Diabetes Medical Guidelines Task Force (American Association of Clinical Endocrinologists and the American College of Endocrinology). The American Association of Clinical Endocrinologists medical guidelines for the management of diabetes mellitus: The AACE system of intensive diabetes self-management—2002 update. *Endocrine Practice* (Vol. 8, Suppl. 1) January/February 2002.

11. ADA. Tests of Glycemia in Diabetes [Position Statement]. *Diabetes Care*. 1999, (S1), 7779. Available at: http://diabetes.bio-rad.com/html/story.html#testing.

12. Thomas J, Doherty SM. HIV infection—A risk factor for osteoporosis. *JAIDS*. H33(3):281–291. July 1, 2003.

13. Glesby MJ. Bone disorders in human immunodeficiency virus infection *CID*. 2003; 37(Suppl 2):S91–S95.

14. Hobar C. Osteoporosis. Emedicine.com. Available at: http://www.emedicine.com/med/topic1693.htm#section~treatment.

15. NHLBI Obesity Education Initiative Expert Panel on the Identification, Evaluation, and Treatment of Overweight and Obesity in Adults. The practical guide to identification, evaluation, and treatment of overweight and obesity in adults. NIH Publication Number 00-4084. October 2000. Available at: http://www.nhlbi.nih.gov/guidelines/obesity/prctgd_b.pdf .

16. Schwenk A, Breuer P, Kremer G, Ward L. Clinical assessment of HIV-associated lipodystrophy syndrome: bioelectrical impedance analysis, anthropometry and clinical scores. *Clin Nutr*. June 2001;20(3):243–249.

17. Bartlett, J. Pocket guide to adult HIV/AIDS treatment. January 2005. Available at: http://hopkins-aids.edu/publications/pocketguide/pocketgd0105.pdf .

18. Bartlett J. Johns Hopkins HIV guide. Lipodystrophy and Metabolic Complications by J. Cofrancesco. Available at: http://hopkins-hivguide.org/ .

19. Kotler D. Lipodystrophy: What is going on? *PRN Notebook*. March 2005 (Vol. 10, No. 1) Available at: http://www.prn.org/prn_nb_cntnt/vol10/num1/kotler_frm.htm.

20. Passalaris JD, Sepkowitz KA, Glesby MJ. Coronary artery disease and human immunodeficiency virus. *CID*. 2000; 31:787–797.

21. Dube MP, et al. Preliminary guidelines for the evaluation and management of dyslipidemia in HIV-infected adults receiving antiretroviral therapy. Recommendations of the Adult ACTG Cardiovascular Disease Focus Group. *CID*. 2000;31:1216–1224.

22. Dube MP. Disorders of glucose metabolism in patients infected with human immunodeficiency virus. *CID*. 2000; 31:1467–1475.

23. Grinspoon S, Carr A. Cardiovascular risk and body-fat abnormalities in HIV-infected adults. *NEJM*. 352; 48–62.

24. Joly V, Flandre P, Meiffredy V, et al. Assessment of lipodystrophy in patients previously exposed to AZT, ddI, or ddC, but naive for d4T and protease inhibitors, and randomized between 36 d4T/3TC/indinavir and AZT/3TC/indinavir (NOVAVIR trial). 8th Conference on Retroviruses and Opportunistic Infections. February 4–8, 2001. Chicago. Abstract 539.

Section III

Systemic Manifestations

10

Gastrointestinal Manifestations of HIV

Sandra G. Gompf, MD, FACP
Assistant Clinical Professor, Division of Infectious and Tropical Diseases
University of South Florida College of Medicine, Tampa
Section Chief, James A. Haley Veterans Hospital, Tampa

Esophageal Disease Causing Dysphagia and/or Odynophagia

CANDIDA (Also see Chapter 19, Fungal Infections)

- Most common cause of esophageal symptoms
- Infrequently associated with fever
- Empiric diagnosis and treatment acceptable, especially with a triad of thrush, odynophagia, and CD4 ≤ 100 cells/mm^3
- Definitive diagnosis through endoscopy if empiric treatment fails
- **Treatment**
    - Fluconazole 200 mg po qd, up to 800 mg qd, for 3 weeks
    - Optimize antiretroviral therapy/reconstitute immunity
- Maintenance for frequent recurrences with fluconazole 200 mg po qd; alternative includes itraconazole 100-200mg/d oral solution,
- Fluconazole-refractory candidiasis is possible with recurrent treatment AND continuous suppression (no advantage to either); treatment alternatives:
    - Itraconazole $\geq$200mg/d po bid
    - Voriconazole 200mg po bid
    - Caspofungin 70mg x 1, then 50mg/d IV
    - IV Amphotericin B 0.3-0.7 mg/kg IV qd for 10 to 14 days
    - Consider antifungal susceptibility testing

CYTOMEGALOVIRUS (Also see Chapter 18, Cytomegalovirus Infection)

- Usually focal pain associated with fever
- Biopsy of erythema, erosions, or ulcers required
- Culture not recommended secondary to high rate of false positives
- **Treatment**
    - Valganciclovir 900mg po bid for 2-3 weeks **or**
    - Ganciclovir 5 mg/kg IV bid for 2-3 weeks **or**
    - Foscarnet 40-60 mg/kg q 8h for 2-3 weeks
- Maintenance treatment if recurs with IV, ganciclovir, or oral valganciclovir

HERPES SIMPLEX VIRUS (Also see Chapter 17, Sexually Transmitted Diseases)

- Often associated with oral ulcerations
- Usually focal pain with infrequent fever
- Brush, biopsy or culture of erythema, or ulcerations or erosions necessary for diagnosis
- **Treatment**
    - Acyclovir 200-800 mg po 5x/d or 5-10 mg/kg IV q8h for 10 days
- Maintenance treatment for recurrences with acyclovir 200-400 mg po 3-5x daily or
    - Valacyclovir 1000 mg po bid x 7-10 d first episode; 500 mg po bid x 3d for recurrences
    - Maintenance with 500 mg – 1000 mg qd

APHTHOUS ULCERS

- Usually focal pain with infrequent association of fever
- Diagnosis based on negative studies for Candida, HSV, CMV, and other pathogens via biopsy, brushing or culture
- **Treatment**
    - Prednisone 40 mg po qd for 7 to 14 days, then taper 10 mg/wk or slower
    - Thalidomide 200 mg po qd (requires provider and patient registration in the System for Thalidomide Education and Prescribing Safety (S.T.E.P.S) program via the manufacturer, Celegene, at 1-888-4-Celgene. For more information visit:
      http://www.celgene.com/steps/index.htm

OTHER CAUSES

- Drug-induced
    - AZT
    - ddC
- Infection
    - M. avium
    - TB
    - Cryptosporidia
    - P. carinii
    - Primary HIV infection
    - Histoplasmosis

- Tumor
  - ◆ Kaposi's sarcoma
  - ◆ Lymphoma
  - ◆ Medication or food related
  - ◆ Gastroesophageal reflux disease (heartburn + regurgitation and dysphagia)
  - ◆ Opportunistic infection or tumor
    - Common
      - · Candida sp.
    - Less common
      - · HSV, CMV, idiopathic (aphthous)
    - Rare
      - · TB, *M. avium*, histoplasmosis, PCP, cryptosporidia, Kaposi's sarcoma, lymphoma

Figure 1. Odynophagia in Patients with AIDS

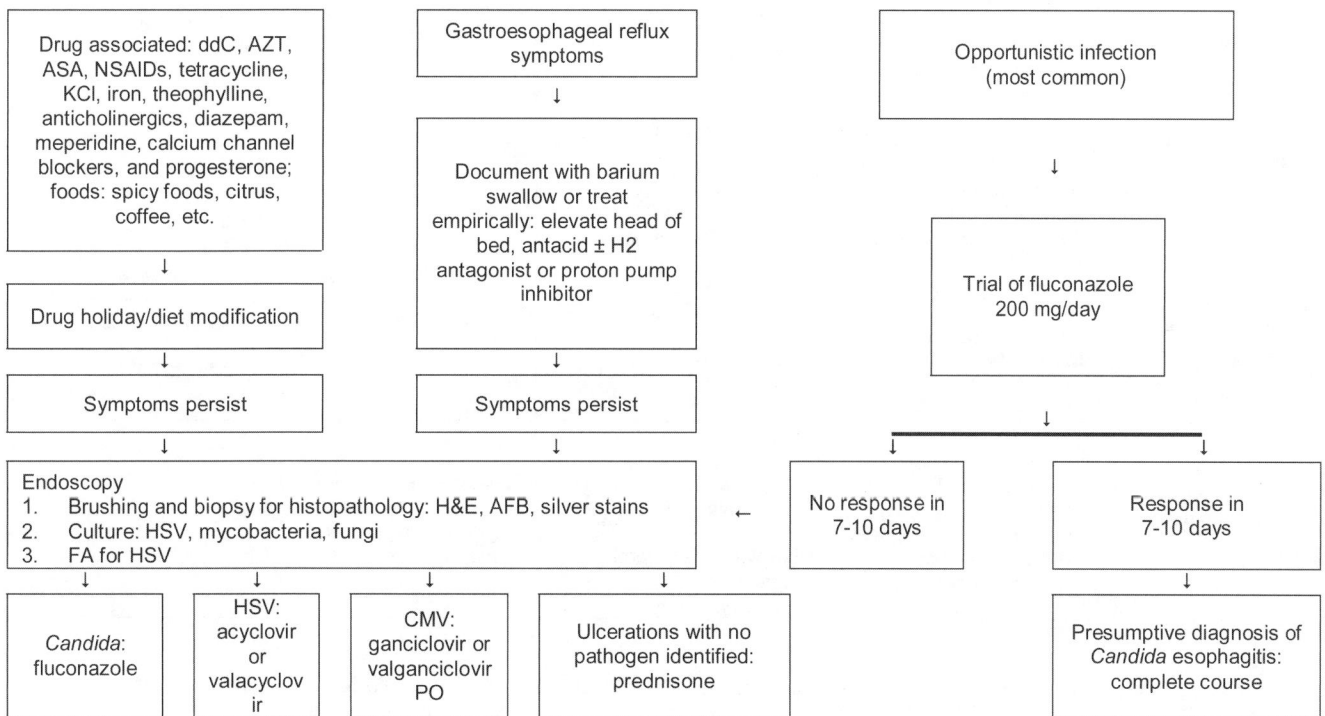

Drug associated: ddC, AZT, ASA, NSAIDs, tetracycline, KCl, iron, theophylline, anticholinergics, diazepam, meperidine, calcium channel blockers, and progesterone; foods: spicy foods, citrus, coffee, etc.	Gastroesophageal reflux symptoms	Opportunistic infection (most common)
↓	↓	↓
Drug holiday/diet modification	Document with barium swallow or treat empirically: elevate head of bed, antacid ± H2 antagonist or proton pump inhibitor	Trial of fluconazole 200 mg/day
↓	↓	↓
Symptoms persist	Symptoms persist	No response in 7-10 days / Response in 7-10 days

Endoscopy
1. Brushing and biopsy for histopathology: H&E, AFB, silver stains
2. Culture: HSV, mycobacteria, fungi
3. FA for HSV

Candida: fluconazole	HSV: acyclovir or valacyclovir	CMV: ganciclovir or valganciclovir PO	Ulcerations with no pathogen identified: prednisone	Presumptive diagnosis of *Candida* esophagitis: complete course

Table 1. Esophageal Disease in Patients with AIDS [1]

	CANDIDA	CYTOMEGALOVIRUS (CMV)	HERPES SIMPLEX VIRUS (HSV)	APHTHOUS ULCERS
Frequency as cause of symptoms	50-70%	10-20%	2-5%	10-20%
CLINICAL FEATURES				
Dysphagia	+++	+	+	+
Odynophagia	++	+++	+++	+++
Thrush	50-70%	< 25%	< 25%	< 25%
Oral ulcers	Rare	Uncommon	Often	Uncommon
Pain	Diffuse	Focal	Focal	Focal
Fever	Infrequent	Often	Infrequent	Infrequent
DIAGNOSIS (SEE NOTES 2–4 BELOW)				
Endoscopy	Usually treated empirically Pseudomembranous plaques, may involve entire esophagus	Biopsy required for treatment Erythema and erosions/ulcers single or multiple discrete lesions, often distal	Biopsy required for treatment Erythema and erosions/ulcers usually small, coalescing, shallow	Similar in appearance and location to CMV ulcers
Microbiology	Brush: yeast and pseudomycelia on KOH prep or PAS See footnote 4 Culture with sensitivities may be useful with suspected resistance	Biopsy: intracellular inclusions and/or positive culture; Highest yield with histopath of biopsy and culture. Culture is often not recommended due to false positives	Brush/biopsy: intracytoplasmic inclusions/multinucleate giant cells, FA stain, and/or positive culture	Negative studies for *Candida*, HSV, CMV, and other diagnoses
TREATMENT				
Acute	Fluconazole 200 mg/day po; up to 800 mg/day Ketoconazole 200-400/day po Ampho B 0.3-0.7 mg/kg IV Efficacy of fluconazole is 85% (*Ann Int Med* 1993;118:825); see footnote 5 See footnote 6 if refractory disease	Valganciclovir 900 mg po BID for 2-3 weeks Ganciclovir 5 mg/kg IV bid x 2 to 3 weeks Foscarnet 40-60 mg/kg IV q8h x 2-3 weeks Efficacy of antiviral treatment is 75%	Acyclovir 200-800 mg po 5x/day or 5 mg/kg IV q8h x 2-3 weeks	Prednisone 40 mg/day po x 7–14 days, then taper 10 mg/week or slower Thalidomide 200 mg/day po (*BJM* 1989;298:432; *J Infect Dis* 1999;180:61)
Maintenance	Fluconazole 100–200 mg/day po (indicated with frequent or severe recurrences) Lower dose or less frequent dosing may induce resistance development	Maintenance treatment arbitrary May await relapse; then ganciclovir, 5 mg/kg/day IV Possible role for oral ganciclovir or valganciclovir	Maintenance treatment arbitrary: acyclovir 200–400 mg po 3–5x daily	

NOTES:

1. One-third of AIDS patients develop esophageal symptoms (*Gut* 1989;30:1033). Esophageal ulcers are usually due to CMV (45%), or they are idiopathic/aphthous ulcers (40%); HSV accounts for only 5% (*Ann Intern Med* 1995;122:143).

2. Diagnostic studies may include barium swallow, but diagnostic yield is low (20-30%) compared with esophagoscopy; with endoscopy a diagnosis is established in about 70-95% (*Arch Intern Med* 1991;151:1567). Response to empiric treatment often precludes need for endoscopic diagnosis of fungal esophagitis.

3. Other diagnostic considerations: drug-induced dysphagia (*Am J Med* 1988;88:512), including AZT (*Ann Intern Med* 1990;162:65) and ddC; infection, including *M. avium*, TB, cryptosporidia, *P. carinii*, primary HIV infection (acute retroviral syndrome), histoplasmosis; and tumor, including KS or lymphoma (*BMJ* 1988;296:92; *Gastrointest Endosc* 1986;32:96).

4. Esophageal brushing: nonendoscopic method to establish the diagnosis of candida esophagitis. Procedure is: pharyngeal anesthesia ➡ 16 French nasogastral tube inserted to distal esophagus ➡ sheathed sterile brush extended through tube ➡ brushing is done during withdrawal ➡ brushings for cytopath and fungal stain (*Arch Intern Med* 1991;151:1567; *Gastrointest Endosc* 1989;35:102). This procedure is inadequate to establish other diagnoses.

5. Fluconazole is the preferred treatment for *Candida* because of established efficacy, more predictable absorption, and fewer drug interactions compared with ketoconazole and itraconazole.

6. Fluconazole-refractory candidiasis is possible with recurrent treatment OR continuous suppression (no advantage to either); treatment alternatives include itraconazole ≥200mg/d, voriconazole 200mg PO BID, caspofungin 70mg x 1, then 50mg/d IV, or IV Amphotericin B 0.3-0.7 mg/kg IV qd for 10 to 14 days; consider antifungal susceptibility testing.

Diarrhea

- Occurs in up to 80% of persons with AIDS
- An infectious cause can be identified in 60–80% of cases
- Motility disorders and bacterial overgrowth may be factors in the cause of diarrhea when no other pathogen is identified.

Figure 2. Diagnostic Algorithm for Acute* Diarrhea

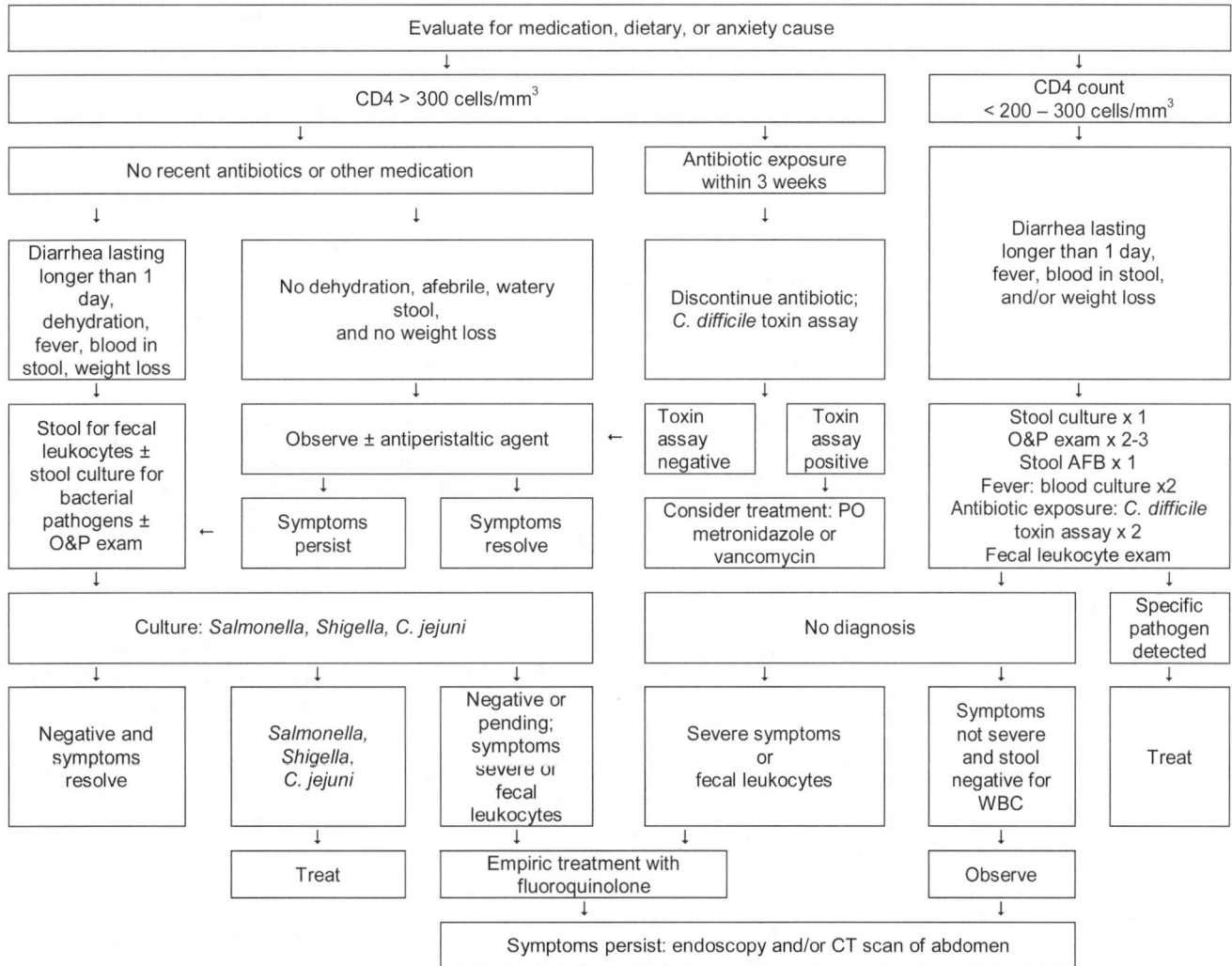

Evaluate for medication, dietary, or anxiety cause

```
                                                                    ↓                                    ↓
┌─────────────────────────────────────────────────────────┐  ┌──────────────────────┐
│            CD4 > 300 cells/mm³                           │  │     CD4 count          │
│                                                          │  │  < 200 – 300 cells/mm³ │
└─────────────────────────────────────────────────────────┘  └──────────────────────┘
        ↓                           ↓               ↓                    ↓
```

No recent antibiotics or other medication	Antibiotic exposure within 3 weeks	Diarrhea lasting longer than 1 day, fever, blood in stool, and/or weight loss

Diarrhea lasting longer than 1 day, dehydration, fever, blood in stool, weight loss	No dehydration, afebrile, watery stool, and no weight loss	Discontinue antibiotic; *C. difficile* toxin assay	

Stool for fecal leukocytes ± stool culture for bacterial pathogens ± O&P exam	←	Observe ± antiperistaltic agent	Toxin assay negative	Toxin assay positive	←	Stool culture x 1 O&P exam x 2-3 Stool AFB x 1 Fever: blood culture x2 Antibiotic exposure: *C. difficile* toxin assay x 2 Fecal leukocyte exam

		Symptoms persist	Symptoms resolve	Consider treatment: PO metronidazole or vancomycin	

Culture: *Salmonella, Shigella, C. jejuni*	No diagnosis	Specific pathogen detected

Negative and symptoms resolve	*Salmonella, Shigella, C. jejuni*	Negative or pending; symptoms severe or fecal leukocytes	Severe symptoms or fecal leukocytes	Symptoms not severe and stool negative for WBC	Treat

	Treat	Empiric treatment with fluoroquinolone		Observe	

Symptoms persist: endoscopy and/or CT scan of abdomen

*Defined as ≥ 3 loose or watery stools for 3 to 10 days.

Table 2. Acute Diarrhea in Patients with AIDS

AGENT	FREQUENCY*	CLINICAL FEATURES	DIAGNOSIS	TREATMENT
Campylobacter jejuni	4–8%	Watery diarrhea or bloody flux Fever Fecal leukocytes variable Any CD4 count	Stool culture Most labs cannot detect *C. cinaedi, C. fennelli*, etc.	Erythromycin 500 mg po qid x ≥ 5 days
Clostridium difficile	10–15%	Watery diarrhea Fecal WBCs variable Fever and leukocytosis common Antibacterial agent nearly always, especially clindamycin, ampicillin, and cephalosporins Any CD4 count	Endoscopy: PMC, colitis, or normal Stool toxin assay: tissue culture or EIA preferred CT scan: colitis with thickened mucosa	Withdraw offending antibiotic if possible Metronidazole 250 mg po qid or 500 mg po tid x 10–14 days Vancomycin 125 mg po qid x 10–14 days Antiperistaltic agents (Lomotil® or loperamide) are contraindicated
Enteric viruses	15–30%	Watery diarrhea Acute, but 1/3 become chronic Any CD4 count	Major agents: adenovirus, astrovirus, picornavirus, Calicivirus (*N. Engl J Med* 1993;329:14) Clinical labs cannot detect these viruses	Supportive treatment: Lomotil® or loperamide
Idiopathic	25–40%	Variable noninfectious causes Rule out medications, dietary, irritable bowel syndrome Any CD4 count	Negative studies including culture, O&P exam, and *C. difficile* toxin assay	Severe acute diarrhea: Ciprofloxacin 500 mg po bid or ofloxacin 200-300 mg po bid x 5 days ± metronidazole (*Arch Intern Med* 1990;150-541; *Ann Intern Med* 1992;117:202; *Clin Infect Dis* 2001;32:331)
Salmonella	5–15%	Watery diarrhea Fever Fecal WBCs variable Any CD4 count	Stool culture Blood culture	Ciprofloxacin 500 mg po bid x 14 days TMP-SMX 1-2 DS po bid x 14 days 3rd generation cephalosporin such as cefotaxime 4-8 g IV/day divided q4–8h x 14 days or ceftriaxone 2 g IV/day x 14 days Treatment may need to be extended to ≥ 4 weeks
Shigella	1–3%	Watery diarrhea or bloody flux Fever Fecal WBCs common Any CD4 count	Stool culture	Ciprofloxacin 500 mg po bid x 3 days TMP-SMX 1 DS po bid x 3 days
Yersinia	-	Watery diarrhea	Stool culture	TMP-SMZ 1 DS po BID x 14 days Ciprofloxacin 500 mg po bid x 14 days Doxycycline + aminoglycoside if bacteremia

*Among patients with acute diarrhea

Figure 3. Diagnostic Algorithm for Chronic* Diarrhea (CD4 Count < 300 Cells/mm^3)

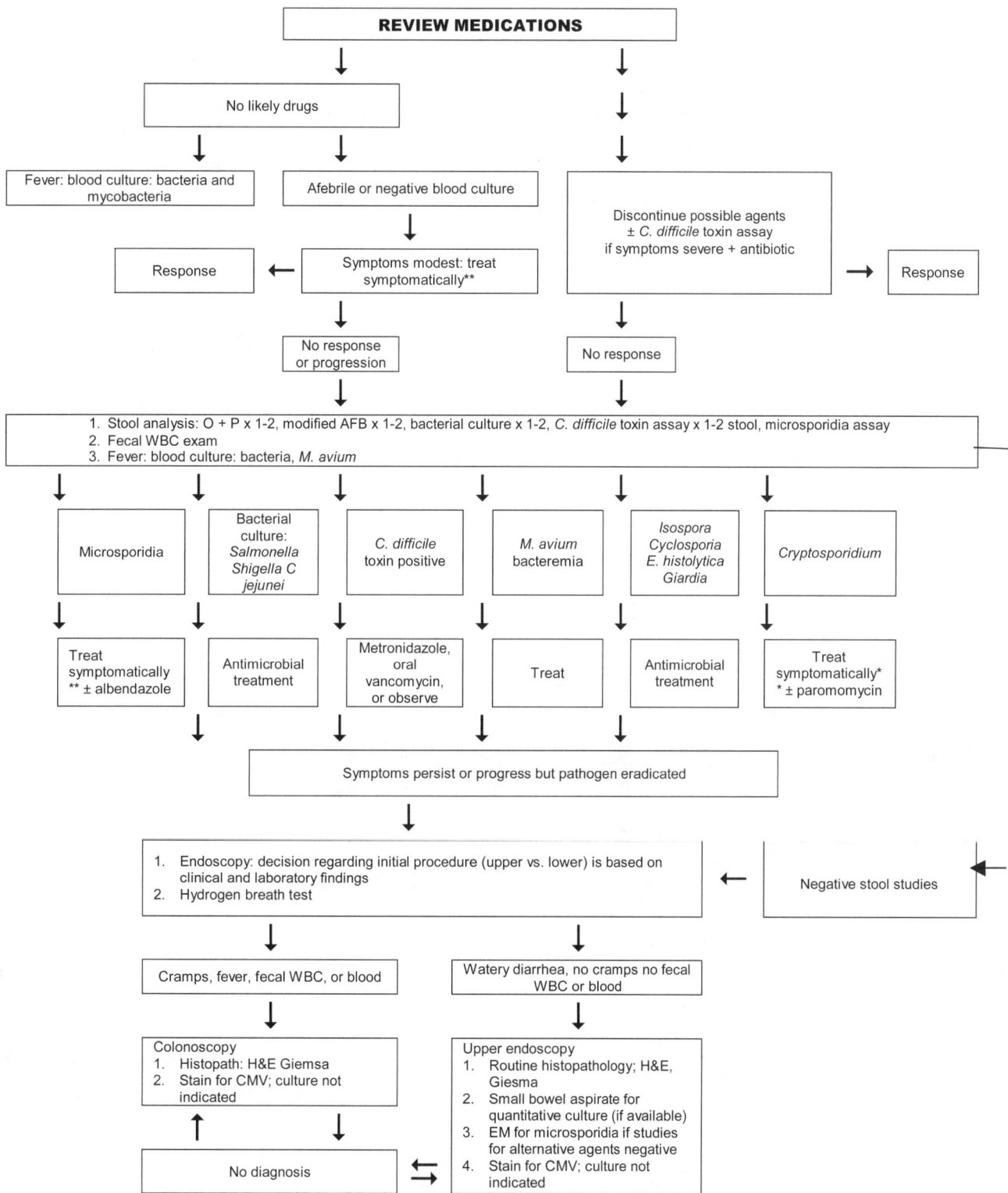

REVIEW MEDICATIONS

No likely drugs

Fever: blood culture: bacteria and mycobacteria

Afebrile or negative blood culture

Discontinue possible agents ± *C. difficile* toxin assay if symptoms severe + antibiotic

Response

Symptoms modest: treat symptomatically**

Response

No response or progression

No response

1. Stool analysis: O + P x 1-2, modified AFB x 1-2, bacterial culture x 1-2, *C. difficile* toxin assay x 1-2 stool, microsporidia assay
2. Fecal WBC exam
3. Fever: blood culture: bacteria, *M. avium*

Microsporidia

Bacterial culture: *Salmonella Shigella C jejunei*

C. difficile toxin positive

M. avium bacteremia

Isospora Cyclosporia E. histolytica Giardia

Cryptosporidium

Treat symptomatically ** ± albendazole

Antimicrobial treatment

Metronidazole, oral vancomycin, or observe

Treat

Antimicrobial treatment

Treat symptomatically* * ± paromomycin

Symptoms persist or progress but pathogen eradicated

1. Endoscopy: decision regarding initial procedure (upper vs. lower) is based on clinical and laboratory findings
2. Hydrogen breath test

Negative stool studies

Cramps, fever, fecal WBC, or blood

Watery diarrhea, no cramps no fecal WBC or blood

Colonoscopy
1. Histopath: H&E Giemsa
2. Stain for CMV; culture not indicated

Upper endoscopy
1. Routine histopathology; H&E, Giesma
2. Small bowel aspirate for quantitative culture (if available)
3. EM for microsporidia if studies for alternative agents negative
4. Stain for CMV; culture not indicated

No diagnosis

* Defined as > 2–3 loose or watery stools/day for ≥ 30 days.
** Frequent small feedings, bland foods, avoid caffeine; low-lactose, low-fat, high-fiber diet. Supplement with polymeric formulas and antiperistaltic agents (loperamide or Lomotil® progressing to tincture of opium or octreotide) as necessary.

Table 3. Chronic Infectious Diarrhea in Patients with AIDS

AGENT	FREQUENCY*	CLINICAL FEATURES	DIAGNOSIS	TREATMENT
Cryptosporidia	10–30%	Enteritis Watery diarrhea No fecal WBCs Fever variable Malabsorption Wasting Large stool volume with abdominal pain Remitting symptoms for months CD4 < 200 CD4 < 150 is associated with recurrent or chronic disease	AFB smear of stool to show oocyst of 4–6 μm	Paromomycin 1000 mg bid or 500 mg po bid x 7 days; efficacy is marginal Best results are with HAART Nitazoxanide 1000 mg/day (not FDA-approved) Azithromycin 600 mg/day + paromomycin (above doses) x ≥ 4 weeks Nutritional support plus Lomotil®; may require parenteral hyperalimentation
Cyclospora cayetanensis	< 1%	Enteritis Watery diarrhea CD4 count < 100 cells/mm^3	Stool AFB smear: resembles cryptosporidia	TMP-SMX 1 DS bid x 3 days
Cytomegalovirus	15–40%	Colitis and/or enteritis Fecal WBC and/or blood Cramps Fever Watery diarrhea ± blood May cause perforation Hemorrhage, toxic megacolon, ulceration CD4 < 50	Biopsy to show intranuclear inclusion bodies, preferably with inflammation, vasculitis CT scan: segmental or pancolitis ± enteritis	Valganciclovir 900 mg po BID x 3 weeks, then 900mg po qd Ganciclovir 5 mg/kg IV bid x 2-3 weeks, then 5 mg/kg/day Foscarnet 40-60 mg/kg IV q8h 2 x weeks, then 90 mg/kg/day Results of treatment variable (*Ann Intern Men* 1990;112:505; *J Infect Dis* 1993;167:278); foscarnet and ganciclovir are equally effective (*J Infect Dis* 1995;172:622)
Entamoeba histolytica	1–3%	Colitis Bloody stools Cramps No fecal WBCs (bloody stools) Most are asymptomatic carriers Any CD4 count	Stool O&P exam	Metronidazole 750 mg po or IV tid x 5–10 days + iodoquinol (diiodohydroxyquin) 650 mg po tid x 20 days or metronidazole + paromomycin 500 mg po qid x 7 days
Giardia lamblia	1–3%	Enteritis Watery diarrhea ± malabsorption, bloating Flatulence Any CD4 count	Stool O&P exam	Metronidazole 250 mg po tid x 10 days
Idiopathic (pathogen-negative)	20–30%	Usually low-volume diarrhea that resolves spontaneously or is controlled with antimotility agents (*Gut* 195;36:283) Typically not associated with significant weight loss and often resolves spontaneously	Biopsy shows villus atrophy, cryptosporidium hyperplasia/no identifiable cause despite endoscopy with biopsy and EM for microsporidia (*Clin Infect Dis* 1992;15:726) These histologic changes are unlikely to explain diarrhea since they are seen in symptom-free persons with HIV (*Lancet* 1996;348:379) with pathogen-negative persistent large volume diarrhea, must rule out KS and lymphoma	Supportive care: Lomotil® or loperamide, nutritional support.
Isospora belli	1–3%	Enteritis Watery diarrhea No fecal WBCs No Fever Wasting Malabsorption CD4 < 100	AFB smear of stool Oocytes: 20-30 μm	TMP-SMX 2 DS po bid x 2-4 weeks Pyrimethamine 50–75 mg/day po + leucovorin po 5–10 mg/day for 1 month
Microsporidia *Enterocytozoon bieneusi Enterocytozoon intestinalis*	15–30%	Enteritis Watery diarrhea No fecal WBCs Fever uncommon Remitting disease over months Malabsorption Wasting CD4 < 100	Special trichrome stain described (*N Engl J Med* 1992;326:326:161) Calcofluor stain	E. intestinalis: Albendazole 400-800 mg po bid or metronidazole 500mg tid x ≥ 3 weeks E. bieneusi: fumagillin 60mg po qd for 14 days found effective (*N Engl J Med* 2002;346:1963-69); not FDA approved
Mycobacterium avium complex	10–20%	Enteritis Watery diarrhea No fecal WBCs Fever and wasting common Diffuse abdominal pain in late stage CD4 < 50	Positive blood cultures for *M. avium* complex; biopsy may show changes such as Whipple's disease, but with AFB CT scan may b supportive: hepatosplenomegaly, adenopathy, and thickened small bowel	Clarithromycin 500 mg po bid + ethambutol 15 mg/kg/day Azithromycin 600 mg/day + ethambutol 15 mg/kg/day ± rifabutin 300 mg/day (caution regarding interaction of rifabutin with NNRTIs and PIs)

* Frequency among patients with advanced HIV infection and chronic diarrhea defined as > 2–3 loose or watery stools/day for ≥ 30 days.

Table 4. Percentage of GI Side Effects by Drug

	RETROVIR® (zidovudine, AZT, ZDV)	VIDEX® (didanosine, ddI)	HIVID® (zalcitabine, ddC)	EPIVIR® (lamivudine, 3TC)	ZERIT® (stavudine, d4T)	EMTRIVA® (emtricitabine, FTC)	VIRAMUNE® (nevirapine, NVP)	RESCRIPTOR® (delavirdine, DLV)	SUSTIVA® (efavirenz, EFV)	KALETRA® (lopinavir/ritonavir, KAL)	NORVIR® (ritonavir, RTV)	VIRACEPT® (nelfinavir, NFV)	FORTOVASE® (saquinavir-SGC, SQV)	CRIXIVAN® (indinavir, IDV)	REYATAZ® (atazanavir, ATV)	LEXIVA® (fosamprenvir)
Anorexia	11	10-13		10						< 2	2-8	< 2		2.7		
Diarrhea	12	1-13	2.5	18	50	23	4	11-17	2	10-20	16-24	11-18	15-17	3.3	6-8	34
Dyspepsia	5			5		4-8		< 2	>	< 2	0-5	1-3	8	1.5		
Abdominal Pain	2	0-2	3	9		8-14	3	< 2	2	1-4	6-8	< 2	2-8	16.6	6	5
Januindice															7-8	1.5-2.1%
Nausea	46	31-43	3.4	33	39	13-18	15	3	2	< 2	25-30	1-3	11-18	11.7	10-16	39
Vomiting	6	31-43	3.4	13	39	9	5	< 2	2	< 2	14-18	< 2	1-4	8.4	6	16
Stomatitis		1-6	3	13			1	< 2				< 2				
Abn. LFT		0-3	8.9	1-2	11-13		3-5	< 2	3	1-10	8-10	< 2	1-6	4.9*	2**	6
Pancreatitis			1.1									< 2				
↑Amylase		3		2-3	14				10	2-5			2	2.1		

*11.9% incidence of elevated bilirubin, **35% incidence of elevated bilirubin
SOURCE: Data obtained from 2004 *PDR*
(Note: data obtained is often from clinical trials using combined ARV therapies)

Biliary Tract Disease

Acute cholecystitis	• Usually acalculous and can occur with systemic toxicity
	• Etiologic agents:
	   - CMV
	   - Candida species
	   - Cryptosporidia
	   - Microsporidia
	• Diagnosis:
	   - HIDA scan

Papillary stenosis	• Recurrent episodes of RUQ pain accompanied by transient liver function test abnormalities with or without common bile duct (CBD) dilatation on ultrasonography
	• ERCP confirms diagnosis
	• Etiologic agents:
	   - CMV
	   - Cryptosporidia

Sclerosing cholangitis	• Can involve CBD alone, CBD + ampulla, CBD + intrahepatic ducts, or intrahepatic ducts alone
	• RUQ pain and an elevated alkaline phosphatase
	• ERCP confirms diagnosis
	• Etiologic agents:
	   - CMV
	   - Cryptosporidia

References

1. Libman H, Witzburg R. *HIV Infection – A clinical manual*, 2nd ed. NY: Little, Brown and Company, 1993.

2. Bartlett JG, Merigan T, Bolognesi D, eds. *Textbook of AIDS Medicine*. Baltimore, MD: Williams & Wilkins, 1999.

3. Bartlett JG, Gallant JE, eds. *Medical Management of HIV*. JHU ID @ Lighthouse Point, 2004. Available at http://hopkins-aids.edu/publications/publications.html.

4. Pappas PG, Rex JH, Sobel JD et al. IDSA guidelines for treatment of candidiasis. *CID*. 2004:38:161–189.

5. *Physician's Desk Reference*, 58th ed. Stamford, CT: Thomson Healthcare, 2004.

11

Hematologic Complications

Eknath Naik, MD, PhD
Director, USF-India Center for HIV/AIDS, HEALTH Research and Training
Assistant Professor in Global Health and Internal Medicine
University of South Florida, Tampa

Adapted with permission from Medscape HIV/AIDS http://www.medscape.com/viewprogram/669_pnt.
©2002;Medscape Inc.

Introduction

Hematologic complications of AIDS, which include cytopenias of all major cell lines, were recognized shortly after the first description of AIDS cases. Anemia is found to occur at any stage of HIV disease; however, it's more common with advanced disease.[1,2,4,5] In one study, anemia was found in 70% of patients with AIDS while neutropenia and thrombocytopenia was present in 50% and 40% of patients respectively. [1] As many as 10% of patients present with thrombocytopenia as a first clinical sign.[1,2,3] The etiologies of cytopenias in HIV are varied and will be discussed in this chapter along with diagnostic approaches and treatment strategies.

Effect of HIV on Hematopoiesis

HEMATOPOIETIC PROGENITOR CELLS (CFU-GEMM)

- There is great controversy concerning whether the CFU-GEMM (Colony Forming Unit-Granulocyte, Erythrocyte, Monocyte, and Megakaryocyte) itself can be infected by HIV.
- While results have been conflicting, a mechanism for HIV infection of CD34+ progenitor cells is apparent: as these cells have been shown to carry both the CD4 receptor and the CXCR4 (fusin) coreceptor necessary for HIV-1 viral entry.[8,9] Some degree of infection may occur, leading to the potential for abnormal hematopoiesis.[5,7]
- It is also recognized that the degree and magnitude of CFU-GEMM infection must be relatively minor, as consistent evidence of infection has not been demonstrated, even after extensive study.[6,7,9,10]
- Numerous defects in the growth of committed progenitor cells may occur in the setting of HIV infection.
- As a result of cell surface interactions with the HIV envelope proteins gp 120/160, decreased colony growth of BFU-E, CFU-GM (Colony Forming Unit-Granulocyte Macrophage), CFU-G (Colony

Forming Unit-Granulocyte), and CFU-M (Colony Forming Unit-Macrophage) have all been reported.[2,13]

- Exposure of CD34+ cells to HIV may also promote apoptosis (programmed cell death) in these cells, with marked decrease in colony growth.
- An additional cause of decreased growth of hematopoietic colonies is cytokine dysregulation, with excessive production of the inhibitory cytokines TNF-alpha (Tumor Necrosis Factor) and interferon-gamma (IFN-gamma) by HIV-infected stromal cells in the microenvironment of the marrow.[2,12-14]
- Another factor potentially responsible for decreased colony growth may be an inhibitory factor that has been identified in the serum of some HIV-infected individuals.
- Although infection of the CD34+ progenitor cell by HIV-1 remains controversial, it is clear that stromal elements of the marrow microenvironment can be infected by HIV. These elements include T lymphocytes, fibroblasts, endothelial cells, and macrophages.[2,12-14]
- These HIV-1-infected stromal cells have been shown to produce decreased amounts of G-CSF (Granulocyte-Colony Stimulating Factor) and IL-3, leading to decreased ability to support normal hematopoiesis.
- In addition, anemic patients with HIV infection have been found to have a blunted erythropoietin response, resulting in significant anemia in some individuals.[23]
- In vitro studies by Bahner and colleagues have shown that infection of human marrowstroma by HIV-1 is both required and sufficient for hematopoietic suppression of all blood lines.[24]

HIV-Associated Anemia

EPIDEMIOLOGY

- Anemia is very common in HIV-infected individuals. It occurs in approximately 30% of patients during the initial asymptomatic years of infection and is found in 80–90% of patients over the course of disease.[1,2,25]
- Multistate Adult and Adolescent Spectrum of HIV Disease Surveillance Project.[25]
- Definition of anemia: hemoglobin level < 10 g/dL *or* a physician's diagnosis of anemia.
- 1-year incidence of anemia was 37% among patients with clinical AIDS, 12% among patients with immunologic AIDS, and 3% among HIV-infected individuals with neither clinical nor immunologic AIDS.
- These data confirm the high incidence of anemia among HIV-infected patients at all stages of disease in the pre-HAART era.
- However, in more recent years, use of HAART has been associated with a marked decrease in the development of anemia, and with resolution of pre-existing anemia.[26,27]

Figure 1. Prevalence of Anemia in HIV/AIDS

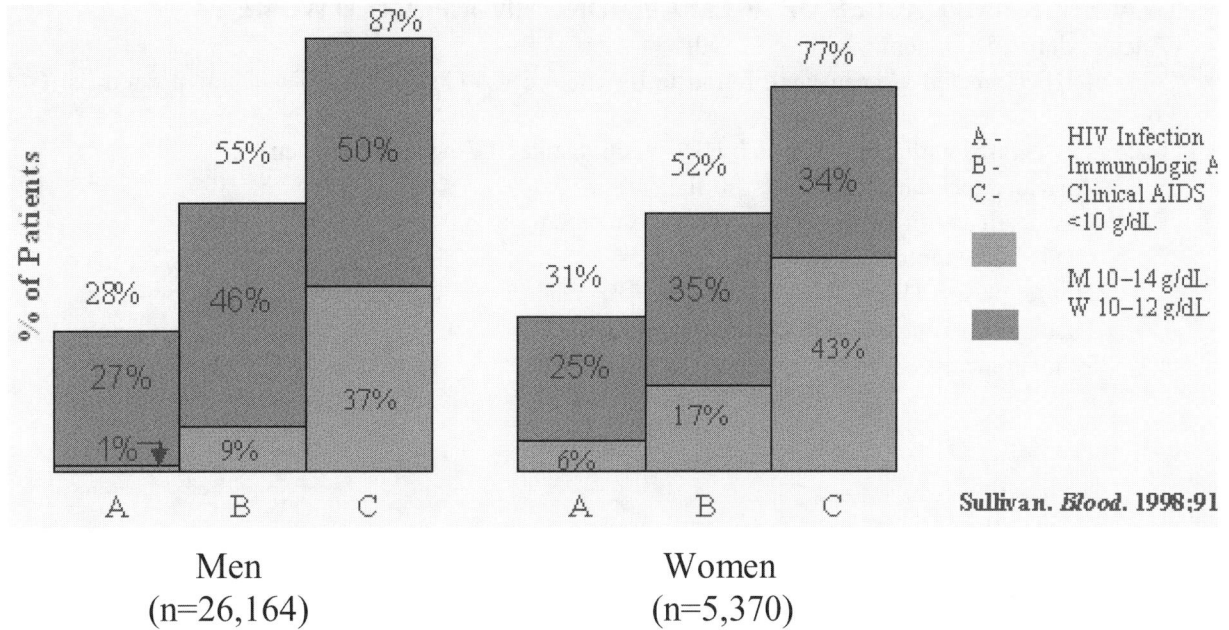

Men
(n=26,164)

Women
(n=5,370)

Figure 2. Prevalence of Anemia in Patients on HAART

	Low Hb (<11 g/dL)	*P* Value Between Groups
CD4 count <200	28.1%	
CD4 count ≥ 200	7.6%	0.001
Women	22%	
Men	10%	0.001
African American	17%	
Hispanic	11%	0.003
White	10%	
Other	8%	

Sharp. *Blood*. 1999;94(10 Suppl 1; Part 2 of 2):8b

PREVALENCE AND CAUSES OF ANEMIA AMONG HIV-INFECTED WOMEN[39]

- Anemia defined as a hemoglobin < 12 g/dL
- 37% of HIV-infected women were found to be anemic vs. 17% of the HIV-negative controls (P < .001)
- Factors associated with anemia in both HIV-positive and HIV-negative women
    - African American and MCV < 80 fl
- Factors associated with anemia in HIV-positive women
    - CD4+ cell counts < 200 cells/mm^3
    - Higher plasma HIV-1 RNA levels
    - History of a clinical AIDS-defining condition
    - Zidovudine use

ETIOLOGY OF ANEMIA

Numerous causes for anemia exist in HIV-infected patients (Table 1).

Table 1. Etiology of Anemia

CAUSE OF ANEMIA	MECHANISM
Decreased RBC production (reticulocyte count low; indirect bilirubin normal or low)	A. Neoplasm infiltrating bone marrow • Lymphoma • Kaposi's sarcoma • Hodgkin's disease • Others B. Infection • *Mycobacterium avium* complex (MAC) • *Mycobacterium tuberculosis* • Cytomegalovirus (CMV) • B19 parvovirus • Fungal infection • Others C. Drugs See Table 2 D. HIV • Abnormal growth of BFU-E • Anemia of chronic disease • Blunted erythropoietin production/response E. Iron deficiency anemia secondary to chronic blood loss
Ineffective production (reticulocyte count low; indirect bilirubin high)	A. Folic acid deficiency • Dietary • Jejunal pathology: malabsorption B. B12 deficiency • Malabsorption in ileum • Gastric pathology with decreased production of intrinsic factor • Production of antibody to intrinsic factor, as in pernicious anemia
Increased RBC destruction, aka hemolysis (reticulocyte count high; indirect bilirubin high)	A. Coombs' positive hemolytic anemia B. Hemophagocytic syndrome C. Thrombotic thrombocytopenic purpura (TTP) D. Disseminated intravascular coagulation (DIC) E. Drugs • Sulfonamides, dapsone • Oxidant drugs in patients with glucose 6-dehydrogenase (G6PD) deficiency

ANEMIA DUE TO DECREASED PRODUCTION OF RBCS

- A decrease in production of RBCs may result from factors suppressing the CFU-GEMM, such as inflammatory cytokines or HIV itself.[1,2]
- In addition, a blunted production of erythropoietin has been documented in anemic HIV-infected patients, similar to the suppression seen in other states of chronic infection or inflammation.[23]

- Antibodies to erythropoietin have also been described in HIV-infected patients with anemia.[28] Infiltration of the marrow by tumor, such as lymphoma,[29] or by infection such as *Mycobacterium avium* complex (MAC), may also lead to the decreased production of RBCs.
- In addition, MAC may be associated with cytokine-induced marrow suppression.
- Involvement of the gastrointestinal (GI) tract by various infections or tumors may lead to chronic blood loss, with eventual iron deficiency anemia.
- Another prominent cause of hypoproliferative anemia in patients with HIV infection is the common use of multiple medications, many of which may cause marrow and/or RBC suppression (Table 2).
- Zidovudine (AZT), one such medication, is uniformly associated with macrocytosis, a condition that can be used as an objective indication that the patient has been compliant with this medication.[30]
- Transfusion-dependent anemia (hemoglobin < 8.5 g/dL) has been reported in approximately 30% of patients with AIDS who are receiving zidovudine at doses of 600 mg/day. However, the incidence of severe anemia is only 1% when the same dose of zidovudine is used in patients with asymptomatic HIV disease.[31]
- While stavudine has also been associated with macrocytosis of RBCs, anemia is not expected as a consequence of this antiretroviral drug.[32]

Table 2. Drugs That Commonly Cause Myelosuppression in the Patient with HIV

Antiretrovirals	Retrovir® (zidovudine, ZDV)
	Epivir® (lamivudine, 3TC)
	Videx® (didanosine, ddI)
	HIVID® (zalcitabine, ddC)
	Zerit® (stavudine, d4T)
Antiviral agents	Cytovene® (ganciclovir)
	Foscavir® (foscarnet)
	Vistide® (cidofovir)
Antifungal agents	Flucytosine
	Amphotericin B
Anti-*Pneumocystis carinii* agents	Sulfonamides
	Trimethoprim
	Pyrimethamine
	Pentamidine
	Dapsone (patients with G6PD deficiency)
Antineoplastic agents	Cyclophosphamide
	Adriamycin® (doxorubicin)
	Methotrexate
	Taxol® (paclitaxel)
	Vinblastine
	Doxil® (liposomal doxorubicin)
	DaunoXome® (liposomal daunorubicin)
Immune response modifiers	Interferon-alpha

- Infection of the marrow by parvovirus B19 is another cause of hypoproliferative anemia in HIV-infected patients, resulting in specific infection of the earliest recognizable RBC precursor, the pronormoblast. [33,34] Thus, while marrow failure, affecting red cells, platelets, and neutrophils, has been described in association with parvovirus B19 infection, a pure RBC aplasia is the usual consequence, with resultant anemia and minimal or absent neutropenia or thrombocytopenia.

- The diagnosis of parvovirus B19 can be made on bone marrow examination with the presence of giant pronormoblasts with clumped basophilic chromatin and clear cytoplasmic vacuoles; diagnosis can be confirmed by *in situ* hybridization using sequence-specific DNA probes for parvovirus B19. Therapy of parvovirus-induced RBC aplasia consists of infusions of intravenous gammaglobulin. Relapse of parvovirus B19-induced RBC aplasia may occur, necessitating re-treatment in some of these individuals.[33,34]

Anemia Due to Increased RBC Destruction (Hemolytic Anemia)

- Increased RBC destruction may be seen in HIV-infected patients with glucose 6-dehydrogenase (G6PD) deficiency who are exposed to oxidant drugs and in HIV-infected patients with disseminated intravascular coagulation (DIC) or with thrombotic thrombocytopenic purpura (TTP);[35]
- Hemophagocytic syndrome has also been described in association with HIV infection, with actual phagocytosis of RBCs by macrophages within the marrow.
- An additional cause of RBC destruction leading to anemia in HIV-infected patients is the development of autoantibodies, with resultant positive Coombs' test and shortened RBC survival. Of interest, presence of antibody coating the RBC surface (positive direct Coombs' test) has been reported in as many as 18% to 77% of HIV-infected patients, although the incidence of actual hemolysis, or RBC destruction, is extremely low.[36-38]
- However, a high incidence of positive direct Coombs' test has also been detected in patients with other hypergammaglobulinemic states, indicating that the positive Coombs' in HIV may simply be secondary to the polyclonal hypergammaglobulinemia known to occur in the setting of HIV infection.[39]

Anemia Due to Ineffective Production of RBCs (B12 and/or folic acid deficiency)

- Folic acid is absorbed in the jejunum and is responsible for one carbon transfer required in the synthesis of DNA. A deficiency of folic acid leads to a megaloblastic anemia, with large oval RBCs in the blood, hypersegmented polys, and a decrease in all 3 lines, with resultant anemia, neutropenia, and thrombocytopenia. Folic acid is found primarily in green, leafy vegetables, and is heat labile.
- Since tissue stores of folate are relatively small, a deficiency of folate from the diet, lasting as little as 6-7 months, may lead to anemia. It is thus apparent that HIV-infected patients who are ill and unable to eat optimally, as well as those with underlying disease of the jejunum, may be unable to absorb sufficient folic acid; this lack of absorption may lead to anemia, neutropenia, and thrombocytopenia.
- In folic acid deficiency, the reticulocyte count is low, while the indirect bilirubin level will be elevated. The MCV of the RBCs will be high. The classic changes of megaloblastic anemia will be detected on examination of the bone marrow, while serum and RBC folate levels will be low.
- Ineffective production of RBCs, with pancytopenia in the blood, elevated indirect bilirubin level, and low reticulocyte count may also be seen in vitamin B12 deficiency. The absorption of B12 requires initial production of intrinsic factor by parietal cells in the stomach, with subsequent absorption of the complex of B12 and intrinsic factor within the ileum. Thus, malabsorption of B12 can occur relatively easily in various disorders of the stomach (e.g. achlorhydria); by production of antibodies to intrinsic factor or to parietal cells ("pernicious anemia"); or by various disorders of the small bowel and ileum (infection, Crohn's disease).
- While B12 deficiency is highly unlikely on a dietary basis alone, patients with HIV infection appear to be prone to B12 malabsorption, presumably due to the myriad of infections and other disorders that may occur in the small intestine of such individuals. Negative vitamin B12 balance has been documented in approximately one third of patients with AIDS, the majority demonstrating defective absorption of the vitamin.[40]
- Diagnosis of B12 deficiency can be made by documenting low serum B12 levels, while the earliest indication of negative B12 balance is the finding of low B12 levels in the blood of patients taking transcobalamin II.[41]
- Monthly administration of parenteral B12 will correct the deficiency as well as the resultant anemia and pancytopenia in the peripheral blood. Since B12 deficiency may also cause neurologic

dysfunction (subacute combined degeneration of the cord), with motor, sensory, and higher cortical dysfunction, the possibility of vitamin B12 deficiency should also be considered in HIV-infected patients with these neurologic symptoms.

Consequences of Anemia in HIV Infection: Decreased Survival

- Four large cohort studies have proven that anemia is an independent risk factor for shorter survival in HIV-infected patients
  - Multistate Adult and Adolescent Spectrum of HIV Disease Surveillance Project
    - Anemia defined as a hemoglobin < than 10 g/dL *or* a physician's diagnosis of anemia
    - Anemia was found to be associated with an increased risk of death in this cohort[25]
      - Relative risk of death for anemic individuals who began the study with CD4+ cell counts > 200 cells/mm^3 was 148% higher than for individuals at the same CD4+ cell count strata without anemia
      - Risk of death was increased by 58% for those who entered the study at CD4+ cell counts < 200 cells/mm^3 and developed anemia
      - Interestingly, the risk of death *decreased* in those patients who recovered from anemia, whatever its cause, while the risk of death remained 170% higher for patients who did not recover from anemia!
  - Moore and colleagues[42]
    - Development of anemia was associated with decreased survival, independent of other prognostic factors
    - Of importance, use of erythropoietin was associated with a *decreased* risk of death, as was use of antiretroviral therapy
  - EuroSIDA study – severe anemia (hemoglobin < 8 g/dL): a strong independent prognostic marker for death, when controlling for CD4+ cell count and plasma HIV-1 RNA level[41]
  - WIHS study of 2056 HIV-infected women: anemia also found to be an independent predictor of shorter survival[42]

Consequences of Anemia in HIV Infection: Disease Progression

- In an attempt to develop a prognostic scoring system for HIV-infected patients receiving HAART, Lundgren and colleagues [45] from the EuroSIDA Study evaluated 2027 patients who started HAART, from among an initial cohort of 8457 subjects. Data were then validated in 2 additional groups of 1946 and 1442 patients, respectively. A total of 9.9% of subjects experienced clinical progression (either a new AIDS-defining illness or death), representing an incidence of 3.9 per 100 person-years.
- On multivariate analysis, 4 factors were found to be independently associated with disease progression:
  - CD4+ cell count
  - HIV-1 viral load
  - History of clinical AIDS before initiation of HAART
  - Level of hemoglobin
- Thus, with mild anemia (hemoglobin of 8-14 g/dL for men, and 8-12 g/dL for women), the relative hazard of disease progression or death was 2.2 (95% CI 1.6-2.9, $P < .0001$), while for severe anemia (hemoglobin < 8 g/dL), the relative hazard was 7.1 (95% CI 2.5-20.1, $P = .0002$).

Relationship between Anemia and HAART

- Recent studies have confirmed the ability of HAART to correct or improve the anemia of HIV infection.
- In a study of 6725 HIV-infected patients from across Europe, Mocroft and colleagues[26] found that HAART was statistically associated with improvement in hemoglobin levels. When used for longer

periods of time, HAART was associated with greater likelihood of correcting anemia. Thus, 65.5% of the cohort was anemic before the use of HAART, 53% were anemic after 6 months of HAART, and 46% were anemic after 12 months of HAART.

- In a study of 905 HIV-infected patients receiving care at the Johns Hopkins Medical Center in Baltimore, HAART use was also shown to be associated with decreased levels of anemia when evaluated on the population level.[27] Normal hemoglobin levels were present in 42% of patients who were taking HAART vs 31% of patients who did not use HAART. In multivariate analysis, use of HAART was strongly associated with freedom from anemia, after adjusting for CD4+ cell count, HIV-1 RNA level, sex, race, history of injection-drug use, and use of various therapies for anemia.

- In the large WIHS study of HIV-infected women, use of HAART for as little as 6 months was statistically associated with resolution of anemia and longer use was associated with more profound improvements.[42]

- Use of HAART has also been associated with prevention of development of anemia, although rather prolonged use (18 months or more) is required.[42]

- HAART may also be associated with an early increase in the prevalence of anemia, with protection occurring only later.[46]

- The mechanisms whereby HAART may protect against development of anemia or correct pre-existing anemia are not yet fully understood. Nonetheless, by decreasing the HIV-1 viral load, one might expect an improvement in the abnormal growth of committed hematopoietic progenitors,[4] a decrease in the level of HIV-1 infection of bone marrow stromal cells,[24] and an improvement in the blunted erythropoietin response, which characterizes chronic HIV infection.[23]

- In addition, Isgro and colleagues [47] showed that HAART was associated with an increase in hematopoietic progenitor cell growth. Further, ritonavir, a protease inhibitor, has been associated with decreased apoptosis of hematopoietic progenitors and direct stimulation of progenitor cell growth in vitro.[46]

Treatment of Anemia in HIV Infection

As indicated above, multiple specific causes of anemia may be encountered in HIV-infected patients. The appropriate therapy of these conditions will depend on the underlying diagnosis.

Figure 3. Simplified Evaluation of Anemia in HIV-Infected Patient

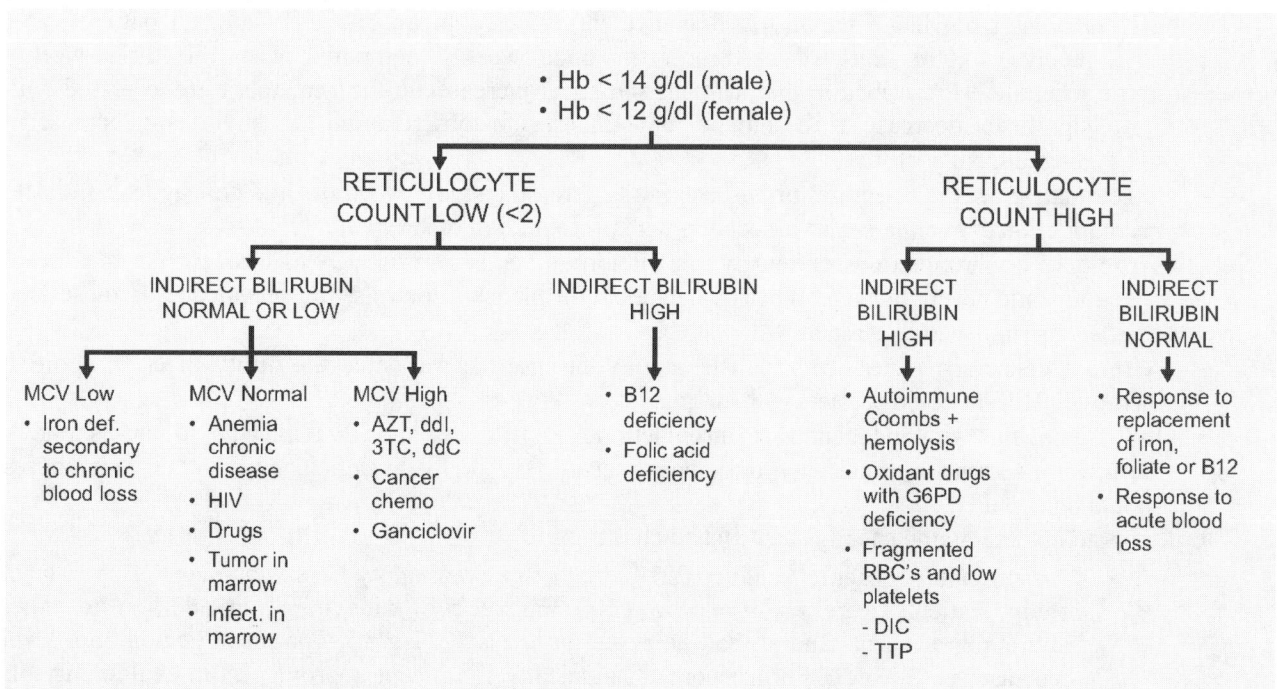

Use of HAART to correct the anemia of HIV infection

As described above, observational cohort studies have documented that efficacious use of HAART may be associated with resolution of preexisting anemia in the majority of patients,[26,27,42,46,47] with improvement expected after approximately 6 months or more of HAART.[26,42]

Erythropoietin

A blunted response to erythropoietin is extremely common in the setting of HIV infection, leading to anemia that can be substantial and requires therapy.[23,40,41]

- HIV-negative
  - Development of anemia usually results in an increased production of erythropoietin in an attempt to correct the anemia
- HIV-positive
  - As the RBC count falls, the normal compensatory erythropoietin response is lost resulting in an inability of the marrow to respond to the anemic state
  - Mechanism of this decreased production of erythropoietin
    - Post-transcriptional defect in production
      - Development of autoantibodies to erythropoietin also described in HIV-infected patients
- Multiple studies have now confirmed the beneficial effect of epoetin alfa (Procrit®) in HIV-infected patients with anemia, in whom marrow function has been suppressed as a result of HIV or of other chronic infectious or inflammatory diseases[40,48-50]
- Epoetin alfa is also effective in treating the anemia due to zidovudine or other medications, including cancer chemotherapy, that suppress the marrow[50]
- Patients with endogenous erythropoietin levels ≤ 500 IU/L are expected to respond to erythropoietin therapy while those with endogenous levels over 500 IU/L are not
- Epoetin alfa Dosing
  - Administer subcutaneously at a dose of 100–200 U/kg body weight, 3 times weekly until normalization of the RBC and then given approximately qw or qow to maintain the desired hemoglobin concentration.
    - Recent trials have demonstrated equivalent efficacy in anemic HIV-infected patients who receive 40,000 units of erythropoietin once weekly compared with the thrice-weekly schedule.[47] Prescribed in this manner, statistical increases in the hematocrit are expected with significant decrease in the number of RBC transfusions required and significant increase in overall quality of life.
  - Recent data from the Spectrum of Disease Study[25] and the study by Moore and colleagues[43] indicate that correction of anemia is also associated with prolongation of survival[23,38]
  - Toxicity to erythropoietin is extremely uncommon and consists primarily of local pain at the site of injection, mild fever, or rash. When compared with placebo controls, the prevalence of these side effects was similar to those seen with placebo.
  - A recent consensus panel of specialists in HIV disease has validated the utility of erythropoietin therapy in HIV-infected patients with anemia.[48]
  - In those patients with endogenous erythropoietin levels less than </= 500 IU/L who do not respond to the drug, a search for occult iron deficiency, serum B12 or folate deficiency or other such causes should be explored.

Erythropoietin therapy impacts the quantity and quality of life
  - Abrams and colleagues[55] studied 221 patients in a community-based, multicenter, open-label study. Patients were taking up to 4200 mg/week of zidovudine in addition to other antiretroviral agents and all had hemoglobin levels < 11 g/dL. The mean hemoglobin level increased by 2.5 g/dL. Furthermore, a statistically significant improvement in total quality-of-

life measures associated with the improvement in hemoglobin level was documented. These improvements were independent of any change in CD4+ cell count.

- Moore and colleagues monitored 2348 HIV-infected patients between 1989 and 1996[40]
  - Of these, 21% developed anemia (hemoglobin < 9.4 g/dL)
  - Development of anemia was associated with shorter survival when controlling for other prognostic factors
  - Notably, use of erythropoietin was associated with a decreased risk of death   (P = .002)[40]
  - Of importance, the risk of death was 170% greater for people who failed to recover from anemia, compared with those in whom the anemia resolved.[25]
- An earlier study by Revicki and colleagues[56] evaluated the effect of erythropoietin on quality of life in 251 patients with HIV infection and anemia, defined as a hematocrit < 30%
  - Correction of anemia, defined as a hematocrit level of 38% or greater with no blood transfusions in the past month, occurred in 34% of the patients by week 24
  - Significant improvement in health satisfaction, global health, energy, and home management were reported by these individuals
- Weekly doses of erythropoietin have also been shown to be efficacious in improving both hemoglobin levels and objective quality-of-life measures in a group of 786 HIV-infected patients treated prospectively[57]
  - In this study, 75% of patients responded with at least a 1-g/dL increase in hemoglobin, with a mean increase over 4 months of 2.7 g/dL. The mean Linear Analogue Scale (LASA) Quality of Life measure increased by 41%, while the MOS-HIV overall quality-of-life measure increased by 37%.

Potential Role of Darbepoetin Alfa

- Darbepoetin alfa, also known as novel erythropoiesis stimulating protein (NESP), stimulates red cell production in the same way as erythropoietin, although it is chemically distinct.
- The presence of an additional sialic acid residue increases its terminal half-life, allowing less frequent dosing than is possible with traditional erythropoietin.
- Recent studies have indicated the efficacy of NESP given at doses of 2.25 or 4.5 mcg/kg once weekly to patients with cancer, in whom approximately 70% to 80% had correction of their hemoglobin to normal levels[58]
- Alternate dosing schedules, with NESP given every 2 or 3 weeks, also appear efficacious[59]
- Although it is not yet licensed for use in HIV/AIDS, multiple prospective studies are currently in progress that seek to define the efficacy and toxicity of NESP in anemic HIV-infected patients
- Results are expected to be similar to those already demonstrated with recombinant human erythropoietin

Blood transfusions

- Periodic blood transfusions may be required to control symptoms in patients with recurrent blood loss or ongoing use of medications that suppress erythropoiesis[52]
- However, transfusions may also be associated with various risks, such as exposure to infectious organisms, alloimmunization, transfusion reactions and febrile, nonhemolytic transfusion reactions[60],
- In a group of 10 HIV-infected subjects,[62] increases in HIV-1 p24 antigen and HIV-1 RNA levels have been documented within 1 to 2 weeks of receiving transfusions. An increased incidence of opportunistic infections has also been documented in this setting[63]
- Of importance, an increased risk of death in HIV-infected subjects who received blood transfusions has also been described[43]
- However, a recent, large prospective trial of 531 patients with HIV and CMV infections, randomized to receive either leukocyte-reduced or unmodified RBC transfusions, found no adverse effect of either type of transfusion in terms of plasma HIV-1 RNA levels, CD4+ cell counts, or plasma cytokine levels.[64] Furthermore, leukocyte-reduced transfusions appeared to offer no benefit over unmodified transfusions in these patients.

- Therefore, it is appropriate to reserve blood transfusions for those HIV-infected patients who require a rapid correction of anemia based on cardiovascular or other symptomatology

Neutropenia

PREVALENCE OF NEUTROPENIA

Neutropenia is present in approximately 10% of patients with early, asymptomatic HIV infection, and in > 50% of individuals with more advanced HIV-related immunodeficiency.[1,2,50]

- Multiple etiologies for neutropenia may be present, either singly or in combination[66]
  - Decreased colony growth of the committed progenitor cell, CFU-GM,[67] may lead to decreased production of both granulocytes and monocytes.
  - Soluble inhibitory substances, produced by HIV-infected cells have been shown to suppress neutrophil production in vitro.[68]
  - Decreased serum levels of G-CSF have been described in HIV-positive subjects with afebrile neutropenia (< 1000 cells/mm^3), indicating relative deficiency of this specific hematopoietic growth factor may also contribute to persistent neutropenia.[69]
  - Myelosuppression and neutropenia may result from any one of several medications commonly used in HIV-infected patients. (Table 2)
  - In addition to absolute neutropenia, patients with HIV infection may also experience decreased function of granulocytes and monocytes.[70]

Risk Factors for Infection in Neutropenic Patients with HIV

- Cancer patients receiving chemotherapy have increased risk of bacterial infection when absolute neutrophil count (ANC) <1000 cells/mm3 and increases again when the ANC < 500 cells/mm^3 [71]
- Several studies have confirmed the same relationships in patients with HIV infection, although the relative risk of infection is somewhat lower in HIV-infected patients when compared with those receiving chemotherapy for cancer at the same level of neutropenia.[72,73]
- Moore and colleagues[74] found that the risk of bacterial infection increased 2.3 fold for HIV-infected individuals with ANCs < 1000 cells/ mm^3 and rose by 7.9-fold in those with ANCs < 500 cells/ mm^3.
- Jacobson and colleagues,[75] who reviewed records from 2047 HIV-positive patients from San Francisco General Hospital's AIDS clinic found that lower ANCs are associated with an increased risk for hospitalization for serious infection. On multivariate analysis, the severity and duration of neutropenia were found to be significant predictors of the incidence of hospitalization for serious bacterial infections.
  - In a study of 62 HIV-infected patients with ANC's ≤1000 cells/mm^3, 24% developed infectious complications, most commonly within 24 hours after the onset of neutropenia.[76] On multivariate analysis, the 3 factors independently associated with infectious complications included: presence of a central venous catheter; neutropenia in the previous 3 months; and, lower nadir of granulocyte count (250 cells/mm^3 in those with infections vs 622 cells/mm^3 in those without). Among patients with medication- associated neutropenia, the most common cause was zidovudine followed by trimethoprim-sulfamethoxazole, and ganciclovir. Neutropenia was less likely to be associated with infection in these patients when compared with individuals who were neutropenic due to the use of cancer chemotherapy.[76]

Impact of Effective Antiretroviral Therapy on Neutropenia

- Recent evidence indicates that highly active antiretroviral therapy (HAART) may be associated with an improvement in leukopenia and neutropenia in treated patients[78]

- A direct stimulatory effect of protease inhibitors on human hematopoiesis recently demonstrated[71] indicating that mild-moderate levels of neutropenia may be managed by use of HAART alone, although several months of therapy are required to achieve the desired effect
- In a group of 66 HIV-infected patients treated with HAART, statistically significant increases in total leukocyte count and absolute granulocyte count were evident after 6 months of therapy. While the ANC also rose during earlier and later time periods during HAART, these differences did not reach statistical significance.[78]
- Sloand and colleagues have recently demonstrated a direct stimulatory effect of protease inhibitors on human hematopoiesis[78]
- These data would indicate that mild to moderate levels of neutropenia may be managed by use of HAART alone, although several months of therapy are required to achieve the desired effect

Use of G-CSF and GM-CSF (Sargramostim, Leukine®) in Neutropenic Patients with HIV Infection

Dose-dependent increases in granulocytes, monocytes, and eosinophils occur [80,81]

- GM-CSF stimulates proliferation, differentiation, and release of these cells from the marrow
- Enhancement of neutrophil function may also be seen with GM-CSF therapy, with increase in superoxide production, increased phagocytosis and intracellular killing by mature granulocytes, and increased antibody-dependent cellular cytotoxicity (ADCC)
- The suggested dose of GM-CSF is 5 mcg/kg/day, administered subcutaneously. After 5 or 6 days, the specific dose is then titrated, dependent on effect (Table 3)
- In early studies, GM-CSF was associated with augmentation in the replication of HIV.[82] However, more recent in vitro studies have indicated that GM-CSF actually inhibits HIV-1 replication in monocytes and macrophages of HIV-infected persons.[83]
- To ascertain the in vivo effect of GM-CSF on HIV-1 replication, Brites and colleagues[84] conducted a randomized placebo-controlled trial of GM-CSF in a group of 105 HIV-infected patients who were also receiving nucleoside analogue reverse transcriptase inhibitor (NRTI) therapy. GM-CSF was given at a dose of 125 mcg twice weekly for 6 months.
- Interestingly, patients randomized to antiretroviral therapy plus GM-CSF achieved a greater reduction in plasma viral load, and were more likely to achieve HIV-1 RNA levels below the limit of detection, and also demonstrated a lower frequency of zidovudine resistance mutations than those who received antiretrovirals plus placebo
- These data confirm that GM-CSF may certainly be used safely in HIV-infected patients receiving antiretroviral therapy, without expectation of any deleterious effect in terms of the underlying HIV infection. Side effects of GM-CSF include an influenza-like syndrome, with fever, bone pain, myalgia, fatigue, malaise, and headache.

G-CSF (Filgrastim, Neupogen®)

- G-CSF has also been shown to raise granulocyte counts in neutropenic patients occurring as a consequence of cancer chemotherapy, antiretroviral and/or anti-infective therapy.[48,85]
  - Use of G-CSF was associated with enhanced functional activity of mature granulocytic progeny. There was a significantly decreased risk of bacteremia (P = .02) and decreased risk of death in patients receiving G-CSF, in those who received antiretroviral agents and in those who received prophylaxis for P carinii pneumonia.[86]
  - When used in the setting of cancer chemotherapy, the hematologic growth factors have been shown to decrease the duration of neutropenia, while also decreasing the mean duration of hospitalization for neutropenic fever
  - While relatively expensive, the growth factors have not been associated with an increase in total healthcare costs!
  - Furthermore, while there is relatively little evidence that overall patient survival has increased as a consequence of G-CSF or GM-CSF,[78] these drugs will allow safer administration of other necessary medications[80,81]

Table 3. Use of Hematopoietic Growth Factors

	ERYTHROPOIETIN (Epoetin alfa, Procrit®)	G-CSF (Filgrastim, Neupogen®)	GM-CSF (Sargramostin, Leukine®)
Indication	Anemia due to HIV, chronic inflammatory or infectious disease, or use of antiretrovirals, anti-infectives and/or cancer chemotherapy	Neutropenia < 1,000 cells/mm^3 due to HIV, anticancer chemotherapy; anti-infective agents	
Evaluation of Hgb and Hct required at baseline	Serum erythropoietin level ≤ 500 IU/L Absence of other causes of anemia		
Initial dosing	100 units/kg SQ 3 times/week or 40,000 units SQ once weekly	1 mcg/kg administered subcutaneously daily	5 mcg/kg administered subcutaneously daily
Subsequent dosing	Titrate as necessary to maintain response (approximately 40,000 U/wk)	Titrate as necessary to maintain response	
Side effects	Pain at injection site Fever	Elevated lactic dehydrogenase Elevated alkaline phosphatase Bone pain	Flu-like syndrome Myalgias Bone pain Fatigue Fever
Targeted effect	Hemoglobin ≥ 11 g/dL in women; ≥ 12 g/dL in men	ANC ≥ 1,000 cells/mm^3	

Thrombocytopenia

- Thrombocytopenia is relatively common during the course of HIV infection. It occurs in approximately 40% of patients and is the first symptom or sign of infection in approximately 10%.[87,88]
- The incidence of thrombocytopenia during one year[88] is 8.7% in patients with clinical AIDS, 3.1% in patients with immunologic AIDS (CD4+ cell count < 200 cells/mm^3) and 1.7% in patients with HIV infection only.
- After controlling for multiple factors (AIDS, CD4+ cell count, anemia, neutropenia, antiviral therapy, receipt of prophylaxis against P carinii), thrombocytopenia is significantly associated with shorter survival.[80] (Risk ratio, 1.7: 95% confidence interval = 1.6-1.8)
- Major cause of thrombocytopenia in HIV disease is idiopathic thrombocytopenic purpura (ITP), in which antibody-coated platelets are removed from the circulation by the macrophages in the spleen.
- The resulting thrombocytopenia may result in bleeding or bruising, predominantly from the mucous membranes or skin
- However, the majority of patients with HIV-related ITP do not actually experience bleeding or have only minor bleeding manifestations[79]
- Likelihood of clinical bleeding is very low until the platelet count < 10,000 cells/mm^3 but potential risk of life-threatening bleeding into the central nervous system does exist in the setting of ITP

MECHANISMS OF THROMBOCYTOPENIA: "DE NOVO" ITP

In usual de novo ITP occurring in people who are not HIV-infected, the disease is caused by the production of antibodies with specificity against certain platelet antigens, such as the IIb/IIIa receptor on the platelet surface. The variable portion of the antibody molecule (Fab) attaches directly to the specific auto-antigen on the platelet surface, while the constant portion of the antibody molecule (Fc) remains free (Figure 4).

Figure 4. Mechanisms of Thrombocytopenia in ITP

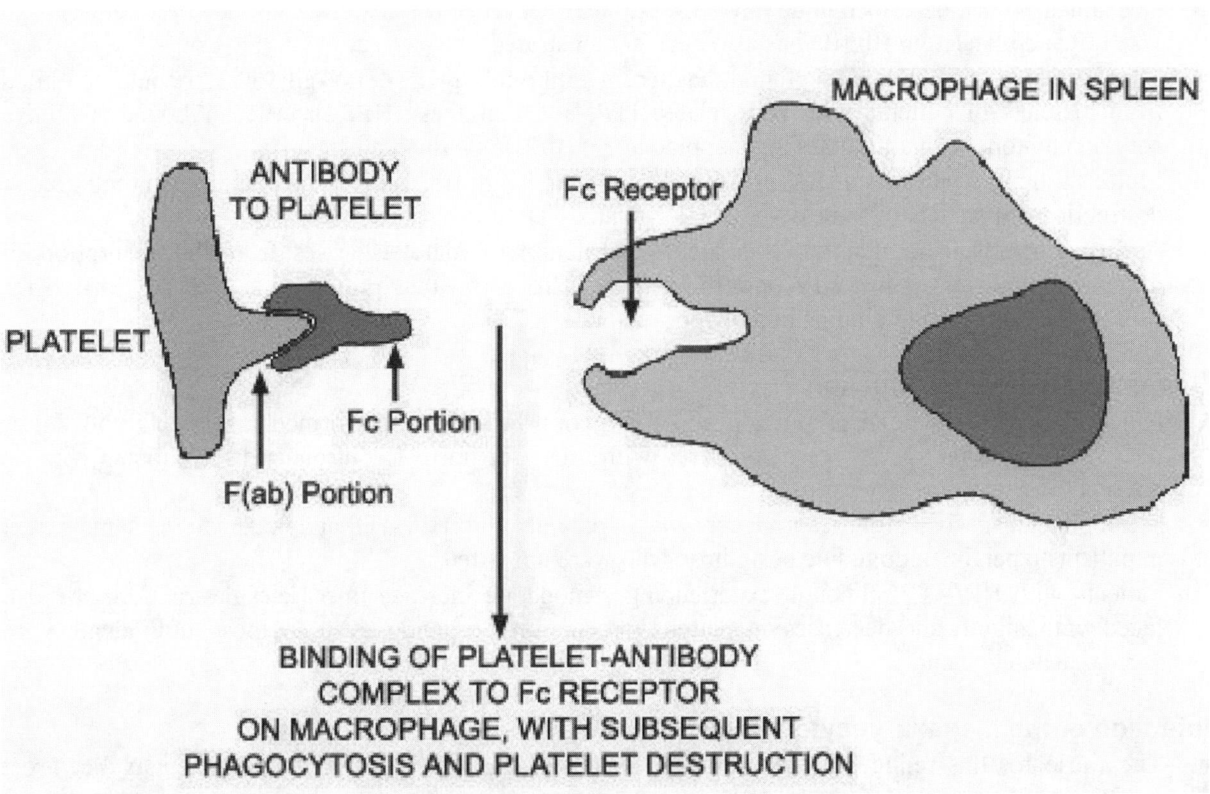

As the platelet travels through the slow circulation of the sinusoids of the spleen, it comes in contact with the macrophages that line these sinusoids. The macrophage possesses receptors for the Fc portion of the antibody molecule, allowing attachment of the platelet-antibody complex to the macrophage, which then internalizes the platelet via phagocytosis. The platelet is destroyed within the macrophage. The resulting thrombocytopenia is thus a consequence of increased peripheral destruction of platelets. In an attempt to overcome this increased rate of platelet destruction, a compensatory increase in platelet production is expected, as demonstrated by increased numbers of megakaryocytes in the marrow.

In most cases, this compensatory increase in platelet production does not fully correct for the increased platelet destruction, and significant thrombocytopenia becomes evident in the peripheral blood.[89] Although the platelet count is low in ITP, it is rather unusual for patients to develop extensive bleeding manifestations. The reason for this finding relates to the fact that new platelets, just released from the marrow, are large and highly functional. Thus, as the normal platelet circulates within the bloodstream during its normal 7- to 10-day life span, it becomes progressively smaller and less functional. In ITP, once the platelet is coated with antibody, it is removed from the circulation rather quickly. As a result, the platelets that are present in the circulation are new, fresh from the marrow, and highly functional. It is for this reason that the usual patient with ITP does not actually experience substantial bleeding.

MECHANISMS OF THROMBOCYTOPENIA IN HIV-RELATED ITP

Increased platelet destruction

- As in de novo ITP, HIV-infected patients with ITP also demonstrate increased platelet destruction via phagocytosis by macrophages in the spleen.[89] In HIV-related ITP, however, several mechanisms for platelet-associated antibody have been described often occurring simultaneously in a given patient.
- Thus, presence of platelet-specific antibodies, immunochemically characterized as anti-glycoprotein (gp) IIb and/or gp-IIIa, have been detected in HIV-infected patients with ITP, indicating a similar mechanism to that described in de novo disease. [90] However, cross-reactive antibody between HIV-gp 160/120 and platelet gp IIb/IIIa has also been demonstrated.[91]
- Thus, Bettaieb and colleagues[91] found that serum antibodies against HIV-gp 160/120 could be eluted from platelets of patients with HIV-related ITP, and that these HIV-specific antibodies shared a common epitope with antibodies against platelet gp IIb/IIIa on the platelet surface
- Molecular mimicry between HIV-gp 160/120 and platelet gp IIb/IIIa may be operative in the immune destruction of platelets in some cases of HIV-related ITP
- A further mechanism of antibody-induced destruction of platelets arises from the absorption of immune complexes against HIV onto the platelet F_c receptor, thus providing a "free" F_c portion for subsequent macrophage binding and phagocytosis

Decreased platelet production

- Kinetic studies of platelet production and destruction have been performed in patients with HIV-related ITP, and the results were compared with those for normal controls and for patients with de novo ITP[89]
- Mean platelet survival significantly decreased in patients with HIV-ITP and occurs to the same extent in patients receiving zidovudine or in those who were untreated
- Patients with HIV-ITP, although experiencing a moderate increase in platelet destruction, are also faced with significant decreases in platelet production occurring even in those individuals with normal platelet counts[89]

Infection of the megakaryocyte by HIV

- The cause for this reduced production of platelets in the setting of HIV infection may be direct infection of the megakaryocyte by HIV
- Thus, Kouri and colleagues[92] first demonstrated that human megakaryocytes bear a CD4 receptor capable of binding HIV-1, while Zucker-Franklin and associates[93] showed that HIV-1 could be internalized by human megakaryocytes. Wang and colleagues[94] have demonstrated the presence of CXCR4, a chemokine receptor known to be important as the coreceptor for HIV on megakaryocytic progenitors, megakaryocytes, and platelets.
- Furthermore, employing in situ hybridization techniques and a 35S HIV riboprobe (antisense to an HIV *env* sequence), HIV transcripts have been detected in megakaryocytes of 5 of 10 patients with HIV-ITP, indicating that the megakaryocyte had been infected by HIV in these cases.[95]
- Expression of viral RNA within the megakaryocytes was also detected in 10 of 10 patients, using in situ hybridization techniques. Specific ultrastructural damage in the HIV-infected megakaryocytes has also been noted, consisting of blebbing and vacuolization of the surface membrane.[96]
- The documentation of significant increases in platelet production after receipt of zidovudine in patients with HIV-ITP[97] would be consistent with the hypothesis that a major mechanism of this disorder is the direct infection of the megakaryocyte by HIV
- Harker and colleagues[98] described 3 chimpanzees, infected with HIV-1, who developed ITP associated with elevated levels of antibody against platelet glycoprotein IIIa
- Use of recombinant pegylated human megakaryocyte growth and development factor (MGDF) was associated with a decline in antiplatelet antibodies in serum, as well as an increase in peripheral blood platelet counts and an increase in the number of megakaryocytes and megakaryocyte progenitors in the marrow.

- These changes would imply that the mechanism of ITP in HIV-infected chimps must also include a component of insufficient compensatory expansion of platelet production, similar to what has been described in HIV-infected humans.

THERAPY FOR HIV-RELATED ITP

Antiretroviral therapy

Zidovudine: high-dose zidovudine (1000 mg per day in divided doses) is advantageous in patients with HIV-ITP[97]

- The Swiss Group for HIV Studies was the first to demonstrate the efficacy of zidovudine therapy in patients with HIV-ITP[97]
- These results were subsequently confirmed by others[99,100]
- The appropriate dose of zidovudine in HIV-ITP was studied by Landonio and colleagues,[101]

Other antiretroviral agents: relatively little known about the efficacy of other reverse transcriptase inhibitors or protease inhibitors in the treatment of HIV-ITP but data indicates that use of effective antiretroviral therapy is clearly the treatment of choice in patients with HIV-related ITP![102,103]

Of importance, Caso and colleagues[104] have recently reported use of HAART in 37 patients with HIV-related ITP. A significant increase in platelet count was observed after 3 months of HAART, independent of the baseline platelet count or the concomitant use of zidovudine. These increases were sustained for at least 6 months. The HAART regimen employed was variable, including indinavir in 60%, saquinavir in 27%, and ritonavir in 14%. In 70% of the treated patients, HIV viral load decreased to nondetectable levels.

These data would indicate that use of effective antiretroviral therapy is clearly the treatment of choice in patients with HIV-related ITP.

Interferon-alpha (IFN-alpha)

- First shown to be efficacious in patients with refractory de novo ITP in 1988[97]
- A prospective, randomized, double-blind, placebo-controlled trial of IFN-alfa, at a dose of 3 million units thrice weekly, given subcutaneously, was subsequently reported by Marroni and colleagues[105] in 15 patients with HIV-related ITP. A platelet response was documented in 66%, with a mean increase of 60,000/mm^3. The average time to response was 3 weeks.
- When interferon therapy was discontinued, platelet counts returned to baseline values within 3 months, indicating the necessity to maintain IFN-alfa therapy over time
- In an attempt to ascertain the mechanisms by which IFN-alfa exerts its effects, Vianelli and associates[106] subsequently treated 13 patients with HIV-ITP, noting a partial response in 53% of subjects. In responding patients, IFN-alfa was demonstrated to prolong platelet survival, while no significant increase in platelet production was noted.

High-dose intravenous gamma globulin (IVIG)

- IVIG, at a dose of 1000-2000 mg/kg, duration has been used effectively in pediatric and adult patients with de novo ITP, resulting in significant rise in platelet counts within 24 to 72 hours in the majority of individuals[107,108]
- Major problem with IVIG appears to be its substantial cost
- In addition, the world supply of IVIG has recently been insufficient to meet the increasing demands imposed by the broader clinical indications for its use
- For these reasons, IVIG often reserved for use in patients who are acutely bleeding and require immediate rise in platelet count and in individuals scheduled for an invasive procedure

Anti-Rh immunoglobulin

- The use of anti-Rh immunoglobulin in nonsplenectomized Rh-positive patients with HIV-related ITP represents another potential mode of therapy.[109]

- "Requirements" for effective therapy with anti-Rh (D)
  - Baseline hemoglobin level adequate to permit a 1–2 gm decrease due to hemolysis, Rh+ patient, and presence of a spleen (the site at which RBCs would be preferentially bound to macrophages and phagocytized)[109,110]
  - Gringeri and associates[109] subsequently confirmed these results, and also studied the use of intramuscular (IM) anti-D immunoglobulin for maintenance treatment after successful induction therapy by the IV route. Patients were asked to self-administer the maintenance anti-Rh, given IM at a dose of 6–13 mcg/kg/week. After induction, 83% of patients had achieved a platelet count > 50,000/mm^3. This response was maintained in 85% over time.
  - More recently, a dose of 75 mcg/kg/day was associated with more rapid and durable responses than 50 mcg/kg/day, when administered in a randomized trial in 27 HIV-negative patients.[111]
- May be used safely and effectively in patients with HIV-related ITP providing an alternative that is approximately **1/10** the cost of high-dose IVIG[109,110]

Danazol (Danocrine®)

- Synthetic steroid that has been used with some success in patients with de novo ITP, at a dose of 400–800 mg po qd [112-114]
- The majority of patients experience a response, with platelet counts rising to > 50,000/mm^3 in approximately 1 to 2 months. Although lower doses (50 mg/day) may also be effective in some patients, the average time to response is prolonged, at 3.5 months.
- Danazol is thought to work via modulation of Fc receptors on the macrophage surface, resulting in fewer available binding sites for antibody-coated platelets
- While no large series of patients with HIV-ITP have been studied, anecdotal reports of efficacy have been described
- In general, however, danazol use is restricted to patients who have failed other standard therapies

Corticosteroids

- Remains the initial therapy of choice in *non-HIV-infected* patients with de novo ITP and at a dose of 1 mg/kg/day are associated with an 80–90% response rate
- Similar results have been documented in patients with HIV-related disease
  - However, immunosuppressive effects of high-dose corticosteroids have made such therapy far from optimal in HIV-infected patients
  - Furthermore, potential development of fulminant Kaposi's sarcoma in HIV-infected homosexual/bisexual men co-infected with human herpes type 8 after use of corticosteroids has further dampened enthusiasm for this therapeutic modality

Splenectomy

- Has been used effectively for years in patients with de novo ITP who are refractory to corticosteroids and is associated with long-term response in approximately 60% of patients
- More recently, Oksenhendler and associates[115] reported long-term experience with splenectomy, performed in 37% of a cohort of 185 patients with HIV-ITP. Splenectomy was eventually performed in 68 such patients, at an average of 13 months from initial diagnosis of HIV-ITP. The mean platelet count presplenectomy was 18,000/mm 3, rising to 223,000/mm^3 postoperatively.
- In comparing the survival or rate of progression to AIDS in the 68 splenectomized patients vs the 117 who did not undergo the procedure, no difference was found, indicating that splenectomy was not associated with more rapid progression of HIV disease.
- Similar conclusions were made by Kemeny and colleagues[116] in a group of 22 patients with HIV-ITP. Again, the procedure was effective in all and was not associated with more rapid progression to AIDS.
- Of importance, however, 5.8% of patients undergoing splenectomy in the series by Oksenhendler and colleagues[115] did experience fulminant infection, consisting of *Streptococcus pneumoniae* meningitis in 2, and *Haemophilus influenzae* sepsis in 1.

- It is thus apparent that patients should undergo prophylactic vaccination before splenectomy, and that such surgery may ultimately be safer in those HIV-infected patients who can still achieve an appropriate antibody response to vaccination against *S pneumoniae* or *H influenzae*.

Summary: Treatment Options and Algorithm

- Many options currently exist to treat patients with HIV-related ITP (Table 4)
- Since patients with platelet counts > 20,000 cells/mm^3 rarely experience clinical bleeding, such patients may actually remain untreated, although the risk for intracerebral bleeding continues to exist and should be monitored

Table 4. Treatment Options in HIV-ITP

1.	Zidovudine (1,000 mg/day in divided doses) Response rate, 70% Best responses with platelets > 20,000/mm^3 at baseline
2.	Other effective antiretroviral agents and combinations
3.	Interferon-alpha
4.	Splenectomy
5.	IVIG or anti-Rh (D), especially useful when rapid response is required for acute bleeding or procedures
6.	Danazol
7.	Corticosteroids
8.	Can potentially leave untreated if platelets > 20,000 cells/mm^3

Thrombotic Disease

Deep venous thrombosis (DVT) in HIV infected individuals has been previous reported and recently, an increased incidence of venous thromboembolic disease has been described in the setting of underlying HIV infection[117-122]

- In the Multistate Adult and Adolescent Spectrum of HIV Disease Surveillance Project sponsored by the CDC, the incidence of thrombosis among 42,935 HIV-infected individuals was found to be 2.6 per 1000 person-years, significantly higher than expected in the general population

Factors predictive of thrombotic disease: age $\geq$ 45 years, CMV retinitis or other infection, other AIDS-defining opportunistic infections, hospitalization (i.e., immobility), use of megestrol acetate, and use of indinavir.[122] Use of other antiretroviral agents, sex, race, and mode of HIV transmission were not associated with an increased risk for thrombosis.

Additional factors that might be etiologic in the thromboembolic disease associated with HIV include acquired protein S deficiency,[123,124] anticardiolipin antibodies,[125] heparin cofactor II deficiency,[126] and others

While clearly not as common as the other hematologic disorders, an increased risk of thrombotic disease is also expected in the setting of HIV infection, and clinicians should be alert to the possibility of venous thrombotic disease in HIV-infected patients.

Conclusion

HIV infection is associated with a myriad of abnormalities related to hematopoiesis.

These include aberrations of various hematopoietic progenitor cells, disturbance of the microenvironment of the bone marrow, and abnormal production of various hematopoietic growth factors that influence blood cell production and function.

In addition, the presence of various infections or malignancies may alter blood cell production, while the numerous medications employed in HIV-infected patients may also affect normal hematopoiesis.

The specific evaluation of patients affected by various cytopenias will depend on the type of blood cell(s) primarily affected, while specific treatment will depend on the specific cause of the disorder, as outlined within the text and tables.

References

1. Mitsuyasu R. *AIDS Clin Review 1993/4*. Marcel Dekker; 1993:189–210.
2. Zon LI, Arkin C, Groopman JE. Hematologic manifestations of the human immunodeficiency virus (HIV). Semin Hematol. 1988; 25:208–219.
2. Moses A, Nelson J, Bagby GC Jr. The influence of human immunodeficiency virus-1 on hematopoiesis. *Blood* 1998; 91:1479–1495.
3. Bagnara GP, Zauli G, Giovanni M, Re MC, Furlini G, LaPlaca M. Early loss of circulating hematopoietic progenitors in HIV-1 infected subjects. *Exp Hematol* 1990; 18:426.
4. Folks TM, Kessler SW, Orenstein JM, et al. Infection and replication of HIV-1 in purified progenitor cells of human bone marrow. *Science* 1988; 242:919–922.
5. Shen H, Cheng T, Preffer FI, et al. Intrinsic human immunodeficiency virus type 1 resistance of hematopoietic stem cells despite coreceptor expression. *J Virol* 1999; 73:728–737.
6. Koka PS, Jamieson BD, Brooks DG, Zack JA. Human immunodeficiency virus type 1 induced hematopoietic inhibition is independent of productive infection of progenitor cells in vivo. *J Virol* 1999; 73:9089–9097.
7. Louache F, Debili N, Narandin A, Coulombel L, Vainchenker W. Expression of CD4+ by human hematopoietic progenitors. *Blood* 1994; 84:3344–3355.
8. Deichmann M, Kronenwett R, Haa R. Expression of the human immunodeficiency virus type 1 co-receptors, CXCR-4 (fusin, LESTR) and CKR-5 in CD34+ hematopoietic progenitor cells. *Blood* 1997; 89:3522–3528.
.9. Molina JM, Scadden DT, Sakaguchi M, et al. Lack of evidence for infection of or effect on growth of hematopoietic progenitor cells after in vivo or in vitro exposure to human immunodeficiency virus. *Blood* 1990; 76:2476–2482.
10. De Luca A, Teofili L, Antinor A, et al. Hematopoietic CD34+ progenitor cells are not infected by HIV-1 in vivo, but show impaired clonogenesis. *Br J Haematol* 1993; 85:20.
11. Schwartz BN, Kessler SW, Rothwell SW, et al. Inhibitory effects of HIV-1 infected stromal cell layers on the production of myeloid progenitor cells in human long term bone barrow cultures. *Exp Hematol* 1994; 22:1288–1296.
12. Moses AU, Williams S, Henevild ML, et al. Human immunodeficiency virus infection of bone marrow endothelium reduces induction of stromal hematopoietic growth factors. *Blood* 1996; 87:919–925.
13. Scadden DT, Zeira M, Woon A, et al. Human immunodeficiency virus infection of human bone marrow stromal fibroblasts. *Blood* 1990; 76:317–322.
14. Henry DH, Beall GN, Benson CA, et al. Recombinant human erythropoietin in the treatment of anemia associated with human immunodeficiency virus infection and zidovudine therapy. *Ann Intern Med* 1992; 117:739–748.
15. Keiser P, Rademacher S, Smith JW, Skiest D, Vadde V. Granulocyte colony stimulating factor use is associated with decreased bacteremia and increased survival in neutropenia HIV-infected patients. *Am J Med*. 1998;104:48–55.
16. Becker AJ, McCulloch EA, Till JE. Cytological demonstration of the clonal nature of spleen colonies derived from transplanted mouse marrow cells. *Nature* 1963; 197:452–454.
17. Spangrude GJ, Heimfeld S, Weissman IL. Purification and characterization of mouse hematopoietic stem cells. *Science* 1988; 241:58–62.

18. Berardi AC, Wang A, Levine JD, Lopez P, Scadden DT. Functional isolation and characterization of human hematopoietic stem cells. *Science* 1995; 267:104–108.

19. Maxwell AP, Lappin TRJ, Johnson CF, et al. Erythropoietin production in kidney tubular cells. *Br J Haematol*.1990; 74:535.

20. Kaushansky K, Lok S, Holly RD, et al. Promotion of megakaryocyte progenitor expansion and differentiation by the c-mpl ligand thrombopoietin. *Nature* 1994; 369:568.

21. Armitage JO. Emerging applications of recombinant human granulocyte-macrophage colony stimulating factor(sargramostim). *Blood* 1998; 92:4491–4508.

22. Spivak JL, Barnes DC, Fuchs E, Quinn TC. Serum immunoreactive erythropoietin in HIV infected patients. *JAMA* 1989; 261:3104–3107.

23. Bahner I, Kearns K, Coutinho S, Leonard EH, Kohn DB. Infection of human marrow stroma by HIV-1 is both required and sufficient for HIV-1 induced hematopoietic suppression in vitro: demonstration by gene-modification of primary human stroma. *Blood* 1997; 90:1787–1798.

24. Sullivan PS, Hanson DL, Chu SY, Jones JL, Ward JW. Epidemiology of anemia in human immunodeficiency virus infected persons: results from the Multistate Adult and Adolescent Spectrum of HIV Disease Surveillance Project. *Blood* 1998; 91:301–308.

25. Mocroft A, Kirk O, Barton SE, et al. Anaemia is an independent predictive marker for clinical prognosis in HIV infected patients from across Europe. *AIDS* 1999; 13:943–950.

26. Moore RD, Forney D. Anemia in HIV infected patients receiving highly active antiretroviral therapy. *J Acquir Immune Defic Syndr* 2002; 29:54–57.

27. Sipsas NV, Kokori SI, Ionnidis JPA, et al. Circulating autoantibodies to erythropoietin are associated with human immunodeficiency virus type 1 related anemia. *J Infect Dis* 1999; 180:2044–2047.

28. Seneviratne LS, Tulpule A, Mummaneni M, et al. Clinical, immunological and pathologic correlates of bone marrow involvement in 253 patients with AIDS-related lymphoma. *Blood* 1998; 92:244A.

29. Walker RE, Parker RI, Kovacs JA, et al. Anemia and erythropoiesis in patients with the acquired immunodeficiency syndrome (AIDS) and Kaposi sarcoma treated with zidovudine. *Ann Intern Med* 1988; 108:372–376.

30. Richman DD, Fischl MA, Grieco MH, et al. The toxicity of azidothymidine (AZT) in the treatment of patients with AIDS and AIDS-related complex: A double-blind, placebo-controlled trial. *NEJM* 1987; 317:192–197.

31. Genne D, Sudre P, Anwar D, et al. Causes of macrocytosis in HIV infected patients not treated with zidovudine. *J InfectDis* 2000; 40:160–163.

32. Anderson LJ. Human parvoviruses. *J Infect Dis* 1990; 161:603–608.

33. Frickhofen N, Abkowitz JL, Safford M, et al. Persistent B19 parvovirus infection in patients infected with human immunodeficiency virus type 1 (HIV-1): a treatable cause of anemia in AIDS. *Ann Intern Med* 1990; 113:926–933.

34. Rarick MU, Espina B, Mocharnuk R, Trilling Y, Levine AM. Thrombotic thrombocytopenic purpura in patients with human immunodeficiency virus infection: a report of three cases and review of the literature. *Am J Hematol* 1992; 40:103.

35. Telen MJ, Roberts KB, Bartlett JA. HIV associated autoimmune hemolytic anemia: report of a case and review of the literature. *AIDS* 1990; 3:933–937.

36. McGinniss MH, Macher AM, Rook AH, Alter HJ. Red cell autoantibodies in patients with acquired immune deficiency syndrome. *Transfusion* 1986; 26:405–409.

37. Gupta S, Licorish K. The Coombs' test and the acquired immunodeficiency syndrome. *Ann Intern Med* 1984; 100:462.

38. Toy PTCY, Reid ME, Burns M. Positive direct antiglobulin test associated with hyperglobulinemia in AIDS. *Am J Hematol* 1985; 19:145–150.

39. Harriman GR, Smith PD, Horne MK, et al. Vitamin B12 malabsorption in patients with acquired immunodeficiency syndrome. *Arch Intern Med* 1989; 149:2039–2041.

40. Herbert V, Fong W, Gulle V, Stopler T. Low holotranscobalamin II is the earliest serum marker for subnormal vitamin B 12 (Cobalamin) absorption in patients with AIDS. *Am J Hematol* 1990; 34:132–139.

41. Levine AM, Berhane K, Masri-Lavine L, et al. Prevalence and correlates of anemia in a large cohort of HIV-infected women: Women's Interagency HIV Study. *J Acquir Immune Defic Syndr* 2001; 26:28–35.

42. Moore RD, Keruly JC, Chaisson RE. Anemia and survival in HIV infection. *J Acquir Immune Defic Syndr Hum Retrovirol* 1998; 19:29–33.

43. Levine A, Berhane K, Sanchez MN, et al. Relationship between highly active anti-retroviral therapy (HAART), anemia and survival in a large cohort of HIV infected women (Women's Interagency HIV Study — WIHS).

Program and abstracts of the XIII International AIDS Conference; July 9–14, 2000; Durban, South Africa. Abstract MoPeB2180.

44. Lundgren JD, Mocroft A, Gatell JM, et al. A clinically prognostic scoring system for patients receiving highly active antiretroviral therapy: Results from the EuroSIDA Study. *J Infect Dis* 2002; 185:178–187.

45. Huang SS, Barbour JD, Deeks SG, et al. Reversal of human immunodeficiency virus type 1 associated hematosuppression by effective antiretroviral therapy. *CID* 2000; 30:504–510.

46. Isgro A, Mezzaroma I, Aiuti A, et al. Recovery of hematopoietic activity in bone marrow from human immunodeficiency virus type 1 infected patients during highly active antiretroviral therapy. *AIDS Res Hum Retroviruses* 2000;16: 1471–1479.

47. Henry DH, Beall GN, Benson CA, et al. Recombinant human erythropoietin in the treatment of anemia associated with human immunodeficiency virus (HIV) infection and zidovudine therapy: Overview of four clinical trials. *Ann Intern Med* 1992; 117:739–748.

48. Demetri G, Wade J, Cella D. Epoetin alfa improves quality of life in cancer patients receiving cytotoxic treatment independent of disease response: prospective clinical trial results. *Blood.* 1997;90:175a.

49. Miles SA. The use of hematopoietic growth factors in HIV infection and AIDS-related malignancies. *Cancer Invest* 1991; 9:229–238.

50. Levine AM, Deyton L, Saag M, et al. Weekly dosing with epoietin alfa in HIV infected patients with anemia: Interim data. Program and abstracts of the 39th Interscience Conference on Antimicrobial Agents and Chemotherapy; September 26–29, 1999; San Francisco, California. Abstract 1313.

51. Volberding P. Consensus statement: anemia in HIV infection—current trends, treatment options, and practice strategies. Anemia in HIV Working Group. *Clin Therapeutics* 2000; 22:1004–1020.

52. Glaspy J, Bukowski R, Steinberg D, Taylor C, Tchekmedyian S, Vadhan-Raj S. Impact of therapy with epoietin alfa on clinical outcomes in patients with nonmyeloid malignancies during cancer chemotherapy in community oncology practice. *J Clin Oncol* 1997; 15:1218–1234.

53. Gabrilove JL, Cleeland CS, Livingston RB, Sarokhan B, Winer E, Einhorn LH. Clinical evaluation of once weekly dosing of epoetin alfa in chemotherapy patients: Improvements in hemoglobin and quality of life are similar to three times weekly dosing. *J Clin Oncol* 2001; 19:2875–2882.

54. Abrams DI, Steinhart C, Frascino R. Epoetin alfa therapy for anemia in HIV infected patients: impact on quality of life. *Int J STD AIDS* 2000; 11:659–665.

55. Revicki DA, Brown RE, Henry DH, et al. Recombinant human erythropoietin and health-related quality of life of AIDS patients with anemia. *J Acquir Immune Defic Syndr Hum Retrovirol* 1994; 7:474–484.

56. Saag MS, Levine AM, Leitz GJ, Bowers PJ. Once weekly epoetin alfa increases hemoglobin and improves quality of life in anemic HIV-positive patients. Program and abstracts of the 39th Annual Meeting of the Infectious Diseases Society of America; October 27, 2001; San Francisco, California. Abstract 708.

57. Smith RE Jr, Jaiyesimi IA, Meza LA, et al. Novel erythropoiesis stimulating protein (NESP) for the treatment of anemia of chronic disease associated with cancer. *Brit J Cancer* 2001; 84:(Suppl 1):24–30.

58. Glaspy J, Jadeja J, Justice G, et al. Darbepoetin alfa administered every 1 or 2 weeks alleviates anemia (with no loss of dose efficiency) in patients with solid tumors. Program and abstracts of the 43rd Annual Meeting of the American Society of Hematology; December 7–11, 2001; Orlando, Florida. Abstract 1256.

59. Jain R. Use of blood transfusion I management of anemia. *Med Clin North Am* 1992; 76:727–744.

60. Snyder EL. Transfusion reactions. In: Hoffman R, Benz EJ Jr, Shattil SH, et al, eds. *Hematology Basic Principles and Practice.* 3rd ed. NY. Churchill Livingstone; 2000: 2300–2310.

61. Mudido PM, Georgs D, Dorazio D, et al. Human immunodeficiency virus type 1 activation after blood transfusion. *Transfusion* 1996; 36:860–865.

62. Sloand E, Kuman P, Klein HJG, Merritt S, Sacher R. Transfusion of blood components to persons infected with human immunodeficiency virus type 1: relationship to opportunistic infection. *Transfusion* 1994; 34:48–53.

63. Collier AC, Kalish LA, Busch MP, et al. Leukocyte reduced red blood cell transfusions in patients with anemia and human immunodeficiency virus infection: the Viral Activation Transfusion Study: a randomized controlled trial. *JAMA* 2001; 285:1592–1601.

64. Vamvakas EC, Blajchman MA. Deleterious clinical effects of transfusion associated immunomodulation: Fact or fiction? *Blood* 2001: 97:1180–1195.

65. Murphy M, Metcalfe P, Waters A. Incidence and mechanism of neutropenia and thrombocytopenia in patients with human immunodeficiency virus infection. *Br J Haematol* 1987; 66:337–340.

66. Bagnara GP, Zauli G, Giovannini M, Re MC, Furlini G, La Placa M. Early loss of circulating hemopoietic progenitors in HIV-1 infected subjects. *Exp Hematol* 1990; 18:426.

67. Leiderman I, Greenberg M, Adelsberg B, et al. A glycoprotein inhibitor of in vitro granulopoiesis associated with AIDS. *Blood* 1987; 70:1267–1272.

68. Mauss S, Steinmetz HT, Willers R, et al. Induction of granulocyte colony-stimulating factor by acute febrile infection but not by neutropenia in HIV seropositive individuals. *J Acquir Immune Defic Syndr Human Retrovirol* 1997; 14:430–434.

69. Elis M, Gupta S, Galant S, et al. Impaired neutrophil function in patients with AIDS or AIDS-related complex: A comprehensive evaluation. *J Infect Dis* 1988; 158:1268–1276.

70. Bodey GP, Buckley M, Sathe US, et al. Qualitative relationships between circulating leukocytes and infection in patients with acute leukemia. *Ann Intern Med* 1966; 64:328–340.

71. Miralles P, Moreno S, Perez-Tascon M, Cosin J, Diaz MD, Bouza E. Fever of uncertain origin in patients infected with the human immunodeficiency virus. *Infect Dis* 1995; 20:872–875.

72. Mayo J, Collazos J, Martinez E. Fever of unknown origin in the HIV infected patient: New scenario for an old problem. *Scand J Infect Dis* 1997; 29:327–336.

73. Moore RD, Keruly J, Chaisson RE, et al. Neutropenia and bacterial infection in acquired immunodeficiency syndrome. *Arch Intern Med* 1995; 155:1965–1970.

74. Jacobson MA, Cohen PT, Liu RC, et al. Risk of hospitalization for serious bacterial infection associated with neutropenia severity in patients with HIV. Program and abstracts of the 11th International Conference on AIDS; July 7–12, 1996; Vancouver, Canada. Abstract 231.

75. Meynard J-L, Guiguet M, Arsac S, et al. Frequency and risk factors of infectious complications in neutropenic patients infected with HIV. *AIDS* 1997; 11:995–998.

76. Moore DAJ, Benepal T, Portsmouth S, Gill J, Gazzard BG. Etiology and natural history of neutropenia in human immunodeficiency virus disease: A prospective study. *CID* 2001; 32:469–476.

77. Huang SS, Barbour JD, Deeks SG, et al. Reversal of human immunodeficiency virus type 1 associated hematosuppression by effective antiretroviral therapy. *CID* 2000; 30:504–510.

78. Sloand EM, Maciejewski J, Kumar P, Kim S, Chaudhuri A, Young N. Protease inhibitors stimulate hematopoiesis and decrease apoptosis and ICE expression in CD34+ cells. *Blood* 2000; 96:2735–2739.

79. Groopman JE and Feder D. Hematopoietic growth factors in AIDS. *Semin Oncol* 1992; 19:408–414.

80. Groopman JE, Mitsuyasu RT, DeLeo MJ, et al. Effect of recombinant human granulocyte-macrophage colony stimulating factor on myelopoiesis in the acquired immunodeficiency syndrome. *NEJM* 1987; 317:593–598.

81. Kaplan L, Kahn J, Crowe S, et al. Clincial and virologic effect of GM-CSF in patients receiving chemotherapy for HIV associated non-Hodgkin's lymphoma: results of a randomized trial. *J Clin Oncol* 1991; 9:929–940.

82. Kedzierska K, Maerz A, Warby T, et al. Granulocyte-macrophage colony stimulating factor inhibits HIV-1 replication in monocyte-derived macrophages. *AIDS* 2000: 14;1739–1748.

83. Brites C, Gilbert MJ, Pedral-Sampaio D, et al. A randomized, placebo-controlled trial of granulocyte-macrophage colony stimulating factor and nucleoside analogue therapy in AIDS. *J Infect Dis* 2000; 182:1531–1535.

84. Kimura S, Matsuda J, Ikematsu S, et al. Efficacy of recombinant human granulocyte colony-stimulating factor on neutropenia in patients with AIDS. *AIDS* 1990; 12:1251–1255.

85. Keiser P, Higgs E, Scanton J. Neutropenia is associated with bacteremia in patients with HIV. *Am J Med Sci* 1996; 312:118–122.

86. Pechere M, Samii K, Hirschel B. HIV related thrombocytopenia. *NEJM* 1993; 328:1785–1786.

87. Sullivan PS, Hanson DL, Chu SY, Jones JL, Ciesielski CA. Surveillance for thrombocytopenia in persons infected with HIV: Results from the Multistate Adult and Adolescent Spectrum of Disease Project. J *Acquir Immune Defic Syndr Hum Retrovirol* 1997; 14:374–379.

88. Ballem PJ, Belzberg A, Devine DV, et al. Kinetic studies of the mechanism of thrombocytopenia in patients with human immunodeficiency virus infection. *NEJM* 1992; 327:1779–1784.

89. Walsh CM, Nardi MA, Karpatkin S. On the mechanism of thrombocytopenic purpura in sexually active homosexual men. *NEJM* 1984; 311:635–639.

90. Bettaieb A, Fromont P, Louache F, et al. Presence of cross-reactive antibody between human immunodeficiency virus (HIV) and platelet glycoproteins in HIV related immune thrombocytopenic purpura. *Blood* 1992; 80:162–169.

91. Kouri Y, Borkowsky W, Nardi M, Karpatkin S, Basch RS. Human megakaryocytes have a CD4+ molecule capable of binding human immunodeficiency virus-1. *Blood* 1993; 81:2664–2670.

92. Zucker-Franklin D, Seremetis S, Heng ZY. Internalization of human immunodeficiency virus type I and other retroviruses by megakaryocytes and platelets. *Blood* 1990; 75:1920–1923.

93. Wang J-F, Liu Z-Y, Groopman JE. The alpha-chemokine receptor CXCR4 is expressed on the megakaryocytic lineage from progenitor to platelets, and modulates migration and adhesion. *Blood* 1998; 92:756–764.

94. Zucker-Franklin D, Cao Y. Megakaryocytes of human immunodeficiency virus-infected individuals express viral RNA. *Proc Natl Acad Sci USA* 1989; 86:5595–5599.

95. Zucker-Franklin D, Termin CS, Cooper MC. Structural changes in the megakaryocytes of patients infected with the human immunodeficiency virus (HIV-1). *Am J Pathol* 1989; 134:1295–1304.

96. Swiss Group for Clinical Studies on AIDS. Zidovudine for the treatment of thrombocytopenia associated with HIV: A prospective study. *Ann Intern Med* 1988; 109:718–721.

97. Harker LA, Marzec UM, Novembre F, et al. Treatment of thrombocytopenia in chimpanzees infected with HIV by pegylated recombinant human megakaryocyte growth and development factor. *Blood* 1998; 91:4427–4433.

98. Oksenhendler E, Bierling P, Farcet JP, et al. Response to therapy in 37 patients with HIV related thrombocytopenic purpura. *Br J Haematol* 1987; 66:49.

99. Oksenhendler E, Bierling P, Ferchal F, Clauvel J-P, Seligmann M. Zidovudine for thrombocytopenic purpura related to human immunodeficiency virus (HIV) infection. *Ann Intern Med* 1989; 110:365–368.

100. Landonio G, Cinque P, Nosari A, et al. Comparison of two dose regimens of zidovudine in an open, randomized, multicenter study for severe HIV related thrombocytopenia. *AIDS* 1993; 7:209–212.

101. Piketty C, Gilquin J, Kazatchkine MD. Successful treatment of HIV related thrombocytopenia with didanosine (ddI). *J Acquir Immune Defic Syndr Hum Retrovirol* 1994; 7:521–522.

102. Tozzi V, Narcisco P, Sebastiani G, Frigiotti D, D'Amato C. Effects of indinavir treatment on platelet and neutrophil counts in patients with advanced HIV disease. *AIDS* 1997; 11:1067–1068.

103. Caso JAA, Mingo CS, Tena JG. Effect of highly active antiretroviral therapy on thrombocytopenia in patients with HIV infection. *NEJM* 1999; 16:1239–1240.

104. Marroni M, Gresele P, Landonio G, et al. Interferon-a is effective in the treatment of HIV-1 related, severe, zidovudine-resistant thrombocytopenia: a prospective, placebo-controlled, double-blind trial. *Ann Intern Med* 1994; 121:423–429.

105. Vianelli N, Catani L, Gugliotta L, et al. Recombinant alpha-interferon 2b in the treatment of HIV related thrombocytopenia. *AIDS* 1993; 7:823–827.

106. Imbach P, d'Apuzzo V, Hirt A, et al. High dose intravenous gammaglobulin for idiopathic thrombocytopenic purpura in childhood. *Lancet* 1981; 1:1228–1231.

107. Bussel JB, Haimi JS. Isolated thrombocytopenia in patients infected with HIV: treatment with intravenous gammaglobulin. *Am J Hematol* 1988; 28:79–84.

108. Gringeri A, Cattaneo M, Santagostino E, Mannucci PM. Intramuscular anti-D immunoglobulins for home treatment of chronic immune thrombocytopenic purpura. *Br J Haematol* 1992; 80:337–340.

109. Oksenhendler E, Bierling P, Brossard Y, et al. Anti-Rh immunoglobulin therapy for human immunodeficiency virus-related immune thrombocytopenic purpura. *Blood* 1988; 71:1499–1502.

110. Newman GC, Novoa MV, Fodero EM, Lesser ML, Woloski BMR, Bussel JB. A dose of 75 ug/kg/d of IV anti-D increases the platelet count more rapidly and for a longer period of time that 50 ug/kg/d in adults with immune thrombocytopenic purpura. *Br J Haematol* 2001; 112:1076–1078.

111. Ahn YS, Mylvaganam R, Garcia RO, et al. Low dose danazol therapy in idiopathic thrombocytopenic purpura. *Ann Intern Med* 1987; 107:177–181.

112. Ahn YS, Harrington WJ, Simon SR, et al. Danazol for the treatment of idiopathic thrombocytopenic purpura. *NEJM* 1983; 308:1396–1399.

113. Schreiber AD, Chien P, Tomaski A, Cines DB. Effect of danazol in immune thrombocytopenic purpura. *NEJM* 1987; 316:503–508.

114. Oksenhendler E, Bierling P, Chevret S, et al. Splenectomy is safe and effective in human immunodeficiency virus related immune thrombocytopenia. *Blood* 1993; 82:29–32.

115. Kemeny MM, Cooke V, Melester TS, et al. Splenectomy in patients with AIDS and AIDS-related complex. *AIDS* 1993; 7:1063–1067.

116. Becker DM, Saunders TJ, Wispelwey B, Schain DC. Case report: venous thromboembolism in AIDS. *Am J Med Sci* 1992; 303;395–397.

117. Roberts SP. Haefs TMP. Central retinal vein occlusion in a middle aged adult with HIV infection. *Optom Vis Sci* 1992; 210:108–111.

118. Tanimowo M. Deep vein thrombosis as a manifestation of acquired immunodeficiency syndrome? A case report. *Cent Afr J Med* 1996; 42:327–328.

119. Narayanan TS, Narawane NM, Phadke AY, Abraham JP. Multiple abdominal venous thrombosis in HIV seropositive patient. *Indian J Gastroenterol* 1998; 17:105–106.

120. Park KL, Marx JL, Lopez PF, Rao NA. Noninfectious branch retinal vein occlusion in HIV-positive patients. *Retina* 1997; 17:162–164.

121. Sullivan PS, Dworkin MS, Jones JL, Hooper CW. Epidemiology of thrombosis in HIV-infected individuals. *AIDS* 2000; 14:321–324.

122. Stahl CP, Wideman CS, Spira TJ, Haff EC, Hixon GJ, Evatt BL. Protein S deficiency in men with long term human immunodeficiency virus infection. *Blood* 1993; 81:1801–1807.

123. Bissuel F, Berruyer M, Causse X, Dechavanne M, Trepo C. Acquired protein S deficiency: correlation with advanced disease in HIV-1 infected patients. *J Acquir Immune Defic Syndr Hum Retrovirol* 1992; 5:484–489.

124. Stimmler MM, Quismorio FP, McGehee WG, Boyen T, Sharma OP. Anticardiolipin antibodies in acquired immunodeficiency syndrome. *Arch Intern Med* 1989; 149:1833–1835.

125. Toulon P, Lamine M, Ledjev I, Guez T, Hollerman MF. Heparin cofactor II deficiency in patients infected with the human immunodeficiency virus. *Throm Haemost* 1993; 70:730–735.

12

Dermatological Manifestations of HIV/AIDS

Marcus A. Conant, MD
Medical Director, Conant Medical Group, San Francisco
Kevin T. Belasco, DO, MS
Resident, Dermatology, Sun Coast Hospital, Largo

Pre-HAART Era

- Numerous and varied opportunistic cutaneous infections and malignancies were common
- DNA viral infections, including molluscum contagiosum, were the most common
- Unusual clinical presentations and manifestations were typical
- Cutaneous diseases were often an indicator of CD4 decline and disease progression
- Biopsy often needed to make definitive diagnosis

HAART ERA

- HIV/AIDS cutaneous disease is often a clue to test for HIV infection
- Recurrence of skin lesions may be indicative of failure of antiretroviral treatment with fall of CD4 count and/or rise in viral load
- Most cutaneous manifestations of HIV infection clear spontaneously with HAART

Dermatological Manifestations of HIV Infection Seen Prior to HAART

- The treatment of choice for all these conditions is to put the patient on aggressive antiretroviral therapy and get their viral load as low as possible as quickly as possible. Consult a standard dermatological text for specific treatment for each of the conditions listed.

Table 1. Dermatological Manifestations of HIV Infection Seen Prior to HAART

Skin Lesion Category	Specific Manifestation	Comments
Acute HIV Exanthem		• Rarely seen • Consider early intervention to preserve cytotoxic T cells
Bacterial Infections • Bacterial infections are very common • Soak cutaneous lesions with sterile saline sponge for 10 minutes prior to culture • Most lesions respond promptly to appropriate topical and systemic treatment	abscesses	• Unusual
	acne	• Common
	actinmycosis	• Rare
	bacillary angiomatosis	• Rare • Treat aggressively with oral erythromycin for 4-5 weeks • Consider Kaposi's sarcoma in the differential diagnosis
	botryomycosis	• Rare
	bullous impetigo	• Common • Treat topically and systemically
	cellulitis	• Common
	chancroid	• Rare
	ecthyma	• Rare
	folliculitis	• Extremely Common • Each pustule will have a hair in the center • Treat with topical and systemic antibiotics
	granuloma inguinale	• Rare
	impetigo	• Common • Culture • Treat with topical and systemic antibiotics • Consider primary Herpes simplex infection
	mycobacterial infection	• Rare
	Staphylococcal scalded skin syndrome	• Rare
	syphilis	• Often missed • Unusual rashes deserve an RPR • Seen in individuals not practicing safer sex
	Aphthous ulcers	• Commonly seen in the oral mucosa
Viral Infections • Viral infections are the most common cutaneous opportunistic disease seen in HIV/AIDS patients	Chickenpox (varicella)	• Rare • Obtain culture for definitive diagnosis
	condyloma acuminatum	• Very common • Refer for anoscopy, pap smear, and aggressive therapy
	cytomegalovirus exanthem	• Rare, may cause retinitis with loss of vision
	Epstein-Barr virus exanthem	• Rare
	herpes simplex	• Very common • Culture to confirm • Use suppressive acyclovir for recurrent outbreaks
	herpes zoster	• Very common • Occasionally recurrent • Culture to confirm diagnosis • Aggressive treatment with acyclovir, valacyclovir, or famciclovir • Do not stop treatment until all lesions have healed
	human papilloma virus (warts)	• Very common • Treat aggressively
	molluscum contagiosum	• Very common • Treat aggressively
	oral hairy leukoplakia	• Topical retin-A solution works well
	vaccinia	• Rare • Follows vaccination
Fungal and Yeast Infections	candidiasis	• Very common • Treat topically and systemically to avoid resistance
	coccidioidomycosis	• Very rare
	cryptococcosis	• Rare, may progress to meningitis if untreated • Mimics molluscum contagiosum
	dermatophytosis	• Very common • Prophylactic therapy will be needed
	histoplasmosis	• Common in the Mississippi Valley
	mucormycosis	• Very rare
	onychomycosis	• Very common
	pruritus ani	• Common • Treat with ketoconazole cream
	Scopulariopsis infection	• Very rare

	seborrheic dermatitis	• Very common • Treat with hydrocortisone cream and ketoconazole cream
	sporotrichosis	• Very rare
Protozoal Infections (biopsy diagnosis)	*Acanthamoeba*	• Extremely rare
	amebiasis/ cryptosporidiosis/ isosporosis	• Extremely rare, often present with chronic GI complaints, including diarrhea
	pneumocystis carinii	• Extremely rare
	toxoplasma	• Extremely rare, neurologic sequelae common
Arthropod Infection	*Demodex* folliculitis	• Common
	scabies	• Very common • Treat sexual and family contacts
Hyperkeratotic Disease	ichthyosis	• Rare
	xerosis	• Very common • Liberal use of moisturizers after bathing
Papulosquamous Disease	lichen planus	• Need biopsy to confirm diagnosis
	palmoplantar keratoderma	• Very rare
	Reiter's syndrome	
	psoriasis	• Moderately common, may be disseminated in HIV/AIDS patients
Eczematous Diseases (see specific disease group above)	dermatophytosis	
	seborrheic dermatitis	
	drug eruptions	
	erythroderma	
	xerotic (asteototic) eczema	
Neoplastic Diseases (all require biopsy to confirm diagnosis)	basal cell carcinoma	
	Bowenoid papulosis	
	Kaposi's sarcoma	• Very common • Treatment of choice is aggressive antiretroviral therapy • Intralesional vinblastine (Velban®) and liquid nitrogen are useful • Topical Panretin (alitretinoin) gel is expensive but beneficial
	lymphoma (b cell, normally)	
	melanoma	
	mycosis fungoides (cutaneous T cell lymphoma)	
	squamous cell carcinoma	
Vascular Lesions	cutis marmorata	
	thrombocytopenic purpura	
	vasculitis	
Hair and Nail Color	alopecia areata	
	changes in nail color	
	nail deformities	
	premature graying	
	telogen effluvium	
	thinning of hair	
Oral Diseases	angular cheilitis	
	aphthosis	
	gingivitis	
	Oral hairy leukoplakia	• Very common, associated with Epstein-Barr virus • See above
	Kaposi's sarcoma	• See above
	black hairy tongue	
Reaction to Medications	TMP-SMX (Bactrim®, Septra®) reaction	• Photodermatitis, fever, morbillifom (measles-like) eruption may occur with or without desquamation • Desensitize patient • Most common drug to cause skin eruptions in HIV-positive patients • Severe cases of hypersensitivity may progress to Stevens-Johnson syndrome
Miscellaneous Disorders	bullous pemphigoid	
	Calciphylaxis	• Associated with renal failure, may be life-threatening
	cervical dysplasia	
	dermatitis herpetiformis	
	dermatomyositis	

	eosinophilic folliculitis	• Very common with extremely low CD4 count • Biopsy needed for a diagnosis • Highly pruritic • Papular pruritic eruption of AIDS (PPE) represents a variant, commonly seen on trunk and extremities
	erythema elevatum diutinum	
	erythema nodosum	
	granuloma annulare	
	lymphocytoma cutis	
	nutritional deficiencies	
	papular pruritic eruption	
	porphyria cutanea tarda	• Associated with phototoxicity
	prurigo nodularis	
	pruritus	• Extremely common • Consider xerosis, eosinophilic folliculitis, bacterial folliculitis, scabies
	pyoderma gangrenosum	
	transient acantholytic dermatosis (Grover's disease)	
	urticaria	• Unusual • Consider drug eruption
	Lipodystrophy syndrome Desquamative cheilitis	• Associated with use of protease inhibitors

Dermatological Manifestations of HIV Infection in Patients Receiving HAART Therapy

- Dermatological diseases are rare if the patient's viral load is undetectable and their CD4 count is rising
- In the unusual situation where one of these diseases appears and the viral load is undetectable, intensify the antiretroviral therapy if the CD4 count does not simultaneously rise. Cutaneous disease in the HIV patient should improve over time as the CD4 count rises, reflecting an overall restoration of immune system integrity. Complete resolution of opportunistic infections, however, may depend on appropriate antibacterial and/or antiviral therapy.

Table 2. Dermatological Manifestations of HIV Infection in Patients Receiving HAART Therapy

Bacterial Infections	Acne	• Benzoyl peroxide wash • Topical clindamycin gel • Systemic antibiotic
	Folliculitis	• See above • Distinguish from eosinophilic folliculitis
	Impetigo	• Culture • Treat with topical and systemic antibiotics • Consider primary Herpes simplex infection
	Syphilis	• Seen in individuals with high-risk sexual encounters and/or multiple sexual partners without barrier protection
Viral Infections	Condyloma acuminata	• Perianal warts are the most commonly seen problem in this population • Appropriate follow-up with anoscopy, pap smear, and aggressive therapy is recommended • Incidence of peri anal squamous cell carcinoma is very high in this group of patients • Aldara® (Imiquimod) cream is beneficial
	Herpes simplex	• Still seen commonly • See above
	Herpes zoster	• Still seen commonly • See above
	Human papilloma virus	• Still seen commonly
Fungal and Yeast Infections	Candida	• Usually seen in individuals with measurable viral load
	Dermatophytosis	• Still seen commonly • Responds to over-the-counter antifungals such as Lamisil® (terbinafine)
	Onychomycosis	• Still very common • Requires systemic treatment to clear and topical treatment to prevent recurrence
	Pruritus ani	• See above
	Seborrheic dermatitis	• See above
Neoplastic Diseases	Basal cell carcinoma	• Superficial spreading subtype is the most common • Mimics a small patch of eczema which has been present for many months, commonly seen on the trunk
	Kaposi's sarcoma	• New lesions are generally seen in individuals with detectable viral load • Progressive therapy with antiretroviral therapy coupled with intralesional vinblastine and/or Panretin® (alitretinoin) gel is extremely effective
	Squamous cell carcinoma	• Particularly common in the anal area in individuals with a prior history of condyloma acuminata
Reaction to Medications	Non-nucleoside reverse transcriptase inhibitors	• Morbilliform and urticarial eruptions are common • Often can treat through to tolerance
	Ziagen® (abacavir) reaction	• Morbiliform eruption 2–5% of patients • Rash alone is not diagnositic for abacavir hypersensitivity reaction • Occasionally fatal reactions have been seen particulary in patients with prior hypersensitivity (which may have gone unrecognized) reaction who have been re-challenged with abacavir
Miscellaneous Diseases	Eosinophilic folliculitis	• Seen as CD4 count rises (immune restoration disease) • Post-corticosteroids on a weekly basis is very effective • Generally ceases when CD4 count rises above 200

Pearls of Wisdom

- Treatment will be far more effective if you can make a definitive diagnosis
- What to do if you don't know what it is:
  - o Stop all topical treatment
  - o Find an early primary lesion
  - o Perform a small 2 or 3 mm punch biopsy and send to a good dermatohisto-pathologist
  - o Remember that a thorough history and physical is vital; always ask the patient with a new rash about recent changes in medications, as well as any drug allergies, pets, and recent international travel
- A final word to the wise
  - o In patients who present with unusual rashes, always consider a possibility of syphilis, drug eruption, or scabies

References

1. Friedman-Kien AE. AIDS and HIV-related diseases. *JAAD* 1990:22:1163–1318.

2. Cockerell C. Human immunodeficiency virus infection and the skin: a crucial interface. *Arch Intern Med* 1991; 1295–1302.

3. Tappero J, Conant M, Wolf S, Berger T. Kaposi's sarcoma, epidemiology, pathogenesis, histology, clinical spectrum, staging criteria and therapy. *JAAD* 1993:28:371–390.

4. Bolognia JL, Jorizzo, JL, Rapini, RP, eds. *Dermatology* New York: Mosby, 2003.

13

Neurological Complications of HIV/AIDS

David Simpson, MD
Professor of Neurology
Director, Clinical Neurophysiology Laboratories
Director, Neuro-AIDS Program
Mount Sinai Medical Center, New York

Introduction

HIV targets many cells, tissues, and organs besides the immune system. Because it is a neurotropic virus, i.e., it has a predilection for cells of the nervous system, HIV enters the central nervous system early and, in as yet unclear ways, leads to many neurological problems. This chapter describes some of the non-infectious, non-malignant neurological complications of chronic HIV infection.

HIV-Associated Dementia (HAD) (adapted from Goldenberg and Boyle[1])

SPECTRUM OF COGNITIVE, MOTOR, AND BEHAVIORAL SYMPTOMS

Mild

HIV-1 Minor Cognitive-Motor Disorder (MCMD)

Moderate-Severe

HIV-Associated Dementia (HAD)
- Subcortical dementia
- Insidious onset
- Absence of focal cognitive deficits
- Global motor deficits
- May be confused with CMV encephalitis (quite rare today)

Epidemiology

Pre-HAART era

–   15–20% of AIDS patients with annual incidence of 7% after a diagnosis of AIDS.

HAART era

–   Incidence difficult to ascertain, depends on whether defining as dementia (5–10%) or minor impairment (higher — approx 20%)

Symptoms

Early: may be subtle!

–   Cognitive:
      o   Mild deficits such as difficulty in remembering recent events, names, and/or problems in concentrating and completing tasks
      o   Mini-mental exam usually normal

–   Motor:
      o   May include clumsiness, slowing of fine motor skills

–   Behavioral:
      o   Social withdrawal, apathy, anhedonia: may be mistaken for depression

Late: may progress to

–   Severe impairment of cognitive function
–   Severe psychomotor retardation
–   Hypersomnia

Diagnosis

History and neuro exam

Exclusion of other causes of altered mental status (i.e., metabolic, infectious, psychologic).

Neuropsychological testing:

–   Mini-mental status exam *rarely* helpful in most cases
–   Neuropsychologic tests helpful to separate organic neurologic from psychologic impairment.
–   HIV dementia scale may be more helpful (see Figure 1)

Figure 1. HIV Dementia Scale

Max Score	Score	
		MEMORY-REGISTRATION Give 4 words to recall to recall (dog, hat, green, peach)[1] 1 s to say each. Then ask the patient all 4 after you have said them.
4	( )	**ATTENTION** Anti-saccadic eye movements: 20 commands. _____errors of 20 trial. ≤3 errors = 4: 4 errors = 3; 5 errors = 2; 6 = 1; > 6 ERRORS = 0.
6	( )	**PSYCHOMOTOR SPEED** Ask the patient to write the alphabet in upper case letters horizontally across the page and record the time: _____s. ≤21 s = 6; 21.1-24 s = 5; 24.1-27 s = 4; 27.1-30 s = 3; 30.1-33 s = 2; 33.1-36 s = 1; >36s = 0.
4	( )	**MEMORY RECALL** Ask the 4 words from registration above. Give 1 point for each correct answer. For words not recalled prompt with a semantic clue, as follows: animal (dog); piece of clothing (hat); color (green); fruit (peach). Give ½ point for each correct answer after prompting.
2	( )	**CONSTRUCTION** Copy the cube below; record time: ____s. <25 s = 2; >35 s = 0; cube wrong = 0.

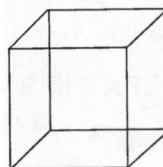

TOTAL SCORE: _____/16

---

[1]In the Dutch version, we used the words *kat* (cat), *hoed* (hat); *geel* (yellow) and *perzik* (peach).

Reprinted with permission from Lippincott, Williams, and Wilkins. Originally appearing in Power C, Selnes OA, Grim JA, McArthur JC. HIV Dementia Scale: A rapid screening test. *Journal of Acquired Immune Deficiency Syndromes.* March 1, 1995; 8(3):273–278.

Radiology
 – Used to exclude other causes of cognitive impairment
 – CT and MR imaging may show diffuse atrophy with enlarged ventricles but not sensitive or specific
 – PET scanning: sometimes shows *hypermetabolism* (early) and cortical and subcortical *hypometabolism* (late)
 – MRI: metabolic profiles correlate with psychological deficits
 – Cerebrospinal fluid analysis
 – Non-specific in HAD, but important to exclude other causes
 – Increasing data on value of CSF VL

Management

Aggressively treat HIV infection with HAART!

 – Believed to be caused by HIV itself rather than some opportunistic pathogen
 – Agents providing best CNS penetration include zidovudine (AZT, Retrovir®), didanosine (ddI, Videx®/Videx EC®), stavudine (d4T, Zerit®), nevirapine (Viramune®), and indinavir (Crixivan®). Efavirenz (Sustiva®) doesn't penetrate CSF well, but seems to control CSF VL
 – Adherence in patients with HAD may be problematic
   •

Psychostimulants:

 – For apathy and psychomotor retardation
   •

Antidepressants:

 – Avoid tricyclics due to possible anticholinergic delirium

Neuropathies (adapted from Price[2])

SENSORY POLYNEUROPATHIES – DISTAL SENSORY POLYNEUROPATHY (DSPN)

Pathogenesis

Probably not caused by HIV itself
More likely secondary mechanisms, i.e. cytokine mediated (TNF)
Primary targets: axon and sensory ganglion cell body rather than myelin sheath

Clinical presentation

Usually symmetric
Usually insidious/progressive
Usually begins in toes and plantar surface of feet and may progress proximally
Paresthesias and pain with preservation of motor function
May be severely debilitating

Diagnosis

By history and clinical presentation
May be impairment of distal sensation and/or reduction of ankle reflexes
Electrodiagnostic testing rarely necessary, but may be used to R/O other problems or if clinical picture is confusing

Treatment

Symptomatic relief

 – Tricyclic antidepressants (e.g., desipramine 10–25 mg qhs and gradually increase dose) — though ACTG trial of **amitriptyline** negative[3]
 – Anticonvulsants
   o Phenytoin, carbamazepine rarely effective (caution regarding drug interactions with PIs and NNRTIs).

o   Gabapentin (Neurontin®) effective in many cases (300–400 mg tid with dose escalation up to max of 3600 mg/day) — due to drowsiness, many start with 300 mg qd x 1 day, then 300 mg bid x 1 day then 300 mg tid

o   Lamotrigine (Lamictal®) reported to be fairly effective in recent clinical trial[4]

- Topical lidocaine (Lidoderm® patch)
- Use of WHO Pain Ladder may be helpful
- Antiarrhythmics (i.e., mexiletine) and capsaicin cream rarely effective
- Opiates — effective in neuropathic pain, with appropriate cautions
- Nerve growth factor
    o   Trial demonstrated modest efficacy for pain reduction, but not currently available[5]
    o   NGF did not show evidence of nerve fiber regeneration in HIV PN

Research agents:

- Topical lidocaine patch
- High concentration capsaicin patch
- Acetyl-L-carnitine
- Prosaptide

TOXIC SENSORY POLYNEUROPATHY

Etiology

Antiretroviral agents most common (zalcitabine > didanosine > stavudine)
Others: dapsone, thalidomide, high doses of vitamin B_6
Possible mitochondrial toxicity

Symptomatology

Same as HIV DSPN

Diagnosis

By history and neurological exam
Relief of symptoms once offending agent is dose-reduced or removed

- May take months but usually within 2 to 3 weeks
- May unmask DSPN

Treatment

Removal of offending agent(s), following cost-benefit analysis
Symptomatic (pain relief)
Pathogenesis-based (research studies)

Motor Polyneuropathies

Acute/subacute (Guillain-Barré (GBS) or acute idiopathic demyelinating polyneuropathy) or *chronic* (chronic idiopathic demyelinating polyneuropathy)

Etiology

Possible autoimmune phenomenon
Mito toxicity (GBS)
CMV (late stage disease)

Clinical presentation

Occurs at any stage of disease
Distal weakness with absent reflexes
Respiratory difficulties and/or autonomic instability in severe cases

Diagnosis

History and physical exam
Electrodiagnostic studies helpful
CSF analysis (⇑ protein, low grade pleocytosis)

Treatment

As per non-HIV-associated diseases (IVIG, plasmapheresis, etc.)
Anti-CMV (late stage)

Myopathies

Etiologies

Inflammatory and non-inflammatory
Mitochondrial toxicity due to nucleoside analogues[6]

Clinical presentation

Proximal muscle weakness

Diagnosis

Clinical features
Laboratory: ⇑ CPK
Electrodiagnostic studies
Histopathologic: helpful

Treatment

Removal of offending agent(s)
Corticosteroid treatment
Multivitamins and minerals (experimental)

Myelopathies

VACUOLAR AND OTHER NON-SEGMENTAL MYELOPATHIES

Characterized by diffuse clinical manifestations with motor deficits predominating
Usually progressive
May be some overlap with HAD

Pathology

Characteristic "foamy" appearance of spinal cord white matter indistinguishable from *subacute combined degeneration* resulting from vitamin B_{12} deficiency

Clinical presentation

Subacute
- – Hyperactive ankle jerks or gait clumsiness
- – Spastic or spastic-ataxic gait that may progress to paraparesis or paraplegia w/o cognitive deficits
- – Sphincter, erectile dysfunction
  - •

Diagnosis

By clinical presentation
Must be differentiated from HTLV-induced disorders
- – HTLV-I-associated myelopathy
- – Tropical spastic paraparesis, HTLV-II
  - •

Treatment

Unknown
Consider treating HIV aggressively

Focal (Segmental) Myelopathies

Much less common
Usually due to diseases causing other focal CNS problems (e.g. VZV infection, toxoplasmosis, primary central nervous system lymphoma)

References

1. Goldenberg D, Boyle B. Psychiatry and HIV: Part 2. *The AIDS Reader*. 2000:10(4):201–204.

2. Price RW. Neurologic disease. In: *AIDS Therapy*. Dolin R, Masur H, Saag MS, eds. Philadelphia, PA: Churchill Livingstone, 1999.

3. Kieburtz K, Simpson DM, and the ACTG 242 Study Team. A randomized trial of amitriptyline and mexiletine for painful neuropathy in HIV infection. *Neurology*. 1998:51:1682–1688.

4. McArthur J. HIV-related peripheral neuropathies and their treatment. 8th Conference on Retroviruses and Opportunistic Infections, February 4–8, 2001, Chicago, IL. Abstract L8. Available at: http//www.retroconference.org/2001/abstracts/abstracts/ abstracts/I8.htm.

5. Simpson DM, Olney R, McArthur JC, Khan A, Godbold J, Ebel-Frommer K. A placebo-controlled trial of lamotrigine for painful HIV-associated neuropathy. *Neurology*. 2000:54:2115–2119.

6. Brinkman K, Smeitink JA, Romijn JA, Reiss P. Mitochondrial toxicity induced by nucleoside-analogue reverse transcriptase inhibitors is a key factor in the pathogenesis of antiretroviral therapy-related lipodystrophy. *Lancet*. 1999:354:112–115.

14

Oral Manifestations

Carol Stewart, DDS, MS
University of Florida, College of Dentistry, Gainesville
Rafael Alfonso, DDS
Ryan White Title I, Miami

Introduction

Establishment and maintenance of oral health is essential for systemic health. Healthy oral tissues and functional dentition help ensure adequate nutrition, positive self-esteem, and enhancement of quality of life.

Screening for dental disease and oral lesions is a component of the initial evaluation (complete history and physical). The oral cavity is often a "window" into the patient's general health status and/or healthcare behavior. Oral lesions are often the first clinical sign of HIV disease; and they may indicate progressing immunosuppression in a patient on HAART. Patients presenting with obvious or suspicious areas of concern should be promptly referred to a dentist for evaluation and treatment. Others should maintain routine evaluation and care every 4–to 6 months as appropriate.

Objectives of Dental Treatment in the HIV/AIDS Patient

- Pain control
- Identification and management of oral lesions
- Elimination of sources of infection
- Stabilization and prevention of tissue destruction
- Preservation of existing oral structures
- Restoration of lost function by means of treatment modalities
- Patient education regarding ongoing oral health maintenance

Specific Dental Recommendations

- After review of medical history and palliation, all patients should have a complete oral exam, full mouth series of radiographs, and a customized treatment plan that addresses objectives listed above.

General Preventive Dental Guidelines

CARIOUS LESIONS

- All carious lesions should be identified and treated appropriately. Teeth with pulpal exposures should be pulp capped, scheduled for endodontic therapy, or extracted. Patients with advanced decay from salivary dysfunction must be instructed to employ dietary modifications (such as avoiding highly carbonated/sugary drinks and candy sweetened with glucose) to retard further caries progression. Other dietary counseling should be performed as appropriate.
  - As xerostomia will enhance development of dental decay, customized fluoride regimens should be provided to minimize caries progression

ACUTE ORAL INFECTIONS

- Acute oral infections should be treated with oral antibiotics. Rapidly progressing intraoral or extraoral facial infections may require referral to a physician for IV antibiotic therapy.

EXTRACTIONS AND INTRAORAL SURGICAL PROCEDURES

- All non-restorable and "hopeless" teeth should be extracted. Hematological disorders such as thrombocytopenia, anemia, leukopenia, or severe immune compromise may require physician referral or prior preparation (such as platelet transfusion or component augmentation) prior to procedures. Caution: if $CD4^+$ count is less than 100 cells/mm^3, evaluate for neutropenia. If absolute neutrophil count is < 500 cells/mm^3, patient should receive antibiotics pre and post surgery and consideration should be given to administer filgrastim (Neupogen$^®$) to stimulate neutrophil production.

PROPHYLACTIC ANTIBIOTIC GUIDELINES

- Patients with history of cardiovascular concerns such as prior heart valve replacement or mitral valve prolapse (MVP), may require prophylactic antibiotic coverage prior to some dental procedures. Table 1 lists the cardiac conditions for which endocarditis prophylaxis is recommended. Table 2 lists the dental procedures for which endocarditis prophylaxis is recommended in patients who have a cardiac condition listed in Table1. (For further details see: Recommendations by the American Heart Association by the Committee on Rheumatic Fever, Endocarditis, and Kawasaki Disease. *JAMA* 1997;1794–1801.)

Table 1. Cardiac Conditions for Which Endocarditis Prophylaxis Is Recommended

High-risk category:

Prosthetic cardiac valves, including bioprosthetic and homograft valves.

Previous bacterial endocarditis

Complex cyanotic congenital heart disease (e.g., single ventricle states, transposition of the great arteries, tetralogy of Fallot)

Surgically constructed systemic pulmonary shunts or conduits

Moderate-risk category:

Most other congenital cardiac malformations (other than above and below)

Acquired valvar dysfunction (e.g., rheumatic heart disease)

Hypertrophic cardiomyopathy

Mitral valve prolapse with valvar regurgitation and/or thickened leaflets[1]

Adapted from *JAMA* 1997;1794–1801.

Table 2. Dental Procedures for Which Endocarditis Prophylaxis Is Recommended[1]

Dental extractions

Periodontal procedures including surgery, scaling, and root planing, probing, and recall maintenance

Dental implant placement and reimplantation of avulsed teeth

Endodontic (root canal) instrumentation or surgery only beyond the apex

Subgingival placement of antibiotic fibers or strips

Initial placement of orthodontic bands but not brackets

Intraligamentary local anesthetic injections

Prophylactic cleaning of teeth or implants where bleeding is anticipated

Adapted from *JAMA* 1997;1794–1801.

Table 3. Prophylactic Regimens for Dental or Oral Procedures

Situation	Agent	Regimen
Standard general prophylaxis	Amoxicillin	Adults: 2.0 g; children[*]: 50 mg/kg orally 1 h before procedure
Unable to take oral medications	Ampicillin	Adults: 2.0 g IM or IV; children[*]: 50 mg/kg IM or IV within 30 min before procedure
Allergic to penicillin	Clindamycin or	Adults: 600 mg; children[*]: 20 mg/kg orally 1 h before procedure
	Cephalexin[†] or cefadroxil[†] or	Adults: 2.0 g; children[*]; 50 mg/kg orally 1 h before procedure
	Azithromycin or clarithromycin	Adults: 500 mg; children[*]: 15 mg/kg orally 1 h before procedure
Allergic to penicillin and unable to take oral medications	Clindamycin or Cefazolin[2]	Adults: 600 mg; children[*]: 20 mg/kg IV within 30 min before procedure Adults: 1.0 g; children[*]: 25 mg/kg IM or IV within 30 min before procedure

Adapted from *JAMA* 1997; 1794–1801.

* Total children's dose should not exceed adult dose.
† Cephalosporins should not be used in individuals with immediate-type hypersensitivity reaction (urticaria, angioedema, or anaphylaxis) to penicillins.

• Patients with history of injection drug use may be at increased risk for cardiac valvular disease.

• Patients with prior joint replacement (prosthetic hips, knees, etc.) may need prophylactic antibiotic coverage. Patients who have had a joint replacement and undergo dental procedures listed in Table 2, are at increased risk of developing hematogenous joint infection. Immunocompromised patients likely maintain this increased risk beyond the 2-year window for which antibiotic prophylaxis is recommended for non-immunocompromised patients. The antibiotic regimens recommended for prophylaxis are the same as those listed in Table 3 for the prevention of endocarditis; however, the macrolide option, although likely to be effective, is not listed in the Advisory Statement for the prevention of joint infections. (See: Advisory Statement. Antibiotic prophylaxis for dental patients with total joint replacement. American Dental Association; American Academy of Orthopaedic Surgeons. *J Am Dent Assoc* 2003 July; 134(7):895–898.)

PERIODONTAL TREATMENT

- At the initial examination, the periodontal status should be evaluated. Based on findings, appropriate treatment and follow-up care plan should be reviewed.

Necrotizing ulcerative periodontitis (NUP)

- Signs and symptoms: Very painful, spontaneous gingival bleeding, loose teeth, and halitosis. A marker of severe immunosuppression.
- Immediate intervention is essential to avoid the typical rapidly progressing tissue necrosis
  - Metronidazole (Flagyl®) 250 mg po tid for 7–14 days   (Caution if severe hepatic disease, alcoholic beverages, or pregnancy) OR
  - Clindamycin 300 mg po q8h
  - Consider addition of antifungal agent in addition to antibiotics
- Gross debridement with topical antiseptic such as povidone-iodine solution and 0.12% chlorhexidine gluconate rinses bid
- Quadrant scaling/root planings (SRP) on follow-up visit as appropriate
- Initial follow-up visits should be frequent until condition is stabilized

Linear gingival erythema (LGE) "red band gingivitis"

- Signs and symptoms: profound red band (1–2 mm) along gingiva where it meets teeth, with mild pain, spontaneous bleeding. Monitor condition as it may progress to NUP.
- Scaling and root planing, with 0.12% chlorhexidine gluconate (Peridex®) rinses bid
- Tooth brushing should be accomplished 2–3 times per day with daily flossing

Periodontal disease class – gingivitis I

- Simple prophylaxis

Periodontal class II, III, IV

- Initiate home care instruction, dietary counseling, debridement, scaling, and root planing as appropriate. Periodontal maintenance schedule and follow-up intervals are determined by the particular condition.

Common Oral Lesions

ORAL CANDIDIASIS OR THRUSH

- Pseudomembranous candidiasis — white patches and plaques on the oral mucosa that can be easily wiped off. Can occur anywhere.
- Erythematous candidiasis — red flat lesions commonly seen on dorsal tongue, hard palate, and sometimes gingiva
- Diagnosis — presumptive, smear, or culture

ORAL HAIRY LEUKOPLAKIA (OHL)

- Painless, raised, ribbed, "hairy" white lesions usually located on the lateral margins of the tongue, can also occur on buccal mucosa
- Biopsy will confirm diagnosis
- Treatment generally not required, unless a cosmetic concern

KAPOSI'S SARCOMA (KS)

- Red, blue, or purplish lesions; flat or nodular; solitary or multiple. Lesions can occur anywhere, but most frequent location is hard palate and gingiva.
- Biopsy of oral lesions necessary to confirm diagnosis. Dentist should notify primary physician or oncologist
- Treatment will vary pending size, location, distribution of lesions, and patient's status as systemic involvement is common

APHTHOUS ULCERS

- Painful eroded areas surrounded by erythema, vary in size from 2 mm to 1–2 cm or larger
- May appear anywhere in mouth, though generally on non-keratinized tissues such as buccal mucosa, soft palate, and tongue
- Biopsy necessary for non-healing ulcers to rule out deep fungal infections and other ulcerative diseases

HERPES SIMPLEX

- Vesicular eruptions on erythematous base, commonly appearing on keratinized mucosa such as the hard palate or gingiva
- In immunocompromised patients, lesions may appear anywhere as seen in primary herpes
- Lesions quickly ulcerate and coalesce into large painful ulcerations
- Diagnosis — culture or smear freshly opened vesicle, or biopsy to rule out other ulcerative diseases

Treatment of Oral Manifestations of HIV Disease (See Table 4)

Consult *PDR* or pharmacology text for full disclosure of indications, contraindications, and adverse reactions.
NOTE: Treatment regimens vary with each patient according to severity of patient's condition and immune status.

Table 4. Therapeutic Agents for Oral Manifestations of HIV Disease

Antifungal	• Nystatin 2% ointment: Apply to commissures of mouth or denture base after meals • Nystatin pastilles (200,000 units, Mycostatin®): Dissolve one tab 5 times daily for 10 days • Clotrimazole troches (10 mg Mycelex®): Dissolve one troche 5 times daily for 14 days • Ketoconazole (systematic, Nizoral®) 200 mg tab po daily with food for 10 days – **NOTE:** Ketoconazole interacts with several antiretroviral medications • Ketoconazole 2% cream (Nizoral® cream)for corners of mouth qid • Fluconazole 100 mg (Diflucan®): As directed by patient's physician. 2 tabs first day, then 1 tab per day for 10–14 days. (Due to development of resistant strains, suppressive therapy is discouraged.) • Chlorhexidine gluconate 0.12% (Peridex®): For maintenance. Rinse ½ ounce for 30 seconds, bid and expectorate (spit out)

Antiviral	Herpes Simplex Virus (HSV):
	    ○ Acyclovir ointment 5% (Zovirax®): Apply q2h to affected area (systemic treatment preferred)
	    ○ Acyclovir (systemic): 400 mg po tid for 7–10 days (for mild/moderate HSV).
	    ○ Valacyclovir (Valtrex®) 1 g bid for 7–10 days
	    ○ Famciclovir (Famvir®): 500 mg bid x 7–10 days
	Herpes Zoster:
	    ○ Acyclovir (systemic): 800 mg po 5x/day for 7–10 days — severe HSV or Herpes Zoster
	    ○ Valacyclovir (Valtrex®) 1 g tid for 7 days
	    ○ Famciclovir (Famvir®): 500 mg tid x 7 days
	If disseminated, in-patient IV acyclovir therapy. Caution with renal impairment. Foscarnet if acyclovir-resistant.

Antibacterial	• Tetracycline suspension (125 mg/5 mL): Rinse with 10 mL for 2 min. qid then expectorate, x 10 days or PRN (May need topical antifungal in conjunction with tetracycline)
Topical steroids for Aphthous Ulcerations	• Fluocinonide ointment 0.05% (Lidex®) 50:50 with Orabase®: Apply to affected areas after meals and at bedtime. • Fluocinonide gel/ointment 0.05% (Lidex®): Apply sparingly to affected areas after meals and at bedtime • Dexamethasone 0.5 mg/5 mL elixir (Decadron®) : Rinse 5 mL for 2 min. qid then expectorate. May be used for multiple lesions when ointment is not feasible.
Antibacterial Agents for Aphthous	• Tetracycline suspension 125 mg/5mL — gargle for 1–2 minutes and expectorate. • Chlorhexidine gluconate 0.12% (Peridex® or Periogard®): Rinse ½ once for 30 seconds, bid (morning and evening) and spit out
Systemic Corticosteroids for Severe Aphthous	• Prednisone (depending on the severity of the lesions); 20–40 mg per day po for 1–2 weeks. Consider biopsy prior to treatment for deep fungal or other organisms. Consult with primary care physician before prescribing systemic steroids.
Topical Anesthetics and Coating Agents for Oral Ulcerations	• Viscous lidocaine 2%: Swish with 5 mL before meals and expectorate. **CAUTION:** gag reflex may be lost; aspiration is possible • Diphenhydramine (Benadryl®) elixir (12.5 mg/5 mL): Swish with 5 mL before meals and expectorate • Diphenhydramine (Benadryl®) elixir + (Kaopectate® or Maalox®), 50/50 mixture: Swish with 5 mL before meals, expectorate • Benzocaine in Orabase®: Apply q4h as needed to affected area. Caution with allergy to esters or Novocain.
HIV related gingivitis and periodontitis	• Povidone-iodine (Betadine®) 10% solution: Used during scaling and root planning • Metronidazole (Flagyl®): 250 mg tid for 7 days or Clindamycin (Cleocin®) 300 mg tid for 7 days. (May prescribe with a fungal agent. Avoid if severe hepatic disease. Avoid alcoholic beverages.) • Chlorhexidine gluconate 0.12% (Peridex® or Periogard®): bid
Xerostomia "Dry Mouth" & Hyposalivation	• Salivary stimulants — sugar free gum, sugar-free hard lozenges • Lubricants — artificial saliva substitutes, and Oral Balance® ointments • Systemic sialogogue – Pilocarpine (Salagen®) Check with physician before prescribing • Fluoride rinses or gel treatment to counter susceptibility to dental decay which results from diminished salivary output and altered salivary protein constituents

SOURCE: Carol M. Stewart DDS, MS Dental Director, Florida/Caribbean AIDS Education and Training Center.

Additional Resources

"Oral Manifestations Associated with HIV/AIDS" pictorial poster available through the Florida/Caribbean AIDS Education and Training Center. To request a copy, call (866) 352-2382 or visit www.faetc.org.

References

1. *Management of the HIV-Infected Adult Patient: Clinical Guidelines for Physicians in Miami-Dade County.* Miami: HIV/AIDS Guidelines Workgroup; July, 2000.

2. 2004 University of Florida College of Dentistry. *HIV/AIDS Oral Health Update.*

3. Glick M. *Dental management of patients with HIV.* Carol Stream, IL: Quintessence Publishing; 1994.

15

HIV-Associated Wasting

Iván Meléndez Rivera, MD, FAAFP, AAHIVS
Assistant Professor, Family Practice Department
Ponce School of Medicine and Family Practice Residency, Dr. Pila Hospital
Director and Founder, Centro ARARAT, Inc, Ponce, Puerto Rico
Clinical Consultant, Ryan White Planning Council and Puerto Rico Juvenile Institutions

Introduction

PRE-HAART ERA

- Malnutrition, weight loss, and wasting have been complications of HIV since the epidemic was first recognized[1]
- Depletions in potassium, body fat, intracellular water, and serum protein concentrations are seen in patients with AIDS[2]
- Decreases in body cell mass (BCM) are seen in asymptomatic patients and are associated with increased hospitalization and diminished quality of life[3]
- Patients with wasting have increased mortality independent of other factors[4-6]
- Weight loss > 5% over a 5-month period is associated with increased mortality and development of OIs[7]

HAART ERA

- A significant decline in mortality, OIs, and hospitalizations has occurred due to HAART[8-10]
- HIV related wasting may be difficult to distinguish from HAART-associated lipoatrophy
- Wasting still exists!
- Nutrition for Healthy Living (NFIIL) study[11]
    - 33.6% of 633 patients met at least one definition of wasting (see Table 1)
    - 48.4% of subjects who were HAART-naïve at entry developed wasting after beginning HAART
- Multiple studies document that depletion of BCM occurs in patients on HAART.[12-16]

THE "WASTED PATIENT" OF TODAY IS PROBABLY DIFFERENT FROM THE ONE OF THE PRE-HAART ERA

- May occur even *without* the loss of body weight[14]
- May occur *despite* adequate virologic and immunologic control[12,13]

Table 1. Definition of HIV-Associated Wasting[54]

Patient must meet one of the following criteria:
- 10% unintentional weight loss over 6 months
- 7.5% unintentional weight loss over 3 months
- 5% BCM loss within 30 days
- In men: BCM < 35% of total body weight (BW) and body mass index (BMI) < 27 kg/m^2
- In women: BCM < 23% of total BW and BMI < 27 kg/m^2
- BMI < 20 kg/m^2

Definition

- HIV-related wasting is not the same as weight loss from starvation
  - Starvation is when caloric intake is well below basal body needs and the body metabolizes stored fat for energy while preserving muscle mass
- HIV-associated wasting, body fat is preserved and lean body mass (LBM) is lost
  - If these patients regain weight, they gain fat, not muscle mass
- CDC definition
  - Involuntary weight loss of more than 10% plus either chronic fever, weakness, or diarrhea lasting for at least 30 days
  - Arbitrary and lacked substantive data
- Expanded definition: see Table 1
  - Takes into consideration body composition changes, gender differences, cultural influences, and changing nature of wasting
  - BCM is the key component of the new definition; healthcare providers must reframe their thinking from mere loss of total body weight
- Definition
  - Oxygen-requiring, carbon dioxide producing, glucose-burning mass of tissues[17]
    - Consists of metabolically active tissue and includes muscle, all organs, CNS, glands, red blood cells, and cells in bone, fascia, tendons, cartilage, and fat and intracellular water
  - Lean body mass (LBM) = BCM + ECM (extracellular mass)
    - **Not** useful in disease because hydration status changes
  - Body mass = BCM + ECM + body fat
    - **NOTE**: Substantial losses of body cell mass can occur while body weight can be maintained or even increase!
- There was a high incidence of AIDS-defining and HIV-related opportunistic infections present either at the time wasting syndrome was diagnosed, or in the period following its diagnosis (CMV, PCP and MAI)
- HIV-related Lipodystrophy:
  - HIV-related lipodystrophy generally consists of fat accumulation in the subcutaneous tissues of the lower trunk (abdominal region), abdominal viscera (visceral obesity), axillary pads (bilateral, symmetric lipomatosis), and dorsocervical region (so-called buffalo hump)

— It also consists of fat loss from the subcutaneous tissues of the lower extremities, upper extremities, buttocks, and face (maxillary, nasolabial, and temporal regions)

— This syndrome appears to be quite distinct from the wasting syndrome of protein-energy malnutrition. Lipodystrophy does not seem to be the result of replacement of lost muscle tissue by fat, and there is evidence that the decrease in mass of the extremities is secondary to the loss of fatty tissue (lipoatrophy). See Chapter 9, Metabolic Complications of HAART, for more information.

Causes

- Anorexia: may be a manifestation of HIV infection, or it may be secondary to a diminished sense of taste and smell
- Malabsorption: may be secondary to either a direct effect of HIV on the GI tract or opportunistic infections of the GI tract, which cause chronic diarrhea
- Altered metabolic state: HIV-infected patients also have increased protein loss from the GI tract because of an altered mucosal barrier, and this loss of protein may well contribute to wasting even if the patient does not have diarrhea

Evaluation

- Complete history and physical (See Chapter 4, Initial Encounter and Subsequent Visits)
- Particular attention directed at assessment of patient's nutritional status
  — Recent weight loss
  —Appetite and caloric intake
  — GI functioning/problems
  —Energy level
  —Activities of daily living (ADLs)
  — Psychosocial factors possibly leading to anorexia
- Evaluation and assessment of concomitant medical and/or psychologic/psychiatric conditions
- Assess body composition
  — Height, weight (at each visit), ideal body weight, and BMI
  — Measure **BCM** by bioimpedance analysis (**BIA**) (every 3 months)
    - Utilizes concept that body is a volume conductor
    - Excellent correlation with gold standards for assessing BCM
    - Easy to perform, quick, painless, results are valid, accurate, and reproducible, and inexpensive!
    - BCM, fat free mass, ECM, ICW (intracellular water volume), ECW (extracellular water volume) may be obtained
    - BCM/ECM ratio has been used for normalization
  — *Changes* in BCM over time are more meaningful than a single measurement in time
  — Several factors may affect BIA testing
    - Patient fluid status: e.g., dehydration, edema, etc.
    - Technical: type of room, electrical interference, temperature, etc.
- Anthropometrics: very helpful but time consuming and evaluator dependent
  —Skinfold thickness

— **Circumference Measurements**: The percentage of fat equals the circumference of the right upper arm and abdomen minus the right forearm (in centimeters) minus 10.2

> Waist to hip circumference ratio
> Mid-upper arm circumference
> Forearm circumference
> Calf circumference

- Other studies like: Nitrogen Balance, CT scan, MRI, DEXA can determine relative gains or losses in the lean body mass
- Laboratory
  — Testosterone (free and total)
  — Albumin
  — Pre-albumin
  —Transferin
  — B-12
  — Lipid profile
  —Lactate levels (if available), can use pH to calculate lactate.
- Routine (See Chapter 4, Initial Encounter and Subsequent Visits)
  —Other labs as directed by a clinical dietician
- For Internet help for the Diagnosis HIV-related lipodystrophy visit http://www.ti3m.com/hiv/default_ld.htm

Management

Table 2. Activities Conducted During Ongoing Visits for Patients with HIV-Associated Wasting

• Perform an interval history and physical examination with the patient undressed
• Measure serial body weights and body composition parameters (body cell mass) using bioimpedance analysis (BIA)
• Monitor antiretroviral therapy and adjust as necessary
• Assess any ongoing medical or psychiatric problems in consultation with outside specialists
• Maintain patient's relationship with registered dietitian as needed
• Measure total and free testosterone on an annual basis or more often as clinically necessary
• Referrals to medical specialists where appropriate

GENERAL:

- Referral to HIV-knowledgeable clinical dietician. (See Chapter 4, Initial Encounter and Subsequent Visits)
- Optimal nutrition is essential to keep up with the increased caloric demands and to decrease the rate of catabolism
  — First goal: provide for the calorie and protein demands
  — Second goal: provide the appropriate nutrient mix. Nutrient mix is typically 50% to 60% carbohydrate, 25% fat, and 20% to 25% protein.

— Excess carbohydrates (CHO) are deleterious and lead to hyperglycemia and excess fat, which acts as a substrate for immunosuppressive mediators

—Protein requirements are 2 to 3 times the RDA, or about 1.5 g/kg body weight per day. The increased protein intake will decrease the net nitrogen losses by increasing the amino acid flow into the protein synthesis channel

— Micronutrients need to be increased to keep up with the increased metabolism and quickly restore deficiencies (See Table 3)

— Lack of key micronutrients, especially thiamine and other B complexes, will allow glucose to go through oxidative phosphorylation resulting in lactate (lactic acid)

— The sudden availability of CHO will exceed down regulated cell demands, necessitating energy for fat production and leading to a further energy deficit

— The most beneficial route for nutritional support is the enteral (oral) route, which is really the only option for outpatients or chronic care patients

— If prior malnutrition has resulted in intestinal mucosal atrophy and malabsorption is present, supplement glutamine, 10 g to 20 g per day

— Oral intake of food is rarely sufficient to meet either energy or protein needs in a catabolic or malnourished patient; therefore, nutritional supplements are invariably needed

— Micronutrient support. (Include organic compounds [vitamins], and inorganic compounds [trace minerals]).

Table 3. Micronutrients

FAT-SOLUBLE VITAMINS[54]	
Vitamin	**Metabolic Function**
Vitamin A (retinol)	Synthesis of rhodopsin, epithelial cell, and bone growth, inflammatory stimulant, wound healing
Vitamin E	Antioxidant in cell membranes
Vitamin D	Regulation of calcium metabolism
Vitamin K	Activates blood clotting factors II, VII, IX, X
WATER-SOLUBLE VITAMINS[54]	
Vitamin	**Metabolic Function**
Thiamin (vitamin B_1)	Oxidative decarboxylation
Riboflavin (vitamin B_2)	Electron transfer during oxidative phosphorylation
Niacin (vitamin B_3)	Nicotinamide-adenine Dinucleotide Electron transfer reactions
Pantothenic acid	Part of coenzyme A
Biotin	Carbon dioxide transfer reactions
Pyridoxine (vitamin B_6)	Transamination and decarboxylation reactions
Folic acid	One carbon transfer reaction
Vitamin B_{12} (cobalamin)	Production of methionine coenzyme A reactions
Ascorbic acid (vitamin C)	Antioxidant in cytosol Collagen synthesis Carnitine production

MICROMINERALS (TRACE MINERALS)[54]	
Mineral	**Metabolic Function**
Chromium	Use of glucose and insulin, potentiates insulin action
Cobalt	Required for vitamin B_{12} synthesis
Copper	Connective tissue development through collagen cross linking
Iodine	Thyroid hormones
Iron	Hemoglobin and oxygen transport Electron transfer in oxidative phosphorylation
Manganese	Procollagen ground substance formation Brain function Neuromuscular function Fatty acid synthesis
Molybdenum	Metabolism of purines, pyrimidines Redox reactions
Selenium	Antioxidant and need for fat metabolism

- **Hydration**. The recommendations for daily fluid intake are as follows:
  — 30 mL to 35 mL per kg body weight
  — Minimum of 1500 mL/day
  — 1 mL to 1.5 mL per calorie consumed
  — Replacement of added losses from disease or medications

SPECIFIC – COMPREHENSIVE APPROACH REQUIRED

- Control viral load and maximize immune function
- Correct immediate causes of wasting
  — OIs
  — Malignancies
  — Diarrhea and other GI problems
  — Psychiatric problems
  — Psycho-social issues: finances, transportation etc.
- Improve nutritional intake (See Chapter 4, Initial Encounter and Subsequent Visits)
  — Specific interventions such as high-protein diets as directed by the clinical dietician
  — May include use of appetite stimulants (see Table 4): will not by themselves improve BCM.[18-22]

Table 4. Appetite Stimulants Used in Patients with HIV Infection

AGENT	TRADE NAME	DOSAGE
Dronabinol	Marinol®	2.5 -10 mg po bid to tid
Megestrol acetate	Megace®	400 mg -800 mg po qd
Lysine	Various	500 mg po daily
Cyproheptadine	Periactin®	4 mg po bid to qid
Prednisone	Various	2.5 -10 mg po qd

Megestrol (Megace) as appetite stimulant will suppress secretion of testosterone, and it will increase body weight by increasing fat stores, not by building protein. If Megestrol is used in men, testosterone should be considered to treat hypogonadism.

- Nutritional supplementation
  — As directed by the clinical dietician
  — May include oral, enteral (uncommon in the HIV-infected individual), or parenteral (rarely used today but may be a temporizing measure)
- Testosterone therapy
  — HIV disease is a catabolic state. Catabolic hormones predominate and the anabolic hormones, growth hormone, and testosterone are decreased in the process. These represent one of the reasons for use of anabolic hormones in wasting syndrome.
  — Testosterone acts on cellular androgenic receptors, (defined in the 1960s) which, in lean mass tissue, lead to cellular amino acid influx and increased protein synthesis. Cells with a high androgenic receptor density include skin fibroblasts and skeletal muscle myocytes.[7]
  — Important for hypogonadal patients
  — May increase lean body mass and muscle strength without adversely affecting viral load and/or CD4+ cell count[23-26]
  — Eugonadal patients
    - Additional benefit when combined with progressive resistance exercise[27], see below
  — Considered safe despite paucity of controlled clinical trials
  — Potential adverse side-effects (generally seen when used in eugonadal men!)
    - Reduction in HDL-cholesterol
    - Acne, hair loss, dsylipidemia, sleep apnea, prostatic enlargement
  — Digital rectal exam and PSA testing should be done prior to and during therapy as well as serial testosterone (total and/or free levels)
  — Several routes of administration, but intramuscular is the preferred. (see Table 5)
  — Use in women is under investigation[56]

Table 5. Testosterone Replacement Therapy for HIV-Infected Hypogonadal Males

ROUTE OF ADMINISTRATION	DOSAGE
Intramuscular (Depo-Testosterone®, Virilon®)	100mg every week **or** 200 mg every 2 weeks or 300 mg every 3 weeks
Transdermal (Androderm®, Testoderm®)	5 mg/day
Topical (AndroGel®)	5 g/qd

- Anabolic androgenic steroids (AAS)
  —Congeners of testosterone with increased anabolic and reduced androgenic effects
  —Generally safe when supervised by a knowledgeable healthcare provider
    - May be contraindicated in patients with hepatic dysfunction/disease
  —Long-term safety and efficacy not known
  — No comparative trials
  — May develop hypertension, which may be controlled by a reduction in the dose of the hormone or, in some cases, by the use of an antihypertensive agent
  — Several small studies with varying results
    - Parenteral: nandralone decanoate ("deca," Deca-durabolin®)
      o Few controlled trials (50–100mg IM every week, no more than 12 weeks)
      o Increases in body weight, lean body mass, and QOL reported[28-30]

- Oral
  - Oxandrolone (Oxandrin®) produced significant increases in weight and body cell mass and significant increases in weight when combined with Progressive Resistance Exercise, (PRE) [31,32]
    - The main contraindications for oxandrolone are hypercalcemia or carcinoma of the male breast or prostate because these tumors have androgenic receptors
  - Oxymethalone (Anadrol-50®) produced weight gain in cachectic patients[33]
- Recombinant human growth hormone (Serostim®, somatropin)[55]
  —Anabolic, anti-catabolic, metabolic, and immunologic properties
  — Placebo-controlled trial produced increases in lean body mass and protein synthesis, improved work capacity and QOL[34,35]
  —Expensive!
  — Administered via parenteral route (3–6mg daily)
  — Generally well tolerated: increased "tissue turgor," myalgias, and glucose intolerance the major side effects
  —Most of the effect reverts when therapy discontinued. (Recommend consideration of a maintenance dose of 1mg daily.)
  — Agents such as glutamine and arginine have been reported to increase HGH release
- Progressive resistance exercise (PRE)
  — Essential in the management of wasting
  — Recommended exercise[53]
    - 90 minutes 3 times a week
      - 5 minutes warm up
      - 20 minutes cycling or other cardiovascular exercise at 70% peak heart rate
      - 60 minutes of resistance training
      - 5 minutes cool down
  — Several studies demonstrated increases in weight, lean body mass, muscle function, and arm and leg strength[36-39]
- Others
  — Excessive production of cytokines postulated to be involved in wasting[40]
  — Cytokine modulators such as thalidomide (Thalomid® increases in BCM, ECF and decrease in nitrogen excretion have been reported) and pentoxyphylline (Trental®) have been evaluated[41-43]

EXPECTED OUTCOMES[44]

—Replacement of lost body cell mass and weight
— Improved physical capabilities and quality of life
— Improved physical appearance
—Decreased frequency of opportunistic infections, hospitalizations, and related complications
— Improved survival

References

1. Mhiri C, Belec L, Di Costanza B, et al. The slim disease in African patients with AIDS. *Trans R Soc Trop Med Hyg* 1992; 86:303-306.

2. Kotler DP, Wang J, Pierson RN. Body composition studies in patients with the acquired immunodeficiency syndrome. *Am J Clin Nutr* 1985; 42:1255-1265.

3. Ott M, Lembcke B, Fischer H, et al. Early changes in body composition in human immunodeficiency virus-infected patients: tetrapolar body impedance analysis indicates significant malnutrition. *Am J Clin Nutr* 1993; 57:15-19.

4. Chlebowski RT, Grosvenor MB, Bernhard NH, et al. Nutritional status, gastrointestinal dysfunction, and survival in patients with AIDS. *Am J Gastroenterol* 1989; 84:1288-1293.

5. Guenter P, Muurahaninen N, Simons G, et al. Relationships among nutritional status, disease progression, and survival in HIV infection. *J Acquir Immune Defic Syndr* 1993; 6:1130-1138.

6. Palenicek JP, Graham NM, He YD, et al. Multicenter AIDS Cohort Study Investigators. Weight loss prior to clinical AIDS as a predictor of survival. *J Acquir Immune Defic Syndr Hum Retrovirol* 1995; 10:366-373.

7. Wheeler DA, Gibert CL, Launer CA, et. al. Weight loss as a predictor of survival and disease progression in HIV infection. *J Acquir Immune Defic Syndr Hum Retrovirol* 1998; 18(1):80-85.

8. Palella FJ Jr, Delaney KM, Moorman AC, et al. Declining morbidity and mortality among patients with advanced human immunodeficiency virus infection. HIV Outpatient Study Investigators. *NEJM* 1998; 338:853-860.

9. Michaels S, Clark R, Kissinger P. Differences in the incidence rates of opportunistic processes before and after the availability of protease inhibitors. In: Program and abstracts of the 5th Conference on Retroviruses and Opportunistic Infections; February 1-5, 1998. Abstract 180.

10. Mocroft A, Sabin CA, Youle M, et al. Changes in AIDS-defining illnesses in a London Clinic, 1987-1998. *J Acquir Immune Defic Synd.* 1999; 21:401-407.

11. Wanke CA, Silva M, Knox TA, et al. Weight loss and wasting remain common complications in individuals infected with human immunodeficiency virus in the era of highly active antiretroviral therapy. *Clin Infect Dis* 2001; 31:803-805.

12. Teixeira A, Leu JC, Honderlick P, et al. Variation in body weight and plasma viral load in HIV patients treated with tritherapy including a protease inhibitor [abstract]. *Nutrition* 1997; 13:269.

13. Zucman D, Teixeira A, Olivieri M, et al. Correlation between body composition, caloric intake and plasma viral load in HIV infected patients [abstract]. *Nutrition* 1997; 13:292.

14. Polsky B, Kotler D, and Steinhart C. HIV-associated wasting in the HAART era: guidelines for assessment, diagnosis, and treatment. *AIDS Patient Care* 2001; 15(8):411-423.

15. Silva M, Skolnik PR, Gorbach SL, et al. The effect of protease inhibitors on weight and body composition in HIV-infected patients. *AIDS* 1998; 12:1645-1651.

16. Lo JC, Mulligan K, Tai VW, et al. "Buffalo hump" in men with HIV-1 infection. *Lancet* 1998; 351:867-870.

17. Torres RA. Treatment of dorsocervical fat pads and truncal adiposity with Serostim (recombinant human growth hormone) in patients with AIDS maintained on HAART. In: Program and abstracts of the 12th World AIDS Conference; Jun3 28 – July 3, 1998; Geneva, Switzerland. Abstract 32164.

18. Moore FD, Olesen KH, McMurrey JD, Parker JHV. *The Body Cell Mass and its Supporting Environment: Body Composition in Health and Disease.* Philadelphia: W.B. Saunders, 1963.

19. Beal JE, Olson R, Laubenstein L, et al. Dronabinol as a treatment for anorexia associated with weight loss in patients with AIDS. *J Pain Symptom Manage* 1995; 10:89-97.

20. Timpone JG, Wright DL, Li N, et al. The safety and pharmacokinetics of single-agent and combination therapy with megestrol acetate and dronabinol for the treatment of HIV wasting syndrome. *AIDS Res Hum Retroviruses.*1997; 13:305-315.

21. Von Roenn JH, Armstrong D, Kotler DP, et al. Megesterol acetate in patients with AIDS-related cachexia. *Ann Intern Med* 1994; 121:393-399.

22. Oster MH, Enders Sr, Samuels SJ, et al. Megesterol acetate in patients with AIDS and cachexia. *Ann Intern Med* 1994; 121:400-408.

23. Summerbell CD, Youle M, et al. Megestrol acetate vs. cyproheptadine in the treatment of weight loss associated with HIV infection. *Int J STD AIDS* 1992; 3:278-280.

24. Bhasin S, Storer TW, Asbel-Sethl N, et al. Effects of testosterone replacement with a nongenital, transdermal system, Androderm, in human immunodeficiency virus-infected men with low testosterone levels. *J Clin Endocrinol Metab* 1998; 83:3155-3162.

25. Grinspoon S, Corcoran C, Askari H, et al. Effects of androgen administration in men with the AIDS wasting syndrome: a randomized, double-blind, placebo-controlled trial. *Ann Intern Med* 1998; 129:18-26.

26. Grinspoon S, Corocoran C, Anderson E, et al. Sustained anabolic effects of long-term androgen administration in men with AIDS wasting. *Clin Infect Dis* 1999; 28:634-636.

27. Coodley GO, Coodley MK. A trial of testosterone therapy for HIV-associated weight loss. *AIDS* 1997; 11:1347-1352.

28. Grinspoon S, Corcoran C, Parlman K, et al. Effects of testosterone and progressive resistance training in eugonadal men with AIDS wasting. A randomized, controlled trial. *Ann Intern Med* 2000; 133:348-355.

29. Gold J, High HA, Li Y, et al. Safety and efficacy of nandrolone decanoate for treatment of wasting in patients with HIV infection. *AIDS* 1996; 10:745-752.

30. Bucher G, Berger DS, Fields-Gardner C, Jones R, Reiter WM. A prospective study on the safety and effect of nandrolone decanoate in HIV-positive patients. In: Program and abstracts of the International Conference on AIDS, July 7-12, 1996; Abstract MoB423.

31. Strawford A, Barbieri T, Neese R, et al. Effects of nandrolone decanoate therapy in borderline hypogonadal men with HIV-associated weight loss. *J Acquir Immune Defic Syndr Hum Retrovirol* 1999; 20(2):137-146.

32. Poles MA, Meller JA, Linn A, Weiss WR, et al. Oxandrolone as a treatment for AIDS-related weight loss and wasting. In: Program and abstracts of the 4th Conference on Retroviruses and Opportunistic Infections, January 22-26, 1997; Abstract 695.

33. Romeyn M, Gunn III N. Resistance exercise and oxandrolone for men with HIV-related weight loss. *JAMA* 2000; 284:176.

34. Hengge UR, Baumann M, Maleba R, et al. Oxymetholone promotes weight gain in patients with advanced human immunodeficiency virus (HIV-1) infection. *Br J Nutr* 1996; 75:129-138.

35. Schambelan M, Mulligan K, Grunfeld C, et al. Recombinant human growth hormone in patients with HIV-associated wasting – a randomized, placebo controlled trial. *Ann Intern Med* 1996; 125:873-882.

36. Waters D, Danska J, Hardy K, et al. Recombinant human growth hormone, insulin-like growth factor 1, and combination therapy in AIDS-associated wasting. A randomized, double-blind, placebo-controlled trial. *Ann Intern Med* 1996; 125:865-872.

37. Bhasin S, Storer TW, Javanbakht M, et al. Testosterone replacement and resistance exercise in HIV-infected men with weight loss and low testosterone levels. *JAMA* 2000; 283:763-770.

38. Spence DW, Galantino ML, Mossberg KA, et al. Progressive resistance exercise effect on muscle function and anthropometer of a select AIDS population. *Arch Phys Med Rehabil* 1990; 71:644-648.

39. Roubenoff R, McDermott A, Wood M, Suri J. Feasibility of increasing lean body mass in HIV-infected adults using progressive resistance training. Presented at the 12th World AIDS Conference, Geneva, Switzerland, June 28 – July 3, 1998. Abstract 42357.

40. Rigsby LW, Dishman RK, Jackson AW, et al. Effects of exercise training on men seropositive for human immunodeficiency virus-1. *Med Sci Sports Exerc* 1992; 24:6-12.

41. Grunfeld C, Feingold KR. Metabolic disturbances and wasting in the acquired immunodeficiency syndrome. *NEJM* 1992; 327:329-337.

42. Haslett P, Hempstead M, Seidman C, et al. The metabolic and immunologic effects of short-term thalidomide treatment of patients infected with the human immunodeficiency virus. *AIDS Res Hum Retroviruses*.1997; 13:1047-1054.

43. Reyes-Teran G, Sierra-Madero JG, Martinez del Cerro V, et al. Effects of thalidomide on HIV-associated wasting syndrome: a randomized, double-blind, placebo-controlled clinical trial. *AIDS*.1996; 10:1501-1507.

44. Dezube BJ, Parde AB, Chapman B, et al. Pentoxifylline decreases tumor necrosis factor expression and serum triglycerides in people with AIDS. *J Acquir Immune Defic Syndr* 1993; 6:787-794.

45. Dworkin MS, Williamson JM; Adult/Adolescent Spectrum of HIV Disease Project. AIDS wasting syndrome: trends, influence on opportunistic infections, and survival. *J Acquir Immune Defic Syndr* 2002; 33:267-273.

46. Kevin Robert Frost, Use of steroids for wasting and lipodystrophy syndromes in HIV/AIDS; *AIDS Reader* 2001; 11(3):130-131..

47. Scevola D, Di Mateo A, Uberti F, et al. Reversal of cachexia in patients treated with potent antiretroviral therapy. *AIDS Reader* 2000; 10:365-375.

48. Fisher K. Wasting and lipodystrophy in patients infected with HIV: a practical approach in clinical practice. *AIDS Reader* 2001; 11(3):132-147.

49. Evans WJ, Roubenoff R, Shevitz A. Exercise and the treatment of wasting: aging and human immunodeficiency virus infection. *Semin Oncol* 1998; 2(suppl 6):112-122.

50. Nemechek PM, Polsky B, Gottlieb MS. Treatment guidelines for HIV-associated wasting. *Mayo Clin Proc* 2000; 75:386-394.

51. Becker K, Lindner C, Frieling T, et al. Intestinal protein leakage in the acquired immunodeficiency syndrome. *J Clin Gastroenterol* 1997; 25:426-428.

52. Kopicko JJ, Momodu I, Adedokum A, et al. Characteristics of HIV-infected men with low serum testosterone levels. *Int J STD AIDS* 1999; 10:817-820.

53. Jones et all. Short term exercise training improves body composition and hyperlipidemia in HIV positive individuals whit lipodystrophy. *AIDS* 2001; 15:2049-2051.

54. Demling RH, DeSanti L. Involuntary weight loss and protein-energy malnutrition: Diagnosis and treatment; *Medscape*. May 30, 2003; Available at http://www.medscape.com/viewprogram/713_index.

55. Evans WJ, Kotler DP. Effect of recombinant human growth hormone on exercise capacity in patients with HIV-associated wasting on HAART. *AIDS Reader* 2005; 15(6):301-314.

56. Testosterone effective for HIV-wasting syndrome in women, *Arch Intern Med* 2004; 164:897-904.

Section IV

Management of Co-Existing Conditions

16

Co-Infection with Hepatitis B & C

Sandra G. Gompf, MD, FACP
Assistant Professor, Infectious and Tropical Medicine
Faculty, Florida/Caribbean AIDS Education and Training Center

Hepatitis B

Introduction

Hepatitis B virus (HBV) infects over 300,000 individuals in the U.S. annually, and 6–10% become chronically infected. While only 25% develop symptomatic disease with jaundice, Hepatitis B causes over 300 deaths per year from fulminant Hepatitis and liver failure. The lifetime risk in the U.S for HBV infection is approximately 5% for the general population, but is up to 100% for groups with high-risk behaviors.

Chronic HBV infection affects 1.25 million individuals in the United States. Like chronic Hepatitis C (HCV), it is generally asymptomatic but results in significant morbidity over 20 to 30 years, including cirrhosis and hepatocellular carcinoma. Morbidity is accelerated by alcohol intake, co-infection with Hepatitis C, co-infection with HIV, or co-infection with HIV and HCV.

VIROLOGY AND NATURAL HISTORY OF HEPATITIS B INFECTION

HBV is transmitted sexually and parenterally via blood-to-blood exposure. HBV is the easiest of the Hepatitis viruses to transmit parenterally, being 10 times more likely to be transmitted than Hepatitis C. It is also 100 times more likely to be transmitted than HIV. Exposure commonly occurs during IV drug abuse with sharing of needles, as well as percutaneous needle stick injuries in healthcare workers. The relative risk of acquiring HBV from a single needle stick is 30% in healthcare workers, and up to 100% of IV drug abusers may be seropositive for HBV.

A member of the *Hepadnavirus* family, HBV is a partially double-stranded DNA virus with a complex life cycle. HBV DNA encodes for four major gene products: S protein, core protein, pre-core protein, and X protein.:
- S protein in the outer envelope is detectable as Hepatitis B surface antigen (HBsAg)
- Core and pre-core proteins yield mature core and Hepatitis B e antigen (HBeAg)
- X protein, which may activate a host growth-related gene

While the virus infects hepatocytes, integrates into the host genome, and actively replicates, the initial phase of HBV infection is asymptomatic, without hepatocellular damage. The second phase may produce symptomatic disease. Core antigen-derived peptide on the hepatocyte surface permits immune recognition and destruction by CD8 lymphocytes, and this immune response may cause a transaminitis. The production of HBe and HBs antibodies heralds the resolution of acute infection and recovery. Anti-HBs after natural infection confers lifetime immunity.

With persistence or chronicity of HBV infection, anti-HBe and anti-HBs are not produced. Chronic HBV is indicated by the persistence of HBsAg and HBV DNA viremia beyond 6 months, and HBe antigenemia is the rule. Asymptomatic fluctuating transaminitis is common. Liver biopsy generally confirms an active necroinflammatory process. The presence of HB core antibody (IgG) alone may indicate latent or "occult" HBV in up to 40% of individuals, as confirmed by a typically low-level HBV viremia. It should be recognized, however, that some false positives may occur in this setting, and use of HBV DNA assays may resolve this question.

HBV persistence is yet to be fully understood. Covalently closed circular DNA (cccDNA), felt to be the stable replicative episome associated with chronic infection, is transcribed to a larger RNA pregenome in the hepatocyte nucleus. Messenger RNA transcripts exit the nucleus and code for dsDNA after reverse transcription in the new viral core. New viral capsids may be released from the cell or recycled into the nucleus to maintain the cccDNA reservoir. Clearance of cccDNA reservoirs from infected cells may hold the key to cure of chronic HBV. While assays for cccDNA are becoming available, the relevance of cccDNA in treatment and follow up of chronic HBV is still under evaluation.

Seven HBV genotypes have been described. The relationship of genotype to geography, virulence, and treatment response is being elucidated. Genotype A appears to be most prevalent in the U.S. Recent data suggests that genotype A may favor response to therapy (lamivudine, tenofovir, or the combination) by 3:1 compared with non-A genotypes in HIV-HBV co-infection.

Precore Variants (HBeAg- mutants)

In general, the individual with acute or chronic Hepatitis is positive for both HBsAg and HBeAg. HBe antigenemia is associated with increased virulence and transmissibility. HBeAg- negative individuals typically have low to no viral replication, low infectivity, and low risk of liver disease. However, some of these individuals have a precore stop codon mutation (G1896A) that abolishes the synthesis of HBeAg; anti-HBe is also ineffective against these mutants. These HBeAg- "precore variants" retain their virulence, are more likely to become chronic, and have a higher rate of relapse after treatment than HBeAg+ strains. They are also associated with a higher risk of hepatocellular cancer. Not surprisingly, precore variants are often resistant to interferon in vitro. Of interest, lamivudine therapy also may promote rapid development of precore and core promoter mutations with persistent low-level viremia in response to selective pressure, despite loss of HBeAg and seroconversion to anti-HBe. These strains are able to protect replication through and after treatment. However, they are less "fit" and revert to wild-type when off of therapy, with relapse of viremia and reversion to HBe antigenemia.

Clearance of HBeAg cannot be used to gauge the success of therapy with precore mutant strains. In any case, as standardization and sensitivity of assays improves, HBV DNA is likely to supplant HBeAg suppression as a marker for disease activity and treatment response.

Table 1. HBV Serologic Markers and Their Interpretation

Diagnosis	HBsAg	Anti-HBs	Anti-HBc (IgM)	Anti-HBc Total	HBeAg	Anti-HBe	HBV DNA
Acute	Pos	Neg	Pos	Neg	Pos	Neg	Pos
Window	Neg	Neg	Pos	Pos/Neg	Neg	Pos	Neg
Resolved/Immune	Neg	Pos	Neg	Pos	Neg	Pos	Neg
Chronic (active)	Pos	Neg	Neg	Pos	Pos	Neg	Pos
Precore variant	Pos	Neg	Neg	Pos	Neg	Neg/Pos	Pos
Vaccinated/Immune	Neg	Pos	Neg	Neg	Neg	Neg	Neg
Occult HBV	Neg	Neg	Neg	Pos	Neg	Neg/Pos	Pos

SCREENING RECOMMENDATIONS FOR HEPATITIS B

All HIV-infected individuals should be questioned regarding HBV risk factors and vaccination history, and all should be screened serologically for HBV. Currently, screening for Hepatitis B should include **HBsAg, HBsAb, and HBcAb**. Individuals who test + for HBsAb may be considered immune to HBV for practical purposes and no further intervention is indicated. **The individual who tests + for HBsAg should undergo further evaluation**, to include:

- Examination for evidence of advanced liver disease
- Alanine aminotransferase (ALT)
- HBeAg
- Anti-HBe
- HBV DNA viral load
- Anti-HDV (Hepatitis delta, see below)
- Hepatitis A IgG

Hepatitis delta (HDV)

The role of HDV co-infection with Hepatitis B should not be underestimated. HDV, an incomplete virus, requires HBV for infection and may co-infect an individual at the same time with HBV. Co-infection typically causes severe acute Hepatitis with a low risk of chronic infection. Of most significance, HDV may superinfect chronic Hepatitis B and cause acute worsening of an otherwise quiescent Hepatitis. When superinfection occurs, HDV typically becomes chronic as well, and dual infection with HBV accelerates and magnifies progression to cirrhosis and hepatoma. Treatment of HDV with high dose interferon is often poorly tolerated and poorly effective, and has not been validated in the HIV-infected population. Transmission risks are the same as for HBV, thus preventive education is important.

Hepatitis A

Acute Hepatitis A superimposed upon chronic Hepatitis B is likely to worsen transaminitis and accelerate progression of liver disease, and may be associated with fulminant Hepatitis. Since this is a preventable infection with typically good responses to vaccination, all patients with chronic Hepatitis B or C should be screened with Hepatitis A IgG and should be vaccinated if found to be seronegative.

Occult Hepatitis B

In individuals who test + for isolated anti-HBc, HBV DNA may be considered, to exclude a false positive test. Occult HBV, defined as an isolated anti-HBc with detectable HBV DNA, may occur more commonly in HIV-infected individuals. However, its clinical significance, and the need for routine HBV

DNA testing or treatment in this situation remains under debate. Based on current knowledge and management algorithms, there is no indication for routine screening of "occult" HBV with HBV DNA, given the added cost and uncertain benefit. However, HBV DNA may be useful in the patient who may be undergoing immunosuppressive therapy (such as cancer chemotherapy), whose HBV may reactivate, in order to determine whether prophylactic anti-HBV treatment should be considered. Also in question is the assumption that the patient with anti-HBc is likely to have sub-detectable anti-HBs and may be able to mount an anamnestic response to acute re-infection with HBV. Recent data may challenge this view, and may reinforce the need for HBV DNA evaluations. Gandhi RT et al reported an overall poor (16%) anti-HBs response to HBV challenge in 69 HIV+/HBsAg-/anti-HBs- subjects; there was no significant difference in antibody response between anti-HBc+ and Anti-HBc- subjects. Further research is necessary, preferably with larger numbers of subjects, and should include screening of these individuals with HBV DNA. No change from the current recommendation may be made based on this study at this time.

HIV-HBV Co-Infection

Among the HIV-infected, up to 95% have serologic evidence of past or current HBV infection. Compared to 5% of the general population with acute HBV, 15% of HIV-infected individuals develop chronic HBV. HIV also increases the likelihood of reactivation at any time in those who "seroconvert" after acute HBV infection. Acute reactivation of HBV may also occur as an immune reconstitution syndrome in patients that begin highly active antiretroviral therapy with advanced immunodeficiency. As might be expected, co-infection with delta agent is 4- to 5-fold more common in the HIV-infected, and HBV itself is likely to be more virulent. HIV-infected individuals are more likely to produce HBe antigen (53% vs. 27% HIV-negative) and high-level HBV viremia, and HBV is increasingly recognized as a cause of cirrhosis and death in the HIV+ population.

Salmon et al elaborated upon this, noting an increasing role of HBV in liver-related deaths. Among 822 HIV-infected individuals co-infected with HCV, HBV, or both, the most common cause of death was liver disease (31%) and AIDS (29%) in HIV/HCV co-infection, and liver disease (22% and 44%, respectively) in HIV/HBV and HIV/HBV/HCV co-infection. Hepatoma was associated with HBV co-infection. Importantly, in this cohort, the risk of death was roughly equal whether CD4 was less than or greater than 200 cells/mm^3.

HBV is accelerated by HIV infection. Co-infection with either HBV or HCV, however, has little effect on antiretroviral therapy changes once it is begun, and early delay in CD4 responses to antiretroviral therapy may not be sustained or have long-term clinical impact. In reverse, the effect of highly active antiretroviral therapy (HAART) upon HBV and HCV has been addressed, with little consensus. Immune reconstitution certainly may reactivate latent Hepatitis B, as well as worsen chronic Hepatitis B or C. This is consistent with observations that poorer (or immature in the case of childhood infection) immune function is often associated with development of chronic but indolent infection. Significant elevations in HBV and HCV viral loads have been observed with the initiation of effective HAART. However, there is no indication for withholding or delaying HAART in the patient co-infected with HBV.

ACUTE HEPATITIS B IN THE HIV-INFECTED PATIENT

Hepatitis B is more likely to cause acute than chronic infection. Acute HBV is symptomatic in approximately 30-50% of cases and is characterized by jaundice, nausea, vomiting, diarrhea, and icterus. Right upper quadrant pain may occur, and transaminases are typically elevated. These symptoms are suggestive of Hepatitis and the differential diagnosis should include screening for Hepatitis A, HCV, HDV, alcohol abuse, biliary obstruction, and medication toxicity. Treatment is typically supportive. A caveat is the case of acute fulminant Hepatitis, where there is consensus that lamivudine should be considered due to the risk of necrosis and acute liver failure.

CHRONIC HEPATITIS B IN THE HIV-INFECTED PATIENT

Assessment for viral activity

Chronic HBV is defined as the presence of HBsAg+ serology and detectable HBV DNA. The literature is limited by the use of nonstandardized DNA assays and quantification units. The current consensus is that results should be expressed in International Units (IU) and decimal log IU/mL, so that log changes may be monitored. In general, 1 IU = 5.4 copies/mL (refer to manufacturer's conversion chart). Assays should be quantitative, and as assays differ in sensitivity, only one assay should be used for monitoring in the same individual. Preferred tests are real-time nucleic acid amplification, and assays should have a low cutoff (80 IU/mL or more) and wide range of detection.

- **ALT levels**
  There is no correlation between ALT level and disease severity, other than the fact that higher levels are associated with worse disease and faster progression of liver disease.

- **HBeAg and anti-HBe**
  HBeAg positivity is associated with high HBV DNA, greater disease severity, and increased transmissibility.

- **Hepatitis A Serology**
  Absence of Hepatitis A IgG indicates need for Hepatitis A vaccination.

Assessment for complications of chronic Hepatitis

- **Liver biopsy**
  The current gold standard for assessing the stage of liver fibrosis and risk of progression to advanced liver disease is liver biopsy. Non-invasive assessment methods, such as Fibro-sure™ and Fibro-Scan™ may be considered as an alternative to biopsy but have not been validated in HIV co-infection. The decision whether to perform liver biopsy may be individualized.

- **Sonography**
  Ultrasound of the liver can assess for cirrhosis, fatty liver, and screen for hepatomas.

- **Alpha-Fetoprotein and hepatocellular carcinoma**
  Note that the sensitivity of alpha-Fetoprotein for hepatocellular carcinoma ranges from 40-60%; this assay is not reliable alone for hepatoma screening. Combined use with other tests, such as sonography, may prove more useful. Hepatoma is often more advanced and multi-focal in HIV-infected individuals when detected, thus a low threshold for screening is important.

Goals of treatment of chronic HBV

Long-term HBsAg clearance and anti-HBs seroconversion is uncommon with treatment of HBV. However, HBV DNA is a more relevant marker of response to therapy and subsequent reduced progression to end-stage liver disease and hepatocellular carcinoma.

Who should be treated for chronic HBV and when?

The HIV co-infected patient raises concerns, including immune status and indications for highly active antiretroviral therapy (HAART), complication of HAART by Hepatitis, and contraindications to treatment. A combination of HBV DNA level, HBe antigenemia, and assessments for liver fibrosis and cirrhosis help guide management. In general, treatment should be considered in patients with high viral loads (Table 2) and abnormal transaminases; the decision may be helped if liver biopsy data is available, especially in the patient with less advanced HIV where progression is less assured. HBeAg negative disease produces lower level viremia and is less likely to respond; relatively high viremia in this setting is more likely associated with progression of disease and greater likelihood of response to treatment.

Table 2. HBe Antigenemia and HBV DNA Cutoffs for the Treatment of Chronic HBV with Evidence of Necroinflammatory Disease

HBeAg +	HBV DNA > 20,000 IU/mL
HBeAg-	HBV DNA > 2,000 IU/mL

If HAART is not indicated, and Hepatitis is mild, watchful waiting is acceptable. Current anti-HBV drugs are also active against HIV, and avoidance of exposure is preferable to prevent future HIV resistance and preservation of antiretroviral options. Interferon-based therapy may be considered for HIV co-infected patients with CD4 counts > 500 cells/mm^3. Data regarding interferon in HIV-HBV co-infection remains limited. Interferons have immunomodulating effects that may reverse fibrosis; however, adverse effects may limit its use.

If HBV DNA levels are high as above and there is evidence of significant liver inflammation and fibrosis, the patient should be treated. While response to therapy may improve with improved immune function or higher CD4 counts, high CD4 counts are not as much of a factor as in HCV in determining when to treat. In general, if HIV is more advanced or the patient is a candidate for HAART, HBV is more likely to progress; thus treatment may be considered for the patient with high viral load and suspected risk for advanced liver disease, without a liver biopsy.

Figure 1 (next page) offers a decision tree summarizing the above approach toward managing chronic HBV in the HIV co-infected individual.

Figure 1. Decision Tree for Managing HBV in the HIV Co-Infected Patient with a +HBsAg

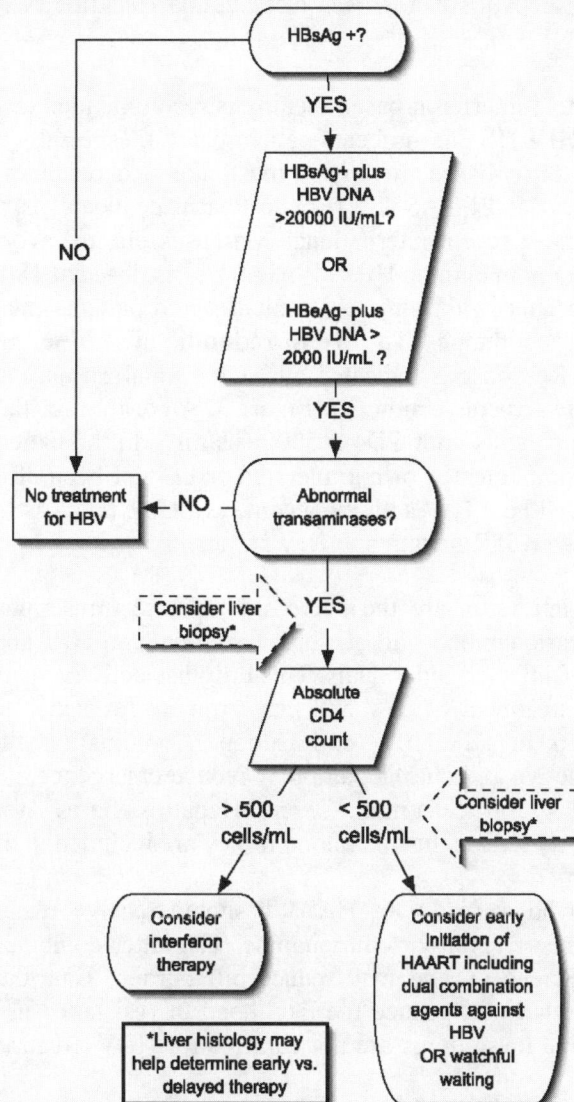

Decision tree for managing HBV in the HIV co-infected patient with a +HBsAg

Cirrhosis

Compensated cirrhosis should be treated with nucleoside analogs if HBV DNA is > 200 IU/mL, and consideration may be given to starting HAART earlier than normally indicated. Combination nucleoside reverse transcriptases are preferred to interferons, as below. Decompensated cirrhosis or end-stage liver disease (Child Pugh stage B or C) should be evaluated for possible liver transplantation.

Treatment of HBV Infection

The patient who is actively abusing ethanol or other substances should be aggressively counseled against it, both to prevent further liver damage and improve response to treatment; treatment is typically deferred until the patient is abstinent for 6 months. Screening for Hepatitis A and C are important because concurrent or superinfecting Hepatitis can worsen disease, and Hepatitis A vaccine should be offered if the patient is not immune.

If HAART is not indicated, interferon-based therapy is recommended (see Figure 2 Interferon-based treatment algorithm for the HIV-HBV co-infected patient below), especially where improvement in liver histology is important. Interferon-based therapy is most likely to result in viral clearance. Pegylated interferon 2-alpha in the form of PEGASYS® (Roche Pharmaceuticals) is currently preferred in HIV-infected individuals by the most recent international consensus due to favorable data and current FDA approval for use as monotherapy in chronic HBV. PEGASYS® is dosed at 180 micrograms SC weekly for 48 weeks. Interferon is associated with numerous toxicities and patients must be carefully screened for contraindications, which are common. **To avoid redundancy, these are fully discussed under Treatment of Hepatitis C**. Response is indicated by ALT normalization, undetectable HBV DNA, and loss of HBeAg with anti-HBe seroconversion (see Figure 3, Algorithm for the treatment of chronic HBV in HIV/HCV co-infection in patients with CD4 > 500 cells/mL). In the patient for whom HAART is not indicated, if interferon is contraindicated or not tolerated or has not been effective in the past, it is most advisable to wait until drugs without HIV activity become available (such as telbivudine, or clevudine), in order to avoid selection for the K65R mutation in HIV strains.

Current alternatives to interferon are the nucleoside reverse transcriptase inhibitors — tenofovir, adefovir, lamivudine, and emtricitabine — all of which have dual anti-HIV/anti-HBV activity. Adefovir is approved for use in non-HIV-infected individuals. This drug has activity against HIV; however, the dose for HBV is insufficient for treatment of HIV and may promote resistance to tenofovir if used. Hence, adefovir should be avoided in HIV/HBV co-infection. Combination therapy with tenofovir and lamivudine is also more effective and durable, and may reduce emergence of resistance in both HIV and HBV. If CD4 counts are < 200 cells/mm^3, severe Hepatitis flares are possible due to immune reconstitution; nucleosides may reduce this likelihood if they are included in the HAART backbone.

Therefore, the patient who is ready for HAART should receive two anti-HIV/anti-HBV agents, typically tenofovir/lamivudine or tenofovir/emtricitabine. The latter combination is available as a single tablet, Truvada™ (Gilead Sciences), and may reduce pill burden. Emtricitabine has pharmacokinetic advantages over lamivudine that may reduce the likelihood of resistance in both HIV and HBV. Since HIV treatment is life long and these drugs are not curative for HBV, treatment with these agents is life long.

Figure 2. Interferon-based Treatment Algorithm for the HIV-HBV Co-Infected Patient

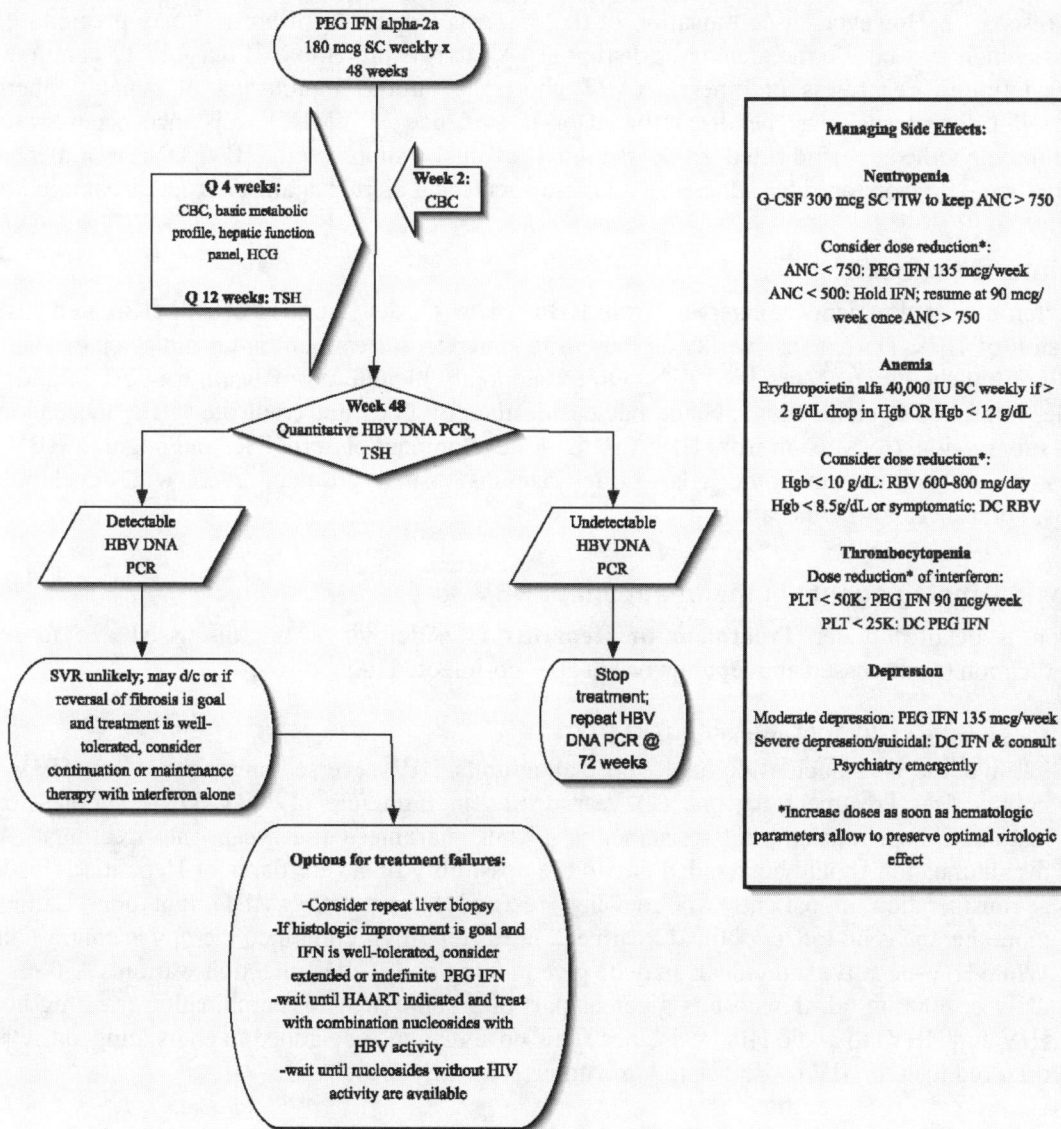

Interferon-based treatment algorithm for the HIV-HBV co-infected patient

PEG IFN alpha-2a
180 mcg SC weekly x
48 weeks

Q 4 weeks:
CBC, basic metabolic
profile, hepatic function
panel, HCG

Q 12 weeks: TSH

Week 2:
CBC

Week 48
Quantitative HBV DNA PCR,
TSH

Detectable
HBV DNA
PCR

Undetectable
HBV DNA
PCR

SVR unlikely; may d/c or if
reversal of fibrosis is goal
and treatment is well-
tolerated, consider
continuation or maintenance
therapy with interferon alone

Stop
treatment;
repeat HBV
DNA PCR @
72 weeks

Options for treatment failures:

-Consider repeat liver biopsy
-If histologic improvement is goal and
IFN is well-tolerated, consider
extended or indefinite PEG IFN
-wait until HAART indicated and treat
with combination nucleosides with
HBV activity
-wait until nucleosides without HIV
activity are available

Managing Side Effects:

Neutropenia
G-CSF 300 mcg SC TIW to keep ANC > 750

Consider dose reduction*:
ANC < 750: PEG IFN 135 mcg/week
ANC < 500: Hold IFN; resume at 90 mcg/
week once ANC > 750

Anemia
Erythropoietin alfa 40,000 IU SC weekly if >
2 g/dL drop in Hgb OR Hgb < 12 g/dL

Consider dose reduction*:
Hgb < 10 g/dL: RBV 600-800 mg/day
Hgb < 8.5g/dL or symptomatic: DC RBV

Thrombocytopenia
Dose reduction* of interferon:
PLT < 50K: PEG IFN 90 mcg/week
PLT < 25K: DC PEG IFN

Depression

Moderate depression: PEG IFN 135 mcg/week
Severe depression/suicidal: DC IFN & consult
Psychiatry emergently

*Increase doses as soon as hematologic
parameters allow to preserve optimal virologic
effect

Resistance to lamivudine (YMDD mutants) and other agents

HBV resistance testing may be performed, where available. Lamivudine resistance is most likely to occur when lamivudine has been used as monotherapy to treat HBV, which has been common until recently. Studies confirm that with HBV monotherapy using lamivudine, over 90% of isolates harbor the YMDD mutation and are resistant by year four. Tenofovir is indicated for treatment of YMDD mutant strains and therefore may be added to a regimen that already includes lamivudine when the HBV DNA PCR > 50,000 copies/mL. Tenofovir has been found to be potent and durable against HBV. Not surprisingly, however, development of tenofovir mutations during long-term monotherapy has been described, with A194T producing a 7.6-fold increase in IC50 from wild-type HBV; the combination of A194T, L180M, and M204V produced a >10-fold increase. As with HIV, combination therapy in Hepatitis is increasingly standard. It may be anticipated that as resistance mutations and assays become standardized, HBV treatment may one day be tailored using resistance testing, but this remains speculative.

Discontinuation of nucleotide reverse transcriptase inhibitors

Discontinuation of nucleoside reverse transcriptase inhibitors may be considered in the rare case of adverse effects (such as peripheral neuropathy or lactic acidosis) or when HAART is being changed due to HIV resistance. However, discontinuation of these agents (especially if abrupt) may precipitate acute Hepatitis, which may be life threatening or disrupt HAART. It is preferable, if feasible, to continue these agents indefinitely regardless of other HAART choices. Cautious monitoring of hepatic function is indicated if these agents must be discontinued or if evidence of YMDD resistance occurs while on lamivudine monotherapy (indicated by a rise in previously suppressed HBV DNA). Patients with Hepatitis should be monitored for adherence on these agents and alerted against abrupt discontinuation.

Endpoints of treatment

For interferon-treated patients, conversion from HBeAg+ to − , development of anti-HBe, and sustained suppression of HBV DNA at 24 weeks or more after interferon treatment is an indicator of successful eradication, but the latter occurs in < 15%. Other endpoints include normalization of ALT, and where available, improved liver histology. Since nucleoside therapy does not eradicate HBV, the endpoint is lifelong suppression. Conversion from HBeAg+ to − , development of anti-HBe, and ongoing HBV DNA suppression is the primary endpoint. HBsAg often remains positive but may revert, with development of anti-HBs, upon successful eradication.

Nucleoside analog agents in the treatment of HBV

Interferon is detailed under **Treatment of Hepatitis C**. Adefovir is not discussed due to relative contraindication (as discussed above) to its use in HIV co-infected individuals.

- **Lamivudine (3TC) / Emtricitabine (FTC)**
  Lamivudine is a nucleoside analogue that inhibits HIV reverse transcriptase and HBV DNA polymerase. Treatment for one (1) year results in high rate of HBV DNA suppression and histologic improvement, but resistance is all but guaranteed four years into treatment. Abrupt discontinuation should be avoided due to the possibility of severe flares of Hepatitis. This is also a consideration in patients who develop resistance with the YMDD mutation. Lamivudine monotherapy is no longer optimal treatment unless tenofovir combined therapy is contraindicated. While HIV-negative individuals may be given 50 mg daily, HIV-infection warrants 150 mg twice daily or 300 mg qd; this dose is given as part of an antiretroviral combination (treating both the HIV and HBV) to avoid HIV resistance. This dose may also be added to an existing antiretroviral drug regimen, if HIV resistance to lamivudine is already present.

  Emtricitabine has similar activity as lamivudine, but has more favorable pharmacokinetics, which may enhance durability. It is supplied alone or in a combination tablet with tenofovir, and dosed at 200 mg orally once daily, as for HIV. Emtricitabine has not been FDA-approved for the treatment of HBV.

- **Tenofovir**
  Tenofovir is a nucleoside analogue with potent inhibition of HBV DNA polymerase. It has activity against YMDD mutants, with a low rate of inducing resistance to itself, and is indicated for lamivudine-resistant strains of HBV. Tenofovir should be used in combination therapy with lamivudine or emtricitabine, dosed as for HIV at 300 mg orally once daily, and may be used in a first-line combination regimen or added to lamivudine or emtricitabine. Tenofovir has not been FDA-approved for the treatment of HBV.

- **Entecavir**
  Entecavir is currently under study in HIV/HBV co-infected individuals. Twenty-four week data from the ETV-038 phase II trial suggests safety and efficacy. Formal recommendations are unavailable for its use in this population.

Prevention of Hepatitis B

Prevention of Hepatitis B is a priority in the public health sector. Education of HIV-infected patients about preventive measures includes condom use, avoidance of IV drug use and sharing injection paraphernalia, as well as other measures to prevent sexual transmission via shared blood and body fluids. As might be expected, public educational efforts regarding safer sex, IV drug use, and needle exchange programs directed at HIV prevention have reduced the rates of HBV over the last two decades. Vaccination and prophylaxis after exposure play key roles in transmission prevention. Universal screening of pregnant women for HBsAg has reduced perinatal transmission by permitting prompt treatment of exposed neonates with Hepatitis B immune globulin and Hepatitis B vaccine.

Hepatitis B vaccine is recommended for all HIV-infected individuals who screen negative for anti-HBs and HBsAg. The likelihood of benefit of vaccination in this population is greater than the risk, especially in preventing HAART interruption, and Hepatitis B vaccination has been found to be cost-effective compared to the costs related to acute Hepatitis B. Clinical studies report induction of protective levels of antibody in at least 90% of healthy adults completing the three dose series. Unfortunately, the response in HIV-infected individuals is far less robust, ranging from 20 to 80% in one study; studies have conflicted as to the role of the CD4 count and immunosuppression with vaccine response, but lower CD4 counts may reduce efficacy. Double-dosed vaccine may improve response based on a recent abstract by Fonseca et al and deserves further investigation. In addition, it is possible that HIV-infected individuals with isolated anti-HBc positivity may not mount an anamnestic response to re-infection; HBV vaccine may be considered in these patients as well, however, data here is limited.

Hepatitis B vaccine is available as Engerix® (Smith Kline Beecham), Recombivax HB® (Merck), and combined with Hepatitis A antibody as Twinrix® (Glaxo Smith Kline). All require a series of three injections given at months 0, 1–2, and 4–6. Anti-HBs titer ≥ 10 mIU/ ml is recognized as conferring protection against HBV. Seroconversion is defined as an antibody titer ≥ 10 mIU/ ml. If seroconversion does not occur (titer < 10 mIU/ ml) after completion of the HBV series, a single booster dose may be considered.

Hepatitis C

Introduction

Approximately 4 million Americans are infected with Hepatitis C, which accounts for 25,000 deaths per year. HCV causes viral persistence and chronic disease in more than 85% of infected patients (90–95% if

HIV co-infected). Over 300,000 Americans with HIV are co-infected with HCV. HCV affects 30–40% of HIV-infected individuals, compared with 2–3% of the general US population. At present, chronic HCV is the most common reason for liver transplantation in the U.S.

Co-infection with HCV does not appear to have a major impact on progression to AIDS, but it has had a major impact on overall mortality. The increase in liver-related mortality in HIV-infected populations reflects the effectiveness of HAART in reducing AIDS-related mortality. HAART was widely adopted by 1997 and has extended the expected life span of HIV mono-infected individuals to nearly normal. Thus, while in 1991 liver-related mortality was only 11% in HIV-infected patients, it is now > 50% and is closely attributable to significant rates of co-infection with viral hepatitides. HCV co-infection is 3 times as likely as HBV co-infection, and is the greater cause of morbidity. While HCV does not appear to accelerate HIV-related mortality or progression, HIV clearly accelerates the progression of HCV-related fibrosis, even independent of the level of immunosuppression. In addition, HCV may complicate antiretroviral therapy, which may be associated with hepatotoxicity.

VIROLOGY AND NATURAL HISTORY OF HEPATITIS C INFECTION

HCV is a single stranded RNA flavivirus with many similarities to HIV. There are at least six genotypes, which vary in geographic distribution. Genotypes 1a, 1b, 2a, 2b, and 3a are most common in blood donors and patients with chronic Hepatitis C from countries in Western Europe and North America. Genotype 1 is prevalent in 75%, versus 25% with non-1 genotypes, and many studies have examined and compared treatment responses in these two groups. It should be noted, however, that genotype 4 occurs in low percentages in the US and responds in similar fashion to genotype 1. Extensive antigenic variation precludes vaccine development, much as it does with HIV, and anti-HCV does not confer immunity. Although a given antibody may be neutralizing against a given antigenic variant, new quasispecies are being produced by the millions daily and allow for immune "escape." Unlike HIV, HCV does not integrate into the host genome, and cure or remission is feasible. The means by which HCV causes liver injury is most likely immune-mediated, and is affected by host immunodeficiency. Iron overload, steatosis, and alcohol are critical co-factors that lead to progressive fibrosis; however, HIV dramatically accelerates progression to end stage liver disease. Concurrent or superinfecting Hepatitis A or B may worsen Hepatitis and long-term prognosis. Typically, cirrhosis develops in 20% of cases after 20 to 30 years of chronic infection, but HIV may shorten this interval to 5 to 10 years, or perhaps less. Hepatocellular carcinoma affects 20% of those with cirrhosis, and those who develop cirrhosis typically decompensate within 5 years. The annual rate of progression to hepatocellular carcinoma after cirrhosis develops is 1–7%. Unlike Hepatitis A and B, acute symptomatic Hepatitis C is uncommon, with silent chronic infection being the norm. When symptoms occur, patients may report fatigue, difficulty concentrating, or right upper quadrant aching.

HCV is predominantly transmitted parenterally, and up to 100% of IV drug abusers are seropositive. HIV enhances the likelihood of transmission. Sexual transmission is inefficient, even in monogamous couples (~1%), but the rate is higher in men who have sex with men. HIV also enhances perinatal transmission of HCV.

Hepatitis A and Hepatitis B

Both acute Hepatitis A and B superimposed upon chronic Hepatitis C are likely to worsen transaminitis and accelerate progression of liver disease, and may be associated with fulminant Hepatitis. Since these are potentially preventable infections, all patients with chronic Hepatitis C should be screened with Hepatitis A IgG and anti-HBs and should be offered vaccination if found to be seronegative for either.

Screening and Assessment for Viral Activity HIV/HCV-infected patient

- **HCV ELISA and HCV RNA PCR**
  All individuals with HIV should be screened for HCV with a sensitive HCV ELISA antibody assay. Anti-HCV positivity may or may not reflect chronic infection, thus seropositive individuals should undergo sensitive (low threshold) HCV RNA PCR testing. Qualitative assays are typically more sensitive than quantitative but some quantitative assays may be as sensitive. Patients with advanced HIV and poor immunity may have falsely negative anti-HCV tests, thus screening with PCR may be considered, especially with unexplained abnormalities of ALT. HCV RNA testing may also be considered if recent infection is suspected (there may be a seronegative window period up to 70 days).

- **HCV Genotyping**
  When HCV RNA PCR confirms the presence of viremia, genotyping is the most powerful predictor of sustained response to therapy. Genotype 1 accounts for the majority of cases and is less likely to respond to treatment, but should not preclude further consideration of treatment.

- **ALT levels**
  ALT levels characteristically fluctuate with chronic HCV, even dipping to normal levels intermittently. There is no correlation between ALT level and disease severity, other than the fact that higher levels are associated with worse disease and faster progression of liver disease.

ASSESSMENT FOR COMPLICATIONS OF CHRONIC HEPATITIS

- **Liver biopsy**
  The current gold standard for assessing the stage of liver fibrosis and risk of progression to advanced liver disease is liver biopsy. Non-invasive assessment methods, such as Fibro-sure™ and Fibro-Scan™ may be considered as an alternative to biopsy but have not been validated in HIV co-infection. The decision whether to perform liver biopsy may be individualized.

- **Sonography**
  An initial ultrasound of the liver can assess for cirrhosis, fatty liver, and screen for hepatocellular carcinoma. In patients known to be cirrhotic, periodic sonography is performed as below, in order to screen for hepatocellular carcinoma.

- **Alpha-fetoprotein and hepatocellular carcinoma**
  The sensitivity of alpha-fetoprotein for hepatocellular carcinoma ranges from 40–60%; this assay is not reliable alone for hepatoma screening. Combined use with other tests, such as sonography, may prove more useful. Hepatocellular carcinoma screening with sonography (with or without alpha-fetoprotein) is typically performed every 3 to 4 months.

- **Extrahepatic manifestations of chronic HCV**
  HCV is associated with several syndromes and may reflect a related autoimmune effect of HCV outside the liver.

  — **Essential mixed cryoglobulinemia (EMC)**
  HCV may be associated with other disorders, including essential mixed cryoglobulinemia. Rash (cutaneous vasculitis) and joint pain are common manifestations, and anti-HCV can be detected in the vessel walls on skin biopsy. While interferon

reduces cryocrit and symptoms, the response is transient. EMC may be associated with glomerulonephritis as below.

— Glomerulonephritis

A membranoproliferative glomerulonephritis may manifest with renal insufficiency and proteinuria that may fall into the nephrotic range. It is often associated with cryoglobulinemia. Interferon may reduce proteinuria. Ribavirin should be avoided in significant renal impairment, as should interferon in patients with creatinine clearance < 50 mL/min.

— Porphyria cutanea tarda (PCT)

PCT is associated with chronic HCV and high ethanol intake. Up to 71% of individuals with PCT are anti-HCV+.

— Lichen planus

This is most commonly found in the oral mucosa, less often on the skin, and may be worsened by interferon.

— Diabetes mellitus and other endocrine disorders

Chronic Hepatitis C is independently predictive of diabetes mellitus. The risk of protease inhibitors in predisposing to glucose intolerance may be worsened by chronic HCV. Hyperglycemia may be exacerbated by interferon.

Hepatitis C is associated with an increased incidence of anti-thyroid antibodies and thyroiditis, independent of interferon therapy. Compared to those with chronic HBV and normal controls, those with chronic HCV are more likely to have elevated anti-thyroglobulin antibodies, and anti-thyroid peroxidase antibodies, as well as TSH-confirmed hypothyroidism. Thyroid disease may be exacerbated by interferon.

— Lymphoma

Lymphoma occurs in increased incidence with chronic HCV, and this is likely to be additive to the risk associated with HIV. Unexplained chronic anemia or cytopenias, unexplained lymphadenopathy, or fever of undetermined origin should prompt evaluation for lymphoma.

GOALS OF TREATMENT OF CHRONIC HCV IN HIV-INFECTED INDIVIDUALS

Sustained HCV RNA PCR clearance ("sustained viral remission," or SVR) and improvement in liver fibrosis and histology are the main goals of HCV treatment. SVR is indicated by negative HCV RNA PCR 6 months after completion of interferon-based therapy, and is associated with reduced progression to end-stage liver disease and hepatocellular carcinoma. Until the advent of pegylated interferons, the response rates to therapy were 15% in HIV-negative populations, and poorer in HIV-infected individuals. Pegylated interferons and ribavirin have doubled the response rates to HCV therapy. The two most commonly used agents for chronic Hepatitis C are pegylated interferon alpha-2a (PEGASYS®, Roche) and pegylated interferon alpha-2b (PEG-Intron®, Schering) both combined with ribavirin. PEGASYS® and Copegus® (ribavirin, Roche) are FDA approved for chronic Hepatitis in HIV-HCV co-infection. The Roche products are therefore currently recommended by international consensus as the combination of choice in HIV-infected individuals, and will be referred to here.

In patients with adequate immunity (CD4 > 200 cells/mm^3), the goal of therapy is eradication of HCV, in addition to delayed liver disease progression, reversal of fibrosis, and prevention of HAART-related toxicity. In those with CD4 counts < 200 cells/mm^3, the goal is less focused on viral eradication.

Who should be treated for chronic HCV and when?

The management of HCV in HIV-infected individuals is very complex, and most patients are best managed by a multidisciplinary team including a hepatologist, HIV specialist, and a mental health professional. The decision to treat the HIV-HCV co-infected patient depends on careful screening for contraindications, stage of liver fibrosis, ALT abnormalities, and CD4 status, particularly given the numerous side effects of interferon-based therapy. Ongoing ethanol and other substance abuse not only hinder response to therapy, but is very likely to preclude adherence. Abstinence for 6 months before initiating interferon-based therapy is prudent.

HCV is most likely to respond at higher CD4 levels, and chronic Hepatitis is more likely to complicate HAART therapy, especially with more hepatotoxic agents. Higher CD4 levels are also associated with slowed progression of liver disease. Therefore, HCV therapy is best prioritized in those with earlier stage HIV infection, especially if HAART is not yet indicated. On the other hand, the patient with advanced HIV should be stabilized from this standpoint first with effective HAART to fully suppress HIV viremia before HCV treatment is attempted.

In the patient without contraindications for therapy, treatment should be considered if ALT is elevated, CD4 is > 350 cells/mm^3, and liver fibrosis is advanced (at least stage 2); some experts would consider treatment with lesser fibrosis if CD4 is high and genotype is 2 or 3, based on best odds for eradication of HCV.

Table 3. Prioritizing HCV Therapy in HIV-Infected Patients

Treat HIV first if:	• CD4 < 350 cells/mm^3 • Plasma HIV RNA PCR > 100,000 copies
Treat HCV first if:	• CD4 > 350 cells/mm^3 • Fibrosis is advanced (especially stage 3 or greater)

Treatment of Hepatitis C

Whereas HCV genotype determines the length of therapy in the HIV-negative individual, Hepatitis C in the HIV-infected individual is treated with combined pegylated interferon and ribavirin therapy for a total of 48 weeks, regardless of genotype. Pegylated interferon-based regimens yield an average SVR rate of 40%, especially in more recent trials enrolling large numbers of patients. Difference in response between these trials appear multifactorial in origin; differences may be attributed to different baseline levels of disease in study participants, as well as differences in attention to adherence and side effect management among studies. Overall, however, it is clear that regimens based on pegylated interferon offer significant benefits over standard interferon regimens, as well as the potential of response rates comparable to those of HIV-negative individuals.

Table 4. Response Rates to Pegylated Interferon and Ribavirin in HIV/HCV-Infected Patients

Study	No. subjects	Treatment Regimen	48 wk %SVR Overall	%SVR Genotype 1/4	%SVR Genotype 2/3	Discontinuations %
RIBAVIC (HNRS HC02) 12/2004 *PEG IFN alpha-2b*	412	*PEG IFN alpha-2b 1.5 mcg/kg Qweek + RBV 800mg QD*	27	17	43	39
ACTG A5071 7/2004 *PEG IFN alpha-2a*	133	*PEG IFN alpha-2a 180 mcg Qweek + RBV 800mg QD*	27	15	60	12
APRICOT 7/2004 *PEG IFN alpha-2a*	868	*PEG IFN alpha-2a 180 mcg Qweek + RBV 600mg QD gradually increased to 1000mg QD*	40	29	70	25
Laguno M et al 9/2004 *PEG IFN alpha-2b*	95	*PEG IFN alpha-2b 1.5 mcg/kg Qweek + RBV 800mg QD*	44	38	47	15

More promising data has been reported recently in the ongoing PRESCO trial, in which Nunez et al have evaluated the efficacy and safety of pegylated interferon alpha-2a plus ribavirin in 542 HIV-HCV co-infected individuals to date. Of interest is the longer duration of treatment, where patients with genotype 1 or 4 are randomized to 12 or 18 months treatment, while those with genotype 2 or 3 are randomized to 6 or 12 months. This trial also updates inclusion and exclusion criteria based on recent guidelines by enrolling those with CD4+ cell counts > 300 cells/mL and excluding concomitant didanosine. End of therapy responses so far are reported at 63% overall, with genotypes 1 and 4 at 50% and 44% respectively, and genotypes 2/3 at 85%. More data is forthcoming.

Despite improvements in HCV therapy, treatment remains somewhat daunting, and clinical trials typically exclude all but ideal therapeutic candidates. Many "real world" patients have relative contraindications to interferon/ribavirin therapy, and results in practice may not reflect those of trials. A thorough discussion about side effects and their management before treatment is important to enhance adherence and response. Pharmaceutical-sponsored patient support programs may be helpful.

Side effects and adverse events associated with interferon

The most common side effects of interferons include flu-like effects and depression. Flu-like effects, which are not life threatening, are worst after the first dose and tend to attenuate somewhat as treatment continues. Nausea, xerosis, hair loss, and poor sleep are not uncommon. Patients may consider taking acetaminophen prior to injections, injecting at bedtime, and injecting on days off work. Fatigue may be worsened by chronic Hepatitis, hypothyroidism, anemia, or depression, thus it may not resolve after treatment ends. Other common reactions include dry skin, alopecia, insomnia, and nausea. Redness and swelling may occur at the injection site.

Depression occurs in up to 60% of patients and may be more common with HIV. It may be related to CNS activation by pro-inflammatory cytokines; interferons may also reduce serotonin. Serotonin reuptake inhibitors are thus the mainstay of treatment in interferon-related depression. Interferon may exacerbate underlying depression, and close monitoring for suicidal ideation is necessary. Attempted and completed suicides have occurred on interferon even without underlying depression, thus caution is indicated on prescreening for treatment.

The neuropsychiatric effects of interferon may worsen those of efavirenz. In addition, many HIV-infected individuals with a history of IV drug use may not accept therapy due to needle aversions.

Other less common side effects of interferon include: pulmonary infiltrates, fibrosis, interstitial pneumonitis, or sarcoidosis, dose-limiting neutropenia (granulocyte stimulating growth factors may permit full dosing) and thrombocytopenia, induction or exacerbation of endocrine and autoimmune disease (prescreen with antinuclear antigen, and monitor glucose and thyroid functions — interferon is contraindicated in autoimmune Hepatitis), serious infections (due to immune modulation), and hepatic decompensation with advanced fibrosis. Hepatic decompensation is more likely in HIV co-infected individuals.

Side effects and adverse events associated with ribavirin

The most common effect of ribavirin is anemia, with a sharp 2 to 3 g/dL drop in hemoglobin possible within the first 2 to 8 weeks. Anemia is predominantly hemolytic, and acute drops are associated with ischemic events in patients with underlying coronary or peripheral arterial vascular disease. Those with significant coronary artery disease should not receive ribavirin.

Ribavirin is a Pregnancy Category X drug, is teratogenic and embryocidal, and may persist in non-plasma compartments for six months after discontinuation. In women of childbearing age, pregnancy testing is done immediately before the start of ribavirin and monthly throughout treatment until six months afterward. Two forms of effective contraception must be used throughout this period by male and female patients on treatment. The US Food and Drug Administration's Ribavirin Pregnancy Registry monitors pregnancy outcomes with ribavirin exposure of either partner during treatment or in the following six months. Cases should be reported to the Registry at 1-800-593-2214.

Interactions with antiretroviral therapy

Ribavirin can inhibit phosphorylation of lamivudine, zidovudine, and stavudine in vitro, but no clinical effect has been observed in HIV co-infected patients. HIV viral loads should be monitored for reduced efficacy of these antiretroviral agents. In addition, absolute CD4 count may drop with initiation of ribavirin, and antiretroviral therapy may need to be initiated in some patients. This effect is transient and does not seem to have longterm effects on HAART.

Didanosine is contraindicated due to increase in active DDI metabolites with ribavirin; pancreatitis, peripheral neuropathy, and lactic acidosis may occur with co-administration.

Zidovudine may cause anemia, and co-administration with ribavirin warrants monitoring; erythropoietin may permit full ribavirin dosing. Most HIV co-infection studies have used doses of ribavirin at 800mg daily due to higher risks of anemia, however, many physicians initiate full doses at 1000-1200mg daily with early erythropoietin "rescue", especially with genotypes 1 and 4. Neutropenia, anemia, and thrombocytopenia are more common in HIV co-infected patients during interferon-ribavirin therapy and are managed with bone marrow stimulants; thrombocytopenia may require reduction of interferon as per product packaging.

Table 5. Considerations in Antiretroviral Therapy When Treating Hepatitis C with Ribavirin

Antiretroviral Agent	Ribavirin Effect	Countermeasures
didanosine (DDI)	Increased DDI metabolites: increase in pancreatitis, neuropathy, lactic acidosis	CONTRAINDICATED if ribavirin is used
zidovudine (AZT) lamivudine (3TC) stavudine (D4T)	Possible reduction of HAART levels	Watch HIV viral loads
zidovudine(AZT)	Potentiation of anemia with ribavirin	Watch closely for anemia, consider erythropoietin early

Pretreatment evaluation (Tables 6 and 7)

HCV genotyping is helpful in that it assists prediction of treatment outcomes. Unlike genotyping in HIV-negative individuals, it is not used to determine duration of therapy in HIV-HCV co-infection. A baseline HCV RNA PCR is necessary for monitoring response.

Liver biopsy may be particularly relevant in HIV-infected patients, where the stage of fibrosis may determine the urgency of therapy.

Screen for ongoing or unstable psychiatric illness, with referral to a mental health specialist in unclear situations or if significant depression warrants. Suicidal or homicidal ideation, or past suicide attempt, are considered contraindications to interferon. In some situations, patients with risk factors or mild to moderate depression should be treated before starting therapy; otherwise, close observation on treatment will permit early treatment with serotonin reuptake inhibitors. Screen for cardiovascular ischemia and significant risks. Prescreening should look for a family or personal history of vascular disease and diabetes, risk factors for the same, and symptoms of unstable vascular disease. Appropriate cardiovascular evaluation may be indicated before treatment. Screen for endocrine disease, including hyperglycemia and thyroid abnormalities, and assure that diabetes and thyroid disease is controlled. Screen for autoimmune diseases and underlying lung disease. Screen for other causes of Hepatitis and hepatocellular carcinoma. Pregnancy prevention must be stressed for the patient and partners; with a woman receiving a urine pregnancy test on the day she is to start treatment.

Currently, the treatment of HCV in patients with advanced renal insufficiency depends on the expected interventions (including renal transplantation), longterm prognosis, and the likelihood of treatment response (genotype, viral load, extent of liver fibrosis, etc). Treatment of HCV after renal transplantation has been associated with increased graft loss. Co-infection with HIV further complicates this decision. In the patient with a creatinine clearance < 50 mL/min, pegylated interferon alpha-2a (PEGASYS®) must be dose-reduced to 135 mcg SC weekly. Ribavirin is contraindicated with a creatinine clearance < 50 mL/min due to increased oral bioavailability, reduced excretion, and inability to remove it by dialysis. Guidelines regarding HCV treatment in this population await study.

Table 6. Contraindications to Hepatitis C Treatment

Interferon	• Severe or unstable psychiatric illness • Neutropenia • Thrombocytopenia • Uncontrolled diabetes or thyroid disease • Autoimmune disease • Current or past malignancy • Serious or uncontrolled infection • History of opportunistic infection • Decompensated cirrhosis
Ribavirin	• Anemia • Severe or unstable cardiovascular or peripheral vascular disease • Pregnancy, planned conception, or uncertain adherence to dual-method contraception • Concurrent didanosine (DDI) therapy • Creatinine clearance < 50 mL/min

Table 7. Prescreening Laboratory and Other Evaluations

- Electrolytes, fasting glucose, BUN, creatinine
- Hepatic transaminases/"liver function tests"
- PT, PTT
- CBC with differential
- ANA
- TSH
- Ferritin, iron, transferrin saturation
- HAV total antibody (or IgG), HBsAg and anti-HBs (to determine need for vaccines)
- Pregnancy testing in women of childbearing potential
- Consider liver sonogram +/- alpha fetoprotein
- Consider liver biopsy

Monitoring of treatment

Refer to **Figure 3,** Algorithm for Treatment of Chronic HCV with Interferon and Ribavirin in HIV/HCV Co-Infection, for details of treatment, dosing, and laboratory monitoring.

Early virologic response predicts SVR. If a greater than 2 log drop in serum HCV RNA is not achieved by week 12 of combination therapy with interferon and ribavirin, treatment may be discontinued. If, on the other hand, an anti-fibrotic effect is a secondary endpoint, treatment may be completed with interferon alone.

Every effort should be made to avoid dose reduction in order to optimize antiviral activity. Folinic acid supplementation may help to ameliorate ribavirin toxicity during the first 12 weeks. Early use of erythropoietin is helpful as well. Granulocyte colony stimulating factor may be used to treat neutropenia related to interferon prior to reduction of dose.

Pregnancy testing should be performed monthly in women of childbearing potential, along with counseling regarding contraception.

Figure 3. Algorithm for Treatment of Chronic HCV with Interferon and Ribavirin
in HIV/HCV Co-Infection

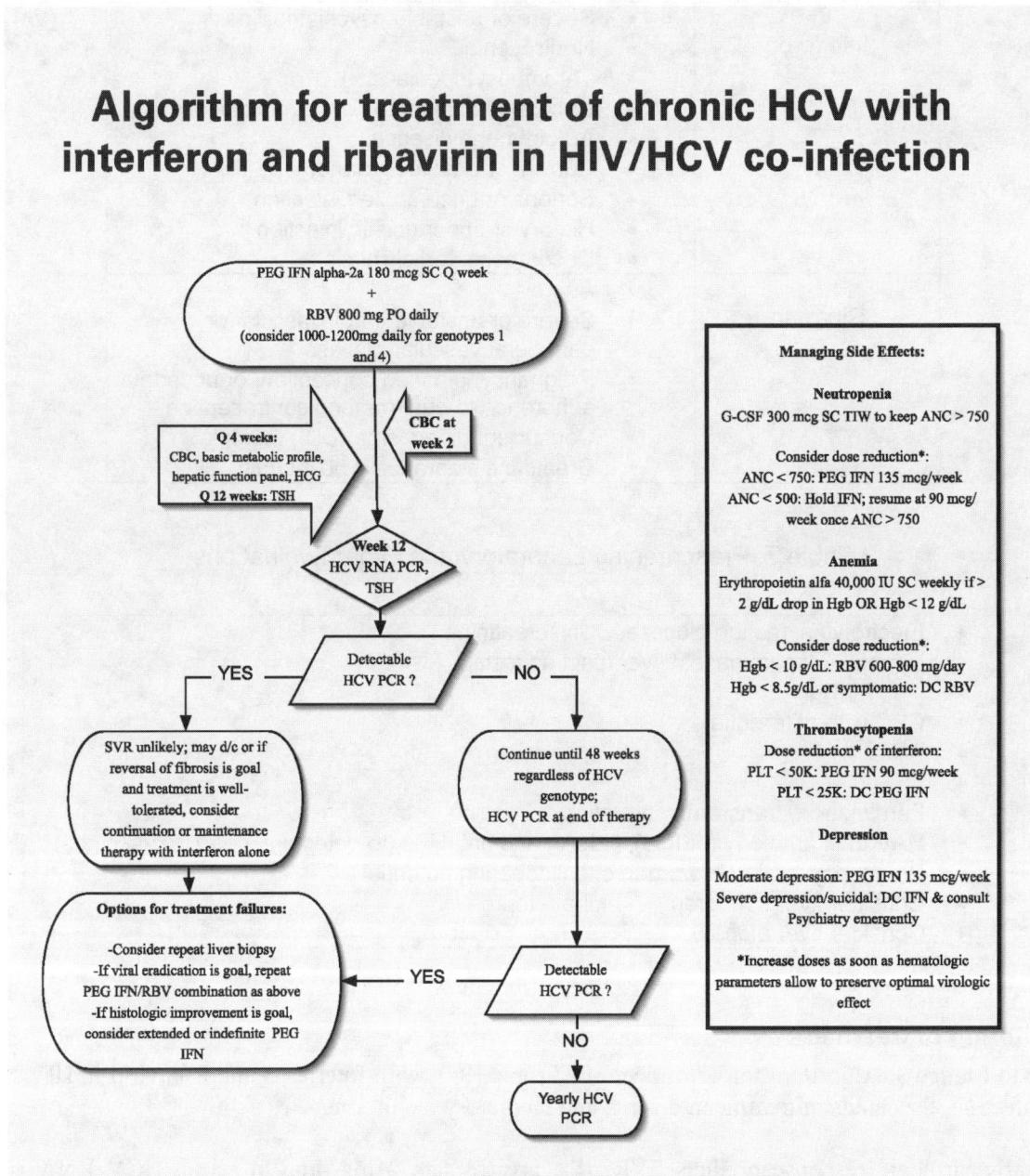

Algorithm for treatment of chronic HCV with interferon and ribavirin in HIV/HCV co-infection

PEG IFN alpha-2a 180 mcg SC Q week
+
RBV 800 mg PO daily
(consider 1000-1200mg daily for genotypes 1 and 4)

Q 4 weeks:
CBC, basic metabolic profile, hepatic function panel, HCG
Q 12 weeks: TSH

CBC at week 2

Week 12
HCV RNA PCR, TSH

Detectable HCV PCR ? — YES / NO

SVR unlikely; may d/c or if reversal of fibrosis is goal and treatment is well-tolerated, consider continuation or maintenance therapy with interferon alone

Continue until 48 weeks regardless of HCV genotype;
HCV PCR at end of therapy

Options for treatment failures:
-Consider repeat liver biopsy
-If viral eradication is goal, repeat PEG IFN/RBV combination as above
-If histologic improvement is goal, consider extended or indefinite PEG IFN

Detectable HCV PCR ? — YES / NO

Yearly HCV PCR

Managing Side Effects:

Neutropenia
G-CSF 300 mcg SC TIW to keep ANC > 750

Consider dose reduction*:
ANC < 750: PEG IFN 135 mcg/week
ANC < 500: Hold IFN; resume at 90 mcg/week once ANC > 750

Anemia
Erythropoietin alfa 40,000 IU SC weekly if > 2 g/dL drop in Hgb OR Hgb < 12 g/dL

Consider dose reduction*:
Hgb < 10 g/dL: RBV 600-800 mg/day
Hgb < 8.5g/dL or symptomatic: DC RBV

Thrombocytopenia
Dose reduction* of interferon:
PLT < 50K: PEG IFN 90 mcg/week
PLT < 25K: DC PEG IFN

Depression
Moderate depression: PEG IFN 135 mcg/week
Severe depression/suicidal: DC IFN & consult Psychiatry emergently

*Increase doses as soon as hematologic parameters allow to preserve optimal virologic effect

Treatment Failure

Failure is defined as non-suppression of HCV viremia by 12 weeks of therapy or redetection of viremia at any point thereafter. If fibrosis reduction is the principal goal of treatment, interferon monotherapy may be continued despite viremia to complete 48 weeks if the patient is otherwise tolerating therapy (longer courses may be considered if chronic suppression or maintenance is felt to be necessary). How long "maintenance therapy" is appropriate in the HIV-HCV co-infected patient remains an unanswered question. Repeat assessment of liver histology may be helpful if the decision to continue seems unclear and may be influenced by the persistence of significant fibrosis.

Recurrence of viremia at the end of 48 weeks or afterwards may be treated with a second 48-week course to reattempt eradication, if the initial course was tolerated. Sustained response rates in HIV-HCV co-infected patients are less likely in this setting but await further study.

The role, complications, and long-term outcomes of liver transplantation in HIV-infected individuals remain a complex subject of investigation.

Conclusion

Optimal management of co-infected patients with advanced fibrosis and treatment failure requires further study, as does 24-week therapy in patients co-infected with HCV genotypes 2 or 3. Most clinicians need clearer guidance in managing adverse events in order to preserve virologic potency in co-infected patients. Despite explosive growth of knowledge in recent years, much has yet to be elucidated in both the fundamentals of Hepatitis C pathogenesis and its complex management in the HIV-HCV co-infected population.

References

1. Gandhi RT, Wurcel A, Lee H, et al. Response to Hepatitis B vaccine in HIV-1–positive subjects who test positive for isolated antibody to Hepatitis B core antigen: Implications for Hepatitis B vaccine strategies. *J Infect Dis* 2005; 191:1435–1441.

2. Salmon-Ceron D, Lewden C, Morlat P, et al. Liver disease as a major cause of death among HIV-infected patients: role of Hepatitis C and B viruses and alcohol. *J Hepatology* 2005; 42(6):799–805.

3. Petoumenos K, Ringland C; Australian HIV Observational Database. Antiretroviral treatment change among HIV, Hepatitis B virus and Hepatitis C virus co-infected patients in the Australian HIV observational database. *HIV Medicine* 2005; 6(3):155–163.

4. Asmuth DM, Busch MP, Laycock ME, et al. Hepatitis B and C viral load changes following initiation of highly active antiretroviral therapy (HAART) in patients with advanced HIV infection. *Antiviral Res* 2004; 63(2):123–131.

5. Chung R, Andersen J, Volberding P, et al. Peginterferon Alfa-2a plus ribavirin versus interferon alfa-2a plus ribavirin for chronic Hepatitis C in HIV co-infected persons. *N Engl J Med* 2004; 351:451–459.

6. Konopnickim D, Mocroft A, de Wit S et al. Hepatitis B and HIV: prevalence, AIDS progression, response to highly active antiretroviral therapy and increased mortality in the EuroSIDA cohort. *AIDS* 2005; 19(6):593–601.

7. Mamta Jain, L Comanor, C White et al. Hepatitis B genotype A is associated with response to lamivudine or tenofovir in HBV/HIV-co-infected patients. 12th Conference on Retroviruses and Opportunistic Infections. February 22–25, 2005. Boston, MA. Abstract 934.

8. Alberti A, Clumeck N, Collins S, et al. Short Statement of the First European Consensus Conference on the Treatment of Chronic Hepatitis C and B in HIV Co-infected Patients (March 1–2, 2005, Paris, France). *J Hepatology* 2005; 42(5):615–624.

9. Pessoa MG. Entecavir in HIV/HBV co-infected patients: Safety and efficacy in a Phase II study (ETV-038). 12th Conference on Retroviruses and Opportunistic Infections. February 22–25, 2005. Boston, MA.

10. Thio CL, Seaberg EC, Skolasky R Jr, et al.; Multicenter AIDS Cohort Study. HIV-1, Hepatitis B virus, and risk of liver-related mortality in the Multicenter Cohort Study (MACS). *Lancet* 2002; 360:1921–1926.

11. Bonacini M, Louie S, Bzowej N, Wohl AR. Survival in patients with HIV infection and viral Hepatitis B or C: a cohort study. *AIDS* 2004; 18:2039–2045.

12. Sulkowski MS, Moore RD, Mehta SH, et al. Hepatitis C and progression of HIV disease. *JAMA* 2002; 288:199–206.

13. Tedaldi EM, Baker RK, Moorman AC, et al. Influence of coinfection with Hepatitis C virus on morbidity and mortality due to human immunodeficiency virus infection in the era of highly active antiretroviral therapy. *Clin Infect Dis* 2003; 36:3637.

14. Law WP, Duncombe CJ, Mahanontharit A, et al; HIV-NAT cohort. Impact of viral Hepatitis co-infection on response to antiretroviral therapy and HIV disease progression in the HIV-NAT cohort. *AIDS* 2004 ; 18(8):1169–1177.

15. Lacombe K, Gozlan J, Boelle PY, et al. Long-term Hepatitis B virus dynamics in HIV-Hepatitis B virus-co-infected patients treated with tenofovir disoproxil fumarate. *AIDS* 19(9):907–915. June 10, 2005.

16. Laguno M, Murillas J, Blanco JL, et al. Peginterferon alfa-2b plus ribavirin compared with interferon alfa-2b plus ribavirin for treatment of HIV/HCV co-infected patients. *AIDS* September 3, 2004; 18(13):27–36.

17. Nunez M, Maida I, Berdun MA, et al. Efficacy and safety of pegylated interferon alpha-2a plus ribavirin for the treatment of chronic Hepatitis C in HIV-coinfected patients: The PRESCO trial. Program and abstracts of the 44th Interscience Conference of Antimicrobial Agents and Chemotherapy; October 30–November 2, 2004; Washington, DC. Abstract V-1148.

18. Perez-Olmeda M, Martín-Carbonero L, Rios P, Núñez M, González-Lahoz J, Soriano V. Predictive value of early virological response (12 weeks) to pegylated interferon plus ribavirin in HIV-HCV coinfected patients. 10th Conference on Retroviruses and Opportunistic Infections. Boston, February 2003. Abstract 842.

19. Perez-Olmeda M, Nunez M, Romero M, Soriano V. Pegylated IFN-a2b plus ribavirin as therapy for chronic Hepatitis C in HIV-infected patients. *AIDS* 2003; 17:1023–1028.

20. Perronne C, Carrat F, Bani S. Ribavic Trial (Anrs HC02): A controlled randomized trial of pegylated-interferon ALFA-2B plus ribavirin versus interferon ALFA2B plus ribavirin for the initial treatment of chronic Hepatitis c in hiv co-infected patients: Preliminary results. In: 14th World AIDS Conference. Barcelona, Spain, July 7–12, 2002. Abstract LBOR16.

21. Sheldon J, Klausen G, Mauss S, Lutz T, Tacke F, Soriano V. Genotypic changes in HBV-DNA of HBV/HIV co-infected patients after long-term exposure to tenofovir. Program and abstracts of the 44th Interscience Conference of Antimicrobial Agents and Chemotherapy; October 30–November 2, 2004; Washington, DC. Abstract V-1154.

22. Soriano V, Puoti M, Sulkowski M, et al. Care of patients with Hepatitis C and HIV co-infection. Update recommendations from the HIV-HCV International Panel. *AIDS* 2004; 18:1–12.

23. Torriani FJ, Rodriguez-Torres M, Roickstroh JK, et al; APRICOT Study Group. Peginterferon Alfa-2a plus ribavirin for chronic Hepatitis C virus infection in HIV-infected patients. *N Engl J Med* 2004 July 29: 351(5):438–450.

24. Voigt E, Schulz C, Klausen G, Mauss S, Rockstroh J. Pegylated interferon alpha 2b plus ribavirin for treatment of chronic Hepatitis C in HIV-coinfected patients: A German multicenter trial. Program and abstracts of the 44th Interscience Conference of Antimicrobial Agents and Chemotherapy; October 30–November 2, 2004; Washington, DC. Abstract V-785.

17

Sexually Transmitted Diseases

John F. Toney, MD

Associate Professor of Medicine, University of South Florida, College of Medicine
Medical Director, Southeast Region STD/HIV Prevention Training Center
CDC National Network of STD/HIV Prevention Training Centers

Introduction

Sexually transmitted diseases (STDs) remain among the most common infections in the United States. Of the top 10 most frequently reported infections, five are STDs. Most Americans are unaware of the extent of the STD epidemic, however, because many infections are asymptomatic, and because social stigma prevents open discussion of the topic. The silent nature of the STD epidemic is perhaps its greatest public health threat, as people continue to underestimate their risk or forgo testing because they have no symptoms. In addition, a potentially deadly aspect of STDs is the link to HIV. STD infections increase susceptibility to acquiring HIV. Clearly the continued spread of STDs is costly in terms of both health care dollars and human suffering. However, many effective treatments and prevention strategies exist that can help stop the STD epidemic if we understand who is affected and the cost-effectiveness of prevention.

Americans of every age and every geographic, racial, cultural, socioeconomic, and religious background are affected by STDs. Infections such as herpes simplex and human papilloma virus (HPV) are so prevalent that almost everyone is at risk, and many are already infected. More than half of teens ages 15 to 19 have had sex, and these teens are at high risk for STDs. About a quarter of all new cases of STDs occur in teens; two-thirds of cases occur in people ages 15 to 24. By age 24, at least one in three sexually active people will have contracted an STD.

The incidence of STDs among men who have sex with men (MSM) declined substantially during the early 1980s as a result of a decrease in sexual risk behavior. However, high-risk behaviors and STDs among MSM have been increasing recently in many cities. MSM are at increased risk for multiple STDs, including HIV infection, syphilis, gonorrhea, chlamydia, genital herpes, Hepatitis B, and Hepatitis A.

Numerous reports document high rates of STDs among MSM that appear to be associated with a resurgence in unsafe sexual practices. Syphilis rates are increasing nationwide among MSM. The CDC has estimated that over 40% of all cases of primary and secondary syphilis in 2002 were among MSM. In

San Francisco, where the number of cases of early syphilis increased 10-fold between 1998 and 2002, 88% of all cases in 2002 were among MSM, two-thirds who were co-infected with HIV. In a study reviewing syphilis transmission in Chicago during 1998-2002, enhanced surveillance during 2000-2002 revealed 13.7% of primary and secondary syphilis cases were attributed to oral sex, including 20.3% of cases among MSM. Recently, in response to increasing prevalence of syphilis in MSM in Florida, the Florida Department of Health, Bureau of STD Prevention and Control, developed initiatives that focused public syphilis awareness through various media resources; expanded access to men's health services; and enhanced syphilis and other STD education/training for public and private healthcare providers, STD program field staff, and community representatives. The Florida syphilis initiative resulted in extraordinary community involvement in syphilis control efforts.

Rates of gonorrhea have also been increasing in MSM, and treatment has become complicated by the rapidly emerging problem with fluoroquinolone antibiotic resistance *Neisseria gonorrhoeae* in the US. Asymptomatic anal HPV infection has been detected in 30% to 48% of MSM who are not HIV-infected and in up to 65% of HIV-infected MSM. A recent multicenter study among a group of MSM at high risk for STD/HIV demonstrated a mean anal HPV infection prevalence of 57%, with no significant geographic or age variation. There is an association between anal squamous intraepithelial lesions (SIL) and HPV, with HIV-infected men being at higher risk of anal SIL. Anal cytology screening for these changes has been implemented in many clinical settings.

The continued high rates of multiple STDs among MSM underscore the importance and need for the delivery of comprehensive STD prevention services in both public and private sectors. A brief review of clinical examination findings and possible specimen collection in men is found in Table 1 and recommendations from the CDC on screening for STDs in a population at-risk or with HIV infection is reviewed in Table 2. However, clinical and preventive services for MSM often do not provide integrated services to prevent all of the STDs affecting this population. In addition, despite recommendations to vaccinate MSM to prevent Hepatitis A and Hepatitis B, vaccination coverage in this population is low. Clinicians are strongly urged to implement STD assessment and screening into their patient's clinical care.

Table 1. Important Findings at Examination and Specimen Collection in Men

Anatomic Site	Signs	Specimens
Skin		
Face, trunk, legs, forearms and palms	Lesions or rashes consistent with secondary syphilis or disseminated molluscum.	Serology for syphilis
Oral		
Lips, tongue, tonsils, hard & soft palate, buccal mucosal, gums	Mucous patches, orolabial herpes, primary syphilis lesions, signs of pharyngitis, warts.	Swab of tonsils and posterior oropharynx for gonorrhea culture (and consider chlamydia, if culture is available). If mucus patches, syphilis serology. Herpes culture or PCR if herpes suspect.
Lymph Nodes		
Axillary, cervical, epitrochlear, inguinal/femoral lymph nodes	Adenopathy.	Serology for syphilis, HIV
Genitals		
Pubic Hair	Lice or nits.	Hair for nits or lice examination
Skin of the penis, scrotum, and perineum	Lesions or eruptions consistent with primary or secondary syphilis, herpes, condylomata acuminata, molluscum contagiousum, or scabies.	Special testing (e.g. darkfield or HSV culture/PCR) of lesions if present. If international travel (or partner has international travel), consider evaluation for LGV (PCR of involved area for L-serotypes of *C. trachomatis*), chancroid (special media culture of ulcer), or granuloma inguinale (touch/crush prep).
Urethral meatus	Papular lesions consistent with intraurethral warts; discharge (following urethral stripping of the penis). Occasionally meatal ulceration.	Intra-urethral swab (inserted 2-3 cm) or urine for gonorrhea and Chlamydia testing. Gram stain of urethral smear if available. If trichomonas urethritis is suspected, first void urine (concentrated 10x) for trichomonads, or urethral swab/urine for trichomonas culture. HSV culture/PCR if ulcer present; if history possibly consistent with genital HSV, consider type-specific herpes antibody testing.
Testes and epididymis	Swelling or tenderness consistent with epididymis.	Intra-urethral swab (inserted 2-3 cm) or urine for gonorrhea and Chlamydia testing. Gram stain of urethral smear if available
Ano-Rectal		
Skin of the anus	Ulcerations, condyloma or other lesions	Rectal swab for gonorrhea culture (and chlamydia culture if available). Anoscopic exam and specimen collection should be considered in patients with rectal symptoms and recent history of anal receptive sex. Consider performing anal cytology; if abnormal, perform high-resolution anoscopy (HRA). Also consider LGV proctocolitis and send specimen for *C. trachomatis* PCR.

Table 2 Suggested STD Screening in Individuals at Risk or With HIV infection

STD	TEST	COMMENT
Syphilis	Serology with nontreponemal tests (RPR or VDRL)	Confirm positive result with serum treponemal test (FTA-ABS, TPPA)
Trichomoniasis	Saline microscopy of vaginal fluid, culture, antigen detection test	
Genital herpes	Type-specific serology (consider)	Genital herpes increases genital HIV shedding
Gonorrhea		
• **Women**	NAAT on cervical swab or urine Culture or other non-NAAT assay of cervical swab	NAAT include PCR, SDA, TMA; most sensitive tests (>90% vs. 70%) Non-NAAT include culture, unamplified DNA probe, antigen detection tests
• **Men**	NAAT of urine or urethral swab Culture or other non-NAAT assay of urethral swab	NAAT only test performed on urine Collect first 15-30 cc of urine stream without cleansing urethral meatus
• **Both**	Culture of rectal or pharyngeal swab (NAAT if locally validated)	Depends on reported sexual exposure at these sites

SOURCE: Adapted from the CDC National Network of STD/HIV Prevention Training Centers (NNPTC) "Incorporating HIV Prevention into the Medical Care of Persons Living with HIV" Training modules – Module One 2005 and *MMWR*. 2003; 52:RR-12.

Sexually Transmitted Genital Ulcerative Diseases

The diagnosis of the etiology of genital ulceration can be challenging to the health care practitioner. A variety of both infectious and noninfectious diseases are associated with genital ulceration. In this review, the term *genital ulcer* means the presence of one or more discrete interruptions of the mucosal or cutaneous surfaces involving the genitals, perineum, or surrounding tissues with the adjoining skin and mucous membranes being normal. Genital ulcer disease has emerged as a potent risk factor for acquisition, and probably for transmission, of HIV infection. The most common sexually transmitted infections that result in ulceration of the genitalia are syphilis, and herpes simplex, with chancroid, lymphogranuloma venereum, and granuloma inguinale uncommonly recognized endemically in the United States.

Genital ulcers are generally divided into diseases that cause painful ulceration and those responsible for painless ulcers. Obtaining this information from the patient is clinically very valuable, as some of these diseases may resemble each other visually. Among the most common errors clinicians make in the diagnosis of genital ulcer disease are failure to test lesions for herpes simplex virus and failure to perform syphilis serology. These errors are common because many genital ulcers lack the "typical" appearances of the common STDs, or because the clinician does not take an adequate sexual behavior history to determine whether the patient is at risk for STDs. Syphilis, lymphogranuloma venereum, and granuloma inguinale are usually associated with painless ulcers, whereas painful ulcers generally result from infections with herpes simplex and chancroid.

SYPHILIS

Of the bacterial infections causing painless ulcers, syphilis is the most common. The stages of syphilis are described as primary disease, secondary syphilis, latent syphilis, and tertiary or late syphilis. Latent and tertiary syphilis do not have genital ulceration as part of their presentation and will not be discussed here. Primary syphilis, caused by the spirochete *Treponema pallidum*, classically presents with a genital ulcer called a chancre; however, ulcerative lesions are occasionally seen in secondary syphilis. The classical chancre is firm, often quite indurated with a "rubbery" feel, and has a clean, nonpurulent base. It is usually nontender or only mildly painful. Most chancres occur on the penis in men and on the labia or near the vaginal introitus in women, but any sexually exposed site can be involved, and chancres of the anus, perineum, and mouth are fairly common. The appearance of a chancre is highly variable, and it is suggested that all patients with a genital ulcer whose lesions are not classical for genital herpes (which will be described later) must be evaluated for syphilis. Bilateral inguinal lymphadenopathy is common. The enlarged nodes typically are mildly tender and nonfluctuant and the overlying skin is not erythematous. Fever, malaise, generalized lymphadenopathy, headache, and other systemic manifestations are common in secondary, but not primary, syphilis. Some patients with early secondary syphilis present with a persistent chancre. Latent (or "hidden") syphilis implies positive syphilis serology without clinical manifestations. If seroconversion occurs within one year, the term early latent syphilis is used. If seroconversion occurs after more than one year, or the duration from infection to seroconversion is unknown, it is termed late latent syphilis.

There are two types of testing for syphilis in presence of genital ulcer; a darkfield examination and serologic testing. If serous fluid can be obtained from the ulcer by gently pressing the ulcer between the gloved finger and thumb, it can be examined under a darkfield microscope for spirochetes. Syphilitic chancres are positive for spirochetes in over 50% of patients. Serologic testing may be negative in early primary syphilis.

Serologic testing for syphilis uses initial screening with nontreponemal tests, either the Venereal Disease Research Laboratory (or VDRL) test or rapid plasma reagin (RPR) test. If the initial screening test is positive, confirmation with a treponemal test (either the fluorescent treponemal antibody absorption [FTA-abs] test or *Treponema pallidum* particle agglutination [TP-PA]), test should be performed. The nontreponemal serum titers correlate well with disease activity, and often become negative with treatment. However, titers may remain positive at low levels after treatment, so that even with adequate treatment, some patients may not revert to seronegativity. In general, treponemal tests are sensitive and specific for the first infection, but they usually remain positive for patient's lifetime and cannot be used to monitor therapy. Some HIV-infected patients can have atypical serologic test results (i.e., unusually high, unusually low, or fluctuating titers). If a patient has clinical manifestations that suggest early syphilis, but the syphilis serologic tests do not correlate, the use of other tests (e.g., biopsy and direct microscopy) should be considered. However, for most HIV-infected patients, serologic tests are accurate and reliable for the diagnosis of syphilis and for following the response to treatment.

Recommended therapy for primary and secondary syphilis is benzathine penicillin G 2.4 million units intramuscularly given as a single dose. If the patient has a penicillin allergy, doxycycline 100 mg orally twice a day for 14 days can be given to nonpregnant patients. Treatment using a single 2 gram dose of azithromycin to treat lesion syphilis has resulted in treatment failures due to macrolide high-level resistance in San Francisco, and is not presently recommended unless there is no other recourse. The treatment for early latent syphilis is the same as primary and secondary syphilis. Recommendations for treating late latent syphilis in nonallergic patients who have normal CSF examinations (if performed) include benzathine penicillin G 7.2 million units total, administered as three doses of 2.4 million units IM at one-week intervals. For nonpregnant patients who have late latent syphilis and are allergic to penicillin, doxycycline 100 mg orally for four weeks is recommended. For the treatment of neurosyphilis, aqueous crystalline penicillin G 18–24 million units a day, administered as 3–4 million units IV every 4 hours for 10 to 14 days is recommended. For unclear cases, especially with discordant clinical and serologic findings, consultation with an expert in the management of syphilis is suggested.

HIV-infected patients should be evaluated clinically and serologically for treatment failure at 3, 6, 9, 12, and 24 months after therapy. Although of unproven benefit, some experts recommend a CSF examination after therapy (i.e., at 6 months). HIV-infected patients who meet the criteria for treatment failure should be managed the same as HIV-negative patients (i.e., a CSF examination and re-treatment). CSF examination and re-treatment also should be strongly considered for patients whose non-treponemal test titer does not decrease 4-fold within 6 to 12 months. Most experts would re-treat patients with benzathine penicillin G 7.2 million units total, administered as 3 doses of 2.4 million units IM at 1-week intervals if CSF examination is normal. Treatment for neurosyphilis as described above should be instituted in patients with a CSF examination consistent with neurosyphilis.

GENITAL HERPES (HSV)

Genital herpes is by far the most common cause of painful genital ulcer disease in North America. Over the past two decades, the number of cases attributed to herpes has risen and the number in which no cause could be determined has declined, as improved diagnostic tools for herpes simplex virus infection have been instituted. About 90% of genital herpes cases are caused by type 2 HSV (HSV-2), the remainder by the type 1 virus (HSV-1), which more commonly causes orolabial herpes. Following infection, the virus persists in a latent state in dorsal nerve root ganglia, with a lifelong potential for reactivation, which results in recurrent mucocutaneous lesions and the potential for transmission to sexual partners. The clinical manifestations of genital herpes are highly variable and are influenced by previous infection with either HSV-1 or HSV-2. Evolving clinical and epidemiologic data have shown that many genital HSV-2 infections, perhaps a substantial majority, are entirely asymptomatic or cause only mild symptoms that patients do not notice or do not recognize. Clusters of vesicles, pustules, or superficial ulcers involving the genitals, anus, perineum, or surrounding areas are classic presentations, but other less clinically apparent manifestations of genital HSV can occur and are more common in most persons. These lesions generally heal by crusting, which is a favorable sign, and complete resolution of lesions routinely takes 5 to 14 days. If healing of documented herpes lesions takes longer than 4 weeks without a known reason, concomitant infection with the HIV should be investigated.

The initial infection in a person never previously infected with either type of HSV (termed primary genital herpes) is commonly associated with bilateral inguinal, firm, tender, and nonfluctuant lymphadenopathy. It is also associated with cervicitis in women and urethritis in men, localized neuropathy (like transient bladder dysfunction), aseptic meningitis, malaise, headache, or fever. These findings can be clues to the diagnosis, but their absence is not helpful. Isolation of HSV is not complex by viral diagnostic standards and most commercial and hospital laboratories can perform the test. Results are typically available in 48 to 72 hours, but treatment, if planned, should not be delayed awaiting culture results. If culture is not available, the direct fluorescent antibody test of ulcer material can be used. The Tzanck test, performed by staining lesion scrapings by either the Wright-Giemsa or Papanicolaou method for cytologic examination, has poor sensitivity, especially in ulcerated lesions. It can help confirm the diagnosis of clinically obvious herpes with intact vesicles, but has little utility in the workup of ulcerated lesions. HSV PCR is becoming more available commercially, and can offer potential information with confusing atypical presentations of HSV, especially with asymptomatic shedding.

Herpes serology has a role in diagnosis, but usually in patients who are culture negative and have an elusive diagnosis. Older commercially available tests (crude HSV antigen) do not accurately distinguish HSV-1 from HSV-2 antibody, despite claims to the contrary by the tests' manufacturers and some laboratories. New superior type-specific (surface HSV glycoprotein-G or "gG") HSV testing is currently commercially available and highly recommended when the serodiagnosis of HSV is considered. A recent evidence-based review of the utility of the type-specific HSV serology was published by Guerry et al in *Clinical Infectious Diseases*. Positive serology during an apparent first episode indicates prior primary infection that may not have been clinically apparent. If resources are limited, the clinician may elect not to perform a test for herpes.

The treatment of genital herpes involves using an antiviral agent, such as acyclovir, famciclovir, or valacyclovir. Patients with frequent outbreaks of genital herpes, severe or prolonged outbreaks, or where outbreaks cause mental health problems (such as acquiring genital herpes by rape) should be considered for suppressive treatment. Patients with a first clinical episode of genital herpes should receive either oral acyclovir 200 mg five times a day, acyclovir 400 mg three times a day, famciclovir 250 mg orally three times a day, or valacyclovir 1 g orally twice a day for 7 to 10 days or until the lesions resolve. Patients with severe disease may require intravenous acyclovir 5–10 mg/kg of body weight dosed every eight hours in patients with normal renal function. For recurrent episodes in HIV-infected patients, episodic therapy with one of the following treatment regimens is recommended: acyclovir 200 mg by mouth 5 times a day, acyclovir 400 mg by mouth 3 times a day, acyclovir 800 mg by mouth 2 times a day, famciclovir 500 mg orally twice a day, or valacyclovir 1 g orally twice a day for 5 to 10 days. Optimal benefits from treatment are reported when acyclovir is begun very early in the outbreak. Daily suppressive therapy is an alternative treatment regimen for patients with regular and frequent HSV recurrences. Recommended regimens for daily suppressive therapy in HIV-infected patients include oral acyclovir 400 mg 2 times a day, famciclovir 500 mg twice a day, or valacyclovir 500 mg orally twice a day. These suppressive regimens are efficient in preventing outbreaks and reduce asymptomatic viral shedding, but are more expensive than the episodic regimens since therapy is given daily for months to years. Patients should be cautioned that they may still shed live herpes virus despite being on therapy and could be potentially infectious to others, even without clinically apparent lesions. Patients with acyclovir-resistant strains may require therapy with intravenous foscarnet or topical cidofovir gel (not commercially available in US). For a reference on compounding topical cidofovir see Goldblum and Zabawski, Compounding of Topical Cidofovir.

CHANCROID

Chancroid, a disease caused by a fastidious Gram-negative bacterium named *Haemophilus ducreyi,* is one of the classical venereal diseases, uncommon in the United States, but can be "imported" by international travelers (or their sex partners) who may become exposed. The ulcer was historically called a "soft chancre," reflecting its nonindurated nature as compared with syphilis. Most lesions occur on the penis, especially under the foreskin in uncircumcised men, and near the introitus in women. Typically one to three lesions are present, but there may be more. Although most ulcers are round or oval, the shape may be very irregular. The edges are erythematous and may be undermined, the base typically is covered with purulent exudate, and the lesion is usually very tender. However, some cases are clinically mild or even trivial. Up to two thirds of patients with chancroid have inguinal lymphadenopathy; in these, about half have unilateral and half have bilateral involvement. The overlying skin is usually erythematous and the adenopathy often becomes fluctuant (the "bubo"), an important characteristic in differentiating chancroid from syphilis or herpes. Untreated, and sometimes despite effective antibiotic therapy, the fluctuant lymph node ruptures and drains spontaneously. Despite the highly inflammatory nature of the local manifestations, chancroid is rarely associated with fever or other systemic manifestations. If the clinical appearance of the lesion suggests chancroid, or if the patient has been sexually active in a setting where chancroid has been reported in the past few years, a culture for *H. ducreyi* should be done on the lesion and, if there is fluctuant lymphadenopathy, on a needle aspirate from the lymph node. Unfortunately, *H. ducreyi* is difficult to isolate, even by highly experienced laboratories, and special media are required.

Currently recommended regimens for the treatment of chancroid include azithromycin 1 g orally in a single dose, ceftriaxone 250 mg IM single dose, erythromycin base 500 mg orally 4 times a day for 7 days, or ciprofloxacin 500 mg orally twice daily for 3 days. Patients with advanced disease should receive more than single-dose therapy, as the failure rate in this group is higher.

LYMPHOGRANULOMA VENEREUM

Lymphogranuloma venereum (LGV), a rare disease in the United States, is caused by the invasive L1, L2, or L3 serovars of *Chlamydia trachomatis*. The most frequent clinical manifestation of LGV among heterosexual men is tender inguinal and/or femoral lymphadenopathy that is commonly unilateral. The disease may initially start as a small generally painless vesicle or papule that erodes into a small superficial ulcer. The patient may not notice the initial lesions. Women and homosexually active men may have proctocolitis or inflammatory involvement of perirectal or perianal lymphatic tissues that can result in fistulas and strictures. Recent reports of LGV proctocolitis, especially in MSM, have recently been reported in Europe, with some of these cases caused by a new serotype (L2b). Treatment cures infection and prevents ongoing tissue damage, although tissue reaction can result in scarring. Buboes may require aspiration through intact skin or incision and drainage to prevent the formation of inguinal/femoral ulcerations. The diagnosis is usually made serologically and by exclusion of other genital ulcerative and adenopathy-producing diseases.

Doxycycline 100 mg orally twice a day for at least 21 days is the preferred treatment. Alternatively, Erythromycin base 500 mg orally four times a day for at least 21 days can be used. The activity of azithromycin against LGV strains of *C. trachomatis* suggests that it may be effective in multiple doses over 2 to 3 weeks, but clinical data regarding its use are lacking.

GRANULOMA INGUINALE (DONOVANOSIS)

Granuloma inguinale, a rare disease in the United States, is caused by the intracellular Gram negative bacterium *Klebsiella granulomatis*. The disease is endemic in certain tropical and developing areas, including India, Papua New Guinea, central Australia, and southern Africa. The disease presents clinically as painless, progressive, ulcerative lesions without regional lymphadenopathy. The lesions are highly vascular (i.e., a beefy red appearance) and bleed easily on contact. The causative organism cannot be cultured on standard microbiologic media, and diagnosis requires visualization of dark-staining Donovan bodies on tissue crush preparation or biopsy. A secondary bacterial infection might develop in the lesions, or the lesions might be co-infected with another sexually transmitted pathogen. Treatment appears to halt progressive destruction of tissue, although prolonged duration of therapy often is required to enable granulation and re-epithelialization of the ulcers. Relapse can occur 6 to 18 months later despite effective initial therapy.

Recommended regimens for treating granuloma inguinale include one double-strength trimethoprim-sulfamethoxazole tablet orally twice a day for a minimum of 3 weeks or doxycycline 100 mg orally twice a day for a minimum of 3 weeks. Therapy should be continued until all lesions have healed completely.

Sexually Transmitted Diseases Characterized by Genital Discharges

Diseases causing infection of the male and female genitalia and occasionally other body sites continue to confront clinicians in their daily practices. The causes of these infections resulting in genital discharge may produce a single disease process or they may interact together. Frequent causes of urethritis in men result from infections with *Chlamydia trachomatis*, *Neisseria gonorrhea*, and genital mycoplasmas. Female infections, commonly involving the vagina, cervix, ascending reproductive structures and less frequently the urethra, encounter the same infectious pathogens as men and, in addition, acquire additional agents such as *Trichomonas vaginalis*, *Candida* species, *Gardnerella vaginalis*, and anaerobic bacteria. Many of these diseases have serious outcomes, such as sterility and ectopic pregnancy, if not rapidly recognized and treated.

CHLAMYDIA

The most common clinical syndrome caused by *C. trachomatis* in male patients is nongonococcal urethritis. Nonspecific urethritis is another common but incorrectly used term for this infection. The disease is characterized by the gradual onset of mild dysuria and a slight mucoid urethral discharge. Not surprisingly, patients who have this syndrome believe that they have gonorrhea. Experienced clinicians can often diagnose nongonococcal urethritis on clinical grounds based on the relatively mild symptoms, the scant discharge which sometimes must be manually stripped from the urethra, and the color of the discharge, which is usually gray or clear rather than the yellow or green that is generally seen with gonococcal urethritis. These clinical criteria lack sensitivity and specificity and usually require the use of simple laboratory testing for confirmation of the clinical impression. Urethral inflammation is defined as the presence of an average of 5 or more polymorphonuclear leukocytes in a Gram stained smear of urethral discharge per oil-immersion field or 15 or more polymorphonuclear leukocytes per high-dry field in the spun sediment of a 5- to 10-milliliter specimen of first-voided urine.

Complications of urethral chlamydial infections in men are uncommon, but occasionally epididymitis may occur. In fact, *C. trachomatis* is the most common cause of epididymitis in men less than 35 years of age. Rarely, urethral chlamydial infection may result in Reiter's syndrome, a systemic illness involving the joints and mucous membranes which is seen almost exclusively in men, most of whom are positive for HLA B27 or related antigens. Enteric Gram-negative bacteria such as Shigella and Salmonella also precipitate this disease. Patients with Reiter's syndrome who have not had gastrointestinal symptoms prior to onset of their joint disease and who have evidence of urethral inflammation either clinically or by Gram stain should be treated with a minimum of a one-week course of doxycycline, since several studies have indicated that approximate 50% are infected with *C. trachomatis*. Their regular sexual partners should also be treated to prevent reinfection.

Though most chlamydial infections in women do not produce clinical signs, various clinical syndromes associated with the presence of the organism have been described. *Chlamydia* can be most commonly isolated from the endocervical canal and is associated with endocervicitis that is characterized by a hypertrophic follicular ectropion surrounding the cervical os and a purulent endocervical discharge. Pap smears may show severe inflammatory changes. Some studies have suggested that biopsy-proven cervical dysplasia may be associated with the presence of *Chlamydia* but these observations require further substantiation. Regardless, mildly abnormal pap smears may revert to normal after treatment for *Chlamydia*.

Occasionally *C. trachomatis* may ascend into the fallopian tubes resulting in pelvic inflammatory disease. The best evidence for the association of *C. trachomatis* with this condition comes from studies done in Scandinavia where the organism has been isolated from fallopian tube biopsy specimens obtained through the laparoscope in 30% to 40% of clinically diagnosed women. For this reason, the CDC presently recommends that all women being treated for pelvic inflammatory disease receive at least one antibiotic which is active against *C. trachomatis*. One major concern is that persistent fallopian tube infection by this organism and subsequent tubal scarring may result in structural infertility or ectopic pregnancy. Whether or not a woman with acute PID will remain fertile or perhaps develop an ectopic pregnancy depends on how seriously her tubes are damaged. In cases of mild tubal disease, effective antibiotic therapy may prevent further damage. In a few cases of pelvic inflammatory disease, it appears that the organism may invade the peritoneal cavity more extensively resulting in perihepatitis.

Nonculture methods have been introduced for the detection of *C. trachomatis* in genital secretions. Fluorescent microscopy, enzyme immunoassay, and nucleic acid hybridization (including nonamplified DNA probe and nucleic-acid amplication tests [NAAT], including polymerase chain reaction [PCR], transcription mediated amplification [TMA], and strand displacement amplification [SDA] testing) are commercially available. The fluorescent microscopic method is highly dependent upon the skill of the technician reading the smears as well as the quality of the microscope used. Fluorescent testing can be done rapidly and economically in laboratories where relatively few specimens are processed; however, if it is not performed according to exact standards, the test lacks sensitivity and may have an unacceptably high rate of false positives. Although less dependent upon technician skill, the enzyme immunoassay method fails to detect 10% to 20% of culture-positive patients and gives false-positive results in as many as 5% of normal uninfected individuals. The clinician should be aware of these problems to avoid under- or over-diagnosing chlamydial infections. More recently, DNA probe and NAAT testing have become and are highly recommended. The sensitivities and specificities of these tests rival chlamydia culture, and, with NAAT offer the potential of diagnosing chlamydia infection using urine specimens.

Fortunately, chlamydial infections are easily treated once recognized. Strains of *C. trachomatis* are uniformly susceptible to tetracyclines and macrolide antibiotics and, as yet, there is no evidence for the emergence of resistance to these antibiotics. The usual course for treating uncomplicated chlamydia infection is doxycycline 100 mg twice a day for a total of seven days. Azithromycin 1 g orally as a single dose is also effective but more expensive. Ofloxacin, a quinolone antibiotic, may also be used to treat *Chlamydia* infections at a dose of 300 mg orally twice a day for seven days. Additional options recommended by the CDC guidelines are levofloxacin 500 mg by mouth once a day for seven days or erythromycin 500 mg by mouth four times a day for seven days. If compliance can be assured and reinfection prevented by partner treatment or abstinence from sexual activity, treatment failures with the above regimens are rare

GONORRHEA

Gonorrhea is the second-most frequently reported STD in the United States. Although behavioral changes among high-risk groups have had an impact, demographic factors are probably equally important. Urethritis is the most common gonococcal infection syndrome in men. Purulent discharge followed by dysuria usually occurs within one week of infection; however, approximately 5% of infected men never develop any signs or symptoms. The major differential diagnosis is gonococcal versus non-gonococcal urethritis, which is differentiated by a Gram stain and culture or DNA probe of the urethral exudate.

In women, the initial gonococcal infection most frequently presents as cervicitis. Purulent exudate often can be detected by a careful visual speculum examination. Infected women may have nonspecific complaints such as increased vaginal discharge, abnormal menses (increased flow or dysmenorrhea, for example), dyspareunia, or dysuria. Labial tenderness and Bartholin's / Skene's gland abscesses are less frequent signs of infection. In women, fifty percent or more are asymptomatic at presentation, but is dependant on the clinical setting. The diagnosis of gonococcal cervicitis is made by culture or DNA probe.

The most serious complication of gonorrhea in women is pelvic inflammatory disease, or PID. Other major causes of PID are *Chlamydia trachomatis* (which is a common co-infection with gonorrhea), streptococci, and anaerobes. Ascending infection from the endocervix through the uterine cavity to the fallopian tubes usually occurs within one to two menstrual cycles in 10% to 20% of women with untreated or undertreated gonococcal infection. However, as many as 50% of those with endocervical gonorrhea may have upper-tract signs such as adnexal tenderness at initial evaluation. PID is actually a spectrum of soft-tissue infections, including endometritis and salpingitis. Tubal scarring, the major long-term sequela of PID, leads to increased potential for repeated episodes of PID, increased incidence of tubal infertility, and higher risk of developing ectopic pregnancy.

Although a diagnosis of PID can be confirmed only by laparoscopy, documenting lower abdominal pain, abnormal cervical or vaginal discharge, and tenderness on bimanual exam often makes the clinical diagnosis. Fever occurs in only half the cases. On bimanual examination, the signs in PID are uterine traction tenderness, adnexal tenderness, or adnexal enlargement. However, laparoscopic studies have demonstrated clinicopathologic correlation in only two-thirds of cases. Therefore, careful clinical observation of the patient is extremely important.

The recommended regimen for the treatment of uncomplicated gonococcal infection, as recommended by the CDC, include ceftriaxone 125 mg intramuscularly as a single dose, or cefixime 400 mg orally as a single dose, or ciprofloxacin 500 mg orally as a single dose, or ofloxacin 300 mg orally as a single dose, or levofloxacin 250 mg orally as a single dose plus treatment for possible chlamydia coinfection. Currently, however, gonorrhea in MSM has been found to be increasingly resistant to fluoroquinolone (FQ) antibiotics, and a recent CDC MMWR advises against treatment using FQ in this population, unless antibiotic susceptibility testing demonstrates FQ susceptibility. The CDC-recommended treatment of PID for inpatients includes either cefoxitin 2 g intravenously every 6 hours or cefotetan 2 g intravenously every 12 hours plus doxycycline 100 mg intravenously or orally twice daily; alternatively, clindamycin plus gentamicin intravenously is effective. Outpatient PID therapy consists of either oral ofloxacin 400 mg twice daily or levofloxacin 500 mg orally once daily for 14 days plus metronidazole 500 mg orally twice daily for 14 days, or alternatively ceftriaxone 250 mg intramuscularly as a single dose plus doxycycline 100 mg orally twice daily for 14 days.

VAGINITIS

In women, a vaginal discharge is one of the most common reasons that patients visit a physician's office. The symptoms of vaginitis may often be misdiagnosed as a urinary tract infection. **Bacterial vaginosis** (BV), which commonly causes a homogenous vaginal discharge, may also be associated with a disagreeable genital odor described as musty or fishy in character, and about 15% can experience vaginal irritation. This condition is caused by the replacement of resident lactobacilli, which maintain the acidity of the vagina, with an overgrowth of several bacteria, including *Gardnerella vaginalis*, *Mobiluncus* species, other anaerobic bacteria, and *Mycoplasma hominis*. BV generally is felt not to be sexually transmitted, but occurs occasionally after intercourse, which can be related to an increase in vaginal pH produced by semen. The diagnosis of bacterial vaginosis is made by the presence of three of the following conditions: a characteristic vaginal discharge; a vaginal pH of greater than 4.5; a positive amine odor test (this was called a "sniff test" or "whiff test" in the past); and "clue" cells being seen on a wet mount or Gram stain of the vaginal discharge. Vaginal cultures are not useful in the diagnosis of bacterial vaginosis as *Gardnerella* may be present in the vagina in approximately 50% of normal women.

The CDC-recommended regimen for treating bacterial vaginosis in nonpregnant women is either oral metronidazole 500 mg twice a day for 7 days, clindamycin cream 2%, one full applicator (5 g) intravaginally at bedtime for 7 days, or metronidazole gel 0.75%, one full applicator (5 g) intravaginally once a day for 5 days.

Vaginal infection due to **candidiasis** may cause a vaginal discharge as well as vulvovaginitis. The usual etiology is *Candida albicans*, but other yeast may occasionally precipitate the disease. This disease, like BV, is usually not acquired by sexual transmission. Predisposing factors for this disease include diabetes mellitus, HIV infection, antibiotic therapy, use of birth control pills, pregnancy, immunosuppresssant medications, obesity, and possibly tight clothing. Symptoms of *Candidia* vulvovaginitis include vulvar or vaginal itching or burning, dyspareunia, and external dysuria. These symptoms may be intensified 1 week prior to menses. Satellite lesions may be noted surrounding the localized erythema seen on physical examination of patients with *Candidia* vulvovaginitis and helps clinically to make the diagnosis. Laboratory examination used in the evaluation of *Candidia* vulvovaginitis includes either a Gram stain or a wet mount using potassium hydroxide to evaluate the specimen for budding yeast and pseudohyphae. A positive vaginal culture for *Candida* without symptoms is not adequate to diagnose vulvovaginitis.

The treatment of *Candidia* vulvovaginitis revolves around the use of topical vaginal azole antifungals. A wide variety of these agents are available, including butoconazole, clotrimazole, miconazole, tioconazole, and terconazole, with multiple dosing regimens used preferentially unless the disease is uncomplicated mild-to-moderate vulvovaginitis. Oral fluconazole given as a 150 mg tablet can be used as a single-dose regimen, although this regimen may be less effective in HIV-positive women. See Chapter

40, Management of HIV/AIDS in Women, for specific drugs and regimens used in the treatment of vulvovaginitis.

Trichomoniasis is caused by the protozoan *Trichomonas vaginalis*. The majority of men infected with *T. vaginalis* are asymptomatic, but women generally have some symptoms. Among women, *T. vaginalis* typically causes a diffuse, malodorous, yellow-green vaginal discharge with vulvar irritation. There is recent evidence of a possible relationship between vaginal trichomoniasis and adverse pregnancy outcomes, particularly premature rupture of the membranes and preterm delivery. Although *T. vaginalis* is not an invasive protozoan, it can cause punctate ulcerations, usually seen on the cervix ("strawberry cervix").

The recommended regimen to treat trichomoniasis is metronidazole 2 g orally in a single dose. Alternatively, metronidazole 500 mg twice daily for 7 days can be used. Only metronidazole is available in the United States for the treatment of trichomoniasis. In randomized clinical trials, both of the recommended metronidazole regimens have resulted in cure rates of approximately 95%. Treatment of the patient and sex partner results in relief of symptoms, microbiologic cure, and reduction of transmission. Metronidazole gel has been approved for the treatment of bacterial vaginosis but is not indicated in the treatment of trichomoniasis. Earlier preparations of metronidazole for topical vaginal therapy demonstrated low efficacy against trichomoniasis. Tinidazole (Tindamax®) 2 g orally in a single dose recently received FDA approval for treatment of trichomoniasis. Follow-up is unnecessary for men and for women who become asymptomatic after treatment.

In conclusion, the challenge of diagnosing and treating genital diseases caused by the most common venereal infectious agents can be reduced if the clinician takes a careful medical, sexual, and social history, performs a thorough physical examination, and applies appropriate laboratory testing for these sexually transmissible organisms.

References

CDC. Increases in unsafe sex and rectal gonorrhea among men who have sex with men. San Francisco, 1994–1997. *MMWR* 1999; 48:45–48.

Klausner JD, Wong W. Sexually transmitted diseases in men who have sex with men: A clinical review. *Current Infec Dis Report* 2003; 5:135–144.

Collis TK, Celum CL. The clinical manifestations and treatment of sexually transmitted diseases in human immunodeficiency virus-positive men. *Clin Infect Dis* 2001; 32:611–622.

Eng, TR, and Butler, WT, eds. *The Hidden Epidemic: Confronting Sexually Transmitted Diseases*. Washington, D.C.: National Academy Press, 1997.

CDC. Sexually transmitted diseases treatment guidelines 2002. *MMWR* 2002; 51(No. RR-6).

CDC's Four Division "Dear Colleague" letter highlighting the 2002 STD Treatment Guidelines recommendations for MSM. March 8, 2004. CDC Web site. Available at http://www.cdc.gov/ncidod/diseases/hepatitis/msm. Accessed October 2005.

Williams LA, Klausner JD, Whittington WLH, Handsfield HH, Celum C, Holmes KK. Elimination and reintroduction of primary and secondary syphilis. *Am J Public Health* 1999; 89:1093–1097.

CDC. Primary and secondary syphilis among men who have sex with men — New York City, 2001. *MMWR* 2002; 51:853–856.

CDC. Brief Report: Azithromycin treatment failures in syphilis infections — San Francisco, California, 2002–2003. *MMWR* 2004; 53:197–198.

Lynn WA, Lightman S. Syphilis and HIV: A dangerous combination. *Lancet* 2004; 4:456–466.

CDC. Transmission of primary and secondary syphilis by oral sex — Chicago, Illinois, 1998-2002. *MMWR* 2004; 53:966–968.

Schmitt K, Bulecza S, George D, Burns TE, Jordahl L. Florida's multifaceted response for increases in syphilis among MSM: The Miami–Ft. Lauderdale initiative. *Sex Transm Dis* 2005; 32:S19–S23.

Rolfs RT, Joesoef MR, Hendershot EF, et al. A randomized trial of enhanced therapy for early syphilis in patients with and without human immunodeficiency virus infection. *NEJM* 1997; 337:307–314.

CDC. Inadvertent use of Bicillin® C-R to treat syphilis infection — Los Angeles, California, 1999–2004. *MMWR* 2005; 54:217–219.

Lukehart SA, Godornes C, Molini BJ, Sonnett P, Hopkins S, Mulcahy F, Engelman J, Mitchell SJ, Rompalo AM, Marra CM, Klausner JD. Macrolide resistance in *treponema pallidum* in the United States and Ireland. *NEJM* 2004; 351:154–158.

Cohen CE, Winston A, Asboe D, Boag F, Mandalia S, Azadian B, Hawkins DA. Increasing detection of asymptomatic syphilis in HIV patients. *Sex Transm Infect* 2005; 81:217–219.

CDC. Internet use and early syphilis infection among men who have sex with men — San Francisco, California, 1999–2003. *MMWR* 2003; 52:1229–1232.

Klausner J, Wolf W, Fischer-Ponce L, Zolt I, Katz M. Tracing a syphilis epidemic through cyberspace. *JAMA* 2000; 284:485–487.

Rietmeijer CA, Patnaik JL, Judson FN, et al. Increases in gonorrhea and sexual risk behaviors among men who have sex with men: A 12-year trend analysis at the Denver Metro Health Clinic. *Sex Transm Dis* 2003; 30: 562–567.

Cook RL, St George K, Silvestre AJ, et al. Prevalence of chlamydia and gonorrhea among a population of men who have sex with men. *Sex Transm Infect* 2002; 78(3):190–193.

Kahn R, Heffelfinger J, Berman S. Syphilis outbreaks among men who have sex with men: a public health trend of concern. *Sex Transm Dis* 2002; 29:285–287.

Guerry SL, Bauer HM, Klausner JD, Branagan B, Kerndt PR, Allen BG, Bolan G. Recommendations for the selective use of herpes simplex virus type 2 serologic tests. *Clin Inf Dis* 2005; 40:38–45.

Goldblum and Zabawski, Compounding of topical cidofovir. *Arch Dermatol* 2002; 138:267.

CDC. Increases in fluoroquinolone-resistant neisseria gonorrhoeae among men who have sex with men — United States, 2003, and revised recommendations for gonorrhea treatment, 2004. *MMWR* 2004; 53:335–338.

Geisler WM, Whittington WL, Suchland RJ, et al. Epidemiology of anorectal chlamydial and gonococcal infections among men having sex with men in Seattle: Utilizing serovar and auxotype strain typing. *Sex Transm Dis* 2002 ; 29(4):189–95.

Ciemins EL, Flood J, Kent CK, et al. Reexamining the prevalence of chlamydia trachomatis infection among gay men with urethritis: implications for STD policy and HIV prevention activities. *Sex Transm Dis* 2000; 27(5):249–51.

Comparative prevalence, incidence and short-term prognosis of cervical squamous intraepithelial lesions amongst HIV-positive and HIV-negative women. *AIDS* 1998; 12:1047–1056.

Koutsky L. Epidemiology of genital human papilloma virus infection. *Am J Med* 1997; 102(5A):3–8.

Van der Snoek EM, et al. HPV infection in MSM participating in a Dutch gay-cohort study. *Sex Trans Dis* 2003; 30:639–644.

Ching-Hong VP, Vittinghoff E, Cranston RD, et al. Age-related prevalence of anal human papillomavirus infection among sexually active men who have sex with men: The EXPLORE study. *J Infect Dis* 2004; 15;190(12):2070–2076.

Palefsky JM, Holly EA, Hogeboom CJ, et al. Virologic, immunologic, and clinical parameters in the incidence and progression of anal squamous intraepithelial lesions in HIV-positive and HIV-negative homosexual men. *J Acquir Immune Defic Syndr Hum Retrovirol* 1998; 17(4):314–319.

Palefsky JM. Human papillomavirus infection and anogenital neoplasia in human immunodeficiency virus-positive men and women. *J Natl Cancer Inst* 1998; (23):15–20.

Palefsky JM, Minkoff H, Kalish LA, Levine A, Sacks HS, Garcia P, Young M, Melnick S, Miotti P, Burk R. Cervicovaginal human papillomavirus infection in human immunodeficiency virus-1 (HIV)-positive and high-risk HIV-negative women. *J Nat Cancer Instit* 1999; 91:226–236.

Spaargaren J, Fennema HSA, Morré SA, de Vries HJC, Coutinho RA. New lymphogranuloma venereum *chlamydia trachomatis* variant, Amsterdam. *Emerg Infect Dis* 2005; 11:1090–1092. Available at: http://www.cdc.gov/ncidod/EID/vol11no07/04-0883.htm.

Pinto V M, Tancredi MV, Neto AT, Buchalla CM. Sexually transmitted disease/HIV risk behaviour among women who have sex with women. *AIDS* 2005; 19:S64–S69.

Sobel JD. Vaginitis. *NEJM* 1997; 337:1896–1903.

18

Cytomegalovirus Infection

Stephen N. Symes, MD
Assistant Professor, Department of Medicine
Division of Clinical Immunology and Infectious Diseases
University of Miami School of Medicine
Todd S. Wills, MD
Assistant Professor, Division of Infectious Diseases
University of South Florida College of Medicine
Faculty, Florida/Caribbean AIDS Education and Training Center

Introduction

- DNA virus, latent infection reactivates in the setting of immunodeficiency
- CD4+ cell counts typically < 50 cells/mm^3
- Pre-HAART era: CMV disease common and serious complication, seen in 21–44 % of all AIDS patients
- Incidence of CMV end organ disease has decreased by > 75% since widespread use of HAART
- Commonly reported as an immune restoration disorder following initiation of antiretroviral therapy – most often in setting of rapid CD4+ increase and rapid viral load decrease
- May affect the eyes (85%), GI tract (10%), central and peripheral nervous systems, lungs, or adrenal glands.
- Primary prophylaxis is not routinely recommended
- Secondary prophylaxis until CD4+ count greater than 100–150 cells/mm^3 for at least 3 to 6 months (Consultation with ophthalmologist required to assure no active disease. Ongoing regular ophthalmologic exams encouraged.)

Chorioretinitis

- Most common opportunistic infection of the eye in patients with AIDS
- Pathology: viral retinal necrosis, infected retinal cells demonstrate viral inclusions, virus spreads from cell to cell
- Infection may begin in the periphery of the retina, and without antiviral therapy migrates centrally, causing a full thickness retinal necrosis and edema that is later replaced by scar tissue

Symptoms

- Unilateral painless visual loss, with blurring of vision
- Scotomata ("blind spots")
- Floaters
- Photopsia ("flashing lights")
- May be asymptomatic in patients with significant immunosuppression
- Lesions close to the fovea or optic nerve may cause blindness
- Funduscopic examination: white fluffy/cheesy exudates with areas of hemorrhage
- Affected areas of the retina do not regenerate functionally so visual loss is permanent, although some patients have improvement reflecting a decrease in inflammation and edema with treatment

General treatment considerations

Four (4) antiviral agents active against CMV currently available in various forms (See Table 1)

Ganciclovir (iv, oral, implant)

Valganciclovir (oral)

Foscarnet (iv)

Cidofovir (iv)

Fomivirsen – antisense oligonucleotide (intraocular injection)

- Initial therapy for CMV successful for 80–90% of patients in pre-HAART era, but many patients would reactivate despite chronic suppressive therapy with resultant progressive visual loss
- Successful cessation of anti-CMV therapy reported in patients on potent HAART combinations without recurrence of retinitis
- Unilateral intraocular therapy without systemic antiviral therapy does not prevent retinitis in the contralateral eye
- Relapses occur in patients experiencing reductions in CD4 counts to < 50 cells/mm^3, suppressive anti-CMV therapy should be restarted at this point
- Retinal detachment occurs in 25% of patients treated with antiviral therapy; a significant cause of vision loss in these patients

Prophylaxis

Primary

- Patient education
- Regular ophthalmologic evaluations for patients with CD4 < 50/mm^3

Discontinuation of secondary prophylaxis:

- May be considered for patients on HAART with sustained (> 3–6 months) increase in CD4+ cell count to > 100–150 cells/mm^3 in consultation and with ongoing examinations with the ophthalmologist

Gastrointestinal disease

GENERAL OVERVIEW

- Decreased incidence with the availability of HAART
- Patients with CMV gastrointestinal disease often have prior or concurrent retinitis, all such individuals should be screened for active eye disease

- May affect all areas of luminal gastrointestinal tract and extraluminal organs including the biliary tract and pancreas

Pathology

- Histological features include mucosal inflammation, tissue necrosis, and vascular endothelial involvement
- Large cells with intranuclear and sometimes intracytoplasmic inclusions ("owl's eye") are present on biopsy, and stains for CMV antigen in biopsy specimens are sensitive and specific

Diagnosis

- Fever common
- CD4+ cell count is usually < 50 cells/mm^3
- Histological evidence of invasive CMV disease necessary to establish diagnosis as viral cultures of mucosal biopsies or brushings may only represent mucosal CMV shedding

Clinical Entities

CMV stomatitis or esophagitis
- Odynophagia; large deep ulcers are visualized by barium swallow or endoscopy
- Must be differentiated from herpes simplex virus (HSV) and idiopathic oral ulceration (aphthous ulcers)

CMV gastritis and duodenitis
- Substernal burning or epigastric pain and tenderness
- Patients may have upper GI bleeding, with coffee grounds or hematemesis, melena or heme-positive stools
- Perforation with peritonitis may also occur

CMV small bowel disease
- May cause diarrhea and generalized abdominal pain

CMV colitis
- Usually presents with fever, multiple small volume heme-positive stools, associated with burning pain with each bowel movement, tenesmus with proctitis
- Hematochezia and perforation may occur
- Mucosal ulceration on colonoscopy and biopsy showing invasive CMV disease is diagnostic

CMV cholangitis or hepatitis (AIDS cholangipathy)
- Presents with right upper quadrant pain, tenderness and fever
- Laboratory findings: elevated transaminases, alkaline phosphatase elevations out of proportion to other liver function test changes
- ERCP may reveal proximal biliary dilatation and possible sphincter of Oddi stricture. Differential diagnosis includes mycobacterium avium complex, cryptosporidium, and microsporidia. Biliary fluid may be sampled for diagnosis during ERCP

CMV pancreatitis
- Reported rarely

Treatment

- Without treatment hemorrhage or perforation of hollow organs may occur
- Antiviral therapy with intravenous ganciclovir, foscarnet, or cidofovir should be administered for 2 to 6 weeks. Valganciclovir may be used if GI absorption is not compromised.
- Chronic maintenance therapy not recommended because time to relapse does not appear to be affected
- HAART with immune restoration is an effective way of controlling CMV disease in the gastrointestinal tract
- Must screen for ophthalmologic disease which requires a longer therapy course and administration of secondary prophylaxis

Neurologic Disease

GENERAL OVERVIEW

- Wide spectrum of disease: encephalitis/ventriculitis, transverse myelitis, polyradiculopathy, rarely mass lesions
- Symptoms determined by anatomic location
- Patients typically have concurrent or prior CMV disease — especially retinitis
- Median survival time despite treatment only 3 months in the pre-HAART era

Clinical Entities

CMV encephalitis
Signs/symptoms

- Fever
- Delirium
- Confusion
- Focal neurologic deficits

Clinical

- Imaging by CT or MRI may show periventricular changes and meningeal enhancement, but are not specific for CMV
- Characterized by microglial nodules or focal parenchymal necrosis
- Spinal fluid often normal but PCR for CMV antigen or DNA both sensitive and specific. Viral cultures for CMV in the CSF often negative.
- Obtundation over several weeks followed by death in patients who fail to respond to treatment
- Must differentiate from AIDS dementia which usually follows a more indolent course

CMV myelitis

- Should be suspected in patients with prior CMV disease elsewhere
- Usual presentation of lower extremity weakness and hyperactive reflexes; may also develop sensory level involvement
- MRI or contrast CT of the spinal cord will show enhancement; biopsy may be needed to confirm the diagnosis

CMV radiculomyelopathy

- Occurs in patients with advanced HIV disease and prior CMV elsewhere

- Characterized by progressive lower extremity weakness and decreased or absent reflexes on neurologic exam
- Diagnosis supported by nerve root thickening on MRI or contrast CT and nerve conduction studies consistent with radiculopathy
- CSF may show a polymorphonuclear pleocytosis, with negative bacterial gram stain and culture
- Flaccid paraplegia and urinary retention may eventually develop even with treatment

CMV mononeuritis multiplex
- Characterized by multifocal or asymmetric sensory and motor deficits in the major peripheral or cranial nerves
- Biopsy confirms the diagnosis

Treatment — CMV Neurologic Disease

- IV monotherapy with ganciclovir, foscarnet or cidofovir therapy for 3-6 weeks recommended
- Case reports suggest that dual therapy with foscarnet and ganciclovir associated with a better outcome but with increased toxicity
- Oral therapy with valganciclovir yet to be fully evaluated

CMV Pneumonia

- CMV frequently isolated in bronchial washings and pulmonary secretions
- Causes disease in HIV-infected patients less frequently than in organ transplant patients; however, evidence of invasive CMV lung disease found in 17% of AIDS patients in autopsy series
- Patients may have diffuse interstitial infiltrates on CXR, with arterial blood gas (ABGs) showing moderate to severe hypoxia and increased alveolar-arterial gradient

Diagnosis
- Based on histological changes of invasive CMV disease on biopsy in absence of other pathogens
- Often found associated with *Pneumocystis jiroveci* pneumonia (PCP), patients usually respond to treatment for PCP alone
- Treatment of CMV isolated in pulmonary specimens is not recommended in asymptomatic patients or when concomitant pathogens present
- Treatment should be reserved for highly suspicious cases and/or evidence of invasive CMV disease on biopsy specimens
- Addition of CMV specific intravenous immune globulin to standard antiviral therapy may improve outcomes in CMV pneumonia/pneumonitis

Adrenalitis

- A rare cause of illness of late-stage HIV infection
- CMV found in adrenal glands in up to 84% of AIDS patients in autopsy series
- Results in adrenal insufficiency with symptoms of weakness, wasting and even shock with hyperkalemia – may mimic sepsis
- Inflammation of the adrenals on imaging studies may be seen
- Fasting cortisol levels and ACTH stimulation test should be performed
- Responds to antiviral therapy in case reports

Table 1. Available Treatments for CMV Retinitis①.

	IV GANCICLOVIR (CYTOVENE®)	IV FOSCARNET SODIUM (FOSCAVIR®)	COMBINATION IV GANCICLOVIR AND IV FOSCARNET SODIUM
Median time to first retinitis progression, in days (by retinal photography where available)②	47-104	53-93	129
Dosing regimen	Standard Induction: 5 mg/kg q12h for 14-21 d Maintenance: 5 mg/kg qd High-dose/intensive for refractory disease Induction: 7.5 mg/kg q12h for 14-21d Maintenance: 10 mg/kg qd Note: dosage should be adjusted for creatinine clearance < 70 mL/min (see Table 2) Administration at a constant rate over 1 hour.	Induction: 90 mg/kg q12h for 14-21 d Maintenance: 90-120 mg/kg qd Note: dosage should be recalculated according to dose-reduction algorithm in package insert (see Tables 4 and 5) based on most current serum creatinine); 500-100 mL of 0.9% saline solution with each dose Administration rate should not exceed 60 mg/kg/dose/hour	Prior ganciclovir: Induction: foscarnet 90 mg/kg q12h and ganciclovir 5 mg/kg qd for 14-21 d Maintenance: foscarnet 90-120 mg/kg, ganciclovir 5 mg/kg qd Prior foscarnet sodium: Induction: ganciclovir 5 mg/kg q12h foscarnet 90-120 mg/kg qd for 14-21 d Maintenance: ganciclovir 5 mg/kg qd and foscarnet 90-120 mg/kg qd Reinduction: ganciclovir 5 mg/kg q12h and foscarnet 90 mg/kg q12h for 14-21 days Ganciclovir[0] should be administered at a constant rate over 1 hour. Foscarnet administration rate should not exceed 60mg/kg/dose/hour
Select adverse effects	Neutropenia; anemia; thrombocytopenia; catheter sepsis	Nephrotoxicity; electrolyte abnormalities; anemia; catheter sepsis; nausea/irritability;	Same as IV ganciclovir and IV foscarnet
Important drug interactions	↑ Neutropenia and anemia with zidovudine, cancer chemotherapy ↑ Didanosine levels	↑ Nephrotoxicity with other nephrotoxic drugs, e.g., amphotericin B, aminoglycosides, IV pentamidine	Same as IV ganciclovir and IV foscarnet
Adjunctive therapy	G-CSF/GM-CSF effective for neutropenia; epoetin alfa (Procrit®) for anemia	IV or oral hydration essential; potassium, calcium, magnesium supplements, antiemetics may be required	Same as IV ganciclovir and IV foscarnet
Advantages	Systemic therapy; anti-HSV activity	Systemic therapy; anti-HSV (acyclovir-resistant) activity; anti-HIV activity	Increased efficacy compared with either IV ganciclovir or IV foscarnet alone; improved response for relapsed disease
Disadvantages	Hematologic toxicity; requires at least daily infusions; indwelling catheter	Nephrotoxicity; requires at least daily infusions/indwelling catheter; supplemental hydration required; prolonged infusion time; requires infusion pump or controlled rate infusion device	Same as IV ganciclovir and IV foscarnet; prolonged daily infusion time and impact on quality of life
Monitoring requirements	Induction therapy: a) CBC with differential, platelet count weekly (twice weekly if baseline ANC < 1,000 cells/mm³ or platelet count < 50,000 cells/mm³; b) serum creatinine weekly Maintenance therapy: a) CBC with differential, platelet count weekly; b) serum creatinine every 2-4 weeks	Induction therapy: a) serum creatinine twice weekly; must be used to recalculate dosage if change in creatinine level occurs; b) serum Ca⁺⁺, albumin, Mg⁺⁺, phosphorous, and K⁺ twice weekly c) hemoglobin and hematocrit weekly Maintenance therapy: a) serum creatinine weekly; b) serum Ca⁺⁺, albumin, Mg⁺⁺, phosphorous, and K⁺ weekly; c) hemoglobin and hematocrit every 2-4 weeks	Same as both IV ganciclovir and IV foscarnet
Precautions and contraindications	ANC < 500 cells/mm³ Platelet count < 25,000 cells/mm³ Hgb < 8 g/dL	Concomitant use with other nephrotoxic drugs (e.g., amphotericin B, aminoglycosides, or IV pentamidine) or in patients with preexisting moderate to severe renal insufficiency (serum creatinine > 1.9 mg/dL) or creatinine clearance (< 50 mL/min)	Same as IV ganciclovir and IV foscarnet

① CMV indicates cytomegalovirus; IV, intravenous; ↑, increased; NSAID, nonsteroidal anti-inflammatory drugs; G-CSF, granulocyte colony-stimulating factor; GM-CSF, granulocyte-macrophage colony-stimulating factor; HSV, herpes simplex virus; HIV, human immunodeficiency virus; CBC, complete blood cell count; WBC, white blood cell count, and ANC, absolute neutrophil count.

② Times to progression of CMV retinitis are from the start of induction treatment for IV ganciclovir, IV foscarnet, combination IV ganciclovir and IV foscarnet, intraocular ganciclovir insert, and IV cidofovir, and from start of maintenance treatment for IV then oral ganciclovir.

③ Zidovudine dose should be reduced by 50% or withheld on the day of infusion only. Rifampin, ketoprofen, chlorpropamide, dapsone, methotrexate, trimethoprim-sulfamethoxazole, zalcitabine, and NSAID should be withheld on the day of dosing only.

④ Some experts recommend monitoring intraocular pressure and slitlamp examination prior to each IV cidofovir infusion.

Table 1 (continued)

IV THEN ORAL GANCICLOVIR (CYTOVENE®)	INTRAOCULAR GANCICLOVIR IMPLANT (VITRASERT®)	IV CIDOFOVIR (VISTIDE®)	PO VALGANCICLOVIR (VALCYTE®)
29-53	216-226	64-120	Unknown
Induction: same as IV ganciclovir Maintenance: 3000-6000 mg/d in 3 divided doses with food Note: dose reduction recommended for creatinine clearance < 70 mL/min (see Table 3)	Surgical: Intraocular implantation via pars plana of ganciclovir (4.5 mg) implant releasing 1 µg/h (duration: 6-8 mo; then replacement required every 5-8 mo) Concomitant system anti-CMV therapy recommended; oral ganciclovir maintenance dosing of 4500 mg/d in 3 divided doses	Induction: 5 mg/kg every week for 2 weeks Maintenance: 5 mg/kg every 2 weeks (Note: dose reduction to 3 mg/kg for ↑ serum creatinine by [0.3-0.4 mg/dL] above baseline [see below]; all doses given with probenecid and IV fluid) Note: The following are essential to minimize renal toxicity: Hydration with NS 1 L over 1-2 hours immediately prior to initiation of infusion and probenecid 2g po 3 hours prior to initiation of infusion. Post-infusion: NS 1L over 1 to 3 hours (as tolerated) and probenecid 1g po 2 and 8 hours after completion of cidofovir administration.	Induction: 900 mg po bid with food x 21 days Maintenance: 900 mg po qd with food Dosage reductions necessary for patients with renal dysfunction (See Table 6)
Neutropenia; diarrhea/nausea	Surgical complications: transient blurred vision; infection; hemorrhage	Nephrotoxicity; neutropenia; probenecid adverse effects (rash, fever, nausea, fatigue); uveitis; alopecia; hypotonia	Same as IV ganciclovir
Same as IV ganciclovir		↑ Nephrotoxicity with other nephrotoxic drugs, e.g., amphotericin B, aminoglycosides, IV pentamidine, NSAID Probenecid: ↑ Level of most proximal tubular-excreted drugs③	Interactions similar to IV ganciclovir: ↑ ddl Auc by approximately 70% when co-administered.
Same as IV ganciclovir	Systemic anti-CMV therapy recommended (oral ganciclovir, 4500 mg/d)	Probenecid and IV hydration essential; antiemetic, antihistamine, acetaminophen premedication commonly used for probenecid toxicity	Same as IV ganciclovir
Systemic therapy; oral administration; less catheter/sepsis complications	Longest time to retinitis progression in treated eye; no IV dosing or catheter required	Systemic therapy; no indwelling catheter required; infrequent dosing	Improved bioavailability over oral ganciclovir, avoids IV therapy
Faster time to retinitis progression; high pill count; poor oral bioavailability (6%); rarely used due to availability of valganciclovir	↑ Fellow eye and extraocular disease; requires surgery; postintraocular surgical complications	Requires probenecid and IV hydration; probenecid toxicity; nephrotoxicity (may be prolonged)	Hematologic toxicity
Induction therapy: IV ganciclovir Maintenance therapy: oral ganciclovir a) CBC with differential, platelet count every 2 weeks; b) serum creatinine every 2-4 weeks	No specific laboratory monitoring required for implant; if oral ganciclovir therapy is added, follow monitoring guidelines as outlined	Within 48 h prior to each induction and maintenance dose a) serum creatinine quantitative proteinuria; b) WBC with differential cell count; monitor intraocular pressure and slitlamp examination at least monthly④	Same as IV ganciclovir
Use with caution in patients with immediately sight-threatening (zone 1) retinitis	External ocular or nasolacrimal infection; patients with ↑ risk of postoperative intraocular infection	Same as IV foscarnet except parameters are baseline serum creatinine level > (> 1.5 mg/dL) or creatinine clearance (< 55 mL/min), or 2+ proteinuria (after IV fluid) Discontinue therapy for 3+ proteinuria, if serum creatinine level increases by (0.5 mg/dL) above baseline, or if intraocular pressure decreases by 50% of baseline value	ANC < 500 cells/mm³ Platelet count < 25,000 cells/mm³ Hgb < 8 g/dL

Adapted from Table 2 in Whitley, RJ, et al. Guidelines for the Treatment of Cytomegalovirus Disease in Patients with AIDS in the Era of Potent Antiretroviral Therapy. *Archives of Internal Medicine*. May 11 1998; 158:962–963.

Table 2. Dosing Adjustment of IV Ganciclovir (Cytovene®)*

Creatinine Clearance (mL/min)	Cytovene®--IV Induction Dose (mg/kg)	Dosing Interval (hours)	Cytovene®-IV Maintenance Dose (mg/kg)	DosingInterval (hours)
≥70	5	12	5	24
50-69	2.5	12	2.5	24
25-49	2.5	24	1.25	24
10-24	1.25	24	0.625	24
<10	1.25	3x/wk (tiw) following hemodialysis	0.625	3x/wk (tiw) following hemodialysis

*Package insert accessed 11/15/05: http://www.rocheusa.com/products/cytovene/pi.pdf

Table 3. Dosing Adjustment for Ganciclovir (Cytovene®) Oral*

Creatinine Clearance mL/min	Cytovene® Capsule Dosages
≥70	1000 mg tid or 500 mg q3h, 6x/day
50-69	1500 mg qd or 500 mg tid
25-49	1000 mg qd or 500 mg bid
10-24	500 mg qd
<10	500 mg 3x/wk (tiw) following hemodialysis

*Package insert accessed 11/15/05: http://www.rocheusa.com/products/cytovene/pi.pdf

Table 4. Foscarnet (Foscavir®) Renal Dosing Guide – Induction*

	CMV: Equivalent to	
CrCl (mL/min/kg)	180 mg/kg/day total (60 mg/kg Q8h)	(90 mg/kg Q12h)
> 1.4	60 Q8h	90 Q12h
>1.0–1.4	45 Q8h	70 Q12h
>0.8–1.0	**50 Q12h**	50 Q12h
>0.6–0.8	**40 Q12h**	**80 Q24h**
>0.5–0.6	60 Q24h	**60 Q24h**
≥0.4–0.5	50 Q24h	**50 Q24h**
<0.4	Not Recommended	Not Recommended

*Package insert accessed 11/15/05: http://www.astrazeneca-us.com/cgibin/azpi.asp?product=Foscavir

Table 5. Foscarnet (Foscavir®) Renal Dosing Guide – Maintenance*

	CMV: Equivalent to	
CrCl (mL/min/kg)	90 mg/kg/day (once daily)	120 mg/kg/day (once daily)
>1.4	90 Q24h	120 Q24h
>1.0-1.4	70 Q24h	90 Q24h
>0.8-1.0	50 Q24h	65 Q24h
>0.6-0.8	**80 Q48h**	**105Q48h**
>0.5-0.6	**60 Q48h**	**80 Q48h**
≥0.4-0.5	**50 Q48h**	**65 Q48h**
<0.4	Not Recommended	Not Recommended

*Package insert accessed 11/15/05: http://www.astrazeneca-us.com/cgibin/azpi.asp?product=Foscavir

Table 6. Valganciclovir (Valcyte®) Renal Dosage Adjustments*

CrCL (mL/min)	Induction Dose	Maintenance Dose
≥ 60	900 mg bid	900 mg qd
40-59	450 mg bid	450 mg qd
25-39	450 mg qd	450 mg q48h
10-24	450 mg q48h	450 mg twice weekly
≤ 10	Cannot use valganciclovir; use renal dose-adjusted IV ganciclovir	

*Package insert accessed 2/27/06: http://www.rocheusa.com/products/valcyte/pi.pdf

References

1. Cinque P, Scarpellini P, et al. Diagnosis of central nervous system complications in HIV-infected patients: cerebrospinal fluid analysis by the polymerase chain reaction. *AIDS* 1997; 11:1—17.

2. Daniel M, et al. Oral ganciclovir for patients with cytomegalovirus retinitis treated with a ganciclovir implant. *NEJM* 1999; 340:1063–1070.

3. Guidelines for the treatment of cytomegalovirus diseases in patients with AIDS in the era of potent antiretroviral therapy. *Arch Intern Med* 1998; 158:957–969.

4. Jacobson M. Cytomegalovirus disease. In: *AIDS Therapy* Dolin R, Masur H, Saag M, Eds. New York, NY: Churchill Livingstone; 1999;456–471.

5. Jacobson MA. Treatment of cytomegalovirus retinitis in patients with the acquired immunodeficiency syndrome. *NEJM* 1997; 337(2):105–114.

6. Musch D, Martin D, et al. Treatment of cytomegalovirus retinitis with a sustained release ganciclovir implant. *NEJM* 1997; 337:83–90.

7. Muhlhofer A, Jung C, Gross M. Successful treatment with ganciclovir of an HIV patent with adrenal insufficiency. *Eur J Med Res* 1997; 2(11) 469–472.

8. Aries SP, Schaaf B. (2005) HIV and pulmonary diseases. In: C. Hoffmann, BS Kamps (eds.). *HIV Medicine 2005*. Paris: Flying Publisher.

19

Fungal Infections

Jose N. Moreno, MD
Professor of Medicine
Division of Clinical Immunology and Infectious Diseases
Department of Medicine
University of Miami School of Medicine

Introduction

- Fungal infections are one of the major complications of HIV infection and may be the first HIV-related opportunistic infection to occur.
- The most common fungal infections that affect patients with HIV are candidiasis, cryptococcosis, aspergillosis, and the endemic mycoses including histoplasmosis in the Midwest, coccidiomycosis in the Southwest, and penicilliosis in South East Asia

Candida

Epidemiology

- Candida infection in AIDS is almost exclusively mucosal
- Candida virulence seems to be site specific
- Systemic invasion is a rare and late event
- Pre-HAART era:
  - 50–70% of HIV-infected patients developed mucosal candidiasis
  - 33% had recurrent disease
  - 20–40% developed esophageal disease (advanced AIDS with CD4+ counts < 50 cells/mm^3)
- Since the advent of HAART the incidence of new candida infections has decreased 60–80%
- 30–40% of HIV infected women will develop vulvovaginal candidiasis which can be severe and persistent.
- *C. albicans* causes 100% of initial episodes of mucosal candidiasis

- When recurrent disease occurs:
  - 50% will be the same candida strain
  - 50% will be a new strain
- *Candida glabrata*, *Candida parapsilosis*: cause infection in patients with advanced disease and prior exposure to antifungal agents (especially azoles)
- *Candida dubliniensis* has been implicated in patients with HIV infection and is more likely to acquire resistance to the azoles (particularly fluconazole)

Clinical features

- Oral candidiasis (thrush) types:
  - **Pseudomembranous candidiasis**:
    - White exudative plaques, cottage-cheese-like on the palate, tonsils or buccal mucosa; can be scraped with a tongue depressor with bleeding
  - **Erythematous candidiasis**:
    - Flat, red, atrophic plaques on the mucosal surface
  - **Hypertrophic candidiasis**:
    - Non-scrapeable, raised plaques similar to hairy leukoplakia that involves the lower surface of the tongue and palate or buccal mucosa
- Angular cheilitis:
  - Fissured, crusted lesions which may ulcerate at the corner of the mouth causing pain, burning or difficulty opening the mouth
  - Scraping of the lesions and examination with KOH wet mount gram stain will show characteristic budding yeast
- Vulvovaginal candidiasis
  - Manifested as:
    - Vaginal itching
    - Burning
    - Vaginal discharge
  - Vaginal exam shows cottage cheese-like material
NOTE: See Chapter 40, "Management of HIV/AIDS in Women," for clinical features and treatment of vulvovaginal candidiasis.
- Esophageal candidiasis
  - Manifested as:
    - Dysphagia
    - Odynophagia
  - Endoscopy reveals pseudomembranes, erosions, and/or ulcers of the esophagus
  - Combination of oral candidiasis and esophageal symptoms both sensitive and specific for predicting esophageal involvement
  - Patients with a presumptive diagnosis of esophageal candidiasis
    - Treat empirically with antifungal therapy for 7 days
    - If no response, perform endoscopy to rule out other conditions such as herpes esophagitis, cytomegalovirus esophagitis, idiopathic ulcers, or resistant candidiasis

Treatment

- Local versus systemic treatment
  - Both are usually effective (see Table 1)

- Symptoms tend to respond more rapidly to systemic agents
- Topical agents are less likely to have mycological clearance at the end of treatment
- Nystatin seems to be less effective than other topical agents
- Systemic agents
  - Similar effectiveness: 75–100% response rates
  - Equivalent relapse rates
  - Fluconazole and itraconazole preferred over ketoconazole in advanced disease
    - Ketoconazole needs acid pH to be absorbed
    - Achlorhydria may be a problem in patients with advanced disease
  - Fluconazole and itraconazole have equivalent activity for esophagitis due to *C. albicans*
  - Azole treatment may be ineffective in advanced disease
    - Intravenous amphotericin B 0.3–0.5 mg/kg/day x 7 to 14 day or liposomal amphotericin B preparations 3–5 mg/kg/d IV for patients not responding to azole treatment
    - <u>Azole antifungals</u> **contraindicated** in pregnant women, (craniofacial and skeletal malformations)

Table 1. Treatment Options for Oral or Esophageal Candidiasis

AGENT	FORMULATION	DOSAGE
Amphotericin	IV infusion oral suspension	0.3–0.5 mg/kg per day 100 mg/mL 1–5mL qid (1mL) (No longer commercially available in US; needs to be compounded by a pharmacy)
Clotrimazole	Troche	10 mg (1 troche) 5 times daily
Fluconazole	tablet, oral suspension	50–100 mg qd 200–400 mg qd①
Itraconazole	oral solution	200 mg (20 mL) po qd or 100 mg (10mL) bid
Ketoconazole	tablet or 2% cream	200 mg qd 400–600 mg qd① Apply cream to corners of mouth qid
Nystatin	oral suspension of pastille or Ointment	400–600,000 units (4–6 mL) qid 1–2 pastilles qid Apply ointment to commissures of mouth after meals

① Esophageal disease

Recurrent mucosal candidiasis

- Treat each episode as it occurs
- May use suppressive therapy, fluconazole, 100–200 mg/d in patients with recurrent symptomatic disease
- Risk of developing azole resistant disease with the use of suppressive therapy

Vulvovaginal candidiasis

- Treatment with topical preparations preferred (See Chapter 40, "Management of HIV/AIDS in Women")
- Single dose fluconazole (150 mg) also effective

Resistant candidiasis

- 5–7% of patients with advanced disease developed fluconazole resistance prior to HAART
- Prevalence is less common since introduction of HAART
- Risk factors for development of resistant candidiasis:

- Advanced disease (CD4+ count < 50 cells/mm^3)
- Extensive prior use of fluconazole
- Isolates more likely to be species other than *C. albicans*
- Disease tends to be more progressive and symptomatic
- Treatment
  - Therapy is unsatisfactory
  - Improve immune function with potent antiretroviral therapy
  - Higher dose fluconazole (800 mg/d) in patients with intermediate susceptibility
  - Itraconazole cyclodextrin oral formulation (solution), 100 mg/ 10mL po bid on an empty stomach (60% success). This treatment is short lived, however, if maintenance not given (oral solution preferred over capsules due to bioavailability).
  - Amphotericin B – oral suspension (40% success) — not generally available in US (needs to be compounded by a pharmacy).
  - Amphotericin B – parenteral administration
  - If amphotericin B fails, consider caspofungin (Cancidas®) 70 mg IV x 1, then 50 mg IV qd (new echinocandin antifungal)
  - Caspofungin is at least as effective as amphotericin B for the treatment of invasive candidiasis, and less toxic.
  - Voriconazole is as effective as fluconazole and can reduce the risk of candida esophagitis and cryptococcosis.
    - **CAUTION** regarding drug interactions with voriconazole and ARVs (due to significant ↓ in voriconazole levels, **it is contraindicated with ritonavir and efavirenz**
  - Consider other investigational agents

Table 2. Treatment Options for Resistant Oral or Esophageal Candidiasis

AGENT	FORMULATION	DOSAGE
Caspofungin	IV infusion	70 mg on day one followed by 50 mg a day (reduced to 35mg a day with moderate hepatitic insufficiency)
Voriconazole	IV infusion	Loading dose 6mg/kg Q 12 hours x 1 d. Maintenance 3 mg kg Q 12 hours
	Oral	≥ 40 kg: 200 mg po q12h <40 kg: 100mg po q12h

Cryptococcus

Epidemiology

- Pre–HAART
  - 4–8% of patients developed cryptococcal meningitis
  - Approximately 5% patients in the Western world developed disseminated cryptococcosis
  - 10–20% mortality
- 2 varieties exist:
  - *C. neoformans*, variety neoformans A&D

- *C. neoformans* variety B&C (gatti)
- Most of the infections in HIV-infected patients is caused by *C. neoformans*, variety neoformans
- Disease more prevalent in Sub-Saharan Africa
- Usually occurs when CD4+ count < 100 cells/mm^3
- Unclear if cryptococcal infection in AIDS patients represents acute primary infection or reactivation

Clinical manifestations

- Most common presentations are sub-acute meningitis or meningo-encephalitis
- Patient may have symptoms for days or even weeks prior to presentation
  - Fever (85%)
  - Headache (77%)
  - Sweats (40%)
  - Visual changes (20%)
  - Mental status changes (10%)
  - Dyspnea (10%)
- Classic symptoms for meningitis such as stiff neck and photophobia occur in 25%–33% (the majority of patients do not present with nuchal rigidity).

Diagnosis

- CSF: cerebrospinal fluid analysis may show:
  - Positive India ink (80%)
  - High opening pressure (> 20 cm H$_2$0 in 70%)
  - Decreased glucose (50%)
  - Elevated 40–400 cells/mm^3 leukocytes (21%)
  - High protein (55%)
  - Eosinophilic pleocytosis (rarely)
  - Positive cryptococcal antigen (> 95% both in CSF and in serum)
  - Positive culture
  - CSF abnormalities are frequently minimal or absent in AIDS patients
  - 20% of patients: no clear abnormality in CSF profile
  - Cryptococcal antigen in the CSF (+) in > 90% of patients
  - Normal CSF *does not* exclude the possibility if (+) CSF cryptococcal antigen
- Blood
  - Serum cryptococcal antigen (+) in 95–99% of cases
  - Positive blood culture

Factors associated with a poor prognosis

- Altered mental status
- Increased opening pressure in the CSF
- < 20 WBC in CSF
- Low glucose
- Positive India ink
- Positive blood culture
- High cryptococcal antigen titer
- Hyponatremia

Complications

- 40% have significant residual neurologic sequelae including

- Visual loss
- Cranial nerves palsies
- Significant motor impairment
- Personality changes
- Decreased mental function (chronic brain syndrome)
- Hydrocephalus can cause late complications or death even when infection is cured

CAUTION: With HAART symptoms of acute meningitis may return (immune reconstitution).

Treatment

Acute infection: amphotericin B, 0.7 mg/kg/day IV + flucytosine (5-FC) 25 mg/kg po q6h x 2 weeks

Follow with: fluconazole 400 mg po qd x 8 weeks and then switch to maintenance/suppressive therapy of fluconazole 200 mg pd qd.

- Lipid amphotericin B formulations: alternative in patients intolerant to regular amphotericin B
  - Liposomal amphotericin B (Ambisome®) 4mg/kg IV or amphotericin B lipid complex (Abelcet®) 5 mg/kg IV daily for 14 days.
- Addition of flucytosine
  - Decreases risk of relapse
  - Does not reduce mortality
  - Does not speed recovery
- With treatment mycologic response is 70% and mortality rate is <10%
  - Initial therapy with fluconazole or itraconazole: only a 50% response rate
- Maintenance/suppressive therapy may be discontinued in patients with a sustained increase in CD4+ counts (e.g. > 6 months) to > 100-200 cells/mm3, in response to HAART if they have completed their initial therapy and have no symptoms or signs attributable to these pathogens (CIII).
- Maintenance therapy should be reinitiated if the CD4+ T-lymphocyte count decreases to < 100-200 cells/µL (AIII)

Mild cases (Cryptococcal antigen < 1:1024 and WBCs in the CSF > 20 cells/mm^3): fluconazole 400-800 mg + flucytosine as initial combination may be an alternative in some patients

Considerations

- If opening pressure normal (<200 mm H_2O) repeating lumbar puncture after two weeks of therapy is recommended to exclude elevated pressure and evaluate culture status
- Patients with CSF opening pressure > 25 cm of H_2O need repeat lumbar punctures to reduce pressure
- Patients with elevated baseline opening pressures should have daily lumbar punctures removing approximately 30 mL of CSF until the pressure has decreased by 50%
- Daily lumbar puncture can be discontinued once the opening pressure has been normal for several days
- No data to support treatment with acetazolamide
- Clinical utility of mannitol (1.5–2 g/kg) for increased ICP is unknown
- The role of corticosteroid use is unknown and remains controversial. In MSG/ACTG trial, corticosteroids were associated with mycological and clinical failure as well as early death but the patients receiving same treatment had the most severe disease.

Endemic Mycoses

HISTOPLASMOSIS

Epidemiology

- *Histoplasma capsulatum*: dimorphic fungus endemic in:
  - Mississippi and Ohio River Valley in North America
  - Certain areas of Central and South America
  - Caribbean
- Occurs sporadically in persons with history of travel to endemic areas
- Frequently seen in Miami-Dade area of Florida due to high number of immigrants from endemic areas
- Occurs in patients with low CD4+ cell counts (< 100 cells/mm^3)

Clinical manifestations

- <u>Normal host</u>: usually asymptomatic or self limited disease presenting as mild respiratory illness; some patients may develop disease that mimics tuberculosis
- In <u>HIV/AIDS</u>: severe disseminated disease
- <u>Clinical Features</u>:
  - Fever (95%)
  - Weight loss (90%)
  - Anemia (70%)
  - Pulmonary disease (50%)
  - Lymphadenopathy (50%)
  - Skin lesions (5–10%)
  - Acute septic shock-like syndrome (5–10%)
  - Meningitis (1%)
  - Oral ulcers (1%)
  - GI ulcer (uncommon)

Diagnosis

- Peripheral blood smear may show intracellular organism (40%)
- Blood culture by lysis centrifugation > 90% positive
- Anti-*H.capsulatum* antibodies (by immunodiffusion and complement fixation) 70–80% positivity
- Positive histoplasma antigen in serum or urine > 95% (extremely sensitive and specific)
  - Test for antigen may be falsely negative in patients with mild clinical manifestations or with localized sites of dissemination (GI or skin)
  - False positive in patients with other mycosis *(blastomyces dermatitidis, Penicillium mameffel, and paraccoidial braziliensis)*
- Skin biopsy
- Bone marrow aspirate and biopsy
- Skin test for histoplasma **not** useful as diagnostic test
- Some patients may present with bilateral interstitial infiltrates on chest x-ray and high LDH mimicking PCP

Differential diagnosis

- Tuberculosis
- Pneumocystis carinii
- Visceral Leishmaniasis (fever, hepato-splenomegaly, pancytopenia)
- Lymphoma
- Fungal infections (paracoccidiomycosis, blastomycosis, cryptococcosis)

Treatment

Induction

- For moderate to severe disease, lipid base amphotericin: Liposomal amphotericin B 3 mg/kg/IV x 14 days. Then suppressive therapy with itraconazole 200mg a day or amphotericin B 0.5–1 mg/kg/day for 1 to 2 weeks until there is clinical resolution (defervescence and improvement in skin lesions).
- For less severe disease itraconazole 300 mg bid x 3d then 200 mg bid x 12 weeks or 400 mg a day x 12 weeks (85% to 90% response) then 200 mg a day. Not recommended for meningitis. Can be given IV if patient unable to take po.

Maintenance: Indefinite treatment with itraconazole 200 mg po bid

Prophylaxis: Primary prophylaxis with itraconazole 200 mg po bid may be considered for patients with CD4+ counts < 100 cells/mm^3 who are living in hyperendemic areas (≥ 10 cases per 100 patient-years)..

- Controversial; clinical trials indicate itraconazole can reduce the frequency of histoplasmosis among patients with advanced HIV living in endemic areas, but no survival benefit was observed. (DHHS Guidelines)
- Concern of possibility of developing azole resistance, drug-drug interactions, and drug-related adverse events.
- Incidence of histoplasmosis is decreasing in the face of adequate antiretroviral therapy.

Secondary Prophylaxis: Although patients on HAART with systemic mycosis whose CD4+ lymphocytes count increases to > 100 cells/ml might be at low risk for recurrence of systemic mycosis, the number of patients who have been evaluated are insufficient to warrant a recommendation to discontinue prophylaxis. Itraconazole 200 mg bid should be continued.

COCCIDIOIDOMYCOSIS

Epidemiology

- Endemic in Southwestern USA (California, New Mexico, Western Texas), Central and South America
- Infections in humans arise from inhalation of windborne arthrospores

Clinical manifestations

- Non-immunosuppressed host:
  - Primary infection is symptomatic in 40% (mild influenza-like illness to severe pneumonia)
  - Mild self-limited infection may come to medical attention because of clusters of hypersensitivity reactions
    - Erythema nodosum
    - Erythema multiforme
    - Toxic erythema
    - Arthralgia
    - Conjunctivitis
    - Episcleritis

- In patients with HIV/AIDS:
  - Fever (95%)
  - Pulmonary disease (90%)
  - Weight loss (60%)
  - Anemia (50%)
  - Hepatosplenomegaly (10–20%)
  - Lymphadenopathy (10%)
  - Meningitis (10%)
  - Acute septic shock like syndrome (5–10%)
  - Skin lesions (5%)
  - Most common in patients with CD4<50/mm^3
  - Usual presentation is disseminated disease or meningitis

Diagnosis

- Culture of tissue specimen or biopsy with histopathological examination
  - Bone marrow aspirate/biopsy
  - Biopsy material from lungs, skin lesions
- Serology
  - Coccidioidal serology: positive in 75% of patients
  - Disseminated infection: may have negative serology in 25% of cases
- Chest X-ray may show
  - Infiltrate
  - Hilar lymphadenopathy
  - Pleural effusion
  - Thin wall cavity
  - Coccidioma
- CBC may show mild eosinophilia
- Positive complement fixation in the unconcentrated CSF: diagnostic of meningitis
- Skin test as diagnostic tool **not** useful

Treatment

Table 3. Treatment for Coccidiomycosis*

	PRIMARY	SECONDARY
Uncomplicated Pulmonary Disease	fluconazole 400–800 mg/d or itraconazole 200-400 mg/d for 3-6 mos *amphotericin B is treatment of choice during pregnancy 2° teratogenic effects of azoles	fluconazole 400 mg/d or itraconazole 200 mg/d
Diffuse Pneumonia	IV amphotericin B, 0.5-1 mg/kg/d until clinical improvement is noted (usually 500-1,000 mg total dose)	fluconazole 400 mg po/d or itraconazole 200 mg bid po/d
Meningitis	fluconazole 800-1000 mg po/d (preferred) or itraconazole 400–600 mg po bid until clinical improvement is noted	fluconazole 400 mg po/d or itraconazole 200 mg po/d

*Adapted from *Clinical Infectious Diseases*, 2000; 30:658-661©2000 ISDA

- Intrathecal amphotericin B should be added for coccidioidomycosis meningitis that fails to respond to fluconazole
- Focal lesions often require debridement or drainage.
- Extrapulmonary: Treat ≥ year and 2 to 6 months post clinical improvement.
- Cure rate to amphotericin B 50–70%
- Response to azoles is similar.
- Relapse rate 40%.
- Relapse rate are increased if CF titer is > 1:256 or if negative coccidioidin skin test.
- Follow CF titer after treatment, rising titer warrant 1 re-treatment.
- Lifelong suppressive therapy is recommended using either fluconazole 400 mg daily or itraconazole 200 mg twice daily.
- The number of patients who have been evaluated are insufficient to warrant a recommendation to discontinue prophylaxis when CD4+ increases to > 100 cells/mm^3 in response to HAART
- Primary prophylaxis is not recommended

ASPERGILLOSIS

Epidemiology

- Ubiquitous in the environment, growing on dead leaves, stored grain, compost piles and other decaying vegetation
- *Aspergillus fumigatus* is the most common pathogen
- Infection with *Aspergillus* species is increasingly reported with advanced HIV disease
- Factors associated with increased risk for invasive aspergillosis
  - Neutropenia
  - Use of corticosteroids
  - Broad spectrum antibiotics
  - Prior pneumonia (especially PCP)
  - Low CD4+ cell count
  - Other AIDS-defining opportunistic infection(s)

Clinical manifestations

- Two major syndromes predominate:
  - Respiratory Tract Disease
    - Clinical Presentation
      - Cough
      - Shortness of breath
      - Fever
      - Chest pain
      - Hemoptysis
    - Chest radiography or CT scanning demonstrates
      - Nodular infiltrate
      - Localized or diffuse
      - Commonly cavitates (which gives characteristic air crescent appearance)
      - Small pleural based lesions with straight edge and surrounding attenuation "halo sign" (short lives less than 5 days).
    - Diagnosis
      - *Definitive* diagnosis requires biopsy demonstrating fungal invasion

- *Presumptive* diagnosis
  - Pulmonary symptoms
  - Chest x-ray abnormalities
  - (+) aspergillus in smear or culture of sputum or bronchial secretion

Classification to diagnose Aspergillosis

Definite = positive histology + positive culture or positive culture from a normally sterile site. Probable = two positive cultures of sputum or one positive bronchoscopy + appropriate host (AIDS, prednisone, ANC < 500)
Halo sign on CT scan is highly suggestive.

- CNS Disease
  - Clinical features
    - Symptoms and signs of a mass lesion
    - Features of stroke (due to invasion of blood vessels)
    - Seizures
    - Hemiparesis
  - Diagnosis
    - CT or MRI of the head
      - Single or multiple lesions usually non-enhancing with surrounding edema
      - Bony invasion common: disease may have spread from adjacent sinuses

Treatment
- Preferred: (invasive disease) Voriconazole, 6 mg/kg IV q 12h x 2, then 4 mg/kg IV q 12 h >1 week, then 200 mg bid. Treatment should continue for life or until immune reconstitution is evidenced.
- Alternative: Amphotericin B 1.0 mg/kg/day or lipid formulation dosed at 5.0 mg/kg or Voriconazole above dose + caspofungin 70 mg IV day 1, thcn 50 mg IV qd
  NOTE: voriconazole AUC ↓ 80% by EFV or RTV (400 mg bid); monitor closely or consider higher voriconazole dose, or add AmBisome or caspofungin
- Promising investigational azoles include posaconazole and ravuconazole

FUNGAL RHINOSINUSITIS
- Five basic diagnostic categories of fungal rhinosinusitis disorder are currently recognized. They can be differentiated from each other by histopathologic findings
  - Three types of fungal rhinosinusitis are true tissue invasive infectious diseases:
    - Acute necrotizing fungal rhinosinusitis
    - Chronic invasive fungal rhinosinusitis
    - Granulomatous (indolent) fungal rhinosinusitis
  - Two are non tissue invasive
    - Sinus mycetoma
    - Allergic fungal sinusitis
- Acute necrotizing fungal rhinosinusitis
  - Usually occurs in immunocompromised patients

- Immunodeficiency disorder
- Diabetes mellitus
- Cancer
- Cytotoxic chemotherapy
- Prolonged stays in intensive care unit.
- Bone marrow transplant.

- Infection may initially present with:
    - Paranasal anesthesia
    - Fever, facial pain, swelling; headaches
    - Nasal eschar spreading through the mucosa into juxtaposed soft tissue and bone
    - Histopathology showed widespread necrosis of all involved structures and inflammatory infiltrate consisting of variable numbers of giant cells, lymphocytes, and neutrophils.
    - Special stains (Gomori or periodic acid schiff).
    - Shows fungal hyphae invading mucosa blood vessel and bone.
    - Aspergillus, mucor, and rhizopus are common offending organism but any fungus can
    - cause it.
- Treatment is urgent
    - Involves urgent wide surgical debridement.
    - Intravenous antifungal drugs (such as Amphotericin B or Voriconazole).
    - Referral to Infectious Disease for dosing and monitoring
    - Correction of underlying predisposing immune compromise.

Chronic Invasive Fungal Sinusitis

- Presents as less fulminating and less necrotizing than acute necrotizing fungal sinusitis
- May occur in immunocompromised patients and diabetes mellitus
- Histopathology shows fungal invasion into the mucosa and chronic inflammatory infiltrates of lymphocytes; giant cells and necrotizing granulomas
- Treatment involves surgical debridement and systemic antifungal drugs
- Referral to Infection Disease is necessary as the infection is difficult to treat and carries a poor prognosis

Chronic Granulomatous Fungal Sinusitis

- Is usually found in immunocompetent patients presenting with hypertrophic sinusitis
- Mucosal invasive fungi are usually encapsulated with surrounding granulomas
- Widespread tissues necrosis; angio invasion or polymorphonuclear infiltrates are not seen
- Two forms occur:
    - A more chronic and recurrent type occurs in Sudan usually due to aspergillus fumigatus and requires surgical debridement and antifungal drugs
    - The other form is usually found incidentally on surgical histopathology from unremarkable hypertrophic sinus disease surgery. It is characterized as a more limited microinvasion of the superficial mucosa and has been suggested to be the sinus equivalent of bronchocentric granulomatosis as usually seen with allergic fungal sinusitis
- Treatment with proper surgical mucosal resection seems to be adequate, although oral antifungal drugs have often been given post-operatively to eliminate potential residual infection
- Prognosis is good

Fungal Ball (Sinus mycetoma)

- An extramucosal accumulation of many degenerating hyphae pressed into a mass or ball within the sinus cavity
- Usually one sinus is involved
- Previous sinus fungal infection, oral sinus fistula or previous cancer therapy may be risk factors for the disease
- It has been reported in 3.7% of all chronic inflammatory sinusitis cases going to surgery
- Surgical removal of the fungal ball along with adequate resection of any associated obstruction or significantly diseased sino-nasal mucosa seems to be curative
- Antifungal drugs are usually not indicated unless a tissue invasive form of fungi, rhinosinusitis is also positive

Allergic Fungal Sinusitis (AFS)

- Is a non-tissue invasive fungal process.
- Represents an allergic/hypersensitivity response to the presence of extramucosal fungi within the sinus cavity
- Overall 5 to 10% incidence of all cases of hypertrophic sinusitis going to surgery
- Patients tend to be young, atopic and immunocompetent
- Presents clinically with hypertrophic sinusitis
- Nasal polyps are reported in most cases (usually unilateral but may be bilateral)
- A prior history of sinus surgery is usual. (AFS is highly recurrent and might not have been previously recognized)
- Headache, paranasal fullness, or purulent discharge occurs frequently
- Increase of inhalant atopy (77 to 100%)
- Fungal specific IgE as detected by skin test or RAST is present in all patients
- Total serum IgE is usually elevated range 5,000 IU or more (mean 600 IU but AFS can be seen with a normal total serum IgE)
- Peripheral eosinophilia or high sedimentation rate is usually not seen
- Sinus CT always shows evidence of chronic sinusitis sometimes unilateral but usually with multiple sinus involvement
- Hyperattenuated signal on CT can be caused by inspissated allergic mucin or fungal hyphae
- Extra sinus extension of AFS is caused by bone resorption from the expanding allergic mucin mass and is not caused by invasion fungal sinus mucosa bone or other tissues
  - The risk of developing a true invasive fungal infection in the immunocompetent host is very small. In the immunocompromised host the most serious sequelae of allergic fungal sinusitis is brain invasion

Histopathology
- Nasal polyps.
- Characteristic inspissated peanut buttery tan to dark green mucin seen on surgery
- Hematoxylin and eosin stain shows hypertrophic sinus mucosa containing chronic inflammatory infiltrates of small lymphocytes, plasma cells, and eosinophils
- Epithelium is frequently desquamated and the basement membrane is thickened
- There should be no evidence of mucosal necrosis, granuloma, or giant cells

- Although earlier studies associated AFS with aspergillus fumigatus as the main etiologic agent, most cases are caused by one of the pigmented forms of dematiaceous fungi:
  - Bipolaris spicifera
  - Exserohilum rostratum
  - Curvularia lunata
  - Alternaria
- Bipolaris spicifera and Curvularia lunata are the most common AFS causing fungi reported overall
- Some patients may have allergic mucin which is negative for fungal hyphae
- Negative surgical sinus culture
- They have similar clinical findings to allergic fungal sinusitis
- They are non atopic and may have aspirin/NSAID hypersensitivity
- The name suggested for this condition has been "eosinophilic mucin rhinosinusitis"

Diagnosis

The diagnosis of allergic fungal sinusitis requires four diagnostic criteria

1. Surgically obtained characteristic inspissated allergic mucin (histologically or grossly at surgery)
2. Presence of fungal hyphae on allergic mucin or fungal staining or a properly obtained surgical sinus culture positive in an otherwise characteristic patient
3. There should be no histopathologic evidence of mucosal fungal invasion, mucosal necrosis, granulomas or giant cell formation
4. Other fungal rhinosinusitis disorders must be excluded

The following are clinical findings that are always present and support the diagnosis of AFS:

- An abnormal CT scan
- Fungal specific IgE
- Positive allergy skin test to fungal organisms
- Positive RAST
- IgG to the etiologic fungus
- Presence of atopy to common aero allergens
- Immunocompetence

If you obtain allergic mucosa with the presence of fungal hyphae without evidence of tissue invasion or other fungal rhinosinusitis, the diagnosis of AFS can still be made but only if the four diagnostic criteria are also met

Treatment

- Adequate sinus surgery
- Oral corticosteroid
- Removal of allergic mucosa
- Toxic systemic antifungal agents should be avoided
- Systemic antifungal therapy has not been shown to be significantly effective in primary treatment of either allergic fungal sinusitis or allergic bronchopulmonary aspergillosis
- Several recent controlled studies on allergic bronchopulmonary aspergillosis show oral itraconazole as having an additional benefit
- Long term itraconazole may be used after repeated surgical drainage to help prevent another recurrence

- Questionable results have been obtained in a few reported cases in which oral antifungal agents have been used in the treatment of allergic fungal sinusitis. More studies are required to determine whether such dual therapy is superior to corticosteroid alone.
  - There are no published studies using antifungal nasal spray or sinus lavage in allergic fungal sinusitis.
  - Two recent studies suggested clinical benefit of using amphotericin B sinonasal lavage in non-allergic fungal sinusitis patients with hypertrophic sinusitis, but treatment control was not used.
  - One study using saline control or tobramycin for hypertrophic sinusitis found the saline to be superior to tobramycin.

PENICILLIOSIS

Epidemiology

- *Penicillium marneffei* is a dimorphic fungi endemic in:
  - Southeast Asia
  - Thailand
  - Vietnam
  - Indonesia
  - Northern China

Clinical manifestations

- Fever (99%)
- Anemia (75%)
- Skin lesions (75%)
- Weight loss (75%)
- Fungemia (50%)
- Hepatosplenomegaly (50%)
- Lymphadenopathy (50%)
- Pulmonary disease (50%)
- Acute septic shock-like syndrome (5–10%)
- Meningitis very rare

Diagnosis

- Blood culture
- Skin biopsy

Treatment

- Amphotericin B with or without flucytosine (78 – 97 % success rate) Amphotericin B 0.6 – 1.0 mg/kg/day x 2 to 4 weeks, then itraconazole oral solution 200 mg po bid x 10 weeks.
  - Shortened hospital stay
  - More rapid clearance of fungemia than with itraconazole
- For mild to moderately severe: itraconazole 200 mg po bid.
- Itraconazole (75% effective)
- Fluconazole (37% effective)
- Lifelong prophylaxis with itraconazole 200 mg po qd

General Considerations in Using Amphotericin B Formulations

Formulations:

- Formulation with deoxycholate (Fungizone)

- In three lipid associated formulations
  - Only one liposomal formulation-liposomal amphotericin B (AmBisome®)
  - Two other preparations are aggregates of lipid rather than liposomal
    - Amphotericin B colloidal dispersion (Amphotec®; this product is rarely used due to higher rates of adverse effects
    - Amphotericin B lipid complex (Abelcet®)

- Tolerance to one product does not always translate to tolerance to another
- It is important that the physician use unambiguous names when prescribing these products
- The table and text below provide a summary of the most commonly used amphotericin B products.

Table 4: Summary of the Most Commonly Used Amphotericin B Products

PRODUCT	Conventional Amphotericin B (convAmB)	Amphotericin Lipid Complex (ABLC)	Liposomal Amphotericin B
BRAND NAME	Fungizone®	Abelcet®	Ambisome®
DOSE	0.5-1.5 mg/kg/day-depending on infection type	5 mg/kg/day	5 mg/kg/day
ADMINISTRATION	Mix with D5W ONLY to a maximum concentration of 0.1 mg/ml; Infuse over 4-6 hours (if tolerated, can decrease infusion time to 1-2 hours); shake bag every 2 hours during infusion; no need to protect from light during infusion; in-line filter not recommended.	Mix with D5W ONLY to a maximum concentration of 1 mg/ml; infuse at a maximum rate of 2.5 mg/kg/hour; shake bag every 2 hours during infusion (can decrease infusion time to 1 hour if tolerated); no need to protect from light; in-line filter not recommended.	Mix with D5W ONLY to a maximum concentration of 1-2 mg/ml; infuse over 2 hours (can decrease infusion time to 1 hour if tolerated); no need to protect from light during infusion; in-line filter generally not recommended but can be considered if mean pore size is ≥ 1 μm
SIDE EFFECTS	See text below		
MONITORING	CBC, serum creatinine electrolytes (frequency determined on case by case basis)		
MANAGEMENT/PREVENTION OF SIDE EFFECTS	Sodium loading with 1l of normal saline prior to infusion may decrease nephrotoxicity (most important for convAmB); acetaminophen with diphenhydramine, ibuprofen or other non-steroidal as pre-medications or hydrocortisone in infusion may diminish infusion reactions; meperidine can be used for rigors; potassium and/or magnesium supplementation may be needed for electrolyte abnormalities		
ADVANTAGES/ DISADVANTAGES	Lower cost; higher rates of nephrotoxicity and infusion reactions	Less nephrotoxicity and infusion reactions compared to convAmB; higher cost	Less infusion reactions compared to convAmB and less nephrotoxicity compared to convAmB and ABLC; higher cost than convAmB and ABLC

Table adapted from Lacy CF, Armstrong LL, Goldman MP, Lance LL., eds. *Drug Information Handbook 13th Edition.* Hudson, OH: Lexi-Comp, Inc: 2005.

Lipid Associated Formulations

Are better tolerated than Amphotericin B deoxycholate.

- Reduces the frequency and severity of acute amphotericin B deoxycholate-related infusion reactions
- Reduced nephrotoxicity

- The exception to the above is Amphotericin B Colloidal Dispersion (ABCD) which generally shows acute infusion related reaction similar Amphotericin B deoxycholate
- Can be used in patients with pre-existing renal dysfunction or in patients who develop renal dysfunction while receiving amphotericin B deoxycholate

Liposomal Amphotericin (AmBisome)

- A triad of infusion related reactions can occur:
  - Chest pain, dyspnea hypoxia
  - Severe pain in the abdomen, flank or legs
  - Flushing and urticaria which usually occurs within the first five minutes of the infusion and is apparently unrelated to infusion speed

ACUTE REACTIONS TO AMPHOTERICIN B

- 30 to 45 minutes after beginning the first few amphotericin B deoxycholate infusions:
  - Chills, fever, tachycardia, may occur at the peak in 15 to 30 minutes of therapy onset and slowly abate over 2 to 4 hours. This reaction will occur at the same time with each infusion and thus can be prevented with pre-medication.
- Patients with underlying cardiac or pulmonary disease may have hypoxemia
- These reactions are less common in children, in patients receiving corticosteroids, and with most of the lipid-based amphotericin B formulations
- Subsequent infusion of the same dose cause progressively milder reaction
- Pre-medication with acetaminophen or ibuprofen or the addition of hydrocortisone 25 to 50mg in the infusion can diminish the reactions
- Meperidine given early in a chill or pre-chill shortens or abates the rigor but may cause nausea or emesis
- Although not universally recommended, a test dose of 1mg given over 15 minutes is not required may be considered to assess subsequent reaction over 1 hour before deciding whether to use full dose of at least (0.5mg/ kg)
- Patients with rapidly progressive mycosis should receive a full therapeutic dose within 24 hours whether or not a test dose was given
- Equally important the reaction should not be confused with anaphylactic reactions (true allergic reactions are extremely rare) or otherwise considered a contraindication for further administration of amphotericin B deoxycholate

Nephrotoxicity

- Amphotericin B deoxycholate causes a dose dependent decrease in glomerular filtration rate.
- Direct vasoconstriction effects on the afferent renal arterioles results in reduced glomerular and tubular blood flow.
- Other primary or secondary effect in the kidney are:
  - Potassium, magnesium, bicarbonate wasting.
  - Decreased erythroprotein production.

- Permanent loss of renal function is related to the total dose, not the level of temporary azotemia, and is due to disruption of the tubular basement membrane and loss of function of nephron units.
- Sodium loading with one liter of normal saline before amphotericin B deoxycholate has been associated with a reduction in nephrotoxicity in some but not in all studies.
- Potassium wasting requires supplements of oral or intravenous potassium.
- Renal tubular acidosis from bicarbonate wasting rarely requires base replacement.
- Other drugs that promote acidosis may act synergistically.
- Azotemia caused by amphotericin is often worse in patients taking nephrotoxic drug such as:
    - Cyclosporin
    - Amino glycosides
- The following magnify the management problem associated with amphotericin B-azotemia.
    - Hypotension
    - Intravascular volume depletion
    - Renal transplantation
    - Pre existing renal diseases
- Renal toxicities are lessened by the use of lipid associated formulations.
- Adult with no other renal disease have an average serum creatinine level of 2 to 3 mg/dl at therapeutic dose. Therapy should not be withheld unless azotemia exceeds this level. Lipid based amphotericin B products can be used if patient has pre-existing renal dysfunction or develops renal dysfunction while receiving amphotericin B deoxycholate (i.e. conventional amphotericin B)
- Attempting to give amphotericin B deoxycholate to an adult without causing azotemia usually leads to inadequate therapy.
- Total daily dose should never exceed 1.5mg/kg
- Monitoring should include CBC, serum creatinine and serum electrolytes.

OTHER CHRONIC TOXICITY

- Nausea, anorexia, vomiting are common.
- Normocytic, normochronic anemia, due to decrease in erythropoietin.
- The hematocrit rarely declines to 20 to 25% unless some other cause of anemia is present.
- Rarely thrombocytopenia, modest leukopenia, coagulopathy, hemorrhagic enteritis, arrhythmia, tinnitus, vertigo, encephalopathy, seizures, hemolysis, dysesthesias of the feet.

References

1. Butt MA, Scerpella EG, Moreno JN, Fischl MA. Increase in the frequency of histoplasmosis caused by HIV infection. Infectious Diseases Society of America 35th Annual Meeting, September 13–16, 1997, San Francisco, CA. Abstract 534.

2. Chuck SL, Sande MA. Infection with cryptococcus neoformans in the acquired immunodeficiency syndrome. *NEJM* 1989; 321:794–797.

3. Diamond RD. Cryptococcus neoformans. In: *Principles and Practice of Infection Diseases*, 7th ed. Mandell GL, Bennett JE. Dulin R, eds. New York: Churchill Livingstone; 2000; 2707–2717.

4. Fichtenbaum CJ. Candidiasis. In: *AIDS Therapy*. Dolin R, Massur H, Saag M, eds. New York: Churchill Livingstone; 1999, 400–429.

5. Powderly WG. Cryptococcus. In: *AIDS Therapy*. Dolin R; Massur H, Saag M, eds. New York: Churchill Livingstone; 1999, 400–429.

6. Powderly WG. Fungal Infections: Diagnosis and Management in Patients with HIV Disease. Available at: www.medscape.com/medscape/HIV/Clinicalmgmt/cm.v06/pnt-cm.v06.html.

7. Schurling SR, Kortinga HC, Frosch BM, Muhlschgelef F. The role of candida dubliniensis in oral candidiasis in human immunodeficiency virus infected individuals. *Crit Rev Microbiol* 2000; 26(1):59–68.

8. Tansuphaswadikul S, Sitawaein S, Artomprasanga S. Amphotericin B combined with itraconazole is superior to amphotericin B alone in cryptococcal meningitis. 12th World AIDS Conference, 1998, Geneva, Switzerland. Abstract 22226.

9. Taylor BN, Fischtenbaum C, Saavedra Metal. *In vivo* virulence of candida albicans isolates causing mucosal infections in people infected with the human immunodeficiency virus. *J of Infect Dis* 2000; 182:955–958.

10. Wheat J. Histoplasmosis. In: *AIDS Therapy*. Dulin R, Mandell Saag M, eds. New York: Churchill Livingstone; 1999; 412–421.

11. July 2001: Draft – 2001 USPHS/IDSA guidelines for the prevention of opportunistic infections in persons infected with human immunodeficiency virus. US Public Health Service (USPHS) and Infectious Diseases Society of America (IDSA USPHS/IDSA Prevention of Opportunistic Infection Working Group. Available at: www.medscape.com/home/topics/aids/directories/diraids. Accessed September 27, 2001.

12. Gilbert DN, Moellering RC , Eliopoulos GM, Sande MA, eds. *The Sanford Guide to Antimicrobial Therapy*. 34th ed. Hyde Park, VT: Antimicrobial Therapy, Inc.; 2004.

13. Ostrosky-Zeichner L, Rex JH. Declaring war on aspergillus. *Medscape*. Available at: htt://www.medscape.com/view program/824 pnt. Accessed November 23, 2004.

14. Nelson PW, Lozano-Chiu M, Rex JH. Comparison of caspofungin and amphotericin B for invasive Candidiasis. *NEJM* 2002; 347;2020–2029.

15. Singer N. Treatment of opportunistic mycosis how long is long enough. *Lancet* November 2003(3); Number 11.

16. Bartlett JG, Gallant JE. 2003 *Medical Management of HIV Infection*. Baltimore, MD: Johns Hopkins University School of Medicine; 2003.

17. Rex JH, Steven DA. In: Mandell GL, Bennett JE, Dolin R, eds. *Principles and Practice of Infectious Diseases*. 6th ed. Philadelphia, PA: Churchill Livingstone; 2005;502–507.

18. Schubert MS Allergic Fungal Sinusitis. *Otolaryngologic Clinic of North America* 2004; 37;301–326.

19. Bartlett JG, Gallant JE. *Medical Management of HIV Infection*, Baltimore, MD: Johns Hopkins University School of Medicine; 2001; 267–268.

20. Hospenthal DR. Uncommon Fungi. In: Mandell GL, Bennett JE, Dolin R, eds. *Principles and Practice of Infectious Diseases*. 6th ed. Philadelphia, PA: Churchill Livingstone; 2005;3068–3079.

20

Mycobacterium Avium Complex (MAC)

Allen E. Rodriguez, MD
Associate Professor of Clinical Medicine
Clinical Immunology Section, Division of Infectious Disease
University of Miami School of Medicine, Jackson Memorial Medical Center

Epidemiology and Pathogenesis

- Also known as Mycobacterium Avium Intracellulare (MAI)
- MAC ubiquitous in nature: frequently isolated from soil, water and food
- There are no specific recommendations regarding avoidance of exposure
- Usually affects people with advanced AIDS and low CD4+ cell count (less than 50 cells/mm^3)
- Median CD4+ cell count of patients developing MAC is 10 cells/mm^3
- Incidence of MAC bacteremia increases in proportion to the amount of time passed since diagnosis of AIDS
- Development of disseminated MAC (DMAC) correlates with increased mortality
- Most patients developing MAC acquire it from the environment and show no sign of localized infection prior to development of DMAC
- Colonization with the organism predisposes patient to the development of DMAC. Respiratory and gastrointestinal colonization: positive predictive value for dissemination.
- Can affect any organ. Most commonly affected sites are lymph nodes, liver, spleen, GI tract, lungs, and bone marrow

Table 1. The Natural History of DMAC in AIDS May be Summarized as Follows

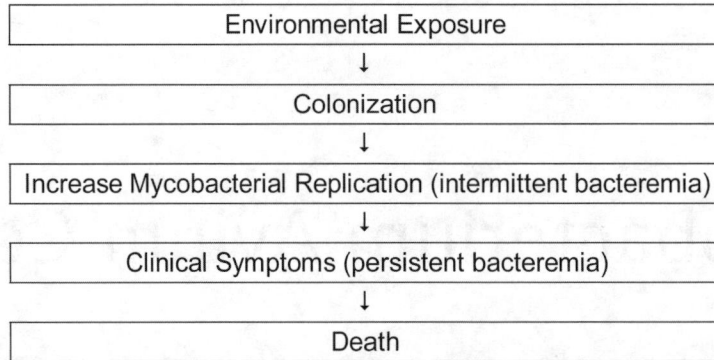

Environmental Exposure

↓

Colonization

↓

Increase Mycobacterial Replication (intermittent bacteremia)

↓

Clinical Symptoms (persistent bacteremia)

↓

Death

CLINICAL PRESENTATION

Table 2. The Frequency of Signs and Symptoms Associated with DMAC

SYMPTOM/SIGN	% OF POSITIVE PATIENTS
Fever	87
Night sweats	78
Diarrhea	47
Weight loss	38
Lymphadenopathy	37
Abdominal pain	35
Nausea/vomiting	26
Hepatosplenomegaly	24

DIAGNOSIS

- Usually straightforward and can be established reliably by obtaining blood cultures
- Inoculation of blood into BACTEC medium: usually positive in 8 to 14 days
- Once there is sufficient growth, speciation can be made using Gen-Probe
- Can also be diagnosed by culture of the bone marrow, lymph nodes, or liver

TREATMENT

- Goals of therapy in the treatment of DMAC are:
  - To reduce or eradicate MAC bacteremia
  - To improve quality of life and improve survival

- Treatment as well as prophylaxis for MAC has been shown to improve survival in patients with AIDS. The following is the currently recommended therapy for MAC:
  - First choice
    - Clarithromycin 500 mg po bid, plus ethambutol 15 mg/kg po qd with or without rifabutin 300 mg po qd*
  - Alternative
    - Azithromycin 500 mg po qd plus ethambutol 15 mg/kg po qd with or without rifabutin 300 mg po qd* (Some use azithromycin 600 mg qd but 500 mg qd [either with 500 mg or 250 mg tablets] is cheaper.)

(*NOTE: Dose modification of rifabutin is required with most antiretroviral regimens. See Chapter 6 or Chapter 21 for dosing rifabutin with antiretroviral agents.)

- Secondary prophylaxis for MAC consists of the same therapy
- Primary prophylaxis for MAC recommended with patients with a CD4+ cell count of < 50 cells/mm^3. Recommendation is based on the assumption that DMAC as well as tuberculosis have been excluded prior to beginning chemoprophylaxis.
  - First Choice
    - Azithromycin 1200 mg po qweek or clarithromycin 500 mg po bid
  - Alternatives
    - Rifabutin 300 mg po qd*
    - Azithromycin 1200 mg po qweek plus rifabutin 300 mg po qd*

(*NOTE: Dose modification of rifabutin is required with most antiretroviral regimens. See Chapter 6 or Chapter 21 for dosing rifabutin with antiretroviral agents.)

- Discontinuation of primary prophylaxis
  - Primary MAC prophylaxis should be discontinued among adult patents who have responded to HAART with an increase in CD4+ T lymphocyte counts to > 100 cells/mm^3 for > 3 months
- Discontinuation of secondary prophylaxis
  - Secondary prophylaxis for disseminated MAC can be discontinued among patients with a sustained (> 6 months) increase in CD4 counts in response to HAART if they have completed 12 months of MAC therapy and have no symptoms attributable to MAC.

References

1. 2002 USPHS/IDSA Guidelines for the prevention of opportunistic infections in persons infected with human immunodeficiency virus. *MMWR* June 14, 2002; 51(RR-08).

2. Benson CA, Ellner JJ. Mycobacterium avium complex infection in AIDS; advances in theory and practice. *Clin Infect Dis* 1993; 17:7–20.

3. Currier JS, Williams PL, et al. Discontinuation of mycobacterium avium complex prophylaxis in patients with antiretroviral therapy-induced increases in CD4 cell count. *Annals of Int Med* 2000; 7: 493–503.

4. Kovacs JA, Masur H. Prophylaxis against opportunistic infections in patients with human immunodeficiency virus infection. *NEJM* 2000; 19:1416–1425.

5. EL-Sadr WM, Burman WJ, et al. Discontinuation of prophylaxis fro Mycobacterium avium complex disease in HIV-infected patents who have a response to antiretroviral therapy. *NEJM* 2000; 342: 1085–1092.

21

Mycobacterium Tuberculosis

Elena S. Hollender, MD
Director, Clinical Services
A.G. Holley State Hospital
Jerry Jean Stambaugh, PharmD
Pharmacy Director
A.G. Holley State Hospital
Karen V. Farrell RN, BSN, RM
Executive Nursing Director and
Director of Education
A.G. Holley State Hospital
David Ashkin, MD
Florida TB Controller
A.G. Holley State Hospital

Michael Lauzardo, MD
Senior Physician
A.G. Holley State Hospital
Tanira Ferreira, MD
Senior Physician
A.G. Holley State Hospital
Masahiro Narita, MD
Tuberculosis Control Program
Public Health
Seattle and King County, Washington.
David Beall, PhD
Head, Mycobacteriology Laboratory
Florida Department of Health
Bureau of Laboratories

Pathogenesis and Transmission

- Caused by Mycobacterium tuberculosis complex (consisting of *M. tuberculosis*, *M. bovis*, *M. africanum*, *M. microti and M. canetti*)
- Most commonly spread through droplet nuclei coughed up by persons with untreated TB disease of the lungs or larynx
- 2 stages:
  - Latent TB infection (LTBI)
    - Patients with latent TB infection are asymptomatic and not contagious but have the potential to develop active disease.
    - Patients co-infected with HIV can develop clinical disease at rate of up to 8% per year if untreated for latent TB infection.
  - Active disease
    - Patients with active disease are usually symptomatic and contagious
    - TB disease may be lethal if not or inadequately treated and may subsequently develop resistance and further spread of the disease

- Lungs are the most common site for TB, however, extrapulmonary disease is common with HIV co-infection (~30% extrapulmonary alone, approx. 30% extrapulmonary and pulmonary concurrently)
  - o Lymphatic tuberculosis
  - o Miliary disease (disseminated tuberculosis)

LATENT TUBERCULOSIS INFECTION

Diagnosis

- PPD skin testing (tuberculin skin testing, TST, with purified protein derivative PPD) utilizing the Mantoux Method (multiple puncture tests are not acceptable alternatives)
- Annual PPD testing for patients with HIV infection is recommended. Significantly immunosuppressed HIV positive individuals may have a false negative PPD. Some authors suggest repeating PPD testing 3 to 6 months after initiation of ART (antiretroviral therapy) or once the immune system has been restored.
- ≥ 5 mm of induration (don't measure erythema) on tuberculin skin testing is considered positive for TB infection in HIV infected individuals
- HIV-infected individuals with a documented history of a positive PPD (> 5mm) who have not previously completed treatment should be considered for LTBI therapy.
- Always rule out active disease in a patient with a positive PPD or symptoms compatible with active TB disease before starting treatment for latent TB infection. Use:
  - o Chest X-ray
  - o Sputum for AFB smear, culture and nucleic acid amplification (if clinically indicated)
  - o Evaluation for active extrapulmonary disease if clinically appropriate
- Routine anergy testing **is not recommended**
- A whole blood interferon γ (IFN-γ) assay, the quantiferon-TB test is a promising *in vitro* diagnostic test for LTBI that has potential advantages over the tuberculosis skin test (TST), See reference #8. However, as this test relies on an immunologic response, it may not be useful in the immunocompromised such as HIV infection and as such is not currently recommended for use in such groups.

Treatment (See Tables 1, 2, and 3)

- INH therapy for 9 months is the preferred regimen.
- Rifampin daily for four months is an alternative when INH cannot be used.
- Short course with Rifampin/PZA for two months should only be considered in HIV positive individuals at high risk if other alternatives cannot be used. Consultation with an expert should be performed prior to initiating this regimen (see Figure 1 – Consultation Resources).
- Significantly immunosuppressed HIV positive individuals (CD4 < 200) who are PPD negative and at risk for TB may be considered for LTBI therapy. High-risk groups may include: History of close TB contact, immigrants from endemic TB countries, residents of correctional facilities and homeless.

ACTIVE TUBERCULOSIS DISEASE

Clinical Characteristics

- Usually prolonged
  - o Productive cough with or without hemoptysis
  - o Fever, chills, night sweats, lethargy, anorexia, weight loss
  - o Lymphadenopathy, especially in HIV infected individuals

Diagnosis

- Chest X-Ray (up to 30% of HIV infected individuals with active TB will have no infiltrates on CXR; cavitation is uncommon -may only have hilar or mediastinal adenopathy or no abnormalities at all)
- **NOTE**: Anyone with the following symptoms should be isolated and a CXR performed promptly (with sputum studies if clinically appropriate) to attempt to rule out active TB disease
  - Unexplained cough (more than 3 weeks)
  - Unexplained cough with fever (more than 3 days)
  - Unexplained pleuritic chest pain, hemoptysis and/or dyspnea
  - Unexplained fever, night sweats, weight loss
- Sputum smear for acid fast bacilli
  - Only positive in ~50% of patients with active pulmonary disease
- Sputum for TB culture and susceptibility
  - Only positive in 80-90% of patients with active TB disease
  - 10–20% of patients with active disease will have Clinical or Culture Negative TB (negative cultures but signs and/or symptoms compatible with TB, a CXR compatible with TB, a positive PPD and when started on anti-TB therapy clinically respond)
- Nucleic Acid Amplification (e.g., PCR or MTD)
  - Results back in < 8 hours after test performed
  - Over 98% specific on smear (+) cases
  - 70–80% sensitive on multiple adequate smear (-) specimens

NOTE: The Florida Department of Health TB Laboratory in Jacksonville is offering this test FREE of charge, 7 days a week, if requested, and sent to laboratory. For more information call the Bureau of Laboratories at 904-791-1630 or contact the TB Hotline at 800-4TB-INFO.

- **NOTE:** A high index of clinical suspicion for extrapulmonary disease should be maintained in HIV positive patients with risk factors for TB and if indicated, appropriate diagnostic studies performed.
- **NOTE:** When a patient is diagnosed with TB, remember to call the local health department so that they can screen all contacts, especially children and other immunocompromised hosts in the patient's environment
- **NOTE:** Active TB is an AIDS-defining infection.

Treatment (See Tables 2, 3, and 4)

- Directly observed therapy (DOT) is considered the community standard of care for patients with HIV and active TB disease in the state of Florida. Every effort should be made to provide DOT. All options to overcome barriers to DOT should be explored (Call TB Physicians Network or Local Health Department for use of enablers and incentives).
- Those that cannot be treated by DOT should be observed closely for adherence and response to therapy and should be prescribed combination pills (e.g., Rifamate® which is rifampin and isoniazid or Rifater® which is isoniazid, rifampin and pyrazinamide) to prevent the development of resistance.
- There is a once weekly continuation phase regimen with rifapentine and INH that can be used in select non-HIV infected patients. This regimen is ***contraindicated*** in HIV-infected patients.

Multidrug Resistant Mycobacterium Tuberculosis (MDR-TB)

- Defined as resistance to at least INH and rifampin. The most common cause of MDR-TB is *nonadherence.*
- May be lethal in up to 50% of cases and these MDR strains may be transmitted to close contacts
- Treat with *at least* 2 but preferably 3 or more drugs (including an aminoglycoside) to which the individual is found to be susceptible, for at least 12 months after cultures become negative
- Clinical consultation is strongly recommended (See Figure 1)

Figure 1. Consultation Resources

A.G. Holley/SNTC TB Hotline
Phone: 800-4TB-INFO (800-482-4636)
Website: www.doh.state.fl.us (look under A.G. Holley) or www.agholley.com
Free 24 hours/7 days a week clinical consultation
.

Southeast National TB Center (SNTC)
Phone: 352-265-7682 (FLA-265-SNTC)
Resource for TB training, education and medical consultation.

Florida Bureau of Laboratories
Phone: 904-791-1630
Website: www.doh.state.fl.us (look under laboratory services)
Resource for laboratory issues.

Florida Bureau of TB and Refugee Health
Phone: 850-245-4350
Website: www.doh.state.fl.us (look under tuberculosis)
Programmatic and information resource.

CDC Division of TB Elimination
Phone: 404-639-8140
Website: www.cdcnpin.org (look under tuberculosis)
Resource for guidelines and research concerning TB.

Florida/Caribbean AIDS Education and Training Center
Website:www.faetc.org/online
Comprehensive Multimedia Lecture on HIV/TB with downloadable valuable resources and references

Table 1. Regimens for Treatment of Latent TB Infection for Adults with HIV Infection

RATING① (EVIDENCE)②	DRUG (SEE TABLE 2 FOR DOSAGES)	INTERVAL AND DURATION	MONITORING	COMMENTS
A (II)	INH③④	Daily for 9 months	• Clinical monitoring monthly • Liver function tests (LFT's)⑤ at baseline, and monthly in all HIV-infected patients	**Rule out Active Disease before beginning therapy for Latent Infection.** • In HIV infected patients, INH may be administered concurrently with nucleoside reverse transcriptase inhibitors (NRTIs), protease inhibitors,non-nucleoside reverse transcriptase inhibitors (NNRTIs), or fusion inhibitors • Hepatitis risk increases with age and alcohol consumption. • Pyridoxine (vitamin B₆ 10-25 mg/d) might prevent peripheral neuropathy and central nervous system effects. • Directly Observed Therapy (DOT) must be used when twice-weekly dosing is used.
B (II)	INH③④	2 times/week for 9 months		
B(III)	Rifampin	Daily for 4 months in Adults, Daily for 6 months in children	Clinical monitoring monthly Complete blood count, platelets, and liver function tests⑤ at baseline in selected cases and repeat measurements at 2, 4, 6, and 8 weeks.	**Rule out Active Disease before beginning therapy for Latent Infection.** • See note below (under ⑥) on use of this regimen with certain NNRTIs or protease inhibitors • May also be offered to persons who are contacts of patients with INH resistant, rifampin susceptible TB • Decreases levels of many other drugs • Might permanently discolor contact lenses

① I = randomized clinical trial data; II = data from clinical trials that are not randomized or were conducted in other populations; III = expert opinion
② A = preferred; B = acceptable alternative;
③ Recommended regimen for children < 18 years of age
④ Recommended regimen for pregnant women
⑤ AST or ALT and serum bilirubin
⑥ Protease Inhibitors or NNRTIs should generally not be used with rifampin-containing regimens; rifabutin can be used as an alternative for patients treated with these medications—see Table 3 for full details

SOURCE: Adapted from American Thoracic Society/Centers for Disease Control. Targeted Tuberculin Testing and Treatment of Latent TB Infection. *Am J of Resp Crit Care Med.* 2000;161:S221-S247 and Targeted Tuberculin Skin Testing and Treatment of Latent Tuberculosis Infection in Children and Adolescents: Pediatric Tuberculosis Collaborative Group. *Pediatrics* 2004; 114;1175–1201.

Table 2. Medications for the Treatment of TB and Latent TB Infection

DRUG	DOSE IN MG/KG (MAXIMUM DOSE)						ADVERSE REACTONS	MONITORING	COMMENTS
	DAILY		2 TIMES/WEEK①		3 TIMES/WEEK①				
	children	adults	children	adults	children	adults			
INH	10-15② (300 mg)	5 (300 mg)	20-30 (900 mg)	15 (900 mg)	20-30 (900 mg)	15 (900 mg)	Hepatic enzyme elevation Hepatitis Peripheral neuropathy Mild effects on central nervous system Drug Interactions	Baseline measurements for adults: •hepatic enzymes Repeat measurements: •if baseline results are abnormal •if patient is at high risk for adverse reactions •if patient has symptoms of adverse reactions	Hepatitis risk increases with age and alcohol consumption Pyridoxine can prevent peripheral neuropathy
RIF	10-20 (600 mg)	10 (600 mg)	10-20 (600 mg)	10 (600 mg)	10-20 (600 mg)	10 (600 mg)	GI upset Drug Interactions Hepatitis Bleeding problems Flu-like symptoms Rash	Baseline measurements for adults: •CBC and platelets •hepatic enzymes Repeat measurements: •if baseline results are abnormal •if patient has symptoms of adverse reactions Monitor for decreased antiretroviral activity if taken with ART	See Table 3 when administered with ART Significant interactions with: •methadone •birth control pills •many other drugs e.g. PIs Colors body fluids orange May permanently discolor soft contact lenses
RFB	–	5 (450 mg)③	–	5 (450 mg)③	–	5 (450 mg)③	Rash Hepatitis Fever Thrombocytopenia with increased levels of rifabutin: •Severe arthralgias •Uveitis •Leukopenia	Baseline measurements for adults: •CBC and platelets •hepatic enzymes Repeat measurements: •if baseline results are abnormal •if patient has symptoms of adverse reactions Monitor for decreased antiretroviral activity if taken with ART	See Table 3 when administered with ART Significant interactions with: •methadone •birth control pills •many other drugs Colors body fluids orange May permanently discolor soft contact lenses
PZA	15-30 (2 g)	15-30 (2 g)	50-70 (4 g)	50-70 (4 g)	50-70 (3 g)	50-70 (3 g)	Hepatitis Rash GI Upset Joint aches Hyperuricemia Gout (rare)	Baseline measurements for adults: •uric acid •hepatic enzymes Repeat measurements: •if baseline results are abnormal •if patient has symptoms of adverse reactions	Treat hyperuricemia only if patient has symptoms. Reduce dose in patients with renal dysfunction.
EMB	15-25 (1000 mg)	15-25 (1600 mg)	50 (2.5 g)	50 (4 g)	25-30 (2.4 g)	25-30 (2.4 g)	Optic neuritis	Baseline and monthly tests: •visual acuity •color vision	Generally not recommended for children too young to be monitored for changes in vision unless TB is drug resistant. Reduce dose in patients with renal dysfunction.
SM	20-40 (1 g)	15 (1 g) or 10 (.75g) for age over 60	20 (1.5 g)	25-30 (1.5 g)	20 (1.5 g)	25-30 (1.5 g)	Ototoxicity (hearing loss or vestibular dysfunction) Renal toxicity	Baseline and repeat as needed: • hearing • kidney function	Avoid or reduce dose in adults > 60 years old or in individuals with renal disease.

ART = antiretroviral therapy   DOT = Directly Observed Therapy   EMB = ethambutol   INH = isoniazid
PZA = pyrazinamide RFB = rifabutin   RIF = rifampin   SM = streptomycin
① All regimens administered 2-3 times a week should be used with DOT
② When children are being treated for active disease, the dose of INH should be 10 mg/kg when used in combination with rifampin.
③ 450 mg max when used with efavirenz, otherwise 300 mg max
NOTE: Children < 12 years old. Adjust weight-based dosages as weight changes

SOURCE: Adapted from American Thoracic Society/Centers for Disease Control/Infectious Disease Society of America. Treatment of Tuberculosis. *Am J Respir Crit Care Med* 2003; 167:603–662. American Thoracic Society/Centers for Disease Control. Targeted Tuberculin Testing and Treatment of Latent TB Infection. *Am J of Resp Crit Care Med* 2000; 161:S221–S247. Centers for Disease Control and Prevention. Prevention and Treatment of Tuberculosis Among Patients Infected with Human Immunodeficiency Virus: Principles of Therapy and Revised Recommendations. *MMWR* 1998; 47(No. RR-20): 1–56. American Thoracic Society/Centers for Disease Control and Prevention. Treatment of Tuberculosis and Tuberculosis Infection in Adults and Children. *Am J Respir Crit Care Med* 1994; 149:1359–1374. Lawrence RM. Tuberculosis in Children. In: Rom WN, Garay S, and editors. *Tuberculosis*. 1st ed. Boston: Little, Brown and Company; 1996. p. 683. American Thoracic Society, Centers for Disease Control and Infectious Diseases Society. Treatment of Tuberculosis, *MMWR* June 20, 2003;52(RR11);1–77.

Table 3. Recommendations for Co-Administering Different Antiretroviral Drugs With the Antimycobacterial Drugs Rifabutin and Rifampin

ANTIRETROVIRAL	USE IN COMBINATION WITH RIFABUTIN	USE IN COMBINATION WITH RIFAMPIN	COMMENTS
Protease Inhibitors (PIs)			
Agenerase® **Amprenavir** **Lexiva®** **Fosamprenavir**	Yes	No	Co-administration of amprenavir or fosamprenavir with a reduced daily dose of rifabutin (150 mg) or with the usual dose of rifabutin (300 mg 3 times per week) is a possibility but there is no published clinical experience. Co-administration of amprenavir or fosamprenavir with rifampin is not recommended because rifampin markedly decreases concentrations of amprenavir.
Atazanavir	Yes	No	There is limited, but favorable, clinical experience with co-administration of atazanavir with a reduced daily dose of rifabutin (150 mg) every other day or 3 times per week.
Crixivan® **Indinavir**	Yes	No	There is limited, but favorable, clinical experience with co-administration of indinavir① with a reduced daily dose of rifabutin (150 mg) or with the usual dose of rifabutin (300 mg 3 times per week) and increase indinavir to 1000 mg q8 hours. Co-administration of indinavir with rifampin is not recommended because rifampin markedly decreases concentrations of indinavir.
Kaletra (lopinavir/ritonavir)	Probably	Probably	If the combination of lopinavir/ritonavir and rifabutin is used, then a substantially reduced-dose rifabutin regimen (150 mg 3 times per week) is recommended. Co-administration of lopinavir/ritonavir with usual-dose rifampin (600 mg daily or 3 times per week) is a possibility, only when additional ritonavir is added.
Viracept® **Nelfinavir**	Yes	No	There is limited, but favorable, clinical experience with co-administration of nelfinavir 1000mg q8 hours② with a reduced daily dose of rifabutin (150 mg) or with the usual dose of rifabutin (300 mg 3 times per week). Co-administration of nelfinavir with rifampin is not recommended because rifampin markedly decreases concentrations of nelfinavir.
Norvir® **Ritonavir**	Probably	Probably	If the combination of ritonavir and rifabutin is used, then a substantially reduced-dose rifabutin regimen (150 mg 3 times per week) is recommended. Co-administration of ritonavir with usual-dose rifampin (600 mg daily or 3 times per week) is a possibility, though pharmacokinetic data and clinical experience are limited.
Saquinavir③			
Invirase® hard-gel capsules (HGC)	Possibly④ if antiretroviral regimen also includes ritonavir	Possibly if antiretroviral regimen also includes ritonavir	The combination of saquinavir SGC or saquinavir HGC and ritonavir, co administered with 1) usual-dose rifampin (600 mg daily or 3 times per week), or 2) reduced-dose rifabutin (150 mg 3 times per week) is a possibility. However, the pharmacokinetic data and clinical experience for these combinations is limited.
Fortovase® soft-gel capsules (SGC)	Probably⑤	Possibly, if antiretroviral regimen also includes ritonavir	Co-administration of saquinavir HGC or saquinavir SGC with rifampin (in the absence of ritonavir) is not recommended because rifampin markedly decreases concentrations of saquinavir. Fortovase® no longer available in U.S.
Non-Nucleoside Reverse Transcriptase Inhibitors (NNRTIs)			
Rescriptor® **Delavirdine**	No	No	Contraindicated because of the marked decrease in concentrations of delavirdine when administered with either rifabutin or rifampin
Sustiva® **Efavirenz**	Yes	Yes	Co-administration of efavirenz with increased-dose rifabutin (450 mg or 600 mg daily, or 600 mg 2 or 3 times per week). Co-administration of an increased efavirenz⑥ dose (800mg daily) with usual-dose rifampin (600 mg daily, or 2 or 3 times per week).
Viramune® **Nevirapine**	Yes	Possibly	Co-administration of nevirapine with usual-dose rifabutin (300 mg daily or 3 times per week) is a possibility based on pharmacokinetic study data. Data are insufficient to assess whether dose adjustments are necessary when rifampin is co administered with nevirapine. Therefore, rifampin and nevirapine should be used only in combination if clearly indicated and with careful monitoring.

① Usual recommended dose is 800 mg every 8 hours. Some experts recommend increasing the indinavir dose to 1000–1200 mg every 8 hours if indinavir is used in combination with rifabutin.

②Usual recommended dose is 750 mg 3 times per day or 1250 mg twice daily. Some experts recommend increasing the nelfinavir dose to 1000 mg if the 3-times-per-day dosing is used and nelfinavir is used in combination with rifabutin.

③ Usual recommended doses are 400 mg 2 times per day for each of these protease inhibitors with 400 mg of ritonavir; other dosing regimens under investigation may also be used.

④ Despite limited data and clinical experience, the use of this combination is potentially successful.

⑤Based on available data and clinical experience, the successful use of this combination is likely.

⑥ Usual recommended dose is 600 mg daily. Some experts recommend increasing the efavirenz dose to 800 mg daily if efavirenz is used in combination with rifampin.

SOURCE: Center for Disease Control and Prevention. Updated Guidelines for the use of Rifabutin or Rifampin for the Treatment and Prevention of Tuberculosis among HIV-infected Patients Taking Protease Inhibitors or Nonnucleoside Reverse Transcriptase Inhibitors. *MMWR* 2004; 49(9):185–189. American Thoracic Society/Centers for Disease Control/Infectious Disease Society of America. Treatment of Tuberculosis. *Am J Respir Crit Care Med* 2003; 167:603–662.

Table 4. Treatment Regimens for HIV-Related TB

6-MONTH RIFAMYCIN-BASED THERAPY FOR TB SUSCEPTIBLE TO INH, RIF AND PZA①						
RATING② (Evidence)③	INDUCTION PHASE		CONTINUATION PHASE		CONSIDERATION FOR HIV THERAPY	COMMENTS
	DRUGS	INTERVAL & DURATION	DRUGS	INTERVAL & DURATION		
A (II)	INH + (RIF or RFB) + PZA + (EMB or SM) ④	Daily for 2 months or daily for 2 weeks, then 2-3 times/week for 6 weeks (intermittent therapy should be administered by DOT)⁵	INH + (RIF or RFB)	Daily or 2-3 times/week for 4 months (intermittent therapy should be administered by DOT) ⑤	See Table 3 for co-administration with antiretroviral therapy.	

DOT = directly observed therapy   EMB = ethambutol   INH = isoniazid   PZA = pyrazinamide   RIF = rifampin   RFB = rifabutin   SM = streptomycin

① Duration of therapy should be prolonged for patients with delayed response to therapy. If still culture positive on a sputum collected after 2 months of therapy, patient should be assessed for non-adherence, malabsorption or drug resistance and therapy should be prolonged for **at least** 4 months after cultures become negative. **Consultation with a specialist is strongly advised in these cases.**

② A = preferred

③ II = data from clinical trials that are not randomized or were conducted in other populations; III = expert opinion.

④ EMB or SM may be stopped after susceptibility test results indicate susceptibility to INH and RIF.

⑤ Twice weekly regimens should NOT be used in patients with CD4⁺ counts < 100 cells/mm³

SOURCE: Adapted from American Thoracic Society/Centers for Disease Control/Infectious Disease Society of America. Treatment of Tuberculosis *Am J Respir Crit Care Med* 2003; 167:603–662.

References

1. American Thoracic Society/CDC. Control of tuberculosis in the United States. *Am Rev Respir Dis* 1992; 146:1623–1633.

2. American Thoracic Society/CDC. Diagnostic Standards and classification of tuberculosis in adults and children. *Am J Respir Crit Care Med* 2000; 161:1376–1395.

3. American Thoracic Society/CDC. Targeted tuberculin testing and treatment of latent tuberculosis infection. *Am J Respir Crit Care Med* 2000; 161:S221–S247.

4. American Thoracic Society/CDC. Treatment of tuberculosis and tuberculosis infection in adults and children. *Am J Respir Crit Care Med* 2003; 167:603–662.

5. CDC. Prevention and Treatment of tuberculosis among patients infected with human immunodeficiency virus: principles of therapy and revised recommendations. *MMWR* 1998; 47(RR-20)1–52.

6. CDC. Updated guidelines for the use of rifabutin or rifampin for the treatment and prevention of tuberculosis among HIV-infected patients taking protease inhibitors or nonnucleoside reverse transcriptase inhibitors. *MMWR* 2000; 49(9) 185–189.

7. Narita M, Stambaugh JJ, Hollender ES, Jones D, Pitchenik AE, Ashkin D. Use of rifabutin with protease inhibitors for human immunodeficiency virus-infected patients with tuberculosis. *Clin Infect Dis* 2000; 30(5):779–783.

8. Mazurek GH, LoBue PA, Daley CL, et al. Comparison of whole-blood interferon γ assay with tuberculin skin testing for detecting latent *mycobacterium tuberculosis* infection. *JAMA* October 10, 2001; 287(14):1740–1747.

22

Pneumocystis Pneumonia (PCP)

Luis A. Espinoza, MD
Assistant Professor of Clinical Medicine
Clinical Immunology Section, Division of Infectious Diseases
University of Miami School of Medicine, Jackson Memorial Hospital

Epidemiology

- First reported by Chagas in 1909 as a morphologic form of *Trypanosoma cruzi*
- Most children develop anti-*Pneumocystis* antibodies early in life
- Infection may occur as a reactivation or infection proximal to the time of the disease
- *Pneumocystis* has worldwide distribution among humans and has been detected in a variety of animals. It has host specificity
- *Pneumocystis* in humans is due to *P.jiroveci*, different from *P. carinii* that is one of the two *Pneumocystis* species found only in rats
- *P. jiroveci* is difficult to find in the environment and has not been found in nonhuman hosts. It is absent or present at very low levels in healthy adults. In contrast, it is fairly common in immunocompromised individuals.
- PCP is one of the leading causes of illness and death in persons with impaired immunity

Microbiology

- *Pneumocystis* is classified as a fungus based on DNA analysis
- Different to other fungi since it lacks ergosterol. The echinocandin and papulocandin antifungal agents block *Pneumocystis* cyst formation
- *Pneumocystis* organisms have demonstrated host-species specificity
- DNA sequence polymorphisms are observed suggesting that numerous strains of *P. jiroveci* exist

Pathogenesis and Pathology

- Usually remains confined to the lungs in more than 95% of the cases. May also infect lymph nodes, spleen, liver, retina, skin, and bone marrow.
- Host factors that predispose to the infection involve defects in cellular and humoral immunity
- *Pneumocystis* is acquired by airborne route and takes up residence in the alveoli adhering to type I cells. In immunocompromised hosts it propagates and fills the alveoli. It results in increased alveolar-capillary permeability and damage to type I cells. There is alteration on the pulmonary surfactant and, in severe disease, may include interstitial edema, fibrosis, and hyaline membrane formation. As a

typical reparative response from the host there are hypertrophy of alveolar type II cells and a mild mononuclear cell interstitial infiltrate. As a result there is hypoxemia, increased work of breathing, and progression to respiratory failure.

Clinical Features

- Clinical picture is quite variable. Most patients are usually ill for two to three weeks
- Progressive dyspnea is the most characteristic feature
- Dry cough, tachycardia, tachypnea, cyanosis, and low-grade fever are other common accompanying manifestations
- Lung auscultation is usually unremarkable, although PCP can mimic asthma
- Increased frequency of pneumothorax is seen in patients who received aerosolized pentamidine
- Arterial blood gas demonstrates hypoxia, increased alveolar-arterial gradient and respiratory alkalosis. Desaturation of > 5% on exercise is a reliable and quick test. Elevated lactate dehydrogenase (LDH) may be seen although it is not specific for PCP.
- Chest radiography classically shows fine, bilateral, diffuse, symmetrical infiltrates beginning in the perihilar regions. Early in the disease the chest radiography may be normal. Other presentations include unilateral infiltrates, cavitary lesions, nodular densities, cystic formation, pleural effusion, pneumothorax, and pneumomediastinum.
- High-resolution computerized tomography is more sensitive than chest radiography in the diagnosis of PCP. Typically it will show a mosaic pattern ground-glass shadowing.

Diagnosis

- Must be based on specific identification of the organism by histopathologic staining (Wright-Giemsa, methenamine silver, Papanicolaou, Diff-Quic). Other tests include the use of monoclonal antibody techniques, and DNA amplification by PCR.
- Sputum induction with nebulized saline has wide variety of success. In seven prospective studies, sputum induction demonstrated 55.5% sensitivity and 98.6% specificity. Sensitivity and specificity are significantly higher with the use of monoclonal antibodies, in induced-sputum samples, than with cytochemical stains.
- Examination of oral washes by a sensitive PCR assay is also a promising technique to diagnose PCP
- Severe depletion of the levels of S-adenosylmethionine in plasma may be a helpful tool in the diagnosis and monitoring the course of the treatment for PCP in the future
- Fiber optic bronchoscopy with bronchoalveolar lavage has > 90% sensitivity and 100% specificity. Transbronchial biopsy and open lung biopsy are other more invasive alternatives.

Treatment

MILD TO MODERATE PCP: PaO2 ≥ 70 mm Hg or A-a gradient ≤ 35 mm Hg
- Recommended
    - Trimethoprim-sulfamethoxazole (TMP-SMZ): 15–20 mg/kg daily of TMP component divided every 6–8 hours po for 21 days. Dose adjust for CrCl 15-30, decrease dose 50%. If CrCl< 15, avoid use.
- Alternatives
    - Dapsone 100 mg po daily plus trimethoprim15 mg/kg po daily in 3 divided doses.
    - Atovaquone suspension 750 mg po twice daily taken with food.

o Clindamycin 300–450 mg q6h (600–900 mg IV q 6h – 8h) plus primaquine 15–30 mg of base po daily
o Trimetrexate 45 mg/m^2 or 1.2 mg/kg IV qd with leucovorin 20 mg/ m^2 or 0.5 mg/kg IV or po q6h. Leucovorin must be continued for 3 days after the last trimetrexate dose. The addition of dapsone or sulfamethoxazole or sulfadiazine might improve efficacy.

SEVERE PCP: PaO2 ≤ 70 mm Hg or A-a gradient ≥ 35 mm Hg
- Recommended*
    o TMP-SMZ: 15–20 mg/kg/day of TMP component divided every 6–8 hours, IV. Add prednisone (in the first 72 hours) 40 mg orally twice daily for 5 days, then 40 mg/day for another five days, then 20 mg/day another five days, and 10 mg/day for the last five days.
- Alternatives*
    Prednisone as above plus one of the following:
    o Clindamycin 600 mg every 8 hours IV and primaquine 15-30 mg po qd.
    o Pentamidine 4 mg/kg/day IV infused over AT LEAST 60 minutes. This is usually the alternative drug of second choice for severe cases.
    o Trimetrexate 45 mg/m²/day IV plus folinic acid 20 mg/m² every 6 hours po or IV.
*Duration of therapy generally 21 days but should be based on resolution of signs and symptoms.

Prophylaxis

PRIMARY PROPHYLAXIS

- Indicated for persons with a CD4 count of less than 200 cells/mm^3 (or less than 14%) or those with oropharyngeal candidiasis.
    o TMP-SMZ one DS tablet po daily or three times a week, or one single-strength tablet po daily (preferred).
    o Dapsone 100 mg po daily.
    o Dapsone 50 mg po daily with pyrimethamine 50 mg po weekly plus leucovorin 25 mg po weekly.
    o Atovaquone suspension 1500 mg po qd.
    o Aerosolized pentamidine 300 mg every four weeks administered via Respirgard II™ nebulizer.
- Primary prophylaxis should be discontinued in patients on HAART whose CD4 counts are above 200 cells/mm^3 for at least three months. It should be reintroduced if CD4 count decreases to <200 cells/mm$^{3.}$

SECONDARY PROPHYLAXIS OR CHRONIC MAINTENANCE THERAPY

- Patients with history of PCP should have chemoprophylaxis with any of the above regimens for life unless immune reconstitution occurs
- It may be discontinued in patients whose CD4 count has increased to > 200 cells/mm^3 for at least three months in response to HAART. It should be re-started if CD4 count decreases to < 200 cells/mm^3 or if PCP recurred at a CD4 count > 200 cells/mm^3.

SPECIAL CONSIDERATIONS DURING PREGNANCY

- Neonatal care providers should be informed if sulfa or dapsone therapy are used near term delivery due to a theoretical risk of hyperbilirubinemia and kernicterus
- Pentamidine is embryotoxic but not teratogenic

- Trimetrexate should not be used due to teratogenicity
- If corticosteroids used in the 3rd trimester, monitor glucose levels
- Rates of preterm labor and preterm delivery are increased with pneumonia in pregnancy

References

1. Stringer JR, Beard CB, Miller RF, Wakefield, AE. A new name (*pneumocystis jiroveci*) for *pneumocystis* from humans. *Emerg Infect Dis* 2002; 8:891–896.
2. Walzer PD. Pneumocystis carinii infection. En: Fauci AS, ed. Harrison's Principles of Internal Medicine. 14th ed. New York: McGraw-Hill, 1998; p. 1161-1163
3. Gomez DaRosa I. *Pneumocystis Carinii* Pneumonia (PCP). *HIV/AIDS Primary Care Guide* Steinhart C, Orrick JJ, Simpson K, eds. Gainesville; University of Florida. 2002:143–146.
4. Barry SM, Johnson MA. *Pneumocystis carinii* pneumonia: a review of current issues in diagnosis and management. *HIV Medicine (UK)* 2001; 2:123–132.
5. Limper AH, Martin WJ III: *Pneumocystis carinii*: Inhibition of lung cell growth mediated by parasite attachment. *J Clin Invest* 1990; 85:391.
6. Fishman J. Radiological approaches to the diagnosis of *Pneumocystis carinii* pneumonitis. *Pneumocystis carinii Pneumonia*. Walzer PD, ed. New York: Dekker. 1994:415–436.
7. Raviglione M. Extrapulmonary Pneumocystosis: The first 50 cases. *Rev Infect Dis* 1990; 12:1127–1138.
8. 2001 USPHS/IDSA guidelines for the prevention of opportunistic infections in persons infected with human immunodeficiency virus. *MMWR* November 28, 2001:8–10.
9. Cruciani M, Marcati P, Malena M, Bosco O, Serpelloni G, Mengoli C. Meta-analysis of diagnostic procedures for *Pneumocystis carinii* pneumonia in HIV-1 infected patients. *Eur Resp J* October 2002; 20(4): 982–989.
10. Weller IV, Williams IG. ABC of AIDS: Treatment of infections. *BMJ* 2001. June 2; 322:1350–1351.
11. Gagnon S, Boota AM, Fischl MA, Baier H, La Voie L. Corticosteroids as adjunctive therapy for severe *Pneumocystis carinii* pneumonia in the acquired immunodeficiency syndrome. A double-blind, placebo-controlled trial. *NEJM* 1990; 323(21):1444–1450.
12. Fishman, JA. Prevention of Infection Caused by *Pneumocystis carinii* in Transplant Recipients. *CID* 2001; 33:1397–1405.
13. Frame P. *Pneumocystis carinii* infection and AIDS. *Management of the HIV-Infected Patient*. Crowe S, Hoy J, Mills J, eds. New York: Cambridge University Press; 1966; 298–315.
14. Weverling GJ, Mocroft A, Ledergerber B, et al. Discontinuation of *Pneumocystis carinii* pneumonia prophylaxis after start of highly active antiretroviral therapy in HIV-1 infection. EuroSIDA Study Group. *Lancet* 1999; 353:1293–1298.
15. Skelly M, Hoffman J, Fabbri M, Holzman RS, Clarkson AB Jr, Merali S. S-adenosylmethionine concentration in diagnosis of *Pneumocystis carinii* pneumonia [Research letter]. *Lancet* April 12, 2003; 361:1267–1268.
16. Fischer S, Gill VJ, Kovacs J, Miele P, Keary J, et al. the use of oral washes to diagnose *Pneumocystis carinii* pneumonia: A blinded prospective study using a polymerase chain reaction-based detection system [Concise communication]. *J of Infect Dis* December 1, 2001; 184:1485–1488.
17. Treating opportunistic infections among HIV-infected adults and adolescents. Recommendations from CDC, the National Institutes of Health, and the HIV Medicine Association/Infections Diseases Society of America. *MMWR* December 17, 2004; 53/ RR-15.
18. Henry Masur. *Pneumocystosis. AIDS Therapy*. Dolin R, Masur H, Saag M, eds. Philadelphia: Churchill Livingstone; 1999:291–306.
19. AAHIVM. *Opportunistic infections, preferred and alternative treatments. HIV Medicine Self-Directed Study Guide*. Vol. 1. Los Angeles: The American Academy of HIV Medicine; 2003 :22–26.
20. Thomas CF Jr, Limper AH. Pneumocystis Pneumonia. *NEJM* 2004; 350:2487–2498 (table 2).

23

Toxoplasmosis

Luis A. Espinoza, MD
Assistant Professor of Clinical Medicine
Clinical Immunology Section, Division of Infectious Diseases
University of Miami School of Medicine, Jackson Memorial Hospital

Epidemiology

- *Toxoplasma gondii* is among the most prevalent causes of latent infection of the central nervous system (CNS) throughout the world.
- *T gondii* is a protozoan parasite that exists in three forms: proliferative (tachyzoite), tissue cyst, and oocyst.
- *T gondii* infects all mammals, but felines are the definitive hosts.
- Toxoplasmic encephalitis (TE) is the most common cause of focal CNS lesions in patients with HIV infection, occurring in 3–10% of cases in the US and up to 50% of cases in Europe and Africa.
- TE is both preventable and treatable.
- TE occurs in 10–50% of HIV-infected patients who are seropositive for antibodies to *T gondii* and who have CD4 count < 100 cells/mm^3. The greatest risk is among patients with a CD4+ T lymphocyte count < 50 cells/mm^3.
- Humans acquire the infection orally although *T gondii* may cause fetal infection in mothers who are exposed to it during gestation.
- In the US the prevalence of latent infection is 10–40%. In some European countries is as high as 70%.
- The highest risk for HIV-infected patients with latent infection is when CD4 count is below 100 cells/mm^3.
- Without prophylaxis the 12-month incidence of TE was approximately 33%.

Pathogenesis

- *T gondii* occurs in three different forms: the oocyst (shed in feline feces), the tachyzoite (obligatory intracellular parasite, which is the invasive form that proliferates during acute infection), and the tissue cyst (appears in mammals tissue such as brain, myocardium, and skeletal muscle; it is the form in which infection remains latent within the human host). The tissue cysts are also present in animal flesh and can transmit disease if meat is undercooked (specifically lamb, beef, venison, and pork).
- After oral ingestion it is carried as latent infection without causing disease. IgG and IgM are produced following an infection with *T gondii*.
- Cell mediated immunity may be the critical determinate in controlling toxoplasmosis with assistance of humoral response but it is not fully protective. Interferon gamma is an absolute requirement for resistance against acquired infection with *T gondii* and development of Toxoplasmic encephalitis during the late stage of the infection.
- TE in AIDS patients is most likely from reactivation of latent infection. The most common affected area is the basal ganglia but other lesions may involve cerebellar and brain stem areas. Outside the CNS, the lungs, retina, and myocardium may also be affected.

Clinical Manifestations

- The most common presentation in AIDS patients is encephalitis, representing approximately 80% of the cases. Other manifestations include *Toxoplasma* chorioretinitis, and less common pneumonitis and myocarditis.
- In TE the presentations may include global encephalitis with altered mental status (75%), focal neurological deficits (70%), headache (50%), fever (45%), seizures (30%), weakness, or cranial nerve abnormalities. The onset of symptoms is subacute in most cases.

Diagnostic Options

- Contrast-enhanced CT or MRI scans:
  - Usually multiple bilateral cerebral lesions (rarely single lesions).
  - Most common location is in the basal ganglia, and ring-enhances after IV contrast.
  - MRI is more sensitive and may show many more lesions; in follow-up it is advisable to compare similar radiologic studies.
  - Single-Photon emission CT (SPECT), Positron Emission Tomography and MR spectroscopy can be used to help to differentiate TE from CNS lymphoma.
- Serologic assays: IgG antibodies to *Toxoplasma* are usually present 1 to 2 weeks after acquisition of the infection and usually persist for life, even in advanced AIDS; a negative *Toxoplasma* IgG antibody makes the diagnosis less likely. With the newest assays a very small percentage of patients will have no demonstrable antibody at the time of diagnosis. IgM antibodies are usually absent.
- Polymerase Chain Reaction: PCR amplification has been successful in detecting *T gondii* DNA in body fluids and tissues for the diagnosis of congenital, ocular, cerebral and disseminated toxoplasmosis. If anti-toxoplasma therapy has been started, the results of PCR are usually negative.

- Histologic diagnosis: The presence of tachyzoites in tissue sections or smears of body fluids establishes the diagnosis of active infection. The immunoperoxidase method is sensitive and specific since it uses antisera to *T gondii.*
- Differential diagnosis: CNS lymphoma, fungal infection such as cryptococcosis, TB, Chagas disease, bacterial abscess, and rarely PML (PML lesions typically involve white matter rather than gray matter and are noncontrast enhancing with no mass effect).

Treatment

Patients with ring-enhancing brain lesions on CT scan or MRI along with positive IgG antibody to *T gondii*, and CD4 count below 200 cells/mm^3 should receive empiric therapy. A clinical and radiological response to the specific therapy will support the diagnosis of TE. Patients who fail to show a radiographic or clinical response within 2 weeks of therapy should have a brain biopsy performed. If the biopsy confirms TE, a switch to an alternative therapy should be considered.

Initial Therapy – for at least 6 weeks:
- Preferred regimen: Pyrimethamine 200 mg po as a loading dose, followed by 50 mg (< 60 kg body weight) to 75 mg (≥ 60 kg) po qd, plus leucovorin (folinic acid) 10–20 mg per day (can increase ≥ 50 mg) po qd, + sulfadiazine 1000 (< 60 kg) to 1500 mg (≥ 60 kg) po q 6h
- Alternatives:
  - Pyrimethamine + leucovorin (as above) + clindamycin 600 mg IV or po q6h (preferred alternative)
  - TMP-SMX (5 mg/kg TMP and 25 mg/kg SMX) IV or po bid
- Other alternatives: :
  - Pyrimethamine + leucovorin (dosed as above) + one of the following:
    - Dapsone 100 mg po qd
    - Clarithromycin 500 mg po bid
    - Azithromycin 900-1200 mg po qd
    - Atovaquone 1500 mg po bid with meals or nutritional supplements
  - Atovaquone + sulfadiazine
  - Atovaquone alone if intolerant of both pyrimethamine and sulfadiazine. Plasma level of ≥ 18.5 µg/mL is associated with improved response rate.
- Adjunctive steroids should be used only if there is a mass effect or significant edema.
- Pregnancy: treatment should be the same as in nonpregnant adults. Pyrimethamine has not been associated with birth defects in limited human data to this date.

Maintenance (suppressive) therapy (should be lifelong unless immune reconstitution occurs)
- Pyrimethamine 25 – 50 mg po qd + leucovorin 10–25 mg po qd, + sulfadiazine 500–1000 mg po q6h (preferred)
- Alternatives (the relapse rate on these regimens is approximately 25%):
  - Clindamycin: 300–450 mg po q6–8h + pyrimethamine + leucovorin dosed as above
  - Atovaquone: 750 mg po q6–12h ± pyrimethamine 25 mg po qd + leucovorin 10 mg po qd
- If at least 6 weeks of therapy have been completed, AND the patient has been asymptomatic for signs and symptoms of TE, AND there has been a sustained CD4+ >200 cells/mm^3 for ≥ 6 months in response to antiretroviral therapy, cessation of chronic suppressive therapy can be considered. Repeating MRI is recommended to assure resolution of any mass lesion or contrast enhancing lesion.
- Restart secondary prophylaxis if CD4+ decreases to <200 cells/mm^3

Prophylaxis

Prevention of Exposure
- HIV-infected persons should be tested for IgG antibody to *Toxoplasma* to detect latent infection
- HIV-infected persons who lack IgG antibody to *Toxoplasma* should be advised not to eat raw or undercooked meat, particularly lamb, beef, or pork, which needs to be cooked to an internal temperature of 165–170° F.
- Wash hands after contact with raw meat, after gardening, and after other contact with soil
- Wash fruits and vegetables before eating them raw
- Cat owners should change litter box daily (preferably done by HIV-negative non-pregnant person), and wash hands thoroughly after changing the litter box. Keep the cat indoors, do not adopt or handle stray cats, and feed the cat canned or dried commercial food. If table food is fed, it must be well cooked.

Primary Prophylaxis
- Patients who are seropositive for *Toxoplasma* and have a CD4 count < 100 cells/mm^3 should receive prophylaxis against TE
    - TMP-SMX one DS tablet po qd (preferred)
    - Dapsone: 50 mg po qd + pyrimethamine 50 mg po qweek + leucovorin 25 mg po qweek
    - Dapsone: 200 mg po + pyrimethamine 75 mg po + leucovorin 25 mg po qweek
    - Atovaquone: 1500 mg po qd ± pyrimethamine 25 mg po qd plus leucovorin 10 mg po qd
- Primary prophylaxis should be discontinued in patients who responded to HAART with an increase in CD4 count to > 200 cells/mm^3 for at least 3 months. Prophylaxis should be reintroduced if the CD4 count decreases to < 100-200 cells/ mm^3

Secondary Prophylaxis or Chronic Maintenance Therapy
- Patients should receive lifelong suppressive therapy (as above) after completing initial therapy for TE unless immune reconstitution occurs as a consequence of HAART.
- Suppressive therapy may be discontinued in patients who after completion of initial therapy for TE remain without signs or symptoms of TE, and have sustained increase in the CD4 count > 200 cells/ mm^3 for more than six months following HAART. Some authors will recommend imaging studies prior to discontinuation of chronic maintenance therapy. This should be reintroduced if the CD4 count decreases to < 200 cells/mm^3.

Special Considerations During Pregnancy
- Treatment is same as nonpregnant adult
- Pyrimethamine has been associated with birth defects in animals, but not to date in humans
- Pediatric providers should be notified if sulfadiazine is continued until delivery for risk of neonatal hyperbilirubinemia and kernicterus
- Risk of transmission to fetus for chronic maternal infection is low.
- Case reports of fetal infection have occurred with reactivation of chronic infection
- US examination of the fetus evaluating for hydrocephalus, cerebral calcifications and growth restriction is recommended for women with primary or symptomatic reactivation of toxo during therapy.

References

1. Israelski DM, Remington JS. AIDS-Associated toxoplasmosis. In: Sande ME, Volberding PA, eds. *The Medical Management of AIDS*. Philadelphia:W.B. Saunders, 1992;319–345.
2. Katlama C. *Toxoplasma gondii* infection in AIDS. In: Crowe S, Holy J, Mills J, eds. *Management of the HIV-Infected Patient*. New York: Cambridge University Press, 1996:318–325.
3. Gomez DaRosa I. *Toxoplasmosis*. In: Steinhart C, Orrick JJ, Simpson K, eds. *HIV/AIDS Primary Care Guide*. University of Florida, Gainesville, FL. 2002:147–149.
4. Chaisson RE, Bishai W. The management of *pneumocystis carinii*, toxoplasmosis, and HSV infections in patients with HIV disease. Clinical Update, July 16, 1999. Available at: www.medscape.com/viewprogram/666. Accessed April 25, 2003
5. 2001 USPHS/IDSA guidelines for the prevention of opportunistic infections in persons infected with human immunodeficiency virus. *MMWR* November 28, 2001:13–15.
6. Suzuki Y. Immunopathogenesis of cerebral toxoplasmosis. *J of Infect Dis* December 1, 2002;186:S234–240.
7. Willis MS, Southern P, Latimer MJ. Toxoplasma infection: Making the best use of laboratory tests. *Infect Med* 2002;19(11):522–532.
8. Montoya JG, Remington JS. *Toxoplasma gondii*. In: Mandell GL, Douglas R, Bennet JE, eds. *Principles and Practice of Infectious Diseases*. New York: Churchill Livingstone; 2000;2858–2881.
9. Richards FO Jr, Kovacs JA, Luft BJ. Preventing toxoplasmic encephalitis in persons infected with human immunodeficiency virus. *Clin Infect Dis* 1995; 21(suppl 1):S49–S56.
10. Vasa CV, Tang I, Glatt AE. Prophylaxis of opportunistic infections in the HIV-infected patients in the HAART era. *Infect Med* 19(10): 452–460, 2002.
11. Menendez JA, Lilien DA, Nanda A, Polin RS. Use of fluorodeoxyglucose-positron emission tomography for the differentiation of cerebral lesions in patients with acquired immunodeficiency syndrome. *Neurosurg Focus* 2000; 8(2).
12. Luft BJ, Remington JS: Toxoplasmic encephalitis in AIDS. *Clin Infect Dis*. 1992;15:211–222.
13. Ramsey RG, Gean AD. Neuroimaging of AIDS. I. Central Nervous system toxoplasmosis. *Neuroimag Clin N Am* 1997;7: 171–186.
14. Cohen BA. Neurologic manifestations of toxoplasmosis in AIDS. *Semin Neurol* 1999; 19(2):201–11.
15. Kirk O, Reiss P, Uberti-Foppa C, Bickel M, Gerstoft J, et al. Safe interruption of maintenance therapy with four common HIV-associated opportunistic pathogens during potent antiretroviral therapy (Abstract). *Ann of Intern Med* August 20, 2002; 137:239–250.
16. Montoya JG. Laboratory diagnosis of *toxoplasma gondii* infection and toxoplasmosis. *J of Infect Dis* 2002; 185(Suppl 1):S73–82.
17. Treating opportunistic infections among HIV-infected adults and adolescents, Recommendations from CDC, the National Institutes of Health, and the HIV Medicine Association/Infectious Disease Society of America; *MMWR* December 17, 2004; Vol. 52;No. RR-15.

24

Progressive Multifocal Leukoencephalopathy (PML)

Stephen N. Symes, MD
Assistant Professor, Department of Medicine
Division of Clinical Immunology and Infectious Diseases,
University of Miami School of Medicine
Jeffrey Beal, MD
Clinical Director, Florida/Caribbean AIDS Education and Training Center

Introduction

- Rare demyelinating disease seen exclusively in immunocompromised patients
- Caused by the human polyomavirus, JC virus, named for the patient from whom it was first isolated
- Results from reactivation of latent infection
- Seen in up to 4–5% of patients with HIV infection before the availability of potent antiretroviral therapy.
- Incidence of PML has not decreased significantly with HAART
- PML should be considered in patients with progressive neurologic dysfunction in the absence of fever
- Prognosis before HAART very poor
    - Median survival from diagnosis was 2.6 to 4 months in over 90% of affected patients
    - < 7% of patients had a more protracted course, with spontaneous remissions described usually in patients with higher CD4 counts
- Mortality rate of PML in the era of HAART is 30–50% during the first 3 months. Good prognostic factors:
    - Beginning HAART at PML diagnosis (i.e., patients naïve to ARV therapy)
    - CD4 cell count >100 cells/mm^3

Clinical

- Characteristic presentation of sub-acute onset of focal neurologic deficit, generally without fever or headache
  - Hemiparesis, sensory loss, and visual field defects, as well as ataxia, aphasia, and cranial nerve deficits
- Plaque-like asymmetrical lesions involving cerebral white matter destroy corticospinal and coticobulbar nerve tract
- Cerebellar and brainstem involvement can occur, but spinal cord involvement rare
- Course is generally rapidly progressive over weeks with new deficits and lesions leading to severe dementia, cortical blindness, quadraparesis and coma with vegetative signs
- Immune reconstitution inflammatory syndrome related PML (inflammatory form of PML)
  - Presents shortly after initiation of HAART onset
  - Believed to be an inflammatory form of PML
  - Accounts for up to 18% of cases
  - Usually a favorable outcome
  - Differs from usual PML:
    - Contrast enhancement on neuroimaging studies
    - Presence of mononuclear cells in the lesions on pathologic exam

Radiographic Features

- Abnormalities on CT scan are hypodense, asymmetric white matter lesions without mass effect, that rarely enhance
- MRI is more sensitive than CT scan with lesions appearing as single or multiple large or small bright areas on T2- weighted images, again without edema or contrast enhancement
  - Findings suggestive but not specific and can be seen with lymphoma, HIV dementia
  - MR spectroscopy is under investigation as a diagnostic tool
- Inflammatory forms of PML contrast enhance on neuroimaging

Diagnosis

- Brain biopsy, either open or stereotactic, has been the definitive procedure
  - Characterized by multiple areas of demyelination, oligodendrocytes showing large, deeply staining nuclei with basophilic inclusions, and reactive astrocytosis. Characteristically devoid of lymphoplasmacytic infiltrates
  - Inflammatory forms of PML contain mononuclear cells in the lesions
- Cerebrospinal fluid typically benign, but PCR for JC virus DNA in the CSF is highly specific (92–100%) and fairly sensitive (74–92%) for PML
- Neuro AIDS study in 2000–2002, 35 out of 84 patients (41.7%) presenting with clinical and neuroradiological criteria consistent with PML were JCV DNA PCR negative. This is felt to be due to the less severely immunocompromised state of patients on HAART therapy prior to diagnosis.

Treatment

- Despite isolated reports and small case studies, ACTG 243 study designed primarily to evaluate the efficacy of cytosine arabinoside (Ara-C) showed that the drug administered either IV or intrathecally did not improve the prognosis of patients with PML. (Study was completed before protease inhibitors became widely available)
- Clinical trials using topotecan (a topoisomerase inhibitor with activity against JC virus) revealed the medication to be poorly tolerated-severe anemia, leukopenia, and thrombocytopenia were frequent side effects
- Cidofovir (an antiviral agent with activity against JC virus) appears to have no additional benefit over HAART administration alone in varied clinical trials and case reports to date.
- HAART at present is the most effective treatment for PML resulting in stabilization and reversal of PML lesions in those who respond. The use of ARVs that penetrate the blood brain barrier is a reasonable treatment plan but remains to date unproven in efficacy.

References

1. Albrecht H, Hoffman C, et al. Highly active antiretroviral therapy significantly improves the prognosis of patients with HIV-associated progressive multifocal leukoencephalopathy. *AIDS* 1998;12:1149.

2. Berger J, Kasovitz B, et al. Progressive multifocal leukoencephalopathy associated with human immunodeficiency virus infection. A review of the literature with a report of sixteen cases. *Ann Intern Med* 1987;107:78.

3. Cinque P, Scarpellini P, et al. Diagnosis of central nervous system complications in HIV-infected patients: cerebrospinal fluid analysis by the polymerase chain reaction. *AIDS* 1997;11:1–17.

4. Demeter L. Clinical Manifestations of JC, BK, and Other Polyomavirus Infections. UpToDate Producers. Monograph on CD-ROM. Ver 8.2. Wellesley, June, 2000.

5. Hall C, Dafni U, et al. Failure of cytarabine in progressive multifocal leukoencephalopathy associated with human immunodeficiency virus infection. *NEJM* 1998;338:1345–1380.

6. Hall CD. JC Virus neurologic infection. In: *AIDS Therapy*. Dolin R, Masur H, Saag M, Eds. New York, NY: Churchill Livingstone; 1999; 565–572.

7. Koralnik, Igor J. New insights into progressive multifocal leukoencephalopathy. *Current Opinion in Neurology* 2004;17:365–370.

8. Paola, Cinque, et al. The effect of highly active antiretroviral therapy-induced immune reconstitution on development and outcome of progressive multifocal leukoencephalopathy: Study of 43 cases with review of the literature. *Journal of NeuroVirology* 2003; 9(suppl. 1):73–80,

25

Kaposi's Sarcoma (KS)

Charurut Somboonwit, MD
Senior Physician, Polk County Health Department
Assistant Professor, Infectious Diseases and Tropical Medicine
University of South Florida, Tampa
Lynette J. Menezes, PhD
Director of International Programs and Assistant Professor
Infectious Diseases and International Medicine
University of South Florida, Tampa

Introduction

In 1872, Moriz Kaposi described an unusual skin tumor in five elderly men. Until the HIV/AIDS era, it was a rare tumor found classically in elderly men of Eastern European and Mediterranean origin. In 1981, Kaposi's sarcoma (KS) became one of the first recognized manifestations of AIDS.

In 1994, Chang et al, described its etiologic agent, human herpes virus 8 (HHV-8, also known as KS-associated herpes virus).[1]

Clinical Variants

There are four clinical variants that have identical histologic features, but differ in terms of their epidemiology, sites of involvement, and rates of progression:

CLASSIC

- Classic KS is an indolent cutaneous proliferative disease that mainly affects elderly men of Eastern European or Mediterranean origin.

ENDEMIC

- The endemic form is seen in Africa among both children and adults, especially in sub-Saharan Africa and is not typically related to immune deficiency.

ORGAN TRANSPLANT-ASSOCIATED

- Organ transplant-associated KS occurs in solid organ transplant recipients, particularly among liver transplant recipients.[2]

EPIDEMIC OR AIDS-ASSOCIATED

- Epidemic or AIDS-associated KS is the most common tumor in HIV-infected patients, and is labeled an AIDS-defining illness by the Centers for Disease Control and Prevention (CDC). It is more aggressive than the classic form, and far more common in AIDS patients than in the general population (20,000-fold), and more common than in other immunosuppressed patients (300-fold).[3]

Epidemiology

- KS is generally under reported

- The incidence at diagnosis of AIDS declined from 31% in 1985 to 13% in 1990

- Male to female ratio is 15:1

- Sexual contact is the important route of transmission. The seroprevalence for HHV-8 is higher among men who have sex with men (MSM) than heterosexual drug users, female commercial sex workers, and hemophiliacs.[4,5]

- There is no single sexual behavior identified as the most risky for HHV-8 transmission. However, four factors are associated with higher risk of KS: HIV infection, increasing HHV-8 titer, the presence of HHV-8 viremia and lack of neutralizing antibody.[4,6,7]

Pathogenesis

- HHV-8 is a member of the gamma-herpesviridae subfamily of viruses, which are notable for their ability to transform cells resulting in neoplasia.

  o Other diseases associated with HHV-8 in HIV-infected patients are: primary effusion lymphoma and Multicentric Castleman disease.[8]

- The abnormal proliferation of vascular endothelium is associated with a number of growth factors. HHV-8 is primarily localized to the spindle and endothelial cells of KS lesions and those cells are thought to be neoplastic cells with abnormal proliferation of spindle shape cells, leukocytic infiltration, and neovascularization of aberrant proliferation of small vessels.

o Three histologic features are characteristic of KS: angiogenesis, inflammation, and proliferation.[9, 10, 11]

- Co-infection of HHV-8 and HIV markedly increases the risk of KS. HIV infection may promote HHV-8 replication indirectly by impairing host immunity. There is evidence that HAART can lead to regression of KS lesions.[12,13] Moreover, HIV may have a direct role in tumorigenesis through cytokine production. The exact mechanism of how HHV-8 induces KS remains unclear.

Clinical Manifestation

The clinical course of KS ranges from minimal disease to severe disease

CUTANEOUS KS

- Skin involvement is usually painless, non-pruritic, variable in size and shape. Color may vary by vascularity from erythematous, violaceous to brown. Occasionally, a yellow perilesional halo may be seen. The lesions are most often on lower extremities, face (especially nose), oral mucosa, and genitalia. Lymphadema may be present.

ORAL CAVITY KS

- Occurs in about one third of patients with KS. These lesions can be easily traumatized causing pain, bleeding, ulceration, and secondary infection. Occasionally, they can impair speech and the patient's nutritional status.

GASTROINTESTINAL KS

- Occurs in about 40% of KS patients at diagnosis, but the number doubles when autopsied. This form of KS can present with or without cutaneous manifestation. Presentations range from asymptomatic, weight loss, abdominal pain, nausea/vomiting, diarrhea, bleeding, malabsorption, or obstruction. Lesions may be limited to the mucosa, and may be invasive or disseminated.[14]

PULMONARY KS

- Patients may present with cough, shortness of breath, fever, hemoptysis, or chest pain. Radiographic findings vary from normal to non specific findings including interstitial/alveolar infiltration, nodules, effusion, and adenopathy. Presumptive diagnosis may be made by bronchoscopic findings showing cherry-red raised lesions.[15,16]

OTHER ORGAN INVOLVEMENT

Other possible organ involvement includes lymph nodes, liver, pancreas, heart, testes, and bone marrow.[17]

Diagnosis

Presumptive diagnosis of KS can be made clinically. Confirmed diagnosis should be made whenever possible by biopsy of the lesion.

The most important differential diagnosis of KS is bacillary angiomatosis. It should be considered especially in patients with systemic symptoms or rapidly progressing lesions. Biopsy of bacillary angiomatosis lesions can mimic KS by neovascularization, but Bartonella sp. can be identified by using Warthin-Starry silver stain.[18]

STAGING

- The most utilized staging system for AIDS-related KS is the one by the AIDS Clinical Trial Group (ACTG) (see Table 1). This system categorized patients into good or poor prognosis by using these parameters: Extent of tumor (T), Immune status (I), and severity of systemic illness (S).[18]

Table 1. ACTG Staging Classification for AIDS-related KS

	Good risk (0) — all of the following	Poor risk (1) —any of the following
Tumor-T	T0 - confined to the skin and/or lymph node and/or minimal oral disease (non nodular disease confined to the palate)	T1- Tumor associated edema or ulceration, extensive oral KS, Gastrointestinal KS, KS in other non-nodal viscera
Immune system-I	I0-CD4 $\geq$ 200 cells/mm^3	I1-CD4 < 200 cells/mm^3
Systemic illness-S	S0- no history of opportunistic infection(OI), thrush or B symptoms*, Karnofsky performance status $\geq$ 70	S1-History of OI, and/or thrush, B symptoms, Karnofsky performance status < 70. Other AIDS related illness(i.e., lymphoma, neurological disease)

*B symptoms are unexplained fever, night sweats, and more than 10% involuntary weight loss, and persistent diarrhea more than 2 weeks.

Treatment

HAART

- HAART is an important component in the treatment of KS and should be administered as soon as possible to maximize virologic response.

- Although there is no known curative treatment for KS, the major goals of treatment are palliation of symptoms — size reduction, decreased edema, minimized effect on organ function, reduce psychological stigma, and prevention of disease progression.

- HAART with or without direct treatment of KS still plays the major role in the management of KS.

- Previous studies of KS patients on HAART without direct KS treatment show no progression of KS lesions and a reduction of HHV-8 viremia.[8,19]

HAART AND LOCALIZED TREATMENT

Patients with slowly progressing minimal disease (e.g., patients with < 25 cutaneous lesions), are best treated by HAART and localized treatment. The goal of localized treatment is cosmetic.

- Alitretinoin (9-cis retinoic acid, Parentin® gel) is the only topical, self-administered treatment for KS. Most patients require at least 4 to 8 weeks of therapy before seeing any response. Skin irritation is a common side effect.[20]

- Intralesional vinblastine helps lesions to regress, although lesions usually do not resolve completely. Multiple injections may be required when larger lesions are present.[21]

- Radiation therapy palliates symptomatic disease that is too extensive to be treated with intralesional chemotherapy. The response in AIDS-related KS is not as durable as in classic KS.[22]

CHEMOTHERAPY

Chemotherapy is generally accepted as the recommended treatment in patients with widespread skin disease (> 25 lesions), extensive cutaneous disease not responsive to local treatment, extensive edema, and symptomatic internal organ involvement.

- Liposomal anthracyclines - pegylated liposomal doxorubicin and liposomal daunorubicin are the two recently approved liposomal anthracyclines that serve as the first line of systemic treatment for KS. They are at least as effective as conventional chemotherapy including bleomycin and vincristine. Moreover, they have better toxicity profiles; in particular, the liposomal formulation decreases cardiotoxicity and allows more cumulative doses in each patient. Their side effects are generally mild.[23, 24, 25]

- Pacitaxel (Taxol®) is the newest chemotherapeutic agent for KS and serves as a second line agent. It has more toxicities than liposomal anthracyclines. Toxicities include thrombocytopenia, neutropenia, and hypersensitivity reaction. Pacitaxel is metabolized through the cytochrome P450 enzyme system and may interact with agents that affect these enzymes. Although no dosage adjustment recommendations can be made, caution should be used especially when co-administered with protease inhibitors.[26]

POTENTIAL FUTURE DEVELOPMENTS IN THERAPY

- Interferon-alfa is a biologic agent that reduces progression in about a third of the patients with AIDS-related KS, though it is more commonly used in patients with skin ailments.

- Angiogenesis inhibitors such as thalidomide and human chorionic gonadotropin (HCG).

- Imatinib, a tyrosine kinase inhibitor traditionally used in patients with chronic myelogeous leukemia, has shown to have promise in treating AIDS-related KS.[27]

Prevention

Currently, HAART with restoration of the immune response is the best tool to both prevent KS in HIV patients and to reduce progression to severe KS disease. Effective antiviral chemotherapy directed against HHV-8 is not yet available.

References

1. Chang Y, Cesarman E, Pessin M, et al. Identification of herpesvirus like DNA sequences in AIDS-associated Kaposi's sarcoma. *Science* 1994; 266:1865.
2. Farge D. Kaposi's sarcoma in organ transplant recipients. *Eur J Med* 1993; 2:339.
3. Beral V, Peterman TA, Berkelman RL, et al. KS among persons with AIDS: A sexually transmitted infection? *Lancet* 1990; 335:123.
4. Martin JN, Ganem DE, Osmond DH, Page-Shafer KA, Macrae D, Kedes DH. Sexually transmission and the natural history of human herpesvirus 8 infection. *NEJM* 1998; 338:948.
5. Cannon MJ, Dollard SC, Smitrh DK, et al. Blood-borne and sexual transmission of human herpesvirus 8 in woman with or at risk of human immunodeficiency virus infection. *NEJM* 2001; 344:637.
6. Rezza G, Andreoni M, Dorrucci M, et al. Human herpesvirus 8 seropositivity and risk of Kaposi's sarcoma and other acquired immunodeficiency syndrome related diseases. *J Natl Cancer Inst* 1999; 91:1468.
7. Sitas F, Carrara H, Beral V, et al. Antibodies against human herpesvirus 8 in black south African patients with cancer. *NEJM* 1999; 340:1863.
8. Cannon MJ, Laney AS, Pellett PE. Human herpes virus 8: Current issues. *Clin Infect Dis* 2004; 37:82.
9. Boshoff C, Schulz TF, Kennedy MM, et al. Kaposi's sarcoma-associated herpesvirus infects endothelial and spindle cells. *Nat Med* 1995; 1:1274.
10. Li JJ, Huang YQ, Cockerell CJ, et al. Localization of human herpes-like virus type 8 in vascular endothelial cells and perivascular spindle-shaped cells of Kaposi's sarcoma lesions by in situ hybridization. *Am J Pathol* 1996; 1:1741.
11. Stakus KA, Zhoung W, Gebhard K, et al. Kaposi's sarcoma associated herpesvirus gene expression in endothelial tumor cells. *J Virol* 1997; 71:715.
12. Mendez JC, Paya CV. Kaposi's sarcoma and transplantation. *Herpes* 2000; 7:18.
13. Denzig JB, Brandt LJ, Reinus JF, et al. Gastrointestinal malignancies in patients with AIDS. *Am J Gastroenterol* 1991; 86:715.
14. Gill PS, Akil B, Colletti P, et al. Kaposi's sarcoma: Clinical findings and result of therapy. *Am J Med* 1989; 87:57.
15. Roux FJ, Bancal C, Dombret MC, et al. Pulmonary Kaposi's sarcoma revealed by a solitary nodule in a patient with acquired immunodeficiency syndrome. *Am J Respir Crit Care Med* 1994; 149:1041.
16. Ioachim HL, Adsey V, Giancitti FR, et al. Kaposi sarcoma of internal organs: a multiparameter study of 86 cases. *Cancer* 1995; 75:1376.
17. Koehler JE, Sanchez MA, Garrido CS, et al. Molecular epidemiology of Bartonella infections in patients with bacillary angiomatosis-peliosis. *NEJM* 1997; 337:1876.
18. Krown SE. Testa MA, Huang J. AIDS-related KS: prospective validation of the AIDS clinical trial group staging classification. *J Clin Oncol* 1997; 15:3085.
19. Antman K, Chang Y. Kaposi's sarcoma. *NEJM* 2000; 342:1027.

20. Walmsley S, Northflet DW, Molesky B, et al. Treatment of AIDS-related cutaneous Kaposi's sarcoma with topical alitetinoin gel. *J Acquir Immune Defic Syndr* 1999; 22:235.
21. Epstein JB. Treatment of oral Kaposi's sarcoma with intralesional vinblastine. *Cancer* 1993; 71:1722.
22. Swift PS. The role of radiation therapy in the management of HIV related Kaposi's sarcoma. *Hematol Oncol Clin North Am* 1996; 22:286.
23. Northfelt DW, Dezube BJ, Thommes JA, et al. Pegylated-liposomal doxorubicin versus doxorubicin, bleomycin and vincristine in the treatment of AIDS related Kaposi's sarcoma. *J Clin Oncol* 1998; 16:2445.
24. Stewart S, Jaablonowski H, Goebel FD, et al. Randomize comparative trial of pegylated liposomal doxorubicin and vincristine in the treatment of AIDS related Kaposi's sarcoma. *J Clin Oncol*.1998; 16:683.
25. Marie Young A, Dhillon BJ, Bower M. Cardiotoxicity after liposomal anthracycline. *Lancet Oncol* 1997; 15:653.
26. Schwartz JD, Howard W, Scadden, DT. Potential interaction of antiretroviral therapy with pacitaxel in patients with AIDS related Kaposi's sarcoma. *AIDS* 1999; 13:283
27. Koon HB, Bubley GJ, Pantanowitz L, et al. Imatinib-induced regression of AIDS related Kaposi's sarcoma. *J Clin Oncol* 2005; 23:982.

26

AIDS-Related Lymphoma (ARL)

Igor Melnychuk, MD
Fellow, Division of Infectious Disease and Tropical Medicine
University of South Florida, Tampa
Manuel Guerra, MD
Senior Attending Physician, Division of Hematology/Oncology
Department of Medicine, Mercy Hospital, Miami

Epidemiology

- In 1984, Non-Hodgkin's Lymphoma (NHL) was described as one of the diseases with increased incidence/risk in the AIDS population
- AIDS-related lymphoma (ARL) represents the second most frequent cancer associated with AIDS after Kaposi's sarcoma
- Lymphoma is a late manifestation of HIV disease
    - Serves as an initial AIDS-defining condition in almost 16% of patients
    - Majority of patients have relatively low CD4+ cell counts (less than 200 cells/mm3)
- ARL is more common in men than in women
- All age groups are affected, and lymphoma is the most common malignancy in HIV-infected children
- May see increased incidence with patients' life expectancy increasing in era of HAART

Pathology

- ARL consists almost exclusively of B-cell tumors that are characterized by extreme clinical aggressiveness
- Diffuse large cell lymphomas (large non-cleaved cell lymphoma, immunoblastic plasmacytoid lymphoma, CD-30-positive anaplastic large B cell lymphoma)
- Small non-cleaved (either Burkitt's or Burkitt's like)
- Histological overlap is common in systemic AIDS-NHL
- The HIV-associated lymphomas can be categorized into:
    — Primary central nervous system lymphoma (PCNSL)
    — Systemic lymphoma

— Primary effusion lymphoma (PEL), formerly called body cavity lymphoma

— Plasmablastic lymphoma of the oral cavity

- PCNSL represents 20% of all NHL cases in AIDS patients and is the second most frequent CNS mass lesion seen in adults with AIDS
- PCNSL has been reported to have a 100% association with Epstein-Barr virus (EBV) while systemic ARL has 30–50% association with EBV
- PEL has been associated with co-infection with Human Herpes Virus Type-8 (HHV-8)

Clinical Presentation

SYSTEMIC LYMPHOMA

- Aggressive lymphoma that is frequently extranodal and usually seen in advanced stage disease
- Vast majority of patients with systemic lymphoma (82%) present with B-type symptoms (fever, night sweats and weight loss more then 10% of basal body weight) that may mimic other infections, such as MAC, CMV, TB, cryptococcosis etc.
- Lymphadenopathy should be differentiated from reactive lymphadenopathy seen with HIV infection
  — Reactive splenomegaly may be seen in 6% of HIV-infected patients with reactive lymphadenopathy
- Most common sites of AIDS-NHL are CNS, gastrointestinal tract, bone marrow, and liver
  — Bone marrow
    - Approximately 20% of patients with ARL have associated cytopenia and occasional bone pain
  — Gastrointestinal tract
    - Occurs in 4–28% of patients with lymphoma and presents with abdominal pain, anorexia, nausea, vomiting or changes in bowel movements
    - Abdominal distention or an abdominal mass may be noted
    - Stomach and small intestine are the sites most frequently involved
    - Involvement of the rectum and/or perianal regions are not uncommon
  — Oral cavity
    - ARL may be present in the oral cavity, with involvement of the maxilla, mandible, or gums
  — Skin or subcutaneous areas
    - May present with nodules or large mass lesions
  — Lung
    - May present with SOB, and/or hemoptysis, with radiological findings of pleural effusion, mass lesions or other parenchymal abnormalities
  — Liver involvement
    - Seen in 9–26% of ARL

PRIMARY CNS LYMPHOMA

- Patients with PCNSL usually do not have lymphoma outside of CNS
- Lower median CD4+ cell count (usually < 50 cells/mm$^{3)}$ and a worse survival time (2.5 mo to 6 mo) without therapy

- Its incidence in HIV-infected individuals is 1000-fold higher then in general population even though it decreased after introduction of highly active antiretroviral therapy (HAART)
- Patients may present with headaches, seizures, focal neurological deficits, altered mental status, and changes in behavior
- Correct diagnosis is a challenge as clinical and radiological presentation of cerebral toxoplasmosis and primary CNS lymphoma may be indistinguishable
- Early brain biopsy (done within a week) is recommended, especially if the patient has negative toxoplasmosa serology

PRIMARY EFFUSION LYMPHOMA (former Body Cavity Lymphoma)

- Rare and accounts for 5% of all AIDS-NHL
- Displays peculiar tropism of the serous body cavities and grows in the ascitic fluid, pleural and pericardial effusions
- Infection of the tumor clone by HHV-8 is universal. Frequent coinfection with EBV.
- Survival is 2 to 6 months, even with chemotherapy
- Occasionally, complete remission is seen with HAART

Diagnostic Evaluation

Laboratory

- *CBC* – To differentiate possible bone marrow involvement versus HIV itself
- *LDH* – High levels associated with more aggressive disease
- *Elevated alkaline phosphatase* – usually associated with liver involvement
- *Elevated uric acid* has been associated with high-grade lymphoma
- *CSF EBV PCR* — may be helpful in diagnosing primary CNS lymphoma
- *Serum Toxoplasma IgG and Cryptococcal Ag* — are used in differentiating cerebral toxoplasmosis and cryptococcal meningitis from PCNS lymphoma

CT scan

- Should be routinely performed for proper staging of systemic lymphoma

Gallium scan

- Assists in possible differentiation of ARL from reactive lymphadenopathy

Fluorodeoxyglucose positron emission topography (FDG-PET)

- Initial studies demonstrated markedly improved specificity in comparison to CT scanning
- Has already proven useful in differentiating lymphoma from other pathologic processes of the brain in patients with AIDS

MRI of the brain with gadolinium

- Useful in differentiating lymphoma from progressive multifocal leukoencephalopathy (PML)

Thallium SPECT scanning

- Useful in helping to differentiate primary AIDS-CNS lymphoma from toxoplasmosis

- Negative thallium SPECT scan along with negative CSF EBV PCR makes diagnosis of PCNSL unlikely

Diagnostic Procedures

Excisional biopsy is the gold standard

Bone marrow biopsy

- Must be performed in all patients with ARL
- Helpful in staging, determines bone marrow reserves when considering treatment plans involving chemotherapy

Lumbar puncture

- Should be performed routinely in all ARL patients
- Able to detect up to 23% of patients with malignant cells in the CSF
- Flow cytometry immunophenotyping is 25% more sensitive in detecting malignant cells of PCNSL than conventional cytomorphological methods
- Evaluation of EBV DNA is useful as its presence is seen in 100% of AIDS-PCNSL. (Yet positive CSF PCR for EBV is not diagnostic of PCNSL)

Prognostic Factors for Survival

Several factors are associated with shorter survival in patients with ARL

- CD4+ cell count < 100 cells/mm^3
- Elevated LDH levels
- Stage III or IV disease
- Age > 35 years
- Poor performance status
- Primary CNS lymphoma
- History of prior AIDS-defining condition
- History of intravenous drug use

Use of HAART is associated with longer survival in patients with ARL

Treatment (Non-CNS NHL)

- Systemic chemotherapy indicated
- Standard dose CHOP (cyclophosphamide, doxorubicin, vincristine, and prednisone) or dose adjusted EPOCH (etoposide, prednisolone, vincristine, cyclophosphamide, and doxorubicin) are most frequently used regimens
- Rituximab with cyclophosphamide, doxorubicin and etoposide is an effective regimen, yet associated with increased mortality from infections
- Toxicities from HAART and chemotherapy are largely the same as the ones with chemotherapy alone
- It is generally recommended that zidovudine not be used during chemotherapy as there is potential for significant anemia

- Withholding HAART while undergoing chemotherapy may result in increased mortality from opportunistic infections
- HAART independently improves survival in ARL
- Attainment of virologic control is not mandatory for achievement of complete response to chemotherapy
- Relapsed/refractory AIDS lymphoma
- Around half of all patients with HIV-NHL need second-line chemotherapy as a result of progression or relapse of their lymphoma
- Cisplatin-based salvage regimens were associated with improved results in one study
- High-dose chemotherapy and peripheral stem cell rescue has shown promising results as salvage therapy

Treatment (CNS-NHL)

- Initiation of HAART is strongly recommended
- High dose methotrexate with leucovorin rescue and concomitant HAART is the mainstay of treatment. The overall median survival is 10 months.
- Radiation therapy is reserved for patients with refractory or recurrent disease
- Radiation therapy or combined-modality therapy (conventional chemotherapy and radiotherapy) result in short survival time (2 to 5 months)
- Combination of zidovudine, ganciclovir, and interleukin-2 has been demonstrated to be efficacious in one small study

References

1. Aboulafia DM, Pantanowitz L, Dezube BJ, et al. AIDS-related non-Hodgkin lymphoma: still a problem in the era of HAART. *AIDS Read* 2004; Nov; 14(11):605–617.
2. Baumgartner JE, Rachlin JR, et al. Primary central nervous system lymphoma: natural history and response to radiation therapy in 55 patients with AIDS. *J Neurosurg* 1990; 73:206–211.
3. Beral V, Peterman T, et al. AIDS-associated non-Hodgkin Lymphoma. *Lancet* 1991; 337:805–809.
4. Cohen J, Powderly WG. *Infectious Diseases.* Vol 2, 2nd ed. Philadelphia: Elsevier Inc. Mosby, 2004:1314–1317.
5. Fine HA, Mayer RJ. Primary central nervous lymphoma. *Ann of Int Med* 1993; 119(11):1093–1104.
6. Gabarre J, Marcelin AG, Azar N, Choquet S, Levy Y, Tubiana R, Charlotte F, Norol F, Calvez V, Spina M, Vernant JP, Autran B, Leblond V, et al. High-dose therapy plus autologous hematopoietic stem cell transplantation for human immunodeficiency virus (HIV)-related lymphoma: results and impact on HIV disease. *Haematologica* 2004; Sep; 89(9):1100–1108.
7. Gaidano G, Carbone A. Pathogenesis of AIDS-related lymphomas: Molecular and histogenetic heterogeneity. *Am J Pathol* 1998; 152:623–630.
8. Gallardo FG, Moreno V, Babe J, Cobo J, Rios M, Gomez MV, et al. Brain SPECT with 201-thallium in AIDS patients. *Rev Esp Med Nucl* 2001; Oct; 20(6):439–442.
9. Hartge P, Devesa SS, et al. Hodgkin's and non-Hodgkin's lymphoma. *Cancer Surv* 1994; 20:423–453.
10. Hoffman C, Wolf E, Fatkenheuer G, Buhk T, Stoehr A, Plettenberg A, Stellbrink HJ, Jaeger H, Siebert U, Horst HA, et al. Response to highly active antiretroviral therapy strongly predicts outcome in patients with AIDS-related lymphoma. *AIDS* 2003; Jul 4; 17(10):1521–1529.
11. Ivers LC, Kim AY, Sax PE, et al. Predictive value of polymerase chain reaction of cerebrospinal fluid for detection of Epstein-Barr virus to establish the diagnosis of HIV-related primary central nervous system lymphoma. *Clin Infect Dis.* 2004; Nov 1; 39(9):1396–1397; author reply 1397–1398.

12. Levine AM, AIDS-related lymphoma. *Blood* 1992; 80:8–20.

13. Lim ST, Levine AM, et al. Recent advances in acquired immunodeficiency syndrome (AIDS)-related lymphoma. *Cancer J Clin* 2005; 55:229–241.

14. Little RF, Pittaluga S, Grant N, et al. Highly effective treatment of acquired immunodeficiency syndrome-related lymphoma with dose-adjusted EPOCH: impact of antiretroviral therapy suspension and tumor biology. *Blood* 2003; 12: 4653–4659.

15. Mandell GL, Bennett JE, Dolin R. *Mandell, Douglas, and Bennett's Principles and Practice of Infectious Disease.* Vol 1, 6th ed. Philadelphia; Elsevier Inc. 2005;1604–1609.

16. Molina A, Zaia J, Krishnan A, et al. Treatment of human immunodeficiency virus-related lymphoma with haematopoietic stem cell transplantation. *Blood Rev* 2003; Dec; 17(4):249–258.

17. Newell ME, Hoy JF, Cooper SG, DeGraaff B, Grulich AE, Bryant M, Millar JL, Brew BJ, Quinn DI, et al. Human immunodeficiency virus-related primary central nervous system lymphoma: factors influencing survival in 111 patients. *Cancer* 2004; Jun 15; 100(12):2627–2636.

18. Noy A, et al. Update in HIV-associated lymphoma. *Curr Opin Onco.* 2004; Sep; 16(5):450–454.

19. Oksenhendler E, Clauvel JP, Jouveshomme S. Complete remission of a primary effusion lymphoma with antiretroviral therapy. *Am J Hemato.* 1998; 3:266.

20. Re A, Cattaneo C, Michieli M, Casari S, Spina M, Rupolo M, Allione B, Nosari A, Schiantarelli C, Vigano M, Izzi I, Ferremi P, Lanfranchi A, Mazzucato M, Carosi G Tirelli U, Rossi G, et al. High-dose therapy and autologous peripheral-blood stem-cell transplantation as salvage treatment for HIV-associated lymphoma in patients receiving highly active antiretroviral therapy. *J Clin Oncol* 2003; Dec 1; 21(23):4423–4427. [Epub2003 Oct 27]

21. Serrano D, Carrion R, Balsalobre P, Miralles P, Berenguer J, Buno I, Gomez-Pineda A, Ribera JM, Conde E, Diez-Martin JL, et al. HIV-associated lymphoma successfully treated with peripheral blood stem cell transplantation. *Exp Hematol* 2005. Apr; 33(4):487–494.

22. Skiest DJ, Crosby C, et al. Survival is prolonged by highly active antiretroviral therapy in AIDS patients with primary central nervous system lymphoma. *AIDS* 2003; Aug 15; 17(12):1787–1793.

23. Spina M, Jaeger U, Sparano JA, Talamini R, Simonelli C, Michieli M, Rossi G, Nigra E, Berretta M, Cattaneo C, Rieger AC, Vaccher E, Tirelli U, et al. Rituzimab plus infusional cyclophosphamide doxorubicin, and etoposide in HIV-associated non-Hodgkin lymphoma: Pooled results from 3 phase 2 trials. *Blood* 2005; Mar 1; 105(5):1891–1897. [Epub 2004, Nov 18]

24. Spina M, Tirelli U, et al. HIV-related non-Hodgkin's lymphoma (HIV-NHL) in the era of highly active antiretroviral therapy (HAART): Some still unanswered questions for clinical management. *Ann Oncol* 2004; July; 15(7): 993–995.

25. Srinivasan S, Takeshita K, Holkova B, Czuczman MS, Miller K, Bernstein ZP, Driscoll D, Chanan-Khan A, et al. Clinical characteristics of gastrointestinal lymphomas associated with AIDS (GI-ARL) and the impact of HAART. *HIV Clin Trials* 2004; May–Jun; 5(3):140–145.

26. Stebbing J, Marvin V, Bower M, et al. The evidence-based treatment of AIDS-related non-Hodgkin's lymphoma. *Cancer Treat Rev* 2004; May; 30(3):249–253.

27. Straus DJ, et al. HIV-associated lymphoma: promising new results, but with toxicity. *Blood.* 2005;Mar 1;105(5):1842.

28. Subira D, Gorgolas M, Castanon S, Serrano C, Roman A, Rivs F, Tomas JF et al. Advantages of flow cytometry immunophenotyping for the diagnosis of central nervous system non-Hodgkin's lymphoma in AIDS patients. *HIV Med* 2005; Jan;6(1):21–26.

29. Vaccher E, Spina M, di Gennaro G, et al. Concomitant CHOP chemotherapy and highly active antiretroviral therapy (HAART) in patients with HIV-related non-Hodgkin's lymphoma. *Cancer* 2001; 91:155–163.

30. Wolf T, Brodt HR, Fichtlscherer S, Mantzsch K, Hoelzer D, Helm EB, Mitrou PS, Chow KU, et al. Changing incidence and prognostic factors of survival in AIDS-related non-Hodgkin's lymphoma in the era of highly active antiretroviral therapy (HAART). *Leukemia and Lymphoma* 2005; Feb; 46(2):207–215.

31. Yarchoan R, Tosato G, Little RF, et al. Therapy insight: AIDS-related malignancies—the influence of antiviral therapy on pathogenesis and management. *Nat Clin Pract Oncol* 2005; Aug; 2(8):406–415; quiz 423.

32. Ziegler JL, Beckstead JA, et al. NHL in 90 homosexual men: Relation to generalized lymphadenopathy and the acquired immunodeficiency syndrome. *NEJM* 1984; 311(9):565–570.

27

Identifying and Treating Depression, Anxiety, and Dementia

Charles F. Clark, MD, MPH
Clinical Associate Professor
Michael G. Dow, PhD
Professor
Michael D. Knox, PhD
Distinguished University Professor
Department of Mental Health Law and Policy
Louis de la Parte Florida Mental Health Institute
University of South Florida, Tampa

Introduction

HIV-infected individuals frequently experience mental health symptoms requiring special focus and attention. This chapter will clarify the relationships among HIV disease and mental health conditions and will describe pharmacological treatment approaches. The three mental health conditions that will be discussed are depression, anxiety, and control of behavior in dementia.

Identifying Depression/Anxiety Symptoms

Although diagnostic criteria for depression and anxiety have been well operationalized in the current *Diagnostic and Statistical Manual of Mental Disorders* (*DSM-IV-TR*), many of these symptoms may be overlooked since some of these same symptoms are associated with HIV disease.

Table 1. Overlap of Depression Symptoms with HIV Disease Symptoms
Differential Diagnosis

SYMPTOM	PRIMARILY ASSOCIATED WITH DEPRESSION	ASSOCIATED WITH BOTH CONDITIONS
Weight loss		X
Decreased appetite		X
Somatic concerns		X
Tiredness or lethargy		X
Insomnia		X
Memory problems		X (only later stage of HIV)
Concentration problems		X (only later stage of HIV)
Irritability	X	(some in later stage of HIV)
Decreased interest or pleasure	X	(some in later stage of HIV)
Depressed mood, sadness	X	
Weight gain	X	
Hypersomnia	X	
Social withdrawal	X	
Guilt	X	
Hopelessness	X	
Suicidal ideation or behavior	X	

Table 2. Overlap of Anxiety Symptoms with HIV Symptoms — Differential Diagnosis

SYMPTOM	PRIMARILY ASSOCIATED WITH ANXIETY	ASSOCIATED WITH BOTH CONDITIONS
Sweating		X
Insomnia		X
Nausea or abdominal distress		X
Hot flushes		X
Chills	X	
Dizziness or light-headed feeling	X	
Fear	X	
Vigilance	X	
Chest pain	X	
Increased heart rate	X	
Social avoidance	X	
Panic attacks	X	

Differentiating Dementia and Pseudo-Dementia

HIV-related dementia is a very common occurrence, especially in the later stages of HIV infection (see the section on Neurological Complications in Chapter 13). However, it is well known that severe depression and anxiety can reduce cognitive performance and may produce a clinical presentation that is sometimes called "pseudo-dementia." Both neurological and neuropsychological assessment methods can be very helpful in differentiating the functional versus organic limitations that are present in these conditions. Absent such information, or when the results of these assessments are equivocal, there are a number of clinical indicators that may be helpful to logically determine which condition is more likely. Table 3 provides some of these guidelines.

Table 3. Differentiating Dementia and Pseudo-Dementia

COGNITIVE DEFICITS	PRIMARILY ASSOCIATED WITH DEPRESSION/ANXIETY (PSEUDO-DEMENTIA)	PRIMARILY ASSOCIATED WITH DEMENTIA	USUALLY ASSOCIATED WITH BOTH CONDITIONS
Gradual onset		X	
Sudden onset	X		
Improvement with treatment	X		
Aware of and acknowledges deficits	X		
Focused (narrow and specific) deficits		X	
Widespread attention and concentration deficits	X		
Memory difficulty			X
Type of deficit or severity of deficit varies from day to day	X		

General Considerations for Pharmacological Treatment

Many HIV-infected patients tolerate psychotropic medications poorly, and do best on lower than normal doses. They are much like the elderly in this respect. For this reason, most recommended starting and maximum doses suggested in this chapter are lower than usual. Because these patients are on multiple medications given multiple times a day, adherence is a major issue. Consequently, the normal recommendation is to give each psychotropic medication only once a day or as few times a day as is required by pharmacokinetic considerations. Long-acting forms of medication are also chosen for this reason.

Of particular concern are the *tricyclic antidepressants*. The "tricyclics" are good sedating drugs, may reduce chronic pain, and dampen anxiety in addition to treating depression. Unfortunately, they are strong anti-cholinergic agents and interfere with cognitive functioning even at low doses. Most HIV-infected patients with depression cannot tolerate effective antidepressant doses, with the possible exception of nortriptyline.

MAO Inhibitors are not recommended for the treatment of any condition. They interact dangerously with many drugs and foods. HIV-infected patients should not have their lives further complicated by complex dietary restrictions that must be rigidly followed.

Depression is best treated with Selective Serotonin Reuptake Inhibitors (SSRIs), as they are safe, have milder and fewer side effects than tricyclics, act as rapidly as the tricyclics, and are given once a day. However, they do not assist sleep. Serotonin/Norepinephrine Reuptake Inhibitors (SNRIs) are frequently used if the SSRI fails or if chronic pain is a simultaneous problem.

For a depressed person with sleep difficulties, which is frequently the case, Remeron may be used by itself or in combination with an SSRI. Trazodone (Desyrel®) is very sedating in low to moderate doses and is probably the most commonly used non-benzodiazepine for sleep. Low doses of tricyclics have a similar effect. Benzodiazepines and their newer relatives zolpidem (Ambien®) and zaleplon (Sonata®) are effective, but habituating. They decrease social control much like alcohol and may make drug abuse worse. Cognitive and behavior therapy techniques can be helpful as an adjunct to medication (increasing activity, cognitive restructuring, identifying and refuting negative beliefs and attributions, etc.).

Anxiety in these patients is difficult to treat both effectively and safely. All of the benzodiazepines can relieve anxiety within one hour. However, they are quickly habituating and withdrawal is difficult. Often, when treating persons with a history of drug or alcohol addiction, obtaining the benzodiazepine becomes the primary focus of the patient-physician encounter. There is no perfect solution for this problem. Buspirone (BuSpar®) is effective in only a modest percentage of patients and is generally rejected by those who have previously taken benzodiazepines. Behavioral techniques may be helpful for some patients (relaxation, cognitive restructuring, temporal or environmental control of worry, etc.).

Anxiety can also be effectively treated with SSRIs in doses similar to the treatment of depression. However, as with their use in treating depression, the SSRIs require 2 to 6 weeks to begin to have an effect on anxiety, and may take months to achieve acceptable target symptom control. Ideally, one should give benzodiazepines in as low a dose as possible to provide initial relief while gradually working up to an effective dose of the SSRI. The benzodiazepine should then be tapered and stopped. Unfortunately, many patients do not take the SSRI regularly and resist stopping the benzodiazepine.

As cognitive functioning declines with the onset of dementia, medication to control unacceptable or dangerous behavior improves the lives of the caregivers as well as the patients. Major tranquilizers in low doses have been widely used for this purpose. The newer "atypical" agents have become the standard of care. Chlorpromazine (Thorazine®), thioridazine (Mellaril®), and similar older agents interfere with cognition due to their strong anti-cholinergic effects while haloperidol (Haldol®) may cause intolerable restlessness or movement disorders. The "atypicals" olanzapine (Zyprexa®), risperidone (Risperdal®), ziprasidone (Geodon®), and quetiapine (Seroquel®) are equally good at controlling target symptoms, have fewer and less severe side effects and rarely cause movement disorders.

Many HIV-infected patients acquired their infection secondary to their involvement with drug addiction. Many patients will continue to use alcohol, cocaine, methamphetamine, heroin, cannabis, and/or a variety of sedatives. All of the medications recommended in Table 4 can be used in the presence of these substances with relative safety. Note however, that Ritalin and Dexadrine are stimulants like cocaine and methamphetamine. Those that have sedating effects should be given with caution in persons known to be sedative/hypnotic addicts, but they are unlikely to cause serious problems unless taken in overdose with other sedating substances. Reduced risk of overdose is another reason to favor SSRIs over tricyclics, and a reason that benzodiazepines are included in this list and barbiturates are not. Barbiturates were the standard treatment for anxiety many years ago. While effective and well tolerated, they are addicting and frequently produce seizures on abrupt withdrawal. They are lethal in modest overdose and are the recommended treatment for physician-assisted suicide and for self-induced suicide. In contrast, with their benzodiazepine replacements, the lethal dose is 50 to 100 times the therapeutic dose. Meprobamate (Miltown®) is not recommended because of similarity to barbiturates including withdrawal seizures and lethality.

As a group, the protease inhibitors (PIs) are potent liver enzyme inhibitors, although they are in some cases inducers. Most of the medications described in this chapter affect these enzymes in some way. Although precaution should be used when combining many of these agents with protease inhibitors, none of those listed in this chapter are contraindicated. The nonnucleoside reverse transcriptase inhibitors may also induce or inhibit some of the P450 enzymes, but to a more modest degree, while the nucleoside reverse transcriptase inhibitors have little effect. Indeed, with most patients on multiple antiretroviral drug combinations, it would be impossible to predict their effect on the blood level of the psychotropic drug and vice versa. The solution is to identify target symptoms and then begin with a low dose of medication, raising it slowly until control is established. Blood levels (when available) should be obtained if there is any reason to suspect toxicity. It is also important to recognize that the dose of the psychotropic medication may have to be changed in response to changes in antiretroviral medications, although specific dosage adjustments cannot generally be recommended.

The following sections provide detailed information about the use of specific medications for the treatment of depression, anxiety, and dementia among HIV-infected individuals.

Use of Anti-Depressant Medications

1. Fluoxetine (Prozac,® Prozac Weekly®)

GENERAL INFORMATION	This is the most frequently used drug for the treatment of depression. It has traditionally been given once each day but was recently approved for once weekly dosing. Occasional missed doses are not a problem as effects last about 2 weeks due to irreversible enzyme inhibition. Due to its long half-life, there is no discontinuation syndrome when Prozac® is stopped abruptly. It can be given to suicidal patients, as it is unlikely to cause death from overdose. It is also effective in reducing anxiety, panic disorder, and obsessive-compulsive symptoms. Despite early press reports to the contrary, Prozac® has not been shown to cause murderous rage or suicidal ideation.
CONTRAINDICATIONS	Hypersensitivity to the drug.
DOSE	10–20 mg in the morning for the treatment of most depressions. In those who respond poorly, it can be increased in 10 mg increments every 6 weeks up to 60 mg a day. Prozac weekly® (90 mg capsule) has been given following initial treatment and response to Prozac® 20 mg once daily. Prozac weekly® should be administered 7 days following the last dose of Prozac® 20 mg.
SIDE EFFECTS	May cause insomnia if given in the evening. Some patients experience anxiety or nausea or headache (treat with acetaminophen), which generally clears in 1 to 2 weeks. Decreased interest in sex and difficulty obtaining an erection are probably the most common reasons for discontinuation, as is true for the entire class of SSRIs. Bupropion (Wellbutrin XL®) 100 mg once or twice a day can be added if sexual side effects are problematic.
CESSATION	Stop treatment or reduce dose or change to another medication if anxiety, restlessness, or persistent nausea occurs.
DRUG INTERACTIONS	Prozac® is metabolized by CYP2D6 and inhibits this enzyme as well as CYP3A4. The PIs ritonavir (Norvir®) and lopinavir/ritonavir (Kaletra®) may significantly elevate Prozac® blood levels. Begin therapy at 10 mg/day and increase cautiously. It may increase the blood levels of phenytoin (Dilantin®), carbamazepine (Tegretol®), imipramine (Tofranil®), and amitriptyline (Elavil®). Due to the risk of arrhythmias, do not administer thioridazine (Mellaril®) with Prozac® or within 5 weeks of Prozac® discontinuation. Do not use with St. John's wort. May displace other drugs that are tightly bound to proteins such as digoxin (Lanoxin®) and warfarin (Coumadin®).

2. Paroxetine (Paxil,® Paxil CR,® Pexeva®)

GENERAL INFORMATION	Very short-acting SSRI, which is as effective in treating depression as the other SSRIs. This medication becomes effective in 2 to 6 weeks. Its effects persist for only 36 hours, so missed doses hurt therapeutic effectiveness and can lead to a flu-like discontinuation syndrome. For that reason the newer long-acting CR formulation is preferred. It can be given to suicidal patients since it is unlikely to cause death from an overdose. It is also effective in treating social anxiety, generalized anxiety, and panic disorder.
CONTRAINDICATIONS	Hypersensitivity to the drug.
DOSE	Paroxetine (Paxil CR®): 12.5–25 mg each morning. May be increased in 12.5 mg increments every 6 weeks to a maximum daily dose of 62.5 mg.
SIDE EFFECTS	May cause insomnia if given in the evening. Some patients experience mild anxiety or nausea or headache (treat with acetaminophen). This generally clears in 1 to 2 weeks. When discontinuing Paxil®, taper the dose over 2 weeks. Otherwise, a discontinuation syndrome with nausea, vomiting, electric shock-like pains in the extremities, headache, and decreased cognition may occur. Decreased interest in sex and ejaculatory difficulties are probably the most common reasons for discontinuation. If this occurs, add bupropion (Wellbutrin XL®) 100 mg once or twice a day.
CESSATION	Stop treatment or reduce dose or change to another medication if anxiety, restlessness, or persistent nausea occurs.
DRUG INTERACTIONS	The PIs ritonavir (Norvir®) and lopinavir/ritonavir (Kaletra®) may significantly elevate Paxil® blood levels. Begin therapy at 10 mg/day and increase cautiously. The other PIs may have a similar but milder effect. Paxil® is predominantly metabolized by CYP2D6 which is inhibited by ritonavir. Paxil® may decrease digoxin levels (mechanism unknown) and increase warfarin (Coumadin®) and phenytoin (Dilantin®) levels. Do not use with St. John's wort.

3. Sertraline (Zoloft®)

GENERAL INFORMATION	Short-acting SSRI. May be the drug of choice for the treatment of depression as it has the least interaction of any SSRI with other medications. This medication becomes effective in 2 to 6 weeks. It is given once a day and missed doses are a problem as a flu-like discontinuation syndrome can occur. It can be given to suicidal patients since it is unlikely to cause death from overdose. It is also effective in treating generalized anxiety, panic disorder, and obsessive-compulsive disorder.
CONTRAINDICATIONS	Hypersensitivity to the drug.
DOSE	25 mg each morning. May be increased in 25 mg increments every 6 weeks to a maximum of 200 mg.
SIDE EFFECTS	Diarrhea and nausea occur in many patients, so the dose should be started low and increased slowly. Headache may occur and can be treated with acetaminophen. Taper over 2 weeks if discontinued. Otherwise, a discontinuation syndrome with nausea, vomiting, electric shock-like pains in the extremities, headache, and decreased cognition may occur. Decreased interest in sex and difficulty obtaining an erection are probably the most common reasons for discontinuation, as is true for the entire class of SSRIs. If this occurs, add bupropion (Wellbutrin XL®) 100 mg once or twice a day.
CESSATION	Stop treatment or reduce dose or change to another medication if diarrhea and nausea occur.
DRUG INTERACTIONS	Sertraline (Zoloft®) is metabolized by the CYP3A4 and CYP2D6 enzyme systems. All of the PIs and the NNRTI delavirdine may elevate Zoloft® blood levels. Begin therapy at 25 mg/day and increase cautiously.

4. Citalopram (Celexa®) or Escitalopram (Lexapro®)

GENERAL INFORMATION	Celexa® is a racemic mixture of citalopram. Escitalopram is the active isomer of citalopram. The dose of Lexapro® is exactly half the dose of Celexa.® The effects and side effects are identical. This is a case of clever marketing with a drug whose patent has expired. Most recently introduced of the SSRIs, although Celexa® was used for many years in Europe. It is as effective as the others in the class for the treatment of depression. Celexa has not been demonstrated to be effective in the treatment of anxiety, panic, and obsessive-compulsive disorder. It is unlikely to cause death from overdose. The medication becomes effective in 2 to 6 weeks.
CONTRAINDICATIONS	Hypersensitivity to the drug.
DOSE	Doses are given for citalopram (Celexa®): 20 mg each day increasing to 40 mg each day after at least one week. If it causes somnolence, give in the evening. May be increased by 20 mg at 6-week intervals until target symptoms are controlled to a maximum of 60 mg each day.
SIDE EFFECTS	Anxiety, agitation, dizziness, and nausea may occur unless started at a low dose. Unlike the other SSRIs, the low starting dose is rarely effective, so it is important to move routinely to the full dose. Decreased interest in sex or difficulty obtaining an erection is a common reason for discontinuation of the medication. If sexual problems occur, they can be treated with bupropion (Wellbutrin XL®) 100 mg once or twice a day. Stop treatment or change to another medication if restlessness, anxiety, or persistent nausea occurs.
DRUG INTERACTIONS	Celexa® levels may be increased by ketoconazole, itraconazole, and macrolide antibiotics. The PIs may increase Celexa® blood levels. Celexa® is metabolized by the CYP3A4 and CYP2C19 enzymes.

5. Bupropion Extended Release (Wellbutrin XL®)

GENERAL INFORMATION	This medication appears to improve depression by increasing the amount of available dopamine. Under the name Zyban®, it is sold to assist smoking cessation. It does not decrease sexual feelings or performance and counteracts that effect when caused by SSRIs. This is a very short-acting drug, so the XL form is preferred. The drug may cause seizures on as little as 600 mg/day.
CONTRAINDICATIONS	Do not use in patients with seizure disorder, prior diagnosis of bulimia, following myocardial infarction, or with known hypersensitivity to the drug.
DOSE	Bupropion Extended Release (Wellbutrin XL®) 75 mg each morning. May increase by 75 mg every 6 weeks until target symptoms controlled or maximum dose of 450 mg per day is reached.
SIDE EFFECTS	May cause insomnia if given in the evening. Anxiety, nausea, confusion, euphoria, weight loss, hypertension, and seizures may occur.
CESSATION	Stop treatment or reduce dose or change to another medication if seizures, arrhythmia, hypertension, or intractable headache occurs.
DRUG INTERACTIONS	The PIs ritonavir (Norvir®) and lopinavir/ritonavir (Kaletra®) may significantly elevate Wellbutrin® blood levels. Begin therapy at 100 mg SR/day and increase cautiously. The other PIs may have a similar but milder effect. There is increased risk of adverse reactions with phenothiazines, levodopa, or tricyclic antidepressants.

6. Amitriptyline (Elavil®)

GENERAL INFORMATION	Tricyclic antidepressant widely used for mitigating chronic pain and to provide nighttime sedation as well as to treat depression. Full antidepressant dosage is often very sedating. Moreover, this medication can be quite lethal in overdose. These are the primary reasons amitriptyline has been largely replaced by the SSRIs for the treatment of depression.
CONTRAINDICATIONS	Do not use in a patient with recent myocardial infarction or where orthostatic hypotension would be hazardous. Co-administration with clonidine (Catapres®) may cause a hypertensive crisis. Avoid use with suicidal patients.
DOSE	Antidepressant doses are from 50–300 mg. Pain and sedation doses range from 10–100 mg. Always start low and work dose up in small increments every 4 weeks, as side effects are very prominent. Give as single dose in the evening as it is quite sedating and the effects last for more than 36 hours.
SIDE EFFECTS	Sedation, dry mouth, orthostatic hypotension, blurred vision, and constipation occur in most patients, but are generally tolerable. May cause significant cognitive impairment. Abrupt withdrawal of the medication may cause headache, nausea, and malaise for 2 weeks. May cause increased photosensitivity.
CESSATION	Stop treatment or reduce dose or change to another medication if increased intraocular pressure, urinary retention, gastric distress, heart block, cognitive impairment, or extrapyramidal reactions occur.
DRUG INTERACTIONS	The TCAs are metabolized by CYP2D6, which is inhibited by ritonavir (Norvir®). The PIs Norvir® and lopinavir/ritonavir (Kaletra®) may significantly elevate amitriptyline (Elavil®) blood levels. Begin therapy at a low dose and increase cautiously. The other PIs may have a similar but milder effect. SSRIs may increase Elavil® blood levels, so use reduced amounts if Elavil® if being added to depression treatment for nighttime sedation or chronic pain. May cause excessive sedation with barbiturates.

7. Imipramine (Tofranil®)

GENERAL INFORMATION	This tricyclic antidepressant is so sedating that full antidepressant doses may be difficult to tolerate. This difficulty along with the lethal nature of overdose, are the main reasons this medication has largely been replaced by the SSRIs.
CONTRAINDICATIONS	Do not use in a patient with recent myocardial infarction or with any condition where orthostatic hypotension would be hazardous.
DOSE	Effective antidepressant dose is 50–300 mg a day. Always start low, generally 25–50 mg, and work dose up in 25 mg increments every 4 weeks, as side effects are often prominent. Give as a single dose in the evening as it is quite sedating and the effects last for more than 36 hours.
SIDE EFFECTS	Sedation, dry mouth, orthostatic hypotension, blurred vision, and constipation occur in most patients, but are generally tolerable. May cause significant cognitive impairment. Abrupt withdrawal of the medication may cause headache, nausea, and malaise for 2 weeks. May cause increased photosensitivity.
CESSATION	Stop treatment or reduce dose or change to another medication if increased intraocular pressure, urinary retention, gastric distress, heart block, cognitive impairment, or extrapyramidal reactions occur.
DRUG INTERACTIONS	The PIs ritonavir (Norvir®) and lopinavir/ritonavir (Kaletra®) may significantly elevate imipramine (Tofranil®) blood levels. Begin therapy at a low dose and increase cautiously. The other PIs may have a similar but milder effect. SSRIs may increase Tofranil® blood levels, so use reduced amounts if it is being added to depression treatment for nighttime sedation. May cause excessive sedation with barbiturates.

8. Nortriptyline (Pamelor®)

GENERAL INFORMATION	Tricyclic antidepressant with fewer sedation and anticholinergic effects than amitriptyline (Elavil®) and imipramine (Tofranil®). May be helpful with chronic pain but can be lethal in overdose.
CONTRAINDICATIONS	Do not use in a patient with recent myocardial infarction or with any condition where orthostatic hypotension would be hazardous. Avoid use in suicidal patients.
DOSE	Effective antidepressant dose is 30–150 mg a day. Always start low, generally 10–25 mg, and work dose up in 25 mg increments every 4 weeks to a maximum of 150 mg, as side effects are prominent. Give as single dose anytime during the day. There is a therapeutic ceiling effect such that large doses may decrease effectiveness. Check blood level to verify that it is within the therapeutic window of 50–150 mg/mL if target symptoms are not yet controlled.
SIDE EFFECTS	Sedation, dry mouth, orthostatic hypotension, blurred vision, and constipation occur in most patients, but are generally tolerable. May cause significant cognitive impairment. Abrupt withdrawal of the medication may cause headache, nausea, and malaise for 2 weeks. May cause increased photosensitivity.
CESSATION	Stop treatment or reduce dose or change to another medication if increased intraocular pressure, urinary retention, gastric distress, heart block, cognitive impairment, or extrapyramidal reactions occur.
DRUG INTERACTIONS	The PIs ritonavir (Norvir®) and lopinavir/ritonavir (Kaletra®) may significantly elevate nortriptyline (Pamelor®) blood levels. Begin therapy at a low dose and increase cautiously, checking blood levels to remain within the therapeutic window. The other PIs may have a similar but milder effect. Use with SSRIs increases Pamelor® blood levels, so use reduced amounts if it is being added to depression treatment. May cause excessive sedation with barbiturates.

9. Nefazodone (Serzone®)

GENERAL INFORMATION	Cases of life threatening liver failure have been reported in patients treated with Serzone®. In otherwise normal patients, liver enzymes can be monitored to make certain that the drug is not causing harm. Many patients with AIDS are on medications that may also raise liver enzymes making the care of the patient unduly complex. **CAUTION: This agent has been removed from the market in the US.**

10. Mirtazapine (Remeron®, Remeron® SolTab)

GENERAL INFORMATION	Unique class of antidepressant. Main action is through inhibition of presynaptic alpha$_2$-receptors leading to an increase in norepinephrine release. It also inhibits histamine receptors. May be useful in patients with anxiety or insomnia co-existing with depression.
CONTRAINDICATIONS	Hypersensitivity to the drug.
DOSE	Initial dose is 15 mg po qhs. Dose can be increased by 15 mg at a minimum of 2-week intervals up to a maximum dose of 45 mg po qhs. Unlike other drugs, the lowest dose, 15 mg, appears to be the most sedating.
SIDE EFFECTS	This medication can cause drowsiness, dry mouth, increased appetite, weight gain, and dizziness.
CESSATION	
DRUG INTERACTIONS	Use with caution with other agents that potential the action of serotonin (e.g., SSRIs, TCAs, serotonin receptor agonists used for migraines). Metabolized by multiple CYP enzymes (2D6, 1A2, 3A4). Although limited clinical drug interaction information is available, clinically significant interactions are unlikely due to the multiple metabolism pathways. Use with caution with other sedating agents such as alcohol, barbiturates, and benzodiazepines.

11. Venlafaxine (Effexor®), Venlafaxine Extended Release (Effexor XR®)

GENERAL INFORMATION	This drug is generally used after the patient has failed to improve on an SSRI. It is sometimes characterized as a tricyclic without the sedation and memory impairment as it elevates serotonin, norepinephrine, and to some extent dopamine. ALWAYS use the XR formulation if possible as it is much better tolerated and can be given once a day. It is effective in generalized anxiety disorder at the same doses used to treat depression. Relatively safe in overdose. It may have some benefit in patients with chronic pain.
CONTRAINDICATIONS	Hypersensitivity to the drug or poorly controlled hypertension.
DOSE	Start at 37.5 mg XR each morning and increase by this amount at intervals of at least 4 days. Most patients will respond between 150 and 225 mg XR per day in 2 to 6 weeks. Some patients may require as much as 375 mg, and this dose should not be exceeded.
SIDE EFFECTS	Monitor blood pressure, especially after each increase, as it can cause sustained dose dependent hypertension. Nausea and vomiting, nervousness, insomnia, and headache are the most likely side effects to cause discontinuation. They occur much more frequently with the regular formulation than with the XR formulation. Stop treatment if hypertension is poorly controlled. Use with caution in patients who are underweight since anorexia can be seen.
CESSATION	Reduce the dose or switch to another medication if insomnia, agitation, or anorexia occurs.
DRUG INTERACTIONS	Do not use with stimulants. The PIs ritonavir (Norvir®) and lopinavir/ritonavir (Kaletra®) may significantly increase venlafaxine (Effexor®) levels while the other PIs may increase levels to a lesser degree. Effexor XR® is primarily metabolized by the CYP2D6 and CYP3A4 enzymes. In a study of 9 healthy volunteers, Effexor® resulted in a 78% decrease in the AUC of a single 800 mg oral dose of the PI indinavir (Crixivan®) and a 36% decrease in Crixivan® Cmax. The clinical significance of this interaction is unknown.

12. Duloxetine (Cymbalta®)

GENERAL INFORMATION	Serotonin-Norepinephrine Reuptake Inhibitor similar to venlafaxine. It is approved by the FDA for treatment of pain due to diabetic neuropathy and will probably help other types of chronic pain. Nausea is frequent at the beginning of treatment so start with the 30 mg dose and increase as tolerated to 60 mg.
CONTRAINDICATIONS	Hypersensitivity to the drug or poorly controlled hypertension.
DOSE	Usual adult dose is 40–60 mg per day given once daily or in 2 divided doses.
SIDE EFFECTS	Most common adverse effects are nausea, vomiting, constipation, and dry mouth. Monitor blood pressure when initiating therapy or increasing dose, especially in those with pre existing hypertension.
CESSATION	Reduce the dose or switch to another medication if insomnia, agitation, or anorexia occurs.
DRUG INTERACTIONS	Duloxetine is mainly metabolized by CYP2D6, duloxetine levels may be increased by the PIs ritonavir (Norvir®) and lopinavir/ritonavir (Kaletra®). Duloxetine also inhibits the CYP2D6 enzyme and can increase levels of other drugs metabolized by this enzyme (e.g., TCAs and some antipsychotics).

13. Methylphenidate Sustained Release (Ritalin SR®)

GENERAL INFORMATION	This stimulant may treat mild cognitive impairment and depression with psychomotor slowing. It may get the patient up and going when malaise and helplessness are prominent. Beneficial effects are typically apparent within 7 days. This is a drug of abuse and should be used cautiously with individuals who have a history of drug or alcohol abuse.
CONTRAINDICATIONS	Do not use following myocardial infarction or when hypertension may be hazardous.
DOSE	20 mg SR in the morning. Effects typically last 8 to 12 hours. Sometimes an additional 20 mg SR may have to be given at noon, but may interfere with sleep. No more than 60 mg/day should be administered.
SIDE EFFECTS	May cause irritability, anxiety, agitation, headache, dizziness, and drowsiness. Interferes with sleep if given late in the day, and suppresses appetite. May increase the possibility of seizures.
CESSATION	Stop treatment or reduce dose or change to another medication if seizures, ticks, dyskinesia, stereotyped movements, abnormal movements of any kind, or hypertension occurs.
DRUG INTERACTIONS	The PIs ritonavir (Norvir®) and lopinavir/ritonavir (Kaletra®) may significantly elevate Ritalin® blood levels. Begin therapy at a low dose and increase cautiously. The other PIs may have a similar but milder effect. May decrease antihypertensive medication effects. Will increase blood levels of tricyclic antidepressants and PIs.

14. Dextroamphetamine (Dexedrine Spansule® or Dextroamphetamine® –long acting)

GENERAL INFORMATION	This stimulant may treat mild cognitive impairment and depression with psychomotor slowing. It may get the patient up and going when malaise and helplessness are prominent. Beneficial effect is apparent within 7 days. **CAUTION: This is a drug of abuse and should be used cautiously with individuals who have a history of substance abuse.**
CONTRAINDICATIONS	Do not use following myocardial infarction or if hypertension is present.
DOSE	5–15 mg dextroamphetamine (Spansule®) in the morning. Effect lasts for 12 hours. Sometimes a second Spansule® may have to be given at noon, but that may interfere with sleep. Dose may be increased weekly to maximum of 45 mg/day.
SIDE EFFECTS	May cause euphoria, dysphoria, irritability, anxiety, restlessness, and headache. May interfere with sleep (Spansule® effect lasts 12 hours), and suppresses appetite. May increase the possibility of seizures.
CESSATION	Stop treatment or reduce dose or change to another medication if seizures, ticks, dyskinesia, stereotyped movements, or hypertension occurs.
DRUG INTERACTIONS	The PIs ritonavir (Norvir®) and lopinavir/ritonavir (Kaletra®) may significantly elevate amphetamine blood levels. Begin therapy at a low dose and increase cautiously. The other PIs may have a similar but milder effect. May decrease antihypertensive medication effects. Haloperidol (Haldol®) and the phenothiazines block the effect of amphetamine. Tricyclic antidepressants may dangerously increase the concentration of amphetamine in the brain and should not be given simultaneously.

Use of Antianxiety Medications

1. Buspirone (BuSpar®)

GENERAL INFORMATION	This drug has no potential for abuse. Onset of beneficial effects occurs in 2–4 weeks. The medication may be stopped abruptly with no adverse effects. Must be given multiple times a day as the effect lasts 8 hours at most. Patients previously on benzodiazepines typically complain that it is ineffective.
CONTRAINDICATIONS	Known hypersensitivity to the drug.
DOSE	Begin at 5 mg tid and increase weekly by 5 mg per day increments until effective or to maximum of 15 mg qid (60 mg per day).
SIDE EFFECTS	Dizziness, dry mouth, nausea, fatigue, blurred vision, and light-headedness.
CESSATION	Stop treatment or reduce dose or change to another medication if side effects are excessive.
DRUG INTERACTIONS	The PIs ritonavir (Norvir®) and lopinavir/ritonavir (Kaletra®) may significantly elevate BuSpar® blood levels. Begin therapy at 2.5 mg bid and increase cautiously. The other PIs may have a similar but milder effect. BuSpar® may cause CNS depression when combined with alcohol or barbiturates. BuSpar® is primarily metabolized by the CYP3A4 enzyme system.

2. Hydroxyzine (Atarax®)

GENERAL INFORMATION	This is a piperazine antihistamine. It has no abuse potential and can be abruptly discontinued. Its effects are immediate and brief. It should be taken qid as the effect persists for only 6 hours. It may cause cognitive impairment.
CONTRAINDICATIONS	Early pregnancy and breastfeeding patients.
DOSE	10–25 mg qid. Dose may be increased daily to a maximum of 100 mg qid.
SIDE EFFECTS	Drowsiness, dry mouth, involuntary motor activity, and confusion after drowsiness.
CESSATION	Stop treatment or reduce dose or change to another medication if side effects are significant.
DRUG INTERACTIONS	Increased CNS depression when given with other sedatives or alcohol.

3. Trazodone (Desyrel®)

GENERAL INFORMATION	Safe drug without abuse potential given for nighttime sedation and immediate mild antianxiety effect. Technically sold as an antidepressant, but the antidepressant dose of 200–400 mg a day is so sedating that few can tolerate it. Frequently used as sleeping aide and antianxiety drug in depressed patients whose primary treatment is an SSRI. It may impair cognitive functioning.
CONTRAINDICATIONS	Hypersensitivity to the drug.
DOSE	25–50 mg hs increasing weekly by increments of 25 mg until satisfactory sleep is attained. May be given bid or qid in anxious patients to a maximum dose of 200 mg per day.
SIDE EFFECTS	Drowsiness, dizziness, dry mouth, constipation, urinary retention, confusion, nightmares, and vivid dreams.
CESSATION	Stop treatment or reduce dose or change to another medication if side effects are excessive. Priapism is a medical emergency.
DRUG INTERACTIONS	The PIs ritonavir (Norvir®) and lopinavir/ritonavir (Kaletra®) may significantly elevate trazodone levels. Use cautiously with a lower starting dose. The other PIs may have a similar but milder effect. Antihypertensive drug effects may be enhanced. It may increase phenytoin (Dilantin®) and digoxin blood levels. Serotonin syndrome may occur with St. John's wort. Trazodone (Desyrel®) is primarily metabolized by the CYP3A4 enzyme system.

4. Diazepam (Valium®)

GENERAL INFORMATION	Effectively stops severe anxiety and panic within one hour, and is long acting because of active metabolites. It is an anticonvulsant, can prevent alcohol withdrawal seizures, and ameliorates DTs. **CAUTION: This is a drug of abuse and is habituating.** It is widely abused by alcohol and drug addicts. Once used for anxiety, patients may resist stopping it and may seek a higher dosage because of drug tolerance.
CONTRAINDICATIONS	It may suppress respiration when combined with alcohol.
DOSE	2–5 mg given bid, or 2–10 mg given as a single hs dose. To prevent DTs or to treat drug withdrawal anxiety use 2–10 mg qid.
SIDE EFFECTS	This drug decreases social inhibition similar to alcohol. It interferes with memory. A person may become drowsy, dizzy, and unsteady after using this medication.
CESSATION	Stop treatment or reduce dose or change to another medication if patient is excessively sleepy.
DRUG INTERACTIONS	The PIs ritonavir (Norvir®) and lopinavir/ritonavir (Kaletra®) may significantly elevate Valium® blood levels. Begin therapy at a low dose and increase cautiously. The other PIs may have a similar but milder effect. Diazepam (Valium®) is metabolized by the CYP2C19 and CYP3A4 enzyme systems. Valium® may increase digoxin levels. Cimetidine (Tagamet®) may increase Valium® levels. Use cautiously with barbiturates as both are sedating.

5. Lorazepam (Ativan®)

GENERAL INFORMATION	Effectively stops severe anxiety and panic within one hour and is medium acting with little accumulation even in persons with liver and renal disease. It is an anticonvulsant, can prevent alcohol withdrawal seizures, and ameliorates DTs. This is a common drug of abuse and is habituating. Once used for anxiety, patients may resist discontinuation. With long-term use, the antianxiety effect may require a slowly increasing dose.
CONTRAINDICATIONS	It may suppress respiration when combined with alcohol.
DOSE	Use 0.5–4 mg bid for anxiety, always keeping the dose as low as possible; 1–4 mg may be used hs to treat anxiety preventing sleep. Do not exceed 10 mg in 24 hours.
SIDE EFFECTS	This drug decreases social inhibition similar to alcohol. It interferes with memory. A person may become drowsy, dizzy, and unsteady.
CESSATION	Stop treatment or reduce dose or change to another medication if patient is excessively sleepy.
DRUG INTERACTIONS	Lorazepam, oxazepam, and temazepam interact with the PIs less than the other benzodiazepines sedative-hypnotics (BZDs) since they have inactive metabolites. May increase digoxin levels. Use cautiously with barbiturates as both are sedating.

6. Alprazolam (Xanax® XR, Xanax®)

GENERAL INFORMATION	Effectively stops severe anxiety and panic within one hour and is short acting. This is a common drug of abuse and is habituating. Once used for anxiety, patients may resist discontinuation. With long-term use, the antianxiety effect may require a slowly increasing dose.
CONTRAINDICATIONS	It may suppress respirations when combined with alcohol. Contraindicated in patients with acute narrow angle glaucoma.
DOSE	1 mg qd to start for anxiety. Usual dose 3–6 mg qd. The short form should not be used as it is more likely to lead to addiction.
SIDE EFFECTS	This drug decreases social inhibition similar to alcohol. It interferes with memory. A person may become drowsy, dizzy, and unsteady.
CESSATION	Stop treatment or reduce dose or change to another medication if patient is excessively sleepy.
DRUG INTERACTIONS	The PIs ritonavir (Norvir®) and lopinavir/ritonavir (Kaletra®) may significantly elevate alprazolam (Xanax®) blood levels. Begin therapy at a low dose and increase cautiously. The other PIs may have a similar but milder effect. May increase digoxin and tricyclic antidepressant levels. Cimetidine (Tagamet®) may increase Xanax® level. Use cautiously with barbiturates as both are sedating.

7. Meprobamate (Miltown®)

GENERAL INFORMATION	**CAUTION: This is a drug of abuse**. It is related to the barbiturates and may cause seizures upon abrupt withdrawal from standard doses. It can be lethal in overdose. It is not recommended for use.

Use of Medications to Control Behavior in Dementia

1. Olanzapine (Zyprexa®) PO tablet, PO wafer (instantly dissolving) and IM

GENERAL INFORMATION	Reduces agitated, aggressive, and psychotic behavior in demented patients with fewer side effects than haloperidol (Haldol®) or the phenothiazines. It may improve cognition. It frequently increases appetite and weight gain, which may or may not be beneficial. May require 4 weeks to be fully effective.
CONTRAINDICATIONS	Known hypersensitivity to the drug.
DOSE	2.5 mg po hs. This is a long-acting medication; no more than once daily dosing is needed. May be increased by 2.5 mg every 4 weeks until target symptoms are controlled or 10 mg per day is reached. May be used up to 20 mg per day to treat overt psychosis. The wafer can be given to patients who attempt to spit out or cheek their medication. For acute control of severe agitation/psychosis, 2.5 to 10 mg IM may be given.
SIDE EFFECTS	May cause somnolence, headache, dizziness, orthostatic hypotension, constipation, and edema. Insulin resistance with or without weight gain may occur and an increased frequency of diabetes has been reported. Has been demonstrated to increase stroke incidence in the demented elderly — effect in HIV dementia is unknown. Despite this problem, this class of medications continues to be the best choice for medication control of behavior in demented persons.
CESSATION	Stop treatment or reduce dose or change to another medication if any type of movement disorder occurs. However, note that olanzapine (Zyprexa®) may be an effective treatment for tardive dyskinesia.
DRUG INTERACTIONS	The PIs ritonavir (Norvir®) and lopinavir/ritonavir (Kaletra®) may reduce the blood level of Zyprexa® through induction of the CYP1A2 enzyme. May potentiate antihypertensives. Antagonizes levodopa.

2. Risperidone (Risperdal®) PO tablet, PO M-tab, IM Risperdal Consta

GENERAL INFORMATION	Reduces agitated, aggressive, and psychotic behavior in demented patients with fewer side effects than haloperidol (Haldol®) or the phenothiazines. May improve cognition. May require 4 weeks to be fully effective.
CONTRAINDICATIONS	Known hypersensitivity to the drug.
DOSE	0.5–1 mg po hs. This is a long-acting medication; no more than daily dosing is necessary. May be increased by 0.5 mg every 4 weeks until target symptoms are controlled or 2 mg per day is reached. May be used up to 4 mg per day to treat overt psychosis. Quickly dissolving M-tab may be given to patients who attempt to spit out or cheek their medication. Effects of IM Risperdal Consta begin 3 weeks after the injection and last for 2 weeks. Given every 2 weeks at 25 or 50 mg, it eliminates the issue of medication compliance.
SIDE EFFECTS	Raises prolactin level. May cause somnolence, headache, dizziness, orthostatic hypotension, and constipation. Above 1 mg it may cause extrapyramidal symptoms. Has been demonstrated to increase stroke incidence in the demented elderly — effect in HIV dementia is unknown. Despite this problem, this class of medications continues to be the best choice for medication control of behavior in demented persons.
CESSATION	Stop treatment or reduce dose or change to another medication if any type of movement disorder occurs. As dose increases, extrapyramidal tremor becomes more likely.
DRUG INTERACTIONS	The PIs ritonavir (Norvir®) and lopinavir/ritonavir (Kaletra®) may significantly elevate Risperidone Risperdal® blood levels. Begin therapy at a low dose and increase cautiously. Nelfinavir (Viracept®) may have a similar but milder effect. (Risperdal®) is primarily metabolized by the CYP2D6 enzyme system. Antagonizes levodopa.

3. Haloperidol (Haldol®)

GENERAL INFORMATION	Reduces agitated, aggressive, and psychotic behavior in demented patients with less sedation than the phenothiazines. However, it is much more likely to cause extrapyramidal symptoms than are the "atypical" antipsychotics. May require 4 weeks to be fully effective.
CONTRAINDICATIONS	Do not use in patients with extrapyramidal symptoms.
DOSE	0.5–1 mg qd. This is a long-acting medication; no more than daily dosing is necessary. May be increased by 0.5 mg every 4 weeks until target symptoms are controlled or 2 mg qd is reached. May be used up to 10 mg qd for overt psychosis. Extrapyramidal symptoms can be treated with benztropine (Cogentin®) 1 mg bid or similar agents, but these interfere with cognition.
SIDE EFFECTS	The most troubling side effects include a sense of inner restlessness, tremor, and Parkinson-like symptoms. Raises prolactin level. May cause somnolence, headache, and constipation.
CESSATION	Stop treatment or reduce dose or change to another medication if neuroleptic malignant syndrome or tardive dyskinesia occurs or extrapyramidal symptoms are troublesome.
DRUG INTERACTIONS	May cause confusion when taken with Lithium.

4. Chlorpromazine (Thorazine®)

GENERAL INFORMATION	Reduces agitated, aggressive, and psychotic behavior in demented patients and simultaneously sedates the patient. Control of symptoms can be accomplished within hours. It may cause cognitive impairment that is disabling.
CONTRAINDICATIONS	Do not use in patients with extrapyramidal symptoms.
DOSE	10–25 mg bid. 10–50 mg hs may insure sleep through the night. Increase weekly by 25 mg until there is effective control of target symptoms or 200 mg per day is reached.
SIDE EFFECTS	Most troubling are orthostatic hypotension and extrapyramidal symptoms. May cause somnolence, dizziness, blurred vision, headache, dry mouth, urinary retention, and constipation.
CESSATION	Stop treatment or reduce dose or change to another medication if neuroleptic malignant syndrome or tardive dyskinesia occurs or extrapyramidal symptoms are troublesome.
DRUG INTERACTIONS	The PIs ritonavir (Norvir®) and lopinavir/ritonavir (Kaletra®) may significantly elevate chlorpromazine (Thorazine®) blood levels. Begin therapy at a low dose and increase cautiously. The other PIs may have a similar but milder effect. Antacids inhibit absorption. May decrease seizure threshold.

5. Thioridazine (Mellaril®)

GENERAL INFORMATION	This medication may dangerously prolong QT interval, which can cause a fatal arrhythmia; its effects are similar to chlorpromazine (Thorazine®). This is particularly true if used with erythromycin or other macrolide antibiotics. Its use is not recommended.

6. Ziprasidone (Geodon®) PO and IM

GENERAL INFORMATION	Reduces agitated, aggressive, and psychotic behavior in demented patients with fewer side effects than haloperidol (Haldol®) or the phenothiazines. It may improve cognition, appears to have some antidepressant properties, and does not cause weight gain or loss. An IM preparation is available that is as effective as IM Haldol® and is much less likely to cause movement disorders. Absorption is greater with food, so give the drug consistently with meals or without meals to maintain a stable blood level.
CONTRAINDICATIONS	Known hypersensitivity to the drug. Ziprasidone (Geodon®) was initially thought to dangerously prolong QT interval, but with extensive clinical experience this has not been a problem. It should not be used in combination with drugs known to prolong the QT interval or in patients with known QT prolongation, recent myocardial infarction, or uncompensated heart failure.
DOSE	20 mg qhs or bid. May be increased by 20 mg every 7 days until target symptoms are controlled or 160 mg per day is reached. May be used up to 240 mg each day to treat overt psychosis. IM dose is 20 mg in a normal size person or 10 mg in a debilitated or elderly person. The IM dose may be repeated in 4 hours.
SIDE EFFECTS	May cause somnolence, postural hypotension, dizziness, and akathisia. This class of drugs has been demonstrated to increase stroke incidence in the demented elderly — effect in HIV dementia is unknown. Despite this problem, this class of medications continues to be the best choice for medication control of behavior in demented persons.
CESSATION	Stop treatment or reduce the dose or change to another medication if any type of movement disorder occurs.
DRUG INTERACTIONS	The PIs, ketoconazole and other CYP3A4 inhibitors may increase Geodon® blood levels, while carbamazepine and phenytoin may reduce the levels as Geodon® is metabolized by the CYP3A4 system. Geodon® does not induce or inhibit the CYP3A4 or any other metabolic pathways and has little effect on the blood levels of other drugs. It may antagonize levodopa.

7. Quetiapine (Seroquel®)

GENERAL INFORMATION	Reduces agitated and aggressive behavior in demented patients. It is quite sedating and may reduce anxiety. May increase appetite, but unlike olanzapine (Zyprexa®), it has not been linked to increased insulin resistance.
CONTRAINDICATIONS	Known hypersensitivity to the drug.
DOSE	25 mg qhs or bid. May be increased by increments of 25 mg every 3 or 4 days until target symptoms are controlled or 600 mg each day is reached.
SIDE EFFECTS	May cause somnolence, dizziness, postural hypotension, increased appetite, and weight gain. Considerable anti-cholinergic effect and abrupt cessation may cause a flu-like syndrome.
CESSATION	Stop treatment or reduce the dose or change to another medication if excessive sedation or any type of movement disorder occurs.
DRUG INTERACTIONS	Quetiapine (Seroquel®) is metabolized by the CYP3A4 isoemzyme. PIs and ketoconazole may increase Seroquel® levels while phenytoin and carbamazepine may decrease Seroquel® levels. Seroquel® itself does not inhibit or induce the isoenzyme.

Use of Medications to Control Insomnia

In addition to agents listed below, trazodone, hydroxyzine, and mirtazapine (discussed above) may also improve insomnia symptoms.

1. Temazepam (Restoril®)

GENERAL INFORMATION	Useful for short-term treatment of insomnia. Short half-life decreases residual next day effects. This is a common drug of abuse and is habituating. Much less expensive then agents described below. CIV controlled substance.
CONTRAINDICATIONS	It may suppress respirations when combined with alcohol. Use with caution in those with pre-existing respiratory depression such as patients with severe COPD, sleep apnea, or uncontrolled asthma. Use with caution in patients with history of substance abuse.
DOSE	Usual adult dose is 15 mg po 30 minutes prior to bedtime. Dose of 7.5 mg may be effective in some patients and some may require maximum dose of 30 mg.
SIDE EFFECTS	This drug decreases social inhibition similar to alcohol. It interferes with memory. A person may become drowsy, dizzy, and unsteady.
CESSATION	Stop treatment or reduce dose or change to another medication if patient is excessively sleepy. Avoid abrupt discontinuation especially in patients on therapy for 2 or more weeks or those with a seizure disorder as withdrawal symptoms may occur.
DRUG INTERACTIONS	Lorazepam (Ativan®), oxazepam (Serax®), and temazepam (Restoril®) interact with the PIs less than the other BZDs since they have inactive metabolites. Use cautiously with other sedating medications such as barbiturates.

2. Zolpidem (Ambien®)

GENERAL INFORMATION	Non-benzodiazepine sedative-hypnotic that is useful for the short-term treatment of insomnia particularly with difficulty falling asleep. Short half-life decreases the potential for residual next day effects but patients may awaken before the night is over. CIV controlled substance.
CONTRAINDICATIONS	It may suppress respirations when combined with alcohol. Use with caution in those with pre-existing respiratory depression such as patients with severe COPD, sleep apnea, or uncontrolled asthma. Use with caution in patients with history of substance abuse.
DOSE	Usually adult dose is 5 mg po immediately prior to bedtime. Some patients may require up to 10 mg. If taken in larger amounts, it behaves as a typical benzodiazepine.
SIDE EFFECTS	This drug decreases social inhibition similar to alcohol. It interferes with memory. A person may become drowsy, dizzy, and unsteady.
CESSATION	Stop treatment or reduce dose or change to another medication if patient is excessively sleepy. Avoid abrupt discontinuation especially in patients on therapy for 2 or more weeks or those with a seizure disorder as withdrawal symptoms may occur.
DRUG INTERACTIONS	Levels may be increased by CYP3A4 inhibitors (e.g., PIs) and decreased by CYP3A4 inducers (e.g., nevirapine). No recommendations on dosage adjustments available. Use cautiously with other sedating medications such as barbiturates.

3. Zaleplon (Sonata®)

GENERAL INFORMATION	Non-benzodiazepine sedative-hypnotic that is useful for the short-term treatment of insomnia. Very short half-life decreases the potential for residual next day effects but patients may awaken before the night is over. CIV controlled substance.
CONTRAINDICATIONS	It may suppress respirations when combined with alcohol. Use with caution in those with pre-existing respiratory depression such as patients with severe COPD, sleep apnea, or uncontrolled asthma. Use with caution in patients with history of substance abuse.
DOSE	Usual dose is 10 mg immediately prior to retiring (dose range is 5–20 mg).
SIDE EFFECTS	This drug decreases social inhibition similar to alcohol. It interferes with memory. A person may become drowsy, dizzy, and unsteady.
CESSATION	Stop treatment or reduce dose or change to another medication if patient is excessively sleepy. Avoid abrupt discontinuation especially in patients on therapy for 2 or more weeks or those with a seizure disorder as withdrawal symptoms may occur.
DRUG INTERACTIONS	Levels may be increased by CYP3A4 inhibitors (e.g., PIs) and decreased by CYP3A4 inducers (e.g., nevirapine). No recommendations on dosage adjustments available. Use cautiously with other sedating medications such as barbiturates.

4. Esopiclone (Lunesta®)

GENERAL INFORMATION	Non-benzodiazepine sedative-hypnotic that is indicated for the treatment of chronic insomnia. Very short half-life decreases the potential for residual next day effects but patients may awaken before the night is over. CIV controlled substance.
CONTRAINDICATIONS	It may suppress respirations when combined with alcohol. Use with caution in those with pre-existing respiratory depression such as patients with severe COPD, sleep apnea, or uncontrolled asthma. Use with caution in patients with history of substance abuse.
DOSE	Usual adult dose is 2 mg po immediately prior to retiring (dose range is 1–3 mg).
SIDE EFFECTS	This drug decreases social inhibition similar to alcohol. It interferes with memory. A person may become drowsy, dizzy and unsteady.
CESSATION	Stop treatment or reduce dose or change to another medication if patient is excessively sleepy. Avoid abrupt discontinuation especially in patients on therapy for 2 or more weeks or those with a seizure disorder as withdrawal symptoms may occur.
DRUG INTERACTIONS	Levels may be increased by CYP3A4 inhibitors (e.g., PIs) and decreased by CYP3A4 inducers (e.g., nevirapine). No recommendations on dosage adjustments available. Use cautiously with other sedating medications such as barbiturates.

References

1. American Psychiatric Association. *Diagnostic and Statistical Manual of Mental Disorders, 4th ed., Text Revision.* Washington, DC: 2000.

2. Batki SL. Buspirone in drug users with AIDS or AIDS-related complex. *J Clin Psychopharmacology* 1990; 10(3):111S–115S.

3. Fernandez F, Levy JK. Psychopharmacology in HIV spectrum disorders. *Psychiatric Clinics of North America* 1994; 17(1).

4. Knox MD, Sparks CH, eds. *HIV and Community Mental Healthcare*. Baltimore, MD: The Johns Hopkins University Press, 1998.

5. *Physicians Desk Reference*. 54th ed. Montvale, NJ: Medical Economics Company, 2000.

6. Rabkin JG, Rabkin R, Harrison W, Wagner G. Effect of imipramine on mood and enumerative measures of immune status in depressed patients with HIV illness. *Am J Psychiatry* 1994; 151:4.

7. Rabkin JG, Wagner GJ, Rabkin R. Fluoxetine treatment for depression in patients with HIV and AIDS: a randomized, placebo-controlled trial. *Am J Psychiatry* 1999; 156:1.

8. Reents S, et al. Clinical Pharmacology, Gold Standard Multimedia Inc. Available at: http://cp.gsm.com. Accessed August 18, 2005.

9. Wagner GJ, Rabkin JG, Rabkin R. Dextroamphetamine as a treatment for depression and low energy in AIDS patients: a pilot study. *J Psychosomatic Research* 1997; 42(4):407–411.

Section V

Pediatrics/
Adolescents

28

Evaluation of the Infant at Risk for HIV Infection

Patricia Emmanuel, MD
Associate Professor of Pediatrics, Department of Pediatrics,
University of South Florida College of Medicine, Tampa

Introduction

Major advances in the prevention of maternal to child transmission of HIV infection have resulted in infection rates of less than 3% in the United States. Despite this progress, clinicians must remain diligent in the diagnosis, treatment, and follow-up of women and their infants to prevent perinatal HIV.

The diagnosis of pediatric HIV-infection is complicated by the presence of maternal antibody, transplacentally acquired, which usually persists in the infant for more than a year. The common laboratory tests used to diagnosis HIV-infection in adults, HIV ELISA and Western Blot, will not differentiate between HIV-infected and uninfected infants. Diagnosis of HIV-infection in children < 18 months of age must rely on laboratory tests that detect either HIV free virus or HIV proviral DNA.[1] Laboratory tests that detect HIV free virus or HIV proviral DNA include PCR amplification and the quantitative plasma viral RNA. Since HIV culture is not readily available, the DNA PCR is the preferred test for HIV detection. The role of assays for circulating HIV RNA in the diagnosis of HIV infection have been studied and are sensitive and specific; however, less is known about whether these tests would be affected by additional antiretroviral prophylaxis in the infant, such as Nevirapine. The quantitative RNA viral load is more sensitive for non-B subtypes of HIV-1.[2] Quantitative RNA viral load should not be used as a confirmatory diagnostic test because of the possibility of false positive results (the test is not FDA approved for diagnosis).[3]

Evaluation of the Newborn at Risk for HIV-Infection (See Figure 1)

The majority of children born to HIV-infected mothers are asymptomatic at birth. The majority of women should be identified prior to delivery. Women who present in labor with unknown status should have rapid testing performed for HIV. A newborn whose mother has no documentation of HIV status in the third trimester of pregnancy (or during labor and delivery) should be screened using a rapid diagnostic test for possible HIV exposure. This should be done as soon as possible after birth (after consent from the guardian), but no later than 6 to 8 hours after birth. Prophylaxis with Zidovudine (ZDV) could be started based on the result of the rapid test while awaiting the results of the more definitive test (HIV antibody ELISA confirmed by Western Blot). If a newborn's antibody test is positive, or if the mother is known to be HIV seropositive, then a DNA PCR should be done to determine if the child is infected. Children who have detectable virus at birth are infected *in utero* and may have a more rapid clinical progression to AIDS.[4] About 50% of infants who are infected can be detected during the first few days of life.[5]

Figure 1. Evaluation of Newborn at Risk of HIV

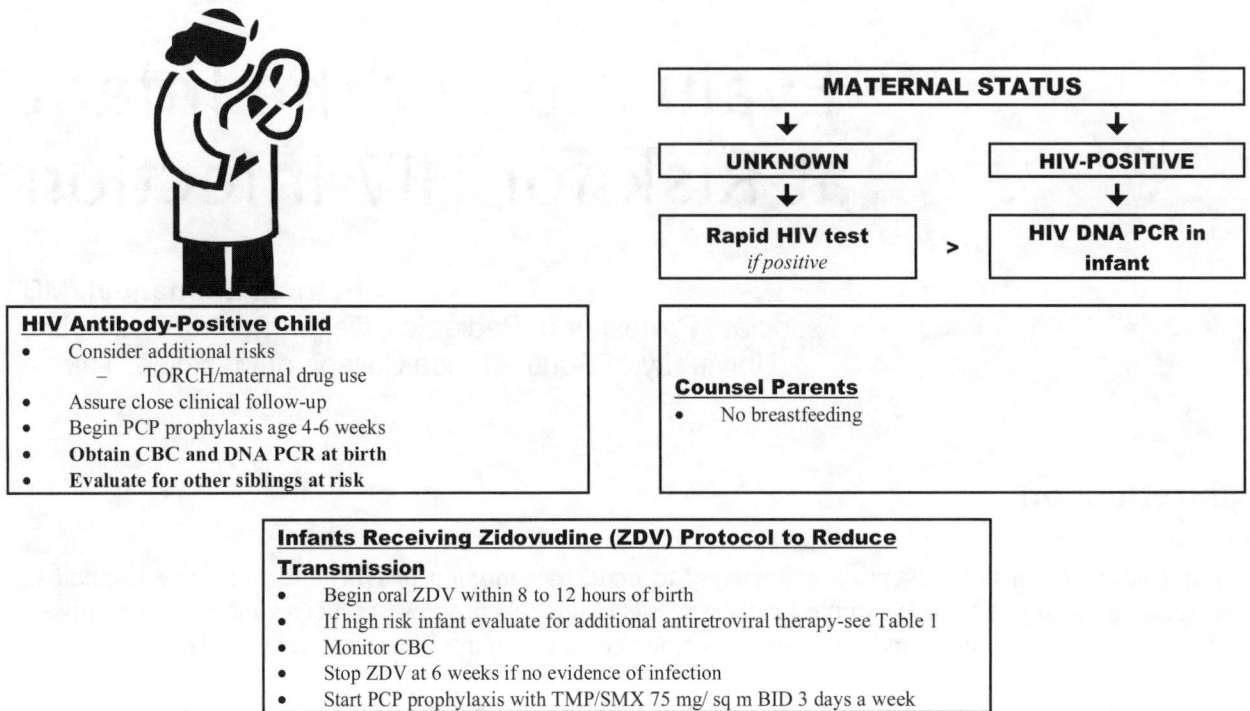

MATERNAL STATUS

UNKNOWN → Rapid HIV test *if positive* > HIV DNA PCR in infant ← HIV-POSITIVE

HIV Antibody-Positive Child
- Consider additional risks
    - TORCH/maternal drug use
- Assure close clinical follow-up
- Begin PCP prophylaxis age 4-6 weeks
- **Obtain CBC and DNA PCR at birth**
- **Evaluate for other siblings at risk**

Counsel Parents
- No breastfeeding

Infants Receiving Zidovudine (ZDV) Protocol to Reduce Transmission
- Begin oral ZDV within 8 to 12 hours of birth
- If high risk infant evaluate for additional antiretroviral therapy-see Table 1
- Monitor CBC
- Stop ZDV at 6 weeks if no evidence of infection
- Start PCP prophylaxis with TMP/SMX 75 mg/ sq m BID 3 days a week

Infants exposed to HIV in utero should be started on Zidovudine prophylaxis within 8 to 12 hours of birth (see first infant regimen in Table 1). Most HIV-infected women will have been on 3 antiretrovirals to control HIV replication during pregnancy. In some patients with viral loads >1000 by RNA PCR late in the pregnancy, an elective C-section may be planned. If a woman has not received antiretrovirals during pregnancy, there are several possible regimens for mother and infant. These are outlined in Table 1. Similarly, if prenatal and intrapartum opportunities are missed, Zidovudine prophylaxis in the infant has been shown to be effective.[6] In addition, one may consider adding an additional antiretroviral and should consult with an expert in the field. The field of prevention of perinatal transmission is rapidly evolving. The most up to date recommendations can be found on the AIDSinfo website: www.aidsinfo.nih.gov.[7]

Table 1. Maternal Intrapartum and Infant Prophylactic Antiretroviral Drug Regimens

Drug	Maternal Dosing	Infant Dosing
Zidovudine (ZDV) Standard Regimen	2 mg/kg IV bolus followed by continuous infusion of 1 mg/kg/h until delivery	2 mg/kg/dose po Q6 h for 6 weeks. If unable to take po: 1.5 mg/kg dose IV Q 6 hours If < 30 weeks gestation, 1.5 mg/kg/dose po Q12 h **OR** 2 mg/kg/dose po Q 12 h for 4 wks then Q 8 hours for 6 weeks If >30 weeks gestation, 1.5 mg/kg/dose IV Q 12 h **OR** 2 mg/kg/dose po Q 12 h for 2 weeks, the Q 8 h for 6 weeks

Regimens when Mother has not received Antiretroviral Therapy during Pregnancy

Drug	Maternal Dosing	Infant Dosing
Zidovudine (ZDV) with Lamivudine (3TC)	ZDV 600 mg po at labor followed by 300 mg Q3h until delivery and 3TC, 150 mg po at labor followed by 150 mg Q12 h	ZDV 4 mg/kg po Q12 h and 3TC 2 mg/kg Q 12 hours for 6 weeks
Zidovudine (ZDV) with Nevirapine (NVP)	ZDV 2 mg/kg IV bolus followed by 1 mg/kg per h until delivery; and NVP single 200 mg dose po at labor onset*	ZDV 2 mg/kg po Q6 hours for 6 weeks and NVP 2 mg/kg po single dose at 48-72 hours.
Nevirapine (NVP)	Single 200 mg dose po at labor*	2 mg/kg po single dose at 48-72 hours

* In order to reduce the development of Nevirapine resistance, if single dose NVP is given to the mother either alone or in combination with ZDV during labor, consideration should be given to adding ZDV/3TC to the maternal regimen for 3 to 7 days as soon as possible.[4] Women who have received highly active antiretroviral therapy during pregnancy should not receive single dose Nevirapine as no benefit has been demonstrated and there is a significant risk of development of Nevirapine resistance.

During the period that the infant's HIV status is indeterminate, aggressive medical intervention is necessary until it is assured that the child is not HIV-infected. Detection of HIV, using DNA PCR should be done at birth, between 4 to 7 weeks of age and 8 to 16 weeks of age. Antiretroviral treatment should be continued and PCP prophylaxis should be initiated in all children at risk for HIV infection regardless of their virologic or immunologic status. The infant's growth and development should be closely monitored and all febrile illnesses aggressively evaluated. Immunizations should be administered according to the recommended schedule. (See Table 2.)

ZDV should be discontinued at 6 weeks of age in infants receiving ZDV to prevent maternal transmission if HIV DNA PCR is negative. The most common short-term side effect of Zidovidine prophylaxis is anemia. This is more common in premature infants and infants who are anemic at birth. A CBC should be checked at birth, 2 to 4 weeks and, if indicated, at 8 weeks of age. The anemia will resolve with discontinuation of Zidovidine. Long-term side effects of ZDV and other antiretrovirals administered to neonates may include mitochondrial toxicity; however, there is still insufficient information in this area. HIV-exposed infants should be monitored for long-term adverse affects.

If the result of the initial HIV PCR is negative, the child should continue to be closely monitored for evidence of HIV infection. Findings suspicious for HIV infection would include:

- – Failure to thrive
- – Lymphadenopathy or hepatosplenomegaly
- – An opportunistic infection associated with HIV
- – A low CD4 lymphocyte count for age
- – Elevated serum immunoglobulins, particularly IgA

If clinical findings suggest HIV infection, then close clinical follow-up is warranted and a repeat PCR determination should be done. If all clinical findings are normal, then a second diagnostic evaluation (PCR) should be carried out at 4 to 7 weeks of age and again at 8 to 16 weeks of age. If those results are negative, then the probability of the child being infected is < 2%. However, the child is not classified as definitively uninfected until after 12 months of age when HIV antibody (ELISA) is tested and is absent.[1] It is not uncommon to have a positive HIV-1 antibody (ELISA) with an indeterminate Western blot at 12 months of age. By 15 to 18 months of age all maternal antibody should disappear. If an at-risk child has laboratory confirmation of HIV infection, then management would follow the guidelines outlined for HIV-infected children. The parents or guardian should be counseled regarding their child's HIV infection and the child evaluated for antiretroviral therapy. The care of an HIV-infected child is complex and consultation with a pediatric HIV specialist is recommended.

Children at risk for HIV infection, but who are shown not to be infected, pose no infectious risk to others, and require only normal well-child medical follow-up. All children born to HIV-infected mothers will require psychosocial support, particularly if and when the mother becomes ill. Potential alternative guardians should be identified and involved in the child's care as early as possible. A primary healthcare provider is essential to the effective medical management of any child at risk for HIV infection.

Infants born to HIV-infected mothers are at risk for other maternally derived infections including toxoplasmosis, hepatitis, syphilis, and CMV. There is a high percentage of HIV infection among women who use cocaine and intravenous drugs. These factors should be considered in the evaluation of the newborn at risk for HIV infection. HIV-infected mothers should be counseled regarding their own healthcare needs and the importance of their health in relation to the well-being of their children. HIV-infected mothers should not breastfeed their infants. The need for prophylactic therapy and the importance of close medical follow-up in the primary care setting should be emphasized. Immunizations should be administered as outlined in Table 2.

Follow-Up Evaluation of the Child at Risk for HIV-Infection from Birth to Age 18 Months

Table 2. Laboratory Monitoring and Immunization for the HIV-Exposed Infant

(Birth to 18 months of age)①

	AGE OF INFANT										
	BIRTH	2 WK	4 WK	6 WK	2 MO	3 MO	4 MO	5 MO	6 MO	12 MO	18 MO
Assess risk of other diseases ②	✖										
Continuation of oral ZDV ③	✖	✖	✖	✖							
CBC and differential leukocyte counts ④	✖		✖⑤		✖		✖				
PCR for HIV DNA and/or viral culture for HIV ⑥	✖		✖⑦				✖				
HIV ELISA/Western Blot										✖	✖
Initiate prophylaxis for PCP					✖	✖	✖	✖			
Immunizations											
Conjugated pneumococcal-PCV-7 (Prevnar®)					✖		✖		✖	✖	
Diphtheria-pertussis-tetanus					✖		✖		✖		
Haemophilus influenzae⑧					✖		✖		✖		
Hepatitis B	✖		✖						✖		
MMR ⑨										✖	
Polio vaccine (IPV)					✖		✖			✖	✖
Varicella ⑩										✖	

① ZDV: zidovudine or AZT; CBC: complete blood count; PCR: polymerase chain reaction

② Test mother or neonate if maternal status for other infections has not been assessed

③ Zidovudine therapy to decrease the risk of HIV infection in the infant is discontinued at 6 weeks of age

④ Premature infants may require more frequent CBC monitoring. CBC and differential leukocyte count should be done to monitor for ZDV toxicity.

⑤ This test can also be done at 6 weeks⑥ Repeat PCR or viral culture immediately if positive to confirm infection. If initial test is negative, repeat test at 4 weeks to 2 months. If clinical status or other laboratory parameters suggest HIV infection, repeat testing earlier than 4 months. If at 4 months the tests are still negative for infection, ongoing serologic follow-up is indicated.⑦ T-cell profile should be repeated at 6 months in infected children and in those whose infection status is unclear at 6 months.⑧ Haemophilus influenzae vaccine schedule may vary depending on which type of vaccine is used⑨ MMR recommended for all HIV-infected children except for immune class 3⑩ Varicella vaccine is not recommended for all HIV-infected children. It should be considered only for HIV-infected children in CDC Class 1 with a CD4+ lymphocyte count of 25% or greater. Eligible children should receive 2 doses of vaccine with a 1 month interval between doses.

References

1. King SM, and the Committee on Pediatric AIDS. Evaluation and treatment of the human immunodeficiency virus-1-exposed infant. *Pediatrics* 2004; 114(2):497–505.

2. Obaro SK, Losikoff P, Harwell J, Pugatch D. Failure of serial human immunodeficiency virus type 1 DNA polymerase chain reactions to identify human immunodeficiency virus type 1 clade A/G. *PIDJ* 2005; 24(2):183–184.

3. Rich JD, Merriman NA, Mylonakis TP, et al. Misdiagnosis of HIV-1 plasma viral load testing: A case series. *Ann Intern Med* 1999; 130:37–39.

4. Bryson YJ, Luzuriaga K, Sullivan JL, Wara DW. Proposed definitions for in utero versus intrapartum transmission of HIV-1. *NEJM* 1997; 175:1029–1038.

5. Midani S, Rathore MH. Polymerase chain reaction testing for early detection of HIV infection in children. 1996; *S Med J* 1997; 90:294–295.

6. Wade NA, et al. Abbreviated regimens of zidovudine prophylaxis & perinatal transmission of the HIV. *NEJM* 1998; 339:20.

7. Public Health Service Task Force Recommendations for Use of Antiretroviral Drugs in Pregnant HIV-1-Infected Women for Maternal Health and Interventions to Reduce Perinatal HIV-1 Transmission in the United States – November 17, 2005. Available at http://aidsinfo.nih.gov/guidelines. Accessed November 17, 2005.

29

Evaluation of the Child with Confirmed HIV Infection

Patricia Emmanuel, MD
Associate Professor of Pediatrics, Department of Pediatrics,
University of South Florida College of Medicine, Tampa

Introduction

HIV infection in infancy should be confirmed as soon as possible by at least 2 positive viral tests, usually HIV DNA PCRs. (See Chapter 28, Evaluation of the Infant at Risk for HIV Infection).[1] Early diagnosis is essential to initiate treatment before immune suppression progresses. In a child over 18 months of age, a diagnosis is established by positive results of either 2 HIV Antibody tests with confirmatory Western Blot assays (WB) or one positive WB and one RNA or DNA PCR. Baseline evaluation of a child with confirmed HIV infection should include a complete clinical exam, complete hemogram including platelet and reticulocyte counts, baseline renal and liver function studies, a chest X-ray, and neurodevelopmental assessment. Many medical centers evaluate the cardiac function by ECG and cardiac ECHO. The HIV plasma viral load (quantitative RNA PCR) should be performed at diagnosis and is often repeated a second time before initiating treatment. One should consider obtaining baseline resistance testing on HIV-infected infants especially if mother was treated during pregnancy.[1] Cases of drug resistant virus transmitted from mother to child have been reported. The results of these studies in conjunction with the blood CD4+ lymphocyte analysis is used to determine the child's clinical stage based on the 1994 CDC Classification System that categorizes children on the basis of clinical and immunologic categories of pediatric HIV disease (see Tables 1 and 2).[2]

The goal of aggressive clinical monitoring in the HIV-infected child is to prevent opportunistic infections, initiate appropriate antiretroviral therapy, and to treat HIV-associated complications early in their course. With the majority of perinatally infected children now entering adolescence, monitoring of short- and long-term complications related to antiretroviral therapy is a critical area with a growing body of literature. All illnesses should be aggressively evaluated. Immunologic function should be monitored every 3 months to assure appropriate institution of prophylaxis and antiretroviral therapy. Especially in infancy, there can be rapid changes in the immunologic and developmental status. Viral loads often peak at 2 to 4 months of age, and are often over 4 logs in the infant. Neurodevelopment assessments should be carried out every 6 months and pulmonary status evaluated at regular intervals. CT or MRI scan can be helpful in monitoring for the presence of neurologic disease.[3] In the era of HAART, neurologic progression can be avoided with early institution of antiretroviral therapy. Growth, development, nutrition, lipid profiles, and urinanalysis should be evaluated at least twice per year to monitor for long-term sequelae. (See Table 3.) The child's TB status should be evaluated yearly. The serologic status of common infections such as hepatitis, toxoplasmosis, EBV, and CMV should be documented and followed if initially negative or with significant immunologic decline. (See Chapter 31, Prevention and Management of Opportunistic Infections.)

Table 1. 1994 CDC Immunologic Categories
Based on age-specific CD4+ T-lymphocyte counts and percent of total lymphocytes

IMMUNOLOGIC CATEGORY	AGE OF CHILD		
	< 12 months	1-5 years	6-12 years
	cells/mm^3 (%)	cells/mm^3 (%)	cells/mm^3 (%)
1. No evidence of suppression	≥ 1500 (≥ 25)	≥ 1,000 (≥ 25)	≥ 500 (≥ 25)
2. Evidence of moderate suppression	750-1499 (15-24)	500-999 (15-24)	200-499 (15-24)
3. Severe suppression	< 750 (< 15)	< 500 (< 15)	<200 (< 15)

Table 2. 1994 CDC Clinical Categories of Pediatric HIV Disease

CATEGORY	SYMPTOMS	DESCRIPTION	
E	Indeterminate Infection	(Confirmed Infection)	
N	None		
A	Minimal	Lymphadenopathy/HSM Dermatitis	Parotitis Recurrent URI
B	Moderate	Pancytopenia❶ Systemic bacterial illness Candidiasis Cardiomyopathy Neonatal CMV Chronic diarrhea HSV stomatitis, pneumonia, esophagitis Recurrent herpes zoster	Leiomyosarcoma Lymphoid interstitial pneumonitis (LIP) Nephropathy Nocardiosis Persistent fever Congenital toxoplasmosis Disseminated varicella
C	Severe	Case definition of AIDS Multiple bacterial infections Extrapulmonary cryptococcosis Cryptosporidiosis diarrhea Esophageal candidiasis Disseminated CMV Encephalopathy❷ Persistent HSV Disseminated histoplasmosis Disseminated TB	Disseminated mycobacterium avium complex (MAI) Pneumocystis carinii pneumonia (PCP) Salmonella sepsis CNS toxoplasmosis Wasting syndrome HIV-associated malignancy: Kaposi's Sarcoma CNS lymphoma B cell lymphoma

❶ Hb < 8 gm/dL, WBC < 1000 cells/mm^3, platelets < 100,000 cells/mm^3

❷ Encephalopathy - loss of developmental milestones, motor deficit, cerebral atrophy

Table 3. Evaluation and Follow-Up of HIV-Infected Children

Initial evaluation	• Confirm infection with repeat PCR or ELISA • Clinical exam and growth evaluation • HIV viral load determination, +/- resistance testing • Baseline T and B cell subsets, CBC with differential and reticulocyte count • Neurodevelopmental evaluation, perform imaging if abnormal • Baseline renal, liver, lipid, heart, and infectious status • Immunoglobulin levels • Determine CDC disease stage
Evaluate every 3-4 months	• Viral load and CD4+ cell count (for prophylaxis and antiretroviral therapy) • CBC, platelet count, LFT, electrolytes, BUN, and Cr
Evaluate every 6 months	• Neurodevelopment assessment, imaging if abnormal • Urinalysis • Lipid panel
Evaluate yearly	• CXR, ECHO, and ECG in symptomatic children (stage B and C) • PPD and anergy panel control • Hepatitis, toxoplasmosis, EBV, and CMV serology

References

1. Centers for Disease Control and Prevention. USPHS Task force guidelines for the use of antiretroviral agents in pediatric HIV infection, March 2005. Available at: http://AIDSinfo.nih.gov.
2. Centers for Disease Control and Prevention 1994 revised classification system for human immunodeficiency virus infection in children less than 13 years of age. *MMWR* 1994; 43(RR-12);1–10.
3. States LJ, Zimmerman RA, Rutstein RM. Imaging of Pediatric Central Nervous System HIV Infection. *Neuroimaging Clinics of North America*. 1997; May; 7(2);321–339.

30

Antiretroviral Therapy in Children

Kimberley Brown, PharmD
Assistant Professor, Department of Pediatrics
Pediatric Infectious Diseases and Immunology
The Rainbow Center for Women, Adolescents, Children and Families
University of Florida, Jacksonville

This chapter summarizes information released by The Working Group on Antiretroviral Therapy and Medical Management of HIV-Infected Children "Guidelines for the Use of Antiretroviral Agents in Pediatric HIV Infection." Clinicians are encouraged to consult the full guidelines at www.aidsinfo.nih.gov.

Introduction

Although the pathogenesis of HIV infection and the general virologic and immunologic principles underlying the use of antiretroviral therapy are similar for all HIV-infected persons, there are unique considerations needed for HIV-infected infants, children, and adolescents, including:

- Acquisition of infection through perinatal exposure for many infected children
- *In utero* exposure to zidovudine (ZDV) and other antiretroviral medications in many perinatally infected children
  - Differences in diagnostic evaluation in perinatal infection
  - Differences in thymic potential and CD4+ T-lymphocyte dynamics in children
- Changes in pharmacokinetic parameters with age caused by the continuing development and maturation of organ systems involved in drug metabolism and clearance
- Differences in the clinical and virologic manifestations of perinatal HIV infection secondary to the occurrence of primary infection in growing, immunologically immature children
- Special considerations associated with adherence to treatment for children and adolescents
- Availability of pediatric formulations

Special Concepts for Using Antiretroviral Therapy in Children

Although some information regarding the efficacy of antiretroviral drugs for children can be extrapolated from clinical trials involving adults, clinical trials for children that evaluate the impact of therapy on specific manifestations of HIV infection in children, including growth, development, and neurologic disease continue to be in development. This does not preclude the use of any approved antiretroviral drug in children.

All antiretroviral drugs approved for treatment of HIV infection may be used for children when indicated – irrespective of labeling notations. However, there is increasing data on the use of specific antiretroviral agents in infants and children.

Management of HIV infection in infants, children, and adolescents is rapidly evolving and becoming increasingly complex; therefore, wherever possible, management of HIV infection in children and adolescents should be directed by a specialist in the treatment of pediatric and adolescent HIV infection. If this is not possible, such experts should be consulted regularly.

Effective management of the complex and diverse needs of HIV-infected infants, children, adolescents, and their families requires a multidisciplinary team approach that includes physicians, nurses, social workers, psychologists, nutritionists, outreach workers, and pharmacists.

Determination of HIV RNA copy number and CD4+ T-lymphocyte levels is essential for monitoring and modifying antiretroviral treatment in infected children and adolescents as well as adults

Healthcare providers considering antiretroviral regimens for children and adolescents should consider certain factors influencing adherence to therapy, including:

- Availability and palatability of pediatric formulations
- Impact of medication schedule on quality of life, including number of medications, frequency of administration, ability to co-administer with other prescribed medications, and need to take with or without food
- Ability of the child's caregiver or the adolescent to administer complex drug regimens and availability of resources that might be effective in facilitating adherence
- Potential for drug interactions
- Ability to meet storage requirements including refrigeration

The choice of antiretroviral regimens should include consideration of factors associated with possible limitation of future treatment options, including the potential for the development of antiretroviral resistance

Monitoring growth and development is essential for the care of HIV-infected children. Growth failure and neurodevelopment deterioration may be specific manifestations of HIV infection in children. Nutritional support therapy is an intervention that affects immune function, quality of life, and bioactivity of antiretroviral drugs.

Recommendations for the Initiation of Antiretroviral Therapy

GENERAL CONSIDERATIONS

Antiretroviral therapy has provided substantial clinical benefit to HIV-infected children with immunologic or clinical symptoms of HIV infection. Studies have demonstrated substantial improvements in neurodevelopment, growth, and immunologic and/or virologic status following initiation of combination antiretroviral therapies. Clinical studies show that combination therapy, particularly regimens that utilize PIs or NNRTIs as part of the combination, is clinically, immunologically, and virologically superior to monotherapy or dual nucleoside combination therapy.

Data from clinical trials that address the effectiveness of antiretroviral therapy in asymptomatic infants and children with normal immune function are not available. However, initiation of therapy early in the course of HIV infection, including during the period of primary infection in the neonate, is theoretically advantageous. Control of viral replication in perinatally-infected infants is inadequate, as demonstrated by the high levels of HIV RNA that are observed during the first 1 to 2 years of life following perinatal infection. Initiation of aggressive antiretroviral therapy during this early period of viral replication could theoretically preserve immune function, diminish viral dissemination, lower the viral set point, and result in improved clinical outcome.

WHEN TO INITIATE THERAPY

Note: Indications for initiation of antiretroviral therapy in post-pubertal HIV-infected adolescents should follow the adult guidelines. See also Chapter 5, Antiretroviral Therapy, for adult guidelines and Chapter 35, Adolescent Issues.

Because of the high risk for rapid progression of HIV disease, all HIV-infected infants <12 months old should be treated, regardless of clinical, immunologic, or virologic parameters. Some intriguing data suggest that the risk of disease progression during the first 2 years of life may be related to maternal clinical, immunologic, and virologic HIV disease status during pregnancy, with more rapid progression in infants born to women with more advanced HIV disease.

Indication for Treating HIV Infected Children >12 months of age

Clinical Category		CD4 percentage		Plasma HIV RNA	Recommendation
AIDS (Clinical Category C)	OR	<15% (Immune Category 3)		Any Value	Treat
Mild to moderate symptoms (Clinical Category A or B)		15–25% (Immune Category 2)	OR	>100,000 copies/mL	Consider Treatment
Asymptomatic (Clinical Category N)	AND	>25% (Immune Category 1)	AND	<100,000 copies/mL	Many experts would **defer therapy** and closely monitor clinical, immune and viral parameters

Therapy should be deferred in situations in which the risk for clinical disease progression is low and other factors (e.g., concern for the durability of response, safety, and adherence) favor postponing treatment. In such cases, the healthcare provider should regularly monitor virologic and immunologic activity, and clinical status. Indications for initiation of antiretroviral therapy in children with HIV infection should be based on:

- Severity of HIV disease and risk of disease progression as determined by presence or history of HIV-related serious or AIDS-defining illnesses (i.e., clinical categories A, B, or C or immune category 2 or 3)
- Immune suppression via absolute CD4+ cell count, percentage, and plasma HIV RNA level. Availability of appropriate (and palatable) drug formulations for the child and pharmacokinetic information on appropriate dosing in the child's age group.
- Potency, complexity (e.g., dosing frequency, food and fluid requirements), and potential short- and long-term adverse effects of the antiretroviral regimen
- Effect of initial regimen choice on later therapeutic options
- Presence of co-morbidity that could affect drug choice, such as tuberculosis, Hepatitis B or C infection, or chronic renal or liver disease
- Dose modification may be required for individuals with significant renal/liver disease
- Potential antiretroviral drug interactions with other medications required by the child
- The ability of the caregiver and child to adhere to the regimen.

Consideration should also be given to obtaining resistance testing prior to initiating therapy in newly diagnosed infants <12 months of age. This is-particularly true if the mother is known or suspected to have drug resistant virus.

CHOICE OF INITIAL ANTIRETROVIRAL THERAPY

Combination therapy is recommended for all infants, children, and adolescents who are treated with antiretroviral agents. Combination therapy slows disease progression and improves survival, results in a greater and more sustained virologic response, and delays development of drug resistant virus. Aggressive antiretroviral therapy for primary perinatal infection with three or four drugs is recommended because it provides the best opportunity to preserve immune function and delay disease progression. The goal of antiretroviral therapy is to maximally suppress viral replication, preferably to undetectable levels.

Based on clinical trials involving infected adults, the preferred regimen is combination therapy with 2 NRTIs and one PI or one NNRTI. Triple NRTI based regimens are reserved for last line due to low potency when compared to other regimens. Recent data using once a day therapy with 2 NRTIs and one NNRTI in children > 3 months of age shows promise.

To date there are 21 antiretroviral agents that are FDA-approved for use in adults with HIV. Twelve of these antiretrovirals also have approval in children. These medications fall into 5 different classes: nucleoside reverse transcriptase inhibitors (NRTIs), nucleotide reverse transcriptase inhibitors (NtRTIs), non-nucleoside reverse transcriptase inhibitors (NNRTIs), protease inhibitors (PIs), and fusion inhibitors.

Nucleoside reverse transcriptase inhibitors include zidovudine (ZDV, AZT, Retrovir®), didanosine (ddI, Videx®, Videx EC®), stavudine (d4T, Zerit®), lamivudine (3TC, Epivir®), emtricitabine (FTC, Emtriva™), abacavir (ABC, Ziagen®), and zalcitabine (ddC, Hivid®). Currently all NRTIs are available as liquid formulations, except emtricitabine, and zalcitabine. Furthermore, there are several fixed dose combinations that are available as solid dosage forms: Combivir (zidovudine/lamivudine®), Trizivir (zidovudine/lamivudine/abacavir®), Epzicom (lamivudine/abacavir™), and Truvada (emtricitabine/tenofovir®). These are difficult to use in small children due to current fixed dose formulations.

Tenofovir (TDF, Viread®) is the only nucleotide reverse transcriptase inhibitor available. Tenofovir differs from nucleoside reverse transcriptase inhibitors because it already contains a phosphate group (therefore, the initial phosphorylation required for NRTIs activation is bypassed). Tenofovir is FDA-approved for use in HIV-infected individuals >18 years of age. Several clinical trials and case reports have documented renal and urinary disorders such as renal failure, Fanconi's Syndrome and nephrogenic diabetes insipidus. Furthermore, in the 903 Study, significantly greater mean percentage reductions in bone mineral density from baseline were observed versus the comparator regimen. Studies in adolescent and pediatric patients are currently underway; however, the safety and efficacy of use in pediatric patients has not been established.

Delavirdine (DLV, Rescriptor®), efavirenz (EFV, Sustiva™) and nevirapine (NVP, Viramune®) make up the class called non-nucleoside reverse transcriptase inhibitors. Nevirapine and efavirenz are FDA-approved for use in pediatrics. Nevirapine is available as a liquid formulation and is recommended to use in children <3 years of age who cannot swallow capsules. Efavirenz is available as capsules, and a liquid formulation is currently under investigation. Delavirdine is not approved for use in pediatrics. Adherence is of paramount importance, since resistance develops quickly after monotherapy and cross-resistance between drugs in this class is common. This class also has a high risk of hypersensitivity reactions such as Stevens-Johnson's syndrome, and rare but potentially life-threatening hepatitis. Those at greatest risk for hepatitis are women with a CD4 count >250 cells/mm^3 and men with a CD4 count >400 cells/mm^3.

Current PIs with formulations appropriate for infants and children who cannot swallow pills include nelfinavir (NFV, Viracept®), ritonavir (RTV, Norvir®), lopinavir/ritonavir (Kaletra®), and amprenavir (AMP, Agenerase®). Indinavir (IDV, Crixivan®), and saquinavir (SQV, hard gel capsule, Invirase®, and soft gel capsule, Fortovase®), are not approved for use in pediatrics, and are not available in liquid formulations. Indinavir is recommended for consideration for children who can tolerate swallowing capsules. Atazanavir, fosamprenavir, and the newly approved tipranavir have only been approved for use in HIV-infected adults and adolescents. Dose optimization studies for children are underway for several protease inhibitors including fosamprenavir, atazanavir, and tipranavir.

Enfuvirtide (T-20, Fuzeon®) is the first FDA-approved fusion inhibitor and the first antiretroviral that is an injection. Enfuvirtide is an amino acid synthetic peptide that interferes with the entry of HIV into CD4 cells by inhibiting fusion of viral and cellular membranes. Enfuvirtide should be used in combination with other antiretrovirals, and has been approved in HIV-infected patients >6 years of age and older. The safety and pharmacokinetics have not been established in pediatric patients < 6 years of age. Enfuvirtide should be reserved for treatment experienced individuals and not for initial therapy.

Table 1. Recommended Antiretroviral Regimens for Initial Therapy
for HIV Infection in Children

REGIMENS	
PI based regimens:§	
Strongly Recommended	Lopinavir/ritonavir *or* nelfinavir *or* ritonavir + Zidovudine **plus** (didanosine **or** lamivudine); **or** (stavudine **plus** lamivudine)
Alternative	Indinavir *or* amprenavir (children ≥4 years old) **+**Zidovudine **plus** (didanosine **or** lamivudine); **or** (stavudine **plus** lamivudine)
NNRTI based regimens: §	
Strongly Recommended	**>3 yrs:** Efavirenz (with or without nelfinavir) + Zidovudine + (didanosine **or** lamivudine); **or** (stavudine + lamivudine) **≤3 yrs or who cannot swallow capsules**: Nevirapine + Zidovudine **+** didanosine **or** lamivudine; **or** stavudine + lamivudine
Alternative	**>3 yrs:** Nevirapine + Zidovudine + didanosine **or** lamivudine; **or** stavudine + lamivudine
NRTI based regimens: †	
Strongly Recommended	None
Alternative	Zidovudine + lamivudine + abacavir
Alternative choices for NRTIs (to use in conjunction with PIs or NNRTIs):	
	Abacavir **plus** (zidovudine **or** lamivudine); **or** didanosine **plus** lamivudine
Use in special circumstances:	
	Stavudine **plus** didanosine; **or** zalcitabine **plus** zidovudine
Insufficient Data:	
	Tenofovir, emtricitabine, atazanavir, fosamprenavir, or tipranavir-containing regimens Enfuvirtide as initial therapy Dual PI containing regimens with the exception of Lopinavir/ritonavir
Not Recommended:‡	
	Zalcitabine **plus** didanosine, stavudine, **or** lamivudine; **or** zidovudine **plus** stavudine Monotherapy except with zidovudine in the first 6 weeks of life

§Evidence of clinical benefit and sustained viral suppression in clinical trials of HIV-infected adults and children
†Durability of viral suppression may be less in adults/children than with strongly recommended regimens
  or may not yet be determined
‡Evidence against use because of overlapping toxicity and/or because use may be virologically undesirable
SOURCE: *Guidelines for the Use of Antiretroviral Agents in Pediatric HIV Infection*, available through the Working Group on Antiretroviral Therapy and Medical Management of HIV-infected Children (http://www.aidsinfo.nih.gov), March 24, 2005.

WHEN TO CHANGE ANTIRETROVIRAL THERAPY

The following four reasons warrant a consideration for change in antiretroviral therapy:
- Failure of current regimen with evidence of disease progression based on virologic, immunologic, or clinical parameters
- Toxicity or intolerance to current regimen
- New data demonstrating that a drug or regimen is superior to the current regimen
- Evidence of resistance or mutations via genotypic or phenotypic data

When therapy must be changed because of treatment failure or suboptimal response to treatment, clinicians should work with families to assess the possible contribution of adherence problems to the failure of the current regimen. Issues regarding adherence should be addressed to increase the likelihood of a successful outcome when initiating a new regimen. These issues are best addressed before therapy is instituted and need to be reinforced during therapy.

Intensive family education, training in the administration of prescribed medications, and discussion of the importance of adherence to the drug regimen should be completed before initiation of new treatment. In addition, frequent patient visits and intensive follow-up during the initial months after a new antiretroviral regimen is started are needed to support and educate the family and to monitor adherence, tolerance, and virologic response to the new regimen.

CHOICE OF A NEW ANTIRETROVIRAL REGIMEN (See Table 2)

• When a therapy is changed because of **toxicity or intolerance**, agents with different toxicity and side-effect profiles should be chosen, when possible. Healthcare providers should have comprehensive knowledge of the toxicity profile of each agent before selecting a new regimen. In the event of drug intolerance, change of a single drug in a multi-drug regimen and, in certain circumstances, dose reductions are permissible options. However, antiretroviral drugs should only be reduced to the lower end of the therapeutic range for those antiretrovirals for which an effective dosing range is known, and adequacy of antiretroviral activity should be confirmed by the monitoring of HIV RNA levels.

• When changing therapy because of **treatment failure**, adherence to therapy should be assessed as a potential cause of failure
• If the patient is adherent to the prescribed drug regimen, assume the development of **drug resistance**. Consider obtaining a genotype and/or phenotype to assess for possible mutations and drug susceptibility. If possible, change at least 2 drugs to new antiretroviral agents. Change in one drug or addition of a drug to a failing regimen is suboptimal. The new regimen should include at least 3 new drugs, if possible. The potential for cross-resistance between antiretroviral drugs should be considered in choosing new drugs, as well as subsequent resistance.
• When considering changing to a **new regimen**, all other medications taken by the patient should be reviewed for possible drug interactions
• A change to a new regimen, especially one containing PIs, must include a discussion of **treatment adherence issues** between the caregivers of the infected child and the healthcare provider. The healthcare provider must recognize that certain medications are difficult to take in combination because of exact and often conflicting requirements with respect to whether they can be taken with food and other antiretrovirals and storage issues
• When changing therapy because of **disease progression** in patient with advanced disease, the patient's quality of life must be considered

Table 2. Considerations for Changing Antiretroviral Therapy for HIV-Infected Children

Note: Partial non-adherence can explain each of the scenarios listed above and must be addressed before making any medication changes

Virologic Considerations	• Less than a minimally acceptable virologic response after 8-12 weeks of therapy. For children receiving antiretroviral therapy with 2 NRTIs and a PI, such a response is defined as a < 10-fold (1.0 log10) decrease from baseline HIV RNA levels. • HIV RNA not suppressed to undetectable levels after 4-6 months of antiretroviral therapy [1] • Repeated detection of HIV RNA in children who initially responded to antiretroviral therapy with • undetectable levels [2] • A reproducible increase in HIV RNA copy number among children who have had a substantial HIV RNA response but still have low levels of detectable HIV RNA. Such an increase would warrant change in therapy if, after initiation of the therapeutic regimen, a > 3-fold (0.5 log10) increase in copy number for children aged ≥ 2 years and a > 5-fold (0.7 log10) increase is observed in children aged < 2 years.
Immunologic considerations	• Change in immunologic classification [3] • For children with CD4+ T-lymphocyte percentages of < 15% (i.e., those in immune category 3), a persistent decline of 5 percentiles or more in CD4+ cell percentage (e.g., from 15% to 10%) • A rapid and substantial decrease in absolute CD4+ T-lymphocyte count (e.g., a > 30% decline in < 6 months)
Clinical considerations	• Progressive neurodevelopmental deterioration • Growth failure defined as persistent decline in weight-growth velocity despite adequate nutritional support • and without other explanation • Disease progression defined as advancement from one pediatric clinical category to another (e.g., from clinical category A to clinical category B) [4]

At least 2 measurements (taken one week apart) should be performed before considering a change in therapy.

1. The initial HIV RNA level of the child at the start of therapy and the level achieved with therapy should be considered when contemplating potential drug changes. For example, an immediate change in therapy may not be warranted if there is a sustained 1.5-2.0 log10 decrease in HIV RNA copy number, even if RNA remains detectable at low levels.
2. More frequent evaluation of HIV RNA levels should be considered if the HIV RNA increase is limited (e.g., if when using an HIV RNA assay with a lower limit of detection of 1,000 copies/mL, there is a ≤ 0.7 log10 increase from undetectable to approximately 5,000 copies/mL in an infant aged < 2 years).
3. Minimal changes in CD4+ T-lymphocyte percentage that may result in change in immunologic category (e.g., from 26% to 24% or 16% to 14%) may not be as concerning as a rapid substantial change in CD4+ percentage within the same immunologic category (e.g., a drop from 35% to 25%).
4. In patients with stable immunologic and virologic parameters, progression from one clinical category to another may not represent an indication to change therapy. Thus, in patients whose disease progression is not associated with neurologic deterioration or growth failure, virologic and immunologic considerations are important in deciding whether to change therapy.

ANTIVIRAL DRUG RESISTANCE TESTING

Failure of antiretroviral drug combinations to achieve durable viral suppression may occur for several reasons including poor adherence, suboptimal drug pharmacokinetics, and the development of drug resistance mutations. The goal of combination antiretroviral therapy should be to maintain suppression of viral replication to below the limits of detection (<50 RNA copies/mL). Genotypic and phenotypic testing for HIV resistance may be useful in guiding initial therapy and in choosing a new treatment regimen. However, the best application of these assays in treatment regimens has not been established for children. If resistance testing is performed it should always be carried out while the child is receiving treatment as the absence of therapy results in viral reversion to wild-type or quasispecies.

The optimal goal of antiretroviral therapy is to reduce plasma HIV RNA to below detection of the most sensitive assay available (<50 copies/mL). Accomplishing this level of viral suppression, while not always possible in perinatally infected infants and children, will reduce the likelihood that genotypic (GT)/phenotypic (PT) resistance will emerge.

Several GT assays are available for detecting specific HIV genetic variants (mutations). They are based on amplification procedures and can usually detect mutations in plasma samples >1,000 copies/mL of HIV RNA. A compilation of the most common HIV-1 mutations selected by currently available antiretroviral agents is available at: http://hiv-web.lanl.gov or http://hivdb.stanford.edu.

PT assays directly measure the ability of the viral isolate to grow in the presence of a drug and measure the 50% or 90% inhibitory concentrations of a drug against the virus *in vitro*, compared to a laboratory strain of wild type virus. The result is expressed as a "fold-change" in susceptibility above a particular cut-off level, below which the virus is assumed to be drug sensitive. These assays have historically been more complex than GT assays but are now available from commercial laboratories.

A method for predicting PT based on the GT is also available. This method matches mutations obtained from the patient sample with a large database of samples for which both genotype and phenotype are known. Thus, the sample is assigned a predicted phenotype susceptibility based on the mean of all the individual samples matching the patient's genotype. The result is expressed as a fold-change. In this assay, both the GT and predicted PT are contained in the test report.

Results of clinical trials with laboratory endpoints in adults have indicated that using genotypic or phenotypic testing to help guide changes in antiretroviral therapy results in a significantly greater, short term, virologic response compared to clinical judgment alone. Although results of similar trials in children are not available, most pediatric experts do not think viral replication in the face of resistance differs between children and adults.

FOR MORE INFORMATION

Guidelines for the Use of Antiretroviral Agents in Pediatric HIV Infection is available through the Working Group on Antiretroviral Therapy and Medical Management of HIV-infected Children. March 24, 2005 **http://www.aidsinfo.nih.gov.**

SPECIFIC ANTIRETROVIRAL AGENTS

The following pages provide detailed information about the currently available antiretroviral medications.

NUCLEOSIDE REVERSE TRANSCRIPTASE INHIBITORS

Abacavir (Ziagen®)

Combination formulations:
Epzicom (3TC 300 mg + ABC 600 mg)
Trizvir (ZDV 300 mg +3TC 150 mg + ABC 300 mg)

SYNONYMS
- GW 1592U89
- ABC

PEDIATRIC FORMULATIONS
- 20 mg/mL
- Strawberry banana flavor

MANUFACTURER/PEDIATRIC APPROVAL
- Glaxo SmithKline, Inc.
- Pediatric labeling: December 17, 1998

ADOLESCENT/ADULT FORMULATION
- 300 mg tablets

NEONATAL DOSE	PEDIATRIC DOSING RANGE	USUAL PEDIATRIC DOSE	ADOLESCENT/ADULT DOSE
1-3mo (investigational) 8mg/kg q12h	8mg/kg bid maximum 300mg q12	8mg/kg bid maximum 300mg q12	>60kg: 300mg bid or 600mg qd

ADVERSE REACTIONS	MANAGEMENT
MOST FREQUENT	
• Nausea and vomiting • Anorexia • Fever • Headache • Fatigue • Rash	• Adjust dose with hepatic impairment • Consult HIV specialist for HSR evaluation
Black Box Warning	PATIENT COUNSELING POINTS
Approximately 8% of patients receiving abacavir develop hypersensitivity reaction (**Black Box Warning**) • Symptoms include , fever, rash, N/V/D, or abdominal pain, fatigue, dyspnea, cough, pharyngitis • Lactic acidosis and severe hepatomegaly with steatosis, including fatal cases, have been reported with the use of nucleoside analogues alone or in combination, including abacavir and other antiretrovirals.	• Fatal hypersensitivity/anaphylaxis has occurred with rechallenge • Take with or without food • Store solution at room temperature

SPECIAL INSTRUCTIONS
Patients and parents should be cautioned about the signs and risks associated with hypersensitivity reactions. A medication guide and warning card should be provided. Patients experiencing a hypersensitivity reaction should be reported to the Abacavir Hypersensitivity Registry (800-270-0425).

DRUG INTERACTIONS –Use with caution if patient is known to use alcohol or methadone
- See Chapter 6, Antiretroviral Drug Interactions

Didanosine (Videx, Videx EC®)

SYNONYMS
- ddI
- Dideoxyinosine

PEDIATRIC FORMULATIONS
- 10 mg/mL pediatric powder for oral solution
- Chalky mint flavor

MANUFACTURER/PEDIATRIC APPROVAL
- Bristol Myers Squibb
- Pediatric labeling: October 9, 1991

ADOLESCENT/ADULT FORMULATION
- 25mg, 50mg, 100mg, and 150mg chewable tablets
- 100mg, 167mg, 250mg, and 375mg powder packets
- 10mg/ml suspension (chalky mandarin orange flavor)
- 125mg, 200mg, 250mg, 400mg delayed release capsules with enteric-coated (EC) beadlets

NEONATAL DOSE	PEDIATRIC DOSING RANGE	USUAL PEDIATRIC DOSE	ADOLESCENT/ADULT DOSE
(2wk-8mo)	(>8mo)	(>8mo)	≥60kg: 200mg bid or 400mg qd
50-100mg/m^2/dose po bid	90-150mg/m^2/dose po bid	120mg/m^2/dose po bid	<60kg: 125mg bid or 250mg qd
Dose with tenofovir (TDF, Viread®)			≥60kg: 250mg qd
			<60kg: 200mg qd

ADVERSE REACTIONS	MANAGEMENT
MOST FREQUENT	
• Nausea and vomiting (7-13%) • Abdominal pain (7-13%) • Diarrhea (81%) LESS FREQUENT • Peripheral neuropathy • Retinal changes and optic neuritis	• Consult HIV specialist • OTC diarrhea remedies • Keep child well hydrated
Black box warning	PATIENT COUNSELING POINTS
• Lactic acidosis and severe hepatomegaly with steatosis, including fatal cases, have been reported with the use of nucleoside analogues alone or in combination, including didanosine and other antiretrovirals. • Fatal and non-fatal pancreatitis have occurred during therapy with didanosine used alone or in combination regimens	• Videx EC must be taken on an empty stomach • Swallow capsules whole • Avoid alcohol while taking Videx • Report any vision changes • Counsel on symptoms of lactic acidosis and pancreatitis • Buffered formulation - avoid other medications at same time (e.g. 2 hours before or 2 hours after)

Warning: Patients with Phenylketonuria: VIDEX Chewable/Dispersible Buffered Tablets contain 36.5mg of phenylalanine

Patients on Sodium-Restricted Diets: VIDEX Buffered Powder for Oral Solution: Each single-dose packet of VIDEX Buffered Powder for Oral Solution contains 1380 mg sodium.

ADMINISTRATION ISSUES
- Requires a high gastric pH for absorption; inactivated by stomach acid
- Contains buffering agents or antacids which decreases the acidity in the stomach
- Food decreases absorption by 55%. Administer one hour before or 2 hours after a meal.
- Non-enteric coated formulations can decrease the absorption of PIs

SOLUTION
- Shake well

- Refrigerate
- Admixture stable for 30 days

DRUG INTERACTIONS – As above, drug levels of didanosine or other drugs may be altered if given at the same time
- See Chapter 6, Antiretroviral Drug Interactions

Lamivudine (Epivir®)

Combination Formulations:
Combivir (ZDV 300 mg + 3TC 150 mg)
Trizvir (ZDV 300 mg + 3TC 150 mg + ABC 300 mg)
Epzicom (3TC 300 mg + ABC 600 mg)

SYNONYMS
- 3TC

PEDIATRIC FORMULATIONS
- 10 mg/mL solution
- Strawberry-banana flavored

MANUFACTURER/PEDIATRIC APPROVAL
- GlaxoSmithKline, Inc.
- Pediatric labeling: September 6, 1996

ADOLESCENT/ADULT FORMULATION
- 150mg, 300mg tablets

NEONATAL DOSE	USUAL PEDIATRIC DOSE	ADOLESCENT/ADULT DOSE
(birth-30days) 2mg/kg/dose po bid	(3mo-16yrs) 4mg/kg/dose po bid; max 150mg bid	≥50kg:150mg po bid or 300mg qd <50kg: 2mg/kg/dose po bid

ADVERSE REACTIONS	MANAGEMENT
MOST FREQUENT • Nausea and vomiting • Abdominal pain • Diarrhea • Fatigue • Headache • Skin rash LESS FREQUENT • Pancreatitis	• Consult HIV specialist • OTC diarrhea remedies • Keep child well hydrated
Black box warning	PATIENT COUNSELING POINTS
• Lactic acidosis and severe hepatomegaly with steatosis, including fatal cases, have been reported with the use of nucleoside analogues alone or in combination, including lamivudine and other antiretrovirals. • Severe acute exacerbations of hepatitis B have been reported in patients who are co-infected with hepatitis B and HIV and have discontinued lamivudine.	• Take with or without food • Counsel on symptoms of lactic acidosis and pancreatitis • Store solution at room temperature and shake well

ADMINISTRATION ISSUES
- Severe acute exacerbations of hepatitis B have been reported in patients who are co-infected with hepatitis B and HIV and have discontinued lamivudine.
Store oral solution at room temperature.

DRUG INTERACTIONS – No known drug-drug interactions
- See Chapter 6, Antiretroviral Drug Interactions

Stavudine (Zerit®)

<u>SYNONYMS</u>
- d4T

<u>PEDIATRIC FORMULATIONS</u>
- 1 mg/mL solution
- Fruit flavored

<u>MANUFACTURER/PEDIATRIC APPROVAL</u>
- Bristol Myers Squibb
- Pediatric labeling: September 9, 1991

<u>ADOLESCENT/ADULT FORMULATION</u>
- 15mg, 20mg, 30mg, and 40mg capsules

NEONATAL DOSE	PEDIATRIC DOSING RANGE	USUAL PEDIATRIC DOSE	ADOLESCENT/ADULT DOSE
(birth-13days)	(<30kg)	(>8mo)	≥60kg: 40mg po bid
0.5mg/kg/dose po bid	1mg/kg/dose po bid	120mg/m²/dose po bid	30-60kg: 30mg po bid

ADVERSE REACTIONS	MANAGEMENT
MOST FREQUENT	
• Nausea and vomiting • Abdominal pain • Diarrhea • Peripheral neuropathy • Lipoatrophy • Headache • Skin rash • Hyperlipidemia	• Consult HIV specialist • OTC diarrhea remedies • Keep child well hydrated • Adjust dose for renal insufficiency • Should not be used with ZDV
Black box warning	PATIENT COUNSELING POINTS
• Lactic acidosis and severe hepatomegaly with steatosis, including fatal cases, have been reported with the use of nucleoside analogues alone or in combination, including didanosine and other antiretrovirals. • Fatal and non-fatal pancreatitis have occurred during therapy with stavudine used alone or in combination regimens	• Take with or without food • Counsel on symptoms of lactic acidosis and pancreatitis • Refrigerate solution and shake well • Discard unused solution after 30 days

<u>DRUG INTERACTIONS</u> - Neurotoxins such as cisplatin, dapsone, didanosine, ethionamide, isoniazid, metronidazole, nitrofurantoin, pentamidine (iv), phenytoin, vincristine, and zalcitabine may exacerbate or ↑ risk of peripheral neuropathy. May ↑ risk of pancreatitis with ddI. May inhibit tubular secretion of stavudine with probenecid. May ↓ antiviral activity with ZDV.
- See Chapter 6, Antiretroviral Drug Interactions

Zalcitabine (Hivid®)

<u>SYNONYMS</u>
- ddC

<u>PEDIATRIC FORMULATIONS</u>
- 0.1 mg/mL syrup (investigational)

<u>MANUFACTURER/PEDIATRIC APPROVAL</u>
- Roche Pharmaceuticals
- No pediatric labeling

<u>ADOLESCENT/ADULT FORMULATION</u>
- 0.375mg, 0.75mg tablets

NEONATAL DOSE	PEDIATRIC DOSING RANGE	USUAL PEDIATRIC DOSE	ADOLESCENT/ADULT DOSE
No data available	0.005-0.01mg/kg po q8h	0.01mg po q8h	0.75mg po q8h

ADVERSE REACTIONS	MANAGEMENT
MOST FREQUENT	
• Nausea and vomiting • Abdominal pain • Diarrhea • Headache • Malaise • Oral/esophageal ulcers • Skin rash • Hematologic toxicity • Peripheral neuropathy • Pancreatitis	• Consult HIV specialist • OTC diarrhea remedies • Keep child well hydrated • Adjust dose for renal insufficiency • Use with caution in patients with pre-existing neuropathy or pre-existing liver disease
Black box warning	PATIENT COUNSELING POINTS
• Lactic acidosis and severe hepatomegaly with steatosis, including fatal cases, have been reported with the use of nucleoside analogues alone or in combination, including zalcitabine and other antiretrovirals. • Fatal and non-fatal pancreatitis have occurred during therapy	• Take on an empty stomach

<u>DRUG INTERACTIONS</u> – Many drug-drug interactions and questionable value as an antiretroviral agent. Use alternative when possible.
- See Chapter 6, Antiretroviral Drug Interactions

Zidovudine (Retrovir®)

SYNONYMS
- AZT, ZDV

Combination Formulations :
Epzicom (3TC 300 mg + ABC 600 mg)
Combivir (ZDV 300 mg + 3TC 150 mg)

PEDIATRIC FORMULATIONS
- 10mg/ml syrup (strawberry flavor)
- 10mg/ml injection

MANUFACTURER/PEDIATRIC APPROVAL
- GlaxoSmithKline
- Pediatric labeling May 1, 1990

ADOLESCENT/ADULT FORMULATION
- 100mg capsules, 300mg tablet

PREMATURE INFANTS	NEONATAL DOSE (< 6 wks age)	PEDIATRIC DOSING RANGE	USUAL PEDIATRIC DOSE	ADOLESCENT/ADULT DOSE
1.5mg/kg IV q12	2mg/kg po q6 hours (starting within 12 hours after birth) 1.5mg/kg IV q6h	90-180mg/m^2/dose po q6-12h	160mg/ m^2/dose po q8h	300mg po bid; 200mg po tid

ADVERSE REACTIONS	MANAGEMENT
MOST FREQUENT	
• Nausea and vomiting • Abdominal pain • Diarrhea • Headache • Malaise • Hematologic toxicity • Asthenia	• Consult HIV specialist • OTC diarrhea remedies • Keep child well hydrated • Use of erythropoietin or filgrastim may be indicated for hematologic toxicity
LESS FREQUENT	
• Myopathy • Myositis	
Black box warning	PATIENT COUNSELING POINTS
• Lactic acidosis and severe hepatomegaly with steatosis, including fatal cases, have been reported with the use of nucleoside analogues alone or in combination, including zidovudine and other antiretrovirals. • Zidovudine has been associated with hematologic toxicity including anemia and neutropenia	• Take with or without food

DRUG INTERACTIONS – As above, hematologic toxicity may be increased when used in combination with other pharmacologic agents.
- See Chapter 6, Antiretroviral Drug Interactions

Tenofovir (Viread®)
Combination Formulation:
Truvada (TDF 300mg + FTC 200mg)

SYNONYMS
- TDF

PEDIATRIC FORMULATIONS
- None

MANUFACTURER/PEDIATRIC APPROVAL
- Gilead Pharmaceuticals
- No pediatric labeling

ADOLESCENT/ADULT FORMULATION
- 300mg tablet

NEONATAL DOSE	PEDIATRIC DOSING RANGE	USUAL PEDIATRIC DOSE	ADOLESCENT/ADULT DOSE
N/A	8mg/kg/dose qd (investigational)	N/A	300mg po qd

ADVERSE REACTIONS	MANAGEMENT
MOST FREQUENT	
• Nausea and vomiting • Abdominal pain • Diarrhea • Headache • Dyspepsea • Renal toxicity • Bone toxicity	• Consult HIV specialist • OTC diarrhea remedies • Keep child well hydrated
Black box warning	**PATIENT COUNSELING POINTS**
• Lactic acidosis and severe hepatomegaly with steatosis, including fatal cases, have been reported with the use of nucleoside analogues alone or in combination, including tenofovir and other antiretrovirals. • Severe acute exacerbations of hepatitis B have been reported in patients who are co-infected with hepatitis B and HIV and have discontinued Tenofovir.	• Take with or without food • Counsel on symptoms of lactic acidosis

DRUG INTERACTIONS - Tenofovir also interacts with didanosine and atazanavir. (See Videx and Reyataz for dosing)
- See Chapter 6, Antiretroviral Drug Interactions

Special Instructions: Use caution in patients with renal insufficiency. Follow dosing guidelines for changes in renal function (drugs that compete for active tubular secretion may change tenofovir concentrations and/or other renally eliminated drugs).

Emtricitabine (Emtriva™)
Combination Formulation:
Truvada (TDF 300mg + FTC 200mg)

SYNONYMS
- FTC

PEDIATRIC FORMULATIONS
- None

MANUFACTURER/PEDIATRIC APPROVAL
- Gilead Pharmaceuticals
- No pediatric labeling

ADOLESCENT/ADULT FORMULATION
- 200mg capsule

NEONATAL DOSE	PEDIATRIC DOSING RANGE	USUAL PEDIATRIC DOSE	ADOLESCENT/ADULT DOSE
N/A	6mg/kg/day (max 200mg qd)	N/A	200mg po qd

ADVERSE REACTIONS	MANAGEMENT
MOST FREQUENT	
• Nausea and vomiting • Abdominal pain • Diarrhea • Headache • Asthenia Hyperpigmentation of palms of hands and soles of feet (usually seen in those with darker pigmented skin)	• Consult HIV specialist • OTC diarrhea remedies • Keep child well hydrated
Black box warning	PATIENT COUNSELING POINTS
• Lactic acidosis and severe hepatomegaly with steatosis, including fatal cases, have been reported with the use of nucleoside analogues alone or in combination, including emtricitabine and other antiretrovirals. • Severe acute exacerbations of hepatitis B have been reported in patients who are co-infected with hepatitis B and HIV and have discontinued Emtricitabine.	• Take with or without food • Counsel on symptoms of lactic acidosis

DRUG INTERACTIONS – No known drug-drug interactions
- See Chapter 6, Antiretroviral Drug Interactions

NON-NUCLEOSIDE REVERSE TRANSCRIPTASE INHIBITORS

Delavirdine (Rescriptor®)

SYNONYMS
- DLV

MANUFACTURER/PEDIATRIC APPROVAL
- Agouron Pharmaceuticals
- No pediatric labeling

PEDIATRIC FORMULATIONS
- None

ADOLESCENT/ADULT FORMULATION
- 100mg tablet, 200mg capsule

Efavirenz (Sustiva®)

SYNONYMS
- EFV

MANUFACTURER/PEDIATRIC APPROVAL
- Dupont Pharmaceuticals
- Pediatric labeling September 21, 1998

PEDIATRIC FORMULATIONS
- 50mg, 100mg, 200mg capsules

ADOLESCENT/ADULT FORMULATION
- 600mg tablet
- 30mg/ml syrup (investigational)

NEONATAL DOSE	PEDIATRIC DOSING RANGE	ADOLESCENT/ADULT DOSE
No data available	10 to <15kg: 200mg po qhs 15 to <20kg: 250mg po qhs 20 to <25kg: 300mg po qhs 25 to <32.5kg: 350mg po qhs 32.5 to <40kg: 400mg po qhs >40kg: 600mg po qhs	600mg po qhs

ADVERSE REACTIONS	MANAGEMENT
MOST FREQUENT	
• Nausea, vomiting, diarrhea • Vivid Dreams • Abdominal pain • Headache • Asthenia • Insomnia • Agitation • Hallucinations	• Consult HIV specialist • OTC diarrhea remedies • Keep child well hydrated
MONITORING	PATIENT COUNSELING POINTS
• Rash-mild to severe; sometimes life threatening. Usually occurs within the first 6 weeks of therapy. Discontinue therapy if rash is severe and do not rechallenge. • Hepatotoxicity: are at greater risk for hepatic events. Greater risk of hepatic adverse effects if associated with elevation in LFTs from baseline. Usually occurs in the first 12 weeks of therapy • Pregnancy category D (do not use in the first trimester of pregnancy) • Adjust dose when used with Kaletra • Monitor lipids closely	• Take with or without food • Take at bedtime to lessen CNS effects • CNS effects usually resolve in 2-4 weeks • Counsel on drug interactions with OTC agents and other agents (i.e. ethinyl estradiol) • Advise to avoid fatty meals with administration • Counsel patients on vivid dreams, dizziness, hallucinations, etc. • Capsules can be opened and added to liquids or foods • Has peppery taste which can be disguised with grape jelly

DRUG INTERACTIONS – EFV is both an inducer and inhibitor of the CYP450 enzyme system and dosage adjustments may be required to avoid adverse drug-drug interactions.
- See Chapter 6, Antiretroviral Drug Interactions

Nevirapine (Viramune®)

SYNONYMS
- NVP

PEDIATRIC FORMULATIONS
- None

MANUFACTURER/PEDIATRIC APPROVAL
- Agouron Pharmaceuticals
- No pediatric labeling

ADOLESCENT/ADULT FORMULATION
- 200mg tablet
- 10mg/ml suspension

NEONATAL DOSE	PEDIATRIC DOSING RANGE	USUAL PEDIATRIC DOSE	ADOLESCENT/ADULT DOSE
5mg/kg qd for 14 days, then 120mg/m^2/dose q12h for 14 days, then 200mg/m^2/dose q12h	2mo-8yrs: 4mg/kg/day for 14 days, then 7mg/kg po bid (max 200mg bid)	8yrs and older:4mg/kg po qd for 14 days, then 4mg/kg po bid (max 200mg bid)	200mg po qd X 14 days, then 200mg po bid

Note: Increase to full dose q12h if no rash or untoward effects

ADVERSE REACTIONS	MANAGEMENT
MOST FREQUENT	
• Nausea and vomiting • Abdominal pain • Diarrhea • Headache • Skin Rash • Sedative Effect	• Consult HIV specialist • OTC diarrhea remedies • Keep child well hydrated
Black box warning	PATIENT COUNSELING POINTS
• Rash-mild to severe; sometimes life threatening. Usually occurs within the first 6 weeks of therapy. Discontinue therapy if rash is severe and do not rechallenge. • Hepatotoxicity: Women with CD4 counts >250 or men with CD4 counts >400 cells/mm^3, and patients with hepatitic B or C co-infection are at greater risk for hepatic events with nevirapine. Greater risk of hepatic adverse effects if associated with elevation in LFTs from baseline. Usually occurs in the first 12 weeks of therapy	• Take with or without food • Counsel on drug interactions with OTC agents and other agents (i.e. ethinyl estradiol) • Shake suspension well and store at room temperature

DRUG INTERACTIONS – NVP is an inducer of the CYP450 enzyme system and dosage adjustments may be required to avoid adverse drug-drug interactions.
- See Chapter 6, Antiretroviral Drug Interactions

PROTEASE INHIBITORS

NOTE : The protease inhibitors are inhibitors of the CYP3A4 system. Adverse drug-drug interactions are common and dosage adjustments may be necessary. Please see Chapter 6, Antiretroviral Drug Interactions.

Amprenavir (Agenerase®)

SYNONYMS
- APV

PEDIATRIC FORMULATIONS
- None

MANUFACTURER/PEDIATRIC APPROVAL
- GlaxoSmithKline
- No pediatric labeling

ADOLESCENT/ADULT FORMULATION
- 15mg/ml solution
- 10mg/ml suspension

NEONATAL DOSE	PEDIATRIC DOSING RANGE	ADOLESCENT/ADULT DOSE
Should not be used in neonates and children <4 years of age due to propylene glycol content	4-16 years and <50 kg: 20mg/kg/dose po bid, max 2400mg qd **or** 15mg/kg/dose po tid, max 2400mg qd **or** 22.5mg/kg/dose po bid (liquid), max 2800mg qd **or** 17mg/kg/dose po tid (liquid), max 2800mg qd	(13-16 yrs old same dosing as adults and adolescents) 1200mg po bid **or** 1200mg + 200mg of RTV qd **or** APV 600mg + RTV 100mg bid **or** 1400mg po bid (liquid)

ADVERSE REACTIONS	MANAGEMENT
MOST FREQUENT	
• Nausea and vomiting • Abdominal pain • Diarrhea • Headache • Perioral paresthesias • Rash • Hyperlipidemia/lipodystrophy • Hyperglycemia	• Consult HIV specialist • OTC diarrhea remedies • Keep child well hydrated
Black box warning	PATIENT COUNSELING POINTS
• Liquid formulation (with propylene glycol) is contraindicated in children <4 years of age, pregnancy, hepatic or renal failure, patients treated with disulfram, or metroniadazole. Do not use unless other PI formulations are not therapeutic options.	• Take with or without food • Counsel on drug interactions with OTC agents and other agents (i.e. ethinyl estradiol) • Shake suspension well and store at room temperature

DRUG INTERACTIONS AND ADMINISTRATION ISSUES
- Amprenavir formulation contains 46 IU/ml Vitamin E and 109 IU Vitamin E per capsule. Excess Vitamin E absorption is associated with creatinuria, decreased platelet function, impaired wound healing, prolongation of the prothrombin time, and hepatomegaly. Patients should not take supplemental Vitamin E.
- The liquid formulation of amprenavir contains propylene glycol. High levels of propylene glycol are associated with hyperosmolarity, lactic acidosis, seizures, and respiratory depression. Neonates, patients with hepatic or renal failure, and children under 4 years should not use amprenavir solution.
- Amprenavir is a sulfonamide. Cross sensitivity between drugs in the sulfonamide class is possible.
- Dosing of the oral solution and capsule are not interchangeable. The bioavailability of the oral solution is 14% less than the capsule.
- Amprenavir can be taken with or without food but should not be taken with high fat meals
- Separate administration of non-enteric coated didanosine or antacids and amprenavir by 2.5 hours
- Capsules should be stored at controlled room temperature
- Adjust dose in hepatic dysfunction; use with caution in patients with moderate to severe hepatic impairment
- See Chapter 6, Antiretroviral Drug Interactions

Atazanavir (Reyataz®)

<u>SYNONYMS</u>
- ATV

<u>PEDIATRIC FORMULATIONS</u>
- None

<u>MANUFACTURER/PEDIATRIC APPROVAL</u>
- Bristol Myers Squibb
- No pediatric labeling

<u>ADOLESCENT/ADULT FORMULATION</u>
- 100mg, 150mg, 200mg capsules

NEONATAL DOSE	PEDIATRIC DOSING RANGE	ADOLESCENT/ADULT DOSE
Not approved for use in infants <3 mo due to the risk of hyperbilirubinemia	Not approved for use, but clinical trials are underway	Tx naïve: 400mg qd Tx exp: 300mg qd + Norvir 100mg qd
Dosing when used with Viread or Sustiva:		300mg qd +Norvir 100mg qd

ADVERSE REACTIONS	MANAGEMENT
MOST FREQUENT	
• Nausea and vomiting • Abdominal pain • Diarrhea • Headache • Jaundice/ Scleral icterus	• Consult HIV specialist • OTC diarrhea remedies • Keep child well hydrated
Warnings/Caution	PATIENT COUNSELING POINTS
• Use caution in patients with a prolonged PR interval or underlying conduction deficit. • Increased unconjugated bilirubin levels (common) • Do not use with proton pump inhibitors	• Take without food • Counsel on drug interactions with OTC agents and other agents (i.e. ethinyl estradiol) • Do not use with proton pump inhibitors. • Interacts with antacids (separate by 2 hours), and H2 blockers (separate by 12 hours)

<u>DRUG INTERACTIONS</u>
- See Chapter 6, Antiretroviral Drug Interactions

Fosamprenavir (Lexiva®)

SYNONYMS
- FPV

PEDIATRIC FORMULATIONS
- None

MANUFACTURER/PEDIATRIC APPROVAL
- GlaxoSmithKline
- No pediatric labeling

ADOLESCENT/ADULT FORMULATION
- 700mg tablet (prodrug equal to 600mg of AMP)

NEONATAL DOSE	PEDIATRIC DOSING RANGE	ADOLESCENT/ADULT DOSE
Not approved for use	Not approved for use, but clinical trials are underway	Tx naïve: 1400mg bid 1400mg qd +Norvir 200mg qd **or** 700mg bid + Norvir 100mg bid **or** Tx exp: 700mg bid + Norvir 100mg bid

Note: Always boost FPV when used with EFV.

ADVERSE REACTIONS	MANAGEMENT
MOST FREQUENT	
• Nausea and vomiting • Abdominal pain • Diarrhea • Headache • Hyperglycemia	• Consult HIV specialist • OTC diarrhea remedies • Keep child well hydrated
Warnings/Caution	PATIENT COUNSELING POINTS
• Amprenavir is a sulfmonamide. Cross reactivity between drugs in the sulfonamide class is possible.	• Take with or without food • Counsel on drug interactions with OTC agents and other agents (i.e. ethinyl estradiol) • Separate antacids or ddI by at least 1 hour before or after FPV.

DRUG INTERACTIONS
- See Chapter 6, Antiretroviral Drug Interactions

Indinavir (Crixivan®)

SYNONYMS
- IDV
- MK-639
- L-735,524

PEDIATRIC FORMULATIONS
- 100 mg capsules

MANUFACTURER/PEDIATRIC APPROVAL
- Merck& Co., Inc.
- Pediatric labeling November 2000

ADOLESCENT/ADULT FORMULATION
- 200 mg, 333 mg, 400 mg capsules

NEONATAL DOSE	PEDIATRIC DOSING RANGE	ADOLESCENT/ADULT DOSE
Not approved for use in infants due to the risk of hyperbilirubinemia	4-15 years of age: 500mg/m2 q8h	800mg q q8h Boosted PI dosing: 400mg bid +Norvir 400mg bid 800mg bid + Norvir 100mg bid for ARV-naïve 800mg bid + Norvir 200mg bid for ARV-exp 600mg bid + Kaletra 3 caps bid NNRTI dosing: 1000mg q8h with EFV or NVP or 800mg bid + Norvir 200mg bid with EFV or NVP

ADVERSE REACTIONS	MANAGEMENT
MOST FREQUENT	
• Nausea and vomiting • Abdominal pain • Diarrhea • Hyperlipidemia/lipodystrophy • Hyperglycemia • Nausea • Abdominal pain • Headache • Hyperbilirubinemia • Oral Ulcers • Nephrolithiasis (Due to crystallization of the drug in the kidney; Onset may occur 1-20 weeks following initiation of therapy)	• Consult HIV specialist • OTC diarrhea remedies • Keep child well hydrated
	PATIENT COUNSELING POINTS
	• Take on an empty stomach (1 hour before meals or 2 hours after meals) • Counsel on drug interactions with OTC agents and other agents (i.e. ethinyl estradiol) • Drink 1-3 liters (1.5 x maintenance) of water daily • Large meals have been shown to reduce bioavailability 60-90% • Separate dose by at least 2 hours from non-enteric coated didanosine and antacids • Capsules should be stored in original container with desiccant

DRUG INTERACTIONS – Do not use with St. John's Wort. IDV is an inhibitor of the CYP450 enzyme system and dosage adjustments may be necessary to avoid adverse drug–drug interactions.
- See Chapter 6, Antiretroviral Drug Interactions

Lopinavir/Ritonavir (Kaletra®)

SYNONYMS
- ABT-53
- LPV/RTV, KAL

PEDIATRIC FORMULATIONS
- Oral solution 80 mg/ml LPV + 20 mg/ml RTV

MANUFACTURER/PEDIATRIC APPROVAL
- Abbott Laboratories
- Pediatric labeling in September 2000

ADOLESCENT/ADULT FORMULATION
- Tablet: 200 mg lopinavir + 50 mg ritonavir
  (Capsules are no longer available)

NEONATAL DOSE	PEDIATRIC DOSING RANGE	USUAL PEDIATRIC DOSE	ADOLESCENT/ADULT DOSE
Not approved for use; clinical trials are underway for children <6mo (investigational dose: 300mg LPV/m^2 bid	7 to < 15 kg 12/3 mg/kg bid 15-40 kg 10/2.5 mg/kg bid 40 kg 400/100 mg bid **Dosing with NVP or EFV:** 7 kg to < 15kg 13/3.25mg/kg bid 15-50 kg 11/2.75 mg/kg bid 50 kg 533/133 mg bid	7 kg to < 15 kg 12/3 mg/kg bid 15-40 kg 10/2.5 mg/kg bid 40 kg 400/100 mg bid **Dosing with NVP or EFV:** 7 kg to < 15kg 13/3.25 mg/kg bid 15-50kg 11/2.75 mg/kg bid 50 kg 533/133 mg bid	400/100 mg (2 tablets or 5 ml) bid **Dosing with NVP or EFV** 600/150 mg bid (3 tablets or 7.5 ml bid)

ADVERSE REACTIONS	MANAGEMENT
MOST FREQUENT	
• Nausea and vomiting • Abdominal pain • Diarrhea • Headache • Perioral paresthesias • Hyperlipidemia/lipodystrophy • Hyperglycemia	• Consult HIV specialist • OTC diarrhea remedies • Keep child well hydrated
PATIENT COUNSELING POINTS	
• Liquid is stable for 60 days if stored at room temperature • Avoid exposure to excessive heat • Administer solution with a calibrated dosing syringe • Separate administration of nonenteric-coated didanosine and lopinavir/ritonavir by 2.5 hours	• Take with food • Counsel on drug interactions with OTC agents and other agents (i.e. ethinyl estradiol) • Shake liquid well • Keep liquid refrigerated • Tablets do not require refrigeration • Mix with milk, chocolate milk, vanilla or chocolate pudding or ice cream • Dull the child's taste buds prior to administration by chewing ice, popsicles, or partially frozen orange or grape juice concentrates • Coat the mouth with peanut butter prior to administration • Administer strong tasting foods (i.e. maple syrup, cheese, or strong-flavored chewing gum) immediately after dose

DRUG INTERACTIONS
- See Chapter 6, Antiretroviral Drug Interactions

Nelfinavir (Viracept®)

<u>SYNONYMS</u>
- NFV
- AG-1343

<u>PEDIATRIC FORMULATIONS</u>
- Powder for oral suspension
- 50 mg/g (one level scoop)
- 200 mg (one level teaspoon)

<u>MANUFACTURER/PEDIATRIC APPROVAL</u>
- Agouron Pharmaceuticals
- Pediatric Labeling March 14, 1997

<u>ADOLESCENT/ADULT FORMULATION</u>
- 250mg, 625mg tablets

NEONATAL DOSE	PEDIATRIC DOSING RANGE	ADOLESCENT/ADULT DOSE
(Birth-6 weeks) 40mg/kg/dose bid (6 weeks to 2 years) no recommended dose	2-13 yrs: 45-55mg/kg bid **or** 25-35mg/kg tid (Max dose 1750 mg bid)	750mg tid **or** 1250mg bid

		Per Dose For TID Dosing (i.e. equivalent to 20-30mg/kg tid)		
Kilograms	Pounds	Scoops	Teaspoons	Tablets
7 to <8.5	15.5 to <18.5	4	1	-
8.5 to <10.5	18.5 to <23	5	1 ¼	-
10.5 to <12	23 to <26.5	6	1 ½	-
12 to <14	26.5 to <31	7	1 ¾	-
14 to <16	31 to <35	8	2	-
16 to <18	35 to <39.5	9	2 ¼	-
18 to 23	39.5 to 50.5	10	2 ½	2
>23	>50.5	15	3 ¾	3

ADVERSE REACTIONS	MANAGEMENT
MOST FREQUENT	
• Nausea and vomiting • Abdominal pain • Diarrhea • Asthenia • Lipid Abnormalities	• Consult HIV specialist • OTC diarrhea remedies • Keep child well hydrated
PATIENT COUNSELING POINTS	
• Loperamide or calcium carbonate can alleviate diarrhea • Powder best mixed with pudding, water, formula, or ice cream; must be used within 6 hours of mixing. Tablets can be dissolved in water, but must be consumed immediately.	• Take with food or a high fat meal • Counsel on drug interactions with OTC agents and other agents (i.e. ethinyl estradiol) • Separate antacids or ddI by at least 1 hour before or after NFV

<u>DRUG INTERACTIONS</u>
- See Chapter 6, Antiretroviral Drug Interactions

Ritonavir (Norvir®)

SYNONYMS
- RTV
- ABT-538

PEDIATRIC FORMULATIONS
- 80mg/ml

MANUFACTURER/PEDIATRIC APPROVAL
- Abbott Laboratories
- Pediatric Labeling March 14, 1997

ADOLESCENT/ADULT FORMULATION
- 100mg soft gel capsules

NEONATAL DOSE	PEDIATRIC DOSING RANGE	USUAL PEDIATRIC DOSE	ADOLESCENT/ADULT DOSE
Not approved for use in neonates/infants under age 1 month. (Investigational dose: 450mg RTV per m^2 twice daily was associated with lower concentrations than observed in adults receiving the standard adult dose)	350-400 mg/m^2 bid To minimize GI toxicity: Initiate therapy at 250mg/m^2 bid X 1 day Then 300mg m^2 bid X 2 day Then 350mg m^2 bid X 1 day Then 400mg m^2 bid thereafter	400 mg/m^2 bid	600mg bid To minimize GI toxicity: • Titrate over 5 days • 300 mg bid x 1 day • 400 mg bid x 2 days • 500 mg bid x 1 day • 600 mg bid

ADVERSE REACTIONS	MANAGEMENT
MOST FREQUENT	
• Nausea and vomiting • Abdominal pain • Diarrhea • Asthenia • Lipid Abnormalities	• Consult HIV specialist • OTC diarrhea remedies • Keep child well hydrated
PATIENT COUNSELING POINTS	
• Mix with milk, chocolate milk, vanilla or chocolate pudding or ice cream • Dull the child's taste buds prior to administration by chewing ice, popsicles, or partially frozen orange or grape juice concentrates • Coat the mouth with peanut butter prior to administration • Administer strong tasting foods (i.e. maple syrup, cheese, or strong-flavored chewing gum) immediately after dose **Black Box Warning**: Co-administration with certain non-sedating antihistamines, sedative hypnotics, antiarrhythmics, or ergot alkaloids may result in serious or life-threatening events.	• Take with food to maximize absorption • Food increases absorption by 15% • Separate administration of non-enteric coated didanosine and ritonavir by 2.5 hours • Capsules should be refrigerated and protected from light (stable for 30 days at room temperature) • Solution must be stored in original container • Solution stable for 30 days if stored at room temperature • Avoid exposure to excessive heat • Administer solution with a calibrated dosing syringe

DRUG INTERACTIONS
- See Chapter 6, Antiretroviral Drug Interactions

Saquinavir (Invirase-HGC, Fortovase-SGC®)

SYNONYMS
- SQV-HGC (Invirase)
- SQV-SGC (Fortavase)

PEDIATRIC FORMULATIONS
- 200mg soft gel capsules
- 200mg hard gel capsules
- 500mg film coated tabs

MANUFACTURER/PEDIATRIC APPROVAL
- Roche Pharmaceuticals
- No pediatric labeling

ADOLESCENT/ADULT FORMULATION
- 200mg soft gel capsules

NEONATAL DOSE	PEDIATRIC DOSING RANGE	ADOLESCENT/ADULT DOSE
Not approved for use	Not approved for use (Clinical trials have shown that doses of 50mg per kg every 8 hours were inadequate to achieve therapeutic SQV levels. Trials are underway in children for use of SQV combined with a second PI.)	1200mg po tid (Fortavase SGC) Unboosted SQV not recommended SQV 1000mg + RTV 100mg bid SQV 1600mg + RTV 200mg qd

ADVERSE REACTIONS	MANAGEMENT
MOST FREQUENT	
• Nausea and vomiting • Abdominal pain • Diarrhea • Asthenia • Lipid Abnormalities • Rash	• Consult HIV specialist • OTC diarrhea remedies • Keep child well hydrated
	PATIENT COUNSELING POINTS
	• Take with food or a high fat meal • Counsel on drug interactions with OTC agents and other agents (i.e. ethinyl estradiol) • Loperamide or calcium carbonate can alleviate diarrhea

ADMINISTRATION
- Invirase and Fortavase are not bioequivalent ; do not use interchangeably.
- SQV should only be used when boosted by ritonavir or another PI.

DRUG INTERACTIONS
- See Chapter 6, Antiretroviral Drug Interactions

Tipranavir(Aptivus®)

SYNONYMS
- TPV

PEDIATRIC FORMULATIONS
- None

MANUFACTURER/PEDIATRIC APPROVAL
- Boehlinger Ingleheim
- No pediatric labeling

ADOLESCENT/ADULT FORMULATION
- 250mg soft gel capsule

NEONATAL DOSE	PEDIATRIC DOSING RANGE	ADOLESCENT/ADULT DOSE
Not approved for use	Not approved for use, but clinical trials are underway	500mg bid +Norvir 200mg bid

ADVERSE REACTIONS	MANAGEMENT
MOST FREQUENT	
• Nausea and vomiting • Abdominal pain • Diarrhea • Headache • Hyperglycemia/hypertriglyceridemia • TPV contains a sulfonamide, cross-reactivity may be present	• Consult HIV specialist • OTC diarrhea remedies • Keep child well hydrated
Black Box Warning:	PATIENT COUNSELING POINTS
• TPV has been associated with reports of clinical hepatitis and hepatic decompensation. Use caution in co-infected patients who have HIV and Hepatitis B or C	• Take with food or a high fat meal • Counsel on drug interactions with OTC agents and other agents (i.e. ethinyl estradiol) • Separate antacids or ddI by at least 1 hour before or after TPV • Store capsules in the refrigerator.

DRUG INTERACTIONS
- See Chapter 6, Antiretroviral Drug Interactions

31

Prevention and Management of Opportunistic Infections in Children

Daniela Chiriboga, MD
Patricia Emmanuel, MD
Department of Pediatrics
University of South Florida College of Medicine, Tampa

Introduction

Disease prevention is important in the medical management of any immunocompromised individual. Dramatic progress in the management of HIV-infected infants and children has been made in the developed world due to initiation of antiretroviral therapy, thus preserving the immune system and preventing opportunistic infections. Despite this, children are still at increased risk for infections due to their immature immune systems, lack of antibody repertoire, and frequent intercurrent illnesses. Ongoing primary care and routine vaccinations are important components of care to maintain health.

The purpose of this chapter is to provide the clinical clues, treatment recommendations and dosing of agents for commonly encountered opportunistic infections in HIV-infected children. Complicated infections may require consultation with an Infectious Disease Specialist. This section also outlines recommendations for pediatric HIV-infected patients for disease prevention in the categories of immunization (active and passive) and recommendations for specific disease states. Some of these guidelines are based upon efficacy data in pediatric patients, others are extrapolations from approaches in the adult HIV-infected patient, and others are derived directly from well-child care recommendations with modification for the pediatric HIV-infected patient. This area is rapidly changing with several new vaccines and medications currently in the approval stage. It is recommended that the guidelines in the Report of the Committee on Infectious Disease of the American Academy of Pediatrics (Red Book) and the USPHS Guidelines for Prevention of Opportunistic Infections be referred to for the most up to date recommendations.[1]

Immunizations and Vaccine Efficacy

With the exception of some live vaccines, most routine immunizations should be given to all HIV-infected and exposed infants according to the schedule recommended by the Advisory Committee on Immunization Practices (ACIP) and the American Academy of Pediatrics (AAP). See Table 1 for recommended schedule. [2]

The efficacy of vaccines in HIV-infected children has been studied in the U.S. as well as the developing world; however, there remains uncertainty in some areas. HIV-infected children may respond poorly to immunizations depending on the status of immune function. Following primary immunization in infancy, 40–95% of HIV-infected children develop protective levels of antibody to diphtheria and tetanus. However, the levels of titers are lower and they wane quicker compared to uninfected children.[3] Response to hepatitis B is also lower compared to controls with 25–50% developing antibody post vaccination. Despite suboptimal vaccine response, there have been few reported vaccine failures with Hepatitis B, Diphtheria, tetanus, or pertussis. There are reports of serious measles disease in immunized children.[4]

In general infected children generate lower geometric means titers following vaccination and these antibody levels decline more rapidly. Symptomatic patients, especially those who have suffered opportunistic infections, are less likely to respond, but response is difficult to predict in individual patients. Where response to vaccination is questioned, specific immune responses may be measured. Patients who lack evidence of immunity after repeated immunization may be considered for intravenous immune globulin (IVIG) therapy and should receive immune globulin on exposure. (See individual disease discussion). One area that is incompletely evaluated is the effect of immune reconstitution on immunization response and protection. How well the immune system responds to vaccination, once the CD4 count recovers with HAART, is still being studied by groups such as the PACTG.[5] An individual's CD4 count at baseline (CD4 nadir) may impact the ultimate response. Immunizations should be initiated as early as possible while the immune system is still intact. If vaccination occurred at a time when CD4 counts were < 200, consideration should be given to repeating some vaccines, such as the Pneumovax, once immune reconstitution has occurred. On-going research is needed to further refine the need for repeat vaccinations, particularly after immune reconstitution.

LIVE VACCINES

Mortality and morbidity of measles is significant and well described in pediatric AIDS patients. Most HIV-infected children tolerate the vaccine well; however, antibody response is impaired. Some studies have correlated this with the degree of CD4 depletion. A case of measles pneumonitis following vaccine in a severely immunocompromised HIV-infected adolescent was described in 2001 prompting the AAP to recommend withholding the vaccine in severely compromised children.[6] Therefore, MMR should not be given to infected children who have profound immunosuppression (immune stage 3) because they respond poorly and there is some risk of complications. In all other cases, measles-mumps-rubella (MMR) vaccination is recommended according to the same schedule as for well children, including vaccination at a younger age during outbreaks. The second dose of MMR can be given as early as 1 month after the first vaccine if there is a need to induce early seroconversion. MMR may be given to household contacts, as components of this vaccine are not transmitted.

In the United States, it is standard to use the Inactivated Polio Vaccine (IPV). In many other countries, oral polio is still utilized, particularly where there is still wild-type polio. Many HIV-infected infants have received the oral polio vaccine (OPV) without consequence; however, two cases of vaccine associated paralytic poliomyelitis (VAPP) have been described in HIV-infected children. The timing of IPV administration is the same for polio vaccination in well children.

Bacillus Calmette-Guerin vaccine (BCG) has been associated with complications in HIV-infected patients. In areas of the world where the risk of tuberculosis is high, the World Health Organization recommends BCG vaccination in asymptomatic HIV-infected infants at risk of acquiring tuberculosis.[7]

Varicella vaccine is recommended for children with CDC stage N or A, and immune class 1 who have a CD4 cell count percentages > 25%. Eligible children should receive 2 doses of varicella vaccine with a 3-month interval between doses. The vaccine is well tolerated and over 60% of HIV-infected subjects develop an antibody response; over 80% demonstrate lymphocyte proliferation in response to the varicella antigen.[8] There are decreased episodes of zoster in vaccinated individuals compared to those with natural disease. Zoster is a major morbidity in infected children. There are no studies on the use of varicella vaccine to prevent zoster in HIV-infected children. It is also recommended that susceptible household members of patients with HIV who are not HIV-infected themselves be given varicella vaccine.

INACTIVATED VACCINES

Routine inactivated vaccines (DTP, Hepatitis B, *Haemophilus influenzae* type b), are recommended for both asymptomatic and symptomatic pediatric HIV-infected patients according to the standard vaccination schedule for children.

Pneumococcal infections are the most common bacterial infections in pediatric HIV-infected patients. The heptavalent conjugated pneumococcal vaccine (Prevnar®) is now recommended for universal use in children < 24 months of age. If there is a local shortage, priority should be given to high-risk infants such as those infected with HIV. The heptavalent vaccine should be given to children < 8 years who are at high risk of invasive disease including all HIV-infected children. In children > 2 years this is a 2-dose series and both symptomatic and asymptomatic HIV-infected patients should still receive the 23-valent pneumococcal vaccine (Pneumovax®) after age 2 years and every 5 years afterward as per the schedule.

Yearly vaccination with the inactivated split influenza vaccine beginning at 6 months of age is recommended for all HIV-infected children, symptomatic and asymptomatic. Influenza vaccination is also recommended for household contacts of HIV-infected patients. Influenza and potentially other vaccines may result in a transient increase in measurable HIV viral load which is *not clinically significant*. The intranasally administered, live, attenuated influenza vaccine (FluMist®) is not approved for use in any HIV-infected child. Studies evaluating this vaccine are ongoing through the Pediatric AIDS Clinical Trials Group (PACTG).

Hepatitis A vaccine is recommended for those children with chronic liver disease, such as Hepatitis B or C co-infection or in children living in regions where there are increased rates of Hepatitis A. It is a two dose series administered 6 months apart.

Table 1. Recommended Childhood and Adolescent Immunization Schedule

Recommended Childhood and Adolescent Immunization Schedule UNITED STATES • 2005

Vaccine ▼ / Age ▶	Birth	1 month	2 months	4 months	6 months	12 months	15 months	18 months	24 months	4–6 years	11–12 years	13–18 years
Hepatitis B[1]	HepB #1	HepB #2				HepB #3					HepB Series	
Diphtheria, Tetanus, Pertussis[2]			DTaP	DTaP	DTaP		DTaP			DTaP	Td	Td
Haemophilus influenzae type b[3]			Hib	Hib	Hib	Hib						
Inactivated Poliovirus			IPV	IPV		IPV				IPV		
Measles, Mumps, Rubella[4]						MMR #1				MMR #2	MMR #2	
Varicella[5]						Varicella				Varicella		
Pneumococcal Conjugate[6]			PCV	PCV	PCV	PCV				PCV	PPV	
Influenza[7]						Influenza (Yearly)				Influenza (Yearly)		
Hepatitis A[8]										Hepatitis A Series		

- - - Vaccines below this line are for selected populations - - -

This schedule indicates the recommended ages for routine administration of currently licensed childhood vaccines, as of December 1, 2004, for children through age 18 years. Any dose not administered at the recommended age should be administered at any subsequent visit when indicated and feasible.

■ Indicates age groups that warrant special effort to administer those vaccines not previously administered. Additional vaccines may be licensed and recommended during the year. Licensed combination vaccines may be used whenever any components of the combination are indicated and other components of the vaccine

are not contraindicated. Providers should consult the manufacturers' package inserts for detailed recommendations. Clinically significant adverse events that follow immunization should be reported to the Vaccine Adverse Event Reporting System (VAERS). Guidance about how to obtain and complete a VAERS form is available at **www.vaers.org** or by telephone, **800-822-7967.**

■ Range of recommended ages   ▨ Only if mother HBsAg(−)
■ Preadolescent assessment   ■ Catch-up immunization

DEPARTMENT OF HEALTH AND HUMAN SERVICES
CENTERS FOR DISEASE CONTROL AND PREVENTION

CDC

The Childhood and Adolescent Immunization Schedule is approved by:
Advisory Committee on Immunization Practices www.cdc.gov/nip/acip
American Academy of Pediatrics www.aap.org
American Academy of Family Physicians www.aafp.org

1. Infants born to Hepatitis B surface antigen (HBsAg) -negative mothers should receive the first dose of Hepatitis B (HepB) at birth and no later than 2 months of age. Infants born to Hepatitis BsAg-positive mothers should receive HepB and 0.5ml of Hepatitis immune globulin (HBIG) within twelve hours of birth at separate sites. The second dose is recommended at 1-2 months and the third dose at 6 months. Infants whose mothers HBsAg status is unknown, should receive HepB within twelve hours of birth. Maternal blood should be drawn at delivery to determine HBsAg status; if the HBsAg test is positive, the infant should receive HBIG as soon as possible (no later than 1 week). All children and adolescents who have not been immunized against hepatitis B should begin the series during any visit. Providers should make special effort to immunize children who were born in areas of the world were hepatitis B infection is endemic.

2. The fourth dose of DTaP may be administered as early as age twelve months, provided 6 months have elapsed, and the child is unlikely to return at 15-18 months. The final dose in the series should be given at >/=4 years. **In Nov-2005, the ACIP recommended that dTap (combination acellular pertussis vaccine) replace the Td booster at the preadolescent visit. Subsequent routine Td boosters are recommended every ten years.**

3. Three Hib conjugate vaccines are licensed for infant use. If PRP-OMP (Pedvax HIB or Comvax) is administered at ages 2 and 4 months, a dose at age 6 months is not required. DTaP/Hib combination products should not be used for primary immunization in infants at ages 2, 4 or 6 months, but can be used as boosters after any Hib vaccine. The final dose in the series should be administered at age >/= 12 months.

4. MMR should not be administered to severely immunocompromised (category 3) children. HIV infected children without severe immunosuppression would routinely receive their first MMR vaccine as soon as

possible after reaching their first birthday. Consideration should be give to administering the second dose of MMR as soon as 1 month after the first dose rather than waiting for school entry.

5. Varicella vaccine should be given to only asymptomatic, nonimmunosupressed children CDC class N1 or A1. Eligible children should receive at least two doses with a 3 month interval between doses. The first dose may be given as early as 12 months of age. There is no recommendation on the use of Varicella vaccine on children who have reconstituted their CD4 count with HAART.

6. Inactivated spilt influenza virus vaccine should be administered to all HIV infected children >/= 6 months of age each year. For children 6 months to 9 years who are receiving the vaccine for the first time, two doses given one >/= 1 month apart are recommended. The intranasal live attenuated influenza vaccine is not recommended for HIV infected persons.

7. Hepatitis A vaccine is recommended for children and adolescents in selected states and high-risk children such as those co-infected with Hepatitis B or C.

Passive Immunization

Children with symptomatic HIV infection (CDC stage B2 or more) respond poorly to immunization and should be considered susceptible in cases of significant exposure regardless of vaccination history. Therefore, they should receive passive immunization when indicated.

Tetanus-prone wounds

All HIV-infected children should receive tetanus immune globulin (TIG) regardless of immunization status: 250 units IM.

Measles exposure✦

If exposed to wild-type measles, all susceptible HIV-infected children and adolescents should be given immune globulin (IG) 0.5 mL/kg (maximum 15 mL) IM. Measles immunization should be delayed 6 months following passive immunization.

Varicella exposure✦

Children with HIV infection, susceptible to Varicella (no history of chicken pox and seronegative for VZV) who are exposed to Varicella should receive Varicella-zoster immune globulin (VZIG) 125 units/10 kg of body weight (maximum 625 units) IM regardless of immune classification. VZIG should be administered as soon as possible and within 96 hours of exposure. There are some reports on the use of acyclovir in HIV-infected children to prevent clinical disease following exposure to Varicella; however, there is insufficient data to recommend this strategy.

✦NOTE: For both measles and varicella exposures, patients who have received intravenous immune globulin (IVIG) within 3 weeks of exposure do not require additional passive immunization. VZIG is considered adequate for prophylaxis for subsequent varicella exposures for 3 weeks after administration.

Intravenous Immune Globulin (IVIG)

Routine IVIG therapy has been evaluated in clinical trials. Such therapy can be considered replacement therapy for deficits in specific humoral immunity and is, in effect, preventative. Routine IVIG (400 mg/kg q 4 weeks) is generally recommended in the following circumstances:

- Documented hypogammaglobulinemia (IgG < 400 mg/µL)
- Recurrent, severe systemic bacterial infections, defined as 2 or more serious infections (i.e., bacteremia, meningitis, pneumonia, sepsis) in a 12-month period
- Children with inability to form antibodies against common antigens (i.e., response to vaccination, childhood infections)

- Children in areas with a high prevalence of measles who have not responded to 2 MMR vaccines one month apart
- Children with bronchiectasis who have not responded to conventional therapies
- Children with immune thrombocytopenia

IVIG has been used in the treatment of severe anemia associated with human parvovirus B19 infection and immune thrombocytopenia.[9] Respiratory Syncytial Virus (RSV) IVIG, not monoclonal RSV antibody can be used in place of standard IVIG in high-risk infants during the RSV season. The dose is 750 mg/kg per month. There is some data to suggest that routine IVIG does not significantly alter outcomes in or lower risk for serious infectious diseases when CD4+ cell counts drop to consistently < 200 cells/mm^3. Initiation of IVIG is not indicated in patients with CD4+ cell counts < 200 cells/mm^3. However, it is not known if withdrawal of IVIG therapy, begun initially according to the above recommendations before the CD4+ cell count falls to very low levels, is appropriate. IVIG may also be less effective in the prevention of serious bacterial infections in patients receiving TMP/SMX prophylaxis. The decision to use IVIG should be made in consultation with a pediatric specialist.[10]

Bacterial Infections

Serious bacterial infections

- Bacterial infections are a common problem in HIV-infected children due to an immature immune system and incomplete antibody repertoire. Recurrent bacterial infections (two systemic infections within two years) are considered an AIDS defining illness in children.
- *Streptococcus pneumoniae* is the most common invasive bacterial pathogen in children with HIV, accounting for more than 50% of blood stream infections. *Hemophilus influenza*e type b infections were also more common in HIV positive children before Hib vaccination was routinely used.
- Pneumococcal infections are more common in HIV positive children than in HIV negative children, with an incidence of 6.1 cases per 100 patient years. This increased incidence is due to poor initial responses to immunization in HIV positive infants and children and later loss of antibody leading to inadequate protection. With the use of the new conjugated pneumococcal vaccine in infancy, rates of invasive disease in HIV-infected children may decrease as has been reported in the general population.
- Clinical presentation is usually similar to HIV negative patients; yet, in severely immunocompromised children, classical signs, symptoms, and lab findings may be absent or misleading.
- Pneumonia is the most common of the serious infections. One third of HIV-infected children who have pneumonia will have recurrent episodes.
- In HIV positive children whose immune systems are not severely compromised, most bacterial infections can be treated with the same antibiotics and doses, as for non HIV-positive children. Clinicians should be aware of the local resistance patterns in their area. Children who have been on prophylactic antibiotics may harbor more resistant strains. For those who are severely immunocompromised, broad spectrum antibiotics should be started empirically   A complete diagnostic evaluation should be done, including less common organisms and opportunistic organisms in the differential diagnosis; depending on the clinical picture and degree of immunosuppression. The work-up should try to identify by culture, PCR or antigen-detection, the infecting organism. Serologic testing should not be relied on for accurate diagnosis depending on the degree of immune suppression.
- As stated above, IVIG is recommended in patients with 2 or more serious infections over a 12-month period.

- Patients with symptomatic HIV infection may also suffer from recurrent otitis media and sinusitis. Some clinicians utilize antibiotic prophylaxis in these cases. HIV-infected patients receiving TMP/SMX prophylaxis may benefit from daily administration during otitis prone periods. Such periods may be seasonal or associated with daycare or school attendance. Prophylaxis is generally continued for one year. Unfortunately, antibiotic prophylaxis greatly increases the risk of selecting antibiotic resistant strains of bacteria (especially with *Streptococcus pneumoniae* and especially in children in daycare). Accordingly, the risk-benefit issues for each patient must be carefully considered.

Mycobacterium Avium Complex (MAC)

- MAC is a common opportunistic infection in pediatric HIV infected patients with advanced disease, and is the initial AIDS defining illness in approximately 5%. *Mycobacterium avium, Mycobacterium intracellulare* and other non-tuberculous mycobacteria are the slow-growing obligate aerobes that make up MAC.

Clinical manifestations

Adults and children above six with CD4 counts below 100 are considered at risk for MAC. Infection may occur at higher CD4 counts in younger children, but is still associated with profound immunosuppression-immune category 3

The disease is usually disseminated and most frequently involves the reticuloendothelial system (lymph nodes, bone marrow, liver, spleen). Findings may include recurrent fever, weight loss, failure to thrive, night sweats, fatigue, chronic diarrhea or malabsorption and abdominal pain. Laboratory abnormalities include anemia, leucopenia, thrombocytopenia, and elevated alkaline phosphatase. Uninfected immunologically intact children can get atypical mycobacterial lymphadenitis. This is a localized infection and will not be covered in this review.

Diagnosis

- Diagnosis is made primarily by mycobacterial culture of organisms from the blood, bone marrow, lymph nodes, or other tissues. AFB stains, from blood culture, bone marrow biopsy, or tissue biopsy of lung, liver, lymph node, etc., can be due to *Mycobacterium tuberculosis* or MAC in HIV infected individuals. Culture is necessary for species identification and susceptibilities should be obtained if possible. Cultures should be obtained prior to initiating prophylaxis or therapy.
- Identification of MAC in stool or the respiratory tract may indicate colonization and not active disease. This result should be interpreted in the context of the clinical presentation (see above) and the degree of immune suppression.

Treatment

- Antimicrobial treatment of MAC is often quite difficult. Multiple drugs are required to prevent development of resistance. The macrolides have been associated with improved outcome and should be included in the regimen. Therapy should be prescribed in conjunction with a specialist in HIV/infectious diseases.[11]
- Initial empiric therapy should include at least two drugs: azithromycin 10 mg/kg qd po (max 500mg) or clarithromycin 15 mg/kg daily divided bid (max 500 mg bid) plus ethambutol 15–20 mg/kg qd po (max 1600mg), and/or Rifabutin 5–10 mg/kg qd po (max 300 mg).
- Ethambutol may cause reversible optic neuritis. Monthly ophthalmologic studies should be followed throughout therapy, along with assessment of visual acuity, red-green color discrimination, and visual fields.
- Both Rifabutin and Clarithromycin have multiple drug interactions; especially with the antiretroviral agents. (See Tables 19 and 20 in the *Guidelines for the Use of Antiretroviral Agents in HIV-1 Infected Adults and Adolescents*, October 29, 2004).

- In adults, Cipro Floxin and IV amikacin have been added in refractory or resistant cases and may be indicated for specific situations in children. This should be decided in conjunction with specialists in HIV and Tuberculosis.

- Treatment should also include optimizing antiretroviral therapy, as an improved immunologic status is important to control the infection

- Clinical improvement occurs during the first 4 to 6 weeks of treatment. Although the infection may be eliminated from blood after 12 weeks of therapy, lifetime chronic suppressive maintenance therapy is recommended for these children. The preferred regime (based on adult guidelines) is a combination of a macrolide with ethambutol, with or without rifabutin.[12]

- Improving the immune system is critical for the treatment and containment of MAC. Either the initiation of HAART or re-addressing the regimen or adherence is an important adjunct to antimicrobial therapy. With successful antiretroviral therapy and CD4 rise, an immune reconstitution inflammatory syndrome (IRIS) can occur. Some clinicians start MAC treatment 1 to 2 weeks prior to starting antiretroviral therapy in order to prevent IRIS.

Prevention

- Children with profound immunosuppression should receive chemoprophylaxis against MAC. Clarithromycin or azithromycin are the preferred prophylactic agents and are well tolerated in children.

- Children with the following CD4+ cell count thresholds should receive prophylaxis:
    - Children > 6 years, < 50 cells/mm^3
    - Children aged 2 to 6 years, < 75 cells/mm^3
    - Children aged 1 to 2 years, < 500 cells/mm^3
    - Children aged < 12 months, < 750 cells/mm^3.

- Azithromycin dosage is 20 mg/kg (maximum adult dosage 1200 mg) q week or 5 mg/kg (maximum 500 mg) po qd

- Clarithromycin dose is 15 mg/kg/day divided in 2 doses, maximum 500 mg po bid. Clarithromycin has many drug interactions as well as increased nausea and GI intolerance.

- Before MAC prophylaxis is started MAC disease should be ruled out by clinical assessment and an AFB blood culture.

- Discontinuation of prophylaxis: In adults and teenagers, MAC prophylaxis should be discontinued once the CD4 count has remained above 100 for a minimum of 3 months. In children, the safety of this practice has not been studied.[13]

Mycobacterium Tuberculosis

- The prevalence of active tuberculosis among HIV-infected individuals is higher than the general population 4% vs. 0.01%. HIV-infected adults have higher rates of extra-pulmonary disease.

- Since children usually acquire TB from an adult contact, many HIV-infected children may be at increased risk for infection

- Unlike other HIV opportunistic infections, TB can present at any time in the course of the disease

Clinical manifestations

- Chest X-ray appearance of TB in children with HIV infection tend to be similar to those in immunocompetent children

- The initial clinical presentation can be non-specific. Children, in general, have more extra-pulmonary manifestations of TB than adults. The clinical picture of tuberculosis can overlap with the systemic signs of disseminated MAC infection.

- As immunodeficiency progresses, the presentation may be altered with atypical infiltrates on radiographic exam and a higher incidence of disseminated disease such as lymph nodes and bone marrow involvement

Diagnosis

- Since there is a high incidence of anergy in HIV-infected patients, the diagnosis of TB may become problematic

- Studies have shown that the tuberculin skin test continues to be of value in this patient population. A TST > 5 mm is considered positive in immunocompromised and/or exposed individuals. Clinicians should be aware that children with active TB can have a negative TST up to 10% of the time. A control skin test is not recommended.

- Special stains for acid fast organisms (AFB stain, acridine orange, etc) and cultures of appropriate specimens including respiratory secretions, gastric aspirates, blood, urine, stool, bone marrow, liver, lymph node, or other tissues should be obtained as clinically indicated.

- Culture of three consecutive morning gastric aspirate samples has a sensitivity of 70% in children. Nasopharyngeal aspirates had a similar sensitivity in one study. Obtaining induced sputums following nebulization with saline in older children (> 7–8 years old) and adolescents is indicated. Bronchoscopy and BAL does not increase the likelihood of diagnosing TB; above the yield of appropriate respiratory cultures or gastric aspirates. [14]

Treatment

- Most HIV-infected adult patients with drug-susceptible TB respond well to anti-TB medications

- Optimal treatment of TB in the pediatric HIV population has yet to be established by controlled trials. Treatment in HIV infected children should follow the same principles of TB therapy in immunocompetent children, except for the need for longer therapy in HIV-infected individuals.

- There is a high risk of dissemination of TB infection in children below age 4 (immunocompetent or immunodeficient); therefore empiric therapy should be initiated as soon as the diagnosis of TB is suspected.

- Therapy should always commence with a 4 drug regimen to be continued for at least 12 months. Specific regimens should be prescribed in conjunction with a specialist in HIV or TB. Ongoing therapy should be coordinated through local Department of Health Tuberculosis Programs, utilizing directly observed therapy (DOT).

- Isoniazid (INH) 10–20 mg/kg/d in one or two doses (max 300mg), rifampin 10-20 mg/kg/day in one or two does (max 600 mg), pyrazinamide 30 mg/kg/day in one or two doses, and streptomycin 20–30 mg/kg/d intramuscular divided in two doses or ethambutol 15 mg/kg/d QD po are recommended for at least the first 2 months. Ethionamide 15–20 mg/kg/d divided in 2–3 doses can be used in place of Ethambutol in cases of CNS disease because of its improved penetration. The INH and rifampin should be continued for one year. Monitor drug interactions between rifampin and the antiretroviral agents. Review all the patient's medications for additive toxicity, especially hepatic.

- The susceptibility pattern of the organism isolated from the contact is very useful in guiding therapy. This information should be actively sought at the time of initial evaluation for tuberculosis. That includes involving the state's DOH Tuberculosis Service for contact testing and information.

Prevention

- All HIV-infected children should be skin tested yearly for tuberculosis with the Mantoux test (5TU-PPD). A positive reaction in HIV-infected children is considered > 5mm induration.

- Patients with intimate household exposure to an active case of pulmonary tuberculosis should receive INH prophylaxis until Mycobacterial tuberculosis is ruled out.

- HIV-infected children and adolescents who are TST positive (> 5mm induration) and have no active pulmonary or disseminated TB (Diagnosis: Latent TB Infection) should receive one year of INH prophylactically at a dose of 10-20 mg/kg/d (max 300 mg) po. Other regimens have been utilized in children for special circumstances. Consult a specialist in tuberculosis for use of alternative regimens.

- Prevention of TB in children is dependent on its prevention in the adult population first.

Fungal Infections

Candidiasis

Clinical Manifestations

- Oral candidiasis (thrush) — if severe can cause dysphagia, oral pain, and a bitter or sour taste in the mouth. White curd-like patches with underlying erythema on the oral mucosa, tongue, and pharynx are the most common finding. Other forms of oral candidiasis include angular chelitis and atrophic, erythematous lesions.

- Diaper dermatitis — often recalcitrant

- May also involve intertriginal areas such as the axillae, neck folds, and the proximal nail beds (paronychia)

- Esophagitis — usually causes odynophagia or dysphagia. Esophageal involvement is quite frequent occurring in approximately 14% of AIDS patients.

- Extension of candidiasis to the laryngeal epiglottis and tracheal mucosa is sometimes noted

- This infection can also occur with any degree of immune suppression, but does occur more frequently with severe immunocompromised states and/or in association with antibiotic use

Diagnosis

- Diagnosis is usually based on history and physical examination for the initiation of empiric therapy.

- If patients with clinical symptoms of esophagitis do not respond to initial therapy then direct visualization of esophageal lesions by endoscopy is the most sensitive diagnostic procedure to confirm candida esophagitis. In these cases, other causes such as co-infection with HSV or CMV or other pathology should be ruled out.

- Wet prep (KOH) and culture for fungus may be used to confirm the diagnosis. Culture and susceptibilities may also be useful in refractory cases where drug resistance may be an issue.

Treatment

- *Thrush* – Early, uncomplicated infection can be treated topically with nystatin solution 100,000 u/mL in a dose of 1-5 mL tid-qid. Clotrimazole troches (10 mg) dissolved orally 4 to 6 times a day, for 10 to 14 days are another alternative.

- Fluconazole 3–6 mg/kg/qd for 7 to 14 days may be required for the treatment of oral candidiasis which does not respond to the previously mentioned measures and can also be used as first line therapy in more severe disease. Itraconazole suspension 2-5 mg/kg once a day or Ketoconazole 5–10 mg/kg once or twice a day can also be used a second line therapy.

- Candidal diaper dermatitis — Nystatin ointment to the affected area qid or ketoconazole cream (Nizoral®) tid-qid

- *Esophageal candidiasis* — mild disease — fluconazole 3–6 mg/kg/qd po or ketoconazole 5–10 mg/kg/d po q12h for a minimum of 14 days. (Ketoconazole may be less effective than fluconazole). In refractory cases, itraconazole cyclodextrin oral solution 5 mg/kg/day for 14 to 21 days is usually effective. Itraconazole capsules should not be used to treat oral or esophageal candidiasis.
- *Esophageal candidiasis* — moderate to severe disease — Fluconazole 3–6 mg/kg/d IV q12h or amphotericin B 0.3 mg/kg/day IV. Echinocandins (caspofungin and micafungin) and voriconazole have also been used but are not yet approved for use in children.
- Recurrences are frequent despite adequate therapy — 81% of all cases of recurrent esophageal candidiasis occur within 10 weeks of stopping therapy

Prevention

- Continuous suppressive therapy (fluconazole) is sometimes given to patients with frequent oral or esophageal candidiasis. Various dosing regimens are used depending on the degree of immune suppression, the patient's hepatic function, concomitant use of other medications with potential hepatotoxicity and the patient's tolerance and compliance with the regimen.
- Regimens include: Fluconazole 3–6 mg/kg/day or ketoconazole 5 mg/kg/qd

Cryptococcosis

- *Cryptococcus neoformans* is a round yeast-like fungus with a polysaccharide capsule. This capsule allows identification by diagnostic testing.
- Cryptococcal infections are infrequent in HIV-infected children. They are associated with severe immune suppression.
- The most common manifestation is meningoencephalitis, with patients presenting with days to weeks of fever, headache and mental status changes
- Skin lesions can also be a presenting manifestation
- Even though CSF cell count, glucose, and protein are usually normal, opening pressures are usually elevated.
- CNS disease can be diagnosed by India ink-stain of the CSF, or cryptococcal antigen detected in the serum, CSF, or in bronchoalveolar lavage fluid.
- The organism can be isolated on fungal cultures of CSF, blood or sputum.

Treatment

- Cryptococcal meningitis, initial therapy — amphotericin B 0.7-1.0 mg/kg/qd IV in combination with 5-Flucytosine (5-FC) 75–100 mg/kg/qd po in 4 divided doses. Therapy often has to be prolonged, but in stable patients one can use two weeks of amphotericin followed by 8 weeks of high dose fluconazole. (Fluconazole 5–6mg/kg/dose bid) Lipid formulations of Amphotericin B have been used and may be better tolerated. Doses from 2–7.5 mg/kg/day have been used.
- Alternative therapies that have been suggested include: intrathecal or intraventricular amphotericin B, miconazole, or fluconazole IV. The efficacy of these therapies in the pediatric population is unknown.
- Because patients with HIV infection cannot be cured of this infection, most should be maintained on suppressive therapy for life, with fluconazole 3–6 mg/kg/day by mouth or amphotericin B 1mg/kg IV once weekly.
- Non-meningeal Cryptococcal disease is most frequently treated with amphotericin at the same dose as for meningitis, but can be treated with fluconazole for the entire period.

- Highly active antiretroviral therapy should be optimized at the same time, to improve immune function and insure resolution of the active cryptococcal infection.

Prevention

- Prophylaxis for cryptococcal meningitis is not generally recommended. Some adult studies have found that fluconazole and itraconazole may reduce the frequency of this disease, but most experts agree that risks of prophylaxis outweigh the benefits.[15] There are no pediatric studies.
- There is no pediatric data to support the discontinuation of secondary prophylaxis following immune reconstitution in children.

Pneumocystis jiroveci Pneumonia (PCP)

Previously called *Pneumocystis carinii,* this organism is now classified as an atypical fungus. It is ubiquitous in the environment, infects humans early in life, and has a trophism for the lungs. Immunocompromised patients are at risk for severe pneumonia.

Clinical Manifestations

- PCP has been the most common AIDS defining illness in children. It is a less common diagnosis since the institution of routine PCP prophylaxis therapy for all HIV-exposed infants, beginning at six (6) weeks of age.
- Most cases occur in children between 3 and 6 months of age regardless of immune status or the presence of HIV infection. In infants and young children with HIV infection; PCP infection and disease occurred even when children had "normal CD4 counts." This prompted the use of early prophylaxis against PCP, for all HIV-exposed infants and the continuation of prophylaxis through the first year of life if HIV infected. Children between one and two years of age are often maintained on PCP prophylaxis if they have moderately or severely low CD4 counts or percentages.
- The risk for PCP disease in older children is based on the degree of immunosuppression. CD4 counts less than 200 or 15% are the major risk factor. Again in younger children and infants, PCP can occur with much higher CD4 counts.
- In HIV-infected infants PCP disease is commonly severe with a high rate of morbidity and mortality.
- Presenting symptoms include fever, cough, dyspnea, and tachypnea. The hallmark of the disease is hypoxemia with an elevated arterial to alveolar gradient. There may be a paucity of lung findings on physical exam.

Diagnosis

- Chest radiograph often shows diffuse bilateral interstitial infiltrates, but the radiologic picture can be highly variable.
- LDH is a non-specific indicator of lung disease but may be very elevated (> 500 or 1000 U/L) in PCP.
- An arterial blood gas showing an A-a gradient may help guide the diagnosis.
- Diagnosis is obtained by evaluation of sputum through silver stain or immunofluorescence staining. PCR has also been developed. Bronchoscopy with bronchoalveolar lavage is often needed to make the diagnosis in infants and children who cannot generate an adequate cough.

Treatment

- Trimethoprim-Sulfamethoxazole (TMP/SMX) is the drug of choice for treatment.

- Mild disease — TMP 20 mg/SMX 100 mg/kg/qd po in divided doses q6-8h. This is rarely done in young children, but could be considered in an adolescent or older child depending on the likelihood of good compliance and follow-up. Most children and especially infants are treated intravenously in hospital for close observation.

- Moderate to severe disease — TMP 15 mg/SMX 75 mg/kg/qd IV in divided doses q6h; may increase to TMP 20 mg/SMX 100 mg/kg/d IV in divided doses q6h.

- Treatment should begin empirically when PCP infection is suspected. Twenty-four to seventy-two (24–72) hours of empiric therapy will not affect the diagnostic yield of bronchoscopy and BAL.

- **Glucocorticosteroids** are indicated if the patient is hypoxic or in respiratory distress, which is the case with most children. Several pediatric studies have demonstrated the benefit of corticosteroids for decreasing morbidity and mortality. The dose range is from 2–4 mg/kg/d of methylprednisolone I.V. administered every 6 to 12 hours for 5 to 14 days and weaned over the subsequent week.

- Alternative therapy for children intolerant of TMP/SMX or who are not improving is Pentamidine – 4 mg/kg/qd I.V. There is little data on other PCP treatment regimens in children such as Atovaquone and Clindamycin/primaquine.

Prevention

- HIV-infected infants less than one month of age are not generally at risk; however, the rates substantially increase with the peak of infection occurring at 4 to 6 months of age. HIV-infected infants can develop symptomatic PCP with relatively high CD4 counts prompting the recommendations that all HIV-infected infants less than one year remain on prophylaxis regardless of immune status. Recommendations for prophylaxis in older pediatric patients are based on the definition of HIV-infection status, age, and CD4+ cell count. PCP prophylaxis of indeterminate infants is recommended until HIV infection and status of immunological function is defined. (See Figure 1 and Table 2.)

Figure 1. Strategy for PCP Prophylaxis

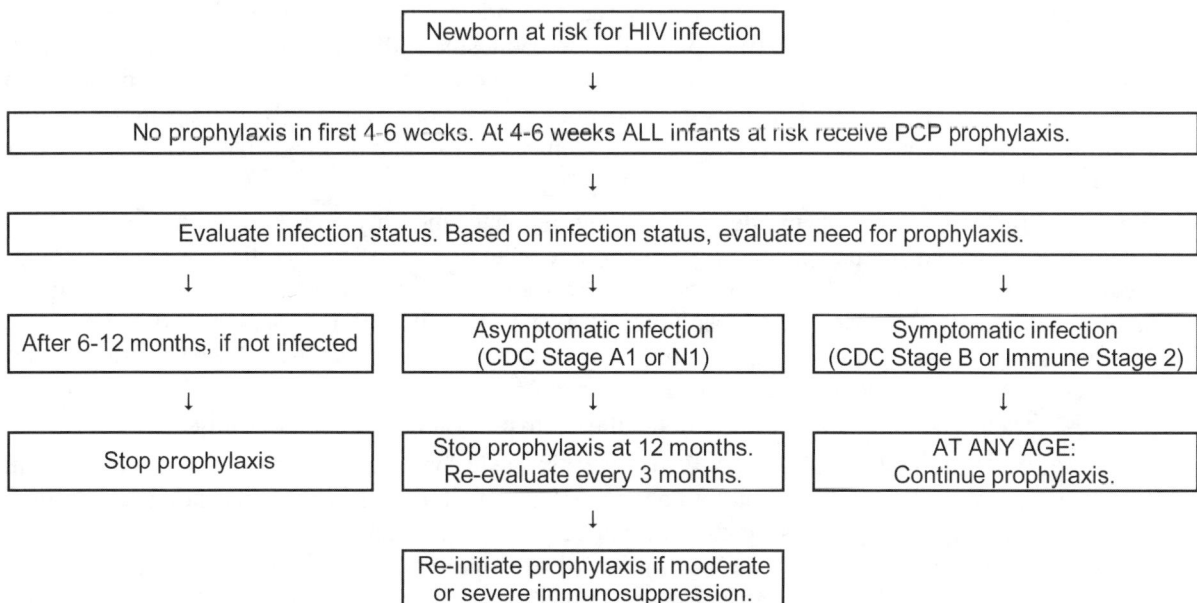

Table 2. Age-Related CD4+ Cell Counts as a Guide for Initiation of PCP Prophylaxis

AGE	CD4+ CELL COUNT AT WHICH TO START PROPHYLAXIS	MEDIAN NORMAL CD4 COUNT
1-11 months	All children at risk	3000 cells/mm^3
12-23 months	< 750 cells/mm^3	2600 cells/mm^3
24 months-5 years	< 500 cells/mm^3	1700 cells/mm^3
6 years and older	< 200 cells/mm^3	1000 cells/mm^3

NOTE:PCP prophylaxis should be started regardless of total CD4+ cell count if:
CD4+ cell % is < 15% of the total CD4+ cell count
Patient has had an episode of PCP

- Trimethoprim-sulfamethoxazole (TMP/SMX) is the most effective choice for PCP prophylaxis. The usual dose used is 150 mg of the TMP component – 750 mg of the SMX component per meter squared per day divided in 2 doses given 3 days per week. Consecutive days are commonly used (i.e., Monday-Tuesday-Wednesday)/an every day schedule is also acceptable. Major toxicities are allergic reactions and rash. These are common in HIV-infected adults, but less in children. Hematologic reactions, especially leukopenia and thrombocytopenia may occur.

- Alternative regimens for patients who do not tolerate TMP/SMX include dapsone, aerosolized pentamidine, intravenous pentamidine, and atovaquone. The relative effectiveness of these regimens is not defined.

- Dapsone (2 mg/kg once daily to a maximum of 100 mg) is usually the agent of first choice if TMP/SMX is not tolerated. It should be used with caution in patients with G6PD deficiency, as dapsone causes hemolysis in these patients. Limited pharmacokinetic data in HIV-infected children suggest less frequent dosing may be adequate due to a half-life of approximately 24 hours, but there is no efficacy data, thus daily dosing is currently recommended. Failures of prophylaxis have occurred with concurrent administration of rifampin and dideoxyinosine (ddI), presumably secondary to drug interactions which decrease the half-life (rifampin) or decrease the absorption (ddI) of dapsone. Toxicities include dose related hemolysis, hematologic reactions (especially leukopenia), "sulfone syndrome" (fever, dermatitis, hepatic dysfunction, methemoglobinemia, and peripheral motor neuropathy).

- Aerosolized pentamidine (300 mg delivered by jet nebulizer monthly) can be used as an alternative for PCP prophylaxis in patients > 5 years of age who can cooperate with respiratory therapy procedures. Aerosol therapy has been shown to be well-tolerated in younger children, but efficacy data is lacking. A drawback of aerosol prophylaxis is that it will not prevent extra-pulmonary pneumocystis disease, and has a higher number of prophylaxis failures. Bronchospasm triggered by this medication can be controlled by beta-adrenergic aerosol therapy. Other toxicities can include dizziness, headache, a burning sensation in the throat, hypoglycemia, and pancreatitis.

- Parenteral pentamidine (4 mg/kg every 2 to 4 weeks) has a long half-life which can result in tissue levels lasting several weeks. Optimal frequency of dosing for prophylaxis has not been defined. Fewer breakthroughs may be associated with dosing every 2 weeks. Theoretically, the parenteral route should be more effective in the prevention of extra-pulmonary pneumocystis disease. A slow intravenous administration is usually used. IM injection may result in sterile abscess formation. Adverse effects may include dizziness, headache, hypotension, hypoglycemia, and pancreatitis.

- Dosing for atovaquone prophylaxis is 30 mg/kg po daily in children above 24 months of age. In children 4 to 24 months of age, the dose is 45 mg/kg daily.

- Breakthrough PCP can occur despite prophylaxis, thus the nature of the prophylaxis should not influence the index of suspicion and diagnostic considerations of PCP.

Discontinuation of prophylaxis

- There have been several adult studies demonstrating that PCP prophylaxis can safely be discontinued in patients responding to highly active antiretroviral therapy (HAART). Thus recommendations now state that primary prophylaxis can be discontinued if patients have a sustained CD4+ cell count of > 200 cells/mm^3 and a sustained reduction in viral load for 3 to 6 months. There is no recommendation to discontinue secondary prophylaxis (patients with a prior episode of PCP) although some studies have shown this to also be safe. The safety of discontinuing prophylaxis in children receiving HAART has not yet been established, but there have been some studies that suggest that this prophylaxis can be safely discontinued once the CD4 count has increased above the age-appropriate CDC threshold.[16] Some concern remains about finding an increase in serious bacterial infections, especially bacterial pneumonias after the discontinuation of PCP prophylaxis. [17] This needs to be studied further.

Protozoal Infections

Toxoplasmosis

- AIDS-defining CNS toxoplasmosis is rare in children. The most common presentation for toxoplasmosis in HIV-infected children is congenital toxoplasmosis. The majority of congenital toxoplasma is asymptomatic with potential late sequelae of retinitis or neurologic impairment. Symptomatic infants can present with multiorgan involvement such as hepatosplenomegaly, thrombocytopenia and rash or primarily CNS disease with hydrocephalus or microcephaly, chorioretinitis and seizures. Infection in older immunocompromised children can involve any organ, although the central nervous system or eyes are most frequently involved. The most common findings in these cases are focal neurologic signs or visual changes.

Diagnosis

- Diagnosis and treatment should be done in conjunction with a pediatric infectious disease specialist.
- Congenital toxoplasmosis can be diagnosed by using enzyme immunoassay or an immunoadsorbent assay to detect Toxoplasma specific antibodies. Specialized Toxoplasma testing is available including PCR and isolation of organisms at specific reference laboratories.

Treatment

- The combination of sulfadiazine and pyrimethamine is the pediatric treatment of choice, but often patients do not tolerate it well.
- Pyrimethamine is started with a loading dose of 2 mg/kg/day for two days and then a maintenance dose of 1 mg/kg/day. The Sulfadiazine dose is 50 mg/kg q 12 hours. Duration of therapy for congenital toxoplasmosis is prolonged and the appropriate duration in HIV infected infants is still to

be determined. In older children, treatment is continued thorough the resolution of symptoms and for 1 to 2 weeks longer. For HIV-infected children, treatment may be continued for their lifetime depending on their degree of immune suppression or 4-6 weeks past the resolution of their symptoms if their CD4 counts are above 200.
- Active chorioretinitis in older children may benefit from the use of corticosteroids.
- Myelosuppressive side effects due to pyrimethamine can often be seen. By adding folinic acid at 5 mg SC (intra-muscularly in young infants) q3 days, this can usually be prevented. Folinic acid (leucovorin) can also be administered orally at a dose of 10–25 mg a day. If bone marrow toxicity

occurs at this dose, a dose of 10 mg SQ q3 days is the alternative.

- Clindamycin or one of the newer macrolides combined with pyrimethamine is another option reported in the adult literature, but not yet studied in infants or children.[18]
- Acute initial therapy usually lasts at least 6 weeks, but lifelong suppressive therapy is usually necessary.

Prevention

- Children who are within the at-risk for PCP (see above) are also at risk for toxoplasma encephalitis and should receive prophylaxis. TMP/SMX, when used at usual doses for PCP prophylaxis, is also effective for preventing toxoplasmosis. Atovaquone may also provide protection, but other alternative drugs used for PCP prophylaxis may not be effective for preventing toxoplasma. Children who are within the at-risk group and are on any drugs other than Atovaquone or TMP/SMX for PCP prophylaxis should have a toxoplasma antibody drawn. If seropositive, they should be on prophylaxis. Pyrimethamine is an alternative to TMP/SMX and Atovaquone for toxoplasmosis prophylaxis, but does not prevent PCP.[19]

Viral Infections

Varicella Zoster Virus (VZV)

- HIV-infected children are at risk for persistent, recurrent, and chronic infections with VZV.

Clinical manifestations

- Zoster occurs in people previously infected with VZV and results from the reactivation of the virus. Children who have low CD4 counts at the time of their primary varicella are at a significantly higher risk of developing zoster (as high as 70%).
- The duration of primary varicella infection may be longer in HIV-infected children. These children are also at higher risk for complications. Severe varicella disease in HIV infected children can involve over 500 skin lesions and the rapid progression of pneumonia.
- Diagnosis should be made by culture or antigen detection from skin lesions or biopsy material in suspected dissemination or from CSF.

Treatment

- Acyclovir is the treatment of choice for varicella in HIV-infected children. It should be initiated as soon as possible after initial lesions appear. Intravenous administration is recommended for children who have moderate or severe immunosuppression, or who have more severe presentations of varicella. (10 mg/kg/dose every 8 hours in children below 1 year old; 500 mg/m2/dose IV every 8 hours in children older than 1 year old). Length of treatment is usually 7 days or until no new lesions have appeared for 24 to 48 hours. Oral dosing (20 mg/kg/dose every 6 hours) can be used in HIV-infected children with normal or slightly decreased CD4 counts, who are able to take oral therapy with insured compliance and follow-up. The maximum dose is 800 mg po qid.
- Oral acyclovir is usually the treatment of choice for zoster for most HIV-infected children. IV administration should be considered in severely immunosuppressed children (CD4<15%), or those with trigeminal nerve and/or eye involvement or multidermatomal or disseminated disease.
- Foscarnet and valacyclovir are alternative treatment options.

Herpes Simplex (HSV)

Clinical manifestations

- HIV-infected children are at risk for more frequent and severe reactivations of HSV disease.
- In neonates, HSV infection may present as disseminated disease, meningo-encephalitis, or skin-eye-mucous membrane disease.
- The most common presentation for HSV in children is orolabial disease. This presents with painful mucosal ulcers, fever, irritability, and lymphadenopathy. Many of these children will have recurrent disease
- Older children with severely compromised immune systems may present with severe local lesions or disseminated infection. The esophagus, CNS, and genitals are other sites that may be infected. Disseminated HSV may present with visceral involvement involving the liver, spleen, lungs, kidney, adrenals, and the brain.

Diagnosis

- *Neonatal disease:* Neonatal disease may be diagnosed by culture of lesions, blood, or swabs of the mouth or nasopharynx. CNS involvement is diagnosed by HSV DNA-PCR of cerebrospinal fluid.
- *Orolabial and disseminated disease in older children:* Diagnosis is based on the typical appearance of the vesicles and ulcers. The virus can usually be isolated in culture or may be diagnosed by IFA or PCR.

Treatment

- *Neonatal disease:* Acyclovir at doses of 20 mg/kg/dose tid. Length of treatment varies by location of disease (21 days for CNS or disseminated disease, 14 days for skin-eye-mucous membrane). Some experts recommend secondary prophylaxis with oral Acyclovir for the first 6 to 12 months of life in all neonates with HSV infection to reduce neurologic sequelae, and recurrence of skin or CNS infection; regardless of HIV status.
- *Orolabial disease:* Treatment for symptomatic orolabial disease is with IV acyclovir (5–10 mg/kg/dose tid) or oral acyclovir (20 mg/kg/dose tid) for 7-14 days. In children with more than 3–6 severe episodes per year, secondary suppressive therapy may be necessary.
- *Disseminated HSV:* IV acyclovir at a dose of 10 mg/kg/dose tid for 21 days.

Prevention

- Patients with frequent recurrences of mucocutaneous HSV disease (defined as 6 or more per year) or HSV esophagitis may benefit from chronic suppressive therapy. Treatment considerations are extrapolated from studies of adults.
- Acyclovir dose for prophylaxis is 200mg tid or 400mg bid. In children, a dose of 300mg/m2 po q8hours or 80mg/kg/day divided tid. Valacyclovir does not have a pediatric indication however can be used in adolescents at a dose of 500 mg bid.

Cytomegalovirus (CMV)

Clinical manifestations

- The most common manifestations of CMV in children are chorioretinitis, esophagitis, pneumonitis, and colitis.
- HIV-infected infants can also be co-infected with CMV which can worsen organ system involvement such as pneumonitis, cardiomyopathy, and encephalopathy.
- HIV disease may also progress more rapidly in children who are co-infected with CMV.
- CMV retinitis may present asymptomatically in younger children. For this reason, routine examination is extremely important. Older children frequently report "floaters" or visual disturbances that prompt a diagnostic, dilated retinal exam.

- Retinoscopy for CMV retinitis is diagnostic, and serial photographs are used to help follow the clinical progression or resolution of disease with therapy.

Diagnosis
- CMV serologies and cultures may indicate infection, but don't necessarily predict disease. CMV positive cultures from biopsy material of the GI tract, lung or from BAL fluid, along with a consistent clinical picture is considered diagnostic.
- Other tests, such as detection of pp65 antigen, PCR and DNA hybridization can be used to identify patients at higher risk to develop clinical disease. Quantification of CMV by PCR from blood, as is utilized in solid organ or bone marrow transplant patients to make clinical treatment decisions, has not been standardized for use in HIV infected individuals.

Treatment
- Initial treatment of disseminated CMV disease and retinitis in HIV-positive children is IV Ganciclovir (5 mg/kg/dose bid). The major side effect is myelosuppression which may require dose interruption or the use of granulocyte stimulating factor. Oral Valganciclovir, the prodrug of ganciclovir, is readily absorbed from the GI tract and is first line therapy for adults with CMV retinitis. An alternative drug for CMV is Foscarnet. The pediatric dose is 60mg/kg/dose every 8 hours. Lifelong maintenance therapy is recommended, but should be managed by a physician with expertise in the management of CMV infection.

Immune Reconstitution Inflammatory Syndrome (IRIS)
- Patients with profound immunosuppression who have an excellent response to antiretroviral therapy with a robust immune reconstitution are at risk for the immune reconstitution inflammatory syndrome.[20] This syndrome has been described less frequently in children but does occur.
- IRIS is a paradoxical deterioration of a pre-existing infection usually due to an aggressive inflammatory response to the pathogen. It has been described most commonly with MAC, TB, CMV retinitis, and Cryptococcus. In children, a herpes zoster outbreak, or a draining infection at the site of an old BCG scar are common manifestations of IRIS.[21]
- It is important to recognize this entity, and to observe for it in individuals who are experiencing a good immunologic response in the days to months after initiating HAART.
- Treatment includes treating the primary infectious disease, continuing HAART and in some cases using anti-inflammatory agents such as steroids. This treatment should be done in consultation with a specialist in HIV.

References

1. USPHS/IDSA. 2001 Guidelines for the prevention of opportunistic infections in persons infected with human immunodeficiency virus. November 2001. Available at: www.aidsinfo.nih.gov.

2. .American Academy of Pediatrics. Active Immunization. In: Pickering LK, ed. *Red Book: 2003 Report of the Committee on Infectious Diseases*. 26th ed. Elk Grove Village, IL: American Academy of Pediatrics; 2003: 24–25.

3. Melvin A, Mohan KM. Response to immunization with measles, tetanus, and haemophilus influenzae type B vaccines in children who have human immunodeficiency virus type 1 infection and are treated with highly active antiretroviral therapy. Pediatrics 2003; 111:e641–644 [epub].

4. Goon P, Cohen B, Jin L, et al. MMR vaccine in HIV-infected children—potential hazards? *Vaccine* 2001; 19:3816–3819.

5. PACTG P1006 The Effects of Highly active Antiretroviral Therapy (HAART) on the Recovery of Immune Function in HIV-Infected Children and young Adults. Version 4.0 http://pactg.s-3.com.

6. American Academy of Pediatrics, Committee on Pediatric AIDS. Measles immunization in HIV-infected children. *Pediatrics* 1999; 103:1057–1060.

7. Moss WJ, Clements CJ, Halsey NA. Immunization of children at risk of infection with human immunodeficiency virus. *Bulletin of the World Health Organization* 2003; 81:61–70.

8. Levin M, Gershon A, Weinberg A, et al. Immunization of HIV-infected children with varicella vaccine. *J Peds* 2001;139:305–310.

9. American Academy of Pediatrics. Passive immunization.. In: Pickering LK, ed. *Red Book: 2003 Report of the Committee on Infectious Diseases*. 26th ed. Elk Grove Village, IL: American Academy of Pediatrics; 2003:56-60.

10. Spector SA, Gerber RD, McGrath N, et al. A controlled trial of IVIG for the prevention of serious bacterial infection in children receiving zidovidine for advanced HIV. *NEJM* 1994; 331:1181–1187.

11. Mofenson L, et al., Treating opportunistic infections among HIV-exposed and infected children. *MMWR*, December 3, 2004; 53(RR14):1–63.

12. 2001 USPHS/IDSA Guidelines for the Prevention of Opportunistic Infections in Persons Infected with Human Immunodeficiency Virus. Available at: www.aidsinfo.nih.gov.

13. 2001 USPHS/IDSA Guidelines for the Prevention of Opportunistic Infections in Persons Infected with Human Immunodeficiency Virus. Available at: www.aidsinfo.nih.gov

14. Mofenson L. et al., Treating opportunistic infections among HIV-exposed and infected children. *MMWR*, December 3, 2004; 53(RR14):1–63.

15. 2001 USPHS/IDSA Guidelines for the Prevention of Opportunistic Infections in Persons Infected with Human Immunodeficiency Virus. Available at: www.aidsinfo.nih.gov.

16. Urschel S, Ramos J, Mellado M et al. Withdrawal of Pneumocystis jirovecii prophylaxis in HIV-infected children under highly active antiretroviral therapy. *AIDS* December 2, 2005; 19(18):2103–2108.

17. Nachman S, Gona P, Dankner W et al. The rate of serious bacterial infections among HIV-infected children with immune reconstitution who have discontinued opportunistic infection prophylaxis. *Pediatrics* April 2005; 115(4):e488–494. March 16, 2005. [epub]

18. 2001 USPHS/IDSA Guidelines for the prevention of opportunistic infections in persons infected with human immunodeficiency virus. Available at: www.aidsinfo.nih.gov.

19. 2001 USPHS/IDSA Guidelines for the prevention of opportunistic infections in persons infected with human immunodeficiency virus. Available at: www.aidsinfo.nih.gov.

20. Shelburne SA, Hamill RJ. The immune reconstitution inflammatory syndrome. *AIDS Rev* 2003, April–June; 5(2) 67–79.

21. Tangsinmankong N, Kamchaisatian W, et al. Varicella zoster as a manifestation of immune restoration syndrome in HIV-infected children. *J Allerg Clin Immunol* April 2004; 113(4); 742–747.

32

Adherence in the Pediatric HIV Population

Ana M. Puga, MD
Children's Diagnostic & Treatment Center, Inc., Fort Lauderdale

Introduction

Highly Active Antiretroviral Therapy (HAART) has made a tremendous impact on the lives of HIV-infected children. The HIV-infected children are living longer, in better health, with decreased morbidity and less frequent hospitalization. Unfortunately, HAART does not provide equal benefits to all children. One factor pivotal to maximizing the benefits of HAART is adherence to the prescribed regimen. Unfortunately, many barriers still exist that make adherence to HAART difficult for children and families. The information below describes these barriers and offers suggestions for improving adherence in the HIV-infected children.

Goals of Adherence[1]

* Suppress viral replication (undetectable < 50 copies/ml)
* Preserve and/or restore immune system function (immune reconstitution)
* Avoid resistance

Importance of Adherence[1]

* Poor medication adherence correlates with virologic failure
* Table 1 (next page) shows the best chance of achieving full therapeutic benefit of HAART required near-perfect adherence, ≥ 95%
* In a 30-day period, an adherence rate of ≥ 95% for a twice-daily regimen is missing only 2 doses!
* In all populations and diseases, approximately 50% of patients fail to self-administer the medications as prescribed

Table 1. A Study of 45 HIV-Infected Adult Patients

MEDICATION ADHERENCE % OF DOSES TAKEN	VIROLOGIC FAILURE % OF PATIENTS
< 80	87%
80-90	47%
> 95	10%

Measuring Adherence[1]

- Problematic due to a lack of accurate tools to measure adherence
  - 2 types of measurements
    - **Direct:** measurement of blood levels of medications
      - Expensive, not covered by insurance, and therapeutic ranges are ill defined in pediatrics
    - **Indirect:** caregiver/patient self-report, interview, pill counts, pharmacy records
      - None of these tools are 100% reliable but they are the most practical especially when used in combination
      - One common approach is to ask the patient to report adherence to specific medications in the previous 3 days, such as "Did you take your morning dose of XX today? How about yesterday, did you take your evening does of XX last night?"

Barriers to Adherence[1,3,4]

- Treating an asymptomatic patient with medications that make him/her feel "sick"
- Failure to disclose the diagnosis to the child and/or family members
- Caregiver and patient knowledge of disease and goals of treatment
- Lack of social support and/or supervision of medication administration
- Caregiver attitudes and cultural beliefs regarding the healthcare system
- Mental illness or drug abuse in household caregivers
- Complex regimens with many pills, many times per day, with dietary restrictions and bad taste
- Complexity of acquiring pharmacy refills
- Illiteracy of caregiver

Clinician Strategies to Support Adherence[1,3,4]

- Education of HIV disease and the goals of therapy as well as feedback regarding lab results and how the patient is doing at achieving the goals.

- Assess comprehension of information given and ask caregiver/patient to explain medication dosing
- Ongoing communication/education regarding side-effects, especially when beginning a new regimen, and subsequent treatment/prevention strategies
- Encourage disclosure of the HIV diagnosis to the child at approximately age 7 or when deemed appropriate
- Instruct parents/caregivers to supervise the child when taking medications even for adolescents.
- Simplify regimens if applicable and tailor regimens to daily activities to enhance convenience
- Use of adherence tools or administration aids: pill crushers, marked and/or color coded oral syringes, medication bottle caps designed for drawing up oral syringes with ease and little mess (i.e., "Adaptacaps®" available in most pharmacies), pill boxes, medication calendar or diary with reward system, auditory reminders/beepers, alarm watches)
- Assess adherence at every visit
- Reassess adherence as a cause of treatment failure before changing a regimen
- Expect relapse and have a relapse plan

Tips for Administration of Bad-Tasting Liquid Formulations[5]

- Medication examples
  - Ritonavir (Norvir®, RTV)
  - Lopinavir/ritonavir (Kaletra®, KAL)
  - Amprenavir (Agenerase®, APV)
- Mask the taste with chocolate syrup, or a couple of ounces of juice or milk
- Dull the taste buds by chewing ice or eating a Popsicle
- Coat mouth with peanut butter prior to taking medications
- Give strong tasting foods immediately after taking medication(s)
  - Maple syrup
    Barbeque sauce
  - Chewing gum
  - Hard candy

Drug-Specific Administration Tips[5]

- Didanosine (Videx®, ddI) liquid
  - Prescribe to be compounded by the pharmacist in cherry or lemon flavored Maalox®
- Efavirenz (Sustiva®, EFV) capsules
  - The capsules may be opened and administered with grape jelly or Pixy Stix® (Pharmacokinetic data of using it in this fashion is limited)
- Nelfinavir (Viracept®, NFV) powder and tablets
  - May mix powder with milk-based products such as formula, milk, pudding, or ice cream
  - Tablets disperse easily in water and have little taste

- Tablet may also be crushed and mixed with milk-based products
- Mixing with acidic foods or juice makes the medication taste bitter

Conclusion

Lifelong adherence to HAART is a formidable task, for all patients. Each child and his/her family have unique barriers to adherence and they need to strive to overcome these barriers. Consequently, the clinician must develop practical strategies to support adherence while utilizing community resources and a multidisciplinary approach to have the best success. This process, while extremely challenging, can be equally rewarding.

References

1. Andrews L. Friedland G. Progress in the HIV therapeutics and the challenges of adherence to antiretroviral therapy. *Inf Dis Clin of N Amer* 2000; 14:1–26.

2. Chesney MA. Factors affecting adherence to antiretroviral therapy. *Clin Inf Dis* 2000; 30(Supp l2):S171–176.

3. Proctor VE, Asrat T, Tompkins DC. Barriers to adherence to highly active antiretroviral therapy as expressed by people living with HIV/AIDS. *AIDS Patient Care and STD's* 1999; 13:535–532.

4. Chesney MA, Ickovics J, Hecht FM, et al. Adherence: a necessity for successful HIV combination therapy. *AIDS* 1999; 13(Supp lA):S271–S278.

5. Guidelines for the use of antiretroviral agents in pediatric HIV infection. January 7, 2000. Working Group on Antiretroviral Therapy and Medical Management of HIV-Infected Children. Available at: www.hivatis.org. Accessed January 7, 2000.

33

Management of Medical Conditions in Children

Gwendolyn B. Scott, MD
Professor and Director, Pediatric Infectious Diseases and Immunology
Department of Pediatrics/Infectious Disease
University of Miami School of Medicine

This chapter will cover the following common problems:
- Acute otitis media
- Sinusitis
- Pneumonia
- Gastroenteritis

Introduction

HIV-infected children can have all the same age appropriate infections as any other child. There are additional considerations that should be included while evaluating an HIV infected child. If an infection is identified, evaluation and management may have to be more aggressive.

Initial considerations in the HIV-infected child with an acute illness should include:
- An assessment of the severity of the illness
- Determining the state of HIV infection. This should include:
  - CDC classification
  - CD4 count
  - Viral load
  - History of prior illnesses
- Being aware of the appropriate use of medications including:
  - Antiretroviral agents
  - PCP prophylaxis
  - Mycobacterial prophylaxis

- It is important to determine:
  - If the patient has been compliant with taking their medications
  - The potential interaction between regularly used medications
  - Those medications which may have been started to treat an acute problem

o The potential myelosuppressive effects of medications that are commonly used to treat HIV infection may blunt the patient's ability to respond to a bacterial infection (i.e., leukopenia associated with ZDV). If this is the case, and you are considering altering the antiretroviral therapy, an HIV specialist should be consulted. In addition, alternative strategies, such as G-CSF therapy should be considered.

o As a rule, if antiretrovirals have to be stopped for any reason, all of the antiretrovirals should be stopped simultaneously

o Consult a pediatric HIV specialist prior to making any changes in medications

General Aspects

- Children with HIV-infection who are asymptomatic and have normal age adjusted CD4 counts will have illnesses that do not differ in character or severity from those seen in uninfected children.

- Children who are **symptomatic**, have **moderate suppression** of CD4 counts, or have AIDS may present with more severe disease and may have a poor response to therapy. These children may have disease caused by less common organisms (i.e., gram-negative enterics). A non-optimal response to traditional therapy may indicate the presence of resistant organisms and require further investigation.

- Children with **severe suppression** of CD4 counts may have disease caused by opportunistic organisms (i.e., aspergillus, Pneumocystis jarovecii, atypical mycobacteria, CMV, and herpes). The clinical presentation in these patients may be atypical and may be severe. These patients are more likely to have persistent or chronic/recurrent infections.

- Consideration should be given to the **total WBC count and to the absolute neutrophil count (ANC)**. HIV-infected children with ANC < 500 cells/mm^3 should be assessed promptly and treated empirically with antibiotics. This is done regardless of the stage of disease or CD4 lymphocyte count.

- Consultation with a pediatric HIV specialist who is familiar with the patient (especially for the most complicated patients with extensive medical histories) can aid in determining the appropriate work-up and management.

Specific Diseases

Otitis media and sinusitis are common infections in both HIV-infected children and uninfected children with normal immune function. However, recurrences are more common in **symptomatic** HIV-infected children. In the immunocompetent child, as well as in the child with HIV infection, *Streptococcus pneumoniae, Hemophilus influenzae, and Moraxella catarrhalis* are the most common bacterial pathogens.

OTITIS MEDIA

Diagnosis

- The diagnosis is based on the same criteria as in non-HIV-infected children
- Tympanocentesis should be considered in children with
  - Toxic appearance
  - Recurrent or persistent disease in those who have failed initial medical therapy

Treatment

- Oral antimicrobial therapy can be used for first episodes of otitis media
  - Standard dosages of antibiotics and length of therapy are recommended.
  - **Amoxicillin** at a standard dose of 45 mg/kg/day or at a higher dose of 90 mg/kg/day if resistant organisms are suspected is the drug of choice.
- Treatment failures should be treated with broader spectrum antibiotics
  - In symptomatic children this treatment may be extended 2 to 3 weeks
- A patient who is systemically ill or toxic appearing should have tympanocentesis performed, tympanic fluid cultures sent and parenteral antibiotic therapy begun
  - Cefuroxime, if meningitis not suspected
  - Ceftriaxone
  - Ceftazidime
  - High dose Ampicillin / Sulbactam, if meningitis is not suspected.
- Retreatment of persistent effusion following symptomatic infection may help prevent recurrences
- Chronic suppurative otitis media should be managed in conjunction with an otolaryngologist. Cultures should be obtained and topical therapy with Ofloxacin drops can be started. If the purulent discharge persists then systemic therapy directed toward *Staphylococcus aureus* and *Pseudomonas aeruginosa* should be started

SINUSITIS

Diagnosis

- The signs and symptoms of acute sinusitis in HIV-infected children are generally indistinguishable from those in uninfected children
- The diagnosis can be made by history and physical exam with upper respiratory symptoms lasting > 10 to 30 days
  - Persistent nasal discharge
  - Cough that is worse at night
  - Low grade fever, headache
  - Facial pain or mild periorbital edema
- Patients with severe CD4 suppression or neutropenia may present with
  - High fever
  - Purulent nasal discharge or nasal ulceration
  - Severe headache
  - Significant periorbital edema
- The indications for obtaining sinus radiographs to confirm the diagnosis of sinusitis in HIV-infected children should be the same as for uninfected children

- CT scans should be considered if complications are suspected or according to clinical circumstances in patients with chronic disease
- Extension of the infection to adjacent bone, orbit, or CNS will occur more frequently in severely immunosuppressed patients
- Patients who have a history of chronic sinusitis may require sinus aspiration for culture
  o This should be done in conjunction with an otolaryngologist
  o Cultures of the fluid may yield unusual organisms such as
    - *Pseudomonas aeruginosa*
    - *Candida albicans*
    - *Aspergillus specie*
    - Gram-negative enterics

Treatment

- Patients who are only mildly ill can be treated with standard outpatient oral antibiotic therapy (i.e., Amoxicillin for 3 weeks). This can be done for symptomatic and asymptomatic patients with HIV infection.
- Patients with chronic disease will usually require treatment with broader spectrum antibiotics for longer periods of time (i.e., Augmentin for 4 to 8 weeks)
- Parenteral therapy may be required in patients with a poor response to oral therapy, for severe disease, and should be considered sooner in the patient with severe immunosuppression

PNEUMONIA

Evaluation (See Figure 1)

- Children who present **only** with signs and symptoms of an **upper respiratory infection (URI)** will likely be infected with the same viruses that occur in non-immunosuppressed patients. There is some evidence that children with HIV infection may have more frequent respiratory tract infections, have prolonged excretion of virus, have more severe infections, and may be infected with more than one virus at a time. This would occur in children with lower CD4 counts. Children with normal CD4 counts can be treated as any other child with an URI; those who are suppressed should be examined carefully for signs of lower respiratory tract involvement and followed more carefully.
- Children who present with signs of **lower respiratory tract infection** should be evaluated with a chest X-ray, CBC, blood culture, and pulse oximetry for measurement of oxygen saturation
- The differential diagnosis should include:
  o Viral pneumonia
  o Mycoplasma pneumonia
  o Bacterial pneumonia, *Streptococcus pneumoniae* is the most common bacterial pathogen.
  o Pneumocystis jiroveci pneumonia (PCP)
  o Lymphoid interstitial pneumonitis (LIP)
  o Mycobacterial pneumonia
  o Fungal pneumonia
- Diffuse bilateral alveolar disease is more likely to be PCP, viral or mycoplasma pneumonia
- Focal infiltrates are more likely to be bacterial or mycobacterial
- Diffuse reticulonodular infiltrates are likely related to LIP and/or fungal diseases
- PCP should be considered in any child with HIV-infection regardless of the stage of infection or CD4 count although PCP occurs more commonly in the child < 1 year of age. PCP can be the presenting illness in previously undiagnosed infants with HIV. Children with suppressed

CD4 counts are more likely to have PCP but children with normal CD4 counts may also get PCP).

- Prophylaxis against PCP is highly effective (though not absolute) if the patient is compliant with the medication. Prophylaxis is indicated for all at risk infants during the first 6 months of life, for all HIV-infected infants for the first year of life and for all children with a prior episode of PCP or who are in immune category 3 (severe immune suppression). An effort should be made to assess compliance with prophylactic regimens.
- Certain clinical features of PCP can be an aid in diagnosis:
    o The classic triad is Tachypnea or dyspnea, fever, and cough
    o Blood gas values usually reveal hypoxemia (PaO_2 levels between 34–73 mm Hg) at the time of presentation. Alveolar-arterial oxygen gradients are usually > 30 mm Hg
    o The lactate dehydrogenase (LDH) levels are usually increased (320–2000 units/liter)
- Early CXR may be normal or reveal only perihilar infiltrates. Progression proceeds peripherally with the apex of the lung being involved last
- An index of suspicion for PCP should prompt a bronchoscopy, bronchoalveolar lavage, and consultation with a specialist in HIV

Figure 1. Evaluation of the HIV-Infected Child with Respiratory Distress

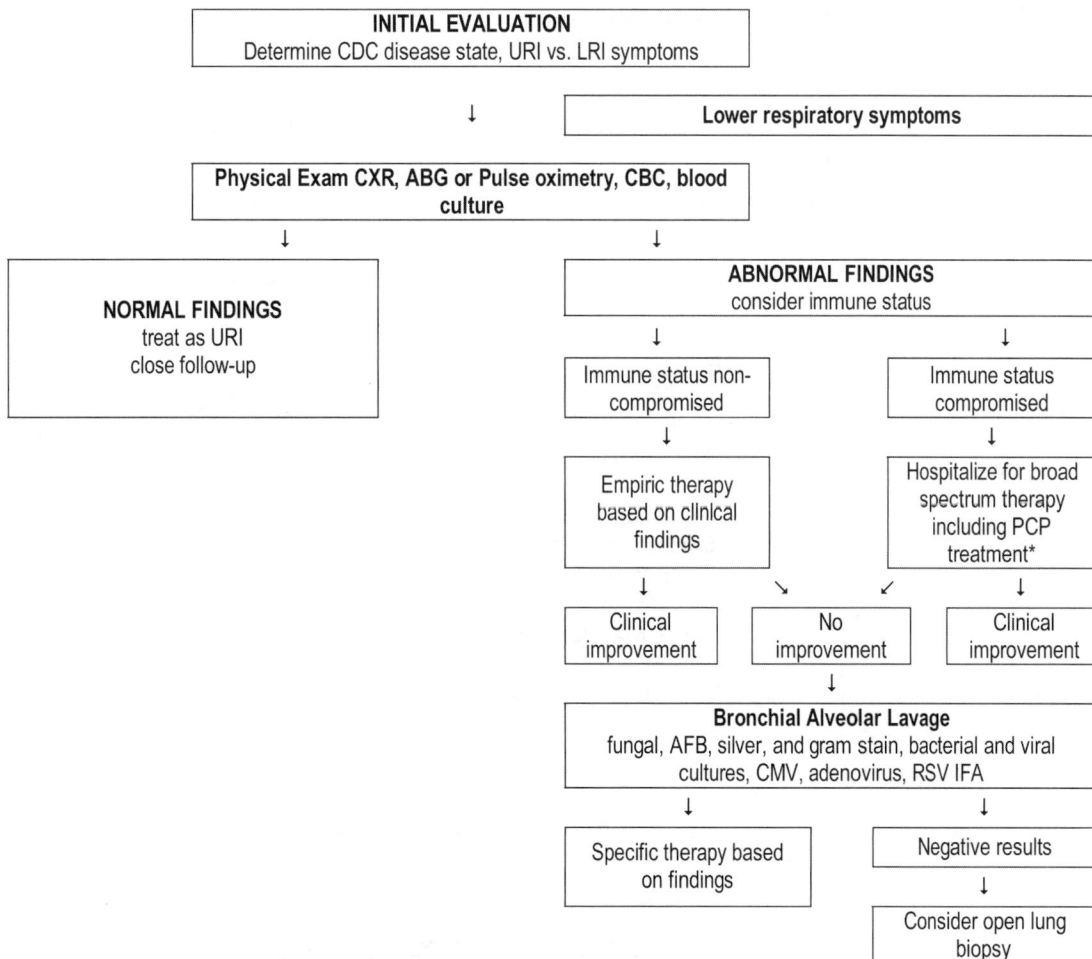

* If PCP, opportunistic infection, unusual bacterial infection suspected or patient is extremely toxic, then bronchoscopy should be scheduled as soon as possible.

GASTROENTERITIS AND DIARRHEA

Most HIV-infected children will experience diarrheal illnesses during the progression of their disease. OIs can be identified as the cause in about 50% of cases.

Evaluation (See Figure 2)
- Initial evaluation should include an estimation of ongoing stool losses.
- Upper tract signs would include:
  - Belching
  - Dyspepsia
  - Symptoms associated with meals
- Lower tract signs include
  - tenesmus
  - mucoid stools
- Low stool pH, elevated stool sodium, and positive stool reducing substances can be seen with small intestine malabsorption
- The presence or absence of blood loss should be verified
- Stool culture should be targeted to the detection of common pathogens or those pathogens known to be associated with HIV infection
  - If studies are negative, then endoscopy and biopsy should be pursued
  - If no treatable pathogen is identified, and diarrhea persists, treatment modalities such as Imodium, Questran, Octreotide and parenteral nutrition should be considered

Figure 2. Clinical Evaluation of the HIV-Infected Child with Diarrhea

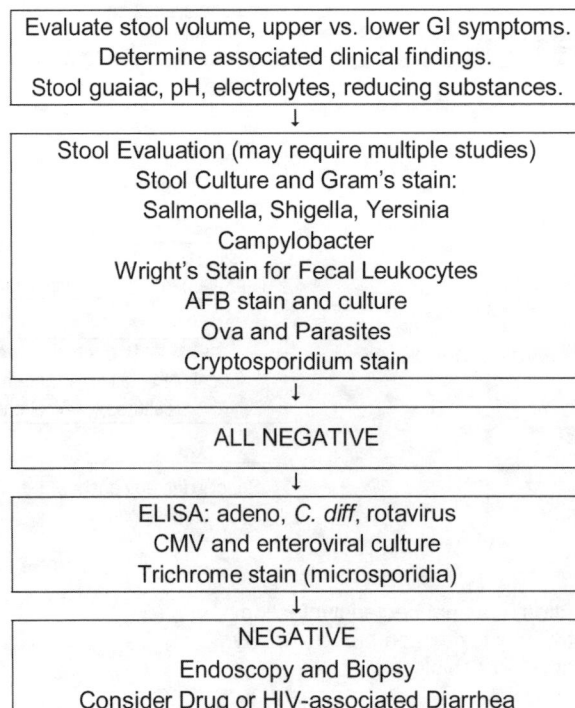

Evaluate stool volume, upper vs. lower GI symptoms.
Determine associated clinical findings.
Stool guaiac, pH, electrolytes, reducing substances.

↓

Stool Evaluation (may require multiple studies)
Stool Culture and Gram's stain:
Salmonella, Shigella, Yersinia
Campylobacter
Wright's Stain for Fecal Leukocytes
AFB stain and culture
Ova and Parasites
Cryptosporidium stain

↓

ALL NEGATIVE

↓

ELISA: adeno, *C. diff*, rotavirus
CMV and enteroviral culture
Trichrome stain (microsporidia)

↓

NEGATIVE
Endoscopy and Biopsy
Consider Drug or HIV-associated Diarrhea

INFECTIOUS CAUSES OF DIARRHEA
COMMONLY ASSOCIATED WITH HIV-INFECTED CHILDREN

PARASITES

Cryptosporidium

Source:	Inhalation or ingestion of oocyst from pets, contaminated water, or person-to-person (day care)
Signs and symptoms:	Large volume secretory diarrhea associated with malabsorption, anorexia, and weight loss
Diagnosis:	Wet prep "O & P," modified Kinyoun acid fast stain, monoclonal antibody based IFA or ELISA, or intestinal biopsy (stool may be negative while biopsy positive)
Treatment:	Nitazoxanide oral suspension has been licensed by the FDA for treatment of C. parvum. Treatment with paromomycin in combination with azithromycin may have some effect. Octreotide may decrease diarrhea.
Comment:	**May cause invasion of biliary epithelium resulting in obstruction of pancreatic duct. Also is a cause of sclerosing cholangitis.** **Oocysts may continue to be shed after symptoms resolve.** Chlorination does not inactivate oocytes, water filtration is necessary

Isospora belli

Source:	Common in tropical and subtropical climates. Humans primary host. Fecal/oral transmission, contaminated water
Signs and symptoms:	Upper GI pathogen, similar to cryptosporidium, but is usually not associated with severe weight loss
Diagnosis:	Wet prep, modified Kinyoun carbolfuchsin and auramine – rhodamine stains of feces or duodenal aspirates or intestinal biopsy
Treatment:	TMP-SMX is the drug of choice. Pyrimethamine may be effective (use in combination with folinic acid)
Comment:	Chlorination does not inactivate oocytes, water filtration is necessary

Microsporidium *(E. bieneusi)*

Source:	Contaminated water, found in invertebrate animals, person to person spread
Signs and symptoms:	Upper GI pathogen, a common etiology for presumed pathogen negative diarrhea, malnutrition, progressive weight loss
Diagnosis:	Intestinal biopsy, electron microscopy
Treatment:	No proven effective treatment. Octreotide may decrease stool output. Highly active antiretroviral therapy with improvement in CD4 can favorably affect the course of disease

Giardia lamblia

Source:	Contaminated water, day care centers, travelers diarrhea
Signs and symptoms:	Bloating, diarrhea, weight loss, cramping abdominal pain
Diagnosis:	Wet prep of stool or duodenal aspirate. Intestinal biopsy is rarely required
Treatment:	Albendazole, 3 day course of Nitazoxanide, quinacrine, furazolidone, or metronidazole

Cyclospora cayetanensis

Source:	Contaminated food and water
Signs and Symptoms:	Profuse, watery, non-bloody diarrhea, vomiting, abdominal pain, fatigue, fever in 50% of cases.
Diagnosis:	Stool O&P using a modified acid fast stain
Treatment:	TMP-SMX, Children with HIV may need higher doses and longer treatment.

BACTERIA

Mycobacterium avium complex (MAC)
Source: Ubiquitous in nature, soil, food, water and animals, Water supply, entry through the intestine
Signs and symptoms: Diarrhea, weight loss, fever, anemia
Diagnosis: AFB stain, mycobacteria culture of stool and blood
Treatment: Multidrug therapy should be initiated and include clarithromycin or azithromycin + ethambutol ± rifabutin. (See previous section on Management of Opportunistic Infections)

Salmonella
Source: Contaminated animal products, contaminated water, contact with infected reptiles, human carriers
Signs and symptoms: Chronic mucoid diarrhea, fever, colitis
Diagnosis: Stool culture, blood culture
Treatment: Ampicillin, Amoxil, TMP/SMX, cefotaxime, ceftriaxone, are recommended for treatment of susceptible strains
Antimicrobial therapy for uncomplicated gastrointestinal disease is recommended for patients with an increased risk for invasive disease including children with HIV

Aeromonas hydrophilia
Source: Contaminated water
Signs and symptoms: Prolonged dysentery-like diarrhea
Diagnosis: Stool culture
Treatment: TMP/SMX, Ceftazidime, Cefepime

Campylobacter
Source: Wild birds, poultry, and animals. Pet associated or day care
Signs and symptoms: Bloody diarrhea, abdominal pain, fever, malaise.
Diagnosis: Stool culture using special media
Treatment: Erythromycin, Azithromycin
Complications: May invade bloodstream

Shigella
Source: Fecal/oral (day care associated), contaminated foods or water
Signs and symptoms: Acute onset diarrhea with fever, abdominal pain, tenesmus, mucoid stools with or without blood, associated with seizures and low wbc counts
Diagnosis: Stool culture, methylene blue stain shows sheets of PMNs
Treatment: TMP/SMX, Ampicillin, parenteral Ceftriaxone
Antimicrobial susceptibility testing is recommended because plasmid related resistance is common
Antidiarrheal compounds are not recommended

VIRUSES

Cytomegalovirus (CMV)
Source: Person-to-person (daycare), vertical transmission
Signs and symptoms: Colitis, fever, abdominal pain
Diagnosis: Viral culture (stool, urine, or blood). Diagnosis of tissue infection usually requires biopsy with demonstration of CMV inclusions in the tissue
Treatment: Ganciclovir

Rotavirus
Source: Person-to-person (day care)
Signs and symptoms: Non bloody diarrhea

Diagnosis: Stool ELISA
Treatment: Supportive care, correct dehydration, Immune globulin oral colostrum with enriched Rotavirus IgG for severe cases. No specific antiviral therapy available

Enteropathic adenovirus
Source: Person-to-person
Signs and symptoms: Upper intestinal diarrhea
Diagnosis: Viral culture, adenovirus antigen test using immunoassays, electron microscopic evaluation of stool.
Treatment: Supportive care, Cidofovir in immunocompromised patients

HIV-related
Source: HIV infection
Signs and symptoms: Chronic, pathogen negative diarrhea and wasting, malabsorption, lactose intolerance
Diagnosis: Exclusion of other causes
Treatment: Combination antiretroviral therapy. (See Chapter 30, Antiretroviral Therapy in Children.)

NON-INFECTIOUS AND OTHER CAUSES OF DIARRHEAL ILLNESS

- Malabsorption, including lactose intolerance
- Lymphoid hyperplasia of the GI tract
- Medications associated with diarrhea:
  - Antibiotics
  - Acyclovir
  - Nystatin solution
  - Ketoconazole
  - Antiretroviral medications

References

1. American Academy of Pediatrics. Adolescents and human immunodeficiency virus infection, the role of the pediatrician in prevention and intervention. *Pediatrics*. January 2001; 107:188–190.
2. American Academy of Pediatrics. Disclosure of illness status to children and adolescents with HIV infection. *Pediatrics*. January 1999; 103:164–166.
3. American Academy of Pediatrics. Human immunodeficiency virus and other blood borne viral pathogens in the athletic setting. *Pediatrics*. December 1999; 104:1400–1403.
4. American Academy of Pediatrics. [chapter title]. In: Pickering LK, ed. Red Book: 2003 Report of the Committee on Infectious Diseases. 26th ed. Elk Grove Village, IL: American Academy of Pediatrics; 2003:360–382.
5. Pediatric and Perinatal Guidelines. Available at: www.aidsinfo.org.
6. Adolescent and Adult Guidelines. Available at: www.aidsinfo.org.
7. American Academy of Pediatrics. Committee on Adolescence Condom Use by Adolescents. *Pediatrics* 2001; 107: 1463–1469.
8. American Academy of Pediatrics. Committee on Pediatric AIDS Postexposure Prophylaxis in Children and Adolescents for Non-Occupational Exposure to Human Immunodeficiency Virus. *Pediatrics* 2003; 111: 1475–1489.
9. American Academy of Pediatrics. Committee on Pediatric AIDS, and Canadian Pediatric Society, Infectious Diseases and Immunization Committee Evaluation and Treatment of the Human Immunodeficiency Virus-1—Exposed Infant. *Pediatrics* 2004; 114: 497–505.
10. American Academy of Pediatrics. Committee on Pediatric AIDS Education of Children With Human Immunodeficiency Virus Infection. *Pediatrics* 2000; 105: 1358–1360.

34

Supportive Care for HIV-Infected Children and Their Families

Gwendolyn B. Scott, MD
Director
Pediatric Infectious Diseases and Immunology
Department of Pediatrics/Infectious Disease
University of Miami School of Medicine
Carol M. Fulton, MSN, ARNP, CPNP
Kathy Letro, RD, LD/N
Pediatric Infectious Diseases and Immunology
Rainbow Center for Women, Adolescent, Children and Families
University of Florida, Jacksonville

Introduction

Nutritional Support of the HIV-Infected Infant and Child

Nutrition plays a very important role in maintaining the well being of the HIV-infected infant. Inadequate weight gain and growth is one of the common problems and can manifest before other symptoms of HIV. Unlike infected adults, infants need to increase their weight; therefore, they are more susceptible at an early stage to develop nutritional deficiencies. This will impact their growth, immunological integrity, and brain development. Nutritional assessment should be performed at every visit, and early recognition of problems and intervention is imperative. Practitioners must identify the multiple factors which contribute to poor growth, including the environment in which the child is being raised.

Studies in the pediatric population have shown that the institution of antiretroviral therapy often results in a significant improvement in growth. In the pediatric population, growth failure is an indication to initiate or change antiretroviral therapy.

FACTORS CONTRIBUTING TO FAILURE TO THRIVE

- Intercurrent illnesses, particularly diarrheal illnesses and subsequent malabsorption
- Increased metabolic needs secondary to fever, cytokine production, and infection
- Decreased intake due to anorexia, dysphagia, nausea or feeding difficulties due to oral thrush, esophagitis or conditions such as encephalopathy
- "Nonorganic" failure to thrive secondary to chaotic home situation, distracted care givers, and/or drug use in the home

NUTRITIONAL ASSESSMENT

- Anthropometric data — weight, height, and head circumference, height for age, weight for age, weight for height plotted on gender specific growth charts, and growth trends monitoring
- Evaluation of weight changes. The definition of AIDS Wasting Syndrome is 10% weight loss. A 1-kilogram weight loss can be all that is needed:

Time Interval	Significant	Severe
1 Week	1 – 2%	>2%
1 Month	5%	>5%
6 Months	10%	>10%

- Interview focusing on detailed dietary intake, intercurrent illnesses, diarrhea, and vomiting
- Periodic laboratory evaluation to include albumin, Fe, B_{12}, Folate, CBC, electrolytes, liver and renal function labs.
- Medication history: to include ART, any medications for opportunistic infections, vitamin and mineral use, and alternative therapies.

CALORIE AND PROTEIN REQUIREMENTS

WEIGHT-AGE*	RDA CALORIES (KCAL/KG)	RDA PROTEIN (GM/KG)
0-6 mos	115	2.2
6-12 mos	105	2.0
1-3 yr	100	1.8
4-6 yr	85	1.5

* Weight-age is the age at which the patient's present weight would be in the 50th percentile.

CALCULATION OF CALORIE AND PROTEIN REQUIREMENTS
DURING CATCH-UP GROWTH

$$\text{Calorie requirements} = \frac{\text{(RDA calories for weight-age) x (ideal wt for ht)}}{\text{(actual weight)}} = \text{kcal/kg}$$

$$\text{Protein requirements} = \frac{\text{(RDA protein for weight-age) x (ideal wt for ht)}}{\text{(actual weight)}} = \text{Gm protein/kg}$$

SOURCE: K M Corrales and S L Uttes, Failure to Thrive. In: Sumour PQ, Kelm K K, and Lange C E. *Handbook of Pediatric Nutrition*, 2nd ed. New York, NY: Aspen Publishers, 1999; 406.

MAXIMIZING ORAL INTAKE

- Assist clients/parents/caregivers in enrolling in all available social services including
  WIC
  Food Stamp programs
  Food Banks
- For infants and children who are not growing well or have failure to thrive, increase caloric density of formula in infants to 24–30 kcal/oz – through addition of other medical nutrients such as carbohydrate sources (Polycose), protein sources (Promod, Meritene) or fat sources (Microlipid)
- Counsel on a high calorie, high protein diet:
  Infants:
    - 150–200 kcal/kg/day
    - 3.0–4.4 g protein/kg/day
  Children:
    - 100–150 kcal/kg/day
    - 1.8–3.6 g protein/kg/day
- Daily vitamin supplement to replace micronutrients that are deficient
- If diarrhea is present:
  Identify and treat enteric infections contributing to weight loss
  Identify and treat for malabsorption if signs and symptoms are present
  Counsel appropriately to minimize diarrhea
  Provide nutrient supplements as appropriate – i.e., Pediasure®, Ensure®, Boost®, Kindercal®, NuBasics,® Carnation Instant Breakfast
- Consider pharmacologic agents to stimulate appetite or anabolism.

WHEN ORAL SUPPLEMENTATION FAILS

- Nasogastric tube feedings can be initiated. In older children nighttime continuous feedings will allow for a normal diet during the day
  In infants, bolus or continuous feeds are often used
    - Complications include
      - Sinusitis
      - GI reflux
      - Aspiration
      - Discomfort
      - Perforation of Viscus
- If use of a feeding tube is required long term, consider placement of a permanent gastrostomy tube

CHOICE OF FORMULAS

- **Polymeric** – intact protein, long chain triglycerides
  Indicated for patients with normal gut function
    - Pediasure®
    - Ensure®
    - Isocal®
    - Boost®
    - Kindercal®
- **Elemental** – peptide or amino acids, medium chain triglycerides as primary fat source
  Indicated in patients with chronic diarrhea or problems with malabsorption
    - Pregestimil®
    - Nutramigen®
    - Vivonex®
    - Alimentum®
    - Peptamen®
- **Fiber-containing formulas** – may act as a binding agent to reduce frequency of stools
    - Jevity®
    - Ensure®
    - Boost® with fiber

INDICATIONS FOR TOTAL PARENTERAL NUTRITION (TPN)

- Severe intractable diarrhea with weight loss
- In the acute setting, during a hospitalization, if enteral feeds are not possible
- Persistent and recurrent pancreatitis

PHARMACOLOGIC MANIPULATIONS TO INCREASE APPETITE

- Periactin® (cyproheptadine HCL) 0.25 to 0.5 mg/kg/day divided q 8–12 hours
  This is an antihistamine which has been found to increase appetite in some children
  Side effects include
    - Drowsiness
    - Dry mouth
    - Potential for increased problems with parotitis
  Should not be used in < 2 years of age
- Marinol® (Dronabinol, THC) 5 mg/m^2/dose, 2.5-5.0 mg twice daily before meals
  Start with lower dose and assess response
  Very little experience in children
  In adults can enhance appetite and decrease nausea
- Megace® (Megestrol acetate)
  Results in weight gain by an increase in body fat mass
  There is little data on the use of this drug in children
  The dose used for stimulation of the appetite and weight gain is 8 mg/kg/day (median dose) with a range between 4 and 12 mg/kg/day
  This drug influences the pituitary-adrenal axis and may cause glucose intolerance and adrenal insufficiency
- Trials involving the use of growth hormone and insulin-like growth factor 2 to enhance growth in children are ongoing

Table 1. Problem Solving for Nutrition

PROBLEM	INTERVENTION
Anorexia	Increase nutrient density of foods High kcal infant formulas Small frequent meals Calorie boosting instructions Nutritional supplements (Pediasure®, Ensure®, Sustacal®, etc.) Zinc supplementation for zinc deficiency appetite stimulants Supplemental tube feedings
Early Satiety	Small frequent meals Consider trial agent to improve GI motility
Oral/esophageal lesions	Topical medications prior to meals Cold foods such as ice-pops given prior to meals Avoid irritating foods, e.g. orange juice, hot spices Good oral hygiene
Food aversion/refusal	Allow child to make food choices among nutritious offerings Encourage child participation in meal preparation present small frequent feedings Encourage finger foods and self-feeding Medications given after or between meals if possible Assess parenting skills Assess eating atmosphere Referral to feeding/speech therapist
Neurologic dysfunction or developmental delay	Modify consistency of food as necessary Bottle or spoon feed as necessary Reduce inconsistencies in care Set up daily routine One (preferably) or at most 2 caretakers
Socioeconomic	Coordination with social work Refer to WIC, soup kitchens, food pantries, food stamps, meal delivery programs

SOURCE: Integrating Nutrition Therapy into Medical Management of Human Immunodeficiency Virus. *Clinical Infectious Diseases*. 2003; 36:S2

Table 2. Food and Water Safety Consideration for Patients with HIV Disease

• Avoid raw animal foods such as uncooked eggs, rare meat, and sushi • Cook meat and eggs thoroughly • Do not use cracked eggs • Thaw frozen foods in the refrigerator or microwave, not at room temperature • Wash fruits and vegetables thoroughly • Keep hot food hot (cooked to 165-212°F and held at 140-165°F) • Keep cold foods cold (refrigerator temperature should be 35-40°F, freezer should be 0°F) • Do not allow foods to stand at temperatures between 45 & 140°F for more than 2 hours • Refrigerate perishable foods immediately upon return from the store.	• Store foods that have been opened in airtight containers or a moisture-/vapor-proof wrap • Don't crowd or over pack foods in the refrigerator • Avoid moldy or spoiled foods • Do not use foods after the recommended expiration date on the label • Always wash hands before handling food • Use different cutting boards for raw and cooked foods • Thoroughly was hands, counters, knives, cutting boards, etc. after handling uncooked foods • Filters removing particles ≤ 1 micron in diameter or boiling H_2O for 1 minute will eliminate waterborne cryptosporidiosis • Do not drink H_2O from lakes or rivers • Do not swim in contaminated water

SOURCE: Hayes, C., et al. Food and Water Safety for Persons Infected with Human Immunodeficiency Virus. *Clinical Infectious Diseases*. 2003; 36:S106-S109

Every Child Deserves a Medical Home

A medical home may be defined as partnership with families to provide primary health care that is accessible, family centered, coordinated through a plan of care that is designed for each patient. It should be comprehensive, providing all aspects of care, continuously through life's transitions (child to adolescent to adult) and is compassionate and culturally effective. Efficient communication between the Primary Care Provider, the patient, his/her family and the extended care team is essential. The child with HIV disease benefits from care that is integrated with well-child and acute care and co-managed with specialists. Care Management is a key to the success of this endeavor.

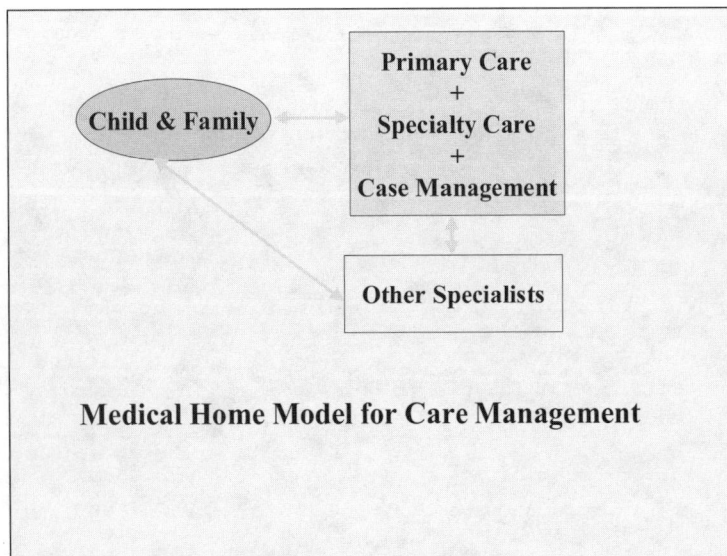

Medical Home Model for Care Management

HIV and Foster Care

The HIV epidemic has profoundly affected the family unit when mothers, fathers, and their children may be infected. Children of mothers who are substance users are more likely to be living with an alternative caregiver. It is estimated that in the year 2000, between 72,000 and 125,000 children and teenagers in the US lost their mothers to HIV/AIDS. Many orphaned children are not HIV-infected but may be at high risk for experiencing a range of developmental and behavioral problems related to difficulties adjusting to loss and abandonment.

- Children entering the system are known to be HIV infected or are at-risk for infection. The following items need to be implemented in order for a child to be placed in a foster care setting:
    - Appointment of a guardian *ad litem* and lawyer for the child
    - Shelter/Foster Placement should ideally be with an HIV-licensed or HIV-trained foster parent
    - Court Order should include:
        - Consent for HIV testing
        - Medical record to be obtained within 48 hours
        - Child to be examined within 48 hours by physician
    - Voluntarily placed children must have accompanying medical records or a contact physician with physician's phone number at time of placement
    - Psychological counseling must be arranged for all children, and psychological support offered for foster parents and other children in the placement home
    - When available, HIV-positive children should be followed by a local HIV specialist and an HIV case manager

Hospice Care and Management of Children with End Stage Disease

Whenever a child is deemed terminal, a DNR needs to be considered, and should be specific regarding resuscitative drugs, intubation and mechanical ventilation, and tube feeding.

Hospice care should be arranged "in-home," if possible, or placement can be at a group home or hospice facility. Not all hospice agencies serve pediatric patients, so careful consideration should be given when selecting the agency for services. For example, if a child requires hospitalization for an acute process, will he/she be admitted to an adult hospice inpatient unit? The caregiver will receive education regarding the hospice concept prior to enrollment into services.

For in-home hospice a 24-hour caregiver must be available. Hospice care will be provided by licensed agencies in the area. If the hospice is not a pediatric hospice, the HIV physician should continue to write orders for pain management.

- Pain management should be on a graded scale
- Hospice care should not negate all other personnel providing support for family. Liaison with these people should be maintained. Hospice care is a collaborative support agency and services are coordinated with the case manager
- At the time of death, patient's physician, case manager, guardian ad litem, lawyer, DCF case worker and the parent (if their rights have not been terminated) should be notified
- Ideally, adolescents in DCF custody should participate in the DNR discussion
- Funeral arrangements should be decided with the DCF case worker at or before the time of hospice placement

References

1. American Academy of Pediatrics. Adolescents and human immunodeficiency virus infection, the role of the pediatrician in prevention and intervention. *Pediatrics* 2001; 107:188–190.

2. American Academy of Pediatrics. Disclosure of illness status to children and adolescents with HIV infection. *Pediatrics* 1999; 103:164–166.

3. American Academy of Pediatrics. Human immunodeficiency virus and other blood borne viral pathogens in the athletic setting. *Pediatrics* 1999; 104:1400–1403.

4. American Academy of Pediatrics. In: Pickering LK, ed. *Red Book: 2003 Report of the Committee on Infectious Diseases*. 26th ed. Elk Grove Village, IL: American Academy of Pediatrics; 2003:360–382.

5. Pediatric and Perinatal Guidelines. Available at: www.aidsinfo.org.

6. Adolescent and Adult Guidelines. Available at: www. aidsinfo.org.

7. American Academy of Pediatrics. Committee on Adolescence Condom Use by Adolescents. *Pediatrics* 2001; 107:1463–1469.

8. American Academy of Pediatrics. Committee on Pediatric AIDS Post-Exposure Prophylaxis in Children and Adolescents for Non-Occupational Exposure to Human Immunodeficiency Virus. *Pediatrics* 2003; 111:1475–1489.

9. American Academy of Pediatrics. Committee on Pediatric AIDS, and Canadian Pediatric Society, Infectious Diseases and Immunization Committee Evaluation and Treatment of the Human Immunodeficiency Virus-1—Exposed Infant. *Pediatrics* 2004; 114:497–505.

10. American Academy of Pediatrics. Committee on Pediatric AIDS Education of Children with Human Immunodeficiency Virus Infection. *Pediatrics* 2000; 105:1358–1360.

11. Integrating Nutrition Therapy into Medical Management of Human Immunodeficiency Virus. *CID* 2003; 36:S2.

12. Hayes, C., et al. Food and Water Safety for Persons Infected with Human Immunodeficiency Virus. *CID* 2003; 36:S106-S109.

35

Adolescent Issues

Lawrence B. Friedman, MD
Professor and Director, Adolescent Medicine
University of Miami School of Medicine, Miami
Jeri A. Dyson, MD
Assistant Professor, Department of Pediatrics, Division of Adolescent Medicine
Rainbow Center for Women Adolescent Children and Families
University of Florida, Jacksonville
Mobeen H. Rathore, MD
Professor and Assistant Chair, Department of Pediatrics
Chief of Infectious Disease and Immunology
Rainbow Center for Women Adolescent Children and Families
University of Florida, Jacksonville

Introduction

Caring for adolescents and young adults with HIV-infection or AIDS may present unique challenges for clinicians. Biologic vulnerability by young age, low financial status, relative educational level, low health literacy, typical feelings of invincibility, and societal power dynamics are real as they relate to health care of HIV-infected youth.[1] Teenager's lack of appreciation of risk for STIs and denial of behaviors that might lead to HIV infection often cause delays in identification of newly acquired cases, subsequent linkage to care, and administration of treatment. Emerging populations of perinatally infected adolescents represent a new challenge in the care of patients with chronic diseases. There are additional issues that should be addressed while caring for perinatally infected school-aged children and adolescents when compared with newly diagnosed cases of HIV. Perinatal HIV infected youth have many similarities with other children diagnosed with chronic childhood diseases. School absenteeism secondary to multiple clinic visits, acute illnesses, and hospitalizations are just some examples of the many social implications of this disease that should be addressed. Adolescents in general experience pressures to assimilate with their peers. The need for perinatally infected youth to take daily medications or undergo procedures to assist in medication administration makes them "different" and is likely to impact self-esteem.[2] This may also account for the low adherence levels providers notice in adolescent patients when compared to younger children and adults.

Epidemiology

The population of HIV-infected individuals in the US who are 13-24 years of age is increasing in numbers, both as youth continue to acquire the infection through behavioral risk factors and survive perinatal transmission. The proportion of young people with AIDS increased from 3.9% of all US AIDS cases in 1999 to 4.7% in 2003.[3] Further, young people represented 12% of all diagnoses of either HIV or AIDS made nationally during the year 2003.[3] Approximately one-half of all new HIV infections in the US occur in individuals less than 25 years of age, disproportionately affecting African-American and Hispanic youth. For youth ages 13 to 19 years old, African-Americans accounted for 66% of the reported AIDS cases and Hispanics for 21%.[4]

Overwhelmingly acquired by heterosexual transmission, young females account for 60% of new HIV cases nationally. Disadvantaged female youth have higher HIV prevalence rates than age-matched males.[5] Adolescent females are at increased risk due to cervical epithelial immaturity and consequent vulnerability to sexually transmitted infections, as well as lack of appreciation of partners' risk factors.[6] For young males, sex with other men is the leading transmission category, increasing from 40% for male teenagers to 64% for young adults 20 to 24 years of age. Many of these young men do not disclose their sexual attractions to or relations with other males, and often report sexual relations with females, as well.[7]

Management

Conversations and interactions with adolescents and young adults can prove frustrating for some professionals. Office décor, hours of operation, employees' attitudes, and presence of other people in waiting rooms all have potential effects on the adolescent's comfort during the health visit. Other selected resources for adolescent care generally are listed at the chapter's end.

Providing clinical care for adolescents and young adults as patients and clients requires an understanding of basic principles of growth and development. Teenagers are neither larger children nor smaller adults, but rather share features of both distinct age designations. Many of these patients have fear of disclosure, lack experience negotiating healthcare systems, and understanding of their healthcare rights, and express discomfort with expectations of behavior. It is also important to note that many of the maturing perinatally infected youth have been managed by an adult caregiver and may be limited in their knowledge of medications, hospitalizations, recent immunizations, other subspecialists involved in their medical care or any additional medical diagnoses they may have. Helping the adolescent patient transition into a more independent patient role will prove successful for future clinic visits. During the transitioning phase, adolescents should be made aware of their special needs as well as be informed on community resources. Studies and experience have shown the importance of providing the transitioning adolescent with support for becoming involved with community links rather than simply referring those patients to community groups. Success with linking these youth to care involves establishing a series of contacts at outreach sites wherein program staff seek to build trusting relationships with youths. With proper transitioning, the team should be able to track the adolescent, identify their need, and address those needs.[8] Remembering that the second decade of life is a dynamic growth process on multiple levels will remind clinicians to view adolescence from a developmental perspective.

With the increasing numbers of perinatally infected adolescents and school-aged children, disclosure of the diagnosis to the patient also becomes an important factor for management as the child transitions into a more responsible role. This will allow the older child and adolescent to participate in the decision-making process when issues of medical care are addressed. Recognition and appreciation of the diagnosis also enables the sexually active patient to further protect themselves and their partners from sexually transmitted infections. Table 1 offers suggestions for clinicians in their contacts with youth.

It is during this adolescent time period that sexual activity usually commences, may be coincident to onset of alcohol and other substance using behaviors, and frequently associated with the altered mental status that accompanies this.[9] For example, among Florida's youth attending high school, 51.3% report having ever been sexually active, with 15.6% admitting to 4 or more sexual partners.[10] Although 88.3% of youth in Florida reported receiving HIV and STD prevention information during school educational activities, only 65.5% reported condom use with most recent sexual intercourse.[10] Information does not necessarily translate to incorporation of protective behaviors by adolescents, however. The problem is heightened with respect to emerging sexuality of perinatally infected teenagers. In addition, there are subpopulations of youth who are at particularly high risk sexually, including those who are homeless, runaway, incarcerated, in foster care, mentally ill, sexually or physically abused, gay or bisexual, or transgender.[11] Homeless or runaway youths pose special concerns that should be addressed during evaluation. Many of these youths will engage in high-risk sexual behaviors as a means to meet their basic needs. Some of these needs include shelter, food, and clothing, which are more important to the youth than seeking medical care for HIV. An interest in these basic elements of life will assist the provider with helping the adolescent properly address their needs as well as help establish the trust between the adolescent patient and the provider that is needed for proper medical care.

These risk-taking behaviors of adolescents have led to the reporting of the highest rates of sexually transmitted infections for the 15 to 24 year age group, another co-factor for HIV transmission.[12] Psychological "tasks" that are normative, and that all youth must negotiate as they mature to adulthood are summarized in Table 2.

Clinical Care

Important current clinical factors, past medical information, and social history surrounding the HIV care of teenagers and young adults are much the same as for other patient age groups (see Section II, Treatment). Specific baseline history from adolescent and young adult patients is suggested in Table 3.

Familiarity with the consent and confidentiality precepts of care for minor patients and clients will assist providers further in the gathering of accurate health information from young people. The clinician-patient relationship allows for privacy, even for youth. Table 4 suggests easy reminders for including complete social history information.[11] Table 5 gives pointers for asking the important sexual history questions for this age group, which often are avoided by clinicians uncomfortable with the subject matter. Age-appropriate vocabulary spoken in a clear and direct language style in privacy is important for gathering accurate details.

Physical examination tips are listed in Table 6. These and particular recommendations for HIV laboratory assessment and routine follow-up are similar for adolescents and young adults as they are for other adults. These have been outlined already in previous chapters.

Counseling on healthy lifestyle practices of regular exercise and/or sports participation; proper nutrition and food choices; adequate rest; avoidance of use of alcohol, tobacco, and other drugs; abstinence and contraception; condom use, secondary prevention, and "safer sex" activities; and use of personal safety devices (seatbelts, bicycle helmets, elbow pads, etc.) all are recommended as harm reduction strategies.

Treatment of HIV and AIDS in youth follows parameters set by the US Department of Health and Human Services. The Guidelines for the Use of Antiretroviral Agents address adolescents in both the Pediatric and Adult versions, with perinatally infected youth generally following the former and behaviorally infected youth following the latter.[13], [14] Dosages of both antiretroviral and OI prophylactic medications are based on Tanner staging of sexual maturation rather than chronological age, due to growth delay commonly seen with perinatally infected cases. In general, pediatric schedules are utilized for Tanner stages I and II, whereas adult schedules are used for Tanner stages IV and V. Monitoring for toxicity and efficacy are important in patients always, but especially for those at the intermediate Tanner stage III for puberty.

Psychological Health Assessment

Depression has been reported as the most common neuropsychological diagnosis affecting these youth.[15] (The cause has been cited as multifactorial; however, other studies have attributed depression and behavioral acting-out to the deleterious effects of deaths of family members and friends. More than half of the older youth have been placed within the care of extended family or orphaned as a result of maternal death. The stigma of HIV leads some families to refrain from disclosing the diagnosis, which may impede the mourning process for the young patient.[2], [16] Given the fact that the patient is also infected and may begin to contemplate his/her own death surrounding the deaths of family and peers, it should be determined how the child is coping with the disease. The amount of social support within the home and from the community (school and friends) may provide some insight into the overall wellness of the perinatally infected youth. Depression in adolescents may take the form of oppositional behavior, mood swings, boredom, or even aggression and anger. These symptoms should be addressed with the patient and the caregiver(s).

In addition to behavioral changes, some adolescents may use illicit or legal drugs as a form of self-medication to mask the depressive symptoms they experience. Providers should be aware of this when evaluating the patient for drug and alcohol use and have a working relationship with drug counselors who are sensitive to the special needs of adolescents. An established referral system makes transition into a drug-counseling program easier for the patient who is willing to seek care in this area.[8] During counseling, the adolescent should be informed of the deleterious effects of combining illicit drugs and alcohol with antiretroviral medications. The drug counselor will be able to assist the medical team in devising a feasible plan for the infected adolescent.

Ancillary Care

Besides attention to usual growth parameters and developmental aspects of pubertal patients with maturing behaviors, assistance with important non-clinical care will also be helpful for youth. Linkage to appropriate specialized healthcare sites with access to qualified professionals for additional services will assist applications for financial and housing benefits, registration for school and employment possibilities, promotion of healthy lifestyle practices, education for STI and HIV prevention, attention to mood and positive psychosocial functioning, encouragement of substance use reduction, and formulation of strategies for treatment adherence. Devoting enough time during appointments for building rapport and providing comprehensive confidential healthcare may form the basis for young people's views concerning future provider-client relationships and healthcare seeking behaviors. These are some of the potential pitfalls that clinicians can avoid in dealing with this age group. The infected adolescent should be cared for with a team approach. Better communication between the primary care provider, subspecialties, and specialized services provides a better chance of achieving a good outcome for the patient.

Table 1. HIV-infected Adolescents Attitudes of Interviewer

- Respect the youth as the patient; his/her parents are not the patient
- Show genuine interest and concern
- Use age-appropriate words and terms
- Avoid slang terms
- Have awareness of your own body language
- Listen with non-judgmental demeanor
- Observe youth's non-verbal communications
- Avoid over-identification and arguments
- Remember the important role of the clinician in the youth's life
- Provide health education, refrain from offering "advice"
- Understand the confidence that parents/guardians place in clinicians

Table 2. HIV-Infected Adolescents Milestones of Adolescent Development

- Body-image/puberty: early adolescence mostly, cognitive changes begin
- Independence/emancipation: ongoing throughout, risk-taking during middle adolescence
- Identity formation (including sexual identity): ongoing throughout
- Future orientation/delineation of functional role: late adolescence mostly, mortality issues

Table 3. HIV-Infected Adolescents Baseline History

HIV Test Date and Type
Mode of HIV Transmission
Previous Source of Healthcare
Current Complaints
Past Medical History
- Symptoms suggestive of acute HIV infection
- Previous hospitalizations or surgeries
- Allergies
- Nutrition (vitamins, nutritional supplements # cans/day)
- Immunizations
- Childhood Illnesses

Medications (herbal treatments/supplements)
Family History (Including knowledge of any other HIV-infected family members, family support, disclosure to family members)
Social History
- Living Situation (Group home, Foster Care)
- Education/Employment status (school performance, days missed, grades/classes repeated, Special Education classes)
- Substance Use (including tobacco, alcohol, injectables, inhalants, pills, hallucinogens, OTC products, etc.)
- Sexual History (see below)
- Activities (Volunteer/Paid Jobs)
- Exercise (involvement in organized sports)
- Mental Health Disorders (including anxiety, depression, suicidal ideation, ADHD.)
- Legal/Criminal Problems
- Health Insurance Status

Table 4. HIV-Infected Adolescents "HEADS" Social History

(adapted from Goldenring, et. al.)[13]

H	**H**ome
E	**E**ducation and/or **E**mployment
E	**E**ating practices
A	**A**ctivities (social including sports/exercise)
D	**D**rugs and other substance use
D	**D**epression and other mental health issues (including suicidal/homicidal ideations)
S	**S**exuality and **S**exual activities
S	**S**afety practices
S	**S**avagery (including violence and criminal involvement)

Table 5. HIV-Infected Adolescents Effective Sexual History-Taking

- Comfort of clinician with confidentiality and privacy precepts
- Non-judgmental questioning style and flexible manner
- Establish with patient the "need to know" aspects of sexual history
- Gender-neutral questions about sexual partners and intimate activities
- Ask patient to self-identify his/her sexual orientation
- Age of sexual debut (if sexually active) and number of lifetime and current partners
- Partner characteristics and sexual practices (i.e., history of IVDU, commercial sex work, sex for favors, etc.)
- Determine if the patient has disclosed his/her HIV status to sexual partner(s)
- Presence of symptoms or signs of genitourinary problems and sexually transmitted infections
- History of sexually transmitted infections, pregnancies, sexual abuse
- Knowledge and use of condoms and other barrier and hormonal contraception
- Menstrual history: age of onset, current pattern, length of cycle, length of menses, number of pads/tampons per day, and inter-menstrual bleeding

Table 6. HIV-Infected Adolescents Comprehensive Physical Examination

Vital Signs (including height and weight growth parameters)
General Appearance
Lymph Nodes
Head
- Hair and scalp
- Eyes (vision and funduscopic exam)
- Ears
- Nose
- Mouth (including tongue, dentition, and gingivae)

Throat
Neck
Chest
Heart
Lungs
Abdomen
Genitourinary Examination
- Sexual maturity rating/Tanner stage
- Lesions or rashes
- Rectal exam (inspection at minimum, as indicated otherwise)
- Pelvic exam (inspection at minimum, as indicated otherwise for sexual activity)

Neurologic Examination
- Orientation
- Mental status
- Gait
- Reflexes

Musculoskeletal Examination
Skin

References

1. Catallozzi MD, Futterman DC. HIV in Adolescents. *Current Infectious Disease Report 2005;* 7: 401–405.

2. Grubman S, Gross E, Lerner-Weiss N, Hernandez M, McSherry G, Hoyt L, Boland M, Oleske J. Older children and adolescents living with perinatally acquired human immunodeficiency virus infection. *Pediatrics* 1995; 95:657–663.

3. Centers for Disease Control and Prevention. *HIV/AIDS Surveillance Report 2003;* 15:1-46, 2004.

4. National Institute of Allergy and Infectious Diseases. HIV Infection in Adolescents and Young Adults in the US. *NIAID Fact Sheet,* Dept. of HHS, July 2005.

5. Valleroy LA, MacKellar DA, Karon JM, Janssen RS, Hayman DR. HIV infection in disadvantaged out-of-school youth: prevalence for US Job Corp entrants, 1990-96. *Journal of AIDS* 1998; 19:67–73.

6. Centers for Disease Control and Prevention. HIV/AIDS among youth. *CDC Fact Sheet,* Dept. of HHS, May 2005.

7. Centers for Disease Control and Prevention. HIV/STD risks in young men who have sex with men who do not disclose their sexual orientation—six US cities, 1994-2000. *MMWR 2003*; 52:81–85.

8. Martinez J, Bell D, Dodds S, Shaw K, Siciliano C, Walker LE, Sotheran JL, Sell RL, Friedman LB, Botwinick G, Johnson R. Transitioning youths into care: Linking Identified HIV-infected youth at outreach sites in the community to hospital-based clinics and or community-base health centers. *Journal of Adolescent Health* 2003; 33S:23–30.

9. National Institute on Drug Abuse. Keep your body healthy—Jack & Jill: Facts about substance abuse and risky sexual behavior. *NIDA Public Service Announcement,* Dept. of HHS, December 2004.

10. Centers for Disease Control and Prevention. Youth risk behavior surveillance—United States 2003. *MMWR* 2004; 53:SS-2.

11. Futterman DC. HIV and AIDS in adolescents. *Adolescent Medicine Clinics* 2004; 15(2):369-391.

12. Centers for Disease Control and Prevention. Sexually Transmitted Diseases Surveillance—2003. Dept. of HHS, September 2004.

13. Goldenring JM and Rosen DR. Getting into adolescent heads: an essential update. *Contemporary Pediatrics* 2004; 21:64.

14. Working Group on Antiretroviral Therapy and Medical Management of HIV-Infected Children. *Guidelines for the Use of Antiretroviral Agents in Pediatric HIV Infection, March 24, 2005.* Department of HHS, http://aidsinfo.nih.gov.

15. Mailky E, Vagnoni J, Rutstein R. School-age children with perinatally acquired HIV infection: Medical and psychosocial issues in a Philadelphia cohort. *AIDS Patient Care and STDs* 2001; 15:575–579.

16. Panel on Clinical Practices for Treatment of HIV Infection. *Guidelines for the Use of Antiretroviral Agents in HIV-1-Infected Adults and Adolescents,* April 7, 2005. Department of HHS, http://aidsinfo.nih.gov.

17. Battles HB and Wiener LS. From Adolescence through Young Adulthood: Psychosocial Adjustment Associated with Longterm Survival of HIV. *Journal of Adolescent Health* 2002; 30(3):161–168.

18. HIV/AIDS Bureau and Special Projects of National Significance. Applying Elements of the Chronic Care Model to HIV/AIDS Clinical Care: Moving CARE Act clients from intensive case management toward self-management. *HRSA Fact Sheet,* Dept. of HHS, August 2005.

19. Rotheram-Borus MJ, et al. Efficacy of a preventive intervention for youths living with HIV. *American Journal of Public Health 2001*; 91(3):400–405.

20. Flynn PM, Rudy BJ, Douglas SD, Lathey J, Spector SA, Martinez J, Silio M, Belzer M, Friedman L, D'Angelo L, McNamara J, Hodge J, Hughes MD, Lindsey JC, and PACTG 381 Study Team. Virologic and immunologic outcomes after 24 weeks in HIV type I-infected adolescents receiving highly active antiretroviral therapy. *JID* 2004; 190:271-279.

21. Johnson RL, Botwinick G, Sell RL, Martinez J, Siciliano C, Friedman LB, Dodds S, Shaw K, Walker LE, Sotheran JL, Bell D. The utilization of treatment and case management services by HIV-infected youth. *Journal of Adolescent Health* 2003; 33(2-Supplement):31–38.

22. Dodds S, Blakley T, Lizzotte JM, Friedman LB, Shaw K, Martinez J, Siciliano C, Walker LE, Sotheran JL, Sell RL, Botwinick G, Johnson RL, Bell D. Retention, adherence, and compliance: Special needs of HIV-infected adolescent girls and young women. *Journal of Adolescent Health* 2003; 33(2-Supplement);39–45.

23. Murphy DA, Durako SD, Muenz L, Wilson CM. Marijuana use among HIV+ and high-risk adolescents: a comparison of self-report through ACASI and urinalysis. *American Journal of Epidemiology* 2000; 152:805–813.

24. Murphy DA, Moscicki AB, Vermund SH, Muenz L. Pyschological distress among HIV-positive adolescents in the REACH Study: Effects of life stress, social support, and coping. *Journal of Adolescent Health* 2001; 27:391–398.

25. Rudy BJ, Wislon CM, Durako S, Moscicki AB, Muenz L, Douglas SD. Peripheral blood lymphocyte subsets in adolescents: a longitudinal analysis from the REACH Project. *Clinical Diagnostic Laboratory Immunology* 2002; 9:959–965.

26. Moscicki AB, Ellenberg JH, Crowley-Nowick P, Darragh TM, Xu J, Fahrat S. Risk of high grade squamous intra-epithelial lesions in HIV infected adolescents. *JID* 2004; 190:1413–1421.

27. Buchaz K, Rogol AD, Lindsey JC, Wilson CM, Hughes MD, Seage GR, Oleske JM, Rogers AS. Delayed onset of pubertal development in children and adolescents with perinatally acquired HIV infection. *Journal of Acquired Immune Deficiency Syndromes* 2003; 33:56–65.

28. Mellins CA, Smith R, O'Driscoll P, Magder LS, Brouwers P, Chase C, Blasini I, Hittleman J, Llorente A, Matzen E. High rates of behavioral problems in perinatally HIV-infected children are not linked to HIV disease. *Pediatrics* 2003; 111;384–393.

Section VI

Special Populations and Other Issues

36

Prevention for Positives

Patricia M. Bryan, RN, BSN, MPH
Coordinator/Trainer, Florida/Caribbean AIDS Education and Training Center
Department of Obstetrics and Gynecology
University of Miami School of Medicine, Miami

Introduction

HIV infection is no doubt one of the most significant challenges to public health this generation has seen. Each year there continue to be upwards of 40,000 new infections reported nationwide. Reports of high sexually transmitted disease (STD) rates in both HIV infected men and women suggest ongoing risky behaviors.[1] Outbreaks of syphilis have been reported among men who have sex with men (MSM), many of whom are HIV infected.[2] This is cause for concern as STDs increase both HIV infectivity and susceptibility. Traditional prevention efforts have focused largely on helping HIV- negative persons stay negative, but have thus far proved insufficient to limit infection rates among adults. If we are to limit the spread of HIV we must also work with persons already infected to decrease rates of unsafe sex and other practices that spread the infection. Through well communicated prevention messages, positive reinforcement for changes to safer sexual practices, referral for substance abuse treatment, referral for partner notification programs and through identification and prompt treatment for STDs, providers can impact further spread of HIV.

The Centers for Disease Control (CDC), the Health Resources Service Administration (HRSA), the National Institutes of Health (NIH), and the Infectious Diseases Society of America (IDSA) have all recommended that providers incorporate fundamentals of HIV prevention in the routine care of persons living with HIV.[3] Over the past few years there has been growing acknowledgment that prevention programs for infected individuals need to be a routine part of care. Not only is this essential but it is also feasible even in settings with limited resources.

Risk Screening and Assessment

The most important step in any intervention is a comprehensive assessment. Both behavioral and clinical risk factors must be considered. A brief initial screen can be used to identify patients needing more intensive assessment, counseling, or referral. All patients should be screened for risk behaviors using a straightforward, non-judgmental approach. Ancillary and support staff can conduct brief interviews before the patient sees the provider. If structured face-to-face interviews are not feasible, then use short self-administered questionnaires in written format or computer-assisted programs. Ask open- ended questions to elicit more information rather than simple yes/no questions. This allows the provider to offer more meaningful prevention counseling. Purposeful probing should yield information on the number and gender of sex partners, HIV status of partners (positive, negative, or unknown), types of sexual activity (oral, vaginal, or anal), condom use, and drug/alcohol use. Some very specific questions suggested in the *MMWR* of July 18, 2003:

- Have you had vaginal or anal intercourse without a condom with anyone?
- What are you doing now that you think may be a risk for transmitting HIV to a partner?
- Have you shared drug injection equipment (needles, syringes, cooker, or cotton) with anyone?

While such questioning may seem to have an "in-your-face" tone, providers seem to have more of a problem with it than patients do. In fact, some patients report greater confidence in their provider's ability to provide quality care when their sexual and STD history are assessed early in their care.[3] Patients are less comfortable discussing sexual risk and illicit drug use if they perceive the provider to be uncomfortable. Some providers ask questions in a more indirect manner such as:

- Some of my patients find it difficult to always practice safe sex. Is that a problem for you?
- Tell me about the challenges you are having staying safe.

It is important for patients to understand that the goal is not for the clinician to become an expert on their private lives but to identify their individual risk factors in order to help them be safe and prevent the spread of disease.

ASSESSING FOR STDS

In the context of transmission prevention, assessing for STDs becomes a central component of medical screening. It is recommended that HIV-infected patients be questioned about symptoms of STDs at the initial visit. Assess for urethral or vaginal discharge, dysuria, bleeding between menstrual periods, genital or anal ulcers or other lesions, anal pain, pruritus, burning, discharge, or bleeding, and for women lower abdominal pain with or without fever. The presence of such signs and symptoms should always prompt diagnostic testing and treatment as indicated, regardless of reported sexual behavior or risk. However, because many STDs are asymptomatic, clinical symptoms are not sensitive for identifying many infections. Laboratory screening strategies to detect asymptomatic STDs should be routine in clinical practice. Syphilis, Chlamydia, and Gonorrhea screening should be repeated *at least annually* if the patient is sexually active or sooner if previous screenings showed the presence of STDs. Screenings should be more often (3- to 6-month intervals) for asymptomatic persons at higher risk. Periodic assessment is also appropriate for patients who report not being sexually active at the time of initial assessment as people's lives, circumstances, and risk factors change over time.

PREVENTION INTERVENTION

A brief behavioral intervention at each clinic visit could, over time, result in patients adopting and maintaining safer practices. This allows for discussions about the patients' responsibility to disclose to their sex and needle-sharing partners, clear up misconceptions, and reinforce risk-reduction activity. Clinician-delivered health messages have proven successful in the past on issues such as smoking and alcohol abuse, depression, weight management, and diet. [4,5,6,7,8] Such discussions can be conducted by any member of the health care team trained to do so; nurse, social workers, case managers, or health educators. Utilize your multi-disciplinary team. Skills vary among staff from different disciplines and the patient may bond more or be more receptive to discussing preventive issues with one team member than another.

Influencing Behavior Change

Behaviorists have identified five essential components that must be present for behavior change to occur. They are knowledge, skills, motivation, resources, and support. To the extent that we can supply these, or facilitate their acquisition, we will be able to influence change. Consider how each factor relates to your patient.

- **KNOWLEDGE:** *Does the patient have accurate knowledge about risky behaviors? Is he/she informed about effective use of condoms?*

- **SKILLS:** *Does the patient have the skills to negotiate safer sex? Does he/she need help with disclosure?*

- **MOTIVATION:** *Does the patient want to protect self and partners? If not, why not? Does the patient think he/she can be successful?*

- **RESOURCES:** *Does the patient have money to pay for condoms? Does he/she know where to get them for free? Is he/she engaged in survival sex? Is he/she being referred to get help with mental illness, domestic violence, substance abuse that impact ability to disclose?*

- **SUPPORT:** *How much support does the patient need? What type of support? Where can he/she get such support?*

Providing information (knowledge) is a first step. Patients need to know that their condom choice should be latex or polyurethane, and to avoid lubricants with nonoxynol 9. Given the failure rate of condoms (2%) when used, emphasize that the only way to prevent sexual transmission is abstinence or refraining from having sex with an infected partner. Of course, the latter risks super infection and does not protect against STDs. Many patients will engage in higher risk behaviors because of the knowledge that a low viral load already reduces transmission risk. Educate patients that in addition to viral load, many other factors including the presence of STDs, trauma, and a host of complicated genetic and immune factors influence the risk of transmission for any sexual act. Thus for a given high risk exposure, it is not possible to predict the probability of HIV transmission with any accuracy. They need to understand that undetectable does not mean non-infectious.

Not all patients will need the same intense information. The message must be tailored to individual need. Avoid making assumptions based on someone's looks, education, or socioeconomic status. Even those who are well educated might not know about specific risks and might need additional resources or referrals.

Wherever the patient is along the continuum of change, risk reduction is a good goal. If the patient exposes one fewer person, whether by increased condom use, fewer sex or needle-sharing partners, or prior disclosure to a potential partner, it is a positive change. Offer encouragement and reinforcement. Remember that change is a slow and incremental process rather than a direct outcome.

Referrals for Additional Services

Some patients may have issues which the clinician will have neither the time nor means to address. Often, achieving behavioral change is dependent on addressing these concerns. For example, while we promote disclosure we must be aware of how complex this can be. In addition to the fears of ostracism and rejection, there may also be legitimate concerns related to abuse and domestic violence. Some clients may benefit from support groups or prevention case management. Others may require multi-session risk reduction counseling.[9]

Partner notification programs are available through local health departments for patients who require them, and all patients should be informed of the availability of these anonymous partner notification services. The CDC recommends a specific model of HIV prevention counseling for persons persisting in risky behaviors.[9, 10, 11]

Patients using IV drugs must be referred for treatment. Methadone maintenance treatment has been shown to reduce risky injection and sexual behaviors, and HIV seroconversion.[12, 13]

Being prepared to make appropriate referrals requires being familiar with resources in your area. Referral guides about HIV prevention and supportive social services can be obtained from local and state health departments.

Suggestions for Your Practice

Limited time and strained resources are ubiquitous concerns across the board. Based on their multi-site study the Partnership for Health program developed by the Keck School of Medicine at USC suggests 3- to 5-minute interventions at each encounter.[14] Structure the clinic or office to support and enhance the prevention initiative. Develop a policy that includes prevention as a priority. Provide periodic in-services and training for your staff.

Use visual cues containing prevention messages, posters, brochures, etc. Utilize all members of the staff. Provide all new patients with printed information about transmission risks. If your population does not read, develop a video presentation that can be viewed while they wait.

Prevention Summary

- Screen risk behaviors
- Identify/ treat STDs
- Educate/Inform/Motivate
- Refer for mental health or substance abuse
- Promote partner notification (if necessary use the Partner Notification Program at your local health department)

Many of these strategies have been used successfully in one form or another. There is no need to reinvent the wheel. Your local AIDS Education and Training Center (AETC) and health department are resources for you. Consider using them.

References

1. Sheer S, Chu PL, Klausner KD, Katz MH, Schwarcz SK. Effect of highly active antiretroviral therapy on diagnoses of sexually transmitted diseases in people with AIDS. *Lancet* 2001; 357: 432–435.

2. CDC. Outbreak of syphilis among men who have sex with men — Southern California, 2000. *MMWR* 2001; 50:117-120.

3. CDC. Incorporating HIV prevention into the medical care of persons living with HIV. *MMWR* 2003; Vol 52, No RR12;1.

4. Lewis CE, Freeman HE, Corey CR. The sexual history-taking and counseling practices of primary care physicians. *West J Med* 1987; 147: 165–167.

5. Hollis JF, Lichtenstein E, Vogt TM, Stevens VJ, Biglan A. Nurse-assisted counseling for smokers in primary care. *Ann Intern Med* 1993; 118:521–525.

6. Ockene JK, Kristeller J, Pbert L, et al. The physician delivered smoking intervention project: can short-term interventions produce long-term effects for a general outpatient population? *Health Psychol* 1994: 13:278–281.

7. Senft RA, Polen MR, Freeborn DK, Hollis JF. Brief intervention in a primary care setting for hazardous drinkers. *Am J of Prev Med* 1997; 13:464–470.

8. Rost K, Nutting PA, Smith J, Werner JJ. Designing and implementing a primary care intervention trial to improve quality and outcome of care for major depression. *Gen Hosp Psychiatry* 2000; 22:66–77.

9. Ockene IS, Herbert JR, et al. Effect of physician-delivered nutrition counseling training and office support program on saturated fat intake, weight, and serum lipid measurements in a hyperlipidemic population; Worchester Area Trial for Counseling in Hyperlipidemia(WATCH). *Arch Intern Med* 1999: 159:725–731.

10. CDC. Revised guidelines for HIV counseling, testing, and referral. *MMWR* 2001; 50(No.RR-19):1–58.

11. Kamb ML, Fishbein M, Douglas JM Jr. et al. Project RESPECT Study Group. Efficacy of risk reduction counseling to prevent human immunodeficiency virus and sexually transmitted diseases: A randomized controlled trial. *JAMA* 1998; 280:1161–1167.

12. Marks G, Burris S, Peterman TA. Reducing sexual transmission of HIV from those who know they are infected: The need for personal and collective responsibility. *AIDS* 1999; 13:297–306.

13. Ball JC, Lange WR, Meyers CP, Friedman SR. Reducing the risk of AIDS through methadone maintenance treatment. *J Health Soc Behav* 1998; 29:214–226.

14. Wells EA, Calsyn DA, Clark LL, Saxon AJ, Jackson TR. Retention in methadone maintenance is associated with reductions in different HIV risk behaviors for women and men. *Am J Drug Alcohol Abuse* 1996; 22:509–521.

15. Richardson JL, Milam J, McCutchan A, Stayonoff S, Bolan R, Weiss J, K, et al. Effect of brief safer-sex counseling by medical providers to HIV-1 seropositive patients: A multi-clinic assessment. *AIDS* 2004; 18;1179–1186.

37

Mother to Child Transmission

Amanda Cotter, MD, MSPH
Assistant Professor
Director of the Perinatal HIV Service
Department of Obstetrics & Gynecology
University of Miami Miller School of Medicine
JoNell Efantis Potter, PhD, ARNP
Assistant Professor
Director of Obstetrics & Gynecology Research & Special Projects Division
University of Miami Miller School of Medicine

Introduction

Perinatal transmission of HIV-1 has been reduced from 25% to less than 2% for a woman who is aware of her HIV infection early in pregnancy as a result of antiretroviral therapy and appropriate obstetric intervention. All women should be screened for HIV prior to delivery, ideally at the first prenatal visit so that antiretroviral therapy can be initiated. However, according to the CDC, approximately 40% of the mothers of the estimated 280–370 HIV-infected infants born in 2000 were not known to have HIV infection before delivery.[2] It is therefore essential to reduce these missed opportunities for identification of HIV-infected pregnant women during the antepartum period when the most effective interventions can be utilized. Consider repeat testing in the third trimester preferably prior to 36 weeks gestation for pregnant women at high risk.[1] These high risk factors include:

- History of a sexually transmitted disease
- Illicit drug use
- Exchange of sex for money or drugs
- Multiple sex partners during pregnancy
- A sex partner known to be HIV positive
- Signs or symptoms suggestive of acute HIV infection at any time during pregnancy
- History of previously declining testing in pregnancy

RAPID HIV TESTING

Routinely offering rapid HIV testing to women whose HIV status is unknown during labor and delivery provides the opportunity to reduce transmission even among women who do not seek care until labor begins. Intrapartum and neonatal antiretroviral prophylaxis can reduce perinatal transmission as much as 50%. A negative rapid HIV test result is definitive. If the rapid HIV test result is positive, the obstetric provider should take the following steps:

- Explain to the woman she may have HIV infection and that her neonate also may be exposed
- Explain that the rapid test result is preliminary and that false positive results are possible
- Assure the woman that a second test is being performed immediately to confirm the positive rapid test result
- With consent initiate antiretroviral prophylaxis without waiting for the results of the confirmatory test to reduce the risk of transmission to the infant
- Advise the woman to postpone breastfeeding until the confirmatory result is available
- Inform the pediatricians of the positive maternal test results so that they may institute neonatal prophylaxis
- If there is a discrepancy in the rapid and confirmatory test, both tests should be repeated
- If the confirmatory test result is negative, all antiretroviral prophylaxis should be stopped.

PERINATAL TRANSMISSION

The perinatal transmission rate in the USA was 21% in 1994; however, this dropped to 11% after implementation of the "076" regimen.[2] Today the risk of perinatal transmission is less than 2% with effective antiretroviral therapy, elective cesarean delivery as appropriate, and formula feeding.

Timing

- In utero transmission is presumed if a specimen taken in the first 48 hours after birth is positive for HIV
- Intrapartum transmission is presumed if a specimen taken in the first week of life in a non-breastfed infant is negative but a later sample is found to be positive.

Mechanisms

In utero transmission accounts for 25–40% of cases
- Most likely transplacental
- Occurs late in gestation although rapid disease progression in infants suggests earlier infection
- Early transmission may result in fetal loss

Intrapartum transmission accounts for 60–75% of cases
- Through maternal-fetal transfusion of blood during labor
- Infant skin or mucous membranes contact with infected blood or other maternal secretions during delivery
- Associated with increased duration of membrane rupture
- Associated with vaginal delivery if the viral load (VL) is greater than 1000 copies/mL

Postpartum transmission
- Risk with breastfeeding is 14% with established infection

PERINATAL TRANSMISSION AND MATERNAL HIV RNA VIRAL LOAD

- There is a strong correlation between maternal VL and risk of transmission even in pregnant women treated with antiretroviral therapy [3-5]
- The risk of transmission in women with undetectable VL is extremely low but transmission has occurred at all levels of VL [6]

- VL levels should be monitored at least every 3 to 4 months or once a trimester to allow for discussion of options for mode of delivery

Breastfeeding

- Women with HIV infection in the USA should not breastfeed and those considering breastfeeding should be aware of their HIV status.
- HIV is commonly found in breast milk, both cell-associated and cell-free.
- The mechanism of transmission is thought to be frequent and prolonged exposure of an infant's oral and GI tract to breast milk.
- Most transmission occurs in the first few weeks and months of life.
- It is important to remember that breastfeeding is the normal practice among many cultural groups in the US, especially among recent immigrants from developing countries.
- A decision not to breastfeed may raise issues regarding confidentiality of a mother's HIV diagnosis and require sensitivity and supportive interventions.

PRECONCEPTUAL COUNSELING

Many women enter pregnancy with a known diagnosis of HIV infection and more than half of those enter the first trimester on antiretroviral therapy.[7] The objective of preconceptual care is to optimize maternal health for pregnancy:

- Initiate or modify ARV therapy to avoid potentially teratogenic agents
- Monitor for therapy associated side effects that could impact maternal and fetal health outcome
- Evaluate and provide prophylaxis for opportunistic infections
- Provide appropriate immunizations
- Optimize maternal nutritional status
- Initiate folic acid supplementation
- Screen and treat for STDs
- Identify risk factors for adverse pregnancy outcome
- Screen for maternal psychological and substance abuse disorders
- Advise how to optimize the chance of conception while minimizing the risk of sexual transmission.

CARE GUIDELINES FOR PREGNANT WOMEN WITH HIV INFECTION

- Monitor CD4 count and HIV-1 RNA levels every trimester to determine the need for antiretroviral therapy for treating the mother's HIV disease, whether to alter therapy, and whether to initiate prophylaxis against opportunistic infections (Table 1)
- Assess risk of disease progression by level of plasma HIV RNA
- Evaluate degree of immunodeficiency by CD4 count
- Document history of prior or current ARV use
- Discuss risk and benefits of therapy
- Develop strategy for management and evaluation of mother and infant
- Discuss plans for postpartum contraception and, if tubal ligation desired, complete paperwork.

GUIDELINES FOR ANTIRETROVIRAL THERAPY IN PREGNANCY

- Use optimal ARVs for the woman's health but consider the potential impact on the fetus (Table 2)
- Offer 3-part ZDV regimen for reducing perinatal transmission in combination with other ARVs
- Discuss preventable risk factors for perinatal transmission
- Support decision making by the woman after discussion of risks and benefits

ANTEPARTUM CARE

History

Complete medical and obstetric/gynecologic history at first prenatal visit.
Subsequent evaluation of possible HIV symptoms should include:
- *General* – persistent fatigue; persistent/frequent fever > 100°F; tender or enlarged lymph nodes; night sweats; weight loss
- *EENT* – Flashes of light, change in vision or loss of vision; persistent sore mouth/throat; oral HSV symptoms; thrush or white patches in mouth/throat; white, frond-like patches on the lateral surfaces of the tongue which do not scrape off (oral hairy leukoplakia); dysphagia and difficulty swallowing; painful swallowing; visual problems
- *Skin* – herpes zoster; a new skin rash; unusual bruises, bumps, or skin discoloration
- *Respiratory* – dyspnea or persistent shortness of breath; a new persistent dry cough
- *GI* – chronic diarrhea; unintentional weight loss; jaundice
- *Genital* – recurrent, refractory vaginal candidiasis; rapid development of cervical dysplasia/squamous intraepithelial lesion
- *Neurologic* – persistent/frequent headaches; problems with coordination/balance; numbing, tingling, or pain in hands, arms, legs, or feet; seizures; inability to think clearly; mental confusion; memory problems

Physical examination

Repeat each trimester and screen for HIV disease progression, especially with a CD4+ < 500 cells/mm³ on no ARV medication:
- *Eyes* – visual fields/funduscopic exam (as indicated; greatest risk if CD4 < 50)
- *Mouth* – gingivitis, thrush, oral hairy leukoplakia, HSV, KS (rare in women)
- *Lymph* – generalized lymphadenopathy
- *Breasts* – masses
- *Lungs* – crackles, rubs, and decreased breath sounds
- *Abdomen* – hepatosplenomegaly
- *Genitalia/anal area* – HSV; candidiasis; HPV; other STDs; evidence of vulvar/cervical abnormalities
- *Extremities* – decreased or increased sensation; weakness
- *Skin* – rash, petechiae, lesions, bruises; xerosis; jaundice; pallor
- *Neurologic* – fine and gross motor impairment; diminished abstract thinking, memory; cranial nerve evaluation

Laboratory Investigations

Prenatal panel and include the following for HIV disease surveillance:
- Hepatitis B and C screening
- HIV RNA by quantitative PCR for baseline viral load, again at 4-8 weeks after initiation of antiretroviral therapy to assess drug efficacy, and in each trimester to assess durability of therapy
- Diabetes screening of patients on protease inhibitors at first contact and at 24-28 weeks gestation
- CBC, differential, platelet count, repeat as indicated by the antiretroviral regimen and potential toxicities
- Serologies :Toxoplasmosis and CMV titers IgG
- Renal profile
- Liver profile
- T-lymphocyte (CD4, CD8, CD4:CD8), repeat in each trimester
- PPD – positive PPD if $\geq$ 5 mm in duration
- STD screening during third trimester or with a change in partners; DNA probe or culture for gonorrhea and/or chlamydia, VDRL; hepatitis B and C if previously negative

Resistance Testing in Pregnancy

The US Public Health Service Task Force recommends resistance testing only:[11]
- if acute HIV infection suspected
- if there is evidence of virologic failure
- if there is suboptimal viral suppression by antiretroviral therapy
- if there is a high likelihood of exposure to resistant virus

While resistance testing has become standard of care in the non-pregnant population, no definitive evidence suggests that it should be routinely performed in pregnancy. However, resistance testing should be performed for the same indications as for nonpregnant patients as listed above. Genotypic assays are more widely available commercially than phenotypic assays, have a quicker turnaround time, and are less expensive. Both require a plasma HIV RNA level above 1000 copies/mL. After initiation of antiretroviral therapy, the viral load should fall by 1 to 2 logs within the first month. If this does not occur despite good adherence, then resistance testing should be performed.

Fetal Assessment
- Assessment of fetal anatomy with level II ultrasound at 18 to 20 weeks.
- Assessment of baseline fetal growth at 28 to 32 weeks gestation.
- Monitor for preterm labor especially if on a PI containing regimen
- Avoid chorionic villus sampling, amniocentesis, percutaneous umbilical blood sampling, and external cephalic version. There is insufficient data concerning the risk of perinatal transmission with these invasive procedures but if deemed necessary by the perinatologist or requested by the woman, aim for an undetectable viral load on antiretroviral therapy.

GUIDELINES FOR ANTIRETROVIRAL THERAPY IN PREGNANCY [8]

HIV-infected pregnant women with no prior antiretroviral therapy
- Recommend 3-part ZDV regimen to reduce transmission for all pregnant women with HIV infection regardless of viral load. (Table 3)

- Recommend combination antiretroviral therapy that includes the 3-part ZDV regimen for women who require treatment with viral load above 1000 copies/mL, regardless of clinical or immunologic status.
- Consider combination antiretroviral therapy for women with a viral load below 1000 copies/mL.
- Consider delaying therapy until after 10 to 12 weeks gestation.

HIV-infected pregnant women entering pregnancy on antiretroviral therapy

- Discuss benefits and risks of her regimen during pregnancy (Table 4)
- Discontinue teratogenic drugs
- Consider continuing or stopping current therapy during first trimester
- If therapy is stopped, restart all drugs simultaneously
- Include ZDV in the regimen
- Recommend ZDV intrapartum and for the neonate
- If suboptimal viral suppression, perform resistance testing while on failing regimen

HIV-infected women with no prior antiretroviral therapy in labor

- Discuss benefits of treatment during labor and for the neonate

Four treatment options (Table 5):

- Intrapartum IV ZDV followed by 6 weeks ZDV for the newborn
- Oral ZDV/3TC for mother at onset and during labor followed by 1 week oral ZDV/3TC for the newborn
- Single dose NVP for mother at onset of labor followed by single dose of NVP for the newborn at 48 to 72 hours of age. The clinical consequence of transient detection of NVP resistant virus following this single dose regimen is uncertain but there are concerns that this could negatively impact the response to subsequent therapy.
- Two-dose NVP regimen as above combined with intrapartum IV ZDV and 6 weeks ZDV for the newborn

Infants born to mothers who have received no antiretroviral therapy antepartum or intrapartum

- Initiate therapy as soon as possible after maternal consent
- Offer the six week neonatal ZDV component
- Begin diagnostic testing of the infant
- Refer to pediatric HIV specialist

Table 1. Prevention of Opportunistic Infections in Pregnancy

Pathogen	Indication	Recommendation
Pneumocystis Jiroveci (formerly carinii)	CD4 < 200	TMP-SMX 1 DS/d
Toxoplasmosis	Anti-toxoplasma IgG positive and CD4 < 100	TMP-SMX 1 DS/d
Mycobacterium avium complex	CD4 < 50	Azithromycin 1200 mg/week
Streptococcus pneumoniae	All patients with CD4 > 200 Revaccinate if initial immunization when CD4<200	Pneumovax® 0.5 mL IM x1
Hepatitis A	Anti-HAV negative (total or IgG)	0.5 mL IM X 2 doses 6 months apart
Hepatitis B	Anti-HBc, Anti-HBs, and HBsAg negative	HBV vaccine series
Influenza	All patients annually	Influenza vaccine 0.5mL IM

NOTE: Consideration should be given to give MMR vaccine immediately post partum to susceptible mothers if they are not significantly immunocompromised.
 HIV infection itself is not an absolute contraindication to MMR vaccine (Ref: MMWR; 51 RR-6:63)

Table 2. Antiretroviral Regimens for HIV Infected Women in Second and Third Trimesters

Standard Antiretroviral Therapy but:

- Include AZT according to 076 protocol

- Treat based upon maternal clinical/immunologic status but avoid efavirenz, hydroxyurea, AZT with d4T, d4T with ddI, amprenavir solution

- Previously untreated pregnant women with VL < 1,000 c/ml and CD4 > 350 cells/mm³ may be treated with AZT monotherapy, AZT with 3TC or HAART

AZT + d4T Pharmacologic antagonism; do not use together
APV oral solution contains propylene glycol which cannot be metabolized in pregnancy
d4T + ddI concerns about lactic acidosis
EFV, hydroxyurea concerns about teratogenicity

Table 3. PACTG 076 Zidovudine (ZDV) Regimen

Time of ZDV Administration	Regimen
Antepartum	Oral administration of 100 mg ZDV five times daily[*], initiated at 14-34 weeks gestation and continued throughout the pregnancy.
Intrapartum	During labor, intravenous administration of ZDV in a one-hour initial dose of 2 mg/kg body weight, followed by a continuous infusion of 1 mg/kg body weight/hour until delivery.
Postpartum	Oral administration of ZDV to the newborn (ZDV syrup at 2 mg/kg body weight/dose every six hours) for the first six weeks of life, beginning at 8-12 hours after birth.

* Oral ZDV administered as 200 mg three times daily or 300 mg twice daily is currently used in general clinical practice and is an acceptable alternative regimen to 100 mg orally five times daily.

Table 4. Antiretroviral Therapy in Pregnancy: Safety and Toxicity

	NRTI		NNRTI		PI	
Recommended agents	Zidovudine Lamivudine	• Efficacy studies and extensive experience • Zidovudine + lamivudine is the recommended dual NRTI backbone	Nevirapine	• No evidence of teratogenicity • Increased risk of liver toxicity in women who start Nevirapine with CD4 >250cells/mm³; in these women, use Nevirapine-based regimens only if benefit outweighs risk • In women with CD4 <250cells/mm³, Nevirapine use acceptable • Monitor closely, especially for first 18 weeks of therapy • No liver toxicity seen with single-dose Nevirapine during labor	Nelfinavir Saquinavir (soft gel capsule)/ ritonavir	• PK studies and extensive experience • Preferred PI for combination therapy • PK studies and moderate experience • Unboosted saquinavir: inadequate drug levels in pregnant women • No PK data on saquinavir hard gel capsule
Alternate agents	Didanosine Emtricitabine Stavudine Abacavir	• Cases of lactic acidosis with didanosine + stavudine; use only if no other alternatives			Indinavir Lopinavir / ritonavir Ritonavir	• Lower drug levels during pregnancy; unboosted indinavir is not recommended • Requires boosting with ritonavir, but optimal dosing in pregnancy is unknown • Concern for possible hyperbilirubinemia in the neonate • Limited experience; study underway • Dosing recommendations not established; may require increased dose during pregnancy • Lower drug levels in pregnancy • Minimal experience
Insufficient data to recommend	Tenofovir	• No studies in human pregnancy; bone toxicity in monkey studies			Amprenavir Atazanavir Fosamprenavir	• No studies in human pregnancy • Oral solution contraindicated (contains propylene glycol) • No studies in human pregnancy • Concern for possible hyperbilirubinemia in the neonate • No studies in human pregnancy
Not recommended	Zalcitabine	• Teratogenic in animals	Efavirenz Delavirdine	• Teratogenic in monkeys; cases of CNS defects in humans • Pregnancy category D • Avoid in first trimester • Avoid in women who may become pregnant • Consider after second trimester only if no alternative • Teratogenic in rodent studies	Tipranavir	• No studies in human pregnancy

Table 5. Antiretroviral Regimens for HIV Infected Women in Labor with No Prior Therapy

Medication(s)	Women	Neonate
Zidovudine (ZDV)	Intrapartum IV ZDV for one hour (2 mg/kg over one hour) followed by continuous infusion until delivery (1 mg/kg/hour).	ZDV syrup (2mg/kg) every 6 hours for 6 weeks beginning 8-12 hours after birth
Zidovudine + Lamivudine (3TC)	ZDV (600mg) and 3TC (150mg) orally at onset of labor, then ZDV (300mg) every 3 hours and 3TC (150mg) every 12 hours	ZDV syrup (4mg/kg) and 3TC (2mg//kg) every 12 hours for 7 days
Nevirapine[1] (NVP)	Single dose of NVP (200mg) orally at onset of labor	Single dose of NVP (2mg/kg) 48-72 hours after birth
Nevirapine + Zidovudine	Intrapartum IV ZDV for one hour (2 mg/kg over one hour) followed by continuous infusion until delivery (1 mg/kg/hour) and NVP (200mg) at labor onset	ZDV syrup (2 mg/kg) every 6 hours for six weeks beginning at 8-12 hours after birth and single dose of NVP (2mg/kg) 48-72 hours after birth

CHANGING ANTIRETROVIRAL THERAPY IN PREGNANCY

When evaluating treatment failure, assessment of adherence to regimen is important. Consideration should be given to changing the antiretroviral regimen if:

- Poor CD4 response
- Drugs with potential teratogenicity
- Poor viral load response
- Poor adherence to regimen
- Evidence of viral resistance

Cesarean Delivery to Reduce Perinatal Transmission

- Use the most recent VL level to counsel a woman regarding mode of delivery
- Risk of perinatal transmission with persistently undetectable VL on antiretroviral therapy is < 2% regardless of mode of delivery
- Women with a VL > 1000 copies/mL should be counseled regarding the potential benefit of scheduled C/S to reduce the risk of transmission
- No evidence of benefit of C/S to reduce transmission after labor or membrane rupture
- Schedule C/S at 38 weeks using LMP and ultrasound estimate of gestational age without assessing fetal lung maturity by amniocentesis
- Honor the woman's decision regarding mode of delivery
- Initiate ZDV infusion for 3 hours prior to C/S and continue until cord clamped
- Women with a low CD4 count may be at increased risk of complications after C/S
- Use of prophylactic antibiotics (narrow spectrum such as a 1st generation cephalosporin) at the time of C/S is generally recommended[12]

Intrapartum care

- Admit in early labor
- Augment labor to expedite delivery
- Maintain universal body fluid precautions for all deliveries
- Administer ZDV IV in labor; 2mg/kg loading dose followed by 1 mg/kg/hr continuously until the umbilical cord is clamped
- Delay amniotomy
- Avoid invasive fetal monitoring
- Inform pediatrician of mother's status
- Bulb suction baby at delivery and wash off maternal secretions as soon as possible after birth

Stopping Antiretroviral Therapy [8]

- Women may interrupt ongoing therapy in early pregnancy because of nausea and vomiting or concerns about first trimester fetal exposure.
- Additionally many pregnant women do not meet criteria for treatment only requiring antiretroviral therapy in pregnancy to prevent perinatal transmission and so stop medication after delivery.
- Before stopping their antiretrovirals, the clinician and the patient should discuss the pros and cons of continuing or discontinuing therapy.
- Patients should stop all drugs simultaneously unless there are significant differences in half lives.
- NNRTIs have long half lives and a low genetic barrier to resistance.
- Resistance may develop quickly after discontinuation of nevirapine-containing regimens.
- For NNRTI containing combination regimens, consider continuing NRTIs for 14- 21 days after stopping NNRTI. (The optimal duration of time to continue NRTIs when discontinuing an NNRTI-containing regimen has not yet been defined. Some would continue for up to 2 weeks since plasma levels of NNRTIs may persist for 2 weeks or longer following discontinuation).

TOXICITY IN PREGNANCY

Monitor for Side Effects
Indications of toxicity that require interrupting or stopping ZDV include:
- Hemoglobin <8g/dL
- Absolute neutrophil count <750 cells/mm^3
- AST or ALT >5x upper limit of normal

Mitochondrial Toxicity and Nucleoside Analog Drugs
- Nucleoside analogues are known to induce mitochondrial dysfunction
- Clinical disorders include neuropathy, cardiomyopathy, myopathy, pancreatitis, hepatic steatosis and lactic acidosis
- Hepatic steatosis and lactic acidosis could be confused with HELLP (Hemolysis, Elevated Liver enzyme levels and Low Platelet count) syndrome characterized by or acute fatty liver of pregnancy
- Pregnant women with HIV on nucleoside analogs should have liver enzymes and electrolytes monitored in the third trimester
- D4T + ddI in combination should be avoided in pregnancy

Nevirapine Rash and Hepatotoxicity
- The risk of NVP associated hepatotoxicity and rash is higher in women especially if CD4 > 250 cells/mm^3
- Women with CD4 < 250 cells/mm^3 may receive NVP
- Women entering pregnancy on an effective NVP containing regimen may continue NVP regardless of CD4 count
- Pregnant women on NVP should have transaminase levels monitored especially in the first 18 weeks of treatment

Efavirenz Teratogenicity
- Now classified as FDA pregnancy category D
- Retrospective case reports of CNS defects in infants of women who received efavirenz at conception and in the first trimester
- Avoid in the first trimester and in women at risk of becoming pregnant

POSTPARTUM CARE
- Comprehensive care and support services are important for women with HIV infection and their families
- Establish ongoing primary care for HIV disease at 3-6 month intervals
- Coordinate care between obstetric and HIV specialists
- Continue antiretroviral therapy if needed for maternal health indications
- Prevent nosocomial infection
- Family planning is critical to the prevention of perinatal transmission
- Monitor for gynecological manifestations associated with disease progression
- Pap smear every 6 months +/- colposcopy
- Mental health and substance abuse treatment as needed

Follow up of infants
- Support for ZDV prophylaxis for 6 weeks

- A baseline CBC should be performed on the newborn before and after 6 weeks of ZDV since anemia is the main complication
- Referral to an HIV specialist
- HIV diagnostic testing to establish or rule out HIV infection as early as possible
- Initiate PCP prophylaxis at 6 weeks
- Long term follow up of HIV and antiretroviral exposed infants

HIV DNA PCR test should be performed on the at risk infant within 3 days of delivery, at 6 to 8 weeks of age, and at 4 to 6 months of age followed by a HIV ELISA at 12 to 15 months.

Definition of an Uninfected Infant:
- Two separate HIV DNA PCR tests negative, one performed after one month of age and the other done at or after 4 months of age in the absence of breast feeding.
- T cell numbers and subsets are normal for age.
- Child is otherwise asymptomatic.
- HIV antibody disappears between 12 and 18 months of age.

Definition of an HIV–Infected Infant:
- Consecutively positive HIV virologic assays on blood taken on two separate days (not cord blood).
- Assays that are acceptable for diagnosis include HIV DNA PCR, Viral culture, HIV RNA PCR.

Referral for Case Management and Psycho-social services
Many women continue to first learn of their HIV status in pregnancy. After delivery both the mother and the infant will need follow-up care, including access to case management and psychosocial support services, ideally through a comprehensive, family centered program. These types of services for families affected by HIV infection are available in many communities provided by the Ryan White Care ACT (Ryan White Title I, III, and IV).

References

1. American College of Obstetricians and Gynecologists. ACOG practice bulletin number 304. Prenatal and perinatal human immunodeficiency virus testing: Expanded recommendations. *Obstet Gynecol* 2004; 104:1119–1124.
2. Connor EM, Sperling RS, Gelber R, et al. Reduction of maternal infant transmission of human immunodeficiency virus type 1 with zidovudine treatment. Pediatric AIDS Clinical Trials Group protocol 076 Study Group. *NEJM* 1994; 331:1173–1180.
3. Garcia PM, Kalish LA, Pitt J, et al. Maternal levels of plasma human immunodeficiency virus type 1 RNA and the risk of perinatal transmission. *NEJM* 1999; 341:394–402.
4. Mofenson LM, Lambert JS, Stiehm ER, et al. Risk factors for perinatal transmission of human immunodeficiency virus type 1 in women treated with zidovudine. *NEJM* 1999; 341:385–393.
5. Shapiro DE, Sperling RS, Coombs RW. Effect of zidovudine on perinatal HIV-1 transmission and maternal viral load. *Lancet* 1999; 354:156.
6. Ioannidis JPA, Abrams EJ, Ammann A, et al. Perinatal transmission of human immunodeficiency virus type 1 by pregnant women with RNA viral loads <1000 copies/mL. *JID* 2001; 183:539–545.
7. Tuomala R, Shapiro D, Samelson R, et al. Antepartum antiretroviral therapy and viral load in 464 HIV infected women in 1998–2000. *Am J Obstet Gynecol* 2000; 182:A285.
8. Public Health Service Task Force. Recommendations for the use of antiretroviral drugs in pregnant HIV-1 infected women for maternal health and interventions to reduce perinatal HIV-1 transmission in the United States 2005. (updated guidelines available http://AIDSinfo.nih.gov).

38

Post-Exposure Prophylaxis for Healthcare Personnel

Susan S. Davis, ARNPC, MSN
Manager, Employee Health, Co-Chair HIV/AIDS Sub-Committee
Mercy Hospital, Miami
Frank Paula, MSN, ARNP
Nurse Practitioner
Mercy Hospital, Miami
D. Stewart MacIntyre, MD
Clinical Professor of Infectious Disease
University of Miami School of Medicine

Introduction

Healthcare personnel (HCP) are at risk for transmission of bloodborne pathogens including HIV, Hepatitis B (HBV), and Hepatitis C (HCV) Percutaneous exposures in the workplace continue to pose the highest risk of transmission. The risk of transmission for each of these pathogens is influenced by the degree of contact with blood as well as the source patient's status[1]. The risk for acquisition of HIV, HBV, and HCV following exposure is affected by the following factors:

- Type of exposure
    - Percutaneous or penetrating sharps-related injuries carry the highest risk for HIV transmission, if the source patient is HIV positive. Other factors affecting percutaneous transmission include:
        - Visible blood on the device
        - Large bore hollow needle
        - Exposure of the device to source patient's vein or artery
    - Mucous membrane
    - Intact or non-intact skin

- The pathogen involved
  - High viral titer
  - HBeAg status of source

- Status of the source (known or unknown HIV, HBV, HCV status)

RISK OF INFECTION AFTER EXPOSURE

HIV

The average risk for infection in HCP as a result of a percutaneous exposure to HIV is 0.3% [1]. The CDC documents that 57 HCP in the United States have seroconverted to HIV following occupational exposures (see Figure 1). Twenty-six had developed AIDS at the time of reporting. The exposures resulting in infection were as follows: 48 had percutaneous (puncture/cut injury) exposure; 5 had mucocutaneous (mucous membrane and/or skin) exposure; 2 had both percutaneous and mucocutaneous exposure; and 2 had an unknown route of exposure. Forty-nine healthcare personnel were exposed to HIV-infected blood; 3 to concentrated virus in a laboratory; 1 to visibly bloody fluid, and 4 to an unspecified fluid [1].

Figure 1. Healthcare Personnel with Documented and Possible Occupationally Acquired AIDS/HIV Infection, By Occupation, as of December 2001

Occupation	Documented	Possible
Nurse	24	35
Laboratory worker, clinical	16	17
Physician, nonsurgical	6	12
Laboratory technician, nonclinical	3	-
Housekeeper/maintenance worker	2	13
Technician, surgical	2	2
Embalmer/morgue technician	1	2
Health aide/attendant	1	15
Respiratory therapist	1	2
Technician, dialysis	1	3
Dental worker, including dentist	-	6
Emergency medical technician/paramedic	-	12
Physician, surgical	-	6
Other technician/therapist	-	9
Other healthcare occupation	-	5
Total	**57**	**139**

[1] Healthcare personnel are defined as those persons, including students and trainees, who have worked in a healthcare, clinical, or HIV laboratory setting at any time since 1978. See *MMWR* 1992; 41:823–825.

Hepatitis B Virus (HBV)

The risk for transmission of HBV in HCP who have received the Hepatitis B vaccination is insignificant. For HCP who have not been vaccinated the risk from a single percutaneous exposure ranges from 6–30% and is dependent on the Hepatitis Be antigen (HBeAg) status of the source patient. Individuals who are HBeAg positive have higher concentrations of HBV in their blood and are more likely to transmit the disease than those who are HBeAg negative. The risk for infection from exposure to non-intact skin is unknown but most probably insignificant[1].

Hepatitis C Virus (HCV)

The average risk for HCV infection after one percutaneous exposure is approximately 1.8%.[1] There have been no documented transmissions in HCP as a result of exposure to intact or non-intact skin. Environmental exposures to HCV are not a significant risk of transmission as with HBV.

Table 1. Expert Consultation Advised

SITUATIONS FOR WHICH EXPERT CONSULTATION FOR HIV POST-EXPOSURE PROPHYLAXIS IS WARRANTED
• Delayed exposure report > 24-36 hours • Unknown source • Known or suspected pregnancy in exposed person • Breastfeeding in the exposed person • Suspected resistance of source virus • Toxicity of initial regimen

US Public Health Service Guidelines

The following guideline quotations are adapted from *The Updated U.S. Public Health Service Guidelines for the Management of Occupational Exposures to HBV, HCV, and HIV and Recommendations for Post-exposure prophylaxis* published in *MMWR* 2001:50 (RR-11). They are intended to guide initial decisions about PEP and should be used in conjunction with other guidance provided in the full report. Call 800-458-5231 to order the full report.

HIV

How to Determine the Need for HIV Post-Exposure Prophylaxis (PEP) After an Occupational Exposure (Revised 9/30/2005)

Recommended HIV post-exposure prophylaxis for percutanious injuries					
	Infection Status of Source				
ExposureType	HIV-Positive Class 1❶	HIV-Positive Class 2 ❶	Source HIV Status Unknown ❷	Unknown Source ❸	Source HIV Negative
Less severe ❹	Recommend basic 2-drug PEP❽	Recommend expanded >3-drug PEP ❽	Generally, no PEP warranted; however, consider basic 2-drug PEP❺, ❽for source with HIV risk factors.	Generally, no PEP warranted; however, consider basic 2-drug PEP❺,❽ in settings where exposure to HIV infected persons is likely. ❻	No PEP warranted
More Severe ❼	Recommend expanded 3-drug PEP❽	Recommend expanded > 3-drug PEP ❽	Generally, no PEP warranted; however, consider basic 2-drug PEP❺,❽ for source with HIV risk factors.❻	Generally, no PEP warranted; however, consider basic 2-drug PEP ❺,❽ in settings where exposure to HIV infected persons is likely. ❻	No PEP warranted
Recommended HIV post-exposure prophylaxis for mucous membranes exposures and nonintact skin exposures❾					
Small volume (e.g., few drops)	Consider basic 2-drug PEP❺ ❽	Recommend basic 2-drug PEP ❽	Generally, no PEP warranted. ❻	Generally, no PEP warranted.	No PEP warranted
Large Volume (e.g., major blood splash)	Recommend basic 2-drug PEP ❽	Recommend expanded >3-drug PEP ❽	Generally, no PEP warranted; however, consider basic 2-drug PEP ❺,❽ for source with HIV risk factors. ❻	Generally, no PEP warranted; however, consider basic 2-drug PEP❺, ❽ in settings where exposure to HIV infected persons is likely.❻	No PEP warranted

❶ HIV-Positive Class 1 - Asymptomatic HIV infection or known low viral load (e.g. <1,500 RNA copies/ml). HIV-Positive, Class 2 – symptomatic HIV infection, AIDS acute seroconversion, or known high viral load. If drug resistance is a concern, obtain expert consultation. Initiation of PEP should not be delayed pending expert consultation.
❷ Source Status unknown (e.g., no prior HIV testing)
❸ Unknown source – (e.g., a needle for a sharps box, sharps in a trash bag)
❹ Less severe – (e.g., suture needle, superficial injury)
❺ PEP is optional and should be based on an individualized decision between the exposed person and the treating clinician
❻ If PEP is initiated and the source later turns out to be HIV-Negative, PEP should be discontinued.
❼More severe- (e.g., large-bore, hollow needle, deep puncture, visible blood on the device, needle used in patient's artery or vein).
❽ See Table 2 on PEP regimens.
❾ Skin exposure follow-up is indicated if there is evidence of dermatitis, abrasion, or open wound

Table 2. PEP Regimens

BASIC REGIMENS		
REGIMEN	ADVANTAGES	DISADVANTAGES
Zidovudine (Retrovir®, ZDV, AZT) 300 mg po bid **+ Lamivudine (Epivir®, 3TC)** 150 mg po bid (also available as **Combivir®**)	• AZT associated with ↓ risk of HIV transmission in CDC study of occupational HIV infection • Experience with AZT for PEP • Serious toxicity rare when used for PEP • Probably a safe regimen for pregnant HCP • Can be given as 1 tablet bid	• Side-effects are common and might result in low adherence • Source patient might have resistant virus
ALTERNATE BASIC REGIMENS		
REGIMEN	ADVANTAGES	DISADVANTAGES
Lamivudine (Epivir®, 3TC) 150 mg po bid **+ Stavudine (Zerit®, d4T)** 40 mg (30 mg if < 60 kg) po bid	• Well tolerated • Serious toxicity rare • Twice daily dosing may improve adherence	• Source patient may have resistant virus
Didanosine (Videx®, chewable buffered tablet; Videx EC®, enteric-coated capsule; ddI) 400 mg (250 mg if < 60 kg) po qd **+ stavudine (Zerit®, d4T)** 40 mg (30 mg if < 60 kg) po bid	• Likely to be effective against HIV strains from source patients who are taking AZT and 3TC	• Old formulation of ddI difficult to tolerate; much better with Videx EC® • Drug interactions with ddI buffered tablet formulation • Serious toxicity (i.e. neuropathy, pancreatitis, or hepatitis) can occur. • Side-effects are common; anticipate diarrhea (less with Videx EC®) and low adherence
EXPANDED REGIMENS: BASIC REGIMEN PLUS ONE OF THE FOLLOWING		
REGIMEN	ADVANTAGES	DISADVANTAGES
Indinavir (Crixivan®, IDV) 800 mg po q8h on an empty stomach	• Potent HIV inhibitor	• Serious toxicity (i.e. nephrolithiasis) can occur; must drink at least 8 glasses of water per day. • Hyperbilirubinemia common; avoid drug during late pregnancy • Many drug interactions
Nelfinavir (Viracept®, NFV) 750 mg po tid or 1250 mg po bid with meal or snack	• Potent HIV inhibitor • Twice daily dosing may improve adherence	• Many drug interactions • May increase the clearance of certain drugs such as oral contraceptives (additional form of contraception required) • Potential for delayed toxicity (oncogenic/teratogenic) is unknown
Efavirenz (Sustiva®, EFV) 600 mg po qhs	• Once daily dosing may improve adherence	• Drug is associated with rash which can be severe and can be difficult to differentiate from acute seroconversion • CNS side-effects (i.e. dizziness, somnolence, insomnia, and/or abnormal dreaming) are common • Should not be used in pregnant women and caution advised in those with childbearing potential due to risk of teratogenicity • Many drug interactions
Abacavir (Ziagen®, ABC), (also available as **Trizivir®**, a combination of AZT, 3TC, and ABC) 300 mg po bid	• Potent HIV inhibitor • Well tolerated in patients with HIV infection	• Severe hypersensitivity reactions can occur (usually within the first 6 weeks)

ARV Agents for Use as PEP Only with Expert Consultation

Ritonavir (Norvir,® RTV)
- Difficult to take; requires dose escalation
- Poor tolerability
- Many drug interactions
- May increase the clearance of oral contraceptives (alternative form of contraception necessary)

Saquinavir (Fortovase,® SQV-soft-gel capsule)
- Relatively poor bioavailability

Amprenavir (Agenerase,® APV)
- Requires that 8 large pills be taken twice daily
- Many drug interactions

Delavirdine (Rescriptor,® DLV)
- Drug is associated with rash that can be severe and difficult to differentiate from acute seroconversion
- Many drug interactions

Lopinavir/Ritonavir (Kaletra,® KAL)
- Many drug interactions

ARV Agents Generally Not Recommended for Use as PEP

Nevirapine (Viramune,® NVP)

- Associated with severe hepatotoxicity (including at least one case of liver failure requiring liver transplant in person taking for PEP)
- Drug is associated with rash which can be severe and can be difficult to differentiate from acute seroconversion
- May increase the clearance of oral contraceptives (alternative form of contraception necessary)

Table 3. HCP Follow Up Post-Exposure

FOLLOW UP OF HEALTHCARE PERSONNEL (HCP) EXPOSED TO KNOWN OR SUSPECTED HIV POSITIVE SOURCES

- HCP should be advised to use precautions to prevent secondary transmission at least during the first 6 – 12 weeks.
  - Avoid blood donations
  - Avoid pregnancy or breastfeeding
  - Unprotected intercourse
- If PEP is prescribed, HCP should be advised of the following:
  - Possible drug toxicities
  - Need for monitoring
  - Possible drug interactions
  - Need for adherence
- Consider reevaluation of exposed HCP 72 hours post-exposure, especially if additional information about the source person becomes available

---

Additional Guidance

- "PEP should be initiated as soon as possible . . . [i.e., within a few hours rather than days]. . . [but] if appropriate for the exposure, PEP should be started even when the interval since exposure exceeds 36 hours" (p.23–26) http://www.cdc.gov/mmwr/PDF/rr/rr5011.pdf

- Although ZDV and 3TC are the recommended agents in a 2-drug regimen, "Individual clinicians may prefer other NRTIs or combinations of other antiretroviral agents based on local knowledge and experience in treating HIV infection and disease" (p.47) http://www.cdc.gov/mmwr/PDF/rr/rr5011.pdf

- "Other considerations [when choosing antiretroviral agents] include pregnancy in the health-care worker and exposure to virus known or suspected to be resistant to the antiretroviral drugs" (p.26) http://www.cdc.gov/mmwr/PDF/rr/rr5011.pdf

- Finally, the National Clinician's Post-Exposure Hotline (PEPLine) is available 24 hours a day, 7 days a week (888-448-4911).

Recommended Post-Exposure Prophylaxis for Exposure to Hepatitis B Virus

Determine Status, Testing, and Treatment for Hepatitis B Virus (HBV) and Hepatitis C Virus (HCV)

The following algorithms and guidelines are adapted from *MMWR* (see References).

Vaccination and antibody response status of exposed worker❶	Treatment		
	Source HBsAg ❷ Positive	Source HBsAg❷ Negative	Source Unknown or not available for testing
Unvaccinated	HBIG❸ x 1 and initiate HB vaccine series❹	Initiate HB vaccine series	Initiate HB vaccine series
Previously vaccinated			
Known responder❺	No treatment	No treatment	No treatment
Known nonresponder❻	HBIG x 1 and initiate HB revaccination series or HBIG x 2❼	No treatment	If know high risk source, treat as if source were HBsAg positive
Antibody response unknown	Test exposed person for anti-HBs❽ 1. If adequate, no treatment is necessary ❺ 2. If inadequate, administer HBIG x 1 and vaccine booster (repeat 3 dose vaccine series)❻	No treatment	Test exposed person for anti-HBs 1. If adequate, no treatment is necessary 2. If inadequate, administer booster (repeat 3 dose vaccine series) and recheck titer in 1-2 months

❶ Persons who have been previously infected with HBV are immune to re-infection and do not require post-exposure prophylaxis.
❷ Hepatitis B surface antigen
❸ Hepatitis B immune globulin; dose 0.06 ml/kg intramuscularly.
❹ Hepatitis B vaccine
❺ A responder is a person with adequate levels of serum antibody to HbsAg (Positive).
❻ A nonresponder is a person with inadequate response to vaccination (Negative).
❼The option of giving one dose HBIG and reinitiating the vaccine series is preferred for nonresponders who have NOT completed a second 3-dose vaccine series. For persons who previously completed a second vaccine series but failed to respond, two doses of HBIG are preferred.
❽Antibody to HBsAg.

Hepatitis C Screening — Post Exposure Follow-Up Algorithm

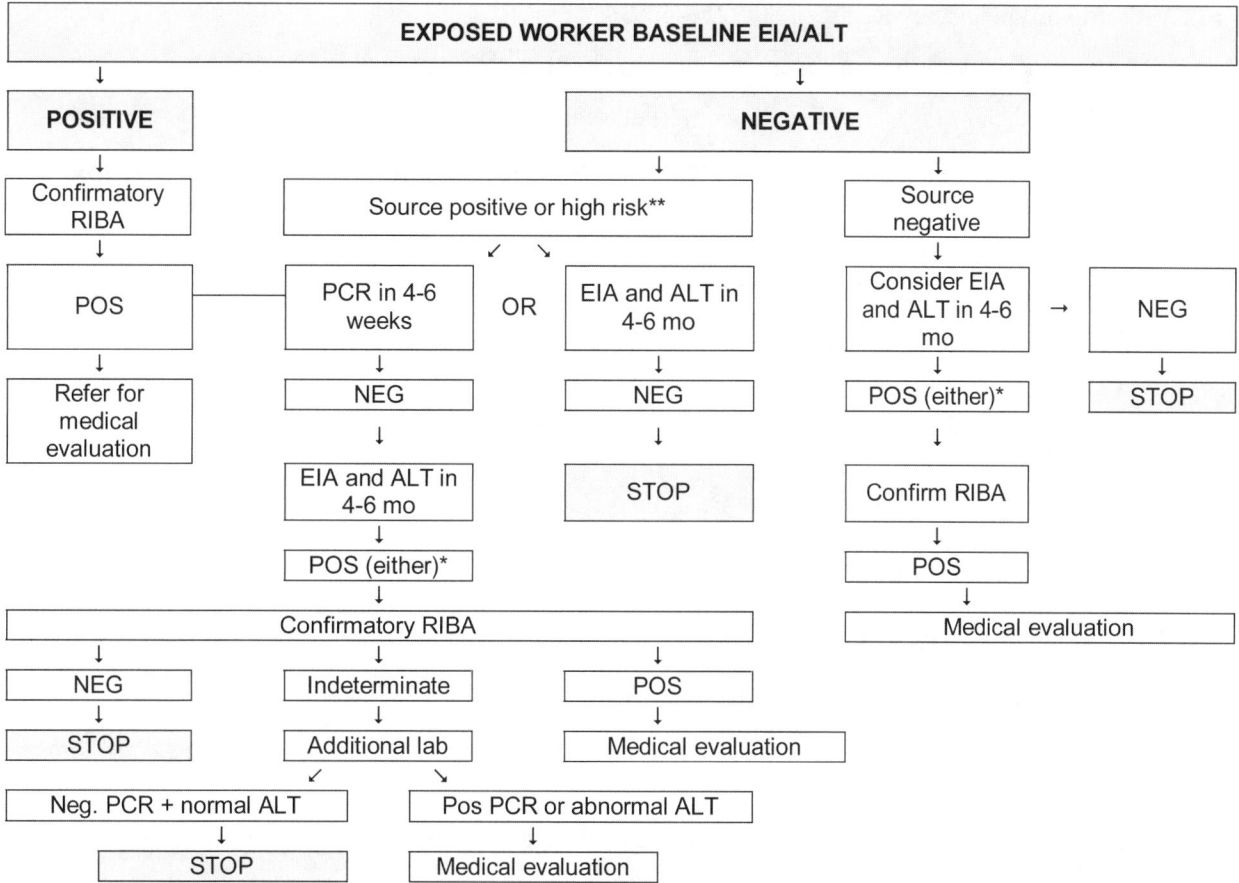

EXPOSED WORKER BASELINE EIA/ALT

POSITIVE   **NEGATIVE**

Confirmatory RIBA   Source positive or high risk**   Source negative

POS   PCR in 4-6 weeks   OR   EIA and ALT in 4-6 mo   Consider EIA and ALT in 4-6 mo   →   NEG

Refer for medical evaluation   NEG   NEG   POS (either)*   STOP

EIA and ALT in 4-6 mo   STOP   Confirm RIBA

POS (either)*   POS

Confirmatory RIBA   Medical evaluation

NEG   Indeterminate   POS

STOP   Additional lab   Medical evaluation

Neg. PCR + normal ALT   Pos PCR or abnormal ALT

STOP   Medical evaluation

*If ALT elevated and nonreactive EIA, refer directly for medical evaluation.
**Criteria for high risk:
Injecting drug users (IDU)
Unexplained elevation of ALT twice normal (discuss with patients/physicians)

For More Information

- National Clinician's Post-Exposure Prophylaxis Hotline (PEPLine): 888-448-4911 (24-hours)

- Antiretroviral pregnancy Registry: 800-258-4263

- FDA (for reporting unusual or severe toxicity to antiretroviral agents): 800-332-1088

- CDC (for reporting HIV seroconversions in health-care workers who received PEP): 800-893-0485

- Centers for Disease Control and Prevention. (1998, September 25). Management of possible sexual, injecting-drug-use, or other nonoccupational exposure to HIV, including considerations related to antiretroviral therapy. *MMWR*, 47(RR-17). Internet: www.cdc.gov.

- Hepatitis Hotline 888-443-7232, Internet: http://www.cdc.gov/hepatitis

- Needlestick! (www.needlestick.org): A Web site to help clinician manage and document occupational exposures.

- Hotline for care of Perinatal HIV Positive Women at San Francisco Hospital: 888-448-8765

Focused Teaching Points

- Report all exposures to employee health and/or your supervisor.
- Do not donate blood, sperm, or organs
- Do not share IV needles, razors, or toothbrushes
- Do not breastfeed
- Abstain from sexual activities that involve the exchange of bodily fluids or use precautions such as barrier devices while undergoing PEP and/or follow up testing.
- If PEP initiated, take every dose on time; report all side effects to medical care provider.

References

1. CDC. Updated US public health service guidelines for the management of occupational exposures to HIV and recommendations for post-exposure prophylaxis. *MMWR 200*1; 50(RR-11):1–42. Available at http://www.cdc.gov/mmwr/preview/mmwrhtml/rr5011a1.htm
2. CDC, Guidelines for laboratory testing and result reporting of antibody to Hepatitis C virus. Alter, M. J, Kuhnert, W.L., Finelli, L. *MMWR*, February 7, 2003; 52(RR03);1–16.
3. CDC. Public Health Service inter-agency guidelines for screening donors of blood, plasma, organs, tissues, and semen for evidence of Hepatitis B and Hepatitis C. *MMWR* 1991; 40(No. RR-4):1–17.Available at:http://www.cdc.gov/ncidod/hip/BLOOD/hivpersonnel.html.
4. CDC. Updated US public health service guidelines for the management of occupational exposures to HIV and recommendations for post-exposure prophylaxis. *MMWR* September 30, 2005: 54 (No. RR09):1–17. Available at: http://www.cdc.gov/mmwr/preview/mmwrhtml/rr5409a1.htm
5. CDC. Recommendations for prevention and control of hepatitis C virus (HCV) infection and HCV-related chronic disease. *MMWR* 1998; 47 (No. RR-19):1–33.
6. CDC. Revised guidelines for HIV counseling, testing, and referral. *MMWR* 2001; 50(No. RR-19):1–53.
7. Kleinman S, Alter H, Busch M, et al. Increased detection of hepatitis C virus (HCV)-infected blood donors by a multiple-antigen HCV enzyme immunoassay. *Transfusion* 1992; 32:805–813.

8. Conry-Cantilena C, VanRaden M, Gibble J, et al. Routes of infection, viremia, and liver disease in blood donors found to have hepatitis C virus infection. *NEJM* 1996; 334:1691–1696.

9. Hyams KC, Riddle J, Rubertone M, et al. Prevalence and incidence of Hepatitis C virus infection in the US military: A seroepidemiologic survey of 21,000 troops. *Am J Epidemiol* 2001; 153:764–770.

10. Alter MJ, Kruszon-Moran D, Nainan OV, et al. Prevalence of Hepatitis C virus infection in the United States, 1988 through 1994. *NEJM* 1999;341: 556–562.

11. CDC. Hepatitis C virus infection among firefighters, emergency medical technicians, and paramedics—Selected locations, United States, 1991–2000. *MMWR* 2000; 49:660–665.

12. Gunn, RA, Murray PJ, Ackers ML, Hardison WGM, Margolis HS. Screening for chronic hepatitis B and C virus infections in an urban sexually transmitted disease clinic: Rationale for integrating services. *Sex Transm Dis* 2001;28:166–170.

39

Non-Occupational Post-Exposure Prophylaxis (nPEP)

Jeffrey Beal, MD
Clinical Director
Florida/Caribbean AIDS Education and Training Center
Associate Professor USF Center for HIV Education and Research
Joanne J. Orrick, PharmD, BCPS
Clinical Assistant Professor
University of Florida Colleges of Nursing and Pharmacy, Gainesville
Faculty, Florida/Caribbean AIDS Education and Training Center

Introduction

Prevention messages (abstinence, condoms, sterile works, etc) are recognized to be the most effective and most cost effective measures for preventing HIV infection, but they are not 100% effective despite our best efforts. Observational studies and case reports in humans all suggest non-occupational post-exposure prophylaxis (nPEP) may be effective. The CDC convened a series of meetings on nPEP with internal and external consultants. In January 2005, they published recommendations on the use and potential efficacy of nPEP in the United States.

The full guidelines can be found at: http://www.aidsinfo.nih.gov/guidelines/nonexposure/NE_012105.pdf.

The report defines non-occupational exposure as "any direct mucosal, percutaneous, or intravenous contact with potentially infectious body fluids that occurs outside perinatal or occupational situations." The body fluids at risk include blood, semen, vaginal secretions, rectal secretions, breast milk, or other body fluids contaminated with visible blood. Animal studies done to date have shown a potential window of opportunity for protection of infection when the exposure has been cervicovaginal. Extrapolating from the animal data, observational studies of nPEP, and recognizing that randomized, placebo controlled clinical trails are unlikely to be performed, recommendations have been made for the clinicians' consideration of treatment if the patient seeks care within 72 hours of exposure.

The benefit of nPEP is the potential to prevent HIV infection. The risks include the potential adverse effects of antiretroviral therapy, the potential to select resistant virus if adherence is poor, and the possible decrease in risk-reduction behaviors based on the perception that post exposure treatment is available.

Available data support the initiation of nPEP in carefully selected patients if the treatment can be initiated within 72 hours of an at-risk exposure. Different nonoccupational exposures are associated with different risks of infection.

Exposure route	Risk per 10,000 exposures to an infected source	Reference
Blood transfusion	9,000	74
Needle-sharing injection-drug use	67	75
Receptive anal intercourse	50	76, 77
Percutaneous needle stick	30	78
Receptive penile-vaginal intercourse	10	76, 77, 79
Insertive anal intercourse	6.5	76, 77
Insertive penile-vaginal intercourse	5	76, 77
Receptive oral intercourse	1	77[†]
Insertive oral intercourse	0.5	77[†]

* Estimates of risk for transmission from sexual exposures assume no condom use.

† Source refers to oral intercourse performed on a man.

MMWR. January 21, 2005; 54(RR02).

The following guidelines help identify those at greatest risk for HIV exposure:

Substantial Risk for HIV Exposure[1]		
Exposure of	With	When
Vagina, rectum, eye, mouth or other nonintact skin, or percutaneous contact	Blood, semen, vaginal secretions, rectal secretions, breast milk or any body fluid that is visibly contaminated with blood	The source is known to be HIV-infected

Negligible Risk for HIV Exposure		
Exposure of	With	Regardless
Vagina, rectum, eye, mouth or other mucous membrane, intact or nonintact skin, or percutaneous contact	Urine, nasal secretions, saliva, sweat, or tears if not visibly contaminated with blood	Of the known or suspected HIV status of the source

1. Adapted from Figure 1 in Antiretroviral Postexposure Prophylaxis After Sexual, Injection-Drug Use, or Other Nonoccupational Exposure to HIV in the United States, January 21, 2005 (www.aidsinfo.nih.gov)

It is important to note that no evidence exists to define what antiretroviral medication or combination of medications is best used in nPEP. Furthermore, no evidence exists that the current standard of 3-drug

HAART regimen is more beneficial than 2 drugs. Determining whether or not to treat a patient following a non-occupational exposure must be individualized. Obtaining the antiretroviral history of the source patient, including the most recent viral load data and past resistance testing results, is essential in trying to determine the best regimen for the exposed patient. When the source patient's HIV status is not known, frank discussions with the patient must guide the selection of antiretroviral therapy. Consideration of the exposure risk is critical, as well as the comfort level of the patient, for the potential risks of antiretroviral therapy. In all cases, the best regimen for the patient is the one that they will take in a compliant fashion.

Due to the lack of available data to dictate otherwise, the antiretroviral regimen chosen for nPEP should be based on the Department of Health and Human Services *Guidelines for the Use of Antiretroviral Agents in HIV-Infected Adults and Adolescents*. See www.aidsinfo.nih.gov (See Chapter 5, Antiretroviral Therapy). The recommended duration of therapy is 28 days. Physicians are encouraged to initially prescribe medications for 3 to 5 days and then see the patient again to refine therapy based upon side effect profile and comfort level of the patient. By then, results of HIV testing should be available if rapid testing was not done.

All patients who are exposed to HIV in the non-occupational setting should have baseline and follow-up testing for HIV infection at, 4 to 6 weeks, 3 months, and 6 months after exposure. It should be remembered as well to include screening for sexually transmitted diseases, hepatitis B and C, and, in females of child-bearing age, pregnancy. All patients at each visit should be reminded of the signs and symptoms of acute retroviral syndrome (refer to Table 1 in Chapter 3, Pathophysiology) and the importance of notifying the clinician if they occur. The clinician should be aware that low-grade transient viremia has occurred in animal studies, and in exposed human case reports, which did not result in HIV infection. Whether this represents an aborted infection or a false positive viral load is not known.

In summary, when faced with a patient who presents within 48 to 72 hours of a potential exposure to HIV, the clinician must assess the risk of the HIV exposure by evaluating the details of the exposure as well as evaluating the HIV status of the source patient, if available. If the HIV risk status is not deemed to be substantial, or the at-risk incident occurred > 72 hours before presenting for evaluation, nPEP is not recommended. If the HIV risk exposure is deemed substantial, baseline HIV testing, STD testing, Hepatitis B and C, and pregnancy testing should be performed. The patient and physician then must discuss the risks and potential benefits of antiretroviral therapy and, if therapy is decided upon, the DHHS Guidelines for choosing antiretroviral therapy in antiretroviral naïve patients should be followed. The patient should be evaluated within 3 to 5 days of beginning antiretroviral therapy, and every 1 to 2 weeks of the 28-day treatment course to assess for medication complications and compliance. All patients should be serially tested for HIV seroconversion at 4 to 6 weeks, 3 months, and 6 months after the risk exposure.

The clinician facing a worried patient who has experienced an at-risk exposure is encouraged to seek expert assistance by calling the PEPline of the National Clinicians' Post-Exposure Prophylaxis Hotline at 888-HIV-4911 (448-4911).

40

Management of HIV/AIDS in Women

Amanda Cotter, MD, MSPH
Assistant Professor
Director of the Perinatal HIV Service, Department of Obstetrics & Gynecology University
of Miami Miller School of Medicine
JoNell Efantis Potter, PhD, ARNP
Assistant Professor
Director of Obstetrics & Gynecology Research & Special Projects Division
University of Miami Miller School of Medicine
Nicoletta Tessler, PsyD
Licensed Psychologist
Department of Psychiatry and Behavioral Sciences
University of Miami Miller School of Medicine

Introduction

The demographic changes in populations infected with HIV in the United States are reflected in the increasing numbers of new infections among women. Racial disparity is most evident among women with a disproportionate number of new infections occurring in African Americans and Hispanics. Nationally the incidence of HIV among women has increased from 4% in the early 1990s to 28% in 2004, according to the CDC. In Florida, women accounted for 24% of reported AIDS cases in 1994 and this figure increased to 30% in 2004.[1] Of the 1741 AIDS cases diagnosed among women in 2004 70% were black, 16% were white, and 12% were Hispanic. Heterosexual contact was responsible for HIV transmission in 90% of the women of childbearing age. This increase in heterosexual transmission among women may be attributed to a lack of knowledge about risk by this mode of transmission and/or failure of disclosure by infected partners. Other contributing factors included domestic violence, poverty, and substance abuse, all of which are more common among at risk women. Increased efforts at screening in prenatal clinics, family planning clinics, STD clinics, emergency rooms, and other sites where women access healthcare services is the first step in identification and prevention of HIV.

Specific populations of women are at increased risk for HIV infection. Adolescents, substance users, and incarcerated women share certain characteristics that may place them at increased risk for HIV infection. Poverty leading to survival sex, which is usually unprotected, is a risk factor for many patients. Intravenous substance abuse may pose an even greater risk for women who are frequently the last to use the shared needles. Correctional inmates and adolescents may have a history of posttraumatic stress disorder as a result of childhood abuse, which may lead to high-risk behavior which, in turn, increases the risk for acquiring HIV infection.

Managing HIV in Women

When women become infected with HIV, they manifest a more heterogeneous viral population than men, which may result in a more diverse immune response.[2] At comparable CD4 counts, women demonstrate viral loads that are 30–50% lower than in men but this difference is most marked after seroconversion and declines with time.[3] Viral loads may be higher in women with advanced disease, but women tend to progress to AIDS at viral loads significantly lower than men. Hence, decisions regarding initiation of antiretroviral therapy should be based primarily on CD4 counts rather than viral load.

One of the most common initial manifestations of HIV infection in women is recurrent vaginal candidiasis.[4] HIV-infected women are also more likely to experience abnormal cervical cytology, more severe pelvic inflammatory disease and vulvovaginal candidiasis, and more frequent outbreaks of herpes infections and bacterial vaginosis than uninfected women.[5-7] The presence, recurrence, and severity of these conditions should heighten the index of suspicion that a woman may be HIV infected.

Differences in how women metabolize drugs may account for sex differences in response to treatment as well as to the development of drug toxicities. Pharmacokinetic variables in women may occur as a result of differences in body weight, fat content, hepatic metabolism, hormonal effects, and pregnancy. Many of the side effects and long-term complications associated with antiretroviral therapy are more common in women than in men. Women are at increased risk for toxicities such as pancreatitis, hepatic steatosis, lactic acidosis, fat accumulation, breast enlargement, decreased bone mineral density, delavirdine- and protease inhibitor-associated rash, intolerance to ritonavir, nelfinavir-associated abdominal pain, nevirapine-associated rash and hepatotoxicity. In contrast, women are at decreased risk for dyslipidemia and nelfinavir-associated diarrhea. Antiretroviral toxicities are important determinants of adherence to an antiretroviral regimen and thus influence the response to treatment.[8, 9]

MANAGEMENT OF HIV-INFECTED WOMEN OF CHILDBEARING AGE

Special considerations must be taken into account when managing HIV in women of childbearing age. Goals of treatment should include:
- Improve overall health and quality of life
- Minimize disease progression
- Minimize unwanted pregnancies
- Prevent heterosexual transmission
- Avoid prescription of medication with teratogenic potential

Contraception for HIV-Infected Women[10]
- See Table 1 for Benefits and Drawbacks of various forms of contraception in HIV-infected women
- Contraception and safe sex counseling is essential

- Barrier methods are required for HIV and STD protection
- Unclear impact of hormonal contraception on viral shedding
- Bioavailability of ethinyl estradiol in contraceptives may be significantly reduced by ritonavir, nelfinavir, or nevirapine
- Nevirapine induces cytochrome P450 metabolism such that ethinyl estradiol levels are subtherapeutic
- Advise patients to back up oral contraceptive methods or tubal ligation with barrier methods

Consistent condom use can serve the dual role of providing contraception and helping reduce the risk of heterosexual transmission. Couples may be less likely to use condoms if oral contraceptives or other nonbarrier methods are used. Unfortunately some of these other forms of contraception may not prevent HIV transmission despite providing protection against pregnancy. Various factors in a couple's history may affect use of condoms such as length of the relationship, existence of any other ongoing relationships, age of the male partner, alcohol, or substance abuse. When both partners are infected, the need for diligent use of condoms to prevent superinfection must be emphasized.

It is important to be aware of the drug interactions between oral contraceptives and antiretroviral therapy. Some of these interactions may compromise the effectiveness of either the oral contraceptive or the antiretroviral agent by lowering drug levels. Specifically amprenavir levels are reduced by oral contraceptives whereas oral contraceptive levels are lowered in patients taking concomitant nevirapine, nelfinavir, ritonavir or ritonavir boosted lopinavir. In contrast levels of oral contraceptives are boosted by efavirenz, amprenavir, and indinavir. (See package inserts)

Table 1. Contraception for the HIV-Infected Woman

METHOD	BENEFIT	DRAWBACK
Male condom	<ul><li>Good protection against STDs and HIV</li><li>Protects partner</li></ul>	<ul><li>Partner cooperation required</li></ul>
Female condom	<ul><li>Good protection against STDs and HIV</li><li>Protects partner</li></ul>	<ul><li>Partner cooperation helpful</li></ul>
Oral contraceptive	<ul><li>Effective if used consistently</li></ul>	<ul><li>No HIV protection for partner</li><li>No STD protection</li><li>Risk of cervical ectopy</li><li>Possible interaction with antibiotics and antiretrovirals</li></ul>
Depo-provera	<ul><li>Effective</li><li>Limited compliance required</li></ul>	<ul><li>No HIV protection for partner</li><li>No STD protection</li></ul>
IUD	<ul><li>Effective</li></ul>	<ul><li>Theoretical risk of uterine infection</li><li>No HIV protection for partner</li><li>No STD protection</li></ul>
Diaphragm	<ul><li>Effective</li><li>Female controlled</li></ul>	<ul><li>Leave in 6-8 hours after ejaculation</li><li>May increase the risk of UTI</li></ul>
Patch	<ul><li>Avoids first pass metabolism</li><li>User friendly</li></ul>	<ul><li>No HIV protection for partner</li><li>No STD protection</li></ul>
Vasectomy	<ul><li>One time procedure</li><li>Permanent</li></ul>	<ul><li>No HIV protection for partner</li><li>No STD protection</li></ul>
Tubal ligation	<ul><li>One time procedure</li><li>Permanent</li></ul>	<ul><li>No HIV protection for partner</li><li>No STD protection</li></ul>

MANAGEMENT ISSUES FOR HIV-INFECTED WOMEN WHO DESIRE PREGNANCY

Until recently HIV infection was seen as a serious contraindication to infertility treatment. Nowadays reproduction is considered a major life activity and refusing to help someone based solely on their HIV status amounts to illegal discrimination.[11] The American College of Obstetricians and Gynecologists (ACOG) states that assisted reproductive techniques should not be denied to HIV-infected couples solely on the basis of their seropositive status.[12] The Ethics committee of the American Society for Reproductive Medicine (ASRM) noted that infertility in HIV-infected couples should be addressed to help prevent transmission between sero-discordant couples who might practice timed unprotected intercourse to conceive.[13] Intrauterine insemination has been successful in establishing pregnancies and avoiding HIV transmission to uninfected partners. Approximately one third of couples achieve pregnancy, which is similar to the pregnancy rate seen in HIV negative infertile couples who undergo this procedure. However patients should be aware of the risk of multiple pregnancies associated with artificial reproduction.

Gynecological Problems

Gynecologic problems are common among HIV-positive women and are frequently present at the time of initial presentation for evaluation and care. Some gynecologic issues are unrelated whereas others are directly related to HIV disease and associated immunosuppression. Still others are associated epidemiologically with HIV because of common risk factors such as sexual behavior or substance abuse.

Women have had the greatest increase in AIDS incidence in recent years and since this disease primarily affects women during their reproductive years, gynecologic and reproductive healthcare will play an increasingly important role in the overall care of HIV-infected women. With improved longevity and quality of life, gynecologic problems will be encountered more commonly or may be more prominent.

Menstrual Problems

Studies of menstrual problems in HIV-infected women offer conflicting evidence.[14, 15] Whether HIV itself or related immunosuppression affects menstrual patterns awaits further research. Hormonal intervention may be offered for heavy bleeding and anemia and to ease discomfort. All menstrual irregularities merit a full evaluation (see Figure 1); do not assume HIV is always the culprit. In the setting of HIV infection, menstrual disorders may be related to confounding variables such as weight loss, chronic disease, substance abuse, and progestational agents used for appetite stimulation or contraception. The impact of antiretroviral therapy on menstruation has not been well studied but excessive menstrual blood loss has been reported with ritonavir.[16]

Figure 1. Algorithm for the Investigation of Menorrhagia

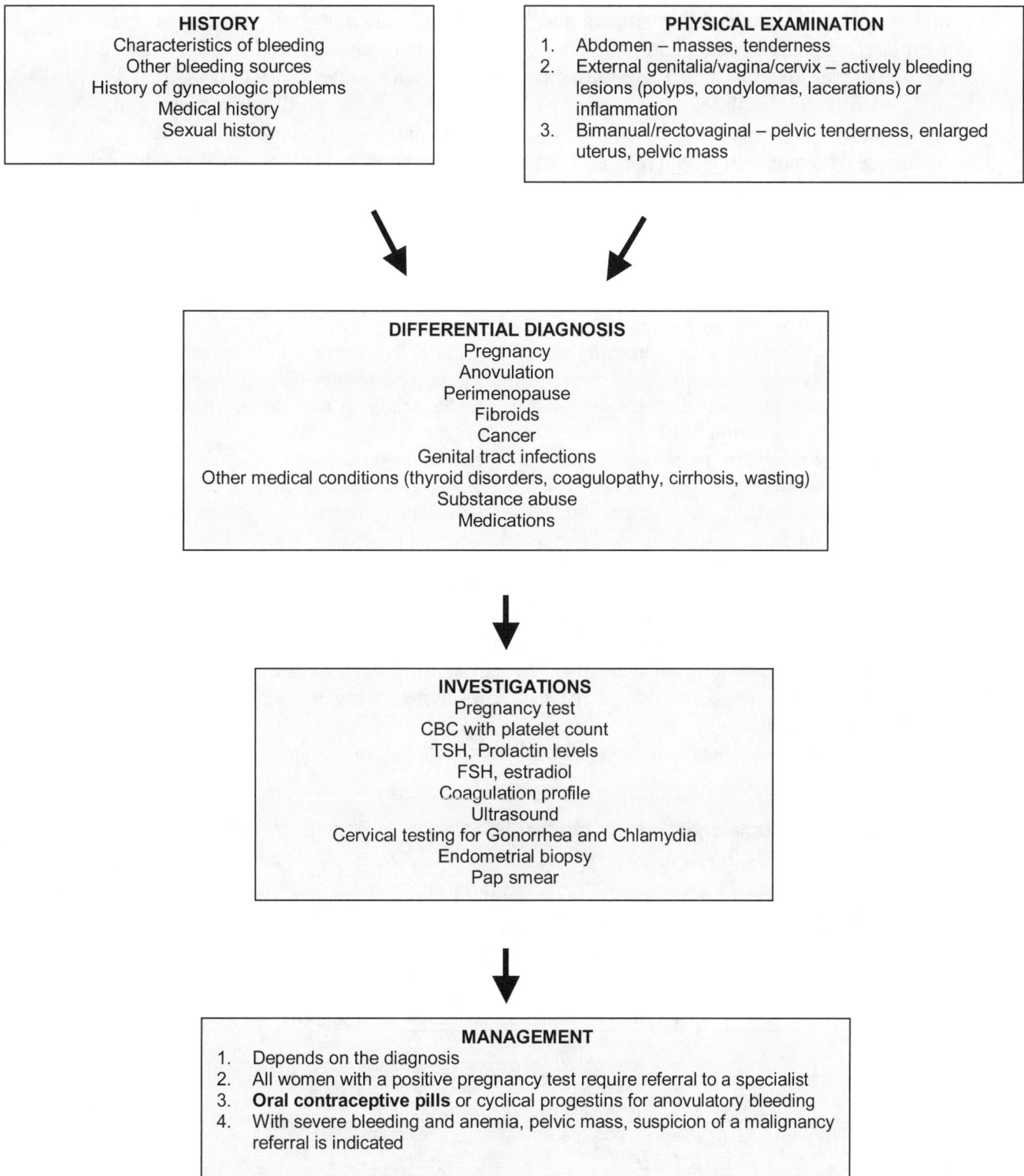

HISTORY
Characteristics of bleeding
Other bleeding sources
History of gynecologic problems
Medical history
Sexual history

PHYSICAL EXAMINATION
1. Abdomen – masses, tenderness
2. External genitalia/vagina/cervix – actively bleeding lesions (polyps, condylomas, lacerations) or inflammation
3. Bimanual/rectovaginal – pelvic tenderness, enlarged uterus, pelvic mass

DIFFERENTIAL DIAGNOSIS
Pregnancy
Anovulation
Perimenopause
Fibroids
Cancer
Genital tract infections
Other medical conditions (thyroid disorders, coagulopathy, cirrhosis, wasting)
Substance abuse
Medications

INVESTIGATIONS
Pregnancy test
CBC with platelet count
TSH, Prolactin levels
FSH, estradiol
Coagulation profile
Ultrasound
Cervical testing for Gonorrhea and Chlamydia
Endometrial biopsy
Pap smear

MANAGEMENT
1. Depends on the diagnosis
2. All women with a positive pregnancy test require referral to a specialist
3. **Oral contraceptive pills** or cyclical progestins for anovulatory bleeding
4. With severe bleeding and anemia, pelvic mass, suspicion of a malignancy referral is indicated

Cervical Dysplasia [17-19]

Abnormal cervical cytology is more common among HIV-infected women and is associated with HPV infection and the degree of immunosuppression. Both the frequency and severity of abnormal Pap smears and histologically-documented dysplasia increase with declining CD4 counts and have also been associated with higher HIV RNA levels. The incidence of abnormal Pap smears is increased with lower CD4 counts. In HIV-infected women, dysplasia is associated with more extensive cervical involvement and is more likely to involve other sites in the lower genital tract. There is an increased incidence of oncogenic HPV types and an increased incidence of biopsy proven cervical dysplasia in HIV-positive women.

Cervical Screening

- Perform a baseline gynecological evaluation with a pelvic examination and Pap smear
- Repeat Pap at 6 months and annually thereafter if normal results. If CD4 count < 200 or symptomatic or prior treatment for cervical dysplasia then repeat every 6 months.
- More aggressive testing is recommended because of a several-fold increase in rates of squamous intraepithelial lesions and a 1.7-fold increase in rates of cervical cancer in young women with HIV
- The severity and frequency of cervical dysplasia increases with progressive immune compromise
- There is a strong association with HIV infection and detectable and persistent HPV infection by oncogenic HPV types associated with cervical cancer; this association increases with progressive immunosuppression.
- HIV positive women should continue to be followed closely for evidence of lower genital tract neoplasia regardless of use of antiretroviral therapy or viral load
- ACOG recommends Pap smears every 3 to 4 months for the first year after treatment of pre-invasive cervical lesions, followed by Pap smears every 6 months.
- Vaginal Pap smears should be obtained after hysterectomy for persistent or recurrent cervical dysplasia
- HIV infection is not an indication for colposcopy in women who have normal Pap tests

Table 2. Recommendations for Intervention Based on Results of Pap Smear[20]

RESULTS	MANAGEMENT
Severe inflammation	• Evaluate for infection • Repeat Pap smear in 2-3 months
ASCUS/ASC-H	• Colposcopy +/- biopsy +/- endocervical sampling • Follow up Pap every 6 months • Repeat colposcopy annually if Pap unchanged
LGSIL	• Colposcopy +/- biopsy • Consider repeat colposcopy annually if Pap unchanged
HGSIL	• Colposcopy, biopsy, endocervical sampling • Treat with LEEP or conization
Invasive carcinoma	• Colposcopy with biopsy or conization • Treat with surgery or radiation

Invasive Cervical Cancer

In 1993, the CDC expanded the case definition of AIDS to include invasive cervical cancer. Women with HIV and cervical cancer tend to be younger and less immunocompromised compared with HIV-positive women with other AIDS-defining conditions. HIV-infected women with invasive cervical cancer appear to present at more advanced stages, may metastasize to unusual locations, have poorer responses to standard therapy, and have higher rates of recurrence and death than their HIV-negative counterparts.

Menopause

As HIV-positive women live longer and more women become infected later in life, menopausal issues become more important to consider. Infected women, like other women, cope with menopause, and may be appropriate candidates for hormonal replacement therapy with the proper indications. Therapies for the prevention of osteoporosis/osteopenia and prevention of coronary artery disease should be discussed. After ruling out any pathology and establishing that hot flashes are not related to infection, standard treatments including hormone replacement can be employed.

Sexually Transmitted Diseases (STDs)

Patients who have gonorrhea, chlamydia, trichomoniasis, or bacterial vaginosis and are infected with HIV should receive the same treatment regimens as those who are HIV negative. The key to successful management of STDs in HIV-infected women is 1) a high index of suspicion 2) prompt diagnosis 3) aggressive treatment 4) prophylaxis when appropriate.

For the latest in STD treatment information, see Chapter 17, Sexually Transmitted Diseases, and the CDC's "Sexually Transmitted Diseases Treatment Guidelines 2002" *MMWR*. 51 (RR-6).

Vulvovaginal Candidiasis

Candidiasis is common among HIV-infected women and may recur frequently when immune status deteriorates. Non-albicans Candida strains are present in 25% of vaginal isolates from women with HIV. For uncomplicated vaginal candidiasis, treatment options, first line treatment is a 7–day course of a topical antifungal. Include a variety of topical antifungals or a single antifungal agent (see CDC guidelines for list of options).

Pelvic Inflammatory Disease

Public health service guidelines note that it is not clear whether immunosuppressed women with PID require more aggressive treatment than other women. An individualized approach to oral versus parenteral therapy is recommended. Indications for inpatient management should include an inadequate response to outpatient therapy, an unclear diagnosis where emergency surgery cannot be ruled out, pregnancy, inability to adhere to outpatient treatment or presence of a tubo-ovarian abscess. With appropriate treatment, the course of PID in HIV-infected women is similar to PID in other women. HIV-infected women with PID have similar symptoms when compared with uninfected controls and although a tubo-ovarian abscess is more common, the response to standard oral and parenteral antibiotics is similar. The microbiological findings are similar except for higher rates of concomitant Mycoplasma hominis, candida, and HPV infections.

Herpes

Herpes is the most prevalent STD in the USA and in HIV-infected women can be more extensive, frequent, prolonged, more painful, atypical in location or appearance, and slower to heal in the presence of immune dysfunction. Viral shedding increases with falling CD4 counts. Most viral shedding is asymptomatic. Herpes is associated with an increased risk for HIV transmission/acquisition. Treat in accordance with standard guidelines. Women with advanced immunosuppression may need higher doses (acyclovir 400 mg po 5 times per day or acyclovir 800 mg 3 times per day) and longer treatment. Consider daily suppressive therapy for women with frequent recurrences (see Chapter 17, Sexually Transmitted Diseases)

PSYCHOLOGICAL ISSUES FOR HIV-INFECTED WOMEN

Many HIV-infected women are coping with mental health problems beyond those associated with living with HIV, including depression, significant posttraumatic stress disorder (PTSD) symptomatology, and substance use disorders. These psychological issues have the potential to disrupt the patient's psychosocial functioning and decrease the patient's quality of life. Many HIV-infected women have high levels of stress that can disrupt adherence to HAART. Management should include both psychological as well as psychiatric intervention

Depression in HIV-Infected Women [21-23]

- Psychiatric morbidity as a result of depressive disorders is common in patients infected with HIV
- Depression is more common among women with HIV infection than among HIV-infected men
- HIV infection may alter mood and conversely, depression may influence the course of HIV-related disease
- Depression has been associated with detrimental effects on immune function and medication adherence in HIV-infected patients
- Depressive disorders, including symptoms of sleep and appetite disturbance, appear to be more common in persons with HIV than in the general population
- Depression in combination with stress can produce declines in immune function
- Self-neglect, forgetfulness, and apathy all potentially result from depression
- Treat depressive disorders in patients with HIV infection in order to improve adherence and limit disease progression
- Use individual and group psychotherapy and cognitive and behavioral therapies in the treatment of depression
- Use antidepressant therapy in HIV-infected patients with major depression
  - Tricyclic antidepressants (TCAs) and selective serotonin-reuptake inhibitors (SSRIs) have both proved beneficial
  - SSRIs preferred because of their larger safety margin
- Interactions between antidepressant and antiretroviral medications must be considered (Refer to American Psychiatric Association, Practice Guideline for the Treatment of Patients with HIV/AIDS, 2000, and Chapter 27, Identifying and Treating Depression, Anxiety, and Dementia.)

Posttraumatic Stress Disorder (PTSD) In Women with HIV [24-28]

PTSD is under diagnosed. It is important to be aware that the post-trauma environment influences rate of PTSD and many HIV-infected women live in environments characterized by poverty, violence, and lack of social support.

- Trauma exposure and PTSD negatively impact immune function and disease progression and are associated with the following behaviors: continued participation in high-risk behaviors; poor adherence to medication regimen; and interference with the benefits of treatments for HIV
- HIV-infected women with PTSD or trauma history show a more rapid decline in CD4+ ratios than women without PTSD.
- Adherence to antiretroviral therapy can be disrupted in PTSD patients as a result of distress, depression, and mistrust
- Use of anxiety management techniques and effective coping training will result in lower levels of distress, better adherence to medication, and higher levels of participation in health-promoting behaviors

MANAGEMENT

Psychological Treatment

- Use a brief mental health screen to alert you to the mental health needs among your HIV-infected female patients
- Conduct a thorough mental health assessment to determine which follow-up services are appropriate and necessary. The following are areas of importance: verbal memory functioning, mental disorders, neurological functioning, general health perception, and cognitive dysfunction
- Increase the patient's assertiveness in interacting with healthcare professionals to gain a greater sense of control in managing medical condition
  - Develop an intervention that increases coping and treatment adherence

Psychiatric Treatment

Identify women at high risk. Problems that may promote risk behavior include: impulse control disorders, hypersexuality, untreated depression, psychotic disorders, substance use disorders, and personality disorders. Assess if psychotropic medication is necessary with special attention to: assessing suicidal ideation, extreme hostility or anger, and self-defeating or self-injurious behavior.

Provide pharmacotherapy and medication management
- Start with lower doses and slower titration
- Try to keep dosing schedules as uncomplicated as possible
- Focus on drug side effects to avoid unnecessary adverse effects
- Psychiatrist should collaborate with primary care provider so that all medications being prescribed are compatible

MENTAL HEALTH INTERVENTION SPECIFIC TO WOMEN IN PREGNANCY

Pregnant women are at even higher risk for mental health problems because of the increased stressors that include: often new diagnosis as a result of prenatal screening, disclosure to partner, concerns about perinatal transmission, unplanned pregnancy, medication adherence in pregnancy, and complexity of a high-risk pregnancy.

Healthcare providers should offer the following to pregnant women:

- Cognitive behavioral and preventative health interventions
- Stress management interventions and coping strategies to promote adaptive coping and reduce distress associated with living with HIV
- Active coping strategies and problem solving skills to address difficulties with disclosure and negotiating relationships
- Anxiety management techniques to help improve adherence in HIV-positive women with PTSD as a result of being diagnosed with HIV
- Postpartum patients should be screened to assess for depressive symptomatology — evaluate the patient's current status and functioning, and determine what follow up services are needed, if appropriate
- Medication can be considered if necessary
- Arrange liaison between outpatient and inpatient teams to transition patients

DOMESTIC VIOLENCE

"As the single most important and most accessed institution in the lives of women, the healthcare setting can provide a unique opportunity to intervene, making it one of the newest and most critical areas of the domestic violence movement today."
(Family Violence Prevention Fund, 2001) [33]

Healthcare Implications [30, 31]

- Women are the most frequent consumers of healthcare services which puts healthcare providers in the best position to identify victims of domestic violence and make appropriate referrals to protect them against further harm
- 92% of physically abused women do not discuss these incidents with their physicians, and 57% do not discuss the incidents with anyone.
- Too few healthcare providers screen for intimate partner violence (IPV). Only 10% of primary care physicians routinely screen for IPV during new patient visits and 9% routinely screen during periodic checkups

Factors Contributing to Risk of Domestic Violence [29, 32]

- **Poverty:** Women with annual household incomes below $10,000 are 3.5 times more likely to suffer abusive violence compared to those with household incomes over $40,000

- – Battered women seem to have higher rates of depression, substance abuse problems, and posttraumatic stress disorder compared to nonabused women
- – Poor women in abusive relationships have complex lives and lack adequate coping resources
- – Intervening to stop violence is only the first step; issues of income, healthcare, both mental and physical care, and housing must also be discussed

- **Psychosocial Stressors:** Families stressed by unemployment, alcohol and/or drug use and HIV illness are more likely to experience violence
- **Pregnancy:** Pregnancy can initiate domestic violence, specifically if the partner is unemployed, or jealous of the child as a rival for the woman's time and attention

  - – Between 25% and 45% of all abused women report being battered during pregnancy
  - – Battering can cause miscarriage, preterm labor, low birth weight of the infant, or other injury to the developing fetus
  - – The stress of abuse also may cause pregnant women to continue harmful behaviors such as smoking and drug or alcohol use

- **Chronic Illness:** Women living with HIV can be at increased rate for intimate partner violence (IPV)
  - – Many HIV-infected women indicate that they have endured emotional, physical, or sexual abuse at some time after their diagnosis

Screening and Assessment [34]

Healthcare facilities serving women need to screen for potential violence. Researchers have developed an effective 2–minute assessment screen for early detection of abuse of women (see Table 3).

Table 3. Abuse Screening Tool

Question	Circle best answer
In general, how would you describe your relationship?	A lot of tension Some tension No tension
Do you and your partner work out arguments with?	Great difficulty Some difficulty No difficulty
Do arguments ever result in you feeling put down or bad about yourself?	Often Sometimes Never
Do arguments ever result in hitting, kicking, or pushing?	Often Sometimes Never
Do you ever feel frightened by what your partner says or does?	Often Sometimes Never
Has your partner ever abused you physically?	Often Sometimes Never
Has your partner ever abused you emotionally?	Often Sometimes Never
Has your partner ever abused you sexually?	Often Sometimes Never

Source: Brown J, Lent B, Brett PJ, et al. Development of the woman abuse screening tool for use in family practice. *Family Medicine* 1996; 28(6) ;422–428.

Potential Indicators of Intimate Partner Violence [31, 33]

- Healthcare providers should be attentive to signs and symptoms of possible IPV, including missed appointments, delay in seeking care, nonspecific somatic complaints and vague or inconsistent explanation of injuries
- Depression and social alienation are common, as are substance abuse
- Poor eye contact by patient and/or partner who is resistant to leave the woman alone with the healthcare provider
- Suicide attempts may be directly related to IPV

Documentation of Suspected Domestic Violence [30]

- Precise thorough documentation of the patient's injuries is crucial in cases of suspected abuse as it serves as objective, third-party evidence useful in legal proceedings
- Medical records for example can assist victims in obtaining a restraining order or qualifying for public housing, welfare, and immigration relief

Guidelines & Interventions for Healthcare Providers [30, 31]

- Healthcare providers should believe any woman who admits being abused for she has shown trust and courage to disclose the facts
- Nonjudgmental interviewing can help build trust and establish a therapeutic alliance

- Guidelines for care of the abused woman (The ABCDES Framework) include the following:

(A) Assure the woman that she is not alone. Isolation enforced by her abusive partner prevents her understanding that others are in a similar situation and that healthcare providers can help
(B) Express the **belief** that violence against the woman is unacceptable in any situation and that is not her fault
(C) Ensure **confidentiality**. She may fear, justifiably, that her abuser will retaliate
(D) Document the case thoroughly
(E) Educate the woman about the cycle of violence (see Table 4) likelihood of reported violence and about her options for ending the abuse
(S) Safety. Help the woman formulate a plan of action for either leaving or remaining in the relationship, which some women do for a variety of reasons. Provide information about available resources such as hotline and shelter numbers. Suggest a quick getaway bag packed with personal items be hidden or left with a neighbor. If possible, the woman should have an extra set of house keys, money, and any legal documents needed for identification

Table 4. The Cycle of Violence [35]

3-Phase Cycle
→ A period of increasing tension, leading to ...   →→ The battery, followed by ...   →→→ A "honeymoon" period of calm and remorse in which the abuser is kind and loving and begs for forgiveness   When stress and conflict begin to build, the cruel cycle begins again. Over time, the first two phases grow longer and the honeymoon phase diminishes and eventually disappears

References

1. Florida Department of Health, Bureau of HIV/AIDS. Data as of 12/31/04. Available at http://www.doh.state.fl.us/Disease_ctrl/aids/trends/trends.html.
2. Long EM, Martin HL, Kreiss JK, et al. Gender differences in HIV-1 diversity at time of infection. *Nature Med* 2000; 6(1):71–75.
3. Napravnik S, Poole C, Thomas JC, Eron JJ. Gender difference in HIV RNA levels: A meta-analysis of published studies. *J Acquir Immune Defic Syndr* 2002; 31(1):11–19.
4. Minkoff HL, DeHovitz JA. Care of women infected with the human immunodeficiency virus. *JAMA* 1991; 266(16):2253–2258.
5. Smith JR, Kitchen VS, Botcherby M, et al. Is HIV infection associated with an increase in the prevalence of cervical neoplasia? *Br J Obstet Gynaecol* 1993; 100 (2):149–153.
6. Korn AP, Landers DV, Green JR, Sweet RL. Pelvic inflammatory disease in human immunodeficiency virus infected women. *Obstet Gynecol* 1993; 82(5): 765–768.
7. Siegel D, Golden E, Washington AE, et al. Prevalence and correlates of herpes simplex infections. The Population-Based AIDS in Multiethnic Neighborhoods Study. *JAMA* 1992; 268(13):1702–1708.
8. Public Health Service Task Force. Recommendations for the use of antiretroviral drugs in pregnant HIV-1 infected women for maternal health and interventions to reduce perinatal HIV-1 transmission in the United States 2005. Updated guidelines available at http://AIDSinfo.nih.gov.
9. Bartlett JG, Gallant JE. Medical Management of HIV infection 2004. Chapter 4 Antiretroviral Therapy, pp 102-112, .Johns Hopkins Medicine, Baltimore, MD. 2004.

10. Hatcher, R. et al., ed. *Contraceptive Technology*, 18th ed. Ardent Media: New York.2004.

11. Americans with Disabilities Act, 1990. Available at http://www.eeoc.gov/ada/

12. American College of Obstetricians and Gynecologists (ACOG). Human immunodeficiency virus. Ethics in Obstetrics and Gynecology. Available at: http://www.acog.org.

13. American Society for Reproductive Medicine (ASRM), Ethics Committee. Human immunodeficiency virus and infertility treatment. *Fertil Steril* 2002; 77(2):218–222.

14. Chirgwin KD, Feldman J, Muneyyira-Delabe O, et al. Menstrual function in human immunodeficiency virus infected women without acquired immunodeficiency syndrome. *J Acquir Immune Defic Syndr Hum Retrovirol* 1996; 12:489–494.

15. Ellerbrock TV, Wright TC, Bush TJ, et al. Characteristics of menstruation in women infected with human immunodeficiency virus. *Obstet Gynecol* 1996; 87(6):1030–1034.

16. Nielsen H. Hypermenorrhea associated with ritonavir. *Lancet* 1999; 353:811–812.

17. Wright TC, Sun XW. Anogenital papillomavirus infection and neoplasia in immunodeficient women. *Obstet Gyncol Clin N Am* 1996; 23:861-893.

18. Sun XW, Kuhn L, Ellerbrock TV, Chiasson MA, Bush TJ. Wright TC. Human papillomavirus infection in women infected with the human immunodeficiency virus. *NEJM* 1997; 337(19):1343–1349.

19. Ahdieh L, Klein RS, Burk R, Cu-Uvin S, Schuman P, Duerr A, et al. Prevalence, incidence and type specific persistence of human papillomavirus in human immunodeficiency virus positive and HIV negative women. *JID* 2001; 184(6):682–690.

20. Abularach S, Anderson J. A guide to the clinical care of women with HIV; 2005 Edition. Available at http://hab.hrsa.gov/publications/womencare05/WG05intro.htm#WG05introa

21. Kimerling R, Clum GA, Wolfe J. Relationships among trauma exposure, chronic posttraumatic stress disorder symptoms, and self-reported health in women. *Journal of Traumatic Stress* 2000; 13:115–128.

22. Tedstone JE, Tarrier N. Posttraumatic stress disorder following medical illness and treatment. *Clinical Psychology Review* 2003; 23(3):409–448.

23. American Psychiatric Association. *Practice Guideline for the Treatment of Patients with HIV/AIDS.* American Psychiatric Publishing, Inc; Arlington, VA. 2000.

24. Penzak SR, Reddy YS, Grimsley SR. Depression in patients with HIV infection. *American Journal of Health-System Pharmacology* 2000; 57:376–386.

25. Cohen MA, Cesar AA, Hoffman RG, Milau V, Carrera G. The impact of PTSD on treatment adherence in persons with HIV infection. *General Hospital Psychiatry* 2001; 23(5):294–296.

26. Delahanty DL, Bogart LM, Figler JL. Posttraumatic stress disorder symptoms, salivary cortisol, medication adherence, and CD4 levels in HIV-positive individuals. *AIDS Care* 2004; 16(2):247–260.

27. Brief DJ, Bollinger AR, Vielhauer MJ, Berger-Greenstein JA, Morgan EE, Brady SM, et al. Understanding the interface of HIV, trauma, post-traumatic stress disorder, and substance use and its implications for health outcomes. *AIDS Care* 2004; 16(1):97–120.

28. Martinez A, Israelski D, Walker C, Koopman C. Posttraumatic stress disorder in women attending human immunodeficiency virus outpatient clinic. *AIDS Patient Care* 2002; 16:283–291.

29. Hartog JP. *Florida's Omnibus AIDS Act: A Brief Legal Guide for Health Professionals.* Jacksonville: Florida Department of Health, Division of Disease Control, Bureau of HIV/AIDS; 1999.

30. Isaac NE, Enos VP. *Documenting Domestic Violence: How Healthcare Providers Can Help Victims.* Washington, DC: National Academy Press; 2001.

31. Lyon E. *Welfare, Poverty, and Abused Women: New Research and Its Implications.* Harrisburg, PA: National Resource Center on Domestic Violence; 2000.

32. Family Violence Prevention Fund. *Model Programs on Health Care and Domestic Violence. National Survey of Managed Care Organizations.* San Francisco: Florida Violence Prevention Fund's National Health Resource Center on Domestic Violence; 2001.

33. Coker A, Smith P, Bethea L et al. Physical health consequences of physical and psychological intimate partner violence. *Archives of Family Medicine* 2000; 9(5): 451–457.

34. Brown J, Lent B, Brett PJ, et al. Development of the woman abuse screening tool for use in family practice. *Family Medicine* 1996; 28(6):422–428.

35. Walker L. *The Battered Woman Syndrome*, Vol. 6. New York: Springer. 1984.

41

Nutrition

Cade Fields-Gardner, MS, RD
Director of Services, The Cutting Edge, Cary, IL.

Introduction

Undernutrition is the primary reason for immune dysfunction in the world today. Nutritional status is a primary consideration to support adequate immune function and to withstand the effects of HIV infection and its treatment.

HIV infection affects nutritional status and vice versa. HIV infection leads to a chronic inflammatory response. Just as with any infection, the degree of response is related to the severity of infection or, in this case, viral load.[1,2] Protein stores are degraded to pool amino acids and make them available for the inflammatory response, initiating a muscle wasting process. Concomitant with the inflammatory response is a diminished appetite, leading to reduced food intake. In addition, gut involvement is common and malabsorption may become a contributing factor to nutritional compromise. With both infectious and malnutrition processes occurring, altered hormonal milieu is common and further complicates chronic HIV infection. These conditions change both macronutrient and micronutrient metabolism in a complex and interrelated series of metabolic events associated with chronic inflammatory diseases, such as HIV infection.

DEFINITIONS

"AIDS Wasting Syndrome" (AWS) is defined by the Centers for Disease Control and Prevention (CDC) as a 10% weight loss for no apparent reason and associated with diarrhea or fever for more than 30 days.[3] While this definition is not based on issues pertaining to HIV infection, it has been used to qualify patients for an AIDS diagnosis in approximately 20% of cases reported both before and after the widespread use of combination antiretroviral (ARV) therapy, often referred to as highly active antiretroviral therapy (HAART). Several researchers have sought to identify independent predictors of survival and morbidity and weight loss appears to be a strong contender.[4,5]

The nomenclature is also unclear. Wasting has commonly been used to designate a cachectic condition in HIV infection, while in other disease states wasting may be used interchangeably with undernutrition. Some evidence suggests that weight losses are initiated by opportunistic or other infections, but that diminished intake in response to infection appears to be a strong predictor of weight loss.[6] Unfortunately, once weight loss has occurred full rehabilitation to baseline appears unlikely.[7]

Refinements to this definition of wasting have been offered, some of which include time-dependent weight loss and body composition criteria.[8] In 1989 evidence was presented to show that the degree of weight loss and the level of body cell mass (muscle and organ tissue) strongly predict survival more reliably than other indicators.[9] However, even weight loss is difficult to relate to outcomes in some cases, especially when body cell mass is preserved during weight losses and body cell mass is not reconstituted reliably with weight gains and ARV therapies.[10]

Relatively new to the scene is body composition alterations collectively known as lipodystrophy syndrome and biochemical abnormalities. These changes both affect and are affected by nutritional status. The development of central fat accumulations is closely related to weight gain and the loss of subcutaneous fat has been related to weight loss episodes. There have been several attempts to classify and define lipodystrophy syndrome to date, without a clear consensus.[11] Additional metabolic alterations include blood lipid alterations, insulin resistance, sex hormone resistance, and other hormonal changes. Both lipodystrophy syndrome and the biochemical alterations have been related to chronic disease and its treatment.[12]

NUTRITION ASSESSMENT

Regardless of definitions, screening and assessment of nutritional status should be a routine undertaking in the clinical care of HIV-infected patients. Nutrition-related screening can include a variety of indicators. The minimum data set will include a carefully measured height and serial measures of weight.

BODY MASS INDEX (BMI)

It has been suggested that Body Mass Index (BMI) (weight in kg/height in m2) is a strong indicator of survival and morbidity. In addition, BMI may be used in resource-limited settings to indicate the appropriate timing for the initiation of antiretroviral (ARV) therapy.[13]

If BMI is below 20 kg/m2 (especially with unintentional weight loss), careful assessment should be pursued. Further evaluation may include additional physical assessment with anthropometry and body composition evaluation to determine patterns of weight compared to the expected or baseline values. This type of evaluation can help determine the type of problem that initiated weight loss and to differentiate cachexia from starvation and from lipodystrophy. For instance, if weight lost is around 2/3 fat tissue then starvation-types of problems should be evaluated, such as appetite loss, malabsorption, and even lack of food access. However, if most of the weight lost is body cell mass, and especially if extracellular tissue (primarily extracellular fluids) is elevated, then an infection should be suspected as an initiator of cachexia. If the weight loss is nearly all fat tissues under the skin, then lipoatrophy should be anticipated.

Additional Measures to Anticipate Nutritional Risk

Additional measures can be used to anticipate nutritional risk and alterations, such as disease status (viral load, CD4, C-reactive protein, cortisol response, and others), risks for complicating disease (diabetes, insulin resistance, markers of cardiovascular disease, hepatic enzymes, renal function markers, elevated lactate levels, and others), and markers of nutritional status and inflammatory process (albumin, pre-albumin, transferrin, ferritin, and others). Each biochemical value can be used as a clue to determine the potential sources of the nutrition-related problem and viable and appropriate interventions.

Food Intake

Food intake should be evaluated if starvation or inappropriate weight gain occurs. In addition, if dietary modulation may be needed to deal with insulin resistance, cardiovascular disease risk, symptoms (diarrhea, nausea/vomiting, anorexia, and others) or other problems then baseline dietary intake may assist in counseling and generating a reasonable intervention.

Review Medications

A review of medications should include potential for nutrient and nutrition-related interactions. The contribution of medications to altered nutritional status and nutrient metabolism is likely because of the types of medications, potential combinations, and long-term polypharmacy, to which most patients are subjected.

Lipodystrophy

Lipodystrophy and altered metabolism may be more common in long-term survivors and especially those who are treated with polypharmacy. Differentiation between central fat accumulation and normal obesity as well as lipoatrophy and more general wasting is important to properly diagnose and match appropriate therapies. Physical changes can be evaluated with serial anthropometry measures and higher-tech measures using dual energy x-ray absorptiometry, magnetic resonance imaging, and computed tomography scans. It may also be valuable to anticipate changes often associated with chronic inflammatory diseases and treatments, such as osteopenia and osteoporosis in nutrition assessment and intervention.

NUTRITION-RELATED INTERVENTIONS

While it remains unknown whether reversing various forms of altered nutritional status will, in fact, improve survival outcomes, it has been suggested that the normalization to and maintenance of good nutritional status is an important factor to limit problems of morbidity and mortality in HIV-infected patients. Nutrition interventions, like other interventions, are varied and matched to assessment factors that help identify problems.

Feeding

If starvation is the primary issue, or even a co-factor in morbidity, then feeding is appropriate. This intervention can include counseling, food access strategies, supplemental feeding, and specialized nutrition support (enteral and/or parenteral feeding). Several strategies can address malabsorption, such as dietary modulation, modified nutrient-containing supplements, enzyme therapies, and nutrition support. Successful candidates for this type of support are those who are expected to rehabilitate their health status to include an anabolic stimulus to assure that body cell mass will be adequately reconstituted to maintain normal body functions.

Appetite Stimulants

With diminished appetite, patients may reduce their food intake resulting in weight loss and wasting. If nutrient-based strategies don't work and indicators suggest that improved nutritional intake will help to reverse weight losses, appetite stimulants have been employed. Examples are megestrol acetate and dronabinol. Anabolic therapies may also improve appetite, possibly partly as a side effect of improved body cell mass levels.

Dietary Modulations

Metabolic abnormalities may also require nutrition-related interventions. Dietary modulations are important features of interventions for insulin resistance, blood lipid abnormalities, oxidative stress, and others. Referral to a dietitian for evaluation and planning within the context of chronic HIV infection is an important adjunctive therapy. Exercise may play an important role in controlling certain metabolic abnormalities, such as insulin resistance and/or cardiovascular risk, and should be included in therapeutic plans along with appropriate medication therapies to achieve normalization.

Hormonal Alterations

Beyond nutrition and exercise, normalized nutrition status may require attention to hormonal alterations. With weight loss of 10% from baseline, or for many other reasons, patients may experience a drop in testosterone levels, which are important to maintain functioning body cell mass tissues. Testosterone replacement is a commonly used therapy to rehabilitate nutritional status and normalize hormonal levels and functions. Testosterone, testosterone analogues, growth hormone, and combinations of these therapies have been used to restore weight and improve body cell mass levels.

Conclusion

Maintaining adequate nutritional status is an important feature of care and treatment of chronic HIV infection and related complications. A reasonable amount of body stores, especially of fluids, body cell mass (muscle and organ tissues), and adequate fat stores are essential to maintain body functions and support survival. Beyond these priorities, consider using micronutrients (vitamins and minerals) and non-nutrient antioxidants and other substances that are important for normal body metabolism.

The most basic interventions will assure that the social and economic issues of adequate food access are addressed. Dietary modulation to complement other medical therapies and as palliative care to reduce adverse effects are examples of nutrition as an adjunctive therapy.

Resources

Fields-Gardner C, Salomon SB, Davis MA. Living Well with HIV/AIDS A Guide to Nutrition. 2nd ed. 2003. ISBN 0-88091-322-3. Available through the American Dietetic Association, Chicago, IL. www.eatright.org

Fields-Gardner C, Fergusson P; American Dietetic Association, Dietitians of Canada. Nutrition intervention in the care of persons with human immunodeficiency virus infection: position of the American Dietetic Association and Dietitians of Canada. *J Am Diet Assoc* 2004; 104(9):1425–1441. Available at: http://www.eatright.org/Member/PolicyInitiatives/index_21020.cfm.

References

1. Batterham MJ, Garsia R, Greenop P. Prevalence and predictors of HIV-associated weight loss in the era of highly active antiretroviral therapy. *Int J STD AIDS* 2002; 13(11):744–747.

2. Ferrando SJ, Rabkin JG, Lin SH, McElhiney M. Increase in body cell mass and decrease in wasting are associated with increasing potency of antiretroviral therapy for HIV infection. *AIDS Patient Care STDS* 2005; 19(4):216–223.

3. Centers for Disease Control and Prevention. Revision of the CDC surveillance case definition for acquired immunodeficiency syndrome. *MMWR* 1987; 36:3–15.

4. Dworkin MS, Williamson JM. AIDS wasting syndrome: trends, influence on opportunistic infections, and survival. Adult/Adolescent Spectrum of HIV Disease Project. *J Acquir Immune Defic Syndr* 2003; 33:267–273.

5. Maas JJ, Dukers N, Krol A, van Amejiden EJ, van Leeuwen R, Roos MT, de Wolf F, Countinho RA, Keet JP. Body mass index course in asymptomatic HIV-infected homosexual men and the predictive value of a decrease of body mass index for progression to AIDS. *J Acquir Immune Defic Syndr Hum Retrovirol* 1998; 19(3):254–259.

6. Macallan DC, Noble C, Baldwin C, Jebb SA, Prentice AM, Coward WA, Sawyer MB, McManus TJ, Griffin GE. Energy expenditure and wasting in human immunodeficiency virus infection. *NEJM* 1995; 333(2):83–88.

7. Macallan DC. Wasting in HIV infection and AIDS. *J Nutr* 1999; 129(1S Suppl):238S–242S.

8. Polsky B, Kotler DP, Steinhart C. HIV-associated wasting in the HAART era: guidelines for assessment, diagnosis, and treatment. *AIDS Patient Care STDS* 2001; 15(8):411–423.

9. Kotler DP, Tierney AR, Wang J, Pierson RN Jr. Magnitude of body-cell-mass depletion and the timing of death from wasting in AIDS. *Am J Clin Nutr* 1989; 50:444–447.

10. Silva M, Skolnik PR, Gorbach SL, Spiegelman D, Wilson IB, Fernandez-DiFranco MG, Knox TA. The effect of protease inhibitors on weight and body composition in HIV-infected patients. *AIDS* 1998; 12:1645–1651.

11. Ioannidis JP, Trikalinos TA, Law M, Carr A. HIV lipodystrophy case definition using artificial neural network modeling. HIV Lipodystrophy Case Definition Study Group. *Antivir Ther* 2003; 8(5):435–441.

12. Lichtenstein KA, Delaney KM, Armon C, Ward DJ, Moorman AC, Wood KC, Holmberg SD. Incidence of and risk factors for lipoatrophy (abnormal fat loss) in ambulatory HIV-1-infected patients. HIV Outpatient Study Investigators. *J Acquir Immune Defic Syndr* 2003; 32(1):48–56.

13. Van Der Sande MA, Van Der Loeff MF, Aveika AA, Sabally S, Togun T, Sarge-Njie R, Alabi AS, Jaye A, Corrah T, Whittle HC. Body mass index at time of HIV diagnosis: A strong and independent predictor of survival. *J Acquir Immune Defic Syndr* 2004; 37(2):1288–1294.